THIRD EDITION

Interviewing in Action in a Multicultural World

Bianca Cody Murphy
Wheaton College

Carolyn Dillon
Boston University

THOMSON
™
BROOKS/COLE

Australia • Brazil • Canada • Mexico • Singapore • Spain • United Kingdom • United States

THOMSON

BROOKS/COLE

Interviewing in Action in a Multicultural World, Third Edition
Bianca Cody Murphy and Carolyn Dillon

Social Work Editor: Dan Alpert
Development Editor: Tangelique Williams
Assistant Editor: Ann Lee Richards
Editorial Assistant: Stephanie Rue
Technology Project Manager: Julie Aguilar
Marketing Manager: Meghan McCullough
Marketing Assistant: Teresa Marino
Marketing Communications Manager: Shemika Britt
Project Manager, Editorial Production: Tanya Nigh
Creative Director: Rob Hugel

Art Director: Vernon Boes
Print Buyer: Nora Massuda
Permissions Editor: Roberta Broyer
Production Service: ICC Macmillan Inc.
Copy Editor: Fred Dahl
Cover Designer: Andy Norris
Cover Image: Rainbow Spectrum ©Digital Art/Corbis
Cover Printer: West Group
Compositor: ICC Macmillan Inc.
Printer: West Group

Thomson Higher Education
10 Davis Drive
Belmont, CA 94002-3098
USA

Library of Congress Control Number: 2006938726

ISBN-13: 978-0-495-09516-3
ISBN-10: 0-495-09516-8

For more information about our products, contact us at:
Thomson Learning Academic Resource Center
1-800-423-0563
For permission to use material from this text or product, submit a request online at
http://www.thomsonrights.com.
Any additional questions about permissions can be submitted by e-mail to
thomsonrights@thomson.com.

To our students

Who taught us how to teach

To our clients

Who taught us how to practice

To our teachers

Who taught us to learn from our students and our clients

Bianca Cody Murphy, Ed.D., is Professor of Psychology at Wheaton College in Norton, Massachusetts. She is a licensed psychologist and has a clinical practice with Newton Psychotherapy Associates. She has conducted numerous workshops and training programs for mental health professionals around the country and has published professional articles and book chapters on clinical work with lesbian and gay clients, on peace psychology, and on families exposed to environmental toxins. Dr. Murphy has served as the Chair of both the Committee on Women and the Board for the Advancement of Psychology in the Public Interest of the American Psychological Association, and she has been President of Psychologists for Social Responsibility. She is the recipient of the Distinguished Professional Contribution Award from the Society for the Psychological Study of Lesbian, Gay, and Bisexual Issues (Division 44) of the American Psychological Association.

Carolyn Dillon, LICSW, is Clinical Professor Emerita, Boston University School of Social Work. She is a Licensed Independent Clinical Social Worker in the Boston, Massachusetts area and has also tutored in English through her local library. She is a member of the National Association of Social Workers and was a longtime affiliate of the Council on Social Work Education and the Massachusetts Society for Clinical Social Work. She has written about how to prevent compassion fatigue through better self-care and stress management and has spoken and consulted widely with social workers in health and mental health settings. She received the Metcalf Award for teaching excellence from Boston University and the Greatest Contribution to Social Work Education award from the Massachusetts Chapter of the National Association of Social Workers. She is the author of *Learning from Mistakes in Clinical Practice.*

Contents

CHAPTER 4
Attending and Listening

CHAPTER 5
Support and Empathy: A Sustaining Presence

CHAPTER 8
Planning for and Evaluating Change

207

CHAPTER 9
Gaining New Perspectives: Helping Clients Feel and See Things Differently

227

CHAPTER 10
Changing Behaviors: Helping Clients Do Things Differently   259

CHAPTER 15
Professional Issues: Ongoing Education and Self-Care

Preface

Interviewing in Action in a Multicultural World emphasizes and illustrates the relational, interactional, and multicultural nature of practice in the twenty-first century. It is based on our RE-VIEW PRACTICE Method of clinical knowledge and skills development. We believe that students can best learn when they read about skills, view seasoned clinicians using the skills with clients, and practice the skills through role-plays and skill application exercises, receiving feedback from instructors and peers. Thus we have developed an integrated learning package whose elements build upon each other. The comprehensive yet easy-to-read text is accompanied by a DVD containing video clips in which real-life clinicians demonstrate and reflect on key skills discussed in each chapter. The Companion Website includes student self-exploration activities, essay questions, Web links, and other resources.

Special Features of the Package

1. *Realistic for today's practice environments.* The text and DVD video clips address the complexity of issues that clinicians confront and the limited time and resources available to them. They also address important issues affecting clinical work, such as managed care, evidence-based practice, and the use of the Internet and other technologies.
2. *Experiential learning.* The book, the Instructor's Manual, and the Companion Website contain almost 300 individual and group exercises for use at home, in class, and in distance learning. They include suggestions for role-plays, personal reflections, essay questions, videotaping activities, classroom discussions, and journaling—all to forward growth in knowledge and in use of self and skills.
3. *Cross-cultural and multicultural.* Multicultural considerations are integrated throughout the book, video clips, Companion Website, and Instructor's Manual. Cultural issues are addressed in all aspects of clinical work from preparation and engagement of clients to endings.
4. *Difference and diversity.* Discussion of the influences and issues of class, gender, ethnicity, sexual orientation, age, spiritual affiliation, and disability are infused throughout text content and are well represented in the DVD video clips, the Companion Website reflection and essay questions, and the Instructor's Manual.
5. *Relationship as well as skills.* Learning how to establish and maintain a productive and caring working alliance is every bit as important to effective work with people as is education about the phases, skills, and mechanics of professional interviewing. The text and video clips highlight the unfolding nature of clinical relationships and the ways in which they can help both clients and clinicians grow and change through mutual feedback and shared responsibility for outcomes.
6. *Beliefs, values, and social norms.* The text and Instructor's Manual exercises and students' own Web-based self-exploration and journaling exercises encourage and assist in their development

of greater awareness of their own values, beliefs, and social norms and how these affect all aspects of their professional relating and work.

7. *Clinician first-person accounts.* The book contains relevant, often touching stories from the field in which seasoned clinicians share personal accounts of their real-life experiences with clients. Students see that the implementation of skills is not always on target as clinicians reflect on what they learned from baffling challenges and memorable missteps. As students are exposed to many different clinicians, in different settings, from different disciplines, with different theoretical orientations, they learn that a practice principle or skill can be actualized in many creative ways, depending on the setting, on the particular needs, background, and culture of the client and on the conditions in the moment or the surround.

8. *Concrete examples.* The text is replete with clinician-client dialogues demonstrating how skills may be implemented. The accompanying video clips show actual clinicians using these skills in clinical situations in which the relationship and the work unfold with varied effects. The clinicians periodically comment on their selective choice and use of skills, comparing effects of skills used at different points in the interview or the work.

9. *Applicability to many disciplines.* Although we use the generic term *clinician* in the text, we provide practice examples from a variety of settings (group home, outpatient clinic, office, home, job, hospital, street corner) and professional roles (employee assistance worker, rehabilitation counselor, social worker, school psychologist, human service worker, drug counselor, milieu therapist, and psychiatric nurse clinician). We believe that more and more practice will occur in interdisciplinary teams and groups and that we need to move toward a shared practice language that can facilitate dialogue and collaboration.

Earlier editions of the book/video learning package have been used by beginning and advanced students of social work, psychology, counseling, human services, and nursing. They have also been used by other professionals wishing to refine or update their knowledge and skills. These disparate learners tell us they have used our materials with a common goal of relating and working more effectively with clients, and we have been very gratified by the positive feedback from them as well as from instructors using our learning package. They tell us that they like the book's lucid explanation of concepts, its down-to-earth language, its realistic practitioner examples and narratives, the chapter exercises and opportunities for students to videotape themselves in action, and the illustrative companion video clips keyed to specific text content. Instructors have commended the Instructor's Manual and its numerous chapter-by-chapter exercises and suggestions for learning activities within instructional groups. Accordingly, all of these mutually enhancing elements have been preserved and expanded in the updating of this third edition.

Students and instructors tell us that this package speaks directly to their own experiences, illustrating how to form and tend effective relationships with clients, carry out thoughtful and productive assessments and develop realistic goals, and begin to evaluate progress and outcomes. They say that they have benefited from content and class discussion about self-disclosure, maintaining one's professional self while remaining human and authentic, and spotting and dealing with inevitable missteps. Instructors and students also like the way the book and video uniquely represent diversity in both clients and clinicians—something they may not see often in educational programs, in agency life, or in learning materials and videos. Instructors and students have also appreciated the absence of clinical jargon, formality, and distance in the text and video clips. The third edition preserves these traditions.

What's New in This Edition

- The learning package now includes two hours of DVD video clips. New video clips have been developed to represent student learning content in Chapter 1 and Chapter 2. In Chapter 2 a diverse group of experienced clinicians talk about issues and challenges they have encountered in their multicultural practice and when facing ethical dilemmas. We have also added a section that now allows students to follow the relationship and work two of the six clinician-client pairs from beginning to end without interruption.

- A new Companion Website incorporates student self-exploration exercises and essay questions, a glossary, and crossword puzzles based on it, Web links, and other resources to enrich clinical learning.

- Chapter 1 has been rewritten to include direct focus on student learning process and developmental milestones on the pathway to becoming a professional clinician. The chapter describes the challenges and satisfactions of a kind of disciplined work that, at its best, leads to the mutual development of both clinician and client. We also elaborate our RE-VIEW PRACTICE Method and the integrative effects of reading, observing, trying out, and exchanging feedback.

- Chapter 2 is new and introduces students to multicultralism and ethics, which we regard as bedrocks of twenty-first century clinical education and practice. Both topics appear throughout the text, but in Chapter 2 students begin their exploration of both topics.

- In the first half of Chapter 2, we highlight the importance of multicultural practice and have students think about identity development, difference, and diversity, as well as multiple dimensions of identity. We discuss the skills and knowledge that clinicians need in order to work in our multicultural world. Multicultural Counseling Competencies are appended to the chapter.

- The second half of Chapter 2 focuses on professional codes of ethics and common ethical dilemmas that clinicians face. We emphasize the importance of ethics in protecting and affirming clients and in guiding clinicians, and we offer frameworks for decision making when dilemmas arise. Sections of actual ethics codes from various professional organizations are included in the text.

- We have deepened our discussion on the structure, content, and process of clinical formulation. We have divided Chapter 6 (formerly Assessment, Goal Setting, and Evaluation) into two new chapters (6 and 7) to provide a more in-depth discussion and illustration of the principles and process skills of assessment, formulation, goal setting, and evaluation. We emphasize the importance of scientific method, reliability and validity of methods and data, and the need for evaluation of the work from start to finish (and frequently thereafter) to identify best practices for serving clients.

- We include new content on writing a psychological report and on appropriate ways to convey diagnostic findings to clients and families. Recognizing that students increasingly work or learn in environments utilizing the DSM, we have enhanced our content on uses and critiques of the DSM, including its Cultural Formulation section.

- A new Chapter 8 (Preparing for and Evaluating Change) elaborates stages of change and core principles of Motivational Interviewing, a widely used strategy for resolving client ambivalence and helping people move toward productive change. From a strengths perpective, "resistance" is reframed as adaptive strategies clients use when feeling cornered, pushed, or ill served.

- In response to colleagues' suggestions, we have added substantial new content on working with feelings, and on helping clients identify, express, or manage their feelings. Chapter 9 is thus retitled "Helping Clients Feel and See Things Differently."

- Since our last edition, millions around the globe have been touched personally by mass traumas. We believe clinicians at all levels of development should be prepared to participate in crisis and trauma assessments and interventions in future. Accordingly, we have added to Chapter 11 new content, readings, and exercises on crisis, its effects, and suggested response strategies in the Instructor's Manual, text, and Companion Website. We also emphasize how critical it is to plan ahead regarding the resources, including language interpreters, that may be needed in the event of large-scale disasters.

- Disability is addressed as a difference or alternative way of being instead of a deficiency requiring professional intervention in every instance. Additional content and readings on disability are integrated into many of the text chapters.

- We have doubled our inclusion of content regarding the importance of spiritual and religious beliefs, practices, and faith-based initiatives in the everyday lives of people around the world. We emphasize the importance of eliciting, assessing, and working with clients' spiritual beliefs, networks, and other resources whenever such actions are appropriate and client-centered. Clinician-client examples illustrate a variety of ways clinicians can show respect and creativity in working with spirituality from a strengths perspective.

- We have added more content, readings, exercises, and examples on working in a multicultural context with clients from different cultural groups in every chapter from beginning to end. For example, we've added a section in Chapter 4 on culture-specific gestures that can misfire or offend in cross-cultural work. In Chapter 14 ("Endings and Transitions"), we include new discussion of how different cultures may benefit from a variety of ending rituals when clinician and client plan respectful endings together.

- There is increased emphasis across the chapters on the wider roles of the clinician as advocate for client services and as social activist working to eliminate oppressive, demoralizing, and traumatizing structures, institutions, and practices that cause or contribute to mental health and family problems.

- We have enhanced content on empirically based practice, treatment by objectives, and Web-based support, information gathering, and education.

About the Book

Chapter-by-Chapter Overview

Chapters 1 and 2 focus on preparing the student for skill development in future chapters. They highlight the history, nature, values, structures, and traditions of clinical practice, and discuss the relational, ethical, and multicultural nature of practice today, emphasizing that self-awareness and knowledge of others different from themselves as crucial to sensitive and informed practice. Chapter 1 focuses on the student's clinical learning pathway and anticipated challenges. We describe our RE-VIEW PRACTICE Method and its integration of read/see/do/get feedback activities that forward learning. In Chapter 2, students prepare for multicultural practice by first exploring their own multiple identities in terms of race, ethnicity, class, sexual orientation, disability, and culture. Chapter 2 includes information on professional codes of ethics and ethical dilemmas they may face in their work with clients.

Chapters 3–5 approach clinical process as a unique kind of talking, with rules, roles, mutual expectations, boundaries, layers, and the requirement of intentional, client-centered behavior on the part of the clinician. Chapter 3 explores planning and preparation for work with clients of varying backgrounds, experiences, communication skills, strengths, and service needs. We discuss special issues related to the great variety of interviewing environments (home, shelter, medical setting, street, agency office, workplace and faith-based sites, scenes of disaster) and review strategies for maintaining clinician safety in high-risk situations. We incorporate a fresh appraisal of confidentiality concerns and steps that can be taken to protect clients and their personal material. In Chapter 4, students learn and practice basic attending and listening skills and learn about the nuances of nonverbal communication. We also address issues for those communicating in a nonnative language, including the use of translators and interpreters. In Chapter 5, we discuss support and empathy as well as empathic failures, noting that empathy is a mutual process. Students learn to develop a sustaining presence that will serve as a holding environment for all ensuing clinical work and to watch for processes that can interfere with empathic responsiveness.

Because clients need to be able to explore and articulate their stories to develop reasonably attainable, meaningful, and practical goals, Chapter 6 addresses skills of exploration and elaboration, discussing the use of well timed questions, prompts, probes, reflection, and other techniques for helping clients elaborate their stories. Care is taken not to press for disclosure when working with people whose family or cultural norms and styles discourage the sharing of personal or intimate information.

Chapters 7 and 8 examine the issues and skills of assessment, goal setting, contracting, and evaluation. In Chapter 7, assessment and formulation frameworks guide students on completing an assessment, conceptualizing their findings, and writing assessment summaries or reports. Students learn how to help clients set goals for their work together based on the formulation. In Chapter 8, we discuss the stages of change. Strengths are actively identified and utilized to animate change work. Motivational Interviewing skills are demonstrated as a means of helping to resolve client ambivalences about change. Students learn about writing treatment plans and establishing working agreements or contracts, as well as about ongoing evaluation of their work together. Students are reminded to be flexible as prospects, situations, or resources change.

Chapters 9 and 10 focus on the skills of helping clients effect desired change in feelings, ideas, and behaviors. Chapter 9 focuses on strategies and skills clinicians can use to help clients recognize, express, and manage feelings while gaining new perspective on their situation and future possibilities. We provide detailed material on developing hunches that may be offered to help clients see and feel things differently, and we urge clinicians to be aware of and careful about the levels of inference in their hunches. Chapter 10 stresses behavioral change and illustrates such skills as modeling, behavioral rehearsal, and reinforcement. Clinical case management roles and advocacy activities are also emphasized as crucial assets in helping clients improve their situations and opportunities.

Chapter 11 reflects our appreciation of the ubiquity of crisis and trauma in the United States and around the world. This chapter differentiates types of crises, including the insidious trauma of racism and other forms of oppression. We discuss the ways we listen to, validate, and help to reempower those affected by trauma, either directly or vicariously. We also discuss vicarious trauma in clinicians and other crisis responders, elaborating on steps we all can take to prevent vicarious trauma so that we remain psychologically and physically fit to carry out roles that ease others' recovery.

Chapters 12 and 13 discuss advanced and thorny relational issues and challenges that can arise in work with clients. We address important issues, challenges, and clinical skills needed to work on the client-clinician relationship itself. Unlike other texts that discuss the relationship in-depth early on to set the stage for engagement of clients, we have purposely delayed detailed discussion of more complex relationship dynamics until learners have mastered some basic skills of engagement, exploration, hunching, and noticing nuances of process as the work unfolds. Chapter 12 integrates constructs from Relational-Cultural theory in discussing the relationship itself as a primary medium and force for growth and change. We provide many examples of relationship maintenance activities and problem resolution process in which clinicians own their own contributions to difficulties as these arise, and encourage client feedback about the clinician's focus, pace, and style of work. Chapter 13 focuses on boundary issues that arise when clinicians are asked to self-disclose, or when activities outside the usual meeting place occasion unplanned contact with clients, or when limits must be set on inappropriate behaviors of clients or unethical behaviors of clinicians or agency personnel.

Chapter 14 prefigures the end of the course by walking students through the issues and tasks of endings and transitions in the work. We discuss the importance of including culturally determined ending rituals. Various kinds of breaks or "planned holidays" in the work are described, and client and clinician reactions to ending are elaborated on and illustrated through examples in the text and the video. Note is taken that, when brief interventions are planned from the outset, ending is always foreshadowed so that it feels like a goal rather than a loss or painful new step. We note that when family and cultural supports have been valued and included all along in interventions, these resources become important sources of ongoing support when the work ends.

Chapter 15 describes the many satisfactions of clinical work, as well as a number of professional needs, challenges, and requirements that learners will face as they move out of educational programs and into the complex "real world" of agency life and professional interactions and responsibilities with clients. We stress the importance of ongoing self-care and self-empathy. Supervision and peer and team collaborations are also emphasized as sources of lifelong learning.

About the DVD

The DVD contains almost 180 minutes of illustrative video clips. Each chapter has companion video clips. Each topical segment is introduced with a brief explanation of its utility, followed by short clips of different clinicians illustrating either a problematic or an effective use of a skill or strategy. Watching and discussing the video segments stimulates interest in reading more about principles and clinician experiences in the text and in trying out ideas in class simulations and conversations with colleagues and instructors.

The video clips allow students to see real clinicians in action. Many people have asked us if the clinician's responses are scripted. They are not. All of the interviewers are seasoned clinicians who demonstrate a variety of different styles of skill used in response to client material. The clips of clinician group discussion of challenges in ethical and multicultural practice in Chapter 2 also lets students see seasoned colleagues spontaneously thinking aloud together about some very difficult issues in practice.

All of the participants reflect the diversity of clinicians and clients. The clinician discussion group and the six clinician-client pairs in the video are from a wide variety of ethnic backgrounds and represent men and women of color and of different ages, abilities, socioeconomic status, sexual orientations, and interpersonal styles.

Video clips follow six clinician-client relationships and their work together from beginning to end. The clinicians use a range of practice principles and skills, and the client stories represent experiences that many students and practitioners work with in a wide variety of practice settings:

- An African-American father dealing with conflict with his adolescent son
- An "out" gay man whose partner (not "out") is hospitalized following an accident
- An isolated, elderly Russian immigrant who has lost her grown daughter to cancer
- An Irish-American teen in a residential setting developing the confidence and skills to return to community life

- An Asian-American woman with mental illness working with her day treatment counselor on social anxieties mobilized at work
- A Latina woman who's been mugged and is now beset by past as well as present reactions to trauma

Clinician comments demonstrate process analysis and ownership of missteps. Clinicians in the DVD clips comment from time to time about what they did and how they felt about it. Students get to hear them discuss their thinking and responses as the work proceeds. Students also get to see that there is more than one "right" way to respond to a client. They learn that they will get to hone their own voice and style over time while working under supervision with a wide variety of clients.

The DVD clips can be used in class or at home. Students report that they enjoy reading and watching video clips at home and have also benefited greatly from watching individual clips in class, as instructors use these to illustrate concepts they are presenting. Home study and viewing have the advantage of freeing up blocks of class time from the watching of videos. This leaves more class time for questions and discussion of reading, text, and video examples, as well as challenges from the field. There is also more time for role-plays and other exercises that advance knowledge, skill application, and confidence.

About the Companion Website

The Companion Website includes over sixty self-exploration exercises and journaling experiences that heighten students' awareness of self and of others with whom students hope to work professionally. Over sixty essay questions then challenge students to go deeper in applying their theoretical understanding developed from readings, class discussions, and role-plays. Students can either store responses to questions in a notebook or journal for later discussion in class or submit them to the instructor over the Internet as part of an assignment.

The Web site also contains a glossary of definitions of the key terms at the end of each text chapter, along with crossword puzzles to be constructed from the key terms and definitions. Other resources and recommendations are available on the Web site as well.

About the Ancillaries

Instructor's Manual

The Instructor's Manual is available on the Instructor's Companion Web site and in portable booklet form. It is filled with good ideas for teaching clinical theory and process and contains almost two hundred activities for use in class or assignments for homework. For instructors new to clinical practice education, we suggest ways to structure time and to use oneself as a model to bring a spirit of collegiality to work with students in class. Each chapter begins with a brief summary of related text chapter content and an outline of text and exercise content. Outlines can be used to frame classroom sessions and to recall key concepts and their elaborative detail.

Demonstration Video

A 10-minute demonstration DVD is also available to instructors. It illustrates how students and instructors can use the book/DVD/Web site package in class, in professional settings, in distance education, and in home learning. It also allows you to "meet" us as we demonstrate our RE-VIEW PRACTICE Method in work with students.

Acknowledgments

We would like to express our continuing appreciation to a number of people. Lisa Gebo was our indispensable editor and imaginative guide for the first two editions of this book. At times we still ask ourselves, "What would Lisa advise?" We are forever grateful for her encouragement, enthusiasm for the project, insightful feedback, and unfailing good humor in helping us give birth to this project.

Dan Alpert has been our very supportive editor and helpmate for this third edition. He has been timely, resourceful, and responsive in shepherding us through the development of our text revision, new DVD, new Companion Website, and updated Instructor's Manual.

We could not have done this package without our longtime friend and collaborator, Nick Kaufman of NKP Media. He was with us from the beginning and we appreciate the art, know-how, and dynamism he has brought to the production of our video clips. His insights, discipline, and wry humor have been immeasurably helpful in the refinement of our learning package over the years. Alan Grazioso, video editor, worked tirelessly with us as we created the new video clips. He is an artist whose meticulous attention to detail has greatly enhanced the project. Terri Cook helped us in the early stages of the video production. We thank Charlie Poey for his care in the design and engineering of the DVD.

We thank the talented clinicians who generously demonstrated their work in the six clinician-client pairs: Maryann Amodeo, Brenda Clarke, Betsy Groves, Joel Hencken, Terry McCandies, Jon Reusser, and Lourdes Rodríguez-Nogués. We are also very grateful for the participation of the seasoned clinician-educators who reflected together on multiculturalism and ethics in professional work: Luz Lopez, Donna McLaughlin, Michael Melendez, and Mojdeh Rohani.

Many friends and colleagues have read the manuscript and given us feedback and advice. We deeply appreciate Robin Buhrke, Ph.D., for her detailed feedback that enriched and improved the second edition of this book and, by extension, this edition as well. We thank Peony Fhagen-Smith, Ph.D., for her insightful comments and discussions on issues of race and identity, and Cassandra Clay, LICSW, for sharing her insights about the assessment process. Many colleagues provided us with resources and forms: Debbie Leshansky Beck, Leah Fygetakis, Peggy Kaufman, Lourdes Rodríguez-Nogués, and Liz Roebuck. Margaret Gardner, librarian at Wheaton College, provided us with a workshop to help us organize our references. We thank former Wheaton students, now colleagues, Liz Brais, Nikaya Becker-Matero, and Alex Young for their help. Finally, we are most grateful to all the students and colleagues who gave us permission to use their stories and first-person accounts.

We extend thanks to the creative team at Wadsworth: Vernon Boes, for artistic and production support; Tanya Nigh, project manager; Ann Richards, assistant editor; Stephanie Rue, editorial assistant; Roberta Broyer, permissions editor; Nora Massuda, print/media buyer; and Julie Aguilar for her skill in creating our Companion Website. Thanks also to Fred Dahl, our copyeditor, for his steady feedback and especially to Jill Traut at ICC Macmillan Inc. who astutely walked us through the production process.

From Bianca Cody Murphy . . .

First and foremost I am indebted to my coauthor Carolyn for her good humor, organization, creativity, stamina, and patience. She made this project fun—we laughed and laughed. My partners at Newton Psychotherapy Associates—Priscilla Ellis, Sarah Greenberg, and Joan Berlin—have greatly shaped the way I think and practice. Over a quarter of a century of peer supervision, love, and laughter have nurtured me as a clinician and as a person. I am grateful for the support of Provost Susanne Woods and my colleagues in the psychology department at Wheaton College, who provided me with a sabbatical while I worked on this edition. In addition to my mother, Bianca R. Cody, and my brother, Joseph T. Cody, I am blessed with an ever-growing family of friends who have supported me over the years: Scott Andonian, Rui Barros, Gail Dewey, Brian Ducharme, Harriet Gordon, Patsy Greene, Sharon Lynn, Ann Maguire, Rita Messing, Lin Reicher, Lourdes Rodríguez-Nogués, and Liz Roebuck. Finally, Sue Buerkel, my partner and soul mate has been my harbor. Her love and support sustain me.

From Carolyn Dillon . . .

I am so thankful for old friends Jim Sellers, Paulina Watson, Toni Tugenberg, Agnes Sector, Julianne Wayne, and Deans Wilma Peebles-Wilkins and Gail Steketee, who have so generously supported me over the many years of this project. It goes without saying that this collaboration with Bianca Cody Murphy has been the opportunity of a lifetime. Through mutual support and feedback, we have integrated our complementary knowledge bases and abilities to elucidate values and ideas we both share. Thanks, all, for deeply enriching my life and purpose.

CHAPTER 1

Becoming a Professional

There have always been people who have helped others cope with difficulties or emotional distress. Culture has always influenced who helps, whom they help, and how they help. At different times and in different cultures, these helpful individuals may have been called shamans, elders, curanderos, healers, wise women, or pastors (Stone, 1997). These people were perceived to have special gifts or talents, and they often received specialized education or training. They were skilled in helping people deal with problems in their lives (Torrey, 1972).

In the twentieth century, a new group of helpers evolved from the urban and rural traditions of assisting people in distress: **professional clinicians.** This group includes human service workers, counselors, social workers, psychologists, milieu therapists, psychiatric nurses, and psychiatrists. Although each of these disciplines has its own philosophy, mission, and emphasis, each requires highly specialized education to prepare clinicians to become effective helpers. As knowledge of human behavior and the social environment has advanced over the last 150 years, this area of professional education has become more organized, scientific, and theory based, integrating learning in school with field-based internships or practicum.

Heavily influenced by advances in medicine, neurology, psychology, anthropology, and sociology, helping professionals created scientific procedures for data collection, intervention planning, and evaluation. Clinical education emphasized an observer's detachment and neutrality with important exceptions. Freud occasionally analyzed friends and students (Roazen, 1992). Jane Addams lived in the settlement house among the poor immigrants with whom she worked (Addams, 1910). Because few services were available for African-American children, social services pioneer Janie Porter Barrett established the Locust St. Settlement for mistreated children in her own home (Barrett, 1926; Peebles Wilkins, 1995). But a gradually emerging emphasis on detachment and "scientific objectivity" contributed to clinicians' distancing themselves more and more from daily interactions with their clients.

A major purpose of clinical education was to develop expertise in helping. As a result, clinicians began to be seen (and to see themselves) as experts. For many, expert status conferred power and prestige and led to a privileging of the clinician's knowledge over that of clients. Employment in the helping professions and the development of clinical service agencies and counseling centers served to amplify position, status, and authority. The media, which both reflect and help create social realities, often portrayed the confused client seeking help from the well dressed, respected authority, creating a dichotomy between the person needing help and the "wise helper." The licensing of clinicians further reinforced an aura of special wisdom and capability, since licensure requires years of formal preparation. It became easy for people to think of clients as empty vessels into which clinicians poured their special knowledge. Ironically, the use of arcane language and complex theory often made this knowledge less accessible to the very people with whom clinicians were trying to communicate.

Clinicians have also become both geographically and economically less accessible. As helpers have become organized and professionalized, they have often moved out of homes, neighborhoods, and street corners and into offices and agencies where their help is shaped by time constraints, bureaucratic procedures, and the income requirements of agencies and clinicians (Iglehart & Becerra, 1995). Today, many clinicians and agencies attempt to overcome this distance and become more accessible through use of technology, such as e-mail, Internet sites that provide resources, teleconferencing, and online support groups. However, Debra Parker-Oliver and George Dimiris (2006) describe the digital divide between the rich and poor and note that the use of these technological advances may themselves limit accessibility for low-income clients.

With the privatization of mental health services and the increase in managed care, clinicians may find their clinical decisions increasingly affected by their own or their agency's financial concerns and pressures. Furthermore, a focus on finances has contributed to an atmosphere of entrepreneurial competition among the various disciplines for power, authority, and clientele. Finally, the ability to pay for services affects basic access to clinical help, as well as the type and amount of help that clients receive (Gorden & Kline,

1997). These financial issues can have a particularly negative effect on people from lower socioeconomic classes (Snowden, 1993).

Western medical models have a long history of explaining and treating emotional distress in physical or medical terms (Mezzich & Kleinman, 1996; Weick, 1983). Clinicians are often trained to diagnose pathology—to find what is wrong or broken and needs to be fixed. In mental health, the mandatory use of the *Diagnostic and Statistical Manual of Mental Disorders (DSM)* (American Psychiatric Association, 2000), with its classifications of symptoms and disorders, exemplifies the emphasis on pathology. Both clinicians and clients may accustom themselves to focusing on problems and difficulties in the client's story and history to the near exclusion of strengths and successes, eliciting what family therapists Michael White and David Epston (1990) call "the problem-saturated narrative" (p. 19). The word *clinical* itself reflects a medical orientation; it is derived from the Greek *klinike,* referring to the work of the physician at the sickbed.

The focus on the "sick individual" has sometimes separated people from their families and other natural helping networks. Clinical work has often focused on issues of individual autonomy and achievement, rather than on connection and collective action for social change. Furthermore, most models of helping, counseling, and psychotherapy were developed by and for white, middle-class, able-bodied, heterosexual males and may not be appropriate for most clients (Ellis & Murphy, 1994; Guadelupe & Lum, 2005; Perez, DeBord & Bieschke, 2000; Stiver, 1991; Sue & Sue, 2003).

As a result of these complex historical forces, what could be a special conversation between two or more people all too frequently becomes a ritualized and formal interview. At times, the voice and strength of the client may seem less important than the voice and strength of the professional. The clinician has become distanced and less accessible, and it sometimes may seem more important to diagnose than to relate.

In contrast, when *we* speak of **clinical interviewing,** we mean a conversation characterized by respect and mutuality, by immediacy and warm presence, and by emphasis on strengths and potential. Because clinical interviewing is essentially relational, it requires ongoing attention to *how* things are said and done, as well as to *what* is said and done. The emphasis on the relationship is at the heart of the "different kind of talking" that is the clinical interview.

EXERCISE 1.1 Characteristics of Helpful People

Think about someone who has helped you in the past—a friend, teacher, neighbor, minister, therapist. Make a list of some of the person's characteristics that you found particularly helpful. Compare your list with those of your colleagues. Of all the helpful characteristics on everyone's list, which ones do you find in yourself and which ones do you want to develop? In your journal, record specific ways in which you need to change to be a more helpful person. List specific steps you would need to take to make the changes.

After an extensive review of the literature, Barbara Okun (1997) summarizes what she considers to be the "qualities, behaviors and knowledge of helpers [that] are most influential in affecting the behaviors, attitudes, and feelings of helpees" (p. 37): self-awareness, gender and cultural awareness, honesty, congruence, ability to communicate, knowledge, and ethical integrity.

While the focus of this book is on the development of professional skills as clinicians, we recognize the important role of those in the growing field of complementary medicine and indigenous helpers. **Complementary medicine** specialists, including acupuncturists, massage therapists, homeopaths, meditation and yoga teachers, energy workers, and spiritual guides, emphasize the harmonious integration of mind and body to achieve well-being. **Indigenous helpers** include gifted neighbors and community members to whom many people turn for advice, consolation, and concrete resources. Melvin Delgado (1997) writes about the importance of beauty parlors in Latino communities as nontraditional settings where mutual sharing and advice giving reduce the stigma of help seeking. "These settings are generally staffed by individuals who share the same ethnic, socioeconomic, and other key factors such as gender and religion as the patrons (maximizing psychological, geographical, and cultural access) and have a primary role that incorporates being a 'helper'" (p. 48). In a similar vein, Robert Taylor and his colleagues (Taylor, Ellison, Chatters, Levin, & Lincoln, 2000) describe the role of the black church as one of the first places people in African-American communities turn for emotional support and concrete resources.

■ The Clinical Interview: A Different Kind of Talking

Becoming a professional clinician can be seen as something that comes easily and naturally, a simple extension of familiar ways of caring and being that we have experienced our whole lives. Yet a clinical interview involves a kind of talking that is different from other conversations and informal helping relationships.

Purpose

Clinical interviewing is purposeful. It requires an intentional focus on the client's story, needs, and goals. This focus distinguishes it from friendly or casual conversation, in which people talk randomly about whatever they wish. Purpose and focus are always informed by assessment—the ongoing gathering of data and impressions that guide all aspects of the work. Clinicians need to stay very clear about the purpose of interviewing to avoid drifting from subject to subject in nonproductive ways. Specific purposes for clinical interviewing vary from client to client and from setting to setting. For example, the purpose may be to help a client cope with debilitating anxiety, to determine a client's eligibility for public assistance, or to help a child adjust to her parents' divorce.

Although there is a general purpose for the overall work together, there may be a number of specific goals for each session. Even if the goals are not explicitly stated, the clinician keeps them in mind. For example, the overall purpose of the work may be to help the client develop stable relationships, but, within a particular session, the goal may be to move into the history of how others in the family handle anger or to discuss why the client has canceled the last three sessions.

Although clinicians have additional reasons for clinical interviewing—to do our job, to earn money, to feel good about ourselves—the guiding purpose is to help clients. Interviewers agree to hold as their primary aim their service obligations to clients over all other interests. This commitment to put clients' needs first is abrogated only in special situations when we are concerned about the imminent safety of clients or others.

Theory

Unlike casual conversation, clinical interviewing is informed by theory. **Theory** refers to a systematic set of principles used to understand and explain observable phenomena. There are numerous schools or models of counseling and psychotherapy. John Prochaska, John Norcross, and Carlo DiClemente (1994) identified over four hundred counseling theories in North America alone. Theory shapes the content and process of clinical interviews. The interviewer's theoretical stance affects the purpose and goals of the interview, as well as how the interviewer listens and responds to the client's story.

A confused or unclear theoretical stance can manifest itself in scattered focus or abrupt shifts in style, which are jarring for the client and can derail purposeful work. At the same time, it is important not to confuse having a theoretical base with orthodoxy. A rigid adherence to theory may impede the flexibility necessary to work with clients and their stories, and it may limit the imagination needed for new theories to evolve.

Your course and field learning will expose you to some widely used and empirically supported theories of counseling and psychotherapy, including cognitive, behavioral, psychodynamic, family systems, crisis intervention, and person-centered theories. Some models of psychotherapy focus more on specific types of skills than others. For example, behavioral therapists focus on helping people to unlearn maladaptive behaviors and to learn more productive ones (Bandura, 1969; Kazdin, 2001; Miltenberger, 2004). Cognitive therapists focus on teaching clients how to combat irrational thoughts (J. Beck, 1995; Berlin, 2002; Ellis & MacLaren, 1998; Meichenbaum, 1996), while client-centered therapists maintain that empathy and relational skills are the central components necessary for therapeutic growth (Rogers, 1957). But all theoretical models require the application of basic interviewing and relational skills, such as those we discuss in this text.

Most theories are thought to apply universally to everyone, but in fact many may not be applicable to the diverse people seeking help. Consequently, a number of writers have proposed theories of multicultural counseling and therapy that emphasize the interactive effects of ethnicity, culture, race, color, class, gender, sexual orientation, spirituality, ability, and age (Atkinson, 2004; Devore & Schlesinger, 1996; Lum, 2004; Ponterotto, Casas, Suzuki, & Alexander, 2001; Sue & Sue, 2003).

Scientific Base

Graduate education in psychology often emphasizes what has been called the **scientist/practitioner model.** David Barlow and Mark Durand (1999) note that clinicians are consumers of science (studying the "latest scientific developments in their field"), evaluators of science ("evaluat[ing] their own assessments or treatment procedures to see if they work"), and creators of science ("conducting research that leads to new procedures useful in practice") (p. 5).

Clinicians study and critically evaluate psychological, biological, and social science research to inform their practice. They also carry out evaluations of programs and procedures to keep improving the services rendered. Clinical practice is increasingly based on evidence from scientific research. Clinicians seek to provide clients with empirically validated programs and methods that have been demonstrated to be effective with particular problems and populations; this effort is sometimes referred to as evidence-based practice (EBP) (Chambless & Hollon, 1998; Chambless et al., 1998; Cournoyer, 2004). However, there is not much research on the applicability of empirically validated therapies to people from different cultures, nor has then been much empirical validation of culturally sensitive therapies (Atkinson, Bui, & Mori, 2001; Lum, 2004; Weaver, 2005).

Structure

In addition to being purposeful and informed by theory, clinical interviews are structured. Both the specific interview and the overall process have a beginning, a middle, and an end, and each phase of the process has its own tasks and emphases. The first and continuing task is to make and sustain a warm, trustful, and collaborative relationship in which clients feel comfortable sharing and elaborating their stories. In the middle phase, clinicians and clients work together to develop new perspectives, skills, and resources from which change can evolve. In the last phase, the review and evaluation of the work and relationship occur, and plans for the future, including follow-up, are discussed.

A second kind of structure is the organization the clinician brings to the clinical interview. At times, clinicians may guide the conversation by the questions we ask, by the issues we respond to, by the subjects we introduce, or by the focus we keep. In addition, we establish rules and norms for behaviors, as well as boundaries around the relationship itself.

Time constraints also impose structure. Clinical interviewing is usually limited to a specified amount of time. The length of any individual meeting, as well as the number of meetings, is usually fixed, especially in **managed care** settings in which clients get a fixed number of visits for defined health or mental health problems. Time limits allow both clinicians and clients to know how much time is available to them for the work they do together. Because meeting time can be a scarce commodity today, it is usually regarded as sacrosanct and inviolable except in extreme circumstances. It should be noted that setting time limits on the length of the clinical interview and the helping relationship is a cultural artifact.

Contract

The participants in a clinical interview enter into a contract. The contract is a working agreement that specifies such things as the participants, purpose, goals, roles, expectations, techniques, time, structure, and cost of care. In evidence-based practice, the contract includes an agreement to carry out the systematic measurement of the client's functional levels. Our findings inform and guide subsequent goals, methods, and activities.

Contracts should be mutually developed so that participants are clear about their responsibilities and commitments, and they should be tailored to the client's style, needs, and language. The specific goals should be realistic and attainable, taking into account the stresses, strengths, and resources in the client's network. The more explicit the contract is, the better it is; the clearer the map is, the more likely the participants will arrive at the desired destination. Due to the shifting realities and resources in people's lives, contracts need to be flexible and subject to renegotiation.

Roles

Clinical interviews usually have two major prescribed roles: that of the client and that of the clinician. The client brings special knowledge of his or her own history and traditions, resources for growth and development, and particular strengths and coping skills. The clinician brings the special knowledge of human behavior, psychological theory, systems theory, and communication skills.

The behavioral components of these roles are complex and varied, and they often overlap. People frequently think of the client as narrating the story while the clinician listens, sustains, and guides. However, in most interviews there is flexibility in behaviors, and, from moment to moment, either participant could be speaking or listening, guiding or following. Although the client is expected to do more of the talking, at times the clinician says more, as when sharing hunches, confronting client behaviors, educating about resources, or detailing necessary procedures. Regardless of participants' behaviors at any given moment, as clinicians, we should always be cognizant of our responsibility to remain focused on the purpose and goals of the interview and on the client's needs. This principle applies whether we are trying to engage gang members on a street corner, listening to a new mother grieve the sudden loss of her baby, or taking an intake phone call from a lonely elderly man threatening to kill himself.

Neither the clinician's nor the client's role comes naturally to people; both clinicians and clients have to be educated about the expectations, responsibilities, and behaviors required by each role. You will learn about the requirements of your roles from academic study, field supervisors, and client feedback. Because clients may have had no experience with clinical interviews before they meet with you, it will be incumbent on you to orient them to roles, procedures, and expectations, inviting questions and feedback to minimize confusion or misunderstandings.

Whenever I begin to work with a new client, I spend part of the first interview talking about the nature of the clinical relationship. I have always liked the feminist therapy analogy that compares the clinician to a midwife. Therapy is explained as a process in which the client gives birth to new parts of herself. Like birth, the process is often painful but very exciting. I see myself as someone who has skills and training to assist her with the birthing process. I stress that I will work with her, sometimes comforting, sometimes supporting, sometimes encouraging as she gives birth.[1]

Labels

Labels and titles also distinguish clinical conversation from other forms of talking. A variety of labels may be used to describe the participants in a clinical interview. At times, the labels for clinicians designate a discipline: mental health counselor, psychologist, social worker, clinical psychiatric nurse, human service worker, psychiatrist, pastoral counselor. At other times, labels are used to try to capture the roles and tasks of particular groups of clinicians: group facilitator, intake worker, case manager. And sometimes labels designate a specialization within a discipline: school counselor, neuropsychologist, geriatric social worker, forensic psychologist.

EXERCISE 1.2   By Any Other Name

Following is a list of terms used to describe the roles of a clinical interviewer. Each may have different meanings or nuances for different people. Apply each term to yourself, and, as you do so, notice any change in your feelings about or perception of yourself or your status as a helper. Record your observations in your journal. If you were a client, how would you feel seeing a professional with each of these labels?

interviewer	case manager
provider	shrink
therapist	life coach
clinician	change agent
counselor	helper
crisis worker	advocate
milieu therapist	analyst

---

[1]Numerous first-person accounts from clinicians in the field are included in this text.

Another category of labels is used to designate people with whom clinicians work: client, patient, member, resident, student, consumer, helpee. At times, the labels connote the setting; persons in a hospital may be called patients, and those in a halfway house may be referred to as residents. At other times, the labels reflect the customs of specific disciplines, agencies, or individuals.

> *I remember when many social workers in the fifties and sixties called their clients "patients" wishing to achieve a professional standing or recognition similar to that of psychiatrists and psychologists. A woman would come to the family service agency seeking housing and financial aid, but, in case conference, she would be described as "the patient." During the activist period of the seventies there was a shift to calling people "clients" to be more egalitarian. In the eighties, people with mental illness and their advocates asked that clients be referred to as "consumers," giving them more power, choice, and initiative in their relationships with governmental and service systems. With the advent of managed care and its medical model, I've noticed a resurgence in the use of the term "patients."*

> *I've worked in a couple of day treatment programs for mentally retarded adults. In one, we called the participants "patients"; in another, "clients"; in another, "club members." I have lots of discussions with colleagues who object to my using the term "patient." They say it reflects a medical model that focuses on illness. They accuse me of being into power dynamics and suggest I call them "clients" instead. I like the word "patient" because for me it implies caring for the other.*

Labels can be helpful in directing people toward specific disciplines, functions, or specialties, but they can be confusing: People with differing labels can all be performing the same roles or functions. The social worker, psychologist, and counselor may all provide counseling or psychotherapy. The client, the patient, the consumer, and the resident may all exhibit similar strengths and problems.

Labels can also obscure the fact that clinicians can have problems at the same time and of the same types as clients do. The distance between labels can appear great, whereas the actual distance between people and their narratives is less so. For example, a clinician may see a client during one hour and then, in the next hour, go to see his or her own therapist.

Labels may be used to express power, prestige, and status. They can also be used to distance, demean, and stereotype. How we connote ourselves and others has an impact on our relationship and interactions with them and on theirs with us. We need to guard against feelings of self-importance and unearned privilege that may be offensive to both clients and colleagues.

A Unique Relationship

Clinical interviewing engenders an intimacy between strangers. Even though the client and clinician have different roles, their unique relationship is like a fishbowl in which both regularly observe and experience the nuances of each other's behaviors and feelings. Just as we observe clients, clients observe us and note our subtle reactions. They observe when we seem focused and present and when we seem distracted and preoccupied. They notice what we attend to and emphasize and what we overlook and ignore. And just as clinicians may sit around and discuss clients in a team conference, clients often sit around and discuss clinicians' mannerisms and idiosyncrasies in great detail. Both clinicians and clients become known to each other in ways that are truly intimate, special, and rare.

I have a client who has noticed that when I sneeze it's usually in a series of three sneezes. I can't believe how attentive he is to my behavior.

Clinical interviewing occurs in the context of a relationship that involves a peculiar kind of mutuality. **Mutuality** refers to the fact that, although the interview focus is on the client's needs, the clinician is also affected by the give-and-take of the relationship. Both people inevitably grow and change through the give-and-take of an authentic and genuine relationship with each other (Jordan, 1991a). The peculiar part of this mutuality is that, while it is mutual, it is not equal. For example, it is chiefly the client who is regularly expected to reveal personal information in exquisite detail, while the clinician discloses personal information only on a very selective basis.

I often talk with clients about this "weird" relationship of therapy. Although clients may not know much about the facts of my personal life, and I usually know a lot about theirs, I still feel as though they know me in a very real and intimate way.

Both the clinician and the client share responsibility for the process and the progress of the work. Yet because of our education, experience, and ethical and legal mandates, we are held accountable for its effectiveness and assume greater responsibility for the safety of the relationship. Furthermore, the relationship frequently entails an unspoken power imbalance due to the authority that many people vest in clinicians because of their professional licensing, status, roles, education, experience, and reputation as knowledgeable and caring people. Clients may attribute a special authority to clinicians working in governmental, armed services, or law enforcement agencies such as courts, protective services, probation, or first responder teams. Finally, the client may literally be paying for the relationship, and the clinician is the one being paid.

I have had clients say, "I can't believe I have to pay someone to listen to me" or "I can't believe I have to pay to have a friend." I gently remind them that they're paying for my skills, not my friendship.

Intentional Use of Self

We pay careful attention to the **intentional use of self** in the interview process. One of the paradoxes of clinical work is that clinicians are asked to be genuine, yet self-aware and deliberate at the same time (Rogers, 1980).

When I'm supervising students, they always ask how to decide when it's okay to be spontaneous and "real" and when it's not. It's one of the hardest things to teach and learn in clinical work. Even after I share my opinions and the theories behind them, students often act spontaneously, doing and saying things without much thought beforehand. They confuse being deliberate with being artificial. It takes a while to learn that one can be both genuine and deliberate.

As much as possible, clinicians behave in considered or deliberate ways. Learning to be purposeful and goal-focused in your responses is one of the continuing challenges as you move from random and spontaneous chatting with clients and others, to saying or asking things for a clinical purpose. At times you may intentionally alter your style or behaviors to support client comfort and growth.

I am usually a very quiet, laid-back kind of counselor. I convey my attentiveness through eye contact, facial expression, and head nods. This usually works well with the clients I see at the clinic. When I was seeing Juan, I realized I had to change my style. He was legally blind and needed more verbal feedback and responsiveness from me.

As clinicians, we also make very deliberate decisions about what we share about ourselves with clients. Personal sharing should occur only if the clinician believes that it forwards the goals of the work and only after careful consideration of its effect on the client. In Chapter 13, we will examine in greater depth issues surrounding personal sharing and disclosure.

Throughout the interview process, we also attend to our own actions and reactions. This attending to self is important for several reasons. First, we need to be aware of what our reactions may convey to clients, both intentionally and unintentionally. Second, the reactions that the client's story evokes in us may provide important information about responses the client may engender in others. Third, introspection increases our own self-knowledge, which is essential to the appropriate use of self in clinical interviewing. In addition, client stories or feelings may stir up the clinician's own old, unfinished business, signaling a need for further attention. One of the most complex tasks that clinicians have to master is that of attending to many things simultaneously.

Listening on Multiple Levels

Any conversation takes place on several levels and has several forms of communication: verbal and nonverbal communication, overt and covert communication, content and process communication, and metacommunication— the messages about the message. In clinical interviewing, clinicians listen intently to all of these types and levels of communication. We listen to what clients say as well as to how they say it. We listen to our own inner process and the relationship process. And we listen to what is happening in the work and what is happening in the surrounding world.

Evaluation

Unlike most conversations, clinical interviewing involves evaluation. Clinicians examine their work session by session to assess the effectiveness of the specific focus, activities, techniques, and uses of self. Progress and process notes, audiocassettes, and videotapes are all helpful. They review their work on a regular basis with supervisors and occasionally with outside consultants who have particular expertise.

Clinicians also engage clients in an ongoing evaluation of how things are going. Clinicians and clients can review the relationship and what has been accomplished through informal check-ins and by using formal progress and outcome measures. These activities allow the clinician and client to document whether measurable positive change is occurring. There is usually a process of formal evaluation at the end of the working relationship. Follow-up evaluations at specified periods after the work has ended can track how well gains from the work are being maintained.

Informed by Ethics and Values

Unlike friendly conversation, clinical interviewing is governed by professional codes of ethics and by laws requiring or prohibiting specific clinician activities. Ethical codes stress the primacy of the service obligation to the client, confidentiality, integrity, and follow-through. They enjoin clinicians from practicing beyond our level of competence and prohibit dual relationships between clinicians and clients. Chapter 2 provides more detailed discussion of ethics and ethical dilemmas.

Clinical interviews should reflect that we value the dignity and worth of all people. They should actively work to identify and eliminate ways of thinking, speaking, or acting that may reflect racism, classism, sexism, ableism, homophobia, religious discrimination, ageism, and other oppressive ideologies. We should convey nonjudgmental acceptance without necessarily approving of specific behaviors.

We believe that clinicians should do more than just think or behave ethically with clients. Ethical codes encourage us to take stands against social forces and institutions that impinge on clients' rights, health, and welfare. We should work in social and economic justice campaigns; fight to end discrimination on the basis of language, country of origin, and cultural practices; and work to change unjust laws and structures that are barriers to client well-being and achievement.

Multiculturalism, Difference, and Diversity

Our society is increasingly pluralistic and multicultural. In our private lives, we are free to decide whether we want to interact with people who differ from us in significant ways or whether we want to carry out our lives mostly with people like ourselves. However, in our professional lives, human service workers regularly interview clients whose class, race, ethnicity, religion, age, language, ability, gender, living situations, cultural practices, values, and norms differ from our own. Note that we do not make assumptions about any clinician's identity. While there is not as much diversity as there should be among those entering and leading our professions (Malgady & Zayas, 2001), gains have been made, and we recognize that clinicians now can be from any country, language, and cultural group, as well as of any race, ethnic group, color, class, size, sexual orientation, spiritual affiliation, physical ability, and age.

Differences are not just limited to cultural differences. You will work with clients who differ from you in terms of age, race, culture, ability, class, gender, family form, sexual orientation, and religion. Knowledge about, experience with, and appreciation of the norms, styles, and strengths within these differences will help you attend to them earlier and more comfortably as you develop as a professional.

We believe that only if we are knowledgeable about and sensitive to a wide range of cultural values, norms, and nuances can we hope to devise appropriate and effective clinical interventions. We discuss issues of multicultural competence in Chapter 2.

EXERCISE 1.3   Your Values and Beliefs

Core values and beliefs are often learned from families and are strongly affected by culture and important reference groups. In your journal, record some of the guiding beliefs and values that are important to you. Do you anticipate that some professional values will challenge your personal beliefs?

Worldview

All clinical interviewing is embedded in a worldview—a system of values and beliefs—that shapes clinical work. A worldview usually has both explicit and implicit elements, both conscious and unconscious influences. We believe it is very important that clinicians use continuing education, supervision, and personal reflection to be aware of the assumptions guiding their professional practice and be able to articulate them clearly.

■ Our Worldview

Our own worldview is both **ecological** and **systemic.** Like all ecological and systemic practitioners, we recognize and appreciate the interactivity and interdependence of all living and nonliving things; we believe that there are biological, psychological, sociocultural, political, economic, spiritual, and environmental influences in what appears to be "individual" human behavior or isolated family interactions (Bateson, 1972; Bronfenbrenner, 1979;

von Bertalanffy, 1968). We believe that people can best be understood in the context of the relationships, resources, and barriers to well-being in their lives. Furthermore, like many ecopsychologists, we believe human beings are affected not only by their relationships with others but also by their relationships with both the animate and inanimate environments (Roszak, Gomes, & Kanner, 1995). Therefore, we pay as much attention to the circumstances and the relationships of our clients, and to the effects of the larger world on them, as we do to their internal processes.

EXAMPLE

Mickey, a drug-abusing teenager, is arrested carrying a gun. In the subsequent court evaluation, it is learned that his mother is a prostitute doing prison time for heroin addiction and shoplifting. His father was killed a few years earlier in a drug raid. The boy lives with an aunt who works two jobs to support many extended kin; however, he often sleeps at friends' apartments, doing and selling drugs, and watching MTV. One could speculate that Mickey's behavior may result from his negative perceptions of self, which he has internalized because of the neglect and abandonment he has experienced at the hands of his adult caregivers. In addition, Mickey suffers from attention deficit disorder related to ingesting lead paint and being exposed to other environmental toxins dumped in his community, and he could be using drugs to calm his symptoms. Several local companies have moved their factories and supermarkets out of the community, leaving few jobs or career prospects in the town other than drug dealing. Furthermore, expanded military expenditures at a time of balanced budgets resulted in the closing of teen programs in his area so that his main opportunity for friendship is gang membership. The clinician working with Mickey needs to recognize all the factors that have an impact on him, including family, friendships, economic trends, corporate policies, political decisions, and environmental pollution.

In clinical interviews, we always listen for **reciprocal influences**—how every member of an interaction influences, and is influenced by, the others. Because of our belief in reciprocal influence, we do not believe that clinicians are "detached," "neutral," or "objective observers." Therefore, we pay special attention to how clients and clinicians influence and affect each other's behaviors in the course of their work together.

Our work is also influenced by the family systems concept of **circular causality** (Bateson, 1979). Events in complex systems often exist as both causes and effects of each other. Clinicians frequently see couples in which each partner blames the other for the troubles in their relationship. For example, one partner showers the other with affection, wishing to become more intimate. The other partner, feeling smothered and invaded, becomes unresponsive and withdrawn. The first partner, alarmed at the distancing, doubles his or her attentions. This dance often goes on indefinitely, ending all too frequently in acrimonious debates about who is doing what to whom. In this example, the first partner may describe the interaction as follows: "My partner pulls away, so I have to chase after him to get close." The second partner may say, "My partner invades me, so I retreat." In trying to make sense of complex related behaviors, people tend to see behaviors as having starting points (causes) and stopping points (effects). However, the choice of a specific event as a starting or stopping point is arbitrary.

Furthermore, we recognize that systems are in constant flux, that life is not homeostatic, and that we are seeing the client at only one point in time. If we enter the relationship with a client at another point, we might see a different person. Clients often make contact with clinicians at a time of crisis, when they are stressed and burdened. What we see is only a snapshot of the person at that difficult moment in time. If we were to see that person at other times, in more supportive circumstances or in more empowered interaction with others, we might describe and respond to the person very differently.

Leslie was a very quiet, shy girl in my office. She was often quite teary and self-effacing. She had almost no self-confidence and was very soft-spoken. When I went to see her on the soccer field, I couldn't believe it was the same girl. She was so sure of herself: She gave orders to the other kids on her team; she laughed and yelled.

Clients may show different aspects of themselves even within the same session. A client may talk about a parent in a regressed, childlike manner and then speak with authoritative confidence when discussing events at work.

We believe that there are **multiple realities,** or differing views about how things are, how they got that way, and how they ought to be. Clinicians need to be careful not to assume that their "reality," or point of view, is more correct or more meaningful than the client's. Each has knowledge and experience that informs and changes the other and the work, validating the strengths of both (Daniel, 2000; Jordan, 2004a).

We believe that all people's ideas are worthy of consideration and that silencing or excluding individuals or groups is the surest road to misunderstanding large segments of human experience. Moreover, clients are sometimes more attuned to both the hard realities and the natural supports of complex environments than clinicians are. Clinicians usually learn a great deal from client knowledge, experience, and perspective.

Experienced clinicians have long observed that, no matter how irrational things may seem to us as outside observers of others' lives, to the people living those lives, the "irrationality" may represent their best adaptation at the moment—a sensible way of negotiating daily life under oppressive circumstances. Clinicians must make continuing efforts to immerse themselves in the client's perspective rather than dragging the client into their own constructions of reality.

We are aware of the growing importance of spirituality in the lives of both clinicians and clients. Spiritual beliefs affect people's worldview—how they make meaning, how they feel about themselves, and how they relate to other people and to the larger world. Spiritual practices can be an important part of a client's plan for change and a resource that can be called on to empower both the client and clinician (Canda, 1997; Canda & Furman, 1999; Hodge, 2003; Walsh, 1999).

Clients often seek clinical help when they are stuck because they have a limited perspective. One of the major goals of therapy is to help clients broaden their perspective, to see things using different lenses, to construct new realities, or to reframe their situations. Indeed, we wish to foster in ourselves and in our clients a growing capacity to appreciate different and even competing perspectives.

> *I often tell clients that we don't have to agree and twin with each other, but we both need to listen with open minds. What appears off target one week may resonate clearly three weeks later. And this cuts both ways. A client may share an idea or an interpretation of an event different from my own, and while at first I may disagree, on reflection I come to see that interpretation as a very novel and helpful take on the situation, and I say that to the client.*

Our perspective is characterized by a deep and abiding belief in the capacity of human beings to grow and change in positive relationships and contexts that activate potentials and provide for the meeting of basic human needs. A **strengths perspective** undergirds all effective clinical intervention. Working within a strengths perspective, we try as frequently as possible to elicit and underscore the often undervalued or unnoticed strengths with which clients have successfully addressed problems (Saleebey, 2005; Weick, Rapp, Sullivan, & Kisthardt, 1989).

Clients often report that professionals have asked them so often to recite what is *not* working that they forget to mention or to value what *has* worked. Clinicians' valuing of unsung acts of valor or achievement, no matter how small, can often fan a spark of hope. Noticing and validating strengths can bring new meaning to clients who have seen themselves (or who have been seen by others) as hopeless, incompetent, or of no importance.

In addition to helping clients gain new perspectives on their circumstances, clinicians may also work with clients to modify their circumstances. We may do so through direct advocacy, such as helping a client get welfare benefits, find day care, or gain access to a training program. We may also advocate for populations, such as when we work on getting legislation passed to fund school lunch programs, support the funding of community day programs for people with Alzheimer's disease, or testify regarding the need for programs for the homeless (Rappaport, 1987).

Finally, we believe that clinicians must work for social change. An old public health adage maintains that, instead of retrieving individual drowning victims one after the other from the river, we must go upriver to determine and eliminate the causes of the drownings. Part of our professional responsibility is to work for the health and mental health of our clients and to prevent conditions that contribute to disease and distress.

A **social justice perspective** informs our professional ethic of care. We believe that we have a social responsibility to work for a more equitable distribution of resources, rights, and opportunities for all people (Swenson, 1998). Clinicians must nourish structures and processes that encourage growth and development and oppose all forms of oppression and environmental degradation.

Activism may be a part of our professional role, such as when we join with other clinicians to work for social change through organizations like Psychologists for Social Responsibility, Social Workers for Peace and Disarmament, and The Public Interest Directorate of the American Psychological Association. At times, we may use our professional skills as volunteers in community agencies or in responding to national disasters.

Following the bombing of the Federal Building in Oklahoma, I was part of a team of clinicians who volunteered to work with child survivors and their families. As an expert on trauma in children, I was glad to offer my services.

I always feel that it is important to do volunteer work using my clinical skills. A couple of years ago, a group of friends and I began a series of support groups for people newly diagnosed with AIDS. Now we are using the same skills to help train peer leaders for a breast cancer support group. I can't tell you how much both experiences have enriched my life and my clinical work.

Our sense of social responsibility also involves personal activism, which leads us to organize, disseminate leaflets, and march. It takes us to state and national capitals to lobby, picket, and become leaders in political bodies that wield real power to effect large-scale change. It stimulates us to speak and write in the media and not only for scholarly meetings and journals.

I was part of a team that conducted research with families about the psychological effects of exposure to nuclear radiation. We interviewed atomic veterans who were exposed during the aboveground atomic testing in the United States. A couple of years later, I went with a group of mental health clinicians to the nuclear test site in Nevada to protest continued underground nuclear testing. We were subsequently arrested with hundreds of other protesters for trespassing on federal property.

■ Learning to be a Professional

Many people decide to become clinicians because they have a strong desire to help others. Some pursue clinical education to advance into leadership roles where they are already employed or to gain new or advanced knowledge and skills as community organizers, activists, and social policy advocates. Gerald Corey and Marianne Schneider Corey (2003) suggest other goals—some conscious, some not—that move people toward clinical careers, including a desire to find and provide answers to problems, to learn more about themselves and their own problems, to make money as therapists, or to gain professional power, prestige, or status.

You may have decided to become a clinician because you have been told that you are a good listener and **natural helper**, who leaves people feeling understood and supported. You may be the "go-to" person for friends or family when problems arise. Perhaps you have prior experience as a community volunteer, Big Brother, Red Cross crisis worker, camp counselor, or hotline staffer. You may have experience in the mental health field, or you may be moving from a career in religious work, business, teaching, law, nursing, or an allied health profession. We all come with a set of strengths, skills, and natural helping styles.

Natural Style

Edward Neukrug and Alan Schwitzer (2006) note that natural helpers can be classified as natural "listeners, analyzers, problem solvers, or challengers" (p. 4). Those who are natural listeners are good at "active listening, empathic understanding, and rapport building" (p. 5). Analyzers are interested in understanding what causes problems for the client: They focus on "case conceptualization, diagnosis, and treatment planning" (p. 6). Problem solvers want to get things done: They "tend to be more directive, attempting to mobilize the person in need to make decisions, take action and decisively change behavior" (p. 6). Finally, challengers believe that they "can quickly push the client into seeing the world in a different manner, and will often confront clients through the use of questions, particularly 'why?' questions" (p. 7).

EXERCISE 1.4 Natural Style

In your journal, describe your own natural style. If others have commented on your helping style, what did they say? Discuss in class what you like about your style and what you might want to change or augment.

Growing from a natural helper into a professional clinician requires engaged interactive learning. Therefore, you can advance your learning best through work in relationships with others. Instructors, fellow students, colleagues, and clients will help you acquire and utilize knowledge and skills and shape your professional values, ethics, and attitudes.

The RE-VIEW PRACTICE Method

We have developed the RE-VIEW PRACTICE Method for acquiring and enhancing the skills of helping. The elements of the method build on and reinforce each other. The RE-VIEW acronym represents the key elements in becoming a more comfortable and informed professional:

- Read about skills, their purpose, and intended effects.
- Explore and discuss the skills in class.

- View instructors and other experienced clinicians employing the skills.
- Implement the skills in videotaped role-play exercises.
- Evaluate your performance.
- Watch your videotapes with others, giving and receiving feedback.

Read

Reading about clinical work is often a first step in formal education. You should read widely about different perspectives on clinical relationships and specific theories from the professional literature in social work, psychology, counseling, psychiatry, and nursing. We also encourage reading in sociology, anthropology, biology, economics, mind-body health, religious and spiritual practices, politics, literature, and history. Since you are dealing with the complexity of people from a variety of backgrounds, experiences, and social contexts, you should read about race, class, disability, sexual orientation, immigration, and gender and age discrimination so that you are well informed and can attend to differences and intragroup variations. We also suggest additional reading from popular literature to help you expand your knowledge base.

Also read about specific skills related to interviewing and helping. This book is designed to walk you through clinician–client work from preparation to ending, discussing the skills commonly used in each work phase and the complexity of issues that can arise in the clinical relationship. Cross-cultural and multicultural practice considerations and skills infuse text content.

Explore

Evaluate what you read judiciously. Rather than just swallowing elegant or compelling theories in which practice is grounded, become a critical thinker. Ann Marie Mumm and Robert Kersting (1997) suggest that **critical thinking** involves dividing theories into their conceptual constructs, assumptions, and hypotheses; understanding the history and context that inform these constructs; and evaluating their strengths, weaknesses, and practice implications.

Skill application is heightened as instructor and classmates provide examples of how, when, with whom, and for what purposes a skill may be useful. Discussion and examples will help you apply skills in meaningful client-centered, nonjudgmental, culturally knowledgeable, and appropriate ways.

Clinical learning also demands self-examination and **introspection**— looking within yourself to appraise the nature, intensity, and meanings of feelings, thoughts, and dynamics that can affect your interviewing behaviors. Learn to articulate your values and beliefs, become aware of your use of self in relationships with clients, and uncover and correct misinformation and bias.

To help you transform accrued information and experience into a humbling yet empowering blend of reflective wisdom, common sense, and compassionate action, we have included a number of activities in the text and on the Companion Website. They contain critical thinking questions to help you reflect on readings and controversial issues, along with self-exploration exercises to surface your personal values and potential blind spots. Many of the activities can be done in class; others can be done at home. We suggest that you keep a journal of your clinical exercise experiences and reflections for discussion in class with instructors and colleagues.

View

An important aspect of learning about the structure, process, and skills of clinical work is to see interviewing in action. One way to accomplish this is to observe supervisors and other highly skilled clinicians at work. With the client's permission, you may be able to observe clinical work through a one-way mirror or sit in on a seasoned colleague's sessions. If you do not have the opportunity to observe clinical work as it occurs, many videotapes and films are available in which clinicians demonstrate skills informed by particular models of therapy.

While watching entire interviews is useful, we agree with Allen and Mary Bradford Ivey (2003) that students learn best by studying "microskills"— the small-skill components of interviewing. The DVD accompanying this text contains clips of six clinicians from diverse backgrounds in clinical relationships with six diverse clients. The clips depict their work as it unfolds over a period as short as one day and as long as a couple of months. Each clip illustrates specific skills keyed to chapter content in the text. At times you will see more than one clinician using the same skill, to illustrate the different ways in which clinicians implement the same skill. In time you too will want to develop your own "voice" and way of implementing specific skills.

We believe it is important to observe as many clinicians as you can to see that clinicians all work somewhat differently, often while applying many similar guiding principles. We are pleased about the increasing number and range of tapes and DVD clips available now showing a range of clinicians using an array of skills and working with a variety of clients. When we were in school, we watched videotapes that almost exclusively showed older white male gurus interviewing depressed white women—not at all representative of the diversity we experienced in our internships.

Implement the Skills

Reading about and viewing skills in action are not sufficient. You must *do the work.* The best way to advance clinical understanding and skills is to work with clients and to get feedback from supervisors. As you begin your work with clients, you need other ways to learn and practice skills. Role-play sessions with students and colleagues can help you prepare for clinical work. If your school or internship site has a video lab or equipment, tape your clinical interactions and view them alone or with others for learning purposes. As your skill and confidence grow, you will begin to develop your own informed style, voice, and way of using specific skills with different clients.

We present a number of role-play exercises in the text and on the Companion Website. Sometimes we present a situation for student "client" and "clinician" to play out. At other times the instructor may play a client with whom you can practice your skills.

Evaluate Performance Together

Continuous reflection on your work is crucial, no matter what stage or level you are at in your training or experience. One very sound way to evaluate and modify your professional style is to make yourself an open and honest recipient of other people's evaluations during your class and field education. Reviewing and rehearing what you said and did is often extremely revealing. Feedback from videotape recordings and direct observation helps us plan and guide further learning and skill development.

In internship case conference presentations, you will get to see senior staff sharing observations and recommendations about interactions that clinicians have had with their clients—why they might have done and said what they did and how to improve on the process. Classroom feedback from role-plays and videotaped dialogues demonstrate how different instructors and classmates make evaluative comments and suggestions. From hearing how others express their feedback and by trying out feedback styles yourself as you comment on your classmates' role-play interactions, you become a better observer of yourself, developing self-observation language from what you have heard others say.

Process recordings constitute a wonderful way to reflect on clinical work. Of the many forms of **process recording,** we suggest writing a verbatim transcript of the interview (role-played or real) on one side of the paper. The other side can contain comments about the process—what you were intending to do, what you were thinking or feeling at a given point in the interview, and what you think the client was thinking or feeling. At the end of the recording, you can summarize new observations about yourself and the client from the interview experience, as well as what you wish you had done or said differently. You can also note questions for supervision and requests for specific help in skill building.

Watch

Reviewing your video and process recordings, both alone and in supervision, provides the opportunity for self-reflection and knowledge building. Observing your own work on video can provide guidance for personal growth because it reveals unhelpful reactions and behaviors in interviews, as well as bias or visible discomfort with certain clients.

Practice, Practice, Practice

The last part of the RE-VIEW PRACTICE Method is practice. While practice does not make you a perfect clinician, it makes you better and better. Learning to be a clinician is a lifelong process of knowledge acquisition and growth in self and skills. So you have to continue your professional development by reading, by practicing with many different clients and supervisors, and by giving and receiving feedback as you watch yourself and others at work, in self-aware and informed interaction with others.

CLIP 1.1
The RE-VIEW
PRACTICE Method

Instructors, fellow students, colleagues, and clients will help you in acquiring and utilizing knowledge and skills, as well as in shaping your professional values, ethics, and attitudes. Though becoming a professional is enjoyable and exciting, you will face many challenges as you begin the learning process.

EXERCISE 1.5   Lights, Camera, Action

Pair up with someone in class. Before you learn more about the skills of helping, videotape yourself trying to have a helpful 10-minute role-play conversation with a peer. Notice how you feel as you watch yourself on tape. Save the tape so that you can see how you change and how you build on your basic strengths throughout the semester.

The Challenges Ahead

Moving from Spontaneous to Intentional

An inextricable part of becoming a clinician is learning to be aware of oneself, the client, the work, and the environment—all at the same time. Clinicians constantly observe, evaluate, and modify their clinical interactions to remain client-centered and goal-focused, and to know where the client is from moment to moment.

This planned use of self and skills requires restraint of some of our natural impulses and feelings. It can be difficult to feel genuine and intentional at the same time. Arnold Lazarus (1981) describes how a clinician friend of his wanted to become a therapist but was so intently focused on "acting like a therapist" that he lost his natural ability to help. Students often comment that they feel phony or awkward when they are thinking so much before they act. The challenge is to become comfortable as both an observant bystander and a genuine human being present in the moment.

Working Under a Microscope

The scrutiny of your knowledge, skills, and relational capacities by teachers, supervisors, and colleagues can be difficult. Trying out new skills while being observed can make beginning clinicians feel paralyzed and aware of every word and move. Many people describe this self-conscious shake-up in confidence and behaviors as they begin to receive supervisory and collegial feedback. You may experience unnecessary worry about whether you are as good as others who seem to have more knowledge, poise, comfort in self-revelation, and ease in role-play and case presentation or who just seem generally better suited for clinical work.

You may discover that your own ethnic or age group is not widely represented in the faculty, internship staff, and student body, and you may feel marginalized or expected to represent your reference group in discussions about diversity. You may be placed in a spotlight and feel self-conscious and even angry when colleagues turn to you expecting you to be the "expert" regarding some aspect of your identity or background.

You may come from a family or culture in which so much focus on yourself would be regarded as self-centered or grandiose, or you may be from a background where the scrutiny of your personal attributes, preparedness, and competence is considered intrusive and inappropriate. However, clinicians come to appreciate that reflecting on personal beliefs and practices and observing and being observed are essential to ensure that they provide effective service to clients. Whereas students might look forward to a day of *less* study and observation, experienced clinicians often ask for *more*, not less, to get fresh perspectives on their work.

Learning That There Is No One "Right" Answer

Prochaska, Norcross, and DiClemente (1994) noted that each of the four hundred systems of psychotherapy they identified espoused its own epistemology as the best frame for interpreting and responding to human needs and problems. As you work with different supervisors or attend different classes, you will hear about many different approaches and sometimes contradictory beliefs about how to help others. Clinical work is rife with theoretical ambiguities and clashes over what constitutes best practice. You may feel some normal exasperation about the lack of one right answer or one way to resolve human problems. However, in time you will discover that patiently struggling with ambiguity may lead to new ideas and new approaches.

You will discover that, due to the great diversity of clients, what is helpful in conceptualizing and responding to one client may not be helpful with another client with similar problems. Furthermore, even when working with one client, you will discover many useful ways of responding to him or her, and each helpful response may lead you down a different path than you anticipated. Your professional education is designed to teach you how to evaluate and distinguish among the many useful ideas and applications in the context of specific cultures, individuals, families, groups, and situations.

Learning from Mistakes

Mistakes are part of all learning, but they can be disconcerting and embarrassing if you are used to doing most things well. Clinicians regularly reflect on their mistakes because mistakes are great teachers and can highlight areas for continued growth and improvement. In setting out in your clinical education, though, it takes trust to believe that instructors and supervisors have your interests at heart when they routinely critique your work. Always keep in mind that "critique" means to identify both the problematic and the positive and constructive aspects of your work.

Also helpful is hearing seasoned colleagues and mentors describing their own bloopers and realizing that mistakes will continue to occur throughout our careers. Seeing others talk comfortably and openly about their mistakes provides relief from secret fears that frequent mistakes make us inherently unsuited for clinical practice.

You may worry about handing in process recordings for practicum supervision because your supervisor will see that you have made the same mistakes that you made twice before and thought you were through making. But this worry is to be expected. "Once we accept mistakes as a human given and not just as personal flaws or too-daunting challenges, we can begin to normalize mistake making as part of a developmental learning curve in the counseling professions" (Dillon, 2003, p. 3).

Dealing with Strong Feelings

While studying to be a clinician you almost certainly will experience strong feelings. Clinical education is not just intellectual learning; it involves the heart as well as the mind. As you read in psychology, social work, and counseling, and as you begin to work with clients, you will hear painful stories and become immersed in human suffering. You may find yourself carrying feelings of sadness, anger, and pain about what you are studying and hearing. Some of what you are learning may touch sore spots or painful issues in your own life. Many of the issues that you discuss in class and that clients face may seem insurmountable because they are related to large-scale social injustice and require structural changes.

Though these feelings can help us understand something of what clients feel, at times your reactions may feel overwhelming and beyond your ability to contain and harness them constructively. Rather than suppressing or avoiding deep feelings, your challenge will be to learn to embrace them, modulate them, and learn from them. You will discover that others often share similar reactions. You can discuss these feelings with colleagues and supervisors to grow as a person and a professional. Clinicians who find that powerful feeling states continually disrupt their work with clients often use personal therapy for understanding and growth just as clients do.

EXERCISE 1.6 Challenges

What do you think will be the hardest part of learning to be a clinician? Will it be having people comment on your strengths and problem areas; giving feedback to other people; meeting new people; responding to people who are angry or sad or who have strong feelings; talking about subjects such as sex, money, and sexual orientation; working with a variety of people who are different from yourself; or something else? Discuss this question in small groups.

■ Conclusion

Becoming a professional clinician is an extremely satisfying and challenging experience. You are starting a lifelong process of learning, interaction, self-observation, and feedback that will shape and reshape your knowledge and skills. In the process of learning to be a clinician, you will need to develop empathy, patience, a durable faith in people and process, the energy to work hard over time, respect for differences, a tolerance for ambiguities, and a sturdy, resilient self that collaborates well with others.

Chapter 2 elaborates further learning challenges, including legal and ethical issues; working with difference and diversity; and developing multicultural knowledge, respect, skills, and relationships within and beyond clinical work.

■ Suggested Readings

We highly recommend the following books about the personal challeges of helping to complement your readings on skill development.

Baird, Brian N. (2004). *The internship, practicum, and field placement handbook: A guide for helping professionals*, (7th Ed.). Upper Saddle River, NJ: Prentice Hall.

Hill, Marcia. (2004). *Diary of a country therapist.* Binghamton, NY: Haworth.

Ram Dass & Gorman, Paul. (1985). *How can I help? Stories and reflections on service.* New York: Knopf.

Ryan, William. (1976). *Blaming the victim.* New York: Vintage.

The following texts provide good overviews of the major schools of clinical practice and counseling theory.

Corey, Gerald. (2005). *Theory and practice of counseling and psychotherapy.* (7th Ed.). Belmont, CA: Wadsworth.

Prochaska, James O., & Norcross, John C. (2007). *Theories of psychotherapy: A transtheoretical approach.* Belmont, CA: Brooks/Cole.

For those interested in an overview of ecological and environmental issues in practice, we recommend the following.

Jacobson, Wendy B. (2001). Beyond therapy: Bringing social work back to human services reform. *Social Work, 46,* 51–61.

Roszak, Theodore, Gomes, Mary E., & Kanner, Allen D. (Eds.). (1995). *Ecopsychology: Restoring the earth, healing the mind.* San Francisco: Sierra Club Books.

■ Self-Explorations

1. Give examples of people you know whose helping style you admire. Where do they fit in Neukrug and Schwitzer's taxonomy of natural styles?

2. Have you ever used acupuncture, herbal treatments, homeopathy, massage, meditation, or any other form of alternative or complementary medicine to help you cope with a physical or emotional problem? Which aspects were different and which were similar to traditional medical or psychological approaches? Why did you choose this type of help and was it useful? Would you use this or another form of alternative help in the future? Why?

3. Has there been a time when after helping someone, you realized that he or she also had helped and changed you in unanticipated ways? What did that person say, do, or embody that helped you? How can that experience help you be a wiser helper in the future?

4. How do your family and friends feel about your decision to enter a helping profession? What reactions or comments of theirs show their support for your decision? What reactions or comments of theirs have challenged or questioned the wisdom of your decision?

5. Have you ever worked for social change or participated in social activism? Describe your original goals, as well as the short-term and long-term effects of this work on both you and the larger community.

6. Discuss instances in which you gave someone feedback about their performance of roles or skills in some undertaking (for example work, sports, volunteering, trying out for a part). How forthright were you able to be in pointing out areas of performance that needed improvement? If you held back suggestions or criticism, why was that? How effective was your feedback in helping that person improve performance?

7. When have you received feedback that helped you to improve role or skill performance? What aspect of the feedback was especially helpful to you? Discuss some feedback you received that was not helpful and explain why.

■ Essay Questions

1. There are many different types of helping professions: social workers, counselors, human service workers, nurses, psychologists. What distinguishes each profession from the others? Visit the Web sites for the

National Association of Social Workers (www.socialworkers.org), the American Counseling Association (www.counseling.org), the American Psychological Association (www.apa.org), and the National Organization for Human Services (www.nationalhumanservices.org). Describe:

a. The focus or mission of the profession.

b. How this profession differs from the other helping professions whose Web sites you visited.

c. The education necessary to become a professional.

d. The respect that society has for members of this profession and why.

2. Do you think clinical work is an art or a science? How much of a role do intuition and personal experience have in clinical work? How might clinical research inform clinical practice and clinical assessment? Based on the material you have read, present thorough arguments on both sides and then draw your conclusion.

3. A "50-minute hour" is an arbitrary construction for the convenience of clinicians and agencies. Do you think clients can be expected to "turn it on" or "turn it off" every week at an appointed time? Discuss the pros and cons of scheduling in this way? Discuss how time-limited and scheduled interviews are culturally constructed.

4. Events in complex systems often exist as both a cause and an effect of each other. The authors give an example of the distancing and pursuing dance in a couple relationship. Give another example that illustrates your understanding of circular causality in systems.

■ Key Terms

Circular causality	Mutuality
Clinical interviewing	Natural helpers
Complementary medicine	Process recording
Critical thinking	Professional clinicians
Ecological	Reciprocal influences
Indigenous helpers	Scientist/practitioner model
Intentional use of self	Social justice perspective
Introspection	Strengths perspective
Managed care	Systemic
Multiple realities	Theory

Responsible Practice:
Difference and Diversity, Values and Ethics

In the last chapter we described a number of ways that clinical interviewing is different from informal or natural helping. In this chapter we focus on two key issues that are the bedrock of responsible practice: (1) attending to multiculturalism, difference, and diversity, and (2) working from a solid base of professional ethics. We chose to address both of these issues in a special chapter because they are essential to effective and responsive practice, and they deserve special emphasis.

Following a review of salient issues and research findings regarding multiculturalism, racism, and identity formation, we discuss guidelines for multicultural practice. We then ask you to think about your own race, ethnicity, and identity and how these may both inform and complicate your work with clients. We introduce you to several important principles and standards of clinical practice ethics codes, asking you to clarify your own values and ethics and to discuss potential ethical dilemmas you might face. While this chapter is a general overview of issues and concerns, in succeeding chapters presenting basic interviewing skills, we discuss specific skills for addressing issues of difference and diversity, as well as skills you can use to implement your ethical stance when dilemmas and challenges arise in your work with clients.

EXERCISE 2.1 I Am What I Am

On a sheet of paper, write the phrase "I am . . ." on 10 different lines. Then go back and quickly complete each sentence with the first thing that comes to mind when you think "I am . . . ."

Review your responses and note how many items refer to identity and how many are related to transient states like being hungry, tired, and the like.

Discuss your answers in small groups. Do others say things about themselves that you might also say about yourself? What can you learn about how you identify yourself?

Is there anything you "are" that you are ambivalent about writing down or discussing aloud?

In what circumstances do you think your answers might change?

■ Multiculturalism, Difference, and Diversity

Multiculturalism

Many professions use the term "multicultural" to describe the increasing diversity of the U.S. population in terms of race and ethnicity. **Culture** refers to a group's shared language, traditions, customs, rituals, history, and expectations of one another. **Ethnicity** refers to the classification of people based on their shared ancestry and culture. **Race** is "the classification of people based on geographic origin and shared physical characteristics like skin color, hair texture and facial features" (Parker & Chambers, 2005, p. 57). Doman Lum (2004) points out that "multiculturalism" implies that cultural groups in the United States now preserve their distinctive identities—their languages, beliefs, customs, religions—and that "these distinctive practices represent enormous cultural wealth . . . [and] are a source of enrichment for society as a whole" (p. 3).

Although the concept of race is socially constructed, people often behave as though there is something essential, innate, or biological about race and ethnicity. Some researchers who found racial differences in characteristics such as intelligence would attribute those differences to presumed genetic or cultural deficiencies of nonwhite people (for example Hernstein & Murray, 1994; Jensen, 1969). In *On the Origin of the Species,* Charles Darwin (1859) hypothesized that whites were superior to blacks to whom he referred as "the lower races." However, scientists currently working on the Human Genome Project have shown that there are no real racial differences: "research on human genome variation increasingly challenges the applicability of the term 'race' to human population groups, raising questions about the validity of inferences made about 'race' in the biomedical and scientific literature" (Royal & Dunstan, 2004, p. S5).

In previous decades, people who were different from the dominant European American ethnocultural groups in the United States were referred to as "ethnic minorities." "**Minority status** denoted a numerically smaller or politically powerless group in relation to a larger, controlling, and dominant majority. Whites were cast as the majority, whereas nonwhites were the minorities" (Lum, 2004, p. 3). However, Victor De La Cancela, Yvonne Jenkins, and Jean Lau Chin (1993) state that the term "minority," used as a label to refer to populations of color, ignores the reality that Caucasians are the numerical minority globally. They go on to say that the use of the term "minority" has "oppressive connotations of disempowerment and poverty that are inappropriate and offensive in the context of African, Latino, Indigenous, and Asian ethnic groups who are becoming economically strong and sociopolitically organized" (p. 7).

> *I hate being referred to as "a minority." I'm Puerto Rican. Being called a "minority" makes me feel like people see me as "inferior." Aren't there more Puerto Ricans in New York City than Swedes? How come they aren't called a minority? People make all kinds of assumptions about minorities—like we're poor, deprived, and depraved.*

> *People call us Asians "the model minority." What the heck does that mean? We're the best of the worst?*

The changing demographics of the United States make it clear that the current Caucasian ethnocultural "majority" will soon be the minority. "By the year 2056, the United States will be a demographic mosaic and the typical resident will trace his or her descent to Africa, Asia, the Latin American world, the Pacific Islands, Arabia—almost anywhere but White Europe" (Comas-Diaz & Greene, 1994, p. 3). Jeanne Slattery (2004) observes that "Euro-Americans are already in the minority in California, Hawaii, and New Mexico" (p. xxiii). Derald Wing Sue and David Sue (2003) note that this "[d]iversification of the United States" is due to two reasons: differential birth rates and immigration. Birth rates among European Americans have declined, while those of other racial and ethnic groups have increased. There are also more documented immigrants, undocumented immigrants, and refugees than at any other time in U.S. history (Lum, 2004). As a nation, we are clearly becoming more mixed in terms of racial and ethnocultural group membership.

There is also a growing awareness that many people are **multiracial** and **multiethnic.** Not until the 2000 census were people able to check more than one box to identify their racial identity. In 2000, 2.4% (over 6.8 million people) checked more than one box to represent their race, but it is estimated that the number is much higher (Lum, 2004). When one considers multiethnic identity, the numbers are even higher. Tiger Woods is often referred to as a "black" golfer, based solely on his skin color. In reality, he is of mixed ancestry and is both multiracial and multiethnic. His mother is Thai, Chinese, and white. His father is black, Native American, and Chinese (Shih & Sanchez, 2005).

*I consider myself black. My father is black and my mother is Puerto Rican, but I some-
how came out looking lily white. People always look at me strangely when I walk into the
Black Student Association meetings.*

EXERCISE 2.2 Your Ethnocultural and Racial Background

In small groups, discuss your racial and ethnocultural background. How do your race
and ethnicity influence your outlook on life—your values, attitudes, and behaviors?
What are the racial and cultural backgrounds of members of your family? Are they
the same as or different from yours? What factors make you feel positive about your
race and ethnicity? Negative? Ambivalent?

Some argue that the concept of multiculturalism includes attention to
more than ethnicity, race, and color. For example, Gilbert Herdt (1992) and
Daniel Harris (1997) have suggested that there is a gay culture with its own
norms, language, rituals, and styles of communication.

Deaf activists describe a deaf culture based on the use of American Sign
Language (ASL) and the use of "vision instead of hearing for getting vital
and incidental information" (Stokoe, 1989, p. 55). Padden (1989) uses an
uppercase D to highlight Deaf people as a cultural group. Others assert
that deafness is a culture and not a disability (Luey, Glass, & Elliot, 1995).
Elizabeth DePoy & Stephen Gilson (2004) assert that thinking of people of
varying abilities "as diverse rather than fitting within categories of 'normal'
and 'not normal' is central" to a strengths approach in working with people
with disabilities (p. 75).

*I'd heard people use the phrase "deaf culture" before, but it wasn't until recently that
I really got it. I was out on a Friday night in an area of town with lots of popular clubs.
It was summer and as I came out of the bar I was in, I walked through a large group of
deaf people—there must have been 200 or so at the outside tables and on the street in front
of the club next door to the one I was in. They were all signing with each other animat-
edly and interacting in small groups of three or four. It was just like the scene I had left
at the club, animated, happy, a bit sexually charged—only it was different. I never
thought before about how deaf people socialize and date in large gatherings like that one,
and it made me want to know more.*

Romel Mackelprang and Richard Salsgiver (1999) argue that there is a
general culture of disability. Although recognizing that people with disabilities are heterogeneous in terms of class, gender, race, ethnicity, and sexual
orientation and have a wide variety of disabilities (spinal cord injury, deafness, blindness), they suggest that the common oppression people with disabilities experience helps to create a "disability culture with shared customs,
traditions, and language" (p. 29). DePoy and Gilson (2004) report that there
is limited empirical support for a "disability culture" but that "those who
believe in such a culture assert that membership in it bestows identity, language, and position vis-à-vis other cultural groups" (p. 79).

Racial and Ethnic Identity

Identity is a term used to describe our self-conceptualization. Identity can reflect how we see ourselves as individuals and how we see ourselves as part of a larger group or community. All identities are **socially constructed,** develop over time with input from a variety of contexts, and have many elements or aspects to them. Tracy Robinson (2005) contends that our identities are **statused** and have particular social meanings: "[I]n both subtle and blatant ways, people who hold membership in higher status groups are valued differently in society than those from lower status groups" (pp. 42–43).

Because of America's history of slavery, racism, and hate crimes against people of color, race has for a long time been a key component of identity for Americans. Janet Helms (1990) contends that racial identity "refers to a sense of group or collective identity based on one's perception that he or she shares a common racial heritage with a particular group" (p. 3).

The earliest work on racial identity development was conducted by William E. Cross Jr. (1971, 1991; Cross & Vandiver, 2001). Cross described a six-stage process in which African-Americans replace negative images (rooted in longtime contextual discrimination and oppression) with positive internal conceptions of themselves as members of a group. There have been a number of other models of racial identity development, largely based on Cross's work: American Indian identity development (Horse, 2001), African-American identity development (Cross & Fhagen-Smith, 2001), Latino identity development (Ferdman & Gallegos, 2001), Asian identity development (Kim, 2001), and a multiracial identity (Fhagen-Smith, 2003; Root, 1996, 2001; Wijeyesinghe, 2001).

Many people believe incorrectly that only people of color have a racial identity. White people often find it difficult to own or talk about their own race and the unearned privilege it often affords them (Daniel, 2000; Guadelupe & Lum, 2005; McIntosh, 1989; Sue, 2003).

Janet Helms (1985, 1990, 1995) has proposed a six-stage model of white racial identity development. Sue and Sue (2003) note that Helms's model of white racial identity is important and valuable because it describes the "'defenses' [and] 'protective strategies,' or what Helms formally labels as 'information processing strategies'. . . which White people use to avoid or assuage anxiety and discomfort about issues of race" (p. 251). Some might suggest that Helms's model of white identity development is about coming to terms with one's privilege as a white person in the United States.

In the first stage, there may be little contact with people of color. The white person is not aware of his or her own race as such and may be oblivious to racism and its impact on others. The person may take what is often called a "colorblind" stance: *I don't see a person's race as an issue—we are all members of the human race."*

In the second stage, disorientation and anxiety can occur as individuals realize that all people really are not treated equally. A self-reflective white person may feel guilt and shame due to a dawning awareness of the in-group privilege of whiteness. The person may face unsettling dilemmas: *"I am not racist, but I don't want my daughter to marry a black man." "I support the need for more diversity in our teachers, I know it is good for kids to have role models of people from different ethnic and racial backgrounds, but I don't think it is fair that I am passed over for a job because I'm a white man."*

In the third stage, to regain a psychological foothold, there is reaffirmation of race-based, distorted beliefs. The person may idealize white attributes and achievements, while devaluing other racial and ethnocultural groups and wondering why they cannot just be "like us." *"Yes, there are fewer people of color in management positions, but that isn't my fault. I've had to work for everything I have gotten. They just don't work hard enough. My father came over from Ireland with just the shirt on his back."*

In the fourth phase, white people who are self-reflective begin to "get it"—that there is racism, that it destructively affects nonwhites, and that they and loved ones have participated in it. This awareness may be very intellectualized. There can be misguided "tolerance" and an at attempt "helping" people of color be—and have—more, "like us." *"I want to help you advance, so let me tell you how we do things here." "You need to tone down your emotions to get ahead."*

In the fifth stage, continued exposure to people of color, as well as exposure to injustices, brings about an earnest search for the meaning of racism in one's own history and current life. Zealotry in race-focused activism is not unusual as efforts are made to compensate for past denial, fear of losing white in-group acceptance, and racist acts. Gradually there is a wish for more and different experience with other cultures. *"Even though I don't like admitting it, I know that I benefit from racism and that, whether I intend to or not, I often act in unconsciously racist ways. It's hard work and it makes me uncomfortable, but I know I have to keep looking at and working on these issues."*

Eventually, in the sixth stage, white people who are motivated to do so consciously work with people of color to be antiracist, experiencing their commonalities with and differences from each other more comfortably and appreciatively. Individuals begin to use their own newly internalized ethical standards to define themselves and the world and to learn to relate, speak, and work publicly against oppression, even if it makes some white friends uncomfortable. *"I will continually speak out about injustices and oppressive acts when I see them and not leave people of color to bear the brunt of that responsibility. I will work with others to fight racism in myself, in others, and in our institutions and policies."*

The racial identity development of clinicians and clients has been a topic of much research (Kwan & Kwong-Liem, 2001; Vinson & Neimeyer, 2000). Renee Middleton and her colleagues conclude that "one factor that may influence multicultural counseling competency is the racial identity development of the practitioner" (Middleton et al., 2005, p. 444).

Difference

Difference and identity are not limited to racial or ethnocultural differences. Almost all of you will work with clients who differ from you in age, gender, family form, religion, class background, and other ways. Many of these differences are an important part of your own and your clients' identities. In their discussion of multiple oppressions, Amy Reynolds and Raechele Pope (1991) noted that people have multiple identities, not just one. Identities may include sexual orientation, age, class, educational level, job, marital or parenting status, important hobbies, and the like.

The **salience of identity** varies over time and circumstances. How you identify and feel about yourself may change depending on the situation. If you are the only person at work without children and people are discussing day care, your identity as a nonparent becomes more salient.

> *I am Irish on St. Patrick's Day and Italian when in Little Italy.*

> *As a retiree, I like to be strong when doing yard work, but when riding the bus to town, I love it when younger people give me their seats.*

> *I love being a biker. I love riding with my friends on the weekend, the camaraderie, and the road action. But lots of people think of bikers as criminals or "no-goods." I don't discuss the fact I am a biker at work.*

William E. Cross, Jr., Lakesha Smith, and Yasser Payne (2002) speak of the complexity of multiple identities:

> Black persons with multi-culturally oriented identities may have as many as three or more attachment or bonding layers (e.g. an individual may be equally attached and bonded to her Blackness, her Puerto Ricanness, and her lesbian identity). This interconnectivity or multiplicity often leads such persons to see things as "connected", or as having connectivity potential, when others see only that which is singular, linear, monoracial, or monocultural (p. 101).

> *I look black and people often assume I am. The other day at work we were talking about Passover and I mentioned I was having a Seder. One of my Jewish colleagues asked me when I converted—As if no black people could be Jewish! I had to explain to him that my father was black and my mother was Jewish.*

Sharon Jones and Marylu McEwen (2001) have developed a conceptual model of **multiple dimensions of identity.** They suggest that we have *a core sense of personal identity* surrounded by intersecting circles that represent various identity dimensions contextualized within such influences as family background, sociocultural conditions, and opportunity systems. (See Figure 2.1)

Diversity within Groups and Invisible Differences

We need to recognize the complexity of people's multiple identities and the variations, permutations, and **diversity** that exist within members of the same group. For example, both clinician and client can be Cambodian, but one is a recent refugee from a poor farm village, while the other is from a wealthy family that came to the United States forty years ago. Clinician and client may both be middle-class professionals now, yet one comes

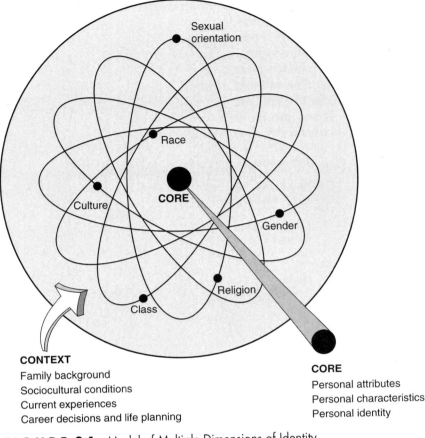

FIGURE 2.1 Model of Multiple Dimensions of Identity

Source: Reprinted with permission from the American College Personnel Association, One Dupont Circle, NW, Suite 300, at the National Center for Higher Education, Washington, DC 20036.

from a working-class background. Both may be Native American, but one is gay.

Sometimes the differences between people are not readily apparent. For example, the client and clinician can have unseen and unspoken **value differences.** Both can be men, but men with different constructions of what it means to be a man. Both can be Catholic, yet each holds different, unexpressed beliefs about gay marriage and abortion. Whether the differences are cultural or not, visible or not, recognized or not, we can be sure that we will all work with clients who are different from us and have different experiences, values, and beliefs than our own.

I was working with a lesbian woman. She was out and politically active. I had even seen her at a National Gay and Lesbian Task Force dinner. I assumed we shared a similar belief system. She was talking about gay marriage, and I was really surprised when she said that she didn't think gay people should adopt children.

Prejudice, Discrimination, and Racism

A **stereotype** is a fixed, oversimplified image we have of members of a group. Stereotyping prevents us from seeing and appreciating both the full range of characteristics of, and the diversity within, the targeted group. Stereotypes very often lead to prejudice. **Prejudice** refers to either positive or negative bias, poorly informed opinions, or unjustified assumptions about individuals who belong to a certain group or fit into a particular category.

EXERCISE 2.3 Stereotypes

In groups of four, make a list of common stereotypes about people who are:

Native American	Arab
Black	Asian
White	Elderly
Latino	Gay
Jewish	Disabled

1. Next to each stereotype, note how much you agree with it using a scale of 1–10.
2. List positive, negative, or neutral aspects of each stereotype.
3. Prepare to discuss with the larger group where the stereotypes come from and how they get reinforced.
4. Think together about what you can do to try to overcome the stereotypes.

Prejudice often leads to discrimination. **Discrimination** is the unfair treatment of people because of prejudice regarding their class, gender, sexual orientation, age, size, ability, or racial, ethnic, and religious group membership. Prejudice is an attitude, whereas discrimination is a behavior. Many people face prejudice and discrimination regularly, and, whether they say so or not, the counseling help they seek is often related to forms of oppression.

Racism is a combination of prejudice and discrimination "that has institutional power behind it" (Mio, Barker Hackett & Tumambing, 2006, p. 147). We find it helpful to think of the distinction that James Jones (1996) makes between three kinds of racism: individual racism, institutional racism, and cultural racism. Individual racism is discriminatory behavior on the part of the individual. Institutional racism refers to social or governmental policies and structures that subordinate people of color. Cultural racism refers to the ways in which the cultures of people of color are denigrated and the culture of the dominant group is imposed on ethnic or racial minorities. In discussing the behavior of individuals, Derald Wing Sue (2003) describes two forms: the *conscious-deliberate* racial oppressor and the *unconscious-unintentional* racial oppressor. Sue suggests that most of us, regardless of our color, are "unintentional racists."

EXERCISE 2.4 Who Can Be Racist?

There is great controversy about the concept of racism and who can be racist. Can people of color be racist? Beverly Daniel Tatum (1997) says that, if you define racism as racial prejudice, everyone can be a racist. But "if one defines racism as a system of advantage based on race, the answer is no. People of color are not racist because they do not systematically benefit from racism" (p. 10). Some theorists argue that since all whites benefit from racism, whether intentionally or unintentionally, all whites are racist. In small groups discuss your reaction to the following statements:

Only whites can be racist.

All whites are racist.

Homophobia, like racism, combines both prejudice and discrimination. Homophobia is the hostility and hatred directed at gay men and lesbian women because of their sexual orientation. **Heterosexism** is "a world-view, a value system that prizes heterosexuality, assumes it is the only appropriate manifestation of love and sexuality, and devalues homosexuality and all that is not heterosexual" (Herek, 1986, p. 925).

Personal Dimensions of Identity

Patricia Arredondo and T. Glauner (1992) developed the Personal Dimensions of Identity model (PDI), which examines how cultural, racial and ethnic identities interact with other dimensions of diversity. The PDI consists of three dimensions:

1. *Dimension A* is a list of generalizable human characteristics—gender, culture, ethnicity, and language. Arredondo et al. (1996) view these characteristics as immutable and suggest that they are relatively fixed at birth.
2. *Dimension C* refers to the global contexts that affect the individual. These include the historical, political, sociocultural, and economic contexts in which we live and over which we have little control.
3. *Dimension B* may be a "consequence" of A and C and may result from the interaction between the "characteristics of the A Dimension and the major historical, political sociocultural and economic legacies of the C Dimension" (Arredondo et al., 1996, p. 50). *Dimension B* includes such variables as educational background, geographic location, relationship status, work experience, and religion.

The PDI illustrates several premises: "a) that we are all multicultural individuals; b) that we all possess a personal, political and historical culture; c) that we are affected by sociocultural, political, environmental, historical events; and d) multiculuralism also intersects with multiple factors of human diversity" (Arredondo et al., 1996, p. 46). Thus, we agree with Paul Pedersen

CLIP 2.1

The Clinician's Identity and Values

(1991) when he suggests that "the construct 'multicultural' becomes generic to all counseling relationships" (p. 7).

Multicultural Practice

Clearly you must prepare yourself for **multicultural practice:** to meet knowledgeably and openly with clients from many cultures, religions, family forms, strengths and challenges, migration stories (be it from one state, one country, or even one gender to another). Research in progress will better define what have been called **cultural competencies** needed for working with colleagues, clients, and community members different from ourselves.

The professional organizations of those who work in human service and mental health all stress the need for clinicians to be aware of multicultural practice issues. The Association for Multicultural Counseling and Development has developed a list of *Multicultural Counseling Competencies,* which have been endorsed by the American Counseling Association (see Appendix 1). The National Association of Social Workers (NASW) has developed *Standards for Cultural Competence in Social Work Practice* (NASW 2001), and the American Psychological Association has developed *Multicultural Guidelines on the Education and Training, Research, Practice and Organizational Change for Psychologists* (APA 2002b).

EXERCISE 2.5 Multicultural Standards

In groups of four, make a list of standards that you think should guide multicultural practice. What specific steps would you need to take to make your clinical work more culturally responsible and responsive? Discuss your conclusions and guidelines with the whole class.

Whether they call them standards, competencies, or guidelines, most researchers suggest that the following three dimensions be addressed in training helping professionals: attitudes and beliefs, knowledge, and skills for the sensitive implementation of interventions (Atkinson, 2004; Constantine & Sue, 2005; Devore & Schlesinger, 1996; Ivey, Ivey, & Simek-Morgan, 2002; Ponterotto, Casas, Suzuki, & Alexander, 2001; Robinson, 2005; Sue, Arredondo, & McDavis, 1992; Sue & Sue, 2003).

1. *As clinicians, we need to be aware of our own ethnic, gender, and cultural heritage.*　We need to be aware of our negative and positive reactions to the values and traditions of other groups and of how our own cultural values affect our worldview. We can enhance our awareness when we live, work, and make friendships with people different from ourselves—people with whom we can discuss our feelings and reactions and with whom we

can exchange honest questions and feedback. These kinds of experiences are still too limited in the lives of many people and must be assiduously developed and nurtured. At the same time, it is important to recognize that we are responsible for our own learning and that we should not always depend on others who are different from ourselves to teach us what we should know about them.

2. ***We need to acquire knowledge about the cultures and customs of the clients with whom we work.***   We need to get information about the specific history and background of the cultural group; about family structures, communication patterns, gender roles, traditions, and values; about the impact of immigration; about the role of spirituality; and so on. We need to explore how culture and ethnicity affect help-seeking behaviors. We must attend to the effects that racism, stigmatization, and discrimination have on our clients' daily lives.

3. ***Finally, we need to use this self-awareness and knowledge to devise flexible strategies for intervention that are effective and congruent with our clients' values.***   We must be aware of bias in research and assessment instruments, and we must design interventions and strategies that are appropriate and linguistically suitable.

EXERCISE 2.6 Matching

In groups of four, discuss the advantages and disadvantages of clinicians working with people who are similar and dissimilar to themselves. Discuss (1) the advantages of working with someone similar, (2) the disadvantages of working with someone similar, (3) the advantages of working with someone different from themselves, (4) the disadvantages of working with someone different from themselves. Which would be hardest for you and why?

CLIP 2.2
Multicultural
Practice

To summarize, multicultural practice recognizes, respects, and responds with informed thoughtfulness to the variety of differences within and between people. It is an important feature of effective clinical relationships and work. We need to stay open to new learning and interpersonal experience, attentive to differences, building knowledge and skills, and engaging in ongoing self-reflection and dialogue with others different from ourselves.

■ Professional Ethics

Ethics is a branch of philosophy that deals with moral judgments and perceptions of right and wrong. A **professional code of ethics** establishes principles and standards of conduct that elucidate the values of a discipline or profession. *Principles* are values that are aspirational in nature, while *standards* consist of prescribed behaviors as well as proscribed conduct.

In our role as helping professionals, we are given a major responsibility: to fulfill the great trust that clients, their families, and society place in us. A major purpose of our codes of ethics is to protect the welfare of individuals and groups coming to us for help. Ethics codes also help us by clarifying our professional responsibilities and providing guidance about most of the situations we will face in our professional roles. Our codes inspire us to adopt high standards of behavior as we render complex and demanding services. Finally, they provide a framework for processing complaints about our professional behavior. Len Sperry (2007) writes that a code of ethics is "more than a set of rules and strategies to avoid legal liability and professional censure. Rather, it is a way of *being* in relationship to clients, supervisees, students, and colleagues that both promotes development and prevents harm" (p. xi).

Each professional clinical association has a published code of ethics: The National Organization of Human Services (NOHS, 1996), American Counseling Association (ACA, 2005), The American Psychological Association (APA, 2002a), and the National Association of Social Workers (NASW, 1999). Membership in these professional organizations is voluntary, but usually a feature of membership is an agreement to become familiar with, and to abide by, the association's ethical code.

Our ethics codes incorporate and reflect carefully chosen societal values and aspirations that our professional organizations hope will serve as enduring benchmarks or **ethical principles** for practice rather than fleeting attitudes. For example, it is hard to imagine a human services ethics code without fundamental ethical guidelines about practicing with respect for the dignity and worth of all people, ensuring the right of clients to participate fully and be well informed in intervention planning, and observing confidentiality in clinician-client conversations. These fundamental values have guided our professions for some time now, but other standards are newer, reflecting changes in society or addressing situations that practitioners had not faced previously. For example, new standards have been written that address the handling of electronic communication over the Internet. Ethics codes are thus updated periodically to incorporate more current wording or thinking, or new issues and value concerns emerging from academic research and professional practice venues.

Many codes of ethics begin with a statement of general principles that foreshadow the standards that follow. For example, NASW lists as overarching principles Service, Social Justice, Dignity and Worth of the Person, Importance of Human Relationships, Integrity, and Competence. These general statements are then followed by enumerated standards of conduct that are enforceable rules for professional conduct.

Ethical standards are quite specific. They detail preferred and proscribed conduct in the major domains of professional practice; for example, the APA has 89 standards of conduct. The clinician who violates ethical standards can be sanctioned by or expelled from the professional association. If the violation is referred to the state licensing board, the clinician may lose his or her license. A professional who violates a state or federal law may also be brought to court for criminal charges or face a civil hearing if a client sues for an ethical violation.

As noted, clinicians are also bound by federal and state laws. Each state develops its own laws to govern professionals and protect consumers. However, ethics codes sometimes hold the professional to a higher standard than the law. For example, Thomas Plante (1999) writes that, while it is illegal to have sex with clients in some states (but not others), such conduct is unethical in all states.

The ethics codes of the various professional associations differ depending on the profession's mission and goals. For example, the APA Code of Ethics has a lot to say about testing, because one of the defining characteristics of psychology is its roots in studying and measuring individual differences. However, most ethics codes address a number of general standards.

EXERCISE 2.7   Ethical Principles

Before reading further about ethical standards, divide into groups of four. Make a list of professional standards that you believe are essential principles for responsible clinical practice. Share your list with the whole class. Compare the list your class developed with the ethics principles of one or more of the professional associations mentioned in the text (adapted from Neukrug & Schwitzer, 2006).

Ethical Dilemmas

While the goal of ethical standards is to provide clear and specific direction, Neukrug and Schwitzer (2006) note that clinicians are often faced with **ethical dilemmas:** (1) sometimes two sections of an ethical code are at odds with each other; (2) agency or institutional policies conflict with an ethical code; (3) the law and an ethical code differ in their requirements; and (4) the clinician's moral values prevent compliance with an ethical code.

Ethics codes themselves often provide some guidance about steps to take to fulfill ethical obligations. For example, the NASW code states: "When such conflicts [such as those cited] occur, social workers must make a responsible effort to resolve the conflict in a manner that is consistent with the values, principles, and standards expressed in this Code. If a reasonable resolution of the conflict does not appear possible, social workers should seek proper consultation before making a decision" (NASW, 1999).

Ethical Decision Making

Sometimes it is easy to decide what is "right" and "wrong" by conforming closely to ethical standards and code guidance statements. However, sometimes the decisions are more complicated. Ethical dilemmas often generate a conflict between a clinician's "tried and true" personal values and the profession's values and ethical obligations. Such dilemmas may involve choosing between two "rights" (for example, a client's right to self-determination and the professional obligation to protect her from self-harming). Ethical dilemmas often stir up anxiety, uncertainty, and ambivalence. Theorists have suggested a number of models to help professionals think about how to make a decision when faced with an ethical dilemma.

Frank Loewenberg, Ralph Dolgolff, and Donna Harrington (2000) describe an "ethical assessment screen" (p. 67), which they feel is a helpful first step in attempting to make an ethical decision:

1. Identify your own personal values in relation to the ethical dilemma.
2. Identify any societal values relevant to the ethical decision.
3. Identify the relevant professional values and ethics.
4. Identify alternative ethical options.
5. Which of the alternative ethical actions options protects to the greatest extent the client's rights and welfare, as well as the rights and welfare of others?
6. Which alternative action protects to the greatest extent possible society's rights and interests?
7. What can you do to minimize any conflicts among 1, 2, and 3? What can you do to minimize any conflicts among 5 and 6?
8. Which alternative action will result in your doing "the least harm" possible?
9. To what extent will alternative actions be efficient, effective, and ethical?
10. Have you considered and weighed both the short-term and long-term ethical consequences of alternative actions?

While the previous models focused only on things the clinician can do, Gerald Corey, Marianne Schneider Corey, and Patrick Callanan (2003, p. 19) propose a seven-step model that involves the client in the process:

1. Recognizing a problem
2. Defining the problem (Collaboration with the client is essential.)
3. Developing solutions with the client
4. Choosing a solution
5. Reviewing the process with the client and rechoosing a solution
6. Implementing and evaluating the solution with the client
7. Continuing reflection

When you are faced with ethical dilemmas, we recommend that you consult with your supervisor or other senior colleagues. Consultation with experienced fellow professionals brings calm and thoughtful brainstorming to the review of the ethical issues and conflicts at hand. Consultation can also help in prioritizing issues that require decisions. Many state professional organizations can provide consultation with a professional or an ethics committee to assist you in thinking through decisions before acting.

CLIP 2.3
Ethical Dilemmas

In the following section, we discuss key ethical standards for clinicians and present some of the ethical dilemmas and questions that you may face in attempting to meet your profession's standards. This discussion is not intended to be all-inclusive or to replace your knowledge of your own professional organization's ethical code. Rather, we wish to highlight important principles and standards that our professions share and give you some examples of dilemmas that often arise in professional life. For each principle, we provide the specific standard as written into one or another of the professional organizations' ethical codes, so that you can experience alternately the conceptualizing language of each profession. In this chapter, we address ethical issues and dilemmas in theory. In later chapters, we describe specific methods for directly responding to clients about such issues.

Professional Standards

Competence

The following is a sample standard from APA (2002):

STANDARD 2. COMPETENCE

2.01 Boundaries of Competence

(a) Psychologists provide services, teach, and conduct research with populations and in areas only within the boundaries of their competence, based on their education, training, supervised experience, consultation, study, or professional experience.

2.03 Maintaining Competence

Psychologists undertake ongoing efforts to develop and maintain their competence.

Clinicians strive to provide the highest-quality service by developing and continually enhancing their knowledge and skills. To be competent in their roles, they must have appropriate education and experience. An important guiding principles for professional codes of ethics is to "do no harm."

Clinicians should not practice outside their area of expertise or beyond their level of competence, to protect consumers from poor or ill informed professional practices. Corey et al. (2003) ask: "What are the boundaries of one's competence, and how do professionals know when they have exceeded them? How can practitioners determine whether they should accept a client if they question their experience and training? What should be the minimal degree requirements for entry to professional counseling? To be competent to practice with a variety of client populations, does a counselor have to be both a generalist and a specialist?" (pp. 294–295).

> *I don't know what it means to be competent. I was working at a clinic and they asked if I would meet with the family of a boy who is dying of cancer. I had only taken one course in the basics of counseling. I wasn't going to do therapy, I was just going to see if they needed any resources I could help them get. But the chances were that they were going to get into their son's condition and how that is affecting them. As a human being, how could I not respond with interest and ask more about how they are coping? How can you learn if you don't practice? But is it ethical to practice on real people?*

This student's question about competence and learning expresses a very common concern of students entering clinical education programs. Clinicians share this concern when they enter more complex and demanding settings than their education prepared them for. Teachers, mentors, and supervisors, indeed, expect that students will learn "on" clients, but they also trust students to absorb knowledge quickly from class and field, as well as to deepen it through supervisory, client, and colleague feedback. Internship sites often have official standards for learning and practice provided by a discipline's national accrediting body. Your supervisor is responsible to make sure that clients are receiving competent care.

One way of measuring and indicating competence is professional certification and licensure. **Certification** is "a voluntary attempt by a group to promote a professional identity. Certification confirms that the practitioner has met a set of standards established by a certification agency" (Corey et al., 2003, p. 308). These standards usually require hundreds of hours of clinical practice experience under the supervision of a similarly certified clinical supervisor, with additional requirements for continuing education. The National Organization for Human Services provides certification for human service providers who have graduated from an accredited undergraduate program and who have met standards similar to those just noted.

Social workers, psychologists, counselors, and marriage and family therapists must usually have a **professional license** in their states to practice clinically. Each state establishes its own unique set of criteria for licensing, including graduate education, specific course work (such as a course on ethics or on child sexual abuse), and a set number of supervised hours of clinical work (some while in graduate school and some following it). In addition, the candidate must pass a test to demonstrate knowledge of advanced practice concepts and methods. Corey et al. (2003) note that "legislative regulation of professionals is proactive because it tends to highlight the uniqueness of an occupation and restricts both the use of the title and the practice of an occupation" (p. 308).

> *In my state, people can't legally say they are social workers unless they are licensed. Independent licensure indicates that you may now work independently because you have the wisdom and experience to do so safely and competently. Part of that wisdom is knowing when you need help and where to find good help. After graduation, I had to take a test to receive licensure at the LCSW level and then work two additional years (several thousand hours) under the supervision of a Licensed Independent Clinical Social Worker and pass yet another advanced exam to receive licensure at the LICSW level. I worked really hard to get that little "I."*

Clinicians are ethically required to enhance their learning and develop new skills and competencies throughout their careers. Along the way, they are constantly informed by new research and creative ideas from the field that generate new methods and approaches (such as dialectical behavioral therapy, motivational interviewing, and mind/body wellness programs). It is their responsibility to keep abreast of changes in the field (we discuss ongoing education and self-care at length in Chapter 15).

EXERCISE 2.8 Competence

In groups of four, discuss the following ethical dilemma:

Tara is a master's level social worker in a community mental health center in a small town in rural West Virginia. A man comes in with his son, who is depressed and said by the father to have been diagnosed with Tourette's Disorder. Tara knows a little about Tourette's and the complications its neurological tics can cause for the person, but she has never worked with anyone diagnosed with it. The nearest large hospital and counseling center is over 200 miles away, and the father says that, because of his work schedule, he cannot take his son there for help. He asks Tara to help him. What should she do?

The American Psychological Association has an ethics code standard that addresses working in an emergency to help people when the clinician does not have much or any real knowledge or experience with the particular kinds of problems they present. We may work with the client so that at least they are not denied all help, but only if we "make a reasonable effort to obtain the competence required by using relevant research, training, consultation, or study" (APA, 2002). In this instance, Tara would seek immediate consultation with her supervisor or their team psychologist or psychiatrist to develop a plan of care that is best for the man and his son.

Informed Consent

The following is a sample standard by the ACA:

ACA Standard A.2.a. Informed Consent

Clients have the freedom to choose whether to enter into or remain in a counseling relationship and need adequate information about the counseling process and the counselor. Counselors have an obligation to review in writing and verbally with clients the rights and responsibilities of both the counselor and the client. Informed consent is an ongoing part of the counseling process, and counselors appropriately document discussions of informed consent throughout the counseling relationship.

A.2.b. Types of Information Needed

Counselors explicitly explain to clients the nature of all services provided. They inform clients about issues such as, but not limited to, the following: the purposes, goals, techniques, procedures, limitations, potential risks, and benefits of services; the counselor's qualifications, credentials, and relevant experience; continuation of services upon the incapacitation or death of a counselor; and other pertinent information. Counselors take steps to ensure that clients understand the implications of diagnosis, the intended use of tests and reports, fees, and billing arrangements. Clients have the right to confidentiality and to be provided with an explanation of its limitations (including how supervisors and/or treatment team professionals are involved); to obtain clear information about their records; to participate in the ongoing counseling plans; and to refuse any services or modality change and to be advised of the consequences of such refusal (ACA, 2005).

Informed consent *ensures that clients are fully informed about the benefits and risks of recommended interventions before they are implemented.* A key purpose of informed consent is to protect the right of clients to self-determination. It provides an opportunity for clients to raise questions about the clinician, the work, and potential outcomes. In most circumstances, clients have the right to refuse or terminate counseling.

Jeffrey Hecker and Geoffrey Thorpe (2005) note that informed consent serves a number of functions. It empowers people by providing them with information that enables them to make wise decisions. It encourages conversation about realistic goals, objectives, and ways to meet them so that clients know what to expect. Informed consent not only protects the client; it may also protect the clinician. "In addition, assuring that clients have understood the goals, methods, and likely outcomes . . . can protect psychologists [and others] from malpractice suits (Roston & Sherrer, 1973)" (Hecker & Thorpe, 2005, p. 163).

Informed consent starts with the initial interview but it is an ongoing process (Corey et al., 2003). After clinicians explain the nature of proposed procedures and their expected benefits and risks, the client is usually asked to read, sign, and date a form affirming a full explanation of procedures, the client's understanding of benefits and risks, and client's agreement to what is planned. If changes in plans or methods are proposed at any time during the intervention, a new informed consent process must proceed them.

Thomas Grisso and Paul Applebaum (1998) believe that, to give informed consent, three conditions are necessary: (1) disclosure of information, (2) client competence to understand the discussion, and (3) voluntariness. Each condition raises a number of potential ethical concerns about informed consent.

In disclosing information, clinicians face two major questions: How accurate is the information? How much should we disclose? The information we have is only as good as the research on which it is based, and some of that research may have serious limitations. Research on the effects of a new treatment for substance abuse, for example, may only have been conducted with a limited sample (adult men) and may not apply to work with adolescents. Laboratory studies on the use of a new method to prevent wandering in people with Alzheimer's Disease may be promising, but are they valid when applied in a community-based program for elderly clients?

Clinicians need to decide whether to recommend treatments that to date have limited empirical support, yet have had some *apparent* success of which clinicians are aware anecdotally. These questions become especially salient when new, experimental treatments are available for use with a client for whom other interventions have not proved very helpful. Still, the clinician's mandate is to fully disclose what *is* known about the experimental intervention to date and what benefits and risks can be expected. This standard is clearly intended to prevent clinicians from hedging on information because they want to try out an intervention and from misleading prospective clients about the risks of interventions because they want to engage them in treatment.

Clinicians engage in thorough discussion with clients about proposed interventions in language that is easily understood. Ethical codes state that we arrange for an interpreter to explain fully the possible risks and benefits of procedures in the primary language of the client if his or her primary language differs from the clinician's. Because of the awe and anxiety that people can sometimes feel in the presence of professional clinicians, they may need time to assimilate the information given them and to digest its implications for their lives. But how much detail does the clinician need to give?

> *How thorough is thorough? I don't want to sound like one of those printouts you get with medication warnings: "Common side effects include hives, asthma, headaches, nose bleeds, rashes."*

> *I remember meeting with an anesthesiologist and going over my informed consent before surgery. He listed all the potential risks—including death. I remember thinking, "Do I need this surgery? Because if I don't, I am out of here. And if I do need it, I don't particularly want to hear everything that can go wrong. It would be good to hear about how it will help."*

Clients usually sign an informed consent form before beginning work together. If the client is not capable of giving informed consent (for example, a minor child or a person with dementia), a court-appointed legal guardian must give informed consent.

To give informed consent, the recipient needs to have the capacity to understand the information. Hecker and Thorpe (2005) suggest that, when people come to see a clinician, they are often struggling with issues that can affect their ability to think clearly and make good decisions. For example, a woman may be seeking help from a human service worker about nursing home care for her mother. However, her distress about her mother's recent fall and her anxiety about having to move her away from her home may prevent her from fully hearing about all the possibilities available.

An interesting conflict about informed consent occurs for clinicians who participate in managed care programs. Corey et al. (2003) note, "Clients have a right to know that managed care programs, with their focus on [cost] containment, may have adverse effects on the quality of care available" (p. 151). They go on to say that some managed care companies have "a gag clause that prohibits them [staff] from sharing any negative information about managed care policies including options not covered by the plan" (p. 151).

Marcia Hill (2004) describes some of the all too common difficulties clinicians can face with managed care companies:

> The client in this case was a man with overwhelming history of recent loss. To top it off, shortly after we started meeting, his wife left him, taking their only child. I had met with this client perhaps ten times by the time of the review, and the (managed care) reviewer said that we had to finish meeting within the next four sessions because, after all, this man was functioning and was able to go to work (p. 205).

EXERCISE 2.9 Managed Care

Marianna Chesholm is a counselor who works full-time in an adolescent drug program. In addition, she has a small private practice in which she sees two or three clients a week. Recently she has become frustrated with managed care companies that approve only three or four sessions at a time and that require her to spend hours each week talking with quality reviewers to obtain additional meetings. She is also concerned that sometimes the type of care that they approve for the client—such as group rather than individual counseling—is not always appropriate. She is considering removing herself from the managed care rolls but is concerned that doing so will limit her practice to people who have private insurance or who are rich enough to pay out of pocket. What should she do?

Multiple Relationships

> The following is a sample standard on multiple relationships from NOHS (1996):
>
> *Statement 6* Human service professionals are aware that in their relationships with clients power and status are unequal. Therefore they recognize that dual or **multiple relationships** may increase the risk of harm to, or exploitation of, clients, and may impair their professional judgment. However, in some communities and situations it may not be feasible to avoid social or other non-professional contact with clients. Human service professionals support the trust implicit in the helping relationship by avoiding dual relationships that may impair professional judgment, increase the risk of harm to clients or lead to exploitation.

Ethics codes caution clinicians against having multiple relationships with clients to protect both clients and the clinical relationship. When a clinician assumes more than one role with a client, it can confuse or hurt the client and the work-focused clinical relationship. While the clinical relationship is mutual, it is not equal. Professional status and helpful roles represent considerable power, both real and symbolic, to clients. That power may easily be abused, even if unintentionally. (We discuss this power differential and strategies for addressing it in later chapters.)

Multiple relationships can occur when the clinician has more than one professional role with a client. Clinicians should not counsel coworkers, students, or others with whom they have a professional relationship. Nor should they hire clients in *their* professional role to do work for them. For example, hiring a client who is an electrician to do wiring in a clinician's home can cause a number of problems. The client may feel anxious about doing the work correctly, might not charge the clinician adequately for the services (to be nice or to show gratitude), or might even discover unwanted information about the clinician.

> *A female colleague of mine wanted to help a client who was very poor and needed money by having him do housework for her. When he saw the messy state of her home and how much picking up after her he had to do for low wages, he eventually quit working for her and quit seeing her for therapy, too. He had lost respect for her after seeing her as a real person.*

Multiple relationships can occur when there is both a personal and a professional role with a client. Clinicians should not see neighbors, friends, or relatives as clients. Good boundaries allow us to work with more objectivity and detachment than we could ever do with a friend or neighbor. Boundaries prevent clients from having to add the clinician's needs to their relational burdens. Relational ethics recommend maintaining the professional relationship as a special, boundaried, work-focused alliance. Carolyn Dillon (1999) has described the clinical relationship as one of the last Western professional venues in which we restrain our own needs and wishes for the sake of another.

Multiple relationships can occur when clients and clinicians socialize together. Clinicians do not usually socialize with clients outside the work setting. Clients can feel uncomfortable observing or being observed by their counselor at, for example, a small dinner party or outing. Clinicians may also feel uncomfortable. While clients may want to see the clinician in informal settings, doing so can confuse the nature of the professional relationship. While most social relationships are mutual with personal information passing back and forth between the participants, the focus of clinicians' work is on the client and little of their personal information is usually shared.

Clinicians limit their relationships not just with clients but also with the people close to them. It might be inappropriate for a clinician to see a colleague's child in counseling or to hire a client's best friend as an attorney. At times we unknowingly find ourselves interacting with friends of clients. In a memorable scene in the TV series *The Sopranos*, Tony Soprano's psychiatrist, Dr. Melfi, sits through a dinner party in which her unknowing friends make fun of Tony Soprano's gaudy Mafia home next door. Tony, who has a crush on Dr. Melfi, watches forlornly from a window in his home while she seems to be having a wonderful time just out of reach. This episode reflects the kind of relational situations that can arise when social overlaps complicate clinical bonds.

Not all social interactions are prohibited. The American Psychological Association's ethical code notes that social interactions in some situations may be beneficial. For example, a clinician might attend a client's graduation or wedding, or the clinician and client might both be involved in a professional or community organization (APA, 2002a).

C L I P 2.4
Multiple
Relationships

In any decisions affecting interactions with clients, we are aware and respectful of clients' needs and rights. We are also mindful of and responsive to cultural differences regarding boundaries.

Prohibition of Sexual Relationships with Clients

> The following is a sample standard from ACA (2005):
>
> Sexual or romantic counselor–client interactions or relationships with current clients, their romantic partners, or their family members are prohibited.

Ethics codes are very clear and unambiguous about one type of multiple relationships: Sexual or romantic relationships with current clients are strictly prohibited. Unfortunately, predatory clinicians may use their knowledge of clients' vulnerabilities to exploit their needs for love and closeness. Because of the serious potential for coercion, manipulation, and exploitation, sexual relationships between clinicians and clients are not only unethical but illegal in many states. While the prohibition of sexual or romantic relationships is one the clearest standards and leaves little room for doubt or confusion, unfortunately the violation of this standard frequently brings clinicians before ethical committees and licensing boards (Pope & Vasquez, 1998). The violation of this standard has hurt many clients, contributing to emotional breakdowns and even suicide. There have been numerous court judgments in favor of clients who have sued their clinicians for having sex with them. Clinicians are also enjoined from engaging in romantic or sexual relationships with important people in the client's life.

Clinicians should not have sex with former clients. The ACA says a romantic or sexual relationship should *never* occur within five years after the end of the professional relationship. The APA ethics code states that there should be at least a two-year interval. But this does not mean that the clinician can terminate counseling, wait a while, and then get involved with a client. The ethical codes state that sexual intimacy with former clients should not occur, "regardless of the interval *except in the most unusual circumstances*" (italics added).

If engaging in a sexual relationship even years after ending the professional relationship, the clinician must:

> bear the burden of demonstrating that there has been no exploitation, in light of all relevant factors, including (1) the amount of time that has passed since therapy terminated; (2) the nature, duration, and intensity of the therapy; (3) the circumstances of termination; (4) the client's/patient's personal history; (5) the client's/patient's current mental status; (6) the likelihood of adverse impact on the client/patient; and (7) any statements or actions made by the therapist during the course of therapy suggesting or inviting the possibility of a post-termination sexual or romantic relationship with the client/patient (APA, 2002a).

Confidentiality

The following is a sample confidentiality standard from NASW (1999):

1.07 Privacy and Confidentiality

(a) Social workers should respect clients' right to privacy. Social workers should not solicit private information from clients unless it is essential to providing services or conducting social work evaluation or research. Once private information is shared, standards of confidentiality apply.

(b) Social workers may disclose confidential information when appropriate with valid consent from a client or a person legally authorized to consent on behalf of a client.

(c) Social workers should protect the confidentiality of all information obtained in the course of professional service, except for compelling professional reasons. The general expectation that social workers will keep information confidential does not apply when disclosure is necessary to prevent serious, foreseeable, and imminent harm to a client or other identifiable person. In all instances, social workers should disclose the least amount of confidential information necessary to achieve the desired purpose; only information that is directly relevant to the purpose for which the disclosure is made should be revealed.

The principle of confidentiality is intended to ensure the privacy of client-clinician communication. **Confidentiality** helps clients disclose to us information about intimate, sensitive and—for them sometimes—shameful topics. They can feel safe to disclose more freely when they have established a trusting relationship with the clinician. Trust is enhanced when clients believe that we will be nonjudgmental and will not disclose anything without their express permission. Very few relationships afford such an opportunity to people, and it is a special aspect of clinical work that clients come to value enormously.

The increasing use of computers and Internet services complicate the practice of confidentiality. Parker-Oliver and Dimiris (2006) note that information on computers is vulnerable to "hackers" who can get into clinicians' files. Furthermore, even after a file is deleted, there can be "hidden files (text residue) left behind"(p. 110). On the other hand, they cite Vernberg and Schuh (2002), who believe that the anonymity of the Internet may protect client confidentiality. Clients may seek support or information when they feel protected from visibility by the Web. For example, Vernberg and Schuh found that clients who were suffering from anal fissures experienced the Internet as a good way to discuss these embarrassing concerns.

Clinicians may breach confidentiality "to prevent serious, foreseeable, and imminent harm to a client or other identifiable person" (ACA, 2005). In fact, helping professionals such as teachers, health care providers, and clinicians are legally mandated to break confidentiality if they determine that the following types of potential for harm exist: (1) The client is at risk for harming self or others, (2) children might be at risk of abuse or neglect, or (3) the abuse of elderly or disabled people is possible. Clinicians can also be compelled to testify in certain legal proceedings, such as at a custody hearing or when the clinician has conducted a court-ordered evaluation prior to trial.

It is important to distinguish confidentiality from privileged communication. **Privileged communication** is the legal protection of confidentiality. Federal and state laws usually protect against forced disclosure during a legal proceeding of confidential information obtained from a **fiduciary relationship,** a relationship based on trust (such as those between doctor and patient, attorney and client, spouses, and psychotherapist and client). Laws about privileged communication vary from state to state and do not apply to all clinicians or in all circumstances. Review with your supervisor or team leaders both federal and state laws about privileged communication in any state in which you are to practice clinically.

If sued by a client, the clinician may then use client materials in his or her defense. Furthermore, insurance companies, quality assurance reviewers, or employers may require information before paying claims. However, in such cases, the clinician is careful to limit the amount of information disclosed, often reporting only the diagnosis and dates of service.

If a client may be dangerous, clinicians have a duty to warn and to protect identifiable potential victims. In a precedent-setting case, a student at the counseling center at The University of California–Berkeley told his psychologist that he was going to kill a former girlfriend when she returned from Brazil. He did not name her, but she was easily identifiable. The clinician told his supervisor about the threat, then called the campus police.

They took the student in for questioning but released him when he seemed rational. He eventually killed the woman, Tatiana Tarasoff. Her parents sued the therapist and the California Board of Regents. Eventually the California Supreme Court found in favor of the parents and said that it was not enough to notify the campus police; the psychologist had to warn the intended victim as well. The case of *Tarasoff v. Regents of the University of California* (1974, 1976) has been the basis for the ethical principle of **duty to warn.** Loewenberg et al. (2000) note that the Tarasoff opinion affirmed that "(p)ublic policy favoring protection of the confidential character of patient-psychotherapist relationships must yield in instances in which disclosure is essential to avert danger to others; the protective privilege ends where the public peril begins" (p. 103).

EXERCISE 2.10 Duty to Warn

Victor is seeing an HIV-affected client who is continuing to have unprotected sex with his girlfriend, who does not know about his diagnosis. The client is unwilling to reveal his HIV status, since he believes he was infected in a one-night stand with a prostitute. He fears his girlfriend would be devastated and would leave him if she knew about the prostitute.

In groups of four discuss what you think Victor should do in this situation. What are his options? Are you aware of any laws related to this dilemma? How did you finally arrive at your decision?

Some agencies have specific limits on confidentiality. Agency limits on confidentiality are different from the legal or ethical limits just discussed. For example, a school system may require clinicians to report all drug usage.

EXERCISE 2.11 Confidentiality

Darren, a 16-year-old junior, is sent to the guidance office because he was in a fight. During their meeting, Darren tells Mike, the school guidance counselor, that he was not really in a fight. Two other students attacked him in the locker room because he is gay. Darren reveals that he just came out and is having sex with his boyfriend Henry, who is also a junior at the school. Darren does not want the counselor to tell his parents because he is sure they will throw him out of the house if they learn he is gay. The school says that all counselors must report student drug use or sexual activity.

In groups of four, discuss the ethics code standards that would guide your thinking if you were the counselor. What personal values would guide you in thinking about this dilemma? Think further about your age now, your teen experiences, and how these would color your decision making. Remember that parents of minor children living at home usually have the right to access their children's school records, including information about any counseling of their child at the school.

Client records are also confidential. The Health Insurance Portability and Accountability Act (HIPAA) limits how much information clinicians can share with others, due to mounting nationwide concerns that technology and the rising power of managed care corporations are leading to the too wide distribution of patient information in health care settings. The release of information to third parties requires informed consent. Clinicians cannot give information to others without the client's permission in writing.

While clinicians are limited in what they can share with others, remember that clients have a legal right to see their records, although a clinician's informal process notes are excluded. Knowing this, clinicians need to think carefully about what and how they write in client records. The NASW code standard 1.08 states:

CLIP 2.5
Confidentiality

Clients should have "reasonable access" to information about them, and that social workers who are concerned that clients' access to their records could cause serious misunderstanding or harm to the client should provide assistance in interpreting the records and consultation with the client regarding the records (NASW, 1999).

Social Justice and Advocacy

The following is a sample from NOHS (1996):

STATEMENT 10 Human service professionals are aware of local, state, and federal laws. They advocate for change in regulations and statutes when such legislation conflicts with ethical guidelines and/or client rights. Where laws are harmful to individuals, groups or communities, human service professionals consider the conflict between the values of obeying the law and the values of serving people and may decide to initiate social action.

STATEMENT 11 Human service professionals keep informed about current social issues as they affect the client and the community. They share that information with clients, groups and community as part of their work.

STATEMENT 12 Human service professionals understand the complex interaction between individuals, their families, the communities in which they live, and society.

STATEMENT 13 Human service professionals act as advocates in addressing unmet client and community needs. Human service professionals provide a mechanism for identifying unmet client needs, calling attention to these needs, and assisting in planning and mobilizing to advocate for those needs at the local community level.

We have a responsibility to advocate for just and equitable public policy. Social justice principles and standards are written into ethics codes to remind clinicians that they should be advocates within the oppressive environments that many clients face every day. **Advocacy** occurs in a number of ways. Clinicians often engage in *direct advocacy for a particular client,* such as helping a client get welfare benefits, find affordable day care, or get into a training program. Clinicians also *advocate for particular issues or populations:* supporting funding of community day programs for people with Alzheimer's disease, testifying about the need for programs for the homeless, or working for legislation to provide school lunch programs for children. On a broader level, we need to recognize the connection between public policy and the services we provide to individuals, groups, and families. We know that poverty, hunger, discrimination, poor housing, insufficient health care, lack of educational opportunities, insufficient day care resources, and unjust labor policies favoring some while restricting others—all affect the well-being of clients.

Professional organizations encourage activism. For example, social work programs require that their students take social welfare policy content; many also require that students participate in some form of community advocacy to prepare for the wider roles of the clinician in social change work. The APA's Public Policy Office is actively involved in many legislative and federal activities, meeting with members of Congress and their staffs, preparing background memos for congressional offices, organizing briefings, and working in coalitions with others. Professional ethical principles and standards suggest that we work as individuals, in groups, with communities, and with clients for political and social change to enhance the rights and well-being of all people.

CLIP 2.6
Words of Wisdom

■ Conclusion

In this chapter, we introduced the key concepts of multiculturally informed and responsive practice grounded in sound professional relationships and ethics. All the chapters that follow deal with specific strategies for attending to difference and diversity and for operationalizing ethical principles in our relationships and work with clients.

By now you are probably quite eager to start learning and practicing interviewing skills with clients. Each of the following chapters focuses on the specific skills used in helping relationships. It is time to start, and we start our work with clients even before we meet.

■ Suggested Readings

The following are useful books on multicultural practice:

Diller, Jerry V. (2004). *Cultural diversity: A primer for the human services.* Belmont, CA: Brooks/Cole.

Lynch, Eleanor W., & Hanson, Marci J. (Eds.). (2004). *Developing cross-cultural competence: A guide for working with children and their families* (3rd Ed.). Baltimore, MD: Brookes.

Murphy, Bianca Cody. (1994). Difference and diversity: Gay and lesbian couples. *Journal of Gay and Lesbian Social Services 1,* 5–31.

Perez, Ruperto, Debord, Kurt A., & Bieschke, Kathleen J. (2000). *Handbook of counseling and psychotherapy with lesbian, gay and bisexual clients.* Washington, DC: American Psychological Association.

Ponterotto, Joseph G., Casas, Manuel J., Suzuki, Lisa A., & Alexander, Charlene M. (Eds.). (2001). *Handbook of multicultural counseling.* Thousand Oaks, CA: Sage.

Robinson, Tracy L. (2005). *The convergence of race ethnicity and gender: Multiple identities in counseling* (2nd Ed.). Upper Saddle River, NJ: Pearson.

Sue, Derald Wing, & Sue, David. (2003). *Counseling the culturally diverse* (4th Ed.). New York: John Wiley.

In addition, we believe everyone should read:

McIntosh, Peggy. (1989). White privilege: Unpacking the invisible knapsack. *Peace and Freedom* (July/August), pp. 10–12.

Sue, Derald Wing. (2003). *Overcoming our racism: The journey to liberation.* San Francisco, CA: Jossey-Bass.

Wise, Tim. (2005). *White like me: Reflections on race from a privileged son.* Brooklyn, NY: Soft Skull Press.

The following articles trace the history, dimensions, and challenges of integrating social justice and clinical work:

Kiselica, Mark S., & Robinson, Michelle. (2001). Bringing advocacy counseling to life: The history, issues, and human drama of social justice work in counseling. *Journal of Counseling and Development 79,* 387–397.

Swenson, Carol R. (1998). Clinical social work's contribution to a social justice perspective. *Social Work 43,* no. 6, 527–537.

An important article on the uses, risks and benefits of technology in clinical work is:

Parker-Oliver, Debra, & Dimiris, George. (2006). Social work informatics: A new specialty. *Social Work 51,* 127–134.

■ Self-Explorations

1. We often take for granted our own assumptions, values, and ways of perceiving the world until we encounter people from another culture. Recall a time when you experienced "culture shock" by traveling to another part of the world or by interacting with someone from another culture and were surprised by some of your own assumptions. If you have not interacted with people from different cultures, think about a book or film in

which you became aware of your own assumptions and discovered that they were not universal. A good book to read about the impact of cultural differences is *The Spirit Catches You and You Fall Down*.

2. Sometimes people find it difficult to have experiences with others who are different from themselves. What experiences have you had with people who are different from yourself? What did you learn from these experiences?

3. We can sometimes enlarge our experiences with people who are different from ourselves by volunteering in a homeless shelter or food pantry, working with people with AIDS, or attending a mosque, synagogue, or church different from our own. What kinds of activities can you engage in to broaden your experiences and friendships? What keeps you from undertaking such activities?

4. Discuss examples of unintentional racism that you have observed or experienced. Remember Derald Wing Sue's assertion that, regardless of race, everyone can be a racist.

5. Identify someone who is different from you in a significant way (race, age, religion, sexual orientation) and from whom you have learned something about his or her culture or experiences. What specifically did you learn? What more would you like to know?

6. Reflect on the people and institutions that contributed to your personal ethical stance prior to undertaking a clinical education. List your own bedrock guiding principle for everyday life, relationships, and work.

7. Describe a situation you witnessed, or were part of, that challenged or brought into question your bedrock values or ethics. What effects did this experience have on your personal ethical development? Would you behave differently today? Why or why not?

■ Essay Questions

1. The APA, ACA, and NASW provide multicultural guidelines for working with diverse populations. Read some guidelines for culturally competent practice. How is culturally competent practice different from just good practice?

2. Do you think clinicians can be value free? Can clinicians be value neutral? How do you think clinicians should handle the issue of values in the clinical relationship?

3. Confidentiality has become much more complicated in the electronic age. Discuss the various ways that technological advances and managed care affect privacy and confidentiality. Can clinicians really offer confidentiality? What should clinicians do to ensure confidentiality?

4. Review the ethical codes of APA, ACA, NASW, or NOHS. Discuss the limits of confidentiality when working with minors.

■ Key Terms

Advocacy	Minority status
Certification	Multicultural practice
Confidentiality	Multiethnic
Culture	Multiple dimensions of identity
Cultural competencies	Multiple relationships
Discrimination	Multiracial
Diversity	Prejudice
Duty to warn	Privileged communication
Ethical dilemmas	Professional code of ethics
Ethical principles	Professional license
Ethical standards	Race
Ethics	Racism
Ethnicity	Salience of identity
Fiduciary relationship	Socially constructed
Heterosexism	Statused
Homophobia	Stereotype
Identity	Value differences
Informed consent	

CHAPTER 3

Getting Started

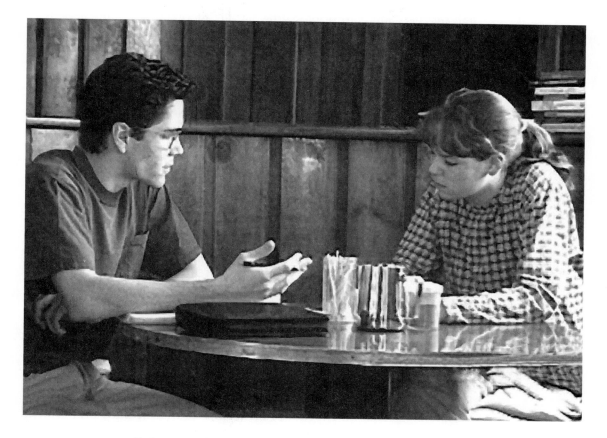

Before you begin working with clients, you have to prepare. In Chapter 2, we laid the foundation for ethical and multicultural practice. In this chapter we talk about how clinicians prepare to meet with clients in a variety of settings and the expectations that both clinicians and clients may bring to their initial encounters. Finally, we discuss ways to begin the clinical interview.

■ The Interview Environment

CLIP 3.1
Variety of Settings

Clinicians interview in a variety of settings. Since the location of the meeting and the physical surroundings affect the aura and process of an interview, it is incumbent on us as clinicians to be thoughtful in setting up our interview environments. Here we refer not simply to arranging an office, but to making every interview space welcoming and accessible to persons with disabilities. Ideally, interviewing environments should be located near the populations served, have office hours that accommodate clients' schedules, be near public transportation, offer child care, provide services in clients' native languages, and offer affordable services scaled to clients' income.

Creating a safe, quiet space for talking reflects an appreciation of the fact that people often share their stories more easily in an atmosphere of privacy and relative calm. Part of preparing for the interview is creating an atmosphere that is quiet and circumscribed enough to be conducive to reflecting and talking together. Such an environment can often be established more easily in office settings in which there is some degree of control over noise and intrusions. Whatever the environment, you should try to surround each unique situation with an invisible **bubble of calm** and focused attention.

The interview ambiance is portable and almost palpable, arising from the clinician's respectful, caring, and attuned presence. It can be experienced on a bus en route to a court hearing, in a kitchen with children and neighbors coming and going, and on a park bench outside a homeless shelter. With few exceptions, our steadiness and thoughtfulness regarding clients' needs and styles act as a containing and soothing environment, no matter the setting for the interview. Clients often experience the relationship as respite and may describe to their clinicians how much they look forward to their time together, or what a "breather from the usual" this encounter is, or how safe and peaceful they feel with us—a unique experience for many. Janet Surrey (1991a) also views this unique good feeling of safety and support as a source of enhanced client agency because relatedness stimulates confidence and initiative.

The Professional Office

Most people think interviews take place in an office, and clinicians may do a lot of thinking about office size, location, comfort, and accessibility. Much has been written about the effects on the interview process of office arrangement and decor, including the presence or absence of the clinician's personal belongings (Kadushin & Kadushin, 1997).

Few clinicians have the opportunity to create their own offices. Interns and clinicians pressed for space in community agencies may share office space and have little control over the physical environment in which they work. Whether we have control over our own office settings, as we might if we were in private practice, or work in an agency where we share space, it is important that we take responsibility for the space in which we work.

> *I had been hired for a new clinic that admitted patients before the physical space was ready. I did counseling sessions in a hallway between two metal file cabinets for 4 weeks. Nervous about confidentiality, I hung a big cardboard sign on one of the drawers: "Counseling in progress. Keep a wide berth."*

We suggest the following guidelines for arranging office setup.

Offices should be private, soundproof, and as free of interruptions as possible. Unfortunately, even these basic requirements for privacy can be hard to meet.

When I was an intern, I was seeing a client at the community mental health center. Our offices were very small with no windows and it really felt like a rabbit warren. One major problem was that at times you could hear clients in other rooms. I remember sitting with a 20-year-old woman who had trouble expressing her feelings. We had been talking about her abusive mother when suddenly through the walls we heard the client next door screaming, "I hate her, I hate her." We both looked at each other, and my client said, "I guess she is mad at her mother." We both laughed. Later I talked at staff meeting about the problem and eventually we bought lots of those little sound machines to mask noise. That worked—for the most part.

Although you may sometimes feel powerless to affect the systems in which you are trained, perceptive interns have often brought about needed change by pointing out problems and working with clients and colleagues to resolve them.

Offices should be accessible to persons with disabilities. There should be ramps and accessible bathrooms. Ideally, there should be phones with TTY (a teletypewriter or text typewriter) so that those who are deaf or hard of hearing can easily communicate with the clinician. Offices should accommodate walkers, wheelchairs, and Seeing Eye dogs. Federal law mandates accessibility in public settings, and professionals may have to work hard to ensure that private practice offices and smaller settings adhere to the guidelines.

Accessibility for people with disabilities is more than physical accommodation. Mackelprang and Salsgiver (1999) recommend a number of guiding principles for clinicians working with people with disabilities. These include maintaining a strengths perspective, recognizing that such clients are "different not deficient," and emphasizing self-determination. We can build all the ramps we want, but we are not truly accessible unless we are also sensitive to and knowledgeable about working with persons with disabilities.

Offices need to be flexible enough to allow both client and therapist a comfortable personal space. Most people have an invisible area around them that serves as a protective barrier. Intrusion into this **personal space** creates discomfort. Personal space varies from person to person, from culture to culture, and from situation to situation. People probably have less need for personal space with a friend than with a stranger. Gender also plays a role; in Western cultures, men tend to leave more interpersonal space between themselves and male strangers than do women with female strangers (Harper, Wiens, & Matarazzo, 1978). Cultural norms also dictate personal space.

Ivey and Ivey (2003) note that most North Americans seem to prefer a conversational space of about an arm's length. "Latino/a people often prefer half that distance, and those from the Middle East may talk practically eyeball to eyeball" (p. 46). The British prefer greater distance than all three. Personal space is often influenced by power dynamics. Those in positions of relatively less power may have their personal space invaded by those with greater power. We try never to invade clients' personal space unless there is no option—for example, if jostled together while riding on a crowded subway, or if a client falls and we reach down to help him or her up, or if we have to assist in restraining someone whose behavior is escalating out of control.

Having movable chairs or furniture helps create a comfortable environment for both client and clinician. When there is a difference in comfort levels about personal space, the clinician should respect the client's needs. However, there are exceptions: The clinician who feels that the client's needs interfere with the ability to attend or to get work done may have to ask the client to move a little. We talk about other issues relating to physical contact and closeness in Chapter 13.

> *In my private practice office, I have two chairs set up with about two and a half feet between them. One time I saw a client who pulled her chair up so close that our knees were touching. I pulled my chair back a little and she moved closer. I felt very uncomfortable with that much closeness. I wondered what it meant but did not feel like making a big deal about it yet. I had only just met her. I noted that she felt comfortable sitting very close and I said that made it hard for me to see her. I said I feel more comfortable with a little more distance between us. I stored the information away for future use.*

Furniture arrangement should reflect equality and respect. Seating should be comfortable, yet not so comfortable that one is likely to fall asleep. The relative height and style of the seats, as well as their position in relationship to each other, should reflect the equality and respect of the client-clinician relationship. Clinicians should have a flexible office arrangement that can accommodate people in wheelchairs and other assistive devices. Although it is important to pay attention to the seating arrangements, remember that it is the sitter, not the seat, who communicates professionalism and respect.

> *I have a colleague who has one of those huge La-Z-Boy recliners for himself and a small folding chair for his clients. I've always wondered how the clients feel about that.*

> *I was working with Karlene, a woman who was somewhat overweight. One day, my usual office was not available. We used another office that had comfortable chairs, but no couch, love seat, or chairs without arms. I didn't notice anything was wrong until she leaned back in her chair and the chair began to tip sideways. I commented on this and suggested that we move to an office with more comfortable seating. I only realized how tight the chair was when she struggled to get out of it. Even though she had been fairly open with me in the past, she said she would not have raised the issue of the chair if I had not brought it up. She cried as she talked about how bad it felt to live in a world where usual things (stores with turnstiles, movie theaters, and airplanes) were not accessible. She later shared that she had interviewed several therapists before deciding to see me. One of the factors that clinched her decision was the sturdy love seat in my office. The experience opened my eyes to the covert discrimination people experience when the world is not designed to be accessible to them.*

> *The first time I worked with a woman in a wheelchair, I quickly removed the chair that normally is placed opposite mine in the office, assuming that she would place her wheelchair in that spot. I thought I was being sensitive. I didn't realize that she might prefer transferring out of her wheelchair to sit in an office chair until she told me. It also reminded me that I should be careful that the furniture in my office be solid and stable enough to support a transfer.*

Many interviewers sit beside the desk, rather than behind it, so that the desk does not create a symbolic barrier. If the desk is placed against the wall and a chair is placed beside the desk, the client seated there can be invited to fill out information on the desktop or work side by side with the clinician on genograms, ecomaps, lifecharts, letters, or artwork. Some clinicians prefer a desk out of the way in a corner, with comfortable chairs placed in the main space of the office. Clinicians concerned about safety may want to place their desks or chairs near the door so that they can exit quickly to summon help in the event of an emergency. If the interviewer has a preferred seat, it should be pointed out to clients while encouraging them to take any other seat they wish.

EXAMPLES

"Mrs. Lindahl, have a seat wherever you would like. Lawrence, feel free to sit on the sofa or any of the chairs."

"Janelle, I'll be sitting here; take any of the other seats you would like."

Clinicians seldom sit on a couch with a client because doing so may suggest a familiarity or informality that may be uncomfortable or inappropriate. In a home visit, however, sitting on a couch may be necessary and appropriate.

After being forced to work behind a desk in a regulation office setting, I devised a living room milieu for my private practice office. I associated the environment with a place for private, intimate talk and hoped my clients would too. I've set up my office with a large window behind me so clients can take a break from looking at me. It also gives a feeling of openness and airiness to the room.

With children, some teens, and some adults, casual seating on the floor may be used as long as clients manifest comfort with this arrangement and there is a clinical reason for it. Children especially appreciate the clinician's willingness to "come down to their size" rather than loom over them. Family therapists, psychodramatists, relaxation trainers, and process group facilitators may all use floor seating from time to time.

Interviewing offices should be able to accommodate unexpected others who may accompany clients to the meeting. The clinician should know where extra chairs can be found if needed and where others may wait comfortably for the client if they are not to be part of the meeting. It goes without saying that attending to the needs of these others is also a way of demonstrating caring to the client.

As in all clinical work, the interviewer considers the possible symbolic meanings of seating arrangements and behaviors noting where the client, group, or family customarily chooses to sit in relation to each other and to the clinician. The choices may signal alliances, the degree of comfort with closeness and distance, and subtle shifts in relationships.

I can often tell what's happening in the midpoint of therapy by the chair the client takes. When we've gotten to the most psychologically affecting material, clients sometimes switch seats. Those needing more intimacy move closer to me; others needing more distance sit farther away.

No matter how the office is arranged, it is important to make sure that the client feels some flexibility in the office seating. You can indicate flexibility in a number of ways. One is by directly asking after the client sits: "Is that okay?" Another is by remaining responsive to reasonable client requests for changes in arrangement.

> *I had brought a client into my office, which has two chairs and a couch in one area and a desk and chair in another. I told her to have a seat wherever she would like and she took a seat on the couch. I took a seat in one of the chairs and angled it a little to face the couch. I asked her my usual pro forma question: "Is that all right?" She responded by jumping off the couch and saying that she felt that the couch was much softer than it looked and that she felt like she sank into it. She said she was glad I had asked because she really did-n't want to sit on the couch and felt uncomfortable about moving. She took the other chair and I turned my chair to face her more directly.*

Office decor should be soothing, not distracting. Warm colors and soft lighting can help create a sense of caring, privacy, and intimacy. However, we are creating a professional environment, not a romantic setting. The lighting should be bright enough for people to see clearly. If possible, have wall hangings and pictures that represent the diversity of cultures served. Try to create an environment that is not too "busy" or disorganized. Individual clinicians have the right to establish their own environments unless an agency dictates or standardizes furnishings. Some clinicians like to display a few personal belongings or pictures of loved ones or pets. Others feel it is more appropriate to have a personally neutral office. Always anticipate the possible effects of displaying personal belongings, and be prepared to respond to questions these may elicit from clients or other visitors.

Two relatively common pieces of office decor are a box of tissues and a clock. Some clinicians place the clock so that it is over the client's shoulder and they can unobtrusively note the time without distracting the client. We have found it useful to have the clock positioned in such a way that both the client and the clinician can easily see it. Sometimes it is helpful to have two clocks—one facing the client, the other facing the clinician—so that both can track time. Some clients feel more in control of the session if they know how much time is left, so that they are able to pace themselves. Others prefer not to see the clock because it reminds them of the arbitrary time limits on the session and on the clinical relationship.

Clinicians who work with children or who do art therapy may display their clients' artwork in the office. Others may place presents from clients in the office. We discuss the implications of client gifts to clinicians in Chapter 13. Gifts from clients raise a number of important questions: What will other clients think about the items? Will clients feel compelled to give the clinician similar presents? If the clinician is hanging one client's drawings, should all clients' drawings be hung? Would this be distracting to others? Where to draw the line?

Make sure that the interview space is not overly cluttered. Avoiding clutter applies to clinicians' desks as well. Having a desk that is relatively clear lets clients know that you have "made room" to see them. On the other hand, it has been suggested that having a messy desk might humanize the clinician in the client's eyes. Of course, we can never fully predict whether a client might find something in or about our offices uncomfortable or even offensive. Clients' reactions to our offices may provide us with important information and can be grist for the mill.

Office decor should be appropriate to the types of clients we see and should reflect the cultures of the people with whom we work. For example, if we are seeing families and children, our offices should have toys and playthings. If we work with Mexican immigrants, we may want to have pictures or posters with Mexican themes. We must be careful about superficial or cosmetic fixes—displaying things just to make an impression.

Try to experience what the office is like from the client's perspective. Sitting in all the available places in the office enables us to consider whether sunlight shines in the client's eyes, what is in the client's line of vision, and whether the chair is comfortable.

Always consider other needs of clients. Is a bathroom available to clients? Is it wheelchair accessible? What about drinking water? Can children play somewhere safely while their parents are being seen? Where can clients hang their coats? Is a phone available for client use? Are clients routinely asked at intake whether they need any special arrangements or accommodations to facilitate the interview process (e.g., child care, translator services, sign language interpretation, ramp entrance)? Weaver (2005) notes that traditional Muslims pray several times a day, so that, out of respect, flexible scheduling should take these practices into account.

Make the best of the situation. Today clinicians often work in less than ideal circumstances. They may share small cubicles with many other people. They may have no privacy, no comfortable chairs, no office decor—not even a place to store their personal belongings. In those situations you need to be as creative as possible. You can arrange schedules so that you and each of your officemates have some time alone to meet with clients—for example, when others are at lunch or out of the office. You can bring in posters or plants from home to make offices look nicer. You can see if other agencies, churches, or schools will give your agency space for private meetings with clients. Finally, you can join with colleagues to lobby administrators for more conducive environments for your work with clients.

> When I was an intern, the office I had was awful. It was dark, had no windows, and had old broken-down furniture with graffiti on the desk. I went to the Christmas Tree Shop and bought some posters, a tablecloth to cover the desk, and two artificial plants. I even found a poster of a field that was hung in a window frame so that it actually gave the impression of a window with a view. And all $18.85!!

> We were so crowded at the mental health center that, with the director's approval, we asked the public library if they would give us a room in their basement where we could meet with clients. They ended up giving us two small rooms. Ironically, some of the people we worked with spent a good part of their day at the library anyway.

> When I was a field supervisor for the school of social work, we placed a student in an ER. The only place they could find for her to write up her case notes was a small anteroom off

the ER where they sometimes left the dead bodies while they waited for their families to arrive. It was awful. Several times she asked for a different space but they said there was none. She called me and the school decided that we could not use that setting for an internship anymore. When we told the ER we would not place students there under those conditions, they cleared a little space for her down the hall.

EXERCISE 3.1 Field Visit

After securing permission to do so, visit an agency where clinical interviews take place. Briefly sit in the waiting area and note what you would observe as a client. Go to one of the offices and sit in all the chairs. In your journal, make notes on what you see and learn. Be aware of privacy, lighting, furniture arrangement, décor, and so on. Do the agency and staff reflect the cultures of the diverse populations they serve? In what ways? Discuss your observations in class.

Out of the Office and onto the Streets

Many clinicians do not see clients primarily in office settings, and many clients may not find an office setting comfortable or safe. To engage clients, we may conduct interviews in their home kitchens, in hospital rooms, on benches outside shelters, over coffee at fast-food restaurants, or in classrooms.

I got a call on intake at the mental health center from a family whose 17-year-old daughter had started to hear voices. My supervisor approved an in-home crisis evaluation to determine whether the girl could be sustained at home. I would be in touch with my supervisor by phone to determine the next steps once in the home. When I arrived, the daughter, dressed in a long wool coat, was fully immersed in a bathtub full of warm water, laughing and singing. She knew I was coming and invited me in "to see I'm just fine." Since she wouldn't leave the tub, I perched on the closed toilet seat and interviewed her there long enough to get a sense of her need for protection. Thus began a relationship that, following her 30-day hospitalization, continued for two and a half years.

Home Visits

There is a lot to learn about clients by meeting with them in their homes. People may behave very differently in their homes than they do in the office; they may be more comfortable, more outgoing—literally, more at home. Clinicians may be able to observe things about the client and his or her situation that are not readily visible in the office, thus expanding their perspective.

As a counseling intern at a suburban mental health clinic, I decided to do a home visit with the family of a 14-year-old adolescent I was seeing. When I arrived at the house, I noticed the striking contrast between the fortresslike outside (gate locked, curtains drawn, double locks on the door) and the absence of doors in any of the rooms inside the house. I began to wonder about family secrets and family boundaries. Later, my client revealed that she was sexually abused by her father.

The home visitor often has a greater opportunity to meet the client's friends and family; see family pictures; note relationships with cherished pets and neighbors that the client may not think to mention in the office; and experience the way the client puts together, develops, and protects living space. Just as we attend carefully to the messages conveyed by our own office arrangements, we also note clients' environments and the messages they convey about the clients and their situations. Culture, income levels, and personal taste all need to be taken into account before making inferences.

Home visits present a number of challenges to the clinician.

- *Clients may live in circumstances different from those of the interviewer—* some may be wealthy, others poor. A variety of factors such as poverty, exploitation, mental illness, and addiction can cause clients to live in inadequate or dilapidated housing lacking basic amenities. Large numbers of extended kin may have to live in two or three rooms. At the other extreme, clinicians visit the homes of wealthy clients living in opulence. Interviewers may thus work in alien and unfamiliar environments, at times feeling uncomfortable or intimidated.

- *The home is not a controlled environment,* nor is it set up to ensure privacy, flexibility, and comfort for interviews the way offices may be. Phone calls, kids waking from naps, elders calling out for help, visitors dropping by—all may seem like intrusions on the interview. We must remember that, as important as our work may seem to us, it is but a small part of many clients' hectic lives and may at times seem to them to be the least important thing they have to worry about.

- *From the client's perspective, the clinician may feel like the intruder, the outsider.* The clinician is the guest and may feel less in control of the environment or the agenda. In some situations, clients may not welcome the clinician and may want him or her to leave their homes. These factors may contribute to the unfortunate reluctance of many professionals to make home visits.

> *Tshanga, a 14-year-old isolated and depressed teen, was referred to family services by her mother "to see if you can find out why she is so sad." Since she would not come to see me, I made several home visits to try to engage her, but she would never let me inside the apartment. My supervisor made me go back for four weeks running and interview her standing outside, talking through the door and feeling ridiculous as neighbors passed in the hallway and stared at me as I talked to an invisible other. I did process recording on each of these visits, and my supervisor treated them like office visits, helping me focus on feelings, use humor, ask about school, inquire about boyfriends, and so on. At about the fifth week, Tshanga suddenly said she would let me come in today, but only if she were allowed to stand on the opposite side of the room. I was very receptive, and this is how our visits went the rest of the year.*

- *Home visits may begin with greetings, social conversation, and sharing coffee or food.* Some clinicians may experience discomfort over the thought that during home visits they are not "doing the work" and are "just socializing." We believe that all these rituals are an integral part of the interview process and may contribute to the development of the positive working alliance. In many cultures, sharing food and informal conversation are an important part of social interaction.

> *Mrs. Lanzarone was not able to meet with me in the office because she had custody of her four grandchildren while her daughter was in prison for selling drugs. So I met with her weekly in the kitchen of her apartment, and I often held one of the kids in my lap while Mrs. L. cooked me Italian food for lunch. At first, I would come away from these sessions exhausted, which helped me understand what Mrs. L. was up against every day. Once I got used to it, I looked forward to our meetings and so did Mrs. L. She called this "Gramma's time."*

- *Home visits may present the clinician with special safety challenges.* Weapons or drugs in the home, when coupled with simmering resentments, can present serious danger. (We discuss safety issues later in this chapter.)

Other Settings

In addition to home visits, interviews may occur in a variety of nonoffice settings. The workplace, the school cafeteria or playground, the shelter, the restaurant, the street corner, the locked facility—all are frequent sites of clinical interventions. Today's practitioners learn to move flexibly and comfortably among locales, tailoring interviewing strategies to the exigencies and advantages of nontraditional sites. For example, from her work with poor single mothers, Janna Malamud Smith (2000) describes accommodating a client with asthma and agoraphobia by driving to her area, parking near her apartment, and interviewing her quite productively in the car.

Major challenges confronting clinicians when we work in a **borrowed environment** include the maintenance of confidentiality and focus, the intrusion of others with different roles and needs, and the pressure of time in an environment whose purposes can shift from moment to moment.

> *It was amazing how much we were able to do at the diner. Russell didn't want anyone in his small town to know that he had AIDS. He was afraid to come to the clinic; so we met at the Busy Bee diner in the next town. We could get a lot done as long as we found a corner table in the back, kept our voices low, and screened out all the hubbub around us by focusing intensely on our work.*

It is crucial to remember that what we see in meetings with a client is only part of the larger picture—snapshots of a person's life at a particular time. To see clients in situations where they are interacting with others may broaden our perspective in unanticipated ways. The quiet teenager in the office may be very outgoing and funny in the playground. The woman suffering from major depression, tearful and seemingly paralyzed during therapy sessions, may still be functioning in superhuman ways in her leadership position at work. Whenever feasible, wise clinicians attempt to see clients in a variety of contexts to get a fuller picture of their strengths and issues. School counselors may observe students in classroom settings. Day treatment staff may observe clients in community meetings. Workers in an adolescent residential treatment center often make home visits to observe the teens interacting with their families. Carel Germain and Alex Gitterman (1996) use the term **lifespace interviews** to describe these informative in vivo transactions.

Safety

Physical Safety

Few issues concern both clients and clinicians today more than physical safety. According to Susan Weinger (2001), OSHA announced in 1996 that "more assaults occur in health care and social service industries than in any other" (p. 3). Weinger cites research predicting that half of all human service workers will experience client violence at some point in their careers. Many clients come from situations characterized by past or present violence, abuse, or neglect. Neighborhoods can be unsafe for travel at the very times busy families are free to come for interviews. Clinicians, too, can worry about physical safety. The violence of home and neighborhood can spill over unpredictably into practice settings, and clinicians need to be prepared for the unexpected (Griffin, 1995).

> *I'll never forget the first time I heard about a clinician who was murdered. I was working at a community center when we received a call that a former colleague of ours had been shot by a client who had come to the clinic with a gun. He killed one psychologist and wounded another.*

> *At my agency, people would be yelling all the time. We became somewhat oblivious to the sound of loud voices. We realized that if a clinician was in trouble and was calling out, no one would pay attention. We decided that we needed a code word that would alert us. We decided to use the word "conference."*

> *I made a visit to a client recovering from an overdose in a hospital in a high-crime neighborhood. She had been a tough client, challenging me constantly, dismissing me as unable to understand her because of our differing backgrounds. When I walked into her hospital room, she was shocked to see me. "You're so little and you come all this way to see me?" she said. We visited for a while, and as I got up to leave, she said, "Now on your way to the subway, walk tall and put your hand in your pocket so they think you have a gun." I laughed but, believe me, I followed her advice. The next time I saw her, the hostility was gone.*

As more and more clinicians conduct interviews in the community, they find themselves in situations in which they fear for their own safety.

> *When I was a counseling intern at an alternative high school, two of my students got into a fight and one, Doreen, had her arm slashed with a knife. After taking her to the hospital and dealing with the police who had been called, I brought Doreen home to her family. Her older sister ran into the bedroom and came out with a gun saying, "We have to kill that bitch who cut you." I was terrified.*

Clinicians need to feel relatively safe to be effective. When feeling personally at risk, they find it hard, if not impossible, to attend to clients and their needs. Clinicians who are too anxious to concentrate will not be able to help others. It is extremely important that you turn to supervisors, colleagues, or consultants when alarm bells go off about physical safety. Do not be embarrassed to ask for help before, during, or after critical incidents. In fact, many agencies have formalized critical incident review processes, whereby staff review incidents together and base future strategies on the learning from each situation.

> *I was seeing a young woman who was a police officer in my private practice in my home. She always had to carry her service revolver with her—even when off duty. I was constantly distracted by it. I didn't worry that she would get angry and use it—I just felt uncomfortable having a gun in my home where my children are. I talked about it with my group practice, and they suggested that I ask her if she would leave her gun locked in the glove compartment or trunk of her car when we met. That was fine with her.*

With regard to physical safety, consider the following cautions:

- Avoid working alone in a building or isolated location, especially after dark. Lighted offices in otherwise darkened buildings can make both clinicians and clients vulnerable targets.
- When you are concerned about the degree of risk involved in a family visit, discuss with supervisors or consultants whether someone should accompany you.
- Let someone at the agency know where you are headed when you leave for visits in the field.
- As a general rule, do not interview people who are intoxicated or who might have weapons on them.
- Carry a cell phone programmed to access emergency help instantly.
- If feeling seriously endangered, leave the situation immediately and get help.

Bradford Sheafor, Charles Horejsi, and Gloria Horejsi (1997) advise clinicians never to touch or turn their backs on people whose escalating rage or fear might lead to an attack. You should also avoid stepping into a dangerous fight between two or more people already out of control. Call for help instead.

> *I didn't tell you what happened before I brought Doreen home and her sister pulled out the gun. I was the counselor in the classroom when another student, Yvette, pulled a knife on Doreen. I remember thinking, "I am the counselor—I should do something about this." I actually stood between the students and tried to talk Yvette into putting her knife away. All the while, Doreen was egging her on. I was lucky Yvette didn't use the knife on me to get to Doreen.*

No one can be completely safe. Clinicians and agencies have to decide what risks they are willing to assume. Address these important practice issues with colleagues, supervisors, and agency or program administrators. Today most schools and court settings, as well as some child protective and health agencies, have security guards posted at entrances so that strangers may not simply wander in. In addition, agencies should have safety and escape plans in case dangerous incidents occur or clients threaten serious harm. Buzzers behind desks, alarms that signal trouble, and coded language signaling for help can all avert harm to both staff and clients.

Other Safety Concerns

Clinicians also need to be concerned about other kinds of safety, not related to the physical environment. Clients may be threatened with harm if they elect to share their stories with a professional. Undocumented immigrants may worry about deportation if they accept services. Battered wives may fear reprisals from spouses if they disclose their abuse. Mothers may fear losing custody of their children if they reveal their lesbianism. It makes little difference to people in crisis whether we are called psychologists, human service workers, counselors, or social workers if what we provide seems to offer more risk than gain. Even clients without such concerns may worry about the confidentiality of the interview process.

Some clients worry that they will be harmed by the clinicians themselves. Unfortunately, these concerns are sometimes justified. As noted in Chapter 2, there has been a steady increase in the number of complaints against clinicians of sexual abuse, physical abuse, and financial exploitation (Pope & Vasquez, 1998; Reamer, 1995).

■ Even Before We Meet

It is human nature to anticipate what people and events will be like before engaging with them. Thinking about encounters in advance may reduce anxiety about the unknown and prepare us to cope with contingencies that may arise from contact with that which is unfamiliar. So, even before we meet, clinicians and clients alike develop expectations about each other and about the relationship.

Clinician Expectations

The Exercise 3.2 helps you identify clinician expectations you may have about clients even before you meet them. Do the exercise, then continue reading.

EXERCISE 3.2 Anticipation

Write down in your journal the ideas that immediately come to mind about the following clients:

- Terry Mahoney is referred to the mental health clinic because of drug abuse.
- Domingo, a high school sophomore, is referred by his teacher because he is failing math.
- A young couple comes to you wanting to talk about the process of artificial insemination.

- Mrs. Giorgio is a 67-year-old woman whose husband has just died.
- Chang Yang is a 33-year-old Chinese immigrant accused of spouse abuse.

It is important to explore the sources of our expectations. Some expectations come from information about the client (such as the client's gender, age, ethnicity, or presenting problem). We refer to these factors as **client information variables.** In Exercise 3.3, see whether your expectations about each client change as information is added or altered. Complete that exercise before reading on.

EXERCISE 3.3   Changing Expectations

- Terry Mahoney is referred to the mental health clinic because of drug abuse. She is a 54-year-old social worker.
- Domingo, a high school sophomore, is referred by his teacher because he is failing math. He is 22 years old and is mentally retarded.
- A young couple comes to you wanting to talk about the process of artificial insemination. They are lesbians who have been in a committed relationship for 7 years.
- Mrs. Giorgio is a 67-year-old woman whose husband has just died. They were married one year ago.
- Chang Yang is a 33-year-old Chinese immigrant accused of spouse abuse. Chang Yang is a woman.

What other variables might shape what you think about these clients? Note the similarities and differences in your reactions once you have additional information.

In answering the last question in Exercise 3.3 you may have focused on other attributes of the client, such as sexual orientation, class, race, ethnicity, family background, diagnosis, or appearance. Much of this information may precede the client into the office.

> *Very seldom do I see a client without having some information about him or her. Often it comes from a phone call with the client in which I learn a little about the reason for the meeting. Sometimes I receive information about the client from the referral source. I am frequently given a case file before I meet the client. I must admit that when I see a very thick case file, I worry that I've been given "a chronic client." I haven't even read any information, but I already have my preformed ideas.*

Clinician Gestalt

Clinician preconceptions about clients based on client information variables are mediated by what we like to think of as the **clinician gestalt.** As you may have already noted, it is not just the information about clients that shapes how clinicians respond to them; it is the information interacting with clinicians' values, beliefs, and past experiences. In turn, their values, beliefs, and experiences are mediated by familial and cultural background, including their own race, gender, class, sexual orientation, ethnicity, age, and physical ability.

Values are also mediated by personal prejudice, xenophobia, misinformation, and stereotyping. Lum (2004) has found that people of color can be reluctant to come to agencies dominated by white professionals because stereotypes, rules, structures, and procedures "can act as a boundary between 'host' and 'visitor'" (p. 152). In anticipating client visits, we must always remember that the larger social context for "minority" populations in the United States is a prevailing climate of color prejudice, gender bias, homophobia, and ethnic and religious discrimination. Hate crimes, mosque and temple desecrations, and church burnings are vivid reminders of the problems that shadow and affect our interactions with each other.

> *I remember my first week of internship at the community mental health center. I was assigned a "young divorced woman with two children coming to the clinic because she was depressed." My picture was of a woman who was 23, with kids about 2 and 4. I was so shocked when I went to the waiting room and found a 39-year-old woman! I was 27 at the time. I realized my supervisor, who is in her fifties, thought of the client as a young woman; but here she was older than I was. Before meeting her, I had pictured myself as older and wiser, even though I didn't have any children and was just starting out. Now here she was, and I was closer in age to her 20-year-old daughter than to her. Suddenly, I felt so nervous.*

Furthermore, the characteristics of individuals and groups obtain meaning within larger social contexts, which include geography, historical period, and prevailing cultural norms. For example, the behavior of a woman who hears voices and talks back to them might have different meaning in different contexts. In sixteenth-century Europe, she may have been called a witch; in twenty-first-century United States, she may be seen as having schizophrenia or as being "perfectly normal," depending on whether her behavior occurs on a subway in New York City or in a Pentecostal church.

EXERCISE 3.4   Clinician Gestalt

In your journal, identify the aspects of your own clinician gestalt that mediate your reaction to or your preconceived ideas about the clients described in Exercises 3.2 and 3.3. These can include your beliefs, cultural heritage, past experiences, gender, class, race, ethnicity, age, sexual orientation, and ability in the larger social context in which you find yourself.

Diagnosis and Labeling

Another type of information that may precede a client into the office is a **diagnosis.** A diagnosis is not a description of a person; rather, it is a shorthand way of referring to a complex set of behaviors and characteristics. At times, diagnoses can be useful in facilitating communication between clinicians, which is essential for research and treatment planning. However, when we reduce the rich complexity of a person to a few behaviors, the diagnosis becomes a label.

Labeling is particularly pernicious because labels can predispose us to categorize people and react to them in formulaic ways. For example, some disability scholars believe that attribution of a disability status and the devaluation of certain diagnosed conditions undermine inclusion, civil rights, and the possibility of being thought of as diverse rather than "abnormal" (DePoy & Gilson, 2004). Sometimes labels cause us to see things, like symptoms, that are not there, and sometimes labels cause us *not* to see things, like strengths, that are there (Szasz, 1960).

In the now famous study conducted by David Rosenhan (1973), eight associates of the researcher acted as if they had a mental illness (schizophrenia) to get themselves admitted to various hospital psychiatric wards. Once admitted to the hospital, each of the mock patients behaved normally. The hospital staff, however, continued to see them as mentally ill, despite their protestations and even though they were no longer manifesting symptoms. Once they had been given a diagnosis—a label—their protestations were defined as further evidence of their mental illness. (Interestingly, the "real patients" on the units could tell that the researchers were not actually mentally ill and did not belong in the hospital.)

Certain diagnoses are particularly stigmatizing. **Stigma** refers to the negative assumptions and biases attached to people because of their membership in particular groups (Goffman, 1963). Judgments about people with particular diagnoses are culturally determined and can reflect the zeitgeist of the times, of the community, or of the agency. The diagnoses may frighten clinicians, constricting their openness and negatively impacting the interview process.

> *An elderly woman called the clinic asking for someone to come out and talk her schizophrenic son into coming out of a closet where he had been holed up for two days. I was on intake and went out with the on-call psychiatrist. I didn't want the doctor to see how anxious I was. I had seen* Psycho *and thought we might be heading into a situation like that one. The man turned out to be a quiet, sad person who began to cry with relief when the doctor said he had come out to help him.*

> *The three supervisors in day treatment told us that most of the women in the Daily Living Group were "borderlines" who would try to manipulate us because we were interns and didn't know any better. They explained the importance of setting firm limits on client behaviors and not giving "these people" extra attention if they did dramatic things. We were very anxious about starting the group and felt irritated with "these women" before we got to know them.*

Diagnoses are usually determined after an extensive process of assessment, which may include observing, testing, interviewing, collecting historical data and life records, and conducting medical exams. Some of the people we see may not have been through an assessment process, but other clients come to us with an already established diagnosis.

EXERCISE 3.5   Diagnosis

In your journal, discuss the ways in which knowing the diagnosis of a client before you meet can be both helpful and problematic.

Preconceived Ideas and Clinical Intuition

Seasoned practitioners may refer to their preconceived ideas as **clinical intuition.** Clinical intuition entails much more than just preconceived ideas. The working hypotheses of the skilled practitioner are developed over time by comparing preconceived ideas and feelings with subsequent experience and learning. However, clinicians must always recognize that, at times, preconceived ideas and clinical intuition may interfere with their ability to be genuinely open to the client's story. In Chapter 9, we discuss the use of clinical intuition and hypothesis building in ongoing work with clients.

Client Expectations

Clients also bring a set of expectations about clinicians and the therapeutic process and environment. These expectations may come from the media, from previous experiences with mental health workers, from the reputation of the agency or setting, or from the information the clients have about the clinician.

The media often show exaggerated or stereotypical representations of "shrinks," social workers, and other counselors. These images are almost exclusively of white, able-bodied, middle-class individuals, like television's Frasier Crane. They may expect the clinician to be helpful, but they may also be aware of sensational stories in the press that report clinicians' sexual and financial exploitation of clients.

Some clients may have had previous interactions with the mental health system. The man with schizophrenia who has seen nine other counselors at the day treatment program may come to see you with the expectation that you, just like the others before you, will be leaving soon. The woman who has received a psychiatric evaluation resulting in the loss of custody of her children may feel hostile and wary before meeting a new clinician. A Mexican-American family may be reluctant to seek help from the school counselor because, in previous encounters with other mental health clinicians, family members felt that the Anglo professionals were condescending and showed no respect for their strong family and community bonds.

Other clients may be reacting to information about the agency's reputation. For example, the factory worker seeking assistance about his troubled adolescent daughter may come to the Employee Assistance Program because his friends have told him that the people there are very helpful. A single mother may resist bringing her children to a homeless shelter because she has heard that it is dangerous.

Clients may also respond to clinician information variables that they know in advance. Knowing that the clinician is a man, a Latino, a social worker, or an intern may influence clients' preconceptions. Just like clinicians, clients react to information about the clinician and their reactions are mediated by their values, beliefs, and personal background in the larger social and cultural context. This is the **client gestalt.**

> *When I was an intern, I was assigned to a white, middle-class woman in her forties who was a survivor of serious physical and sexual abuse. After we had worked together for five years and were in the process of terminating, she told me that when I walked into the waiting room on the first day, she almost walked out. She couldn't imagine how a young black woman from what she guessed to be a working-class background (she was right) could be helpful to her. She said that she was glad she had stayed.*

Cynthia Garcia Coll (Garcia Coll, Cook-Nobles, & Surrey, 1997) suggests that, if an oppressed person meets with a therapist who appears to be from the oppressing group, the person is likely not to expect mutuality. Instead, he or she may experience a power differential, whether it is real or not, "as powerful as if it were real" (p. 180).

EXERCISE 3.6 Client Expectations

Break up into small groups and discuss how you would feel if a client said that he or she did not want to work with you because you were too young or too inexperienced. How would you handle a client who said he had a preference to work with someone who was gay, heterosexual, black, white, Latino, or Catholic? Does the client have a right to ask for a clinician with certain personal characteristics? What about requesting someone with specialized education or training?

Getting Ready

Students wonder about the reasoning behind the "50-minute hour"—why the clinical hour is often reduced to 45 or 50 minutes. We try to reserve a space between clients or engagements for a number of reasons: to jot down notes from the last meeting, to return phone calls, to consult with colleagues, to provide an intellectual and emotional space between the last experience and the one to come, to refresh ourselves between visits, and to prepare for meeting with the next client. Clinicians meeting with clients outside agency settings may use travel time for many of the same purposes.

Attending to Self

Before the actual meeting with the client, experienced clinicians prepare for the meeting in a number of helpful ways. They try to relax. Some take a short walk, some get a breath of fresh air, some stretch, and others meditate to get into a quiet state of readiness. They also try to clear away any impinging thoughts or take care of any personal needs that may affect their ability to attend to the incoming client.

> *I had received a message from the clinic secretary that my son had called. He seldom called me at work, and I knew that if I didn't call him back, I would be sitting with my next Adult Children of Alcoholics (ACOA) group wondering what he wanted. I also knew that, if I called, I might be a minute or two late, and I had to decide whether I should keep my group waiting for two extra minutes or be distracted for the entire 90-minute group meeting. I returned his call.*

> *It took me a long time to realize that all the cups of coffee I was drinking to help me stay awake briefly stimulated me but then caused me to feel sleepy 15 to 20 minutes later. I had to learn to avoid caffeine, chocolate, and heavy meals before working with clients.*

> *I realized after much trial and error that I could competently do five sessions in a row with 15-minute breaks in between. But I found at the end of the day I couldn't calm down fast enough to get to sleep. Now I do no more than three in a row at one time.*

Thinking About the Client

In preparation for meeting with the client for the first time, clinicians should review the information available to them. This information may be in the form of client records; test results; referral forms; intake forms; comments from family, friends, or professionals; symptom checklists; and so on. Box 3.1 shows a sample intake form.

Some clinicians prefer not to have any information before meeting with the client for the first time, but rather, to see the client with fresh eyes so as not to be contaminated by colleagues' judgments. Others feel it is essential to

---

BOX 3.1 Sample Brief Intake Form

- Client name:
- Address and telephone:
- Who referred (self, others) and why:
- Presenting problem(s):
- Strengths and resources:
- Brief description of client and current situation:
- Previous history with service agency and outcome of contact:
- Any immediate crises or action needing to be taken:
- Insurance/payment information:
- Person to call in case of emergency:
- Recommendations:

read all the available material and develop hunches about where to go in the interview.

Whenever possible, *the clinician should review all available material before meeting the client.* Clients need to know that we have done our homework. If the clients have been asked questions, filled out complicated forms, or talked at length with an intake worker, they need to know that we care enough to make use of their information. This is indispensable preparation for a respectful encounter. At the same time, it is important that the clinician understand that these materials may contain omissions and distortions.

Clinicians should not rely solely on such material. We need to have an informed openness. We sustain this openness by not jumping to conclusions and by recognizing that clients may present themselves very differently in the interview situation, from moment to moment, from interview to interview, and from clinician to clinician. People usually react very differently to a person than to a questionnaire. They may reveal themselves more deeply within an unfolding relationship of trust and helpfulness than they do at the beginning of the relationship. Furthermore, a client's situation can change dramatically between intake and first session.

> *I was about to see a client whom the intake worker described as hostile, suspicious, and guarded. When I met with her, she seemed open, comfortable, and self-disclosing. Only later did I learn that she felt very uncomfortable talking with men. The intake worker was a man.*

In addition to reading available materials, *we may need to do extra reading and preparation.* For example, before seeing a client who has just surrendered a child for adoption, we may want to read material about birth mothers and the psychological sequelae of surrendering a child. Before meeting with a young transgendered male, the clinician is wise to read about issues of gender identity and the effects of rigid sex roles, homophobia, and transphobia.

As discussed in Chapter 2, *clinicians often have to prepare for working with people from a culture different from their own.* According to Sam Chan and Evelyn Lee (2004), "intercultural communication difficulties are not simply a matter of different languages, but of different thought patterns, different values, and different communication styles" (p. 271). While being careful not to stereotype, clinicians need to gain background knowledge about the cultures that may affect the client's beliefs and behaviors.

Clinicians may also need to gather resources to share with the client as appropriate. It is often helpful to create a resource file that can be shared by others. Resource files may include lists of contacts in specific areas, community services for particular populations, or copies of articles from the periodical literature. For example, to help a woman deal with her child's adoption, the clinician may want to know about any groups for birth mothers and get the address of Concerned United Birthparents (CUB). When preparing to work with a lesbian woman new to the area, the clinician can identify lesbian support groups and resources in the community and determine whether a gay/lesbian health center or women's bookstore is in the area, in case the client asks about these services.

The available information is used to help the clinician develop **anticipatory empathy.** Empathy is the ability to immerse oneself in another's experience and to imagine the feelings of that person in that situation. (We have a more thorough discussion of empathy in Chapter 5.) Judith Jordan (Miller, Jordan, Stiver, Walker, Surrey, & Eldridge, 2004) defines anticipatory empathy as thinking, in advance of meeting, about each client particularly and about the impact our ways of being are likely to have on him or her. We then adjust our ways accordingly to express that empathy. Lawrence Shulman (2006) emphasizes a similar process, preparatory empathy, involving "tuning in" to "get in touch with the feelings and concerns that the client may bring to the helping encounter" (pp. 57–58).

EXERCISE 3.7   Anticipatory Empathy

Client 1: Helena

Helena is a 39-year-old woman who is an active crack cocaine addict. To support her habit, she has been working as a prostitute. Her 6-month-old baby has just died of pneumonia. She has two other children, ages 2 and 3. You are the protective services worker who has been asked to assess whether the two children should be left in her care. Imagine Helena's experience and the feelings that might arise for her in this situation. What different feelings might Helena be experiencing about the death of her baby? What are some of the feelings Helena might have about her other children? What kind of feelings might Helena have about this upcoming meeting with you as her protective services worker?

Client 2: Jorge

Jorge is a 45-year-old man who has just lost his job in the defense industry. He has a wife with leukemia and two children—a boy age 7 and a girl age 9. He has worked for the plant as a bomb assembly expert for 15 years. He is seeing an employment counselor for help in getting a new job. Imagine Jorge's experience and the feelings that might arise for him in this situation. What pressures might Jorge experience at this time in his life? What are some of the feelings Jorge might have about his wife's leukemia? What feelings and anxieties might Jorge have about losing his job? What expectations might Jorge have of the interview or of the interviewer?

Thinking About the Interview

Because of the many different reasons for interviewing and the different types of interviews, the following interview parameters can help organize thinking in preparation for meeting clients for the first time.

- What is the purpose of the interview? Why am I meeting with this client? Why do I think the client is meeting with me? How might the client's ideas about this meeting be different from mine? How much of the purpose is governed by the agency, by the insurance company or funding source, and by the client's or interviewer's own agenda?
- How might my culture and the client's culture affect the interview?
- What are the time constraints on this interview? How long do we have to meet today?
- How long do we have to work together? Is this a time-limited or an open-ended contract?
- What resources are available to the clinician and the client? What other supports does the agency have? Does the client have extended family, friends, or others available to help?
- Are there any procedural requirements, such as forms to fill out, fees to negotiate, discussion of confidentiality, or permission releases?
- What are the desired outcomes of today's meeting?

Each of these questions is important in focusing the interview. For example, a clinician meeting with a client for a brief 10-minute session may spend little time exploring the details of the client's developmental history. In an agency that requires an intake form to be completed at the end of the interview, a clinician wants to be sure to gather all the information necessary to complete that task. If the purpose of the meeting is to evaluate a third-grader's readiness for special education classes, a clinician may focus on the child's competencies and areas that need remediation.

Watchwords

In addition to thinking about the tasks of the interview, clinicians develop a "mantra of reminders," or **watchwords,** that are particularly important to keep in mind during the interview. These may be simple things, such as reminders about attending behaviors like "Keep good eye contact," "Relax," or "Be honest when you don't know something."

As an interviewer becomes seasoned by experience, education, and supervision, these beginning reminders become second nature, replaced by watchwords about specific relational dynamics or complexities of interview techniques. For example, a clinician who has been working with a family for a while may have to remind herself before the next interview: "You know how anxious you get when this family argues. Remember to stay out of the fray." Approaching an interview with a client who is slow to speak, a clinician may say to himself, "Her mother puts words in her mouth, so leave some pauses for her to initiate talking."

Watchwords usually develop out of supervision, from reading the professional literature, or from direct observation of colleagues at work. They are used to promote careful attentiveness and responsiveness, rather than to admonish or punish.

As a new interviewer, I always felt that I needed to talk or do something when pauses or uncertainties arose in the interview. I still remember a piece of advice a supervisor gave me way back in 1969: "When in doubt, butt out."

But sometimes words are not necessary. An image can replace words as a mantra.

Sometimes as I prepare to see a client for the first time, I imagine that, as I'm sitting in the room with the client, my team is sitting behind me with their hands on my shoulder. That helps me remember that I'm not alone in the work that I'm doing.

Although we have been talking about how clinicians prepare for the first meeting with a client, the process of getting ready—attending to ourselves, to the client, and to the interview—should occur before *all* interviews.

Preparing for subsequent interviews differs little from preparing for the first one: The goals are to create a calm state of mind, screen out intrusions, and prepare for the client by attuning to his or her particular style, circumstances, and focal content of prior sessions. Notes about previous meetings are reviewed, attending to themes, emphases, or notable interview exchanges that may need revisiting in the next or subsequent sessions. Careful attention is given to the ongoing process and to the clinician-client relationship (see Chapters 12 and 13).

C L I P 3.2
Getting Ready

■ Greeting and Welcoming

The interview begins when the clinician greets the client. Clients may have preconceived ideas before meeting the clinician. Later, they may say that they had strong positive or negative feelings about the clinician based on the clinician's manner of speaking when making an appointment by phone or on the promptness with which the clinician responded to an urgent walk-in request to be seen. They may even base their reactions on their accumulated feelings about helping professionals in general.

The Agency as Representative

Often the agency first greets the client. Clinicians should spend time conferring with colleagues about how to create a warm and welcoming entry area appropriate for the cultures the agency serves. When possible, reading materials, pictures, and background music should reflect the local diversity of tastes and interests. While waiting, clients may have the opportunity to observe clinicians as they interact with agency personnel and with other clients, and these observations may color a client's feelings about the agency and the staff. Thus, it is important that staff members be aware of their demeanor and behavior at all times. The time spent in waiting areas also allows clients a first impression of the degree to which the staff and setting are or are not representative of their own ethnicity, culture, and language group. Agency personnel, forms, and public waiting areas can be intimidating.

Public waiting areas present unique problems for the interviewer in maintaining professionalism and confidentiality. While most clinicians enter the waiting area and call out the client's name, clinicians should be aware that this may compromise confidentiality. An alternative might be for clinicians to announce their own names, rather than the client's. For example, a clinician announces, "I'm Kalana Johnson."

What's in a Name?

Styles of address differ from culture to culture, locale to locale, and person to person. In some agencies, informality dictates that clients and staff alike are called by first names; in others, more formality and hierarchy are observed. We recommend that clinicians use clients' formal titles and last names until they say otherwise. At the outset of contact, clients and clinicians should discuss the names by which each prefers to be addressed. Hilary Weaver (2005) notes that this avoids the imposition of power inherent in our deciding what to call people.

> *In my internship at an outpatient unit, we were taught to call our clients by their last names, like Mrs. Huggins or Mr. Ward, as a sign of respect. So I was shocked when I transferred to another outpatient unit and heard my supervisor call her adult client "Billy." She explained that this was the way they did things there. She said it reflected a more laid-back, intimate style. Now I notice that I sometimes call people by their first names, and sometimes by their last. It depends on the situation and what the client and I work out together.*

> *As a geriatric social worker, I have heard many complaints from older women patients who resent being called by their first names by people who don't know them. One woman told me: "It felt disrespectful when, the first time we met, this young boy half my age asked, 'How are you, Bernice?' He didn't ask me what I wanted to be called. I got him back. I said, 'Not bad, Tom.' I read his name from his name badge. He was surprised that I called him by his first name. He was the doctor and wasn't used to this."*

Some clients may anglicize their first or family names because they feel that they may be too difficult for others to pronounce, to avoid discrimination based on ethnicity, or to "fit in" with the mainstream culture. Clinicians should always take the time to learn the pronunciation of clients' names. First and family names have different meanings in different cultures.

> *In most Asian countries, women keep their own family surname when they marry, even though they may often be referred to as the "mother of X" or the "wife of X" in their mother tongue. Do not assume, therefore, that the wife of Mr. "X" will be Mrs. X. You will also find that some women have encountered so much confusion on the part of U.S. government agencies or other social agencies that they have started using their husbands' last names. And even if an Asian woman does use her husband's name, the therapist should find out if it is a true choice or just a way of avoiding lengthy explanations to agency personnel. For example, you could say, "I know you use Mrs. 'X' with your son's teachers but your own name is Mrs. 'Y.' Which would you prefer me to use?" (Chao, 1992, p. 167)*

CLIP 3.3
Greeting and
Welcoming

Christine Chao goes on to state, "Refugees have given up everything they once knew; unless it is their choice, they should not be made to give up their names" (1992, p. 168). No one should be made to give up his or her name. Regardless of the formality or informality of the culture or setting, it is important for the clinician to be respectful of clients' wishes. Clients' preferences should dictate how they are addressed.

■ Opening Lines

Wherever the interview takes place—in the office, at home, on the street—there are a number of helpful ways to begin. Factors that influence the opening style include the meeting location, the people present, the motivation of all participants, the purpose of the meeting, and the time available. Cultural styles are also important to take into account. Some clients may need a more informal period of social exchange at the beginning of the interview to assess the clinician's skill and authenticity, whereas others may prefer a more formal expert-consultee approach (Lum, 2004; Pinderhughes, 1989).

Chao (1992) notes that:

> in Asian families the father can experience a treatment referral as a personal assault on his authority and therefore resist it. Understanding this dictates a careful response: "I meet with fathers the way one head of state meets with another head of state; the ruler has been forced to seek help and must be treated with respect and dignity. . . . I tell the father something about the families of which I am a member, . . . where I obtained my degree, what my training was, where I have worked . . . I let the father know that *he* is the expert in terms of his culture and his country of origin . . . Granted, his kingdom is in trouble, perhaps his subjects are rebelling, but he is still "king" and that position, with all of its responsibilities and stresses, must be acknowledged. I am an ambassador with whom he can consult for possible solutions. I am the guest in his kingdom (pp. 175–176).

EXERCISE 3.8   Opening Lines

You are a counseling intern at a community mental health center. You're about to meet Rich Navic, a 44-year-old depressed man about whom you have no other information. In your journal, write four or five opening lines you might use with him.

Participants, Roles, Tasks, and Time

After a friendly greeting, the interviewer usually begins by acknowledging the names and roles of all present and reviewing either the initial request for help or the reason for the interview. We should use clear language, avoid professional jargon, and clarify our role by giving examples of the types of help provided. Many clients may not know that, in addition to counseling, many clinicians can also provide testing and evaluation. We may serve as teachers and trainers, advocates for services, links to other staff, conflict mediators, and so on.

The clinician clarifies the amount of time available for the initial meeting, as well as the total number of sessions available to the client, so that participants can ready themselves psychologically for time-sensitive conversation. Usually, these issues are all briefly addressed in the first moments of the interview. How a clinician begins the interview may reflect a number of factors, including values, personal style, intent, or goals.

EXAMPLES OF OPENING LINES

"I'm the social work intern on the team, Ngo Diap. I meet with all patients' families to find out how the transplant process has affected everyone. We know how hard and complicated it can be. I also want to talk with you about how to manage when Tim comes home. We have forty minutes to meet today, and we can meet for two more sessions before Tim's discharge. I can also help arrange for VNA and home PT when Tim comes home. You might also be interested in our Wednesday night family group. I could tell you about that later, if you like."

"I understand you wanted to speak to someone about your divorce. I'm a counseling intern here at the center, and I'd be happy to meet with you to see whether I could be of assistance. We have fifty minutes to meet today."

"Thank you for letting me come out to see you, Señora Ramirez. As I said over the phone, I'm the psychologist at Centro Hispano Well-Baby Clinic and I wanted to talk with you about getting Carmelita ready to go to preschool. If it's okay with you, I can stay for about forty-five minutes."

Confidentiality and Its Limits

In the opening lines, it is important for the clinician to share with clients how the information they provide will be used. As discussed in Chapter 2, the clinician must also discuss confidentiality and its limits, lest the client reveal information before understanding its possible consequences. Many agencies have specific handouts that directly address confidentiality and its limits. Box 3.2 contains a sample confidentiality statement.

EXAMPLES OF CONFIDENTIALITY STATEMENTS

"Mrs. Franz, our conversation today is private except that counselors are mandated to disclose information if they feel that the client is a danger to herself or others. I also know that your insurance company is going to want to know your diagnosis and the number and length of visits."

"Most people think that what they tell a social worker is totally confidential. However, we are evaluating your family to decide if your son should live with you or your husband after the divorce. Since we have been asked to do this evaluation for the court, you should know that whatever you tell me can be shared with the judge and with the other lawyers involved in the case."

"Julie, an exception to the confidentiality of our meeting is that, as an intern, I review with my supervisor my conversations with clients to make sure I'm giving you the very best service. Do you have any questions about what I've said about confidentiality?"

B O X 3.2   Important Information About Confidentiality

Massachusetts law requires that I provide you with the following information concerning confidentiality at the initiation of our professional contract. It is important that you understand these issues as we begin our work together. Please review this material carefully so we may discuss any questions or concerns.

In general, the confidentiality of all communications between a client and a clinician is protected by law, and I can only release information about our work to others with your written permission. There are a number of exceptions.

I will ask you to sign this as an indication that you have read and understood the following points, and that we have had an opportunity to discuss any confusion you have about them.

Situations in Which There Is Potential Harm to You or Others

There are some situations in which I am legally required to take action to protect others from harm, even though that requires revealing some information about a client. These situations have rarely arisen. Should such a situation occur, I will make every effort to fully discuss the situation with the client before taking any action.

If I believe that a child, an older person, or a person with a disability is being abused, I must file a report with the appropriate state agency. If a client reveals information that constitutes physician misconduct, I am required to report the physician to the state medical board; however, I will not reveal the client's name or give any information that would allow the client to be identified unless she/he agrees to it.

If I believe that a client is threatening serious bodily harm to another person, I am required to take protective actions, which may include notifying the potential victim, notifying the police, or seeking the client's hospitalization. If a client threatens to harm self, I may be required to seek hospitalization or to contact family members or others who can help provide protection.

Professional Records

I am required to keep appropriate records. Because these records may contain information which can be misinterpreted by a nonclinician, it is my general policy to allow a desirous client to review them only in my presence after the matter has been fully discussed and where both agree that such a review would not interfere with the service. If I decide that reviewing the records would be emotionally damaging, I will be happy to forward a summary to the client's designee.

(continued)

B O X 3.2 *(continued)*

Professional Consultations

I may occasionally find it helpful to consult with professional colleagues to enhance the services that I am able to provide my clients. In these consultations, I make every effort to avoid revealing the identity of my client. The consultant is also legally bound to keep the information confidential. Unless there is a specific clinical reason to do so, I will not inform you that these consultations are taking place.

Insurance Reimbursement

If you expect to receive insurance (third party) reimbursement, be aware that I am required to provide certain information. This information includes clinical diagnosis and in some cases a plan/summary. Clients are entitled to receive a summary of these records, unless I believe that the information would be emotionally damaging. In those cases, the summary can be given to the client's designee. If clients are concerned about the policies of their insurance company, they should check with the appropriate resource before any insurance forms are submitted. The client has the option of not using insurance and paying directly, thereby not creating a record outside this office.

Collection of Overdue Accounts

If a client account is overdue, and suitable arrangements for payment have not been agreed to, I have the option of using legal means to secure payment. Unless questions are raised about the quality of services I have provided, the only information which will be released will be the client's name, the nature of the services, dates of service, and other relevant financial damages.

Legal Proceedings

In most judicial proceedings, clients have the right to prevent me from providing any information about them. However, in child custody proceedings, adoption proceedings, and proceedings in which the client's emotional condition is an important element, a judge may require my testimony if he/she determines that resolution of the issues before him/her require it. Testimony may also be ordered in (1) a legal proceeding relating to psychiatric hospitalization; (2) malpractice and disciplinary proceedings brought against me; (3) court-ordered psychological evaluations; and (4) certain legal cases where the client has died.

I have read this statement about confidentiality and have had an opportunity to discuss any confusion I have about it with my clinician. I understand that I may discuss any concerns about it with my clinician at any time.

Client Signature

Clinician Signature

Date

Client Name (Please print)

Clinician Name (Please print)

Source: Contributed by R. Rasi.

The Internet and other technological developments complicate issues of confidentiality (Gelman, Pollack, & Weiner, 1999). Advances in the delivery and coordination of health and mental health services can allow patient records to be centrally located and available to all of the person's health care providers (Rock & Congress, 1999), potentially to all health care workers in the system. Clinicians often use computers to record and store information about clients. E-mail and cell phone conversations between clinicians and clients and between professionals provide quick and easy access and are rapidly taking the place of phone conversations, but they are not secure. As private health care companies are buying or selling services, they may make information about clients available to prospective buyers.

These organizational and technological changes, together with the demands of managed care companies, create new privacy and confidentiality challenges. Clinicians should not only work within agencies and professional organizations to establish and review policy and procedures to protect client information, but also inform clients that there is no absolute guarantee of privacy or confidentiality in the electronic age.

Client Rights and Responsibilities

Many agencies and clinicians have developed a list of **client rights** and responsibilities, such as the right to see one's record upon request; the right to receive information about the range of available treatments; the right to be treated with respect; and the right to be informed fully and accurately about the procedures, benefits, and possible risks. Frequently, information regarding confidentiality and clients' rights is posted in waiting areas or is available as handouts. However, the clinician should review these issues directly with clients to be sure they are understood. Box 3.3 contains a sample client agreement that spells out client rights.

Focal Opening Lines

Focal opening lines offer an initial framework or guidelines that are especially helpful when clients are new to talking with a professional or when they are feeling confused, overwhelmed, or scattered. These guidelines lend structure to the process without foreclosing client contributions to the direction of the interview. Structure and guidance are also crucial when time is limited and therefore focus and roles need to be developed without delay.

EXAMPLES OF FOCAL OPENING LINES

For the opening lines in the preceding examples, after the routine introductions stating (1) names and roles, (2) the reason for the meeting, and

(3) the time available, the clinician may use focal opening lines such as the following:

"Let's review the plans for Tim's return home."

"Tell me about the circumstances that led to the divorce."

"Let's talk about how Carmelita feels about starting preschool."

Even though they may be ready with their focal opening lines, professionals should remain flexible and ready to respond to the unexpected. Clinicians should always be open to clients' needs and to making culturally appropriate accommodations.

EXAMPLE OF FLEXIBILITY AND ACCOMMODATION

Clinician: Are you Larry Kwan?

Client: Yes.

Clinician: I'm Gaylord Dunes, the social worker from the New Horizons work training program. I've come to the hospital to meet with you today to discuss what our program can offer you after you leave here. If you want, we can meet down the hall where it's quiet. Then you can tell me what you think and ask any questions about the program.

Client: My brother and uncle are coming to pick me up for my weekend pass at home. Can they listen, too? They are out of work also, and our family is suffering from this.

Clinician [recognizing the importance of family in the Asian culture]: Of course, we can all meet together. I have from nine to ten free to talk with you and them. Let me just tell the nurse where we'll be so that your family can join us. Maybe there's more I can help with besides employment.

Nondirective Opening Lines

Nondirective opening lines provide less information, leaving the client a greater opportunity to set the agenda, pace, focus, and tone. Using nondirective opening lines, the clinician begins with introductions, including names and roles, the reason for meeting, and the time available, then provides only minimal prompting to get things started.

EXAMPLES OF NONDIRECTIVE OPENING LINES

"I believe you asked to see one of the social workers this morning."

"Where should we start?"

"What would be most helpful to talk about?"

B O X 3.3   Client Rights

Part of our obligation to our clients is to inform you of the principles of care and your rights as a client of our agency:

- As a person served by this agency, you have the right to a high standard of care.

- You have the right to be treated with courtesy, respect, and dignity.

- You have the right to receive interpreter services to assist in understanding and fully participating in the services offered. If we cannot provide such service, we will make every effort to refer you to a provider who speaks your language or an agency that has interpreters who speak it.

- You should be informed about various services offered and the process by which the decision is reached as to which of these services is/are most helpful to you.

- You may request at any time to know who is responsible for the program that is providing you service and how he/she may be contacted.

- You have the right to ask about the relevant qualifications of the people who are helping you.

- You have the right to review your record. You may exercise this right by providing a written request to review your record, together with your reasons, to the director of the program that is providing you with services.

- You and your clinician should review your treatment plan periodically. You have the right to ask your clinician or the program director for a reevaluation or consultation by another clinician. This may be at your own expense.

- If a medication is prescribed by a physician, you should be informed as to what the medication is, why it is being prescribed, what it is expected to change, and its common side effects.

- If research is being conducted or any experimental procedure is being recommended, you will be informed before being involved in any such study-procedure. You have the right to refuse to participate in any research without jeopardizing your care here. Your written consent must be given before you would be included in any research or experimental procedure.

- If you wish to be referred to another agency or to a private practitioner, we will make every effort to refer you to the most appropriate resources.

- You have the right to receive an explanation of the basis by which your fee is set and to ask for a reevaluation of your fee. You have a right to a copy of the bills or statement of charges submitted to any third party.

- You have the right to receive care in a place free of architectural barriers if you have a limiting physical condition.

_____   _____
Client's Signature   Date
belated   _____
Witness's Signature   Date

_____   Client given copy but did not sign.

_____   Rights explained but client not given copy because

_____

These nondirective openings provide an immediate opportunity to assess client skills in organizing, communicating, and relating to both the clinician and the tasks at hand. However, if we find that the client is unable to respond to nondirective openings, we may need to provide more focus and structure.

Opening Lines Help Set the Tone

CLIP 3.4

Opening Lines

In addition to communicating information, opening lines convey a tone that can have lasting effects on the relationship. Opening lines can communicate warmth, indifference, welcome, aversion, hierarchy, disorganization, comfort, or fear. Sometimes the same opening line may have different meanings for two different clients or to the same client at different times. In Chapter 4, we discuss how tone is conveyed by means other than just words; in Chapters 12 and 13, we talk about the clinical relationship and its important elements and dynamics.

EXERCISE 3.9   Noting Tone

Go back to Exercise 3.8. Review the opening lines you wrote in your journal for Rich Navic.

Were they focal or nondirective?

What tone do you think you conveyed?

What would you change about your opening lines at this point and why?

■ Conclusion

Clinical interviewing can occur in a variety of settings. No matter where the interview takes place, we should carefully prepare for the meeting, getting both the environment and ourselves ready for the encounter. How we greet the client and begin the interview can set the tone for future work. Once initial contact is made, clinicians use a number of basic skills to establish an emphatic relationship to help the client tell his or her story and begin the process of problem solving. The next chapter elaborates the basic skills of attending and accurate listening, skills that are essential to all good clinical interviewing.

■ Suggested Readings

The following article addresses home visits.

Hodges, Vanessa G., & Blythe, Betty J. (1992). Improving service delivery to high-risk families: Home-based practice. *Families in Society: Journal of Contemporary Human Services*, (May): 259–265.

Clinician safety is addressed in:

Weinger, Susan (2001). *Security risk: Preventing client violence against social workers*. Washington, DC: National Association of Social Workers Press.

Critiques of the use of labels and diagnoses appear in the following sources:

Caplan, Paula. (1995). *They say you're crazy: How the world's most powerful psychiatrists decide who's normal*. Reading, MA: Addison-Wesley.

Szasz, Thomas. (1993). Curing, coercing, and claims-making: A reply to critics. *British Journal of Psychiatry, 162,* 797–800.

■ Self-Explorations

1. Which aspects of your nature and presence may make it easy for you to maintain a "bubble of calm" around the interview process? Which may make it harder? Are there environmental or client factors that can jar your calm?

2. Recall that people coming to see clinicians often feel like "strangers in a strange land." Have you ever visited a place or country where the norms, language, customs, and ways of managing time were very different from your own? How did you feel? Which differences pleased or engaged you and which did not?

3. The next time you are in a social situation, be aware of people's personal space preferences. Notice what happens when you move very close to a person. Record the other person's reactions. Then record how you feel when others come very close to you or cross into your personal space. How is your need for personal space influenced by your family and culture?

4. Remember a time when someone called you by your first name and it felt strange to you. In what circumstances do you like to be called by your first name? When do you prefer to be called Mr. or Ms.? What other appellations may be appropriate (e.g., Señor, Madam, Reverend)? Do you have a nickname? Who calls you by that name? In what circumstances do you like to be called by your nickname? When would it feel odd? Think about the professionals with whom you interact. Notice what they call you and what you call them. What did you learn from your observations? In the future, when would you call clients by their first names and when would you call them by their last names or titles? Would you ever call clients by their nicknames?

■ Essay Questions

1. Many people would agree with the statement that clinicians should refuse to work in situations where they feel unsafe. If clinicians refuse to go into situations in which they feel unsafe, how will the people who must live in

those situations ever get clinical help when they need it? Discuss this question with the class.

2. Client rights are easy to grasp but what are "client responsibilities" in clinical work? How do clients find out what their responsibilities are?

3. On the one hand, we have a professional responsibility to get as much information as possible. On the other, we have a growing awareness that many people around the world find it difficult or offensive to reveal intimate or personal information to a stranger. As practitioners, what factors do we need to consider when trying to balance gathering information with respecting people's discomfort in sharing highly personal information?

4. Discuss the pros and cons of focal versus nondirective opening lines.

■ Key Terms

Anticipatory empathy

Borrowed environment

Bubble of calm

Client information variables

Client rights

Clinical intuition

Clinician gestalt

Diagnosis

Focal opening lines

Labeling

Lifespace interviews

Nondirective opening lines

Personal space

Stigma

Watchwords

CHAPTER 4

Attending and Listening

■ Interviews

Interviews are a specific form of conversation, and, like all conversations, they are mutual. Both parties have a stake in the outcome and the influence of each on the other contributes to growth in each. Indeed, dictionary definitions of "interview" include "sight shared by two people" and "a mutual view."

Interviews have many layers of meaning and influence, only some of them apparent to participant-observers. Nowhere is this more true than in cross-cultural communication. If we have learned anything from clinical experience, it is that there are always multiple realities. Individuals speak, listen, and make meaning from their own unique perspectives. Two people may share the same experience, and yet each perceives it uniquely. Individual experience and meaning are mediated by such things as age, race, class, gender, culture, ethnicity, sexual orientation, spiritual and political beliefs, geographic locale, and individual and societal ideologies. However, two people may share similar backgrounds, values, or belief systems, yet experience and interpret things differently because they differ in other important respects.

Therefore, as you go about the task of attending and listening, you need to remember that there are few if any fixed truths or realities, apart from the inevitability of birth and death. Knowledge, beliefs, and practices inevitably change with the passage of time and through the transforming influences of various cultures and groups on each other. Thus we always consider and value multiple perspectives even though they make our task of attending and listening more complex.

In this chapter we focus on attending to verbal and nonverbal content, to the affect that they may signify, and to emergent themes and patterns. In later chapters, we discuss how participants in an interview mutually affect each other.

■ Focused Attending

Clinicians need to create an ambiance of focused attention in which meaningful communication can occur. We attend in order to listen; we listen in order to understand. Understanding contributes to empathy, and empathy engenders a readiness to respond. Thus, focused attending is an essential component of the therapeutic process, consisting of psychological attending and physical attending.

Psychological Attending

The bubble-of-calm attentiveness that the clinician brings to each interview is the result of (1) psychological readiness and openness to the client and (2) the clinician's commitment to creating an environment in which other people feel as welcome, appreciated, and heard as possible. **Psychological attending** involves putting aside personal distractions, worries, and self-concerns to give center stage to the client's story. We think of psychological attending as setting up radar to receive the signals the client is sending.

Psychological attending requires both discipline and flexibility. The client's story and demeanor inevitably arouse responses in the clinician that can distract attention from the client's experience. These "blips" on the radar screen need to be noted. As discussed in Chapter 12, the clinician's reactions to the client's story provide important information and should not simply be dismissed as interference.

Physical Attending

The **posture of attention** is the physical manifestation—literally, the embodiment—of the clinician's interest in and openness to the client, to the story, to the relationship, and to the work to be done together. It readies the interviewer to listen.

Gerard Egan (2006) describes the components of physical attending using the acronym **SOLER:**

S—sit squarely
O—open posture
L—lean forward
E—eye contact
R—relax

EXERCISE 4.1 Physical Attending

This beginning in-class exercise is designed to help you practice basic clinical skills, to allow you to get to know your fellow students, and to begin to develop a relationship with each other. Therefore, you are asked to talk about yourself.

In class, divide into groups of four, with each student assigned role A, B, C, or D. Student A talks to student B about his or her day, why he or she is in the class, or why he or she wants to be a clinician. Student B practices attending behaviors, while students C and D observe and make notes about student B's attending behaviors. If possible, videotape the interaction and, after getting feedback from students C and D, watch the video together. Rotate roles until each student has had the opportunity to be both the speaker and the attending listener. Do not worry about what you say; just focus on your physical behaviors.

Record your thoughts about the exercise in your journal. What did you discover about yourself? Note how comfortable or uncomfortable you felt both when you gave attention and when you received it, as well as when you were an observer.

The clinician adopts a posture of attention to communicate presence, interest, and close following. In a society characterized by rushing and preoccupation, this type of attention can be a unique experience. For many clients, such attending feels reassuring, caring, and desirable. For others, however, this close-attention between strangers may feel inappropriate, invasive, or threatening.

> *My first job was at a family agency where I was taught the importance of eye contact. When I moved on to work with clients with persistent mental illness, my supervisor told me my gaze was too direct and "hot" for clients with low tolerance for contact and that I needed to learn to look away and down briefly, without seeming to drift from the subject. I found this one of the hardest things I ever had to learn.*

Furthermore, attending behaviors are **culture-bound.** What is considered attentive in one culture might be offensive in another. For example, Weaver (2005) asserts that "eye contact is disrespectful in some Latino, Native American, and Asian cultures" (p. 42), especially in the presence of people perceived as authority figures. We cannot emphasize enough the importance of getting to know the expressive nuances of the cultures and people with whom we work.

I was conducting an in-service training for teachers in the local grammar school. One of the Irish Catholic teachers was talking about how disrespectful and stubborn the Vietnamese students were. I asked her to give me an example, and she said: "They never look at me when I talk to them. Even when I tell them to pay attention, they sullenly look away." The Vietnamese translator, who was part of the training, came to see me and told me that for a Vietnamese child to look an adult in the eyes is "like an American child sticking his tongue out at an adult."

It may seem easy to apply Egan's SOLER skills in an office. But because clinical interviewing may take place in a variety of nonoffice contexts, clinicians have to think about how to adapt a posture of attending in those settings. A clinician accompanying a client in a car, bus, or taxi is usually sitting side by side with the client. In such circumstances, a useful way to attend is to look where the client is looking so as to join the client's perspective or position, heightening a sense of connection. In such crowded, side-by-side situations, there may be jostling together and body contact, which may feel uncomfortable. However, remember the *R* in SOLER: to relax and not let the unanticipated create anxiety that distracts from focused attending. We talk more about issues concerning physical contact in Chapter 13.

In a home visit, the client may move around, carrying out tasks while sharing information and feelings. For example, in visiting with a young mother with children at home, we may interview in the kitchen while the mother makes formula, folds laundry, or attends to a child's needs. In such situations, the clinician's comfortable repose acts as a pivot for the client's moving about and often has a calming or settling effect. When a client feels more comfortable pacing about, entering and leaving the room, or attending to the needs of young children, the clinician's stable presence remains a constant in good attending.

I used to interview Janice, a young woman with schizophrenia, in a tiny office on the inpatient unit. She was often not comfortable in close proximity, but I didn't want to talk with her in the dayroom, where others could overhear. I would see her in that little office, but in a different way than I was used to. I would just remain comfortably seated while she paced, walking in and out of the room. Eventually, she would relax some and sit down with me briefly. I was surprised by how much she was able to share with me in this sporadic way.

In group work, family, or team meetings, the interviewer faces the additional challenge of attending to more than one person at the same time. In interview situations with multiple participants, the key is flexible attentiveness. On occasion, the clinician may pan the group, not making extensive or specific eye contact with any one individual. At other times, the clinician may make sequential eye contact with each individual or focus on specific members. It is important that we convey continuous interest in each person by making periodic eye contact with each, even if it is not returned.

Clients also have a posture of attention. Their attending or nonattending behaviors affect clinicians in much the same way that clinicians' behaviors affect clients. In our experience, clinicians are more likely to attend to a client who attends to them in an open and welcoming way. It is not unusual for clinicians to become more anxious, stiff, or self-conscious in the presence of a client who they feel is demonstrating hostility, indifference, or nonattending behaviors. Again, we always need to be careful about misinterpreting client behaviors.

EXERCISE 4.2 Nonattending

Ask a friend to have a conversation with you, and videotape it if you can. After a minute or two of talking, purposefully withdraw your attention. You might look away, look at your watch, cross your arms, or tap your foot. Notice what happens to the conversation. If you videotape the conversation, watch the video together. Ask your friend what it felt like when you stopped attending.

There is no one "right" way to attend. Over time, clinicians learn to communicate attentiveness without rigidly adhering to behavioral guidelines. For example, we can cross our legs, look away, close our eyes, or lean back and still be conveying attentiveness. Moreover, as we get to know our clients better, we adapt our physical attending to their nuances and changing needs.

> *A few years ago, I was working with Oscar, a man who had difficulty talking in therapy. He suffered abuse as a child and was unable to share feelings, fearing that if he expressed them, they would not be validated by the clinician. We talked about this and brainstormed how he could feel more comfortable talking with me. In one session, he shared that he thought he might be able to talk to me if I didn't look at him. We tried different ways of arranging things. When I turned my chair around, Oscar could talk more freely, but he missed my facial expressions, and I had a hard time hearing exactly what he was saying. Through trial and error, we discovered that, if I just closed my eyes, he was able to open up and share feelings he had never shared before. I think it was the act of letting myself be vulnerable that made it safe enough for him to take a chance. With my eyes closed, I felt less secure and found that I had to trust him in a new and challenging way. Emotionally, I joined him in the process of taking a risk, while never leaving my essential role as the therapist. I also discovered that, without visual distraction, I could tune in to his words in a more deliberate and focused way.*

Some clinicians believe that clearing the mind is a prerequisite for physical attending. Others believe that assuming a posture of physical attending helps clear the mind. In our view, psychological and physical attending are exquisitely intertwined and continuously resonate with one another: Psychological attending enhances the physical attending, which enhances psychological attending, and so on.

CLIP 4.1
Attending

■ Clinical Listening

A major task in any interview situation is to listen. Clinical listening is more complicated than just hearing the client's words. **Clinical listening** requires focused attention and alertness to everything going on in the interview and in the relationship. Clinical listening means that we attend to both verbal and nonverbal communication, listening to what clients say, how they say it, and how they feel about what they say. We also listen to what clients *don't* say. We listen for emerging themes and patterns, both during an individual interview and over time. In addition, we listen to the relationship that develops with the client. Equally important, we listen to our own inner process.

What we listen to—and are able to hear—is shaped by our own experiences, our family, our culture, the media, and the zeitgeist. That is why, when a group observes an interview and discusses what happened, each person has a slightly different take. Supervision, process recording, and videotaping are extremely important to clinical learning because they often pick up what we do not hear or notice.

> I remember talking with my supervisor about a client. She asked how the client handled her abortion. I had no idea where this came from. I didn't hear the client say she had an abortion. Then we listened to the tape together, and my supervisor pointed out that the client had said she "had a termination."

What the clinician hears may not be what the client intended. The client may unintentionally reveal something, or the clinician may misinterpret the client's meaning. The factors that contribute to inaccuracies or distortions in listening include a lack of knowledge, a lack of experience, cultural bias, defensive filters, and countertransference. These factors are discussed in Chapter 5.

Nonverbal Communication

People often think of an interview as the words spoken between two or more people. It has been suggested, however, that as much as 65% of what is communicated is nonverbal (Birdwhistell, 1970). **Nonverbal communication** includes physical appearance, body posture, gestures, movements, and facial expressions. Clinicians need to be extremely careful that they do not misperceive the client's nonverbal communication because it can be easily misinterpreted. A helpful practice is to observe the nonverbal communication and later check in with the client about its meaning.

EXERCISE 4.3 *Noting Nonverbal Information*

Break up into groups of four. Focus on person A (who remains silent) and record what information you have about person A that is communicated nonverbally. Compare and contrast your lists. What did you observe? What was the person communicating to you? What were the similarities and differences in what you each observed? How would you interpret what you observed? Note that you are making assumptions that can only be confirmed or corrected later by person A.

Sue and Sue (2003) note that research has shown that African-Americans tend to communicate more nonverbally than white people and trust nonverbal communication more than verbal communication as a true representation of a person's feelings thoughts and feelings. Sue, Ivey, and Pedersen (1996) state that "African Americans are better able to read nonverbal messages (high context) than are their White counterparts and . . . they rely less on verbalizations than on non verbal communication to make a point. Whites on the other hand need greater verbal elaborations to get a point across (D. W. Sue et al., 1996, p. 77).

EXERCISE 4.4   Videotaping a Conversation

Make a 5-minute videotape in which you have a conversation with a colleague. You can talk about yourselves, about your work, or about the experiences of the day. After making the videotape, watch it once with your colleague with the sound on. Note your nonverbal behavior. Watch the tape a second time, without the sound, and again note your nonverbal communication. Did you notice different things? Record in your journal what you learn.

Appearance

When we meet someone for the first time, we often make assumptions about gender, race, ethnicity, sexual orientation, and class based solely on physical appearance. However, these assumptions may or may not be accurate. As noted in Chapter 2, race and ethnicity are social constructions, not absolute characteristics, and people are often multiracial and multiethnic (Root, 1990; Spickard, Fong, & Ewalt, 1995). Within constructed "categories," individuals differ from each other in special ways and, as Robin Cook-Nobles notes, "we are not unidimensional" (Garcia Coll, Cook-Nobles, & Surrey, 1997, p. 186).

Clinicians often use physical appearance, style of dress, demeanor, and hygiene as indicators of clients' functioning, including the ability to care for themselves. Many intake forms have traditionally included dress, manner, and bearing as important diagnostic information. Of course, taking into account personal taste, cultural styles, and the economic realities of clients' lives is always important. A person who enters the agency without a coat during a midwinter snowstorm might be demonstrating disorganization and poor judgment—or might be unable to afford a coat or just unprepared for an unexpected storm.

Body Posture

The body often reveals a lot about mental and emotional states. When people are depressed, they may slouch or walk with their shoulders hunched. When people are happy, they may stand erect and have a "spring in their step."

The connection between body and feeling states has been a topic of great interest in both the psychological and medical fields (Benson & Klipper, 1976; Borysenko, 1987; Lowen, 1975). Will Schutz (1967) notes that the connection between body and feelings is captured in North American colloquialisms such as "lump in the throat," "butterflies in the stomach," "hair-raising," "green with envy," "pain in the neck," and "heartsick." Other cultures also note the connection between mind and body through their choice of words. Carla Bradshaw (1994) notes that since Asians and Asian Americans have a strong tendency to somatize emotional distress, clinicians must carefully attend to physical complaints, according them their rightful place in the clinical encounter.

> *I was working with a Vietnamese woman who came to see me complaining of headaches and wanting to know how to get rid of them. Being Vietnamese-American myself, I knew that her headaches were a way of her telling me about the emotional pain she felt. I told her that I often got headaches when I was worried about my family, and she began to talk about what kinds of things were going on in her head that may have been causing her pain.*

Clinicians should pay attention to the range and fluidity of their clients' body motion. As we get to know our clients, we can observe how they may be feeling from the way they use their bodies. If the presence of disease or disability limits the client's range of motion or use of the body, the clinician, of course, is sensitive to other nuances of expression.

Gestures

Many people gesture when they communicate. People may tap their feet, flail their arms, shrug their shoulders, clench their fists, or wring their hands. Everyone has a unique style of gesturing, and the clinician needs to become familiar with each client's style and learn what each client's particular gestures express.

> *Whenever Kerry was nervous, she would jiggle her hands by her chair. Toni would play with the top button of her blouse, whereas Rob would rub his left wrist with his right thumb, and Concetta would stare up at the clock as though wishing the time to hurry by.*

In addition, we need to be aware that gestures have different meanings in different cultures. Chan and Lee (2004) describe "friendly" North American gestures that can have very unpleasant meaning for some people from Asian cultures:

> The American gesture for "come here" (using the pointing finger with the hand raised and palm inward) is a hostile, aggressive gesture among Southeast Asians or is the manner in which one beckons dogs, lower animals, or an "inferior" person. Similarly, the crossing of the index and middle fingers as a gesture for "good luck," the "V" sign to indicate "peace". The "OK" sign (with curled thumbs and forefinger), or the thumbs up signal all potentially constitute obscene gestures with sexual connotations for Southeast Asians, as well as many other ethnic/national groups (Axtell, 1991, p. 273).

Facial Expression

Participants in conversations tend to pay a lot of attention to the face and facial expressions. People may smile, frown, wrinkle their foreheads, raise their eyebrows, or purse their lips at particular moments in the conversation. Again, we are careful not to overgeneralize or make culturally inappropriate interpretations. For example, Chan and Lee (2004) note:

> In general, the value that is placed on control of emotional expressions contributes to a demeanor among selected Asian groups that is often interpreted by Eurocentric individuals as "flat," "stoic," "enigmatic," or even "inscrutable." Koreans, for example, in keeping with the national character of the "Land of the Morning Calm," may present with a demeanor referred to as my-po-jung (lack of facial expression). Casual smiling and direct eye contact when greeting or interacting with strangers is considered inappropriate (p. 322).

From his research on the expressive styles of various cultures, Doman Lum (2004) finds that many clients feeling despair or anger due to oppression and economic hardship may mask or armor themselves with a flat facial expression in early clinical encounters, defending against feelings of vulnerability. Facial expression may soften and flex as the client experiences respect and mutuality with the clinician.

Clinicians should also be alert to sudden changes in facial coloration or the stress-induced development of hives or facial tics.

> *A cotherapist and I were seeing a heterosexual couple. At the end of the interview, my colleague expressed concern about the wife's emotional state. I hadn't noticed anything particular, so I asked why he was concerned. He said that her arm broke out in hives when we were talking about how they handled anger in the family. Because of where I was seated, I had missed the blotches, which he spotted.*

Eyes—"the windows to the soul"—may tear with sadness, widen with surprise, or narrow with suspicion. Eyes can also reflect organic problems; for example, pupil dilation may signal a tumor or drug use. People convey a lot with their eyes, which may be one reason that they sometimes close their eyes or look down and away so as not to reveal their inner experiences. Clinicians often put a lot of significance on eye contact, noting when it is made or broken. We must be sensitive to cultural and idiosyncratic differences in making and interpreting eye contact. For example, Teresa La Fromboise, Joan Saks Berman, and Balvindar Sohi (1994) recount the Navajo myth about a monster called He-Who-Kills-With-His-Eyes, which they believe "teaches Navajo children to avert their eyes to avoid bringing harm to others" (p. 32).

Some physical conditions can significantly impact bodily posture, gestures, facial expressions, and eye contact. The body movements and functions of some persons with disabilities or who are on certain types of medication are not always voluntary and should not be misconstrued as nonverbal communication. Sometimes it is hard for clinicians to remain focused and at ease in the presence of involuntary body movements or some forms of physical disability. This lack of comfort is easily recognized by clients.

Andrew was a client who had cerebral palsy. I felt very uncomfortable with his jerky movements. I didn't know whether to ask him directly about his condition because I didn't want to make him feel uncomfortable. Ten minutes into the interview, he asked, "Is my shaking distracting? I do it all the time, but more so when I am tired. Usually, I can control it better, but between being tired and somewhat nervous about being here, I know I am shaking like an earthquake."

Clinician Nonverbal Communication

Clinicians also communicate nonverbally through dress, manner, bearing, facial expression, eye contact, gestures, and so on. Clinicians always need to be self-aware in interviews with clients. Perhaps because of early abuse or trauma and because of the perceived power inherent in the clinician's role, many clients may be highly sensitized to nonverbal changes in demeanor. They scan us all the time to see whether we prove to be safe, caring, comfortable, and attentive to them as unique and special. A continuing task of clinical learning is to increase awareness of what we might be conveying at any given moment. We should think about what we want to communicate nonverbally and, whenever we can, have ourselves videotaped in clinical interactions to increase awareness of our styles and mannerisms.

I remember the first time I ever watched myself on videotape. I was shocked to discover that, throughout the entire interview, I kept nodding my head. I looked like one of those dolls you see in the back of a car, whose head keeps bobbing up and down on a spring. I still have to work on only nodding occasionally.

Our facial expressions are often a focus of client attention. While we may be paying attention to our gross body movements (posture, gestures, and head nods), it may be harder to be aware of the subtleties of our facial expressions.

E X E R C I S E 4.5 Facing the Camera

Break up into pairs and have a 10-minute conversation. You may talk about any topic that you wish. For the first 5 minutes, person A is the "face" and the camera focuses on a close-up of person A's face. For the second 5 minutes, the camera focuses on person B's face. After making the video, watch it with two other colleagues and get feedback about your facial expressions. What did you learn about yourself and about others?

When looking at your facial expressions in Exercise 4.5, you become aware of one facial expression at a time. However, when interacting with others, facial expressions are constantly changing. You may smile to convey happiness; however, you may be unaware that you also smile when you are nervous. It is therefore helpful to look at your facial expressions in

C L I P 4.2
Nonverbal
Communication

videotaped conversations. You may not always be conscious of shifts in expression or of the meaning that other people may attribute to your facial expressions. Clients are particularly attuned to the facial expressions of the clinician. That's why in Exercise 4.5 you are asked both to observe your own facial expressions during a conversation and to get feedback from others.

Verbal Communication

Much of what happens in the interview consists of what the client says and what the clinician says. The clinician listens to both the words the client says and how she or he says them. It is amazing how difficult it can be to recall exactly what another person has said.

EXERCISE 4.6 Repeat After Me

Break up into groups of four and assign roles A, B, C, and D. Person A is the speaker and person B is the "parroter." Persons C and D attempt to record verbatim what person A says so that they can correct person B's accuracy. Videotaping the conversation will give you much more accuracy.

Person A begins by saying one sentence. Person B repeats the sentence exactly, using the formula "You said ' . . . .'" Persons C and D report on the accuracy and then watch the video to check it. Since clients seldom talk in single sentences, person A then says two additional sentences, which person B parrots. Finally, person A says three additional sentences that person B attempts to parrot. This is harder than it seems. By watching the video, you can see how much you miss when someone talks to you. Discuss what factors may get in the way of your ability to remember.

Of course, clinicians do not often parrot a client's exact words. We must, however, pay careful attention to the specific words that clients use, because the words may have special and crucial meanings to explore further.

I remember working with a female client who told me about a disagreement she had had with her husband. I said, "So you and Jacques had an argument about money." She said, "No, we had a fight." When I asked her to clarify, she explained that they had come to physical blows. For her, argument implied disagreement, whereas fight implied physical contact. I learned to listen carefully for when she used the word argument and when she used the word fight.

Just as words can be a vehicle of communication, they can also be a barrier. Clients (and clinicians) can use a barrage of words to distract others from topics they wish to avoid. They can also use specialized language or in-group jargon to distance themselves or demean others. Beginning clinicians often feel as though they have to pretend that they understand what the client has said, even when they do not. (This can also happen in supervision or team meetings, when others are using jargon or expressing superior knowledge.) Beginners often hope that, if they just wait and listen, they will catch on. By doing so, they may make faulty assumptions. Even when they honestly think they understand the words clients are using, they may be wrong.

> *In a supervision class, a student from Romania reported a conversation she had with a British patient from a nearby state hospital. The patient told the student that he got "really pissed" the night before. Because she was unfamiliar with American colloquialisms, she asked him what he meant by "pissed." Since I'd read the student's journal and knew what the patient had answered, I asked the other members of the class what they thought he meant. They all assumed he meant he was angry. I then asked the student; she reported that the patient said it meant he had gotten very drunk. In this instance, the student's unfamiliarity with American jargon gave her the permission to ask what the client meant. If she'd understood jargon better, she might not have asked and thus might have misunderstood the client's words.*

Before reading any further, do Exercise 4.7.

EXERCISE 4.7 What Are You Trying to Say?

Define each of the following underlined terms or phrases:

1. Katie was wearing <u>knickers.</u>
2. The project will be finished <u>at the end of the day.</u>
3. A business indicates that there is <u>a backlog</u> at its warehouse.
4. At a meeting, one of the participants suggested <u>tabling the item.</u>
5. A friend of yours tells you that, when she meets her boyfriend, she will <u>fill him in.</u>
6. A friend of yours tells you that his presentation <u>bombed.</u>
7. John was really <u>pissed.</u>

The purpose of this exercise is to demonstrate that, although the same terms or idioms may be used in different cultures, they can have different meanings.

1. America: knee-length trousers
   Britain: women's underpants
2. America: usually taken literally, the end of the working day
   Britain: whenever it gets done—an open-ended finish time
3. America: a list or orders waiting to be filled
   Britain: an overstocked inventory
4. America: put the discussion off until another time
   Britain: discuss the item immediately
5. America: that she will elaborate, clarify, or tell him
   Britain: that she will hit him over the head

6. America: a failure
   Britain: a success
7. America: angry or upset.
   Britain: drunk

From: Hill, G. William, IV (1998) *Activities and Videos for Teaching Cross-Cultural Issues in Psychology*. Retrieved from: http://www.lemoyne.edu/OTRP/otrpresources/otrp_ccissues.html#activities.

Paralinguistic Cues

How clients (and clinicians) say things is as important as *what* they say. **Paralinguistic cues**—the tone and pitch of voice, rate of speech, emphasis, stuttering, sighing, and other vocalizations—are crucial elements of verbal conversation (Hall, 1959; Pope, 1979). There are cultural differences in paralinguistic communications. For example, Terry Tafoya (1989) discusses the sociolinguistic concept of "pause time" and notes that Native Americans often leave a longer space between the ending of one person's statement and the beginning of another's.

EXERCISE 4.8 Paralinguistic Cues

Practice saying the following sentences with different tones, speed, emphasis, and other paralinguistic cues. Demonstrate how the same words can convey different meanings.

Are there any other solutions to this problem?

Tomorrow is Christmas.

Mrs. Jorgensen wants me to come to school tomorrow morning at 7 A.M.

Exercise 4.5 helped you see how you look to clients. Ivey and Ivey (2003) offer a similar exercise (Exercise 4.9) in getting feedback about how you sound.

EXERCISE 4.9 Vocal Qualities

Use a videotape or audiotape for this class exercise. Divide into groups of four. One person becomes the speaker, who tells the others a 2-minute story in a normal tone of voice. With their eyes closed, the others listen for vocal qualities, noting their reactions to the speaker's volume, speech rate, and regional or ethnic accent. The group then provides feedback. Rotate roles until everyone has been the speaker and received feedback. In your journal, record what you have learned.

Adapted from Ivey and Ivey (2003, p. 43).

Silence

Silence is a form of communication, not just a blank space between periods of speech. Clinicians attend to silence, noting when it occurs, its frequency or patterning, and any affective coloration that may accompany it. For example, a client may fall silent after talking about the death of his mother. Another client may be silent because she does not know how to proceed. A third client may sit silently because of a lack of trust. Often, clues about the meaning of silence may be gleaned from the content immediately preceding the silence and the nonverbal communication that may occur during or after it.

Silence may have very different cultural meanings. In North American cultures, a long silence may be a sign of tension or discomfort. However, Virginia–Shirin Sharifzadeh (2004) notes:

> In most Middle Eastern cultures, social interaction and connectedness take precedence over the need for privacy . . . . Whereas for many Americans privacy requires actual physical distance, many Arabs, for example, achieve it by becoming silent and temporarily tuning out in a crowd (Safedi & Valentine, 1985). Such silence and tuning out may be interpreted as rude or as daydreaming by many Americans (pp. 395–396).

Metacommunication

Metacommunication refers to messages about the message, as well as messages about the relationship between the communicators (Bateson, Jackson, & Weakland, 1963). Clinicians attend to the relationship between the verbal and the nonverbal cues and to changes in the client's style of communication. Sometimes verbal, nonverbal, and paralinguistic cues are concordant, as when an angry person says "I'm mad!" in a loud voice while hitting the table with his or her fist. Sometimes they are discordant, as when a client timidly says in a low voice while looking away, "I know I can get that job." Clinicians need to look for how verbal and nonverbal cues do or do not match, paying careful attention to discrepancies, because these may signal ambivalence or important areas for further exploration. Some clinicians think that the nonverbal aspect of communication is more important than the verbal component—that nonverbal communications reveal the client's true feelings. We think that clinicians should take note of any discrepancies, whatever their form, without making too facile an interpretation.

They should also note any changes in the style or manner of communication (such as when a usually animated speaker becomes quiet and soft-spoken or when a client who is usually very attentive looks away a lot). Taking careful note of nuances and alterations of style applies to the clinician's communications also.

EXERCISE 4.10   Communication Discrepancies

Two people go to the center of the room to talk about what it is like to try to make friends when they are all newcomers to a training program. Half the class takes notes on person A and the other half on person B, recording their verbal and non-verbal behaviors and whether they are concordant or discordant. Share your observations with each other. Note the variations in what observers report.

■ Listening to Clients' Stories

Clinicians listen to verbal and nonverbal communications. But what are we listening for? We listen for the behaviors, feelings, thoughts, context, and meanings that constitute the client's story. We also listen to how clients punctuate their stories, emphasize or highlight content and themes, and remember or forget things they shared earlier.

Behaviors

Behaviors are the actions people take in their lives in response to other people, ideas, impulses, feelings, events, or outside stimuli. Clinicians listen for behaviors that are effective and that promote connection with others, as well as for those that *appear* to be self-defeating. (We say "appear" because, early in the work with someone, clinicians do not know what purposes client behaviors may be serving for themselves or for their families or larger systems.) We listen for the extent to which behaviors are impulsive or well thought-out and the degree to which they are elective or driven by inner compulsions, organic factors, external demands, or other people. We also listen for how flexible or rigid behaviors are, as well as how rational or irrational they appear to be in the client's situation. we note the effect that people's behaviors have on each other.

We need to make sure that we accurately understand the meaning of the client's behavior. It is easy to make faulty interpretations of the client's behavior, particularly when our cultural background is different from the client's. For example, a clinician might regard a client's tearing at her clothes and falling to the floor upon news of a death in her family as out-of-control behavior, whereas her family would regard her actions as a culturally appropriate form of grieving.

Feelings or Affect

Clinicians listen for the variety and range of feelings (e.g., sadness, surprise, anger, happiness, anxiety), noting the frequency of each feeling state and which feelings seem to predominate. We listen for the behaviors clients use to express their feelings (e.g., whether anger is expressed through sulking, silence, withdrawing, hitting, threatening, self-harming, throwing objects, or direct angry statements). We listen to discern whether clients can modulate their feelings or whether they feel overwhelmed by them. Expressive styles differ among cultures, families, and locales, and prevailing group norms may dictate that members not express strong personal feelings or conflicts in public or with outsiders. Such expressions might be interpreted as rude, shameful, weak, or aberrant.

Thoughts and Cognitive Style

Clinicians listen for clients' thoughts and cognitive style. We listen to what clients think about—people, things, events, feelings. We listen for the degree to which clients seem to think about their inner lives, external events, or their connections with others. We listen for the degree to which their thoughts are positive and hopeful or negative and pessimistic. We also listen to how they think and how they handle new thoughts or conflicting ideas. Is the thinking flexible? Is it organized and rational? Do thoughts jump from one topic to another? Does the client feel obsessed by particular thoughts? Does the client think concretely or abstractly? Can the client express thoughts openly and directly?

Context

Clinicians listen for the context in which their clients' stories take place. The immediate context consists of the client's personal circumstances: current living arrangements, family and social relationships, economic status, personal history, health, and the particulars of daily life. For example, it is important that the clinician know that a woman's mother was just diagnosed with Alzheimer's disease, which might contribute to her feeling of depression. In another instance, a white clinician must try to appreciate that racial discrimination and being passed over for a promotion could contribute significantly to the suspiciousness and distrust shown by an African-American client.

The immediate context is always embedded in a larger systems context, including economic, social, political, and religious forces and institutions and even global relationships and developments. For example, a woman may be sad and anxious because she lost her job (her immediate context). She lost her job because she could not get reliable day care and often had to leave work to take care of her 2-year-old daughter (the immediate context). One of the reasons she could not find reliable day care was that, as a result of increased defense spending, Congress had to cut federal subsidies to day care providers so that now fewer providers are in her neighborhood (larger systems context).

A number of years ago, I was working with a family in which the parents reported that their daughter was having nightmares about nuclear war. Although my first instinct was to wonder about what "wars" were happening in her "nuclear" family, I also had to consider the fact that she had just seen the movie The Day After, *a dramatic representation of the consequence of nuclear war.*

Similarly, the immediate context can affect larger systems. The woman who lost her job, for example, could organize her neighbors and colleagues (the immediate context) to write Congress to get federal funding for day care programs reinstated (the larger systems context). We listen to how the immediate and larger systems contexts of our clients' lives resonate with and mutually influence each other.

Meaning

Clinicians must listen for how clients interpret or make sense of their situations, feelings, behaviors, and thoughts. How do they understand the way things have evolved in their lives? How do they understand current events? For example, what meaning does a wife attribute to her husband's working late three or four nights a week? Does it mean he is working hard to provide for her and the children? Does it mean she has lost her attractiveness? Does it mean his boss is overly demanding? Does it mean he is having an affair? Does it mean he is afraid of being replaced by a younger, less highly paid staff member unless he overperforms?

Clinicians listen to whether clients are open to alternative meanings and whether they can hold multiple perspectives simultaneously. For example, can a father understand that, although his attention to his son's schoolwork each night means (to him) that he cares, to his son the father's inquiries may mean that he is being critical? Clearly, the components of stories are neither discrete nor static. Thoughts, feelings, behaviors, relationships, events, and meanings constantly interweave and influence each other, and clinicians are always listening for the interactions and influences.

Emphasis

Different theoretical models emphasize different components of the client's story. Behaviorists emphasize behaviors and their reinforcing consequences. Psychodynamic theorists focus on client developmental history and relational dynamics. Cognitive theorists focus on thoughts as causes of feelings and behaviors. Existential and narrative theorists emphasize clients' meaning making. Expressive theorists focus on feelings. Systemic and family theorists pay great attention to the context of behaviors and relationships.

Agencies often oblige clinicians to use information-gathering tools and formats that may shape what they attend to and listen for. For example, evaluation forms for brief treatment increasingly focus on behaviors and behavior change and their reverberating influences.

At the mental health center, my supervisors were always asking me about how my clients felt and how they expressed their feelings in different situations by saying things like, "So how did she feel about that?" When I went to work at a health maintenance organization (HMO), my supervisor asked about behaviors a lot more: "What did he do then?" "Is this a pattern or a one-time thing?" I noticed a subtle change in what I focused on with clients. At the mental health center, my clients used to go through boxes of Kleenex; now I notice that my clients hardly use any!

It is not just theories, agencies, or trends that influence how we listen to the different components of the client's story. We sometimes listen more for behaviors, sometimes more for feelings, sometimes more for events. At other times, we listen more for meanings and emphasis. This flexibility is natural and essential, and it should be guided by client priorities and goals.

EXERCISE 4.11   Listening to the Story

Break up into groups of four. Assign roles A, B, C, and D. If possible, videotape or audiotape the conversations. Person A is the first speaker and person B the first listener. Persons C and D are the first observers. The speaker talks to the listener for 2 minutes and describes an event in his or her life. The listener responds to the speaker in any way he or she chooses. Observers take notes on what the speaker is communicating. It might be helpful to divide a sheet of paper into five columns to record your observations about context, thoughts, feelings, behaviors, and meanings.

After 2 minutes, the listener tries to report what the speaker said about his or her context, thoughts, feelings, behaviors, and meanings. The speaker may correct the listener, and the observers can point out omissions.

Watch the video and compare your observations with what has been captured on tape.

Take 2 minutes to debrief, noting what kinds of things were easier to hear and remember. Rotate roles until everyone has had a chance to be speaker and listener. Record in your journal what you learned.

DVD

CLIP 4.3
Verbal
Communication

It is important to remember the client's story—both the general message and the details and nuances. We listen carefully to remember what clients have shared with us. We listen to understand, and, with the help of supervision, we use this understanding to develop an appropriate focus, empathy, hunches, and plans. Because clients tell us so much in a short period of time, process notes, audiocassettes, videotapes, and observations are all useful for remembering and reflecting on what the client has shared.

■ Listening for Themes and Patterns

People's lives develop rich meaning and complexity, which at times can be organized into themes and patterns. Because the themes and patterns often reflect some of the client's central organizing schemas, clinicians must attend to them as they emerge both in the client's story and in the clinical relationship. Repeating themes and patterns often signal topics important to explore further.

Themes

Themes are repeated sets of ideas, beliefs, and notions. They may be expressed directly and with awareness ("There I go again, blaming myself"). However, they often emerge indirectly and without conscious recognition, as when a client describes a persecuting sibling in one session, a persecuting lover in another, a persecuting employer in another, and annoyance at the clinician for "running the show" in yet another. Clinicians commonly encounter client themes of loss, betrayal, oppression, injustice, hopelessness, and despair, as well as companion themes of courage, persistence, survival, and resistance to oppression.

> *For almost 6 months, I had been working with Johann on problems with self-control at work. It took me that long to realize that in almost every session, he would mention alcohol. For example, he would say: "Last night a couple of us went out for drinks"; "The other day we put away a couple of martinis at lunch"; or in describing a picnic at work, he said, "We polished off a keg of beer."*

EXERCISE 4.12   Say It Again, Sam

Samuel is a 33-year-old Russian immigrant to the United States who lives in a small town in Ohio. He is meeting with a female counselor to discuss employment opportunities. At the beginning of the interview, while talking about work, Sam said that a person who speaks poor English has no chance of advancement in his current job. Later, while discussing his childhood, he said that he never had any of the advantages of his older brothers, who were bigger and stronger than he. As the session was ending, he said that he was sure that the woman clinician did not like him because he was a man. How would you describe the underlying theme of this interview? How would you convey it to Samuel?

Patterns

Patterns are repeated behavioral or affective sequences. Like themes, patterns may have a great impact on clients' daily lives, and clients may be aware or unaware of them. Some common patterns observed in client stories include the avoidance of intimacy, frequent angry outbursts, crying when anxious, addiction to substances or people, and picking inappropriate partners. Other patterns include choosing loyal friends, asserting oneself in adversity, protecting vulnerable others, and using spiritual resources.

Jack Henry came to the job center because he had lost his job. This the fifth job he had lost in 12 years. It turns out that he always gets in conflict with his boss and he eventually leaves in a huff.

The clinician should pay careful attention to themes and patterns that come up during the interview. Sometimes a theme or pattern emerges across a series of interviews, or they may be things the clinician notes during specific interviews or things that the client reveals over time. Some of the patterns are nonverbal.

I noticed that Becky always got teary when she spoke of her mother but seemed strangely cold and intellectualized when she described her father.

Observing themes and patterns is just a first step. We discuss how to use themes and patterns to help people see, feel, and do things differently in Chapters 9 and 10. We also discuss how to comment on themes and patterns within the clinical relationship in Chapter 12.

Themes and patterns can also emerge from clinicians. One clinician may have a tendency to focus on anger rather than on sadness (as a theme), whereas another may start jiggling his foot when anyone talks about sex (a pattern). Clients can observe these themes and patterns in us just as we do in them. As discussed in Chapter 2, supervision and feedback are important in developing greater self-awareness, which can inform our behavior in the interview.

CLIP 4.4
Themes and
Patterns

Dana said, "You always look so uptight when I describe seeing Lynn. It makes me not want to tell you when I see her."

Sonia told me that she could always tell when our time was about to be up because I would reach for my appointment book while she was still talking.

■ Listening to the Relationship

Clinical conversation is much more than words exchanged and feelings shared. The nature of the relationship in which the story unfolds is crucial to its evolution. The maintenance of a positive, supportive relationship is thus a clinical goal in and of itself. We therefore pay careful attention to what happens within the clinical relationship and listen for the thoughts, feelings, and reactions that the interview may arouse in both ourselves and the client.

So there I was—leaning forward, sustaining eye contact, being aware of transference and countertransference, reflecting themes and parallels, trying to respond with sensitivity in my words and tone . . . So there I was trying not to freak out. I have wanted to be a therapist since I was 10 years old. I used to think they just sat back in cozy, expensive chairs and said nice things for 50 minutes a few times a day. I was really wrong. I had a taste of what was ahead, but I had to remind myself I was only just beginning.

In Chapter 13, we discuss the complicated relationship dynamics and the skills used to address them. In the next chapter, however, we discuss the initial development and continuing maintenance of the relationship through clinical support and empathy.

■ Bridging Linguistic Differences

In addition to dealing with how cultural filters affect the ways in which clinicians and clients listen to each other, a specific challenge is trying to bridge linguistic differences when the clinician and client do not share the same primary language.

Talking in a Non-Native Language

The *APA Guidelines for Providers of Psychological Services to Ethnic, Linguistic, and Culturally Diverse Populations* (American Psychological Association, 1990) suggest that "psychologists interact in the language requested by the client and, if this is not feasible, make an appropriate referral" (p. 6). However, clinical work is often conducted in a language other than the client's primary language. For example, a Puerto Rican client with a rudimentary knowledge of English may be asked to speak in English with an Anglo clinician or even to a Puerto Rican clinician raised in the United States whose primary language is English. Communicating complex experiences or emotionally charged issues in a second language can be extremely difficult, especially when talking about things that occurred before the second language was learned.

> *I remember that, when Mercedes and I would talk about things in her childhood, she would often slip into Spanish. At times, she would speak in English, talking about how she missed her mother and father. When I asked her to "say it in Spanish," she said, "Yo extraño a mi mami y papi" and burst into tears.*

It can be particularly productive to ask the client to say a particular word in his or her own native language—words that may carry significant meaning and affect.

> *I have a friend from Puerto Rico who is a very visible, out lesbian. She gives talks around the country about being lesbian. However, she has told me that she isn't "out in Spanish." The word used to denote lesbians in Spanish carries with it such a negative connotation that she can never say it. So she has never come out to her parents, who speak only Spanish.*

Sometimes neither the clinician nor the client is speaking in his or her native language. This can happen when neither speaks the other's language, but both have some facility in a third language. Some impatience, frustration, or misunderstandings may result.

Using Translators and Interpreters

When a clinician is unable to speak the client's preferred language, it is appropriate to refer the client to a clinician who can. If no appropriate clinician is available, a trained interpreter may be used. Most, although not all, deaf clients use American Sign Language (ASL). If the clinician is not proficient in ASL, a sign language interpreter may be used. Many of the same benefits and challenges apply to ASL interpretation as apply to other language interpretation.

Rather than using nonclinical agency staff members who happen to speak the client's language, clinicians should be sure that they have access to people who are trained as **interpreters.** Translators may be exposed to material that is overwhelming or that they are not prepared to deal with appropriately. Interpreters know about the counseling process, confidentiality, and the culture of the clients with whom they will be speaking. Interpreters do not simply translate words but also interpret their meaning in a culturally sensitive way.

The use of an interpreter clearly affects the clinician's ability to listen to and understand the client accurately. Maryann Amodeo and colleagues note that interpreters can perceive and intuit subtle dynamics that the clinician may miss and can provide a sense of connection and support for the client. They further suggest that such collaborations result in capacity building in several ways. Agencies and workers become more knowledgeable about community values, beliefs, and communication styles. Clients who feel better understood and helped may be more willing to seek assistance from the agency. "Interpreters learn more about medicine, mental health, substance abuse, or social service, and about the ways that health and illness are treated in the United States" (Amodeo, Grigg-Saito, & Robb, 1997, p. 78).

However, using interpreters introduces "the additional complexities of a three person relationship" (La Framboise, Berman, and Soh, 1994, p. 53). The clinician has to leave time and space in the conversation for the work of the interpreter, which can interfere with customary pacing and flow. The clinician may feel sidelined while watching the interaction between the client and the interpreter, especially if they appear to be more engaged with each other than with the clinician.

Also, we must attend to what transpires between the interpreter and the client as well as to what transpires between ourselves, the client, and the interpreter. Like clinicians, trained interpreters may have biases or cultural styles that inhibit them from accurately interpreting either the clinician's or the client's comments. Interpreters can also be astute observers of content and process and can provide helpful feedback to the clinician that informs and enhances the work.

I've learned a lot from working with our interpreter Martine. She has taught me so much about Haitian culture. Getting to know her and learning from our interactions together has helped me understand my clients better.

When English is not the native language, we should offer the services of an interpreter, no matter how good the client's use of English appears to be. This is particularly important if the clinician is providing new or technical information, such as assessment results, or discussing a medical procedure (Joe & Malach, 2004).

Whenever possible, family members or others with dual relationships or vested interests should not be used as interpreters because overlapping relationships may affect the validity and reliability of the translation or curtail frank expression of information and feelings.

> *I had a bad experience with an interpreter, which makes me very aware of how carefully you have to prepare before working together with a client. The hospital was attempting to provide counseling support to an unmarried Portuguese teen who had just delivered a baby. Since no one on the staff spoke Portuguese, a Portuguese-speaking priest was invited to serve as an interpreter. I asked the priest to explain to the girl the services that were available to her in the community. The girl burst into tears. I asked the priest why the girl was crying, and he said he felt it was important to begin by reminding the girl that she had committed a mortal sin for which she must ask God's forgiveness.*

Wong (1987, cited in La Framboise et al., 1994) recommends that the clinician meet with an interpreter in "a pre-interview session to build a relationship of trust and to plan the objectives of the interview, the topics to be covered. The clinician and the interpreter should discuss the preferred translation style, whether it be word for word, summarizing or cultural interpretation" (p. 53). Seating arrangements should also be adapted to the needs of ASL clients and interpreters. It is important that a deaf client be able to see the ASL interpreter, although a non-English-speaking client need not necessarily see a language interpreter.

Using Easily Understood Language

Clinicians should use language that clients from many backgrounds and regions can understand. We may see clients who, although newly immigrated, speak English as a second or third language. These clients may not need translators, but we must speak clearly and remember that our southern, Asian-American, or Boston accents may not be easy to understand. We also have to be careful not to use jargon, slang, idioms, or abbreviations.

> *Mra Sabai had recently emigrated from rural Myanmar. She had studied English in school when Myanmar was called Burma and was a British colony. However, she was confused when the social worker said Mra Sabai could wait until the cows came home before DSS would help her. She didn't have any cows. What was DSS anyway? Mra Sabai figured it must be some dairy organization.*

> *Evianne recently left Romania. He wondered what the counselor meant when he suggested he go "the whole nine yards." A yard is about the same length as a meter; he knew that. But what was significant about that particular length?*

■ Conclusion

Clinical work requires careful listening and an accurate perception of what is being transmitted by clients. We carefully attend to the client, listening to verbal and nonverbal communication and paralinguistic cues. We note behaviors, feelings, themes, and patterns as they emerge in the interview, alert for both idiosyncratic, cultural, and locale-specific meanings. Through listening, the relationship develops and the story unfolds. As we discuss in the next chapter, accurate listening is not enough. For effective change to occur, support and empathy are essential.

■ Suggested Readings

A novel that is helpful to understand communication difficulties in cross-cultural context is:

Fadiman, Anne (1997). *The spirit catches you and you fall down*. New York: Farrar, Straus & Giroux.

Cultural issues in verbal and nonverbal communication are discussed in:

Lum, Doman. (2004). *Social work practice and people of color: A process-stage approach*. Belmont, CA: Wadsworth.

The following addresses working with linguistic differences and interpreters.

Amodeo, Maryann, Grigg-Saito, Dorcas, & Robb, Nancy. (1997). Working with foreign language interpreters: Guidelines for substance abuse clinicians and human service practitioners. *Social Work, 15,* 75–97.

■ Self-Explorations

1. Spend 5 minutes in front of a mirror acquainting yourself with the subtleties of your facial expressions. Relax your face completely, noting what your face looks and feels like when you are completely at rest. See how it looks and feels when you are happy, when you are unhappy, when you want to look inquisitive, or when you show disapproval. Record what you learned by observing your facial expressions.

2. Think about people in your life who are "bad" listeners. What do they do? How do you respond when they do it? Are you aware of times when you are a "bad" listener? Explain.

3. Do you pay more attention to what people say or to what people do? How do you reconcile inconsistencies between what a person says and how he or she says it? How might this affect your work with clients?

4. People hold tension in different parts of their bodies (for example, a clenched jaw, shoulder and neck pain, stomach aches). Where do you

experience tension? It is important to identify your own tension centers so that you can use signals from these areas to alert you to personal reactions arising in the interview situation. Have you noticed any ways in which you manifest anxiety when interviewing (for instance, foot jiggling, pen tapping, perspiring, shifting around in seat, losing track of what's being said)?

■ Essay Questions

1. What are the differences between a translator and an interpreter? Discuss the pros and cons of using translators or interpreters when working with people who do not speak the same language as the clinician. What advice would you have for a clinician who needs to work with an interpreter?

2. What is meant by nonverbal and paralinguistic cues? How are they important to the clinician? What are some nonverbal cues that a clinician can give unintentionally to a client?

3. List the five components of physical attending and note other things that clinicians can do to show that they are listening to their clients.

4. People from different cultures may use silence for different purposes. Describe as many reasons as you can why clients may be silent.

■ Key Terms

Clinical listening	Posture of attention
Culture-bound	Psychological attending
Metacommunication	Silence
Nonverbal communication	SOLER
Paralinguistic cues	Themes
Patterns	

CHAPTER 5

Support and Empathy: A Sustaining Presence

■ A Supportive Presence

A supportive presence is crucial to the development of a trusting relationship in which meaningful conversation can occur. The clinician's caring and support cannot be communicated solely through attending and listening. It is also consciously communicated by sensitively timed and orchestrated words, gestures, behaviors, and emotional responses—all of which, together, communicate an active presence and wish to help.

Warmth and Caring

Clinicians must genuinely care about clients and their well-being. It is only common sense that clients will respond more readily to interviewers who are warm and caring than to those who come across as bureaucrats, technicians, or "cold fish." Warmth and caring are often conveyed with a smile, a cordial

119

handshake at the beginning of the interview, close attention to what is being expressed or felt, and the use of appropriate facial expressions and gestures. Some individuals may prefer a detached and distant clinician, but even they usually like to believe that the clinician has some feeling of care for them. More frequently, people rate warmth and caring extremely high when asked to list attributes they would like in a potential clinician, mentor, or adviser (Combs, 1989; Rogers, 1958).

Clinicians may find it difficult to decide how to show caring. On the one hand, we do not want to appear too detached and professional. On the other hand, if we are too saccharine or "touchy-feely," clients may feel put off.

> *One of the things I notice when I am teaching first-year social work students is what I call their "singsong" tone. They often say things like "Oh-h-h, I am so-o-o-o-o sorry to hear that." It reminds me of the behavior and tone of voice often used with small children and older people. That's why I like to have students hear themselves on tape. It also helps if they can sit in on colleagues' interviews to hear how different clinicians "really" sound when they're speaking with clients.*

Warmth and caring are relational processes. These feelings do not arise in a vacuum, but are elicited by thinking about or interacting with other people, animals, music, nature, and the spiritual. To see how you look when attempting to demonstrate warmth and caring, look in a mirror or watch yourself on video.

EXERCISE 5.1   Conveying Warmth and Caring

In class, break up into groups of four. Take turns being the speaker, the responder, and two observers. The speaker tells a story about him- or herself while the responder practices conveying warmth and caring. Observers note the specific behaviors that they think convey warmth and caring. The list can include things like facial expressions, postures, comments, and tone of voice. The observers also make note of any lapses in warmth. If possible, videotape yourselves so that you can observe yourself doing the things you do to communicate warmth and caring. Note that each person may experience and manifest warmth and caring in different ways. In your journal, record what you have learned.

Acceptance

Another important element of sustaining presence is acceptance. Clinicians must be able to appreciate and affirm clients as people without necessarily condoning specific behaviors that might be harmful to themselves or to others. Carl Rogers (1958) refers to this as **unconditional positive regard.** To accept clients as people sounds deceptively simple, but it can be quite difficult when client behaviors either go against societal laws or norms or are in radical conflict with our own professional and personal values or preferred styles of behavior.

Societal Norms

Societal norms are widely held standards of conduct to which all members of a society are expected to adhere. Norms usually dictate what is acceptable and what is not—what the powerful majority in a society defines as "right" and sanctioned or "wrong" and forbidden. Norms are often codified into laws; for example, most societies have laws that prohibit incest, murder, and theft. Usually norms prescribe gender roles, dress, bearing, and speech, and they distinguish what is acceptable in public from what is to be confined to private life.

Clinicians often see clients who have sought out or been referred for help because they have violated social norms or taboos. Sometimes they have broken the law. More often people come because others may believe that their behaviors, although not illegal, violate social norms (e.g., the woman who yells and talks to herself in the subway or the man who prefers to wear women's clothes). People may also consult with a professional when they experience a conflict with social norms, such as the married woman who decides not to have children or the man who is struggling with his sexual attractions toward men.

Some norms endure, whereas others change over time: Dress and gender roles have changed dramatically since the 1950s. People from one age group may cling to "old" norms that may seem outdated to those in other age groups. An older man may think it polite to open the door for women, whereas a young woman may be insulted, believing that he thinks women are weak and need help. Sometimes there is a contradiction between what society prescribes as a standard or norm and what actually happens. In the United States, two-parent families are held up as the norm, but this country actually has one of the highest rates of divorce and single-parent families in the Western Hemisphere. Millions are spent on the war on drugs, while millions are also spent on government subsidies and research grants to the alcohol and tobacco industries.

Every culture defines its own norms. Most societies around the world today, including the United States, are pluralistic—that is, composed of many diverse cultures. Problems can arise when differing cultural norms conflict, especially when one group has more socioeconomic and political power than another. For example, many Native Americans believe in the power of the dead and may attribute misfortunes to the actions of ghosts or spirits, some of whom they may claim to see. A naive or misinformed clinician may interpret these beliefs and reported experiences as delusions or hallucinations.

> An intern reported that the team psychiatrist on the inpatient unit told her to tell a father that he should dress more appropriately when visiting his adolescent daughter. The psychiatrist said that the father was "dressing in a seductive manner with his shirt unbuttoned and gold chains calling attention to his hairy chest." The intern, an Italian American woman, felt this behavior was not seductive but rather represented an Italian father's way of dressing up for a Sunday visit.

Traditional norms in Haiti and several other Caribbean islands may prescribe corporal punishment as an appropriate response to a child's misbehavior and as a sign of caring and concern, whereas in the United States the same kind of hitting might be called child abuse. Lillian Comas-Diaz (personal communication, 1996) states that, although corporal punishment may be acceptable in the native country, the parent living in the United States must be educated about the possible consequences of the behavior here.

Finally, while working to improve our understanding of diverse cultures and their norms, we need to be careful that we do not mistake behaviors due to cultural influence with those that may be due to illness, addiction, antisocial stance, or individual style. We also need to be aware of **culture-bound syndromes**—that is, "recurrent, locality-specific patterns of aberrant behavior and troubling experience that may or may not be linked to a particular DSM-IV-TR diagnostic category" (American Psychiatric Association, 2000, p. 898).

Personal Values

Individual values are cherished beliefs that develop in the context of family and sociocultural influences. Clinicians may value anything from personal autonomy to personal hygiene and can find themselves dismayed or offended by clients who do not share their value systems. We need to be aware of our values and how they influence responses in ways that may leave clients feeling unaccepted. We must be dedicated to being nonjudgmental—unconditionally accepting people for who they are without necessarily accepting all their behaviors. The clinician's nonjudgmental stance leaves clients free to confide openly and honestly without fear of rejection, shaming, or reprisal.

> *Eileen, a 48-year-old woman who had always lived with her family, was discussing whether to move out and get her own apartment. I saw her desire to live alone as a healthy one. I didn't even recognize that living independently was a personal value of mine; I thought it was a sign of "mental health." I believed that adult women should be able to separate from their families to develop autonomy. It wasn't until I talked with a colleague that I realized I had to be careful not to let my values influence our discussion.*

As we work with clients and are exposed to diverse situations and beliefs, we often find our values challenged and changed. A side benefit of clinical work is that our perspective is enlarged so that we both see and appreciate more of the world beyond our own. We stretch and grow through exposure to differences.

> *I used to see the halfway house as a way station where people were supposed to get it together and then move on. After many years of watching dozens of people with mental illness bounce back to the hospital after leaving transitional living programs. I came to realize that, for many isolated people, long-term communal living may be the end goal rather than a "halfway" achievement.*

At other times, we may have cherished values confirmed by the similar beliefs and experiences of clients from diverse cultures, reminding us of the larger universal community of shared human values. At such intersections of shared experience and values, mutuality is often experienced more easily and visibly without the clinician and client thinking of themselves as identical.

EXERCISE 5.2   Personal Values

Think of a time when you found your personal values challenged. Think of a time when your personal values changed. Record each story in your journal. What did you learn about yourself and about others from these experiences? Then, think of a time when you felt forced to go along with values you did not respect. Reflect on that experience and how you might deal with the situation differently now. Why?

Stylistic Differences

Everyone has a personal style—individual habits and preferences expressed in interactions with others. Personal style is often mediated by gender, race, class and economic opportunity, age, sexual orientation, ethnicity, culture, and geographical region. When feeling misunderstood, one angry person raises his or her voice, whereas another bursts into tears. One client may appear stoic, whereas another seems to plead for help constantly. One client waves a pen while talking, whereas another sits rigidly without moving for the entire session.

As you develop professionally, you may find yourself more or less responsive to particular client styles, looking forward to meetings with certain clients and dreading meetings with others.

> *Usually, I can be accepting of most of my clients' behaviors, but Maddie's whiny tone really grated on me. I had to use every trick in the book to remind myself of her pain so as to stay attentive to her story and not just shout, "Stop whining!" Joanne, an intelligent and competent teacher, spent most of the session time asking my opinion of family and life issues, rather than giving her own. I found this extremely annoying as I knew it to be unnecessary, given her capacity to figure things out. But I came to appreciate that, in her family, one never gave an opinion in front of an authority figure—that would be considered disrespectful. It took a while for her to perceive our situation as different and exempt from her family's rules.*

Clinicians also have unique personal styles and preferences. Some are formal and businesslike; others are relaxed and down-to-earth. Some retain a serious demeanor with clients; others take a lighter touch. Some readily reveal themselves to clients; others prefer to present a "blank screen." The important point about the personal styles of clinicians and clients is not that they match perfectly but that they are not so discordant as to constantly distract from the focus of the work or be offensive. It is the clinician's responsibility, not the client's, to try to make the interviewing ambiance as harmonious and supportive to the client as possible. An uncomfortable presence makes for uncomfortable relating and working, and it can wordlessly signal lack of respect, empathy, and attunement to the needs of others.

Norms, values, and personal styles are all interrelated, and sorting out one from another can be hard. Supervision can help beginning clinicians explore their attitudes and values so that they can learn to be accepting of clients even if they do not accept a particular behavior. Although the development of openness, respect for differences, and true acceptance of others is a lifelong task, it is also a clinician's ethical responsibility.

E X E R C I S E 5.3 Clients I Might Find Hard to Accept

Following is a list of clients with different characteristics. In your journal, rank-order them from the easiest to the hardest for you to accept. Discuss what made each one easy or hard for you to accept. In class, discuss in small groups what kinds of clients you would have a hard time accepting and what steps you might take to become more accepting.

Woman having an abortion

Drug-addicted mother

Client who hates professionals

Client who yells in the session when angry

Religious zealot

Husband who is abusing his wife

Transsexual

Person who is a bully

Clergyperson sexually involved with a parishioner he or she is counseling about loneliness

Man who makes racist statements

Person who is very critical

Gay adolescent

Clinical Repose

The clinician's anchored and relaxed presence acts as an island of calm and allows the client to stay self-focused without being distracted by the clinician's needs or anxieties. This repose is central to supportive presence. It provides a clear but unobtrusive **holding environment** for the work and the relationship. Clients come to know that they can count on the clinician to remain centered and steady regardless of events and developments. Even in the face of the unexpected, clinicians try to remain as calm and reliable as possible. The clinical environment is portable and can be constructed almost anywhere to establish safe and supportive conversation. **Clinical repose** is developed with experience and tends to relax, reassure, and open others to the clinical process because it gives them confidence in the helper's reliability.

This repose is expressed by a relaxed, open posture and gaze, along with a calm, confident manner.

As mentioned, in learning how to create a supportive presence, students often complain that they lose their natural warmth and spontaneity; they feel that the restraints imposed by other-centeredness make them self-conscious and interfere with their natural responsiveness. At first, their newly adopted professional tone or detachment may cause loved ones to say, "Quit therapizing me!" With time, experience, and good supervision, clinicians are able to combine informed awareness and appropriate self-control with genuine warmth, caring, and acceptance in a way that feels increasingly comfortable and natural.

EXERCISE 5.4 Clinical Repose

In small groups, discuss any ways in which your clinical presence is different from your manner when you are just being yourself in your private life. Note any things that disrupt your clinical repose. How can you work to enhance your repose and presence? In thinking about repose and presence, what have you learned about yourself? Is your clinical presence beginning to alter the way you carry yourself in your private life? Have people commented on that?

Genuineness

To be effective, support has to be genuine—sincere and free from pretense or hypocrisy. As one of his six necessary and sufficient conditions for change, Carl Rogers (1957) speaks about "genuineness or congruence." By **congruence**, Rogers means that "the therapist is willing to express and be open about any persistent feelings that exist in the relationship. It means avoiding the temptation to hide behind a mask of professionalism" (Rogers & Sanford, 1985, p. 1379). Barbara Okun (1997) writes about the need for clinicians to be honest: "Clinicians can communicate honesty by being open with clients, by answering questions to the best of their ability, and by admitting mistakes or lack of knowledge" (p. 40).

While attempting to communicate a supportive presence, clinicians need to avoid fake smiles, counterfeit approval, and false reassurance (e.g., "Don't worry—things will get better"). Many clients can spot faking easily because they have often been manipulated by the pretenses of others. They may not comment because they need the approval or services that the clinician can offer. Perceptions of inauthenticity undermine confidence in the clinician and impede the development of a trusting relationship.

There is a difference between genuineness and total honesty. A wise French saying, *"Toute la verité n'est pas bonne à dire,"* translates as "The whole truth is not always good to say." To create a supportive presence, we need to be selective, always considering the impact of our remarks and behaviors have on our clients. Subsequently, we do not always say everything we think, but we should think about everything we say. And what we do say, we have to mean. As clinicians, we are always "in role." Although we have to be ourselves, authentic in our role rather than hiding behind it, we also have to be deliberate. For example, we might think that a diagnosis of a particular kind of cancer puts a client at high risk of dying, but we would not say so. The goal is to accompany the client in the moment of his or her experience, not to be a wizard or mind reader.

Availability

Clinicians further support clients by making ourselves easily available. We need to be physically and psychologically accessible. As discussed in Chapter 3, clinicians indicate a willingness to join and work with clients by setting up offices that are welcoming, having hours that fit with clients' needs, being available by phone, and being flexible in setting the frequency and length of sessions. In addition, we demonstrate availability by being culturally responsive and able to provide services in the language of the client's choice. In sum, every effort is made to reduce feelings of distance or alienation.

> *As a social worker in the rehabilitation hospital, I needed to meet with the children of Rachel, a woman in our hospital recovering from a serious stroke. I'd been seeing one daughter each week for 30 minutes or so to provide support as she began to screen nursing homes and come to terms with her mother's chronic disability. When two more daughters became involved, I began to meet with everyone together, including Rachel, for an hour. I had to switch our meeting time to the early evening to accommodate their work and home schedules. I planned our meetings for Wednesdays so that it would be easy for them to stay for the stroke education group that met on Wednesday nights.*

A number of factors constrain the amount of time that clinicians can see clients face to face, such as the client's busy schedule, financial and insurance limitations, and long-distance travel. Clinicians need to be flexible in finding additional ways of being available to clients—in person, by phone, by letter, by fax, on cassette recordings or videotapes, and today even over the Internet by e-mail. An example from a recently developed Telehealth Program illustrates this kind of meaningful flexibility in getting services to clients who are unable to reach them easily otherwise. Dawn McCarty and Catherine Clancy (2002) report that South Carolina has only one psychiatrist fluent in American Sign Language. Videoconferencing has linked her with several mental health centers across the state at given times. She uses sign language in assessing client needs and strengths, recommends follow-up treatments, and, as needed, prescribes medications for deaf patients all over the state.

It is important to discuss with clients the easiest ways to reach us. Some people check e-mail several times a day and others only once a week. Unanswered calls for help pose both therapeutic and liability problems. However, the use of cell phones, fax machines, and computers presents the clinician with the difficult challenge of ensuring confidentiality. These forms of communication are accessible by others, and therefore sensitive material should not be transmitted by these means.

At times in the relationship, the clinician may offer the client more opportunities for contact, such as when the client is going through a particularly difficult time or when the clinician or client believes that the client can make productive use of additional contact. Proposed increases in contact should be reviewed with supervisors in advance because they can have unforeseen consequences. Most clients respond favorably to a goodwill offer of additional visits or "other times you can reach me." Some, however, can abuse the availability, experience it as seductive interest on the part of the clinician, feel too dependent after additional calls or visits, or think the clinician is judging the client as unable to cope or, more seriously, in need of help. The clinician has to note the use the client makes of the added contacts and respond accordingly by discussing any untoward effects of this extension of self and role.

In emergencies or to support clients under duress, clinicians may accompany clients to emergency rooms, court proceedings, hospital admissions, school evaluation meetings, and other places. In Chapter 12, we discuss accompanying clients as a form of clinician influence. Visiting incarcerated clients can also be supportive under well thought-out conditions. We always try to consult with supervisors or senior colleagues on the implications of activities with clients outside the usual scope of the work.

> *I visited Maureen in jail 2 days after she stabbed her husband in front of her two boys. I knew she would be beside herself with guilt and shame, and possibly suicidal. She was also new to the area and had no friends. My supervisor suggested I take her some personal items like a comb, brush, lotion, and some magazines to pass the time. She could not believe I would come "to such a place to see a person like me." I also went to their court hearing and then out to lunch in the neighborhood with her and her husband after he dropped the charges. The agency provided the money for all of these services, seeing it as building the family's view of themselves as "mattering." We really began our deeper family work after that. No one had ever given them the time of day.*

Many other services and arrangements can be set up to support clients between interviews to diminish feelings of isolation or vulnerability. The clinician can establish a safety net that includes family members, friends, on-call staff or hotlines, brief inpatient hospital stays, attendance at Alcoholics Anonymous (AA) or Narcotics Anonymous (NA) meetings, day treatment, sheltered work, respite care, and the like. Positive attitudes of network providers, a readiness to help, the availability of translators as needed, affordable transportation, and well coordinated schedules all make a difference as to whether "supports" feel truly supportive or not.

Validation of the Client's Story

Validation occurs when we endorse and appreciate the realities of the client's story. The clinical encounter may be the first opportunity people have had to feel that their stories are moving and believable and that the details ring true to a witness.

Universalizing is another supporting and validating technique, used to undercut a client's sense of isolation or differentness. In universalizing, we frame our response in such a way as to locate the client as one of a universe of people sharing similar feelings, experiences, or opinions.

EXAMPLES OF UNIVERSALIZING

"A lot of other people share that feeling."

Who wouldn't be nervous in a dark parking lot late at night!

Most working moms like yourself have the same fear you do about being laid off or losing their benefits if they take a maternity leave.

Join the crowd.

Universalizing is not always useful. Some clients may need to feel unique in their experiences or perceptions—the only specialness they may have known. Such clients may respond to universalizing with irritation or disappointment, communicating a feeling that the interviewer just does not understand their unique situation. Others may have experienced aloneness, alienation, or differentness for so long that simple reassurances from the clinician about the commonality of their experiences are insufficient to break up their core sense of alienation. To them, the clinician may appear naive or inattentive to their deep levels of distress. As with all techniques, we watch carefully for the client's response, note it, and explore it further, if necessary.

Identifying and Affirming Strengths

CLIP 5.2
Affirming Client Strengths

Clinicians who hold a strengths perspective recognize clients' courage or persistence in working toward goals. Recognition and confirmation can build self-esteem and initiative. Clients often come to see that the strengths used in one situation are often transferable to other seemingly insurmountable crises of the moment, making problems seem more resolvable. Identifying and affirming client strengths further the development of a supportive presence. As clinicians we can usually validate client strengths more effectively when we are aware of and secure in our own strengths and can appreciate the importance of self-validation.

EXAMPLES OF STRENGTHS PERSPECTIVE RESPONSES BY CLINICIANS

"It's amazing how much you got done with almost no support."

"You said you "ran out on every relationship you ever had, but you've come to see me for three months straight now, and this is a relationship. This relationship counts; it's a very important exception to your stated pattern, and it suggests to me that you do not in fact "run out" on every relationship. Maybe we could take a look at when relationships work for you and when they don't."

"I notice you whizzed right over the statement that, for the first time, when you felt like drinking this week, you increased your AA attendance. That was such an important step. I'd like to hear more about how you made that change happen."

"You say you're embarrassed to talk to me over and over again about your job achievements, but I like to hear about them. I think it's wonderful that things are working out for you now, and, frankly, I think you deserve a little more support for your successes than is out there for you right now."

Provision of Concrete Supports

Clinicians in both agency and private practice often demonstrate support for clients by helping them access needed services. Professional attention to the deleterious effects of poverty, economic dislocation, and institutionalized bias has increased clinicians' appreciation of the importance of providing for the basic human needs of individuals and families. These needs include food, clothing, shelter, adequate financial support, transportation, pathways to education or training, and access to opportunities for recreation and affiliation. Abraham Maslow (1968) outlined a hierarchy of human needs with concrete needs at its foundation. He postulated that, unless these basic human needs are met, people understandably do not develop much beyond the level of profound despair and so may not feel able to take action on their own behalf. It is unrealistic, if not cruel, to ask desperate people to sit around reflecting on their psychological lives and perspectives.

Providing needed resources can be a critical factor in building trust and in developing a therapeutic alliance. Clients often experience us as more respectful of their struggles when we actively help them obtain needed services, such as food stamps, housing, referrals to job training, and so on. We may be perceived as more appreciative of the exigencies of daily life and the bureaucratic snares that often await the person seeking services. A caution is that, although clinicians may at times directly provide needed services or resources, clients' resourcefulness is best developed when they learn how to exercise their own knowledge and skills on behalf of themselves and their loved ones. We agree with the wise saying that, if you give a hungry person a fish, he or she will eat for a day, but if you teach that person to fish, he or she can eat for a lifetime—if there are fish!

Clinicians are ill advised to impulsively offer concrete help if such offers are motivated by rescue fantasies, the wish to be liked, or a client's demands. Such moves frequently backfire, leaving all parties feeling used or betrayed. Lending money (as opposed to helping the client obtain funds) is also an unwise clinician practice, as is giving rides in personal vehicles (because of the risk of injury to the client if there is an accident or if a suicidal or psychotic client jumps out into traffic).

Advocacy

Another very important kind of support, intrinsic to the work clinicians do with people, is advocacy for client rights and opportunities. **Advocacy** takes place when clinicians join with others in political activities and movements in the community to achieve increased rights, protections, access, and opportunities for all people, including but not limited to our clients. As advocates, we also inform agencies or practice groups of important services or amenities that are not available to clients. Clinicians need to work together with colleagues and community groups to improve the conditions within which services are delivered. Advocacy also occurs when clinicians struggle with insurance companies or other payers to get the proper amount and kinds of services for clients. All of these activities have the potential to heighten client morale and hopefulness and to energize the clinical work.

◼ Empathy

DVD

CLIP 5.3

Empathy

Supportive presence is good for starters, but it is not enough to carry clinical process forward from its beginnings of cordiality, interest, and openness. The clinical relationship cannot move forward without empathy—the ability to immerse oneself in another's experience without losing one's own sense of self. **Empathy** requires that the clinician see and experience the world from the client's subjective perspective while maintaining the perspective of an outside observer. It thus requires a constant oscillation between observing the client, feeling and thinking as if one *were* the client, and then feeling and thinking *about* the client's experience. In addition to what it contributes to supportive presence, empathy provides the clinician with important human experience and information on which to base hunches that inform future clinical work.

Empathy is a complex process that is often misunderstood. The following clarifications may be helpful:

1. Empathy is not sympathy. Sympathy is what I feel *toward* you; empathy is what I feel *as* you.
2. Empathy is much more than just putting oneself in the other person's shoes. Empathy requires a shift of perspective. It is not what I would experience *as me* in your shoes; empathy is what I experience *as you* in your shoes.
3. Empathy requires a constant shifting between my experiencing *as you* what you feel and my being able to think *as me* about your experience.

EXERCISE 5.5   Experiencing Empathy

In your journal, record a time when someone really understood you, when they seemed to know exactly what you were feeling—a time when you felt someone's empathy. In class, describe the experience to your colleagues. How do you think that person knew so much about what you were feeling?

Empathy and Human Development

Jean Baker Miller and her colleagues at the Wellesley College Stone Center have written about the development of empathy and mutuality in relationships (Jordan, Kaplan, Miller, Stiver, & Surrey, 1991). They suggest that empathy is developed through mutually engaging exchanges that begin in infancy. Infants and children experience pleasure when they feel they are being accurately seen and heard by their caregivers. They internalize and practice the engaging skills of observing and feeling with others. They receive feedback and praise in relation to the accuracy of their empathic responses, reinforcing their pleasure and increasing their attempts at empathy. Likewise, their caregivers feel and show similar pleasure when on the receiving end of the child's budding caretaking behaviors or when delighting in the child's playing nurse, Mommy, or helper.

> *My 3-year-old daughter noticed that I was sad and she patted my back and said, "Mommy, you're sad today. . . . Do you want my teddy bear?" I said, "Yes, sweetie. I am sad. You are a very good girl to try to take care of Mommy."*

The accuracy and appropriateness of joining with the experiences of others are fine-tuned over time. Basically, one learns empathy by experiencing empathy, by being on the receiving end of empathy. The experience of being accurately seen and heard by another has few equals. Those who have been denied or shortchanged in their experience of empathy *from* others often show little or tenuous empathy *for* others. Those who have been overwhelmed by requests for empathic caregiving may manifest "compassion fatigue" (Figley, 1995). In either situation, people may be less likely to reveal themselves to or care much about others. Moreover, members of oppressed groups may generously empathize with each other but maintain emotional distance as protective armor when with outsiders—including clinicians—who are viewed as members of a subordinating group or culture (Walker & Rosen, 2004).

Developing Clinical Empathy

Empathy is a developmental process that can be consciously fostered and strengthened in adulthood in a number of ways. To think and feel as another person, we need to have a lot of experience with others, and we need to learn about the range of reactions that people have to various situations. Judith

Jordan (2004b) speaks of this developmental process as gaining relational awareness—awareness of what a relationship both provides and requires. We can gain this knowledge by enriching and expanding our own life experiences and by learning about human diversity through experiences with others who are different from us.

A simple and useful technique in establishing empathy with another person is the psychodramatic process of getting into role—taking on the physical and psychological characteristics of the other. We assume the other's posture, manner, tone, and intentions, as well as the dynamics of his or her personal history, family, and cultural experiences.

EXERCISE 5.6   Becoming the Other

Think of an important person in your life, perhaps a member of your family. Get into the role of that person. (For example, let's assume you have taken the role of your sister, Jen, although, of course, you can take the role of anyone you want.) Now, tell the group your name. (In the instructions, we use "Jen." but you can play anyone.) Assume the body posture, tone, and manner of Jen. What are you wearing? Jen, think about how you look, dress, feel, and speak. Remember your history, family, and culture. Give a brief monologue about yourself to the group, Jen, and then let the group interview you in role for 5 minutes to learn more about you. Videotape the monologue.

Group members help each stay in role by using the role name. (For example, "Jen, how do you feel about . . . ?" or "Jen, is that how you speak?" or "Is that how you hold your body, Jen?"). While you are in role, group members may ask you questions about how you feel about current social issues, what is important in your life, or about the relationship between the person you are role playing and you (e.g., between Jen and her sister).

After completing your role-play, talk with the group about the experience. Watch the video together. In your journal, record what you learned about the other person when you took the role. Did you learn anything about yourself? Did you learn anything about your relationship with the person?

This exercise may have been easy because you are familiar with the person you were asked to play. You have a history of interaction and a wealth of information about the person on which to draw. Similarly, as clinicians we need basic background information about the people we work with to build empathy, because empathy is a relational process and cannot occur in a vacuum.

EXERCISE 5.7   Information Builds Empathy

Play Leti. Notice that you cannot do it without some basic information about Leti that helps you get into her role. Write down what kinds of information you would want to have to empathize with her. Compare the information you want about Leti with the information that others might want to know. Note the different kinds of information people seek. You might want to know her age, ethnicity, living situation, and other important circumstances before even trying to empathize. Discuss with others the things that help you, personally, empathize with someone and the things that make empathizing harder for you. Record your reactions in your journal.

One of the tasks of the initial interview—indeed, of all interviews—is to gather necessary and relevant information (to be detailed in Chapters 6 and 7). Sometimes gathering information is easy: from an intake form; the initial telephone call; or comments from friends, family members, or referring persons. Many times, clients themselves readily provide continuing information with which we can identify and use to empathize. When clients are silent or do not talk easily, we still use the empathic process by imagining ourselves as the other to understand why they are expressing themselves through silence rather than through speech. Shulman (2006) regards silence as an important form of communication and speaks of "reaching inside silence" as an important technique in expressing empathy and reengaging the client in verbal exchange.

Students often ask, "How can I be empathic with people whose experiences I've never had and can scarcely relate to?" (Examples could be pregnancy, imprisonment, the death of a child, or from other classes or cultural backgrounds.) To be empathic, we need to both broaden our knowledge of the wide range of human experience and, quite simply, open our hearts.

Clinicians strengthen empathy by trying it out with many different kinds of people and getting differential feedback from them regarding the accuracy and timeliness of our empathic responses. Under the pressures of school or work, it is often easier to socialize with people whose backgrounds and experiences are similar to your own. However, push yourself beyond the familiar and expand the network of those with whom you interact. Social activism in various communities is a great way to meet new people and become familiar with beliefs, values, and experiences different from your own. In-class exercises and group assignments are also designed to enhance your knowledge of other people's experiences and perspectives. Ideally, in the process, you increase your capacity for empathy with a widening range of people in varying situations.

> As a southerner, I had been taught that Catholics were under rigid papal control and that, if Kennedy were elected president, he would be taking orders directly from the Pope. I laugh now to think how incredibly naive this was. It wasn't until I came to social work school and actually became friends with a number of Catholics that I realized that many of my Catholic friends were freer from religious strictures than I was as a southern Methodist. It was also the first time I befriended people of color and worked with people from the inner city. My ideas changed so much as we all shared our stories in role-plays, over lunch, and hanging out after work.

Reading the professional literature and attending conferences are other ways to become better acquainted with the conditions and experiences of many different people. Professional reading can be augmented with novels, plays, autobiographies, and the like. Educational and commercial films, videos, plays, and documentaries offer additional opportunities for learning. For example, the films *Hoop Dreams* and *Crash* may be useful for developing empathy with some inner-city families, while the films *Philadelphia* and *Yesterday* may help people grasp the struggles and challenges of some men and women with AIDS.

EXERCISE 5.8   Expanding Your Capacity for Empathy

This week, read or watch something you think will expand your capacity for empathy. It could be a story about a person with a mental illness, a family from a different culture, or someone struggling with an issue with which you are unfamiliar or uncomfortable. Record in your journal why you chose the topic and what you experienced and learned from it. Also discuss what it would be like for you to be *in* this situation, rather than reading about it or watching it.

You can also broaden your human experiences by volunteering in the community: working at a meal site, senior center, or homeless shelter; helping with a neighborhood campaign for better schools or voter registration; marching for an end to domestic violence; or joining candlelight vigils. All this constitutes the expanded role of the clinician in working for peace, justice, equity, and basic rights for all

> *I did my master's thesis on working with people who were dying. However, it wasn't until many years later, when I volunteered at AIDS Action Committee, that I had any idea of what it might be like to face my own death. Meeting each week with men who had just discovered that they had a life-threatening illness made me much more sensitive to the issues and feelings around death and dying. I moved from "knowing" to "experiencing."*

EXERCISE 5.9   Empathy Role-Plays

Take the role of each of the people described in the following vignettes.

You are Janelle, a 23-year-old African-American mother of two children who has moved to a new neighborhood.

You are Kieran, an Irish Catholic college junior, and you have just been told that you have been cut from the Notre Dame football team.

You are Kim Soong, a 16-year-old adopted daughter from Korea, and your parents just told you they are getting a divorce.

You are Frankie, a 78-year-old widower, and your daughter told you it would be best for you to live in a nursing home.

You are Rosalie, a woman being stalked by her boyfriend.

In your journal, discuss the following: What helped you get into each role? Did you have similar experiences on which to draw? What information and experiences were helpful in taking on each role? Which role was hardest to get into and why?

In the Exercise 5.9, you may have noticed that it was easier to get into some roles than others. It is often harder to get into a role in which we have to take on negative or uncomfortable feelings (e.g., fear, shame) or an identity discredited by others (e.g., gay, welfare recipient, drug user). Empathy can also be difficult if the client's experiences arouse some unfinished business or personally charged issues for the clinician. Clients often notice when clinicians tighten up or detour around such issues.

> *When my client began expressing her sadness about her mother's death, I noticed that I did not want to feel her sadness. Prior to the interview, I had just been at the hospital visiting with a good friend dying of cancer. The moment my client cried, I actually stood up and said, "Please go ahead; don't let me interrupt. I just have to shut the window; it's freezing in here." When I returned to my seat, she changed the subject without skipping a beat.*

A major challenge in empathizing is maintaining self-awareness and centeredness while "feeling as" the other and communicating that feeling effectively. We need to be able to distinguish the client's feelings and experiences from our own. While attempting to be empathic, clinicians need to guard against projection and overidentification with clients. In **projection,** clinicians disavow and repress their own unpleasant or taboo feelings, then attribute the feelings to clients ("I'm not angry—*she* is."). In **overidentification,** clinicians emphasize the similarities between themselves and clients, and minimizing or denying things that would reveal unsettling differences between them. Whereas empathy takes us *toward* client experience, projection and overidentification take us *away* from it, as our defenses arise to protect us from our own inner anxieties about the relationship.

Communicating Empathy in the Relationship

We move from *feeling* empathic to *being* empathic by converting our perceptions, feelings, and intuitions into postures, gestures, sounds, words, and behaviors. The basic methods we use to communicate support and empathy include supportive sounds, mirroring, and empathic echo. These methods incorporate two important components. First, the clinician is the caring other who offers supportive responses as the client reveals his or her story. Second, the clinician is the empathic other who reflects back content, affect, themes, and patterns in the client's story from the client's perspective.

Supportive Sounds

We demonstrate our presence and close attention by making periodic use of **supportive sounds,** such as "ohhh," "mm-hmm," "uh-huh," "yes," "ah," and "I see." These brief utterances mark our active involvement in the client's narrative and are often gently interjected during long narrations by the client. They indicate to the client that we are listening and following the story closely, and they can encourage the client to continue talking.

EXAMPLES OF SUPPORTIVE SOUNDS

Client: It hurt so much when I was dismissed like that.

Clinician: Awww . . .

Client: I didn't want to give my boss the pleasure of seeing me cry.

Clinician: Mmm . . .

Client: I have some ideas about what to do next, though.

Clinician: Good. I'd like to hear them.

Since responses must be genuine to be effective; we make every effort to avoid speaking in a repetitious, hackneyed, or "singsong" manner. In the preceding example, a minimal response suffices to show caring and presence while keeping the clinician out of the way of the story so that the *client's* voice is exercised and validated.

> *One of the first times I listened to myself on tape, I noticed that I kept saying "right" to the client. It wasn't that I was agreeing with her; it was my way of saying "uh-huh." I realized the danger of using that phrase when she said, "My husband is a pain in the ass," and I said, "Right." I suddenly worried that she would go home and tell her husband that her counselor agreed that he was a pain in the ass!*

Mirroring

Mirroring is a physical form of reflection. In mirroring, the clinician matches the client's posture, facial expression, and gestures. For example, if the client is leaning forward, the clinician may also lean forward; if the client is frowning, the clinician may also frown. Mirroring helps us develop empathy for the client's perspective, and it communicates that we are closely following and are "where the client is." We are always careful not to mimic the client or interfere with the natural flow of productive conversation. Imitating or copying the client's every movement can make the client self-conscious and distract attention from the whole person and the emerging details of the story. Mirroring thus involves art as well as technique, and it is a matter of nuance and subtle responding.

As rapport and **synchrony** build between interviewer and client, their postures often become more congruent. Kadushin & Kadushin (1997) note that the client can also unconsciously begin to parallel the clinician's posture, tone, and nonverbals. Clinicians can use this knowledge about synchrony to shape interviewee behaviors by using relaxed posture and comfortable gaze to calm and soothe an overexcited client, for example, or by using exuberant facial expressions and gestures to energize someone about a hard-won success.

EXERCISE 5.10 Mirroring

Watch any ongoing conversation between two people and note how the participants begin to mirror each other nonverbally. Is the synchrony present from the outset? If not, how long does it take to set in, and what forms does it take?

Empathic Echo

Empathic echo refers to a verbal reflection of the client's story—that is, behaviors, thoughts, affect, and meanings in context. For purposes of theoretical discussion, clinicians often distinguish between content and affect, although the two are always interacting at some level. **Reflection of content** involves making statements that accurately represent the client's statements about behaviors, thoughts, and interactions. It can also entail making statements regarding the context or situation in which the client's story is embedded. **Reflection of affect** consists of making statements about the feelings that may wrap around or suffuse the client's content.

Gerard Egan (1998) differentiates between basic and advanced empathy. Basic empathy is the skill of joining the client's perspective and is similar to our concept of the empathic echo. The clinician attempts to reflect content and affect that are the most crucial to the client. The goal of reflection in the empathic echo is to have the client experience the clinician as joining his or her perspective. In Chapter 8, you will learn that reflection techniques are central to motivational interviewing, a set of strategies designed to help clients resolve ambivalences about changing (Miller & Rollnick, 2002).

In **advanced empathy**, the clinician reflects the meaning beneath the surface of the client's awareness. Egan (1998) notes that "as skilled helpers listen intently to clients, they often enough see clearly what clients only half see and hint at" (p. 170). We agree with Egan that one can reflect content and affect for reasons other than to convey basic empathy. As we discuss in later chapters, the clinician can choose to reflect some parts of content or affect to increase clients' awareness of patterns and themes, to confront, to explore, or simply to move the conversation ahead.

Empathic reflection of content.   Reflection of content may seem simple, but it is a lot harder than it sounds, and it involves clinical judgment. The interviewer has to decide whether speaking is appropriate at the moment and, if so, whether to reflect the words themselves or their presumed meanings. We do not always use the same words as the client; more often, we paraphrase what the client has said using similar words and phrases that ideally convey the same meaning.

EXAMPLES OF REFLECTION OF CONTENT

Client: I had my one-year anniversary at AA.

Clinician A [using the same words]: You had your one-year anniversary in AA.

Clinician B [using different words]: You haven't had a drink in a long time.

A risk in using words other than those of the client is that the clinician may choose words that do not convey the same meaning as the client intended. In the preceding example, Clinician B's view that one year is a long time might not correspond with the client's perspective. For the client, the one-year anniversary may be small compared to his cousin's 22 years of sobriety. Also, having one year in AA does not necessarily mean that the client has not had a drink in a year.

Linguistic differences can also complicate accurate reflection. Roger Fisher, William Ury, and Bruce Patton (1991) tell the following story that exemplifies the difficulties:

> The Persian word "compromise" apparently lacks the positive meaning in English of "a midway solution both sides can live with" but has only a negative meaning as in "our integrity was compromised." Similarly the word "mediator" in Persian suggests "meddler," someone who is barging in uninvited. In early 1980, UN Secretary General Waldheim flew to Iran to seek the release of American hostages. His efforts were seriously set back when Iranian television broadcast in Persian a remark he reportedly made on his arrival in Tehran: "I have come as a mediator to work out a compromise" (p. 33).

Reflecting content is further complicated by the fact that people tend to talk in paragraphs, conveying several ideas at once. Human communication is multilayered, and the clinician is constantly making judgments about which of the many pieces of shared content is the most important to reflect at the moment. At different times in the interview or in the working relationship, we reflect and emphasize different pieces of client content to challenge, to help expand awareness, or to develop new perspectives on problems. At this point, we are using reflection as part of the empathic echo; because we are trying only to demonstrate empathy and support, we need to reflect what we believe the *client* sees as the crucial content. Other content is stored for future consideration.

E X A M P L E

> *Client:* I had a terrible day. The bus was late, my daughter was sick, and the boss yelled at me for being late for work again.

There are six pieces of content that could be reflected following this client's statement:

1. Terrible day
2. Late bus
3. Sick daughter
4. Late for work
5. Not the first time late for work
6. Boss yelling

The clinician is free to reflect any of these pieces of content, and three different clinicians might all choose different reflections, depending on the stance or focus each wants to sustain.

E X A M P L E S

> *Clinician A:* Your daughter was sick, the bus was late, and you were yelled at by your boss for being late again. It was a terrible day.
>
> *Clinician B:* You had a terrible day.
>
> *Clinician C:* What a lot of things to cope with in one day!

Clinician A decides to reflect all of what the client said, to acknowledge hearing it while leaving the conversation leadership to the client. Although this may be useful in letting the client know that the clinician heard all that was said and simply wishes the client to continue, just repeating everything the client says time after time can feel tedious and meaningless to both client and clinician. Too many repetitions can dull the liveliness of spontaneity and make the clinical conversation feel too far removed from ordinary exchange. Rarely does anyone just repeat back what someone else has said.

Clinician B notes to herself that the client was late for work "again," which may be an important piece of information to pick up on later, especially if it signals a pattern undermining the client's achievement of stated goals. However, since she is attempting an empathic echo, she reflects what seems most crucial to the client in the moment of this encounter: the "terrible day." She stores the information about being late for work, the boss's yelling, and the daughter's illness, perhaps to make use of them later. Clinician B uses the *first* piece of content because in this instance she feels that it captures the gestalt of the entire communication. At other times, clinicians reflect the *last* piece of content in clients' narratives, just as an encouragement for clients to go further.

Clinician C's response is a summary comment, using words that are different from those of the client. Such a response is an attempt to reflect content *and* tone so as to express and build empathy.

EXERCISE 5.11   Empathic Reflection of Content

Read the following client statements. List the pieces of content—the different ideas—in each statement. Which pieces might you reflect to show empathy or support for the client? Reflect the content in two ways:

1. By using the client's own words

2. By paraphrasing the content or meaning of what the client said

Client A: I am trying to choose between a career with the military or with the police. The military will give me a chance to see the world and experience other cultures. I can also get my B.A. degree for free. But my father and my uncles are all cops.

Client B: I just found out that my aunt is having her kidney removed. My uncle is 86 and is really worried about her. He has high blood pressure and diabetes. I have to find out about nursing care for both of them.

Client C: The kids at school are picking on me. I am the only girl in the shop class. We have to make a model for a tool shed, and no one will be my partner. If I can't get a partner, I'll fail.

Note that you are only reading this and that your experience of the exchange might be different if you actually heard the client's statements, replete with nonverbal, paralinguistic, and metacommunication clues.

Now, instead of reading each statement to yourself, pair up with a colleague and take turns making each statement. Note differences in tone, emphasis, speech rate, and other paralinguistic cues as the speaker and the content change.

Empathic reflection of affect.   Clients can tell us directly how they feel, as when they say, "I'm so proud . . . ," or "I am scared," or "I am so sad that . . . ." Sometimes, though, the words clients use to describe their feelings are ambiguous—for example, "I was upset that I got fired." The term "upset" could mean that the client was sad, worried, angry, embarrassed, or any number of things that we can only imagine unless the client elaborates.

Often the clinician is left to guess what the client feels, combining prior knowledge of the client's habitual patterns and the literal words spoken with the accompanying tone, emphasis, facial and body movements, or feelings. We need to develop a capacity to recognize when feelings are arising, to discern one feeling state from another, and to decide when and when not to focus on them. We also need to familiarize ourselves with the variety of ways in which clients express feelings, coming to appreciate local, cultural, and idiosyncratic styles and influences.

EXAMPLE

Client: I'm so pissed off at my brother for telling my mom I'm pregnant, when I wanted to tell her myself.

Clinician A: You're pregnant and your brother told your mother.

Clinician B: You're mad at your brother.

Clinician C: You're disappointed that you didn't get to tell your mother you're pregnant.

Clinician A decided to reflect content only. She noted two pieces of content: that the client was pregnant and that her brother told her mother. She did not reflect the client's feeling, perhaps because of how the client expressed herself: "pissed off." The clinician may have felt uncomfortable reflecting that term or uncomfortable about getting more anger into the room by focusing on it. Other clinicians might feel that, unless the angry feelings are acknowledged and validated, attempts to focus intellectually on content will not get very far because the client is "so pissed off."

Clinician B reflected that the client was angry with her brother. Note that this clinician used the word "mad" to reflect the client's feeling. Clients may at times use words that we feel uncomfortable reflecting. We have found that it is wiser not to fake comfort; it works better for us to paraphrase the client than to use terms we are not comfortable with. For example, adolescents can use extreme language for purposes of group belongingness or to test or shock adults. Clinicians may try to assume this style and end up seeming and sounding phony.

Clinician C did not reflect the feeling that the client directly expressed—anger. She reflected what she felt the client might also be feeling—disappointment. So even when clients directly express feelings, clinicians attempting empathy may pursue other feelings that, although unspoken, may also be crucial to the client's perspective in the moment.

Each of the preceding reflections takes the conversation in a different direction. Clinician B's response might lead to a focus on the client's relationship with her brother, whereas Clinician C's might lead to concerns about talking with her mother. All the approaches have merit: They are attempts at empathy.

EXERCISE 5.12   Empathic Reflection of Affect

Go back to Exercise 5.11. Describe the different feelings that might go along with the content of each client's statement. Which feelings might you reflect to show empathy or support for the client? Reflect the affect in two different ways. Again, note the additional clues to intent and meaning when you *hear* communication rather than read it.

The empathic echo is more than simply an echo of specific words or feelings. In reflecting either content or affect, clinicians carefully attempt to reflect the way clients understand or make meaning of their situations, feelings, behaviors, or thoughts. We thus reflect not only *what* is said but also *how* it is said—its tone, its coloration, and the metacommunication and paralinguistic cues (described in Chapter 4). We use the empathic echo for several reasons: to show we are listening, to increase the client's feeling of being attended to closely, and to increase the client's feeling of being understood. The empathic echo allows the client to correct any misconceptions the clinician may have.

Empathic Failures

CLIP 5.4
Empathic Failures

Empathic failures occur when clinicians miss the boat and reflect the wrong content, feeling, or meaning. At other times, we may drift from the moment and miss a very important theme or feeling altogether, all the while appearing to listen and nod attentively. Clients often notice when clinicians drift away, and they may signal their awareness by asking, "Now, where was I?" or "What was I talking about when I got off there?"—as though *they* were lost, not us! Another empathic mistake interviewers sometimes make is to confuse one client's story with another's and make a remark about an event or loved one unrelated to the client, hurting the client's feelings. The client may think, "I'm indistinguishable from all the others."

Dillon (2003) has identified many ways that clinicians can make empathic mistakes:

- *Boilerplate empathy.* The clinician uses singsong or stockpiled and overused empathic statements that sound as though they were learned from TV sitcoms rather than from supervisors: "I feel your pain," "Oh, my!" "I see what you're saying."
- *Piling it on.* The clinician makes empathic comments or sounds after almost every client statement. The comments are too numerous, too exaggerated, too childlike in tone, or so repetitious that they feel inauthentic: "Wow," "Awful," "No way," "Oooh," " I feel so bad for you," "Geeee," "You must have felt terrible."
- *Getting the facts wrong.* The clinician says, "This is the anniversary of your brother's suicide . . . an important day." The client says, "No, that was last month."
- *Trivializing via excessive universalizing.* The clinician can make the client feel that a uniquely painful situation is being trivialized as "just one of" a hundred similar instances: "Lots of people feel that way." "You're not alone." "I know lots of women who have lost their husbands."
- *Mistaking personal sharing for empathy.* The clinician shares an experience similar to the client's with the intention of empathizing, but takes the focus away from the client's story: "I've been there myself." "That happened to me and I know how you must feel." "When my father died, I . . . ."

- *No clinician response.* The clinician who is not following closely may miss important moments when an empathic response is sorely needed. The absence of a response at a crucial moment (for example, the clinician simply says "Hmmm" or leaves a silence) can be experienced as a lack of interest.

There is an increased likelihood of empathic misses when the client and clinician come from different ethnic or sociocultural backgrounds (Comas-Diaz & Jacobsen, 1991). Even within the same cultural or ethnic group, people can act on faulty assumptions or generalizations. Empathic failures can also occur when the clinician overidentifies with or idealizes the client or feels some antipathy toward the client. In addition, empathic misses may occur when the client is particularly difficult or when the client demeans, attacks, or sabotages the clinician.

Psychodynamic theorists postulate a process called **countertransference,** in which the clinician unconsciously sees the client as representative of an important figure from the past and behaves toward the client as though the client *were* that person. Countertransference distortion negatively affects the clinician's ability to be empathic because empathy requires the ability to accurately perceive and join with the client's perspective. We discuss the psychodynamic concepts of transference and countertransference in greater detail in Chapter 12.

Clinicians should make use of detailed process recordings, video- and audiotapes, and supervision to understand and, ideally, to change personal feelings, beliefs, and reactions that interfere with empathy and caring. Group supervision is very useful in the mutual sharing and spotting of overidentifications, scapegoating, aversions, and other behaviors that negatively affect clinician empathy. Personal therapy is highly recommended when clinicians continue to have problems with caring, sustainment, and empathy. Those continuing to have serious difficulties with empathy over time may need to conclude that clinical work is not a suitable undertaking for them.

Learning from Empathic Failures

Even when our reflections of content and affect are misguided or wrong, attending to the errors can be extremely important in modeling for clients that mistakes can occur without destroying relationships. Both client and clinician are reminded that the important step in maintaining connection is not the perfection of the participants but the work of sorting things out together in a mutually trusting and accepting bond.

Moreover, mutuality is heightened because the client gets to educate and correct the clinician about what was actually said or what is happening between them so that the customary power imbalance in clinical work is somewhat mitigated through this two-way feedback. We listen for empathic failures, acknowledge them with grace, and thank clients for their patience, reactions, and feedback as we correct our course.

EXAMPLE OF EMPATHIC FAILURE AND CORRECTION

Client: My child has gone off to college. It's really a change in my life.

Clinician: You must feel very sad now that your last child has left home.

Client: Not really. I actually feel relieved to finally have time to spend on myself.

Clinician: So you don't feel sad. You feel relieved, and perhaps excited, that there are new opportunities for you.

Client: Yeah, it *is* very exciting.

I was seeing a client who had been abruptly let go from her company during a downsizing. She said she was incredibly anxious. I started to reflect how worried she must be about economic issues—how she would pay the rent, where she would get a new job, etc. We spent almost the whole session talking about that. The next week, she came in and said that what really had been bothering her was how other people would perceive her. I had missed the point of her anxiety. I immediately acknowledged that I had been thinking that she was worried about money when she was worried about something else. At first, I felt bad. Later, my supervisor pointed out that it was great that she corrected me. I didn't have to be perfect. I had created an atmosphere where she felt comfortable telling me when I was wrong. We really were a team working together. I was trying and she was helping me really understand her.

■ Conclusion

In this chapter, we reviewed two basic elements that sustain clinical work: support and empathy. We communicate support through a reliable clinical presence that provides genuine warmth, caring, acceptance, and validation and that affirms client strengths. We also demonstrate support by being available, by providing concrete services, and by advocating with and for clients.

Empathy is the ability to join the perspective and experience of the client—to feel *with and as* the client while maintaining the position of an observing and communicating other. Clinical empathy can be expressed through supportive sounds, mirroring, and empathic reflection of content and affect. However, as we saw in the clinical examples, clinicians may not be empathic, and attempts at empathy may fail. The conscientious clinician uses every opportunity to develop and sustain the clinical relationship.

In the next chapter, we discuss methods clinicians use within this relationship to help clients further elaborate their stories.

■ Suggested Readings

This is a classic work on the helping relationship.

Rogers, Carl. (1957). The necessary and sufficient conditions of therapeutic personality change. *Journal of Consulting Psychology, 21,* 95–103.

There are a number of excellent works on the process and complications of empathy, including the following:

Coleman, Daniel. (2000). The therapeutic alliance in multicultural practice. *Psychoanalytic Social Work, 7,* 65–90

Comas-Diaz, Lillian, & Jacobsen, Frederick M. (1991). Ethnocultural transference and countertransference in the therapeutic dyad. *American Journal of Orthopsychiatry, 61,* 392–402.

Jordan, Judith V. (1991b). Empathy and self-boundaries. In Judith V. Jordan, Alexandra G. Kaplan, Jean Baker Miller, Irene P. Stiver, & Janet L. Surrey (Eds.), *Women's growth in connection: Writings from the Stone Center* (pp. 67–80). New York: Guilford Press.

■ Self-Explorations

1. What do you think about physical touching in the clinical relationship? How has touching been handled in your family? Are people physically affectionate? How about outside your family? Do people pat each other on the back, hug hello, touch each other in sympathy or in humorous exchanges? Is your culture a "touchy" culture? Do friends touch each other? What about strangers?

2. Make a list of your personal strengths. How important are they to you? How did you learn that each was a strength? Was writing down your strengths easy or hard to do? What familial and cultural messages came up for you as you thought about your own strengths?

3. Sometimes it is hard for the clinician to be fully present with the client and attend to his or her story because of uncomfortable feelings that arise when discussing certain subjects. Do any topics make you uncomfortable or cause you to have difficulty being empathic? What are they? Why are they difficult for you?

■ Essay Questions

1. What are the advantages and disadvantages of clinicians working with people who are similar and dissimilar to themselves? What are (1) the advantages of working with someone similar, (2) the disadvantages of working with someone similar, (3) the advantages of working with someone different, and (4) the disadvantages of working with someone different? Which would be hardest for you and why?

2. Discuss some of the things that may get in the way of a clinician's acceptance of a client. What kinds of things should clinicians do when they find it hard to be supportive of a client?

3. Empathy is key to the development of the clinical relationship. Define empathy and discuss the three components of empathy described in the text.

4. Do you think it is permissible under any circumstance to lend a client money, offer a client a ride, or co-sign a document for a client? When and why? What might be the potential downside of offering such concrete support?

5. Discuss the factors that should be taken into account when deciding whether to extend extra time, appointments, or phone calls to clients. Do you have any examples from your own experiences of "going beyond the usual" with a client?

■ Key Terms

Advanced empathy	Overidentification
Advocacy	Projection
Clinical repose	Reflection of affect
Congruence	Reflection of content
Countertransference	Societal norms
Culture-bound syndromes	Supportive sounds
Empathic echo	Synchrony
Empathic failures	Unconditional positive regard
Empathy	Universalizing
Holding environment	Validation
Mirroring	

CHAPTER 6

Exploration and Elaboration

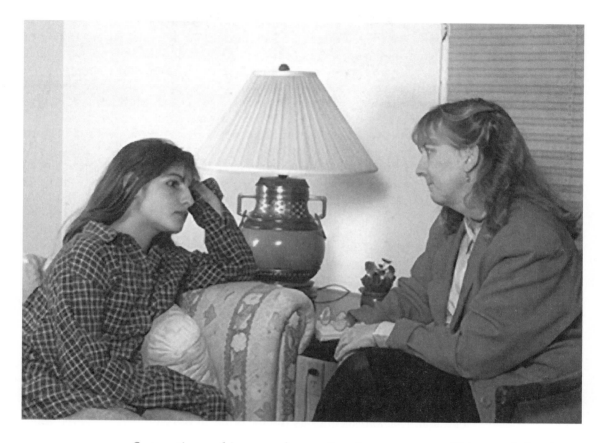

Supportive ambiance and empathy alone are not sufficient to help clients grasp their situation and bring about the changes they desire in themselves or in their lives. In the following chapters, we explore a variety of ways clinicians work together with clients to create change: using exploration, developing hunches and new perspectives, changing old behaviors and learning new ones, using the clinical relationship as a venue for change, and moving to action. In this chapter, we discuss how clinicians can deepen the level of conversation by helping clients explore and elaborate on their stories.

■ Levels of Exploration and Elaboration

Few narratives, especially ones shared with a relative stranger, emerge full-blown all on their own. In addition to creating a supportive relationship, safe space, and congenial tone, the clinician uses the techniques and strategies of exploration and elaboration to elicit and expand on the story. In exploration the clinician gathers initial information through the use of questions, prompts, and probes. In elaboration the clinician encourages the client to expand on the story. Exploration and elaboration help both clinicians and clients. They help clinicians gather new information, clarify ambiguities or uncertainties, raise new issues, and attain a deeper and more accurate understanding of the client. They help clients expand their stories, note and elucidate their meanings, and develop new perspectives. Exploration and elaboration are important to every aspect of clinical work. They are central to the assessment process as clinicians clarify and prioritize presenting problems and assets. However, exploration and elaboration are not limited to the assessment phase; they are also crucial in establishing working agreements and in planning and implementing interventions.

Arnold Lazarus (1971) was the first to describe the layers, or circles, of personal territory. He suggested that people keep their most private thoughts in an inner circle, shared with few others. Dusty Miller (1996) further proposes that interview conversation itself has outer, middle, and inner layers or circles. The *outer circle* houses the opening—sometimes surface—exploratory conversation between people who are just getting to know each other. Outer circle exploration occurs early in the interview, as the client is assessing the clinician's trustworthiness, respectfulness, and reliability. The goals of this outer level of exploration are to develop knowledge of the presenting situation and to establish a relationship of trust and collaboration by talking about subjects that do not push the client too quickly into forbidden or overly distressing topics. It focuses on clarifying the reasons for referral, eliciting the strengths and vulnerabilities of the client and his or her systems, fleshing out client demographics, and spelling out interviewer-client roles and agreements on how to proceed.

The *middle circle* houses more revealing exploration of deeper-level content, conflicts, and feelings as the relationship develops and both the client and the interviewer feel themselves on more secure ground. A shift to the middle circle involves more focused exploration, which may elicit more painful detail, reflection, and affect. Here the clinician may begin to raise topics not yet broached or elaborated on by the client. Whereas the earlier focus often tends to be more about information, middle circle exploration usually elicits more complicated feelings and meaning. Often, more is shared about significant or previously undisclosed behavior patterns, relationship issues, and situation dynamics.

The *inner circle* houses feelings and content about frightening, taboo, or shame-bound areas. This level of exploration brings people into areas of the story that may have been previously unshared with others or that may have been unknown even to the clients themselves. At this level of conversation, clients often discover things about themselves and their relationships with others about which they previously have been unaware. Often a good deal of embarrassment, reluctance, hesitation, and confusion is manifest at this level. Only after trust and talking are well established do most people risk the maximum exposure of the inner circle.

The following examples demonstrate outer, middle, and inner circles of conversation in response to clinician probes. Although the clinician's questions and the client's responses all move from outer to inner circles, often the client's responses have more to do with where the participants are in the interview or in the relationship than with the specific questions the clinician asks. Family and cultural norms about sharing personal information or material that might "shame" the client also affect the client's willingness to disclose information (Chan & Lee, 2004; Sharifzadeh, 2004).

EXAMPLES

Outer Circle Talk

Clinician: Can you tell me something about your work?

Client: I work as a painter for a large painting company. I'm the supervisor for a crew of four. I like the outdoor activity and being my own boss.

Middle Circle Talk

Clinician: You mentioned things you like . . . are there things you don't like?

Client: Well, I find it hard to be the boss sometimes. I'm not really comfortable telling people what to do. I hate it when someone screws up and I have to get after them.

Inner Circle Talk

Clinician: Where do you think this "hating to get after people" comes from?

Client: I always hated being bossed around myself. I was the youngest boy in the family, and my four older brothers were always on my case. I guess I feel that I never want to come across as a bully and make people feel as bad as I did. I never thought about that before . . . . It's weird how something that happened when I was a kid could affect me at work today.

Levels of conversation and exploration are not discrete, and they do not appear in neat sequences, one right after the other. More often, clinicians and clients subtly shift between levels within each interview and from interview to interview. Most interviews begin at the outer circle to "warm up" participants to further exploration and discussion and then move, when they are comfortable, to deeper levels of elaboration. Inner circles of communication usually are not reached until a level of trust has been established between the participants. It is not unusual for clinical interviews to stay at the outer and middle circles for several sessions. In fact, some clinical relationships stay almost entirely at the outer and middle circles and still get very important work done. In addition, a client may be able to work at inner circle levels on topic A, but only outer circle levels on topic B.

The depth and intensity of exploration should always be guided by the clinician's awareness of cultural norms, customs, and taboos. Lum notes Ramon Valle's (1980) suggestion that clinicians spend some start-up time in friendly conversation, or *platica*, when working with Latino clients:

> Latinos are accustomed to mutual extended discussion, which is a recognized form of relationship building. "Platica" stresses mutuality and reciprocity, meaning an open and free exchange of information between two parties. Helper-initiated friendly conversation about the weather, humorous incidents, or recent activities sets the stage for development of a relationship (Lum, 2004, p. 153).

During times of crisis, both clinicians and clients may move rapidly to inner circle conversation without necessarily building the relationship first. Accelerated questioning is often appropriate when the time available is limited and the need for prompt intervention is urgent. Such accelerated probing often occurs in mandated protective service evaluations; for example, a child's insufficiently explained burns, an elderly woman's black eye and broken arm, or the delusion of a person with mentally illness that he is flying between buildings may all be cause for more direct, persistent exploration to protect people from further harm.

Other clients may also move quickly to inner circle conversation, believing that this is what "therapy" is all about and pushing ahead without sufficient awareness of the impact that too much self-disclosure may have on them. At some point in their careers, almost all clinicians have seen the results of rushing into inner circle conversation: overwhelmed clients canceling for a period of time or never coming back, feeling too exposed. We need to be aware that, while frequently the goal of clinical work may be to deepen the level of conversation, deepening is only one goal among many. An equally important goal is to maintain the safety of the clinical experience so that clients do not feel overwhelmed by revealing too much, too soon. Usually, we also try to move the conversation to the middle or outer circles before the interview ends, so that clients are not left feeling overwhelmed or exposed as they return to their community roles and responsibilities.

> *A mentor told me never to do emotional surgery on people if what they needed was a transfusion, and never to do emotional surgery in the session without leaving enough time to suture the client back up before leaving, so they don't go out alone and have an emotional bleed with no tourniquet in sight.*

It is important to note that beginning clinicians often confuse "going deep" with succeeding as an interviewer. In reality, good clinical interviewing can occur even when the interview does not move beyond the outer circle of conversation. The purpose and goals of the contact, as well as the time and resources available, usually have a great influence on the level and duration of clinical conversations. Success is most often measured by the realization of agreed-upon aims and goals, not by the number of painful subjects covered. Indeed, the thoughtful clinician tries to introduce momentary intervals of respite into intense exploratory conversation, carefully helping clients move back and forth between deep immersion and more detached review. Respite protects the client from being overwhelmed and allows the clinician to check in with the client to ensure that the process feels okay to continue.

> *Lupe came into the Rape Crisis Center for her second interview after being assaulted at her high school homecoming party. This time she did not hold back and talked for almost 20 minutes straight, graphically describing the attack, and with a whole lot of crying. This was a different girl than I saw last time, and I think she would have cried and talked the whole time if I hadn't stopped her. At about 20 minutes, I asked if we could stop for a minute so she could catch her breath and check in with me about how it was to share all this with me. First she cried quietly for a time. Then she let out a huge sigh. She held herself and rocked a little. I said we could take our time; there was lots of time for the story to come out. She said she wasn't used to talking so much and apologized for "making me listen to all this." I said this is what we're here for, so women can speak out in safety. She nodded and leaned back against the wall. She said she didn't know what she would have done without this place. In a bit, she described a nightmare no one else wanted to hear.*

The rest of this chapter focuses on techniques clinicians can use to help clients explore or elaborate their stories and move, when appropriate, between conversational levels or circles.

■ Techniques of Exploration and Elaboration

A number of techniques can be used in exploration and elaboration. The most useful are questions, prompts, silence, reflection (including underlining and summarizing), refocusing, and initiating new topics.

Questions and Questioning

Asking questions is one of the most reliable and effective techniques for gathering information, deepening discussion, or broadening focus. Clinicians ask questions about:

- The client's thoughts, feelings, behaviors, and relationships.
- The client's cultural identit(ies), beliefs about help seeking and about what causes problems and how they may be resolved.
- Other people in the client's life (what the client reports that other people feel, think, or do).
- The client's circumstances and the larger social contexts within which the client interacts.
- The client's reactions to the clinician and to experiences in the clinical relationship itself.

In general, interviewers routinely ask more questions in the engagement and assessment phases of work than in others. The aim is to elicit a working sketch of the story and its participants, as well as their strengths, resources, and stressors, as guides for more immediate decision making and planning. The use of many questions early on is particularly prevalent in managed care settings, in which engagement, assessment, planning, and intervention all occur in the first contact. Historically, detailed early questioning has also characterized crisis intervention work, such as protective service evaluations and emergency room interviews (see Chapter 11). A lot of gentle questioning often occurs in initial contacts with clients who present for help but have difficulty expressing themselves.

Asking questions may seem to the novice interviewer an easy, even routine, matter. In reality, asking appropriate and timely questions is one of the hardest clinical skills to master. Good questioning requires sensitivity to where the client is; exquisite timing as to the fit between the question, the moment, and the people present; and conscious self-containment to avoid asking numerous tangential questions that may readily come to mind. Beginning interviewers frequently either ask too many questions (to fill out mandatory forms or because they do not yet know what else to do) or ask too few (because they feel intrusive in asking or feel embarrassed to go more deeply into sensitive or forbidden areas). They can also delve too soon into personal questions before a relationship is established or cultural norms about self-disclosure are clarified, thus appearing disrespectful or rude.

Attitudes toward questioning are often influenced by family and cultural norms and taboos. For example, clients and clinicians both may have been taught that asking personal questions is prying. Again, it is essential that clinicians become familiar not only with the communication norms and styles of the many different cultural and social groups with which we work, but also our own. Hillary Weaver (2005) notes that Native American clients may feel more comfortable and responsive if the clinician demonstrates cultural sensitivity and uses self-disclosure before asking personal questions. Many cultures still educate members not to share feelings with outsiders, not to discuss conflicts outside the family, and not to disclose in-group information that could damage group members or weaken group cohesion.

Our own attitudes toward questioning are similarly influenced by our upbringing, education, and life experience. Clinical theories vary regarding the importance of questioning, and some mentors and supervisors encourage active exploration by the clinician, whereas others do not.

General Principles Regarding the Use of Questioning

1. *Questions should be intentional.* Clinicians should know why they are asking what they are asking. Clinical questions always have to have a purpose, and we should always be aware of the possible effects that each question might have on the client.

2. *Clients should know why questions are being asked and how the answers will be used.* Joe and Malach (2004) suggest that clinicians convey clearly to clients why particular questions will be asked, what the nature of these questions will be, and how answers to them will be helpful in designing appropriate services. They also believe clinicians should invite clients' questions about them or any aspect of the process. Clients should be told that they are free to consult with family members before answering questions. Joe and Malach's discussion of practice principles is for use with Native Americans,

but we believe that their advice is widely applicable to respectful work with all clients. In addition, we like to tell clients that they can decline to answer any question that does not feel right to them.

3. *Clinicians need to be sensitive to cultural attitudes toward questioning.* Every culture, and most families, inculcate norms regarding who can ask what, of whom, in what order, and which questions should be asked only in private or without certain members present. It is imperative that clinicians develop cultural sensitivity and competence in asking questions regarding such subjects as race, class, sex, money, religious beliefs and practices, serious illness, addictions, and family violence. Barbara Okun and her colleagues (Okun, Freed, & Okun, 1999) observe that North Americans are used to "telling it all, exploring it all" even with relative strangers, while many of the world's cultures find this diving-in style shockingly intrusive. Because members of the family or culture are the most expert interpreters of their own meaning systems, they should be asked directly about preferred customs and styles in providing the needed information to outsiders, such as clinicians.

4. *Questions should be well timed.* Clinicians should know why they are asking what they are asking *now*—at this particular time in the interview. The clinician must think about whether it is possible to get the same information by another means that will not disrupt client flow; often it is simply a matter of waiting for the client to disclose more information.

5. *Too much questioning makes the clinician the director.* Gentle guidance and data-gathering questions are inevitable in emergencies and in initial sessions with clients not used to clinical work. As the work evolves, the clinician wants the client's thinking and voice to strengthen through maximum encouragement, participation, expression, and initiation of topic or focus. Too many clinician initiatives lessen this potential for strengthening.

6. *Questions can interrupt concentration.* Although questions are often necessary and helpful, every question, no matter how well intended, interrupts the natural flow of the client's narrative. Few things are more maddening than attempting to tell something to another person and being constantly interrupted by questions that throw the narrator off track.

7. *Flexibility in data gathering is essential.* Sometimes clinicians are forced to ask lots of questions immediately to get the information necessary to make decisions by the end of the meeting. Even in such a situation, we may alter a planned agenda if the client sits down and bursts into tears, comes in and starts shouting, or describes an impending crisis or a personal success. Usually, we explore briefly what is happening rather than abruptly refocusing the conversation to get the planned questions asked. Data gathering merely for filling out forms should come only after showing concern and support for the client, and a data-gathering agenda should always give precedence to situational or psychological emergencies. Clients are more likely to broaden or deepen their stories when they feel calm, safe, and understood.

8. *Good questions can be supportive and therapeutic, as well as useful for gathering data.* Questioning can serve many purposes: to help the client expand the story, to gain new perspectives, to provide more information, or to clarify ambiguity for the clinician. Questions can also be used to support

or underline client strengths or to reflect empathy. For example, "How have you managed so much at once?" is both a real question and an affirmation of client strength. "Will your remarkable courage hold up through this long court process?" performs a validating function, as does a question such as, "You mean there's even more that's happened to you?"

9. *Difficult questions should be introduced carefully.*   Kadushin and Kadushin (1997) suggest that the impact of difficult questions can be mitigated by the use of prefaces or lead-ins that help clients save face, that "universalize problems," or that "raise a client's self-esteem in preparation for dealing with a question which is apt to be self-deflating" (p. 261). For example, you might preface a question by saying: "So many moms have told me they feel alone and pushed to the wall when they strike out at their children. What were you personally feeling before you hit Kendra Lee?"

10. *Too little questioning can make for drift or leave the client at a loss for direction.*   Although an interview can be conducted without the clinician asking a single question, sometimes we may need to help a new, unfocused, or disorganized client by asking gentle questions in plain language, designed to keep things on track when the client starts to wander. A new client may start to talk about her worries about being a mother for the first time, then describe a new mother she saw on TV, then talk about how much cable TV costs, and then talk about the things she watches on cable in the evening when the baby's asleep. Although none of these subjects is "bad" and all are pieces of information about the client and her experience, the goals of the session determine to what degree the clinician reintroduces the original topic by gently asking questions that redirect the client to it.

Clinicians may also need to ask questions for purposes of clarification or to get more information. Too little questioning can occur when the clinician thinks personal questions are becoming too intrusive or does not want the client to feel pushed too soon to reveal difficult material. At other times, we may not ask questions for fear of seeming unempathic ("If I ask a question, she'll think I haven't been following closely and have forgotten her details"). Sometimes the clinician's own unresolved issues may prevent the timely exploration of personally sensitive material.

> My supervisor urged me and urged me, but I just could not ask that lady more details about her divorce right then, and I wasn't ready to have my supervisor or others at work know I was splitting up with my wife then, in much the same way my client was splitting up with her husband. I would go into each session with a plan to ask Ms. Morales more about what had happened, and somehow, the time would just zoom by and it would be the end of the session and I hadn't asked her.

11. *Follow-up questions are often necessary.*   Clinicians need to stay with a line of inquiry long enough to mine it sufficiently for details about content, meaning, or feelings. Sometimes we should ask more follow-up questions regarding something the client has said, but we do not. Sometimes clinicians feel they should know the answer or may have been told the answer before and are embarrassed not to have remembered it. Sometimes they are embarrassed to ask clients what they mean, fearing to appear ignorant when in the not-knowing position.

12. *Clinician questions can be both verbal and nonverbal.* Raising an eyebrow, cocking one's head, responding wide-eyed to statements—these and many other lighthearted responses of the clinician can act as questions to which the client can respond immediately and with goodwill. Such clinician responses represent a warmer, less formal style of probing, and they are best used in the context of a solidly established working relationship. Otherwise clients new to counseling might feel teased or made fun of by facial gestures that they are not familiar with or that may be culturally inappropriate.

13. *Answers to questions can be both verbal and nonverbal.* Clinicians need to listen to both the verbal and nonverbal answers of clients. Sometimes there are discrepancies between the verbal and the nonverbal. Any discrepancies in clients' answers are stored away as potentially important pieces of information for possible future exploration. We also listen for discrepancies between clients' stated intentions (e.g., "I'm going to AA every night next week") and their actual behaviors, which can be known only over time, through exploration ("I only got there once").

14. *Clinicians need to attend to apparent patterns and themes that emerge in client answers to questions.* For example, the repeated exclamation "Am I stupid or what?!" following descriptions of habitual behaviors definitely should be explored further. So should statements like "There I go again" and "I can't believe I let that happen!"

15. *Clinicians need to be aware of what they are not asking.* Clients often notice clinician patterns just as we notice theirs. They often note—sometimes subliminally—which topics we do not ask about (such as racial and cultural differences, sex, money, violence). It is not unusual for clients to protect us by not bringing up subjects about which we have shown uneasiness or embarrassment. It is all too easy for us to say that clients are not talking about certain issues, only to discover through examination of process recordings or videotapes that *we* are not asking about the issues.

16. *Questions can be used as defenses or weapons by both clinician and client.* Questions can be used to diminish or shame the other so that the questioner feels more powerful. The following are examples of hostile questions that are not seeking the answer they appear to solicit.

"What is the point of all this?"

"Is this really what we're here to talk about?"

"Haven't you asked me that enough times?"

"Are you finished yet?"

"You mean you don't know after all this time what the Twelve Steps are?

Closed-Ended and Open-Ended Questions

Questions can be closed-ended or open-ended. **Closed-ended questions** are the more focal of the two types and can usually be answered with a word or two, after which the client characteristically ceases talking and waits for the next question from the clinician. Closed-ended questions often begin with interrogatives such as "do you," "are you," or "have you" and hint at what the interviewer expects the response to be. In contrast, **open-ended questions** give the client more opportunity or flexibility in responding and elaborating. Because open-ended questions keep the client in the driver's seat of the conversation, we usually prefer them. These questions often begin with interrogatives like "what" or "how," but not necessarily.

EXAMPLES

Closed-ended:	Do you live alone?
Open-ended:	What is your living situation?
Closed-ended:	Did that make you sad?
Open-ended:	"How did you feel about that?
Closed-ended:	Did you hit him back?
Open-ended:	What did you do then?
	What happened then?

In the last question, two different open-ended questions are offered. While both allow the client to elaborate the story of being hit by another person, the first is more directive in that it focuses specifically on the *client* and what he or she *did* in response. The second question is more nondirective and allows the client to proceed in any direction. The client could say what he or she did, what he or she felt, or what someone else did or felt.

EXERCISE 6.1 Opening Up Closed-Ended Questions

In small groups, take each of the following questions and think of several other ways you could phrase it as an open-ended question.

"Did that make you feel guilty?"

"Would you stay put or run if he threatened you?"

"Is our work together a help to you?"

"Are those tears telling me you are sad?"

"Are you relieved to have her gone?"

Problems with closed-ended questions. The use of closed-ended questions introduces a number of problems. First, these questions give the client little opportunity or encouragement to expand on the theme at hand because they often suggest single answers such as "yes," "maybe," or "no." Second, with closed-ended questions (as well as too many questions in a row), the clinician keeps the initiative, disempowering the client, who may quickly be conditioned to expect to answer just one question and passively await the next. Reducing the client to the role of mere respondent may inadvertently replicate the experience of far too many clients who historically have been made to feel that they are the objects rather than the subjects of their own lives and stories. Further, by establishing the clinician as expert, closed-ended questions may set up the expectation that, given the answers to the questions, we will be able to solve the client's problem.

Moreover, closed-ended questions often suggest the answer the interviewer expects or prefers—for example, "Did that make you mad?" "Was that when he hung up?" "Are you nervous about our meeting?" The client who sees the interviewer's preference within the question may feel worried about differing with the clinician's point of view or feel irritated by the clinician's "mind reading." In the preceding example, the question "Did you hit him back?" could convey to the client that hitting back is what the clinician thinks the client would or should have done when hit.

At times, though, clinicians *need* to use closed-ended questions. Such questions are essential when agency routine or necessity requires that the clinician get a great deal of information in a very short time to determine immediate eligibility for needed services. We may go through a symptom checklist ("Do you have any sleep problems?"), a benefits enrollment form ("Do you have other sources of income we haven't covered?"), or an emergency room family history ("Has anyone in your family had problems with alcohol?"). Also, closed-ended questions can be imperative in establishing clear assessment or understanding ("Are you thinking of hurting yourself?").

Furthermore, if someone is rambling agitatedly or is getting out of control with fear or confusion, a series of organizing closed-ended questions often provides much needed structure and calming.

EXAMPLE OF PURPOSEFUL

Closed-Ended Questions

Clinician: Do you have a place to sleep tonight, Aaron?

Client: No, no! Do I look like I have any place?

Clinician: Is there anyone I can call to let know you're okay?

Client: Nobody. I don't want nobody to know . . .

Clinician: Do you have any money to buy dinner with while I look for a bed for you?

Client: No . . . I'm flat out.

Clinician: If you're hungry, I can get you a voucher for a cafeteria meal.

Client [relaxes and sits back]: Okay . . . I could stand something hot for a change. Could somebody go with me, though? This is my first time here . . .

Clinician: Can you sit here with me while I make a couple of calls to find a bed? Then I can go with you to the cafeteria.

Client: Yep . . .

E X E R C I S E 6.2 Interviewing Using Questions

Divide into teams of three. Person A is the interviewer, person B the interviewee, and person C the observer. The interviewer asks the interviewee about his or her day. The observer notes all the questions and reviews them to see how many were open-ended and how many were closed-ended. Switch roles. This time the interviewer uses only closed-ended questions. In the final round, switch roles again and use only open-ended questions. Discuss anything from this exercise that you want to keep in mind when asking questions. Record what you learned in your journal.

Tried-and-True Questions

Certain questions remain useful over many decades of experience. They just seem to get easily and directly at the things we need to know to assess, plan, and act wisely in our clinical roles.

E X A M P L E S   O F   T R I E D - A N D - T R U E   Q U E S T I O N S

Reason for coming: What brings you here to see me?

Timing of request: Why are you seeking help now?

Anticipation of the experience: How did you think I might help?

Client as the driver: What would you like to get done today?

Client as the driver: Where would you like to begin?

Elaboration of person-situation information: Can you tell me more about your situation?

Support network: Who else is available as a support or help in this?

Situation dynamics: Who, if anyone, is making things more complicated just now?

Previous experience with professionals: Have you ever spoken with a professional before? If so, how did it go?

Elaboration: Are there other things you haven't mentioned yet that would be important for me to know?

Concretizing the desired outcome: What will we look for to know that the changes you want have actually taken place?

Exploring the influence of others on participation: What do people say about your coming to talk with me?

Checking-in: What's it like for you to be talking about these things with me?

Checking-in: Is the work moving in the way you hoped it would?

Checking-in: How does the work we're doing compare with what you thought it would be like?

Checking-in: Is the pace we're going at okay for you?

Checking-in: Would you let me know if, at any time, we go too fast or get into things you're not comfortable talking about?

Clarifying: Does what I'm saying make sense?

Not knowing: Could you put that in other words so I can understand it better?

Elaboration: Can you say more about that?

Problematic Types of Questions

"Why" questions can be problematic because they often sound judgmental—and they often are. "Why did you do that?" may leave the client feeling defensive. "Why do you feel that way?" can leave clients wondering if their feelings are strange or unnatural. Although at times asking clients to think about motives for their behaviors or feelings might be helpful, we have found that "why" questions rarely work. We prefer to use phrases such as, "What do you make of that?" or "What do you think caused it?" or "As you look back, what do you think was going on?"

Pseudoquestions are often directives or commands disguised as questions. For example, a parent who says, "Are you going to do your homework now?" really means "It's time to do your homework." A clinician who begins a session with the question, "Did you want to pick up where we left off last time?" is actually saying, "Let's pick up where we left off last time."

Double questions occur when we ask the client to respond to more than one question at a time. A confused look on the client's face often indicates uncertainty as to which question to address. Double and even triple questions are not unusual in the interviews of newcomers to clinical work, and occasionally these forms of questions show up in the work of experienced clinicians as well.

EXAMPLES OF DOUBLE QUESTIONS

Clinician A: Tell me about your week. How are the kids doing in school? What's going on at work?

Clinician B: So, are you feeling more depressed? Are you having fights?

Tangential questions veer from the main topic, taking side roads without good reason. These occur when the clinician either is curious about an unrelated detail or does not have a clear focus or direction in mind. The clinician who goes off on too many tangents can create an aura of hopping around aimlessly or of being superficial.

EXAMPLES OF TANGENTIAL QUESTIONS

Client A: I've had the hardest day! We're putting out a new computer program, and everybody was so stressed out.

Clinician A: What kind of computer program is it?

Client B: My mother's new boyfriend moved in with us last week. I don't like him very much.

Clinician B: What day did he move in?

Ratatat questioning barrages the client with one rapid-fire question after another. The questions often impart pressure and do not leave time for in-depth exploration. They may all be on one topic, or they may shift from topic to topic so that no subject is pursued long enough to develop any real depth or meaning. Again, the tone of the meeting is one of superficiality; it seems to lack a clear direction or interest on the clinician's part.

EXAMPLE OF RATATAT QUESTIONING

Note that these ratatat questions are all closed-ended as well.

Clinician: Where did you go to high school?

Client: Sacred Heart.

Clinician: When was that?

Client: Sixty-three.

Clinician: Was it a big school?

Client: Pretty big. I was . . .

Clinician: Did you date while you were there?

Client: Not really.

Clinician: And after that, did you date . . . later on, I mean?

I told my supervisee that I thought she was covering so many subjects in her interviews that it didn't give clients enough time to really get into anything in depth. She didn't agree, so I asked her to videotape her next client session and then watch the interview with a tablet handy so she could count up the number of new subjects introduced by her questions. She was astonished to find that she had asked 37 questions in 45 minutes and had covered a wide array of subjects. She was surprised by both the number of questions she asked and the number of topics introduced.

EXERCISE 6.3 Asking Hard Questions

Break up into small groups and list topics that you personally find difficult to explore. Practice asking the other members of your group two questions about one of your least comfortable topics, those that you would find hard to ask a client. Give each other feedback to assist in reconstructing questions or style so that the questions come across more comfortably. Did your questions elicit what you antici- pated? Record what you learned in your journal.

Prompts

Prompts are brief responses by the clinician that encourage the client to continue with the story or to add to what has been said. Prompts are often given in the form of questions or brief utterances that pick up on the client's last remarks. Prompts are meant to be minimal and to signal the clinician's close fol- lowing of the story and interest in details. Some clients respond well to prompts; others may prefer that the clinician just sit quietly and listen unobtrusively.

EXAMPLES OF COMMON PROMPTS

"Say more about that."

"Could you please expand on that?"

"Uh huh."

"And then . . . ?"

"Please continue . . . "

"Was there more you wanted to say?"

Silence

The clinician's judicious use of silence can help the client explore and elabo- rate. Although silence can also be uncomfortable for both the clinician and the client, sometimes the best way to encourage clients to tell their story is simply to leave room for it to unfold. Clients may use silences to reflect on what has been said, to make choices about where to take the story next, or to experience reactions to what is happening in the moment. Sometimes they may simply not know what to do or say next. If the clinician is too quick or too active in ending a silence, clients—especially those whose experience has already undermined initiative—may be conditioned to sit and wait for the clinician to direct the process.

The meaning of silence and comfort with silence are culturally based. Virginia-Shirin Sharifzadeh (2004) notes that one way many Arabs achieve privacy is "by being silent and temporarily tuning out in a crowd (Sapadi & Valentine, 1985). Such silence and tuning out may be interpreted as rude or daydreaming by many Americans" (pp. 395–396). Chan and Lee (2004) note that "in most cultures throughout the world, individuals *start* talking when they have to; Americans, instead, tend to *stop* talking when they have to" (p. 272). Sharifzadeh (2004) notes that, for those from Middle Eastern cultures, "what is left unsaid is as important as what is said" (p. 405).

Reflection

In addition to helping build empathy (see Chapter 5), reflection can also be used in exploration and elaboration. It can be used as a probe to encourage the client to explore a specific area further. Reflection avoids the problems of too much questioning. Rather than asking a direct question, the clinician can indicate a line of inquiry by reflecting back a specific part of the content or affect in the client's story, thus encouraging continued discussion. Carl Rogers, the founder of person-centered counseling, was a master at using reflection, prompts, and silences to help his clients elaborate and expand on their stories.

EXAMPLES OF REFLECTION

Each clinician helps the client explore or elaborate, and each takes the story in a different direction while encouraging the client to amplify.

Client: You know, I'm not feeling bad for a man of fifty. I have my health, an okay relationship with my wife—although she wouldn't agree. My best buddy just died, but I still hang out with a great group of guys. We go bowling every Friday.

Clinician A: You're feeling that your relationship with your wife is "okay," but you don't think she'd agree.

Clinician B: Your best friend just recently died.

In the **dot-dot-dot reflection** technique, the clinician simply repeats back the last thing said and hangs it, unfinished, in midair for the client to complete. Dot-dot-dot is a very useful technique in any conversation when the client loses track for a moment. It is an unfinished sentence of reflection that, if written out, would appear as triple dots (. . .) indicating an invitation to complete the sentence.

EXAMPLES OF DOT-DOT-DOT REFLECTION

"You came home, fed the puppies, and then you . . . ?"

"You were saying that after you got your GED, you would . . . ?"

"First we talk about Glen; then we . . . ?

Underlining is a special form of reflection. The clinician underscores important content or experience by the strategic use of verbal or nonverbal emphasis. This emphasis is often rendered through tone of voice, facial expression, or emphatic gesture.

EXAMPLES OF UNDERLINING

"So you *did* talk to your partner after all."

"You felt *angry* that your sister didn't lend you the money."

"But I *want* you to give me feedback on this work."

In **summarizing,** the clinician pulls together the major ideas, themes, or patterns that have just been discussed and reflects them to the client. Summarizing is a form of reflection in which the clinician sums up in condensed form what has just been discussed. In pure reflection, we usually repeat only one thing the client has just said. In summarizing, we usually reflect many ideas or themes. During the interview, summarizing can be used as a prompt to help the client further elaborate the story. At the end of the interview, summarizing can be used for closure.

EXAMPLE OF SUMMARIZING

Client: I don't know whether to adopt a baby from China or to wait on this list and try to get an American child. It could be years and I'm not getting any younger.

Clinician: Mm-hmm . . .

Client: My parents want me to wait for an American child. They say you never know the kind of experience a baby might have in overseas orphanages. You could be in for a lot of medical expenses.

Clinician: So they want you to wait?

Client: Yeah, but my friends are even worse. They say I shouldn't wait or I will be too old to handle a child. As it is, I'll be sixty by the time the child graduates from college.

Clinician: I see.

Client: Well, there are going to be layoffs at work, and some of my colleagues keep telling me I should be worried that I will lose my maternity benefits.

Clinician [summarizing]: So it sounds as if a lot of people have ideas about what you should do—your parents, your friends, and the women at work.

Client: Yeah, and what's important is that *I* figure out what *I* want.

CLIP 6.1
Questions,
Prompts, and
Probes

EXERCISE 6.4 Using Reflection Techniques to Explore

In small groups, experience what it is like to interview without using any questions. Each person uses only reflection techniques: prompts, dot-dot-dot, underlining, and summarizing. In the large group, discuss any advantages and disadvantages of using no questions when interviewing.

Refocusing

When the client has left a specific topic or theme that the clinician deems important, the clinician can use the technique of **refocusing**: returning the client to a desired topic by gently inserting it into the conversation again. Sometimes clinicians interject when the client takes a breath, but sometimes we may just have to gently intrude upon a long stream of conversation in which no breaks are apparent.

In fast-paced managed care environments emphasizing brief clinical interventions, the need for highly focused interviewing assumes increasing importance. The clinical conversation focuses on the stated objectives of the interview. Comfort with refocusing assists in this effort, and this comfort can be developed only by using the technique under supervision. The following interjections can be useful in refocusing.

EXAMPLES OF REFOCUSING

"I'm wondering if we can get back to the topic of . . . ."

"Getting back to the requirements of your probation, do you have to . . . ?"

"Earlier we were talking about . . . ."

"Forgive me for interrupting, but I'm not clear what this has to do with our work on your sobriety."

"How is that related to the issue of . . . ?"

"Let's continue with what we were talking about earlier."

"Excuse me, but our time's almost up, and we haven't designed the next steps you wanted to map out today."

Initiating New Topics

At times, clinicians follow the client. At other times, our acquired knowledge of human behavior and person-in-situation dynamics suggests potentially fruitful areas for further exploration not yet introduced by the client. The art of exploration involves learning (1) when to follow and just accompany the client on the journey unfolding and (2) when to introduce and explore new areas.

CLIP 6.2
Refocusing

EXAMPLES OF INTRODUCING NEW TOPICS

"I realize I don't know anything about your relationships with your siblings."

"We haven't talked about how you handle your anger."

"We've discussed your home life but not much about work. Could we talk some about that today?"

■ Important Factors in Effective Exploration and Elaboration

Good exploration concerns itself with many complex issues. While seeming so easy at the outset, effective exploration calls for good timing. The clinician must also be sensitive to the client's tolerance level for both the topic and the depth of exploration, to the client's cognitive capacity and expressive style, and to the state of the clinical relationship. We need to accumulate knowledge of the many ways to encourage and elicit a story: how to use tried-and-true methods of exploration; how to ask questions in the client's language and style; how to maintain a "not-knowing perspective"; how to cushion intensive exploration with sustaining techniques; and how to appreciate and use resistance. Finally, we need to know when to stop pressing for more.

Sensitive Timing

Why am I asking this particular thing, at this particular moment, in the visit or the work?

Every clinician has had the experience of asking something that gets no response, that gets a look of puzzlement, or that goes over like a lead balloon. Typically, we say after the meeting, "I wish I had waited until the client brought that up herself" or "I wish I hadn't interrupted him with that question, which wasn't as important as what he was saying—it really threw him off."

Timing has to do with *what* and *how much to ask, when to ask it,* and *whom to ask.* Part of developing a timing instinct has to do with noticing how different people react to exploration and noticing which behaviors of the interviewer seem to broaden or deepen the conversation instead of shutting it down or causing undue discomfort. The sharing of personal information is framed and timed differently for everyone and is very much shaped by family and cultural norms and taboos. Chan and Lee (2004) speak of the need of Korean families to save face, maintaining the dignity, honor, and self-respect of the individual. "One must anticipate that a family member . . . will be reluctant to initially reveal 'vital' information if this will cause loss of face (Kim, 1996). The helping professional is cautioned against venturing into a frank discussion of specific problem areas too quickly" (p. 280).

Timing has to be considered in each interview, as well as across the sequence of all interviews. It is important to note from first contact how readily and under what circumstances clients share personal information and how accurately and realistically the story seems to be unfolding. Many clients indicate right away, by opening up or closing down, how they feel about questions and probing, and they signal what topics are easier or harder for them to explore. Their behavioral cues assist the clinician's judgments about the timing and dosage of further inquiry. Indeed, the cues can be used to focus further tentative exploration, as when, for example, the clinician might note that the client looks down and blushes anytime dating or sex is mentioned. The client may then elect to say more, to look down and blush again, or simply to stare at the clinician and await her lead. Each of the responses is useful new information.

An important challenge for the clinician is to notice the client's patterns and styles of responding to exploration and to watch carefully for what evolves *following* an exploration. A spontaneous deepening of conversation often indicates growing trust and readiness to share at a more personal level. More deepening or opening up of content or feelings often signals to the clinician that the timing is right to risk middle circle and inner circle exploration. The clinician has to attend carefully to the client's response to any question or probe, to be ready to pick up on the response, or just to store it away. Respect for a client's need to ebb and flow is imperative. No one is "on" all the time in clinical work—neither the clinician nor the client. Sometimes clients signal problems with the clinician's timing by saying things like, "You don't usually push me on stuff like this—you usually let me take my time. Why are you pushing me today?"

Even when trust and safety are well established and evidenced by increased client participation levels, certain material always proves relatively difficult to elicit and develop. Just which material proves difficult varies from person to person, culture to culture, and locale to locale. Again, clinicians should watch what evolves once exploration begins. Clients often manifest unreadiness to proceed with further exploration by protesting the need for it, questioning or criticizing the questioner, demeaning the topic, changing the subject, or abruptly cutting the session short.

I remember Junior just getting up and walking out without a word when I brought up his wife's charging him with incest and asked his reaction to the charges. Later, he told me by phone that he found the question "shocking and disgusting" and that, if that is what I think of him, then he would like to work with someone else in the program.

The State of the Clinical Relationship

Is the relationship strong and trusting enough to bear the questions I'm about to ask? Knowing this client, what is the most respectful way to explore this material?

The level of trust and comfort between clinician and client greatly determines the timing and the substance of exploration. In a good working alliance, all that may be required for exploration is a supportive, empathic milieu and some initial broad questions that set the framework of the meetings. The client takes it from there, in his own style, at her own pace. But people new to each other have to feel each other out, testing for comfort and safety. For example, a lesbian client might not come out to her clinician until the latter has demonstrated trustworthiness and acceptance . The clinical encounter is a fishbowl in which both parties become known to each other in conscious and unconscious ways: the former by listening and watching, the latter by intuitive "radar" honed over years of human interaction. As we have seen, safe and sound work together gradually builds trust, ease, and synchrony.

Every relationship, however, has its ups and downs, and no less so the relationship between clinicians and clients. Clients may at any time balk or react to exploration in unaccustomed ways, perhaps because of increased outside stress or illness, unexpected behaviors on the part of the clinician, or misinterpretation of the clinician's intentions. New topics may suddenly reveal to both client and clinician an unexpected level of sensitivity, apprehension, or shame. Similarly, we may balk at material brought up by the client, leaving both parties feeling awkward and uncomfortable. No conversation just rolls along without stumbling points.

The ongoing work of a good relationship is first to acknowledge stumbling points and then, sort through them together. Rough spots are not a disaster. In fact, they offer possibilities for relationship building and the deepening of conversation. The clinician may want to say simply, "Something's just happened. Let's stop a minute and talk about it. I think it's important not to just let it go by." Here the clinician demonstrates the value of examining the moment and models the skill of addressing things directly with great caring (see Chapter 12).

The Client's Readiness to Explore Charged Areas

Will the material I am about to pursue make things better or worse for the client? If worse, whose interests are served by this inquiry?

As clinical conversations develop, all decisions about exploring charged areas are based on the cumulative assessment of the client's capacities, vulnerabilities, and tolerance for varied content and affects. Our overriding intent is to do nothing to harm or needlessly intrude on the client. For example, a time of increased client stress is not the preferred time to go on fishing expeditions into painful areas, stirring up themes or feelings that only add to the stress already besetting the client. Clinicians should be thinking about what is in the client's best interest at any given moment, weighing the appropriate challenge of new learning against its emotional price.

We prefer the gradual introduction of deeper-level exploration, carefully monitoring and often discussing the client's reactions to advancing exploration. We understand that both clients and clinicians can be traumatized by the detailed recounting of overwhelming stories (McCann & Pearlman, 1990), and we proceed carefully, always asking at the outset of each new session how the client experienced the last session, both right after the session and during the time since. Coping levels and resources (or the lack of them) give us important clues as to client readiness and capacity to continue exploring.

The Client's Cognitive Capacity and Expressive Style

Can I put this in her metaphor or language? How would he say it to me if our positions were reversed?

The kind of exploration and elaboration we do also depends on the client's intelligence, educational level, and cognitive capacities, including the accuracy of perception, reality testing, judgment, logic, abstract and concrete thinking, use of fantasy, insight, and general quickness of mind. Cognitive capacity can be affected by a lack of adequate nourishment, stimulation, soothing, and modeling; trauma; limited educational opportunity; and messages from others that thinking is dangerous. It can also be affected by stress levels, tiredness, biological dysfunction, and mood. Always trying to "be where the client is," the clinician tries to frame prompts, reflections, and questions in a style that follows that of the client, insofar as this feels natural and appropriate to the participants. We generally try to avoid jargon and esoteric language, although we have sat in many meetings in which professionals seem to need to use such language to assert power or expertise. Some terminology may become so common among clinicians that we are not even aware that it is jargon. Still, we try to keep language immediate, simple, encouraging, and respectful of each client's style.

Using the client's **metaphor** (a word or phrase that stands for another similar concept) creates a sense of close following and respect for the way the client frames the world. Sometimes we purposely want to praise the client's special metaphors as a way of making things very clear or as being a real gift that not everyone has. At other times, we listen for frequently used metaphors (e.g., "This is part of my journey," "I'm digging myself in deeper," or "I'm in a stew") and, without noting them out loud, simply use them in the conversation.

When Glen talks about failing at work, he'll say, "I'm on the highway and I'm going fine, but I don't know which exit to get off. What if I get off at the wrong exit? How would I find my way back to the highway?" He constantly uses such metaphors, and I think this tends to work against him sometimes. I follow along with his metaphors for a while, but eventually I start talking more concretely about what interests him, his previous jobs, etc. I think Glen uses metaphors as a way of distancing himself from problems so he doesn't have to deal with them directly.

EXAMPLES OF METAPHORS

"Do you have to take *this* much baggage on your journey?"

"If I were going to dig myself out, I might start by . . . ."

"Tell me more about the vegetables in this particular stew . . . ."

Informed and Respectful Process

Am I maintaining a deliberate, informed, and respectful stance in my explorations with all clients?

Educational and class differences can negatively affect the language that clinicians use with and about clients while exploring and elaborating the story. At times, we have noticed colleagues using pomp, jargon, or flourish in the presence of clients who are famous or wealthy and talking down to poorly educated or non-native speakers. Furthermore, many clinicians seem to feel that it is all right to ask poor or disempowered people anything, while at the same time they may feel extremely uncomfortable and apologetic probing the lives of the rich and famous.

Clinicians may also make mistaken assumptions about groups of people and not explore things as frankly as they should. For example, they may not ask a lesbian woman if she is having safe sex, ask a "good Catholic girl" if she ever had an abortion, or ask a longtime widow in her seventies if she thinks of dating again.

Maintaining the Not-Knowing Position

I'm not really sure what he meant by that; I need to ask about it.

There's a lot about this situation that needs clearing up. I need to explore further before I come to so many conclusions.

I haven't asked about subject x for a long time. I should ask, to see if anything has changed since we last talked about it.

A **not-knowing perspective** has two important aspects: (1) it is okay not to know, and (2) clients often know more than we do about the realities of their experience.

New learners often think they need to show that they know a lot to retain credibility with clients, but comfort with not knowing is absolutely essential for eliciting the client's story. When we do not adequately grasp clients' situations, they often say things like, "I'm not sure you really get what I mean" or "See what I'm saying?"

Surprisingly, to elicit more information, saying "I don't understand" is often more useful than saying "I understand" or "Yes, I know." Such responses from a clinician can be interpreted by clients to mean "enough said," whereas "I'm not sure I understand what you mean" invites the speaker to elaborate, even in different words. We can have brilliant hunches, but we never really understand things until clients spell them out more fully. Even then, clients may add material later that gives completely new meanings to situations or events. No matter how much we think we understand, we must always remember that clients are, and will always remain, the expert on their own lives.

Sustaining Techniques to Cushion Intensive Exploration

What can I do or say at intervals so that the inquiry feels less intrusive and the client feels less vulnerable?

Clinicians try to ensure that feelings of relief and support outweigh any potential feelings of vulnerability or threat from overexposure of personal information. **Sustaining techniques** offer clients support as they open their stories to deeper exploration and elaboration. **Checking-in** is a sustaining technique in which the clinician is really asking how things feel or seem to the client after a period of exploring. Check-ins emphasize to the clinician the importance of the client's feelings, observations, and participation generally. They are like the periodic reading of the road map together or the joint taking of the temperature of the interview. "What's this like for you?" and "How are you doing with this?" are two standard ways of checking in. Another is, "Have we talked enough about this for now? Should we give it a rest for today?"

Another sustaining technique during elaboration work is **crediting client strengths,** especially those shown in sharing the story and unfolding its layers in spite of any pain or risk involved. As long as the clinician is authentic in giving the credit, it can take almost any form: for example, "It takes courage to do what you're doing."

Slowdowns can also be sustaining. They are the verbal equivalent of tapping the brakes and are often framed in such a way as to reduce the speed of the interview: "Take your time now; there's no rush." "You needn't rush this. Give yourself the time you need." Here the clinician models patience and carefulness with self, which is novel for many clients.

Validation of the difficulty of disclosure can also feel sustaining: "This is hard, and I respect your willingness to do it." At other times, we might say, "You've talked about some really painful things today, and I can appreciate the exhaustion from it that you're describing."

Appreciating and Using Resistance

I need to view the client's responses to my inquiry as her best means of protecting herself and her loyalty systems at the moment. The main thing the client is "resisting" is having familiar things taken away or tinkered with in ways that do not yet feel safe. I had best slow down or change course.

When seemingly sensible exploration hits a stone wall of silence, protest, denial of relevance, or refusal to respond, clients are signaling a need for caution and a wish to protect the known in the face of the unknown. Clinicians have historically labeled as "resistance" most refusals to follow the clinician's leads or suggestions. (In psychodynamic theory, the term **resistance** refers to the unconscious defenses against the emergence of painful or forbidden material.) Resistance to clinician questions should not be seen as a negative trait of the client. Clinicians should appreciate clients' needs to protect themselves from questions that might create the upheaval of or threat to their sense of stability. We discuss resistance in more detail in Chapter 8.

When the client balks at further elaboration, the clinician can honor and reframe the balking as sensible: "I think you're absolutely right to stop here for now. It's good to see you being careful of yourself and not just plunging into topics because I suggest them. I don't think we should continue with this topic right now, and I want you to keep on waving me off of anything like this that seems absurd or hurtful." Again, this technique works only when we believe what we are saying. Another response to balking is simply to say something like, "I can see that what I asked doesn't feel right to you; can we stop a minute and talk about it?" This is an example of examining the moment, a skill discussed in Chapter 12.

Enough Is Enough

I need to let this line of questioning or exploration go—at least for now.

Sometimes when clients balk, it may be wise to go down another path or to try exploring with different words on another day or when they signal readiness by introducing a topic akin to the one refused earlier. Sometimes clinicians get "on a mission" and pursue a hunch or an agenda, unable to let go. Such persistence may be required as part of a mandated protective role; for example, when the clinician has reason to fear for the client's safety. It may also arise from the clinician's own needs to be right, to prove a hunch, or to please a supervisor who is pushing for material about which the client is not forthcoming. Interns and new employees are especially vulnerable to pressure from supervisors and consultants to go after information that, in face-to-face contacts with clients, may be impossible or unwise to obtain. Pressuring clients usually makes no sense, feels very unempathic, and often ends in power struggles, cancellations, and the termination of work. Sometimes it ends with the client going to the agency director and requesting another clinician. So it is good to recognize when enough is enough and to let go and move on unless there is imminent risk of harm to the client or to others.

CLIP 6.3
Sustaining
Techniques

■ Conclusion

Exploration and elaboration help the client put ideas and feelings into words so that assets and problems are clarified in ways that make goal setting, planning, and problem solving possible. Information gathered and hunches evolved are distilled into the purpose and focus of working together. Questions, prompts, silence, reflection, refocusing, and initiating new topics are important skills in exploration. Sustaining, watchfulness, and sensitive timing all cushion the sometimes painful process of elaborating the story.

A final point: Clinicians clearly influence the conversation by the areas we choose to explore, by the topics to which we respond and do not respond, and by how we frame exploration or elaboration probes. Good clinical work requires a constant monitoring of our behaviors—our acts of commission and omission and our attempts to understand these actions. Process recordings, clinical notes, and the use of audiotaping and videotaping help us monitor our use of influence so that we can use it intentionally and appropriately, not only in exploration and elaboration but throughout all clinical work.

In Chapters 7 and 8, we see how exploration and data gathering in assessment inform the selection of goals and the work of contracting and evaluation. Periodic evaluations of process and progress are used to keep the work on track toward the achievement of agreed-upon objectives.

■ Suggested Readings

Anderson, Harlene, & Goolishian, Harry. (1992). The client is the expert: A not-knowing approach to therapy. In S. McNamee & Kenneth Gergen (Eds.), *Therapy as a social construction* (pp. 25–39). Newbury Park, CA: Sage.

DeJong, Peter, & Miller, Scott D. (1995). How to interview for client strengths. *Social Work, 40,* 729–736.

The following readings discuss how to ease clients into more trusting and revealing conversations.

Saleebey, Dennis (Ed.). (2005). *The strengths perspective in social work practice* (4th Ed.). Upper Saddle River, NJ: Pearson.

Wachtel, Paul. (1993). *Therapeutic communication: What to say when.* New York: Guilford. (See especially Chapter 6, "Exploration, Not Interrogation.")

■ Self-Explorations

1. Remember a time when someone was asking you about something that you did not want to discuss. What was the topic? How did you feel? In what ways did you indicate that you either did not want to talk about it at all or that you did not want to talk about it further?

2. Think about a time when a friend raised a personal matter that he or she seemed uncomfortable discussing. How did you encourage the person to talk with you? Did you ask direct questions? Did you talk about yourself in a similar situation, hoping he or she would feel more comfortable? Did you change the topic? What did you learn about yourself through this experience?

3. Did your family or culture impose restrictions on the types of questions or topics you could ask other people about? For example, "You shouldn't ask people about their income"? Were there "secrets" or "pseudosecrets" in your family that you were not supposed to ask about?

■ Essay Questions

1. Clinicians can help clients elaborate their stories in many other ways than just asking questions. Describe four additional techniques that can be used to aid in exploration.

2. List several kinds of questions that this chapter suggested that you *not* use. For each kind, describe its potential problematic effects on the client and the interview.

3. What are some of the pros and cons of asking open-ended questions? Under what circumstances is it appropriate to ask closed-ended questions?

4. Discuss five principles of effective exploration.

■ Key Terms

Checking-in	Ratatat questioning
Closed-ended questions	Refocusing
Crediting client strengths	Resistance
Dot-dot-dot reflection	Slowdowns
Double questions	Summarizing
Metaphor	Sustaining techniques
Not-knowing perspective	Tangential questions
Open-ended questions	Timing
Prompts	Underlining
Pseudoquestions	Validation of the difficulty of disclosure

CHAPTER 7

Assessment, Formulation, and Goal Setting

The hospital social worker meeting with a family around a health crisis, the counselor doing case management in the drug treatment program, the outreach worker talking to a teen mother on the street, the psychologist doing individual therapy with a woman who has anxiety attacks—all must have some kind of working agreement with their clients to proceed with the work. Working agreements may be formally written and contractual, or they may be informal, unspoken shared visions of what the relationship and the work will be like. Most working agreements fall somewhere in the middle, having some clearly spelled out understandings and goals and some quiet, shared hopes and intuitions about how things might work out.

Whatever the level of formality and concreteness, working agreements are usually composed of at least four parts: (a) assessment, (b) the setting of goals, (c) the negotiation of contracts to meet these goals, and (d) plans for the periodic evaluation of the work. Throughout the process, the clinician is continuously engaged in building the relationship and hypothesizing about the client's story and the tasks to be accomplished.

■ Assessment

We use the skills of exploration and elaboration to help us assess or make sense of the client's story. Assessment involves gathering and analyzing information about the client, the story to date, and the contextual or larger system influences affecting the client and the story. As Doman Lum (2004) notes, "The term 'assessment' denotes appraisal of the value or worth of a person and situation. Assessment comes from the root 'asset,' which is an item of value or a resource owned" (p. 219). Six classic questions are often used by interviewers to organize their assessment agendas: *Who? What? Where? Why? When? How?* These questions can be used at two levels.

Levels of Assessment

The first level concerns the **process of the assessment** itself. We start with the "why" of assessment because it often predicts "whom" and "how" the clinician assesses.

Why am I doing this assessment? Why has the client presented for help, or why was the client referred?

Who is "the client"? (The client could be a person, family, group, organization, or larger system.) Who should be involved in the assessment process? Who made the referral?

What do I want to know? What information should I gather? What cultural considerations should inform assessment and planning with this client?

How should I gather the information? What methods will be most useful in getting the information? How can the client be actively involved in designing the assessment process?

Where should the initial assessment take place: in the office, home, street, shelter?

When will the client and I have enough understanding to begin to plan and contract?

At the second level, the answers to these questions form the **content of the assessment.** At this level the questions are asked in a different order:

Who are the main participants in the successes and problems of the people or systems I am assessing?

What are the presenting problems, strengths, resources, and needs in this system? What are the potential barriers? What incentives for change can be identified? What will change look like when it is achieved?

Where do the successes and problems most often manifest themselves, and where will effective interventions most likely occur?

Why is the client presenting at this time, and why would the client be interested in continuing beyond the initial meeting?

When did major influencing events take place, and when did the problems begin? When did problems reach the level of precipitating a contact with professionals? When in the client's life am I entering the story?

How can I, the client, or others help at this time?

Formal Clinical Assessment

Clinicians are often asked to do formal, reasonably structured assessments of individuals for the purpose of diagnosis, treatment planning, or research or to determine eligibility for specialized services such as disability assistance payments, residential placement, or inpatient treatment. In formal assessments, we start with what is the problem or issue motivating the client (or others) to seek help.

We evaluate the person's overall functioning, exploring current and past behaviors, relationships, cognitions, affect, and contextual influences. We attempt to understand how these are affected by the client's race, culture, ethnicity, class, gender and sexual orientation, age, abilities, spirituality, and family developmental history and background. We explore for current and past social barriers to well-being and achievement, as well as other stressors. We note client coping mechanisms, strengths, and resources. We look at the person's physical health and well-being, including medications and their effects, and we assess for potential substance abuse. Box 7.1 contains a sample assessment outline (see Compton, Galaway, & Cournoyer [2005]; Hepworth, Rooney, Dewberry Rooney, Strom-Gottfried, & Larsen [2006]; and Lum [2004] for a comprehensive discussion of formal assessment of clients from a variety of cultures). Formal assessments are often repeated both during and at the conclusion of clinical work to evaluate the effectiveness of interventions and to suggest steps to maintain gains in the future.

Clinical assessment need not be limited to individuals. We routinely conduct family assessments in which we evaluate the structures, roles, communication, and overall functioning of the family as a whole, as well as the more specific transactions between family members. A clinician may also assess the dynamics of a classroom, an activity group, a neighborhood gang following a member's death, and so on (see Hepworth et al. [2006]; Kilpatrick & Holland [2003]; and Sue & Sue [2003] for a more thorough discussion of culturally informed family assessment).

At the macro level, professionals also assess agencies, institutions, organizational structures, and forces in the wider community—even systems of ideas and related behaviors, such as classism, sexism, and racism (see Netting, Kettner, & McMurtry, [2003] for a more thorough discussion of macro-level assessment).

As a part of ongoing assessment from an ecological perspective, clinicians must continuously listen for overt and covert barriers to the realization of clients' potentials. We ask about intrapersonal, interpersonal, and societal forces that may hinder the client's problem-solving abilities, growth, and development. For many years, clinical assessment focused almost exclusively on the *intrapersonal*—the individual's characteristics, behavioral patterns, and intrapsychic dynamics. Most clinicians now prominently focus on the *interpersonal,* assessing the client's family support, intimate and work relationships, friendships, and social networks.

Millions of people around the world use spiritual or religious experience and affiliations for guidance, support, and social connection. Researchers

---

BOX 7.1   Outline for Assessment

---

1. Identifying and demographic information
     Name, age, gender
     Sexual orientation, relationship status
     Religion, cultural, or racial identities
     Employment, education, training
     Economic status, including problems or needs
2. Presenting problem or concern
     Current
     History
     Past treatment
3. Strengths and resources
     Coping mechanisms
     Social supports, including friends, cultural, spiritual, community networks
     Motivation and readiness for change
4. Background
     Family history
     Significant developmental events
     Effects of race, culture, sexual orientation, age, class, immigration, and other influences
5. Biopsychosocial stressors
     Previous
     Current or continuing
6. Psychological functioning
     Behavioral observations
     Cognitive or intellectual capacity and skills
     Emotional/affective state and self-regulation
7. Health and biological factors
     Physical health
     Disability
     Medications
     Substance abuse
8. Test results
     Intelligence
     Neuropsychological
     Psychological
9. DSM diagnosis (all five axes)
10. Formulation or conceptualization

have noted the enormous support people find in relationships with a god, goddess, or guiding spirit; with pastors, rabbis, imams, and spiritual healers; and with faith communities (Cascio, 1998; Haight, 1998; Taylor et al., 2000; Walsh, 1999). For example, Haight (1998) found that spiritual socialization can be central to African-American children's healthy development.

At the same time, very few agency assessment forms and protocols contain any reference to or questions about client beliefs about or use of spiritual resources in sustaining and enriching their lives. By not bringing spiritual beliefs into assessment and practice, clinicians may be thought to be signaling that these are not important or appropriate topics in counseling. On the other hand, a good spiritual assessment may turn up instances in which clients have been wounded or excluded by faith communities.

Some very simple assessment questions regarding client spirituality (or its absence) can demonstrate a clinician's respect for spirituality as a potentially renewing and connecting force:

"Do you have any spiritual affiliation or beliefs in which you find hope when you feel alone or down?"

"Is there a special place where you walk or sit to connect with nature or the universe or to get a feeling of acceptance and belongingness?"

"Are there readings, sayings, or poems that lift your spirit when you feel like giving up?"

"Do you meditate or pray or use rituals of any kind to connect you with a force beyond yourself?"

These questions are not thrown at the client in ratatat fashion. They are asked as space arises, when clients are talking about how hard and hopeless life seems at times or when they are describing how little support they feel in daily life. Clients are often very ready to recount for the authentically interested clinician the images and activities they count on to connect and bolster them when things go wrong. On the other hand, some clients occasionally ask why we are probing such matters when their focus is on other concerns.

> *I was asking Rip about strengths and successes in his life because so far, he had only mentioned the problems and stresses. As a part of this inquiry, I asked him if he ever used prayer or meditation to lift his spirits. He replied sarcastically: "I never touch the stuff . . . please don't start on that, I had it stuffed down my throat my whole childhood." Without getting defensive, I simply said that I make it a practice now to ask people if they are spiritual because so many people all over the world call on a higher power or use other spiritual activities when feeling down, but we professionals rarely ask them about these important practices or encourage their use. Rip said he didn't mind me asking about it. He then talked with more feeling about a harsh childhood in which the aunt who raised him was always saying how God would punish him for this or that behavior. He couldn't wait to get away from such a God and is not eager to go back! I appreciated that and asked him tell me more about his "getaway" at 18 . . . a source of pride.*

It is essential that the clinician also consider the impact of such larger social forces as poverty, language barriers, racism, sexism, ableism, and other systems of oppression as potential barriers to the client's growth and development (see DePoy & Gilson [2004]; Garbarino & Abramowitz [1992]; and Hill & Rothblum [1996] for a further discussion of the impact on clients of unjust and marginalizing larger systems).

> *In training, when I saw the documentary* True Colors, *I realized for the first time the way that racism affects the daily interactions of African-Americans in the United States. Watching two men (paired for similarities on education, age, dress, social skills) as they spent a week in a midwestern town doing exactly the same things revealed how the fact that one was black and the other white affected every aspect of their daily lives—from walking into a department store to browse, to renting an apartment.*

Methods of Assessment

Formal clinical assessment uses a variety of methods, including:

1. **Assessment interviews,** such as client self-reports and the clinician's experience in the interview, interviews with family members, and interviews with relevant others
2. **Observation** in a lab, natural setting, or lifespace
3. **Testing,** including intelligence tests, personality tests, symptom checklists, and medical tests
4. **Review of life records,** such as previous treatment notes, school records, health reports, and other written documents

Clinicians need to explain their methods of assessment and obtain signed informed consent forms for any procedures or assessment activities to be undertaken. Because of confidentiality, they should obtain permission releases for any information to be obtained from others. Box 7.2 contains a sample release of information form.

Techniques of Assessment

As discussed in detail in Chapter 6, the techniques of exploration and elaboration are particularly useful in assessment interviewing. These techniques include questioning, prompting, probing, reflecting, summarizing, underlining, refocusing, and initiating new topics.

While most clients come to professional encounters expecting to answer questions, reveal information, and share ideas about their situations, many have no idea of how the process of disclosure and exploration actually *feels*. They may have impressions from others or from the media, but, just like us, they have to carefully feel their way into the process of making themselves known as they become more comfortable with us.

In so doing, they may feel pressured to consider the feelings of significant others who have a stake—spoken or unspoken—in the process. What is revealed during the assessment process may have major consequences and

BOX 7.2 Authorization for Release of Information

Client Name: _____ Date of Birth: _____

Prior to the release of any information, we wish to make you aware that this request may include results of an HIV antibody or antigen test, or records that contain such information, which may be covered by MGL c.241 CMR 180.300. This information may not be copied or transferred to anyone other than the recipient noted below.

Your medical record may contain information about your identity, diagnosis, psychiatric treatment, mental health history, alcohol and drug addiction history, and sexually transmitted disease history. You are hereby granting permission to release this information to the specified provider or facility.

I hereby authorize _____ to:

1. Obtain from:
   Name: _____
   Address: _____
   City/Town: _____
   State: _____ Zip: _____
   Send to:
   Name: _____
   Program: _____
   Agency: _____
   Address: _____
   City/Town: _____
   State: _____ Zip: _____

2. Furnish to other provider/facility:
   Name: _____
   Agency: _____
   Address: _____
   City/Town: _____
   State: _____ Zip: _____

3. The specific information as indicated below:
   _____ Admission/Intake Note
   _____ Discharge Note/Summary of Treatment to Date
   _____ Psychological Test Report

(continued)

B O X 7.2 *(continued)*

_____ Substance Abuse Treatment Records

_____ Health Reports/Records

_____ Lab Reports

_____ School/766 Reports

_____ Birth Records

_____ Verbal Client Status Update/Treatment Coordination

_____ Other (specify)

This authorization shall be considered valid for this express purpose only and will automatically expire ninety (90) days from the date of signature.

_____   _____

Signature of Client or Legal Guardian   Date

_____   _____

Witness   Date

---

can affect relationships, economic supports, living situations, custody rights, and future prospects of all kinds. No wonder, then, that apprehension and caution can manifest themselves during exploration. Krishna Guadalupe and Doman Lum note that, in work with Latino families, rapport building is very important before beginning to probe with assessment questions (2005, p. 373). The same point applies to working with people with Asian roots (Chan & Lee, 2004), with clients from the Middle East (Sharifzadeh, 2004), and with Native American clients (Weaver, 2005).

Sustaining techniques are crucial to assessment to ease the way (see Chapter 5). For example, assessment may proceed smoothly until the clinician asks for permission to send off for records from a psychiatric hospitalization. A client might respond by saying, "So you think I'm mental, too?" This kind of reaction can signal sensitivity to what the clinician thinks or to being judged, a stigma left over from the experience of mental illness, or it can reflect a concern about what the record will reveal. At this point the clinician might stop to explore what meanings the client attaches to the request for hospital records, giving the client a chance to express concerns or even perhaps to share past experience in which having a hospital record worked against him or her. Sympathetic appreciation of the concern, as well as universalizing the fear of stigma and negative consequences, might be very sustaining.

EXAMPLE

Client: So you think I'm mental, too?

Clinician: People sometimes worry that, once someone learns of their hospitalization, they will be viewed as mentally ill.

As another example, a young child (referred for therapy because of his distractibility and impulsivity in the classroom) might be embarrassed to have his play therapist, an admired psychologist, observe him in the classroom as part of the assessment process, worrying about being seen at his most problematic times. The clinician might spend a few moments exploring the child's sensitivity and its attendant fantasies of what would occur during the visit. Then some time might be spent educating the boy about the usefulness of assessment, of getting to see firsthand how things are for him in the class, and exploring the things that might be making it hard for him to focus and learn. Similarly, before including testing in the assessment process, a clinician would educate the client about the tests and about the nature, purpose, and process of the testing situation, then elicit client reactions to all of this information.

Another useful technique might be encouraging the client to assess the clinician as part of the assessment process. Usually in assessments, the clinician asks clients many questions, which can leave them feeling as though they are "in the hot seat." Reminding clients that they are also evaluating the clinician can heighten the sense of collaboration and shared responsibility.

> Sometimes during an assessment interview, I will say to the client: "I've gotten to ask you a lot of questions. Is there anything you would like to ask me?" Clients often ask about my training or about what I think will happen in our work. Sometimes they ask if I think I can help them. If they don't ask anything, I might say, "Sometimes clients want to know if I've had any experience with the kind of problems they're bringing in."

> When I am going to do an assessment observation in a classroom, I often let the child come behind the one-way mirror and watch me as I interact with some of the kids. I say to them, "You can watch me, and then I'll watch you . . . and then let's talk about what we see."

All Interviewing Requires Assessment

Formal assessment procedures are most frequently required in hospitals, outpatient mental health clinics, and forensic and protective services evaluations, but many clinicians work in situations or settings that do not require formal assessment protocols. No matter the setting or task, clinicians must always do some kind of assessment before planning and acting in concert with or on behalf of clients. Street outreach workers may not use a formal standardized test, but they do make assessments of client strengths, weaknesses, styles of interaction, and even cognitive abilities. As noted in Chapter 4, the clinician is also always listening for content, affect, themes and patterns, and contextual influences in the client's story. As clinicians come to appreciate the importance of understanding before responding, assessment becomes second nature.

> *As a social worker, I am always thinking about the "person-in-situation" context. Even when friends ask for advice, I find myself asking all sorts of questions as they talk. I find I am trying to figure out all kinds of things that might be influencing the situation.*

Principles of Assessment

1. *Assessment is an objective and an outcome of initial conversation, as well as an ongoing process guiding clinical interchange.*   It begins immediately when people meet, and it is continuously threaded into ongoing interchange as the story deepens and broadens. The more we know, the more we want to ask or to understand. Moreover, people and their situations change fluidly over time; little remains fixed. Knowing this, we realize that situations and dynamics always merit reexamination along the way because information, people, activities, relationships, and contexts all can change.

2. *A full assessment includes evaluation of the clinician, the relationship, the appropriate services, the surround, and the interface among all of these elements.*   For example, the clinician may ask, "Is this the agency or setting that can provide the best resources for this particular client?" We also continuously assess the motivation of the clinician and the agency to make sure that they are persisting, advocating, and caring about the people they are committed to help.

3. *Assessment should be reliable.*   **Reliability** refers to assessment consistency. When applied to testing, reliability means that the score a person obtains on a particular test should be consistent even if the test is given by different testers or administered at different times (**test-retest reliability**). But reliability is important in all parts of assessment, including observation and diagnosis. "**Interrater reliability** refers to the level of agreement between two observers rating the same behaviors . . . . **Diagnostic reliability** refers to the level of agreement between two or more diagnosticians about whether individuals meet criteria for psychiatric (or other) diagnoses and which diagnosis is primary" (Hecker & Thorpe, 2005, p. 548).

4. *Assessment should be valid.*   **Validity** refers to accuracy—how well the assessment measures what it intends to measure. Does the assessment give us an accurate picture of the individual?

5. *Assessment should be culturally responsive.*   Both the methods used and the areas explored should be sensitive to cultural differences. Guilmet and Whited (1987) suggest that the intake interview with Native American clients should avoid direct questioning and consist of a supportive conversation about the clients' needs, thus requiring more time than usually scheduled. Weaver (2005) notes that many Native Americans believe it is inappropriate to be asked by clinicians in family meetings to speak for absent members, since speaking for another is taboo.

Sue and Sue (1990) note that "White counselors tend to view their client's problems as residing within the individual rather than society" (p. 72). Romero (1983) states that "the majority of mental health problems exhibited by Chicanos are not pathological. Rather they result from a combination of socioeconomic stresses that are compounded by poverty, racism, oppression, [and] lack of access to educational and legal systems and institutions" (p. 91). Thus, the clinician should assess the effects of oppression, racism, bilingualism, ethnic identity conflicts, and other social conditions.

In working with immigrant families, Elaine Congress's (1994) **culturagram** (Figure 7.1) illustrates the complexities of family culture. Its matrix shows the interwoven influences of important family variables, such as the language spoken at home, health beliefs, and contacts with cultural institutions for support. The clinician should ask about all of these influences during interviews over time, rather than barraging the client with them all at once. Client reflections on these influences in daily life often weave together a narrative of coping via empowering connections and traditions.

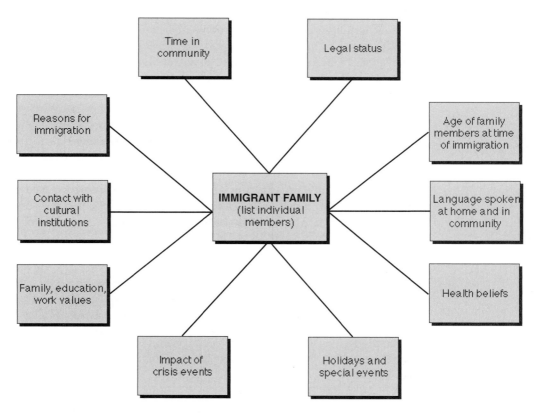

FIGURE 7.1 Culturagram

Source: Elaine Congress (1994) "The use of culturagrams to assess and empower culturally diverse families," *Families in Society: The Journal of Contemporary Human Services, 75,* 531–539. Copyright © 1994 Alliance for Children and Families. Reprinted with Permission.

6. *The more methods and strategies used to assess, the more balanced the understanding we are likely to develop.* When feasible, we like to observe—or at least ask in detail about—functioning across many domains. The woman who stays with a batterer and does not currently "appear" to be able to protect herself or her children from harm may be a leader in her church's women's group or a helpful suicide hotline responder. Perhaps we do not think to ask what she does in her free time because we have already assumed she does not have any. By the same token, observing an adult at a neighborhood meeting or in a home visit or observing a child in a gym or in a classroom may provide much more clarity about skills and limitations than office interaction ever would.

Test information may provide us with new insight into the cognitive strengths of clients so that we may plan our intervention to fit their cognitive style. A physical exam could reveal diabetes, which might be one alternative explanation for the symptoms that the client defines as "anxiety attacks."

Several helpful tools are available to capture and reflect client experience, relationships, and themes or patterns. The **genogram** reflects multigenerational family relationships and patterns. The **ecomap** reflects the nature and extent of reciprocity in relationships with significant others. The **life chart** provides a birth-to-present time line of dates and ages at which major life experiences impacted the client, positively or negatively (see Hartman [1978] and McGoldrick & Shellenberger [1999] for more detailed discussion of the use of these and other assessment tools).

Jeanne Slattery (2004) has devised a "strength-based genogram" (Figure 7.2) to complement traditional genograms, which tend to focus on problems, losses, and conflicts. The **strength-based genogram** clarifies intergenerational models and sources of individual and family assets and accomplishments. An important feature of many immigrant families' assessment narratives are the travails and triumphs in their migrations from distant homelands. Clinicians too rushed to elicit the details of these heroic stories miss a great opportunity to validate client strengths for use another day. The strength-based genogram can be used with individuals, groups, and families. Concentrating on strengths in visual form reminds people of their assets and the many possibilities that these suggest.

EXERCISE 7.1 Your Strength-Based Genogram

Construct your own strength-based genogram based on Slattery's model. Bring your genogram to class. Discuss what effect an intense reflection on strengths and connections had on you. How have your family's strengths contributed to who you are today?

---

7. *Multiple perspectives help in assessment.* We cannot always include as many participants in the assessment process as we would like, but we do understand as clinicians that the more perspectives we include, the greater the likelihood is of adding new dimensions to our understanding. Events are

F I G U R E 7.2 Strength-Based Genogram

Source: From "*Counseling Diverse Clients," Bringing Context into Therapy.* 1st edition by Slattery. 2004. Reprinted with permission of Wadsworth, a division of Thomson Learning: www. thomsonrights.com. Fax 800-730-2215.

experienced differently by all parties to them; each puts an interesting spin on the story and, in doing so, fleshes it out usefully. Often we make the mistake of limiting the number of people in the room for purposes of control, focus, or expediency. Remember that we often sacrifice information and valuable relationships for control.

> *I'd never met with a family before, and I found seeing the parents and their five children awesome. The dad had had a heart attack, and the mom was depressed thinking that he looked older and more tired and might die suddenly. The adolescent kids seemed a little sullen and critical of him for "making Mom wait on you hand and foot." There was a little 4-year-old who ran around the room distracting everyone, so for two or three meetings I had her play outside with the secretary. My supervisor suggested I bring the little girl back in next meeting, and this time ask her what she thought of daddy being sick at home. She looked straight at me and blurted out, "Daddy squished our brother." Mom tried to silence her and looked so uncomfortable. I asked, "How come?" She looked at dad, who paled, but said it was okay. Mom then told me that 10 years before, dad had come home for lunch and, in backing out of the driveway to return to work, he ran over and killed their 2-year-old. Mom said it broke everyone's heart. No one knew what to say next . . . me either.*

8. **What is observed is altered by the presence of the observer and the activities of observation (Maturana, 1978; von Foerster, 1981).** The interviewer has to keep in mind the influence that he or she has on the behaviors of clients and the reciprocal influence they have on him or her.

We were doing interviews on videotape for a research study. Children were observed for two weeks by two different evaluators. When Randy was in the room with Bonita, she was active, made eye contact, and explored the room. On those days when Susie was with her, Bonita sat down in a corner and didn't make eye contact. Needless to say, Randy and Susie each had very different evaluations of Bonita. We also observed that Susie was less active with Bonita than she was when we observed her with other children. We really got a sense of what our teacher meant when she talked about "reciprocal influence."

9. ***Clinicians can be drawn into or "inducted" into systems they are assessing.*** Becoming a participant in the system can undercut the clinician's capacity to see, experience, and accurately report it to outsiders or to colleagues. A blurring of roles can occur when clinicians overidentify with client systems, have strong needs to rescue, or get caught up in unwitting reenactments of old, unresolved scenarios of their own.

A couple of years ago, I was supervising a student, Nadine, at the Department of Family and Children's Services. When one of her clients came to the agency, I thought I could smell alcohol on the client. It became obvious to me that the student was ignoring the fact that the mother was drinking again. When I pointed it out to Nadine and questioned her about why she thought she missed it, she said that she probably didn't see it because she was hoping that the kids would have some stability. If the mother was drinking again, the kids would be sent to separate foster care families. Nadine, just like the kids, really wanted to believe that this time the mother would succeed in sobriety. I thought it was possible that Nadine might have also come from a family where the kids were taught to pretend parents weren't drinking when they actually were.

10. ***Where we carry out our assessments influences the kinds of data we gather.*** People are often much more comfortable in their natural settings than in office or agency settings. On their own ground, they may be more comfortable and open. On the other hand, people threatened in their own environments may relax in an agency, where they feel safe and protected.

11. ***Remember that we are seeing the client only at one particular moment in time.*** At that moment, we are seeing but one frame of an entire movie. The clinician needs to remember that the client who today looks well put together may have been very distressed five years ago, five months ago, or five days ago. The client who is struggling to get an entry-level job today may have been a physicist in his country of origin the year before. Therefore, it is helpful to make sure that we obtain as much information as possible about the whole story to date.

When I started working for the state, I had to go 20 weeks without pay because of civil service complications. I was new in the area, without resources, and it was suggested I apply for temporary public assistance, which I reluctantly did. The intake social worker was incredulous that I was a social worker needing public assistance. I could see she didn't believe me by the frown on her face. I gave her the name of the financial director at my agency to validate my application. She called and got the facts while I sat there. At no time did she show one ounce of care for my plight. I got food stamps and left feeling very embarrassed. It left me very much more understanding of how clients feel judged.

Furthermore, clinicians usually meet clients at a highly stressed time. Because seeking assistance from strangers can be very stressful and can cause clients to regress from previously higher levels of functioning, they can present their stories with more urgency, anxiety, and disorganization than we might see under different conditions. Were we to enter the story at a different time or see the client at a less stressed point in life, we might gain a different perspective.

> *When I was working in a detox setting, we were encouraged not to give alcoholics a personality diagnosis until they had been abstinent for a year or so because their functioning could look so much healthier once they were off drugs for a while. An elderly woman with hallucinations and without family available came into the hospital unable to offer a coherent story. It looked as if she would be transferred out to a state hospital locked unit. However, a nurse took a liking to her and asked me to look in the transfer record from the acute hospital and see if there was anything else that could keep her in rehab. By examining the detailed notations in her transfer record, I was able to determine that she had been a senior seamstress for almost 50 years and was nicknamed "Golden Fingers" for her dexterity. She had always lived independently before her diabetic complications and surgery. Hearing this detail reminded the team that there might be strengths here, once medication helped clear cognition. Sure enough, once clear, this lady proved to be very spunky and verbal and had a longtime taxi driver friend who worked with the team and found her an accessible first-floor apartment in her old neighborhood. People had mistaken her confusion for a permanent impairment. So had she.*

12. **The "assessor" is also being assessed by the client,** whose estimation of the clinician greatly affects what is shared and owned by the client.

> *Lara was a 19-year-old single mother of a 1-year-old son in our Transitional Living Program. She was usually cast as a shy "outsider," and people wondered why she was so shy. One day, as we were hanging out in the kitchen, she told me that she had been attracted to women for a couple of years and that she was afraid that other mothers would find out. She was worried that people might think she was an unfit mother. I thought, "No wonder she's so quiet. She's scared." I asked her what made her tell me. She said she had been watching the way I interacted with the other mothers and I seemed to be pretty open to different things.*

13. **Research informs clinical assessment,** just as it does clinical practice. The clinician uses available research data on human behavior to inform assessment. For example, the clinician who is familiar with the research showing that the lack of economic resources often prompts women to stay in battering situations will ask abused women about their financial supports. The clinician who knows that people who suffer from depression often have, among other symptoms, fitful sleep and early morning awakening will include questions about changes in sleep patterns.

14. **Real understanding involves more than data gathering,** for it brings the heart as well as the mind to bear, and it *involves the intuition as well as the intellect.* Intuition is a "sixth sense" combination of autonomic bodily reactions, perceptions, and insights gained through experience.

> *As a social work instructor, it is often hard to explain to students how to hone intuition and the sensing of things that cannot be rationally explained or aren't empirically derived. I often describe it as getting a "flavor of" something or "having an internal*

beeper go off." I don't want to just have students learn to "listen to their gut," but, on the other hand, if we don't pay attention to it at times, we can really miss important clues for further assessment. Sometimes it involves goose bumps on the arms, a "funny feeling" in the chest or gut, hair standing up on the back of my neck, or a welling up of things I can't name but that I feel are for sure at work in the room or in the person's life. Sometimes I think this ability to "sense" things is a gift that one is born with and can't just be implanted. But I do believe that intuition is nurtured and validated through clinical experience and life experience in general.

■ Conceptualization or Formulation of Assessment Findings

Data gathering is an important part of assessment, but a second and equally important part of assessment is how we pull all the data together into a practical and meaningful guide for work.

On my first job, I hoped to impress my supervisor, a friendly psychiatrist, by handing in a 7-page assessment before supervision so he could see how much information I had gathered about my first client. He started off by saying that I sure had gathered a lot of information and that he just had one question: "So what?" He explained amiably that my assessment had nothing in it to make sense of the woman's request for counseling, to help us understand her described symptoms better. He said that the "so what?" question is short for "so, what's going on here beyond the obvious, and how might we help?" He went on to help me add that "meaning making" piece to my assessment skills.

The integration and analysis of assessment data is called **case conceptualization,** or case formulation. The **formulation** condenses and attributes meaning to all the rich data emerging from the assessment process. It reflects the clinician's interpretations of what the facts imply about past and current functioning of the client system at hand, about future potentials, and about strengths, issues, and dynamics within and between people and their related systems. In formulation or conceptualization work, we look for participants, themes, patterns, and dynamics in the client's story.

We attempt to understand the story in the context of the client's ethnicity, race, culture, class, gender, sexual orientation, age, economic situation, risk factors, and unique background. We weave in any observed effects of discrimination. We hypothesize about the impact of all these factors on the client's beliefs, mood, behaviors, relational interactions, and readiness for change. Strengths are highlighted as assets to be tapped and emphasized in the work to come. Pieces of information gathered begin to be assembled like a big picture puzzle of tentative hunches, interpretations, and conclusions.

In many settings, **multidisciplinary team** meeting time is set aside for case conceptualization. These team formulations benefit from the collaboration of a number of clinical colleagues with specialized knowledge, skills, and biopsychosocial perspectives to assist in better understanding the client.

When I was working at the mental health center we had to have team consultation after every intake. A psychologist might administer personality tests, a neurologist might provide information about MRI results, a social worker might report on a family assessment.

Even if only one person conducted the assessment, it was essential that three out the four disciplines—social worker, psychologist, psychiatrist, psychiatric nurse—be represented at the meeting so that a variety of perspectives could be included in the case formulation. At the end of the team meeting, a formal assessment/formulation report was placed in the client's file.

Clinical social work educator and researcher Cassandra Clay (personal communication, 2006) describes two different clinician stances for assessment and formulation work. First we have to "get up close" in assessment, using empathy, facilitative questions, and support to elicit intimate client assessment information. Then in formulation work, we have to "stand back to get the bigger picture" using moderate detachment, intellect, and informed clinical judgment to tease out interpretations and implications.

Good formulations require **clinical judgment** to select appropriately from many theoretical explanatory models to try to explain the phenomena observed in clients, their stories, and their interactions with the clinician and others. The theory or theories we select shape what we do in the assessment and formulation process: the persons included in the assessment process; the kinds of questions asked and information emphasized or minimized; the way the purpose, goals, and methods of assessment and intervention are spelled out with the client; the language used in conceptualizing the data gathered; and the specific goals and plans for the work.

For example, to try to understand and interpret the situation and behaviors of Mickey (the drug-abusing teenager in Chapter 1), we incorporated knowledge from psychodynamic, family systems, social systems, political, class, and biological theories. That example contained both assessment and formulation statements. We noted that psychodynamic and family theories might attribute Mickey's problem behaviors to individual developmental stressors, family breakdown, and neighborhood violence, when other factors, including federal policy and environmental hazards, might also contribute. Again, it is crucial to know what theoretical lenses we are looking through when we assess, interpret, and speculate about clients' lives and stories, which are extremely complex and contextualized in multiple layers of overt and covert influence.

Levels of Inference

When clinicians develop their formulations, they are making inferences based on the information they have at a given point in time. Michael Nietzel, Douglas Bernstein, Richard Milich, and Geoff Kramer (2002) offer an informative discussion of the **levels of inference** clinicians may use when making hypotheses.

Clinicians who use low levels of inference stay close to the data and do not make major leaps away from the known facts. For example, Helga complains of trouble sleeping through the night. A clinician using low levels of inference might suggest that something was worrying Helga. Clinicians who use moderate levels of inference often base hunches on known correlations between one behavior and another. For example, a clinician using moderate levels of inference might infer that Helga is depressed, knowing that sleep disturbance is often correlated with depression. Clinicians using high levels of inference see the behavior as a sign of some deeper issue or meaning interpreted through the lens of a preferred theoretical model. Such clinicians might hypothesize that Helga was a victim of sexual abuse in her family and the abuse occurred at night, leaving her hypervigilant at night, thus disturbing her sleep.

Nietzel et al. (2002) further suggest that the level of inference is closely related to the clinician's theoretical orientation. Behavioral and humanistic therapists often use low or moderate levels of inference; psychodynamic theorists may use moderate to high levels. High levels of inference can be risky, because they are often based on intuition, personal experience, and speculation. The greater the speculation is, the higher the level of inference becomes. We need to be extremely careful about sharing hunches that are highly speculative in nature. Because of the power invested in professional pronouncements, clinicians can worry or mislead clients who trust such statements more than their own experience. Furthermore, speculations developed on the experience of a clinician in one culture can seem way off base to a client from another culture.

In making a formulation, we draw inferences from the raw data obtained during the assessment process. Separating data from inference takes practice. A clinician might note that Lorenzo's IQ test score is 80 and infer that he has borderline intellectual functioning, when actually on the test day he was stressed out by neighborhood violence, had not slept much all night, and could not think clearly—circumstances not elicited in assessment. A clinician might observe that Mahdia slurred her speech during the initial meeting and infer that she was intoxicated, when it turns out she has had a stroke that is affecting her speech. A clinician might notice that in a family intake the father speaks loudly, interrupts others, and answers questions addressed to other family members, and then infer that he is authoritarian, not understanding that he is behaving as fathers are supposed to behave in his culture.

Making a clear distinction between data and interpretation is important because, as human beings, we can be subject to mistaking our own strongly held opinions and impressions for "facts," thereby misunderstanding clients, their actual situations, triggers, motives, potentials, and assets. Clinicians have to record the specific data and the inferences they have drawn from them rather than record just the inference itself.

EXERCISE 7.2 Moving from Data to Inference

A number of pieces of data follow. What kinds of inferences can you draw from them? What is a low-level inference? What is a high-level inference? On what do you base your inference? Discuss your answers in class.

Jenny is depressed.

Alijah scored 108 on an IQ test.

Holly is 28 and she cuts herself on her arm with a razor.

Sam and Irma have been married for 30 years.

Jim has been stopped for speeding 10 times.

Madela is 23 and has night terrors.

Formal DSM Diagnosis

Health and mental health settings may require that the formulation include a **formal diagnosis.** The **Diagnostic and Statistical Manual (DSM),** developed by the American Psychiatric Association, is currently utilized in the United States and in many other countries to diagnose mental disorders. Another internationally recognized diagnostic classification system is the World Health Organization's **International Classification of Diseases (ICD).** The purpose of having a diagnostic classification system is to provide clinicians from a variety of disciplines with a framework and a common language for assessment, formulation, treatment planning, and research.

The DSM-IV-TR defines a **mental disorder** as a behavior or psychological syndrome (groups of associated features) that is associated with either (1) emotional distress, (2) impaired functioning or disability, or (3) a behavior that puts the person at risk of pain, suffering, disability, death, or loss of freedom. The DSM definition of mental disorders excludes expected or culturally sanctioned responses to a stressful event, such as the loss of a loved one. The DSM also excludes "deviant behavior (e.g. political, religious or sexual)" and "conflicts that are primarily between the individual and society" (American Psychiatric Association, 2000).

The DSM contains over three hundred clinical syndromes or diagnoses of mental disorders, each with a list of specific symptom criteria that must be met before the diagnosis can be given. The DSM attempts to categorize symptoms into discrete diagnostic entities in an effort to discriminate one condition or disorder from another, with the goal of developing increased reliability among clinicians and more effective case formulation, research, and treatment planning. However, a diagnostic system is descriptive, not explanatory. It describes a cluster of symptoms; it does not explain their origins, nor does it discuss treatment approaches. For example, the criteria for Major Depressive Episode are listed in Box 7.3.

The DSM is a **multiaxial diagnostic system** and attempts to provide more information than just a diagnosis. The five axes are described in Box 7.4.

Proponents of a strengths perspective wisely continue to argue caution about reducing people to their symptoms and problems—a process that can stigmatize and mislead, because people are always so much more than their symptoms (Caplan, 1995; Kutchins & Kirk, 1997). Dennis Saleebey (2001) proposes a Diagnostic Strengths Manual with categories whose descriptive "symptoms" are each something the client does well each day. Advanced clinical practice, psychopathology, and abnormal psychology courses present opportunities to learn much more about understanding and applying DSM

BOX 7.3 DSM-IV-TR Criteria for a Major Depressive Episode

A. Five or more of the following symptoms have been present during the same 2-week period and represent a change from previous functioning; at least one of the symptoms is either (1) depressed mood, or (2) loss of interest or pleasure.

1. Depressed mood most of the day, nearly every day as indicated either by subjective report [for example, feels sad or empty] or observation made by others (for example, appears tearful). Note: in children and adolescents, can be irritable mood.

2. Markedly diminished interest or pleasure in all, or almost all, activities of the day, nearly every day.

3. Significant weight loss when not dieting or weight gain (for example, a change of more than 5 percent of body weight in a month), or decrease or increase in appetite nearly every day. Note: in children, consider failure to make expected weight gains.

4. Insomnia or hypersomnia nearly every day.

5. Psychomotor agitation or retardation nearly every day (observable by others).

6. Fatigue or loss of energy nearly every day.

7. Feelings of worthlessness or excessive or inappropriate guilt nearly every day (not merely self reproach or guilt about being sick).

8. Diminished ability to think or concentrate, or indecisiveness, nearly every day.

9. Recurrent thoughts of death (not just fear of dying), or recurrent suicidal ideation without a specific plan, or a suicide attempt or a specific plan for committing suicide

Source: Reprinted with permission from the Diagnostic and Statistical Manual of Mental Disorders, Fourth Edition, Text Revision. (Copyright 2000). American Psychiatric Association.

BOX 7.4 DSM-IV-TR Axes

Axis 1 Clinical Syndromes and Other Conditions That May Be a Focus of Clinical Attention—includes all diagnoses (except those listed in Axis II) or other conditions such as academic problems

Axis II Personality Disorders or Mental Retardation—chronic long-term conditions

Axis III General Medical Conditions—illness that are important to understanding the diagnosis and treatment or that may have a role in causing the disorder

Axis IV Psychosocial and Environmental Problems—problems that may affect diagnosis and treatment

Axis V Global Assessment of Functioning—rating on a scale of 1–100 of how well the person is currently functioning, may also include the highest level of functioning during the past year.

and ICD diagnostic frameworks and about arguments for and against the use of symptom frameworks (Kutchins & Kirk, 1995; Williams & Spitzer, 1995).

People of color, new immigrants, gays, lesbians, transsexuals, people with severe mental illness, and homeless people are among the many people who have been the object of negative, inaccurate, or stigmatizing formulations and diagnoses applied by professionals due to misinformation and lack of experience (Mezzich & Kleinman, 1996; Sue & Sue, 2003; White Kress, Eriksen, Rayle, & Forde, 2005). Research studies of the past twenty years also revealed that white clinicians across many different settings have diagnosed clients of color as having more pathology and poorer prognoses than white people with identical demographics and functional profiles (Baker, 2001; Rollock & Gordon, 2000; Snowden & Cheung, 1990).

There is an extensive controversy about whether DSM diagnoses should be applied cross-culturally. Two important perspectives about the relationship between culture and pychopathology are: **cultural universalism** and **cultural relativism.** According to Joanne Thakker and Tony Ward (1998) "(u)niversalists emphasize the Western biomedical framework to find similarities across cultures" (p. 507). They cite Littlefield's (1990) suggestion that "given the primacy of European psychiatry, local 'psychiatric systems' [are] examined not as self-contained, meaningful and functional patterns in themselves, but as more or less accurate approximations to the 'real' (Western) classification" (Littlefield, 1990, p. 309, cited in Thakker and Ward 1998, p. 507).

On the other hand, relativists assume that culture has a significant impact on mental disorders and, that if cultures vary, there will be differences in psychopathology. "[R]elativists assert that diagnostic categories are essentially abstractions or constructions used to explain psychiatric phenomena within the context of Western culture . . . . Hence they are necessarily limited in their capacity to explain such phenomena in diverse settings" (Thakker & Ward, 1998, p. 508).

Because of frequent cross-cultural misunderstandings and misinterpretation when diagnosing people from other cultures, the DSM (APA, 2000) includes a list of **"culture-bound syndromes"**—abnormal behaviors that are found in some cultures but are rare or unheard of in others. In addition, a **Cultural Formulation** section provides a list and brief discussion of some cultural issues to consider before diagnosing "disorders" in people from cultures different from that of the person diagnosing. The cultural formulation includes the cultural identity of the individual, cultural explanations of the individual's illness, and cultural elements of the relationship between the individual and the clinician (Thakker & Ward, 1998).

Moving Beyond Formal Diagnosis: Motivation, Strengths, and Resources

While formulation may include a DSM diagnosis, a meaningful formulation is much more than the diagnosis alone. It includes recognitions of client strengths and coping mechanisms; motivation and readiness; and community, cultural, spiritual, and social supports.

The formulation often provides tentative prognostic statements regarding expectations for the short, medium, and long term of any work to follow. It usually outlines important implications for intervention suggested by assessment findings and hypotheses, and it contains recommendations for the treatment plan and interventions.

Reformulation and Reconceptualization

The formulation is subject to continuous review and change as we learn more over time about clients and their situation. As assessment continues over time, we may gain new information that requires readjusting our initial conceptualization. As client feelings of comfort and safety increase, supportive clinicians with good listening and elaboration skills often elicit more information, feelings, and details. Our awareness of the tentative nature of our most sacrosanct interpretations and conclusions keeps us humble and open to new understanding, leading to a *re*formulation or *re*conceptualization.

Shifts in information, inferences, and interpretations should be written in the client's record and communicated verbally with involved colleagues. For example, if your colleagues thought that a teen's bulimia might be fueled by her perfectionism, and you have since learned that her parents were suddenly divorcing without warning at the same time as her younger sister was diagnosed with leukemia and their prized pet died of old age, you should share that information with them.

Lum (2004) notes that many new immigrants and people of color with numerous experiences of racist and classist oppression may approach white clinicians with wariness and distrust—wearing a protective psychological mask or armor. Their lack of affect may cause clinicians to misdiagnose them as depressed, bored, or uninterested. Such clients, suspicious of what might be done with their information, might not disclose much, so that the clinician's "big picture" is inaccurate. If upon the establishment of a trusting relationship new information is revealed, understandings about the client need to be reconceptualized, and the treatment plan may need to be altered. Similarly, if the clinician becomes aware of cultural or other biases that influenced the original formulation, the case formulation and sometimes the approach, may need to be adjusted in light of new understanding.

> Hospital staff asked me to assess a 93-year-old African-American woman with pneumonia, whom they described as "noncompliant," resistant to getting well, and probably needing a nursing home to ensure her nutrition and self-care. The patient was refusing meals and existing on tea and toast in early morning and at dinnertime.
>
> When I went to assess the patient, I found her to be annoyed, spunky, and talkative. She proudly stated that she had reached her age by taking only tea and buttered toast and an occasional meal with family and friends. All of her family and most of her friends had by now died from heart attacks and strokes she attributed to "eating too much." She also explained that she has regular visits from the neighborhood health clinic's home health staff. All of this was validated by her church pastor, who visited a day or two later and was "a great fan of Miss E's." After my report back to staff, they had a

better understanding of her. They no longer saw her as resistant and noncompliant and they stopped trying to force her to eat. They recognized that she had faithful support in the community and agreed that she probably would not need a nursing home.

■ Assessment Summaries or Psychological Reports

We conclude the assessment process by writing an intake report, also known as an **assessment summary** or a **psychological report,** in which we summarize assessment findings and case conceptualization. Most licensed agencies, managed care programs, and insurance companies require such a psychological report before treatment planning can begin, then require briefer treatment summaries and progress reports at intervals, to make judgments about the accuracy of case formulation and the benefits (or lack of them) of the intervention.

Reports must be clearly written, avoiding jargon as well as speculation or inference for which there is little or weak evidence. For example, to describe a teen as "acting out" is not helpful. Terms like "acting out" too often connote a "bad" teen who is breaking rules or insulting staff. The clinician should describe the specific behavior in a particular setting and hypothesize possible triggers and consequences contributing to and maintaining it. Clinicians need to understand behavior in the context of its social antecedents and consequences.

Psychological reports usually include identifying and demographic information about the client, along with name, age, gender, sexual orientation, relationship status, and occupation. The report then includes presenting problems or concerns: the reasons for the referral or the reasons the client sought help from the clinician and the history of the presenting issues (how long in development, when and how the problems began, and the nature of their development over time). If the client has seen other providers for help in the past, previous treatment and its effects are summarized.

The report describes the client's background: family developmental history, including family strengths, significant childhood events, meaningful migration stories, cultural and larger systems influences and issues, biopsychosocial stressors, and oppressive forces affecting functioning. A description of a client's overall functioning often includes relational and other behavioral observations, cognitive and intellectual levels and skills, and emotional and affective state and self-regulation. The results of mental status exams or other psychological, intellectual, or neuropsychological tests are included. The report also describes health or biological conditions that may be related to the presenting problem, including medical history and medications and their effects. Also important is any history of substance or drug abuse (Amodeo & Jones, 1997). Most psychological reports require a DSM diagnosis on all five axes.

However, the report should not be exclusively "problem focused," because everyone has strengths, and tapping and enhancing strengths and social resources are important goals of any intervention. Strengths and resources include coping mechanisms; the motivation to work for change; social and spiritual support networks; and agencies and services available in the client's geographic area. The written report culminates in a brief formulation or conceptualization.

Communicating Assessment Findings

Both during and upon completion of an assessment, we discuss our findings and conclusions with the client. This includes sharing with the client the results of any tests or information obtained through interviews with others and reviews of life records or any other material or experience with the client. In sharing this information, we are careful to note and validate the client's strengths, normal developmental issues and challenges, and other areas for potential work.

Communication should be direct, stated in plain language, and interspersed as needed with support and empathic comments. The clinician seeks feedback from the client, listening for thoughts and reactions that may differ from those of the clinician and exploring them further. Discussion of the assessment process and findings helps develop the working alliance as clients and clinicians prepare to set up goals and contracts for their work together.

We believe that it can be helpful to have friends or family members present for the discussion of assessment findings. Writing about Native American families, Joe and Malach (2004) suggest that "when an entire family is included, communication should be directed to the entire group" (p. 129), showing respect for all. However, in working with some matriarchal and patriarchal families, it may be important to direct comments to the elders in the group, signaling respect for cultural traditions. Again, cultural awareness and judgment are required. If uncertain about conversational protocol within a given culture, the clinician should ask the presenting client to whom comments and questions should be addressed.

Clinicians are often uncertain about whether to share a DSM diagnosis. Many authors have written about the stigma of labeling and the problem of self-fulfilling prophecies (Caplan, 1995; Rosenhan, 1973; Torrey, 1972). Some clinicians prefer not to discuss the diagnosis because much of the formal DSM nomenclature ("cyclothymia," "schizoaffective disorder") can be scary or off-putting, and the focus of the moment is on pathology and dysfunction rather than on strengths and possibilities.

However, clients do have a right to ask for their diagnosis and obtain a copy of the contents of their chart or folder. Many have reported feeling very relieved finally to have a name for their experiences. Once a condition or set of experiences is named, clients and family members can obtain more information about "the disorder" from the Internet, public libraries, and other resources such as self-help groups. Clients may be relieved to discover that what seem to be strange and unique feelings or behavioral patterns are actually also experienced by others with whom they now can consult for advice and support.

CLIP 7.1
Assessment and
Formulation

The clinician should discuss diagnoses and related interventions in clear, easily understood language. A reflective comment, such as "You seem to prefer being alone most of the time to interacting with people," is more respectful and meaningful than, "You have what we call schizoid personality." Even more meaningful is a follow-up question, such as, "How do you react to what we have said?"

■ Goal Setting

Desired Outcomes

Goals express the desired outcomes of the working relationship agreed upon by clinician and client. Many human service professionals working in schools and agencies are required to use formalized methods to assess change and progress toward goals. As often as possible, goals should include **desired outcomes** that are observable and measurable and that can be used in assessing the effectiveness of interventions.

EXAMPLE

Goal Outcomes   To improve self-esteem

Client will be able to express opinions and give feedback to others.

Client will tolerate praise and positive feedback.

Client will make more positive statements about self.

Client will demonstrate increased eye contact with others.

Client will identify positive talents and strengths about self.

Client will increase the frequency of speaking with confidence in social situations.

Client will report a decreased fear of rejection.

Client will increase statements of self-acceptance.

Goals are informed by images of how clinicians and clients would like things to be in the future, and they can be either short term or long term. **Short-term goals** can be accomplished relatively quickly, whereas **long-term goals** may take more time. Clinicians can ask clients about their goals by asking future-oriented questions, such as:

"How would you like things to be different?"
"What are your goals for our work together?"

"If our work is successful, what would be changed for you?"
"How would things look if they were the way you wanted them to be?"

Working from a strengths perspective, we are always interested in (a) what clients do well and want to sustain or enhance and (b) what issues need to be addressed or what problems need to be solved. In the assessment process, clinicians and clients assess what skills and resources might be used or developed to help clients reach their goals.

While exploring problem areas presented by clients, clinicians also ask clients what is working for them—what they would like to keep. Sometimes, during the intake, the client and related others may be so caught up in worried or unhappy feelings that positives are left out of their reports or are disqualified as having no real meaning or present relevance.

E X A M P L E

Clinician: Have you ever had any moments when you're not feeling "out of it"?

Client: No . . . um, well, at the gym when I'm working out, I feel better.

Clinician: What is it about working out that helps?

Client: I don't know. I get out of myself, I guess.

Clinician: Anything else about the gym?

Client: I guess I'm with people. I talk to the other guys some days. I don't feel so alone.

Specific and Concrete

Goals flow from assessment findings, and they have to be specific and concrete to provide clear directions for ensuing work together. Clinicians often ask questions, such as:

"What would things look like if you were to achieve your goal?"
"How will we know when we have achieved the goals you want?"

Sometimes clients come in with very concrete and specific goals: "I want to score ten points better in my basketball games" or "Can you help me get into the Jobs Program?" Often, however, they come in with goals that are abstract or are generally stated: "I want to feel better." The clinician then needs to help them be more specific and eventually formulate more concrete goals.

EXAMPLE OF HELPING CLIENTS SET CONCRETE GOALS

Clinician: If our work were successful, what would be different about your son?

Client: Davey wouldn't be so depressed.

Clinician: What would show us that Davey wasn't so depressed?

Client: He would smile more.

Clinician: What else would you notice?

Client: He would play with friends after school instead of just hanging out at home alone.

EXERCISE 7.3 Turning Abstract Goals into Concrete Goals

In your journal, record goals that you have for yourself. Turn these general goals into specific concrete goals with measurable outcomes.

Partializing and Prioritizing

Clinicians help clients partialize goals; we help clients break major goals down into component parts, called **objectives.** Each goal may have many objectives. For example, recovery from alcoholism is a broad goal within which there may be a number of specific objectives: to recognize and own a problem with drinking, to attend AA meetings, to develop friendships with people who are sober, to live in a stable environment. We have to help clients take broad goals and **partialize,** that is, break them down into component parts. In doing so, we take vague or general concepts like "feeling more independent" and identify their defining components so that each can be addressed in the order of its priority in problem resolution.

EXAMPLE OF PARTIALIZING GOALS

Clinician: What goals do you think we should have for our work together?

Client: I want to be more independent.

Clinician: How would that look?

Client: I'd have my own place, my own spending money and schedule.

Clinician: What kinds of things would need to happen for you to be more independent?

Client: I would have to improve my English and get a job.

Often clinicians and clients can see problems as so enormous and lacking in definition that they can feel burdened and overwhelmed. A feeling of hopelessness can suffuse the work. By breaking goals down into concrete objectives and talking about them in simple everyday language, tasks can seem much more achievable and clients can feel much more hopeful.

EXERCISE 7.4 Partializing

The following is a list of goals that clients might have for their work with a clinician. Partialize them into smaller objectives. In your journal, write down the broad goal, and, for each goal, make a list of component objectives. Discuss your list with your fellow students in class.

Freydia is a 27-year-old mother who has been using crack cocaine for 4 years. Her children, ages 7 and 9, have been removed from her care by Child Protective Services and are currently living with her mother. Freydia comes to the drug program saying, "I want to get my children back."

Thomas, a 20-year-old college sophomore, drops out of school. He has just been diagnosed with schizophrenia. His mother has brought him to the day center saying she hopes that "somehow he will be able to get back to college."

Rad is a 49-year-old refugee from Bosnia. He was an engineer in Sarajevo, but now he cleans buildings at night. He does not speak English well. He wants to get certified as an engineer and get a job so he can bring his family to the United States.

We help the client **prioritize** goals and objectives, ranking them in the order of their urgency or importance. The ranking of priorities has to take into account the client's capacity and motivation to work on the selected tasks during and between visits, the likelihood that achieving the objectives will have positive consequences, and the availability of resources required to achieve the objectives.

When feasible, we prioritize a relatively easy goal or objective so that the client can experience mastery, which fuels further efforts. Every effort is made to stage the work so that, when possible, small successes build on one another.

EXAMPLE OF PRIORITIZING

Clinician: What would be your first step in becoming more independent?

Client: Get a job first, I guess; then I can pay my bills.

Clinician: What kinds of things would you have to do to get a job?

Client: Well, I would have to go out on interviews.

Clinician: Are there steps you would need to take before that?

Client: Well, first, I guess I would have to start reading the want ads. I'd have to start buying the paper first.

Priority setting is also affected by the needs and feelings of others in the client's family or social system. Different **stakeholders** may have different goals. For example, Davey's mother wants him to smile more. Davey may want his parents to stop fighting, or he may want his mother to be less concerned about whether he smiles. The parents of Thomas, the young man with schizophrenia, may stipulate that he can live at home only if he stops smoking in the house. Giving up smoking may not be Thomas's goal, but, since he needs to live at home, realistically he has to change his priorities and accommodate his parents' wishes; perhaps all can agree that Thomas can smoke on the back steps. It may even turn out that this "smoking" issue masks other fears regarding his condition.

The demands of the larger society can also intrude on priority setting. Freydia, the woman who wishes her children back, might see getting sober and getting work training as priorities. However, in a conversation with the clinician, Freydia realizes that she is going to have to include a mandated 6-week parenting course in her priorities.

EXERCISE 7.5   Prioritizing

Go back to Exercise 7.3 in your journal. List the strengths and resources that will help you meet the specific goals. Then prioritize the specific goals and objectives. In class, share your goals, objectives, and priorities. Remember to set priorities that:

CLIP 7.2
Developing Goals

- You want.
- Are attainable.
- Are in accord with the resources available.

■ Conclusion

Once assessment and goal setting take place, clinicians and clients make plans to work together for change. This work includes formulating treatment plans (which include specific interventions and strategies for change, along with contracts about who, when, where and how the work of change will be done) and a plan for evaluating whether and how much change has occurred.

■ Suggested Readings

Cowger, Charles. (1997). Assessing client strengths: Assessing client empowerment. In Dennis Saleebey (Ed.), *The strengths perspective in social work practice* (pp. 59–73). New York: Longman.

Delgado, Melvin. (1999). *Social work in nontraditional settings.* New York: Oxford University Press.

Hartman, Ann. (1978). Diagrammatic assessment of family relationships. *Social Casework, 59,* 465–476.

Jordan, Catheleen, & Franklin, Cynthia (Eds.). (2003). *Clinical assessment for social workers: Quantitative and qualitative methods* (2nd Ed.). Chicago: Lyceum.

Lum, Doman. (2004). *Social work practice and people of color: A process-stage approach.* (5th ed.) Belmont, CA: Brooks/Cole. (Includes useful information on culturally responsive assessment.)

Malgady, Robert G., & Zayas, Luis, H. (2001). Cultural and linguistic considerations in psychodiagnosis with Hispanics: The need for an empirically informed process model. *Social Work, 46,* 39–49.

McGoldrick, Monica, and Shellenberger, Sylvia. (1999). *Genograms: Assessment and intervention.* New York: Norton.

Good critiques of the DSM-IV include:

Caplan, Paula. (1995). *They say you're crazy: How the world's most powerful psychiatrists decide who's normal.* Reading, MA: Addison-Wesley

Kutchins, Herb, & Kirk, Stuart. (1997). *Making us crazy: DSM: The psychiatric bible and the creation of mental disorder.* New York: Free Press.

Thakker, Joanne, & Ward, Tony. (1998). Culture and classification: The cross-cultural application of the DSM-IV. *Clinical Psychology Review, 18,* 501–529.

White Kress, Victoria, Eriksen, Karen, Rayle, Andrea Dixon, & Ford, Stephanie J. W. (2005). The DSM-IV-TR and cultures: Considerations for counselors. *Journal of Counseling and Development, 83,* 97–105.

■ Self-Explorations

1. Recall a time when you underwent some type of assessment to receive a service or enter a program. What aspect of the assessment process was comfortable and routine, and what provoked anxiety for you?

2. Have you ever been labeled in a positive way, for example "good athlete," "Dean's List student," "student leader"? What were the labels? Describe their effect on you. Have you ever received unsettling or stigmatizing label, for example "slow learner," "class clown," "low life," "dumb blonde"? What were the labels? Describe their effects on you?

3. Have you or anyone in your family ever received a DSM diagnosis? What were the positive and/or negative effects of having received the diagnosis?

■ Essay Questions

1. What are the sources of and methods for collecting assessment data? What are the strengths and weaknesses of each method?

2. Discuss issues of reliability and validity? What do you think clinicians can do to improve both the reliability and validity of assessment interviews?

3. What factors can negatively affect a clinician's ability to make accurate inferences about a client from assessment data? List and describe three potential biases in clinical inference.

4. Read the suggested readings by Paula Caplan (1995) or Kutchins and Kirk (1995 or 1997). Then discuss the strengths and weaknesses of the DSM-IV-TR.

■ Key Terms

Assessment interviews

Assessment summary

Case conceptualization

Clinical judgment

Content of the assessment

Culturagram

Cultural formulation

Cultural relativism

Cultural universalism

Culture-bound syndromes

Desired outcomes

Diagnostic reliability DSM (Diagnostic and Statistical Manual)

Ecomap

Formal diagnosis

Formulation

Genogram

Goals

ICD (International Classification of Diseases)

Interrater reliability

Levels of inference

Life chart

Life records

Long-term goals

Mental disorder

Multiaxial diagnostic system

Multidisciplinary team

Objectives

Observation

Partialize

Prioritize

Process of the assessment

Psychological report

Reliability

Review of life records

Short-term goals

Stakeholders

Strength-based genogram

Testing

Test-retest reliability

Validity

CHAPTER 8

Planning for and Evaluating Change

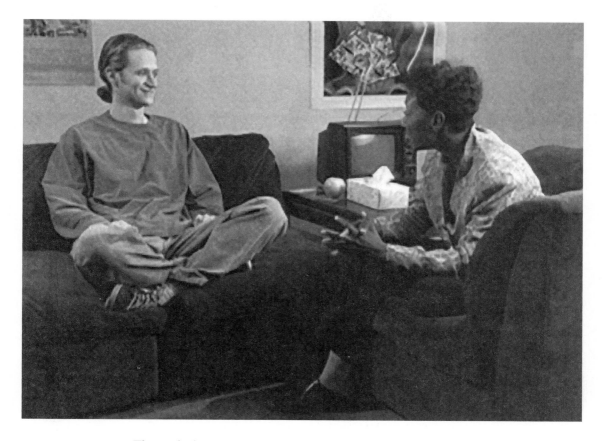

Through the initial assessment and formulation process, the idea of "getting help" now begins to take on form and meaning. People begin to realize that, contrary to expectations, help and change are not prepackaged procedures or supplies the professional "delivers." Instead, the work is collaborative: a supportive, participatory, and dynamic process that clinician and client must coevolve using their own vision, capacities, determination, and resources. Clients realize that they may need to make changes in their familiar ways of thinking, feeling, relating, and behaving. Clinicians realize that they, too, need to make changes in response to the specific styles, pace, assets, and needs of each client. They need to be flexible and willing to adapt familiar approaches so that each client feels more empowered and at ease in the work ahead. Both clinician and client prepare for the time, energy, and personal commitment required to plan and to carry out work together.

During goal setting and treatment planning work, clients realize more clearly than before how promising and helpful the work of change can be. At the same time, they realize that this work may involve some pain and the relinquishing of long familiar habits and relationships. Resulting ambivalences can lead to hesitation and mixed feelings about proceeding. Awareness of the ways in which the process of change unfolds can help clients and those working with them anticipate what may lie ahead.

■ Preparing for Change

Stages of Change

After reviewing and comparing several hundred therapeutic models, Prochaska, Norcross, & DiClemente (1994) noted common components of effective change strategies as well as stages, or phases, of change. They assert that "over 45 percent of clients drop out of psychotherapy prematurely, since treatments too often don't match the stage clients are in" (p. 16). They identified six stages of change (pp. 38–50) and suggest specific activities that can help in each stage.

1. ***Pre-Contemplation.***   People minimize and rationalize their problem behaviors, attributing them to fate, family, and social influences, or genetics. Pre-contemplation is often found in court-mandated referrals and in clients pressured by significant others to "get help or else."

Advice giving, lecturing, and moralizing almost never work with individuals who are not ready to take ownership of behaviors that others see clearly and experience as harmful. Remembering from time to time that it is human to ignore or deny painful realities helps us to remain patient with people who persist in justifying self-defeating behaviors.

Sometimes pre-contemplators can be helped by empathizing with the fix they are in and sympathetically naming possible unsettling consequences if their habits persist. If clients feel accepted for who they are rather than judged for who they are not, they are likely to be more receptive to the information that professionals can provide about the complex nature and multiple causes of problems, the painful consequences of continued behaviors, and examples of strategies and programs that have educated and supported others under similar pressure to change.

At the same time that we want to show support and understanding of the client's anxiety about change, it is important not to become an "enabling helper." That term describes clinicians and other allies of clients who may be tempted to collude with clients' rationalizations of problems because they fear losing the relationship if they address problems directly and forthrightly.

Matilda said it wasn't a big deal that she keeps losing every job. She said employers have always discriminated against her because she is overweight—she's not the "eye candy" that male bosses like to have around. I realized she was two years out of college and had already lost three or four jobs in short order. She was not able to discuss any other things that might have brought trouble on herself. She said she'd only come to see a counselor because she lives at home and her parents put pressure on her to come. I didn't want to make her feel bad about herself, so I didn't push the job topic this time.

. . .

My supervisor told me I wasn't helping Jax by just listening to all of his excuses about why he can't get to school on time, since his mother always gives him a ride to the corner down the street from the school. My supervisor reminded me that Jax had a history of drug use and that he might be meeting up with his old crowd briefly before school. This could put him at risk for using again. She told me to ask him about this possibility but I couldn't do it right away—it just seemed like he would resent me for not trusting or believing him. I wanted to make a relationship with him first by being nonjudgmental—then I could ask him.

2. **Contemplation.** In this stage, the client experiences a dawning awareness of a need for change—but wants change and does not want it at the same time. This ambivalence is manifested in hopeful anticipation mixed with doubt or retreat. We can help clients by encouraging the open discussion of problems and prospects with friends or in social groups, where others are sharing similar stories and detailing strategies that helped them face themselves and their problems and initiate change. Prochaska et al. (1994) also encourage educating clients about the antecedents and consequences of their habitual behaviors so that they can avoid or minimize time spent in triggering relationships or environments.

Clients can be helped to develop and use self-monitoring tools (journals or tracking sheets) and discuss ways to deal with daily temptations and triggers. In-session visualization exercises help clients positively imagine and describe themselves and how their lives will be different in the future, when problematic habits no longer control them. Teaching clients to give themselves positive self-talk for owning behaviors and embarking on change helps them maintain their self-observation and self-restraint in this early phase.

3. **Preparation.** In this stage the person establishes goals for change, outlines small steps, and even sets a time for start-up. This stage is characterized by swings between impulsive leaps forward and slips backward into problematic behaviors. Clinicians can offer support if clients feel embarrassed or have doubts about continuing. Highlighting past successes is helpful in fueling hope and initiative. We can ask clients to tell others about their intended efforts so that they can elicit continuing social support and check-ins from others.

We can also ask clients to recall people they know or have heard of who have experienced the drastic consequences of hurtful patterns (for example, someone who died of alcohol-related cirrhosis), then acknowledge and honor their grit and determination in facing problems head-on and using their self-commitment to change rather than give up. Joining a relevant mutual aid group adds support and coping information during the early stressful period of initiating change behaviors

Anson didn't agree with his male partner's assessment of him as having a drinking problem. Instead, he always laughed and joked at parties about being Irish and loving to "push a few back" in order to lighten up and have fun in a crowd. He came to the counseling center because of recent problems sleeping the night through and hoping we might give him some medication to help with sleep. When I learned in the evaluation that he was having rich dinners late and consuming four or five drinks before and during them, I asked if he would at least give some thought that too much food and drink were part of the sleep problem. He was willing to take home some literature I routinely hand out to older men about weight and heart problems, Type II diabetes, and alcohol and aging. He told me the next visit that he and his partner were both thinking about going to an open AA meeting but wanted to find one outside their area, which might take a little time. I said I was glad to hear it and would look forward to hearing how it went.

4. *Action.*   At this stage the person's planned actions for change proceed more evenly. Goals and steps are kept small and manageable.

We help clients focus on the benefits derived from new behaviors and the lessons they are learning from mastering the inevitable rough spots. Clients need to understand that the temptation to return to familiar habits is normal. They can also predetermine small rewards to give themselves for positive change behaviors. (In subsequent chapters, we discuss specific tools, strategies, and techniques that can help clients substitute new thoughts, feelings, and behaviors for old ones.)

5. *Behavior maintenance.*   Additional support and coping tips are gained from joining support or recovery groups and from getting a sponsor or special friend to talk with during crises or lapses. People may change some relationships and environments to support continued growth. For example, people with drug or alcohol problems may exchange old "using" buddies for clean and sober friends who share their motivation and readiness to change.

Clinicians can provide encouragement and praise while helping clients remain aware of temptations. We can review why these changes have been made so that clients do not forget why they took this hard work on in the first place.

6. *Recycling.*   Change usually involves two steps forward, one step back, because growth is a spiraling rather than a linear process. People may return to the pre-contemplative or maintenance stages often, to reflection and planning, sometimes resuming work at higher levels.

Prochaska et al. (1994) urge people to remember that one lapse is not a relapse and that lapses are human. Advise clients to work each stage one step at a time and to remember that most lasting change takes months and sometimes years. All change work has its ups and downs, and it is crucial that you remain hopeful and encouraging when clients feel like giving up on themselves. They often later describe how much this belief in them kept them going.

Reframing "Resistance" to Change

We know that some clients drop out of the work early on, even during or just after the assessment, realizing that more is required than they are interested in or can commit to at present. Others may agree to planned work, but with ambivalence, self-doubt, or trepidation about consequences. For many years, practitioners have described the lack of motivation, noncompliance, and resistance as major obstacles to change. Whereas these terms were once used to describe the client, we now recognize that environmental and clinician/agency factors greatly affect a client's attitudes toward the work.

Proponents of Relational-Cultural Theory believe that resistance is relational. They suggest that regarding resistance as a flaw in the client overlooks the fact that difficulties in the relationship are often "products of relational disconnections and empathic failures . . . ." They believe that "[m]ovement out of disconnection requires looking at what both the client *and* the therapist bring to the relationship at any particular point" (Comstock, 2004, p. 91).

In addition to relational factors, contextual factors affect continuance. Agency policies, procedures, staff, and location may seem too far removed from a client's experience, language, and comfort zone. Stresses at home and the lack of resources (including transportation and child care) can affect attendance and follow-through. The cost of treatment and medications can be beyond many clients' means. The timing of suggested meetings, when planned around clinicians' availability and schedules, can interfere with other important obligations. Loved ones, feeling threatened by the intended changes, may discourage following through on sessions and planned work. Unexpected local crises and agency cutbacks can also undermine or end planned work.

Building Motivation to Change

William Miller and Stephen Rollnick (2002) define motivation as an interpersonal process, the product of interactions between two people. They point out that clients who appear unmotivated at a given time or with a given clinician or program may go on to change behaviors in the future, given the proper moment, circumstances, advice, and support. Instead of focusing on the presence or absence in clients of motivation or noncompliance with treatment, they suggest **motivational interviewing** strategies to enhance client participation. They believe that all human change involves ambivalence and that it should be no surprise to clinicians that, when we lean on clients to change in the ways we think best for them, they respond with numerous justifications for keeping things as they are.

Techniques for Resolving Ambivalence About Change

Miller and Rollnick (2002) have conducted a number of empirical studies on motivational interviewing. They have found several techniques effective in resolving ambivalence regarding change:

- *A major technique to help people move toward change is the* **decisional balance sheet** (see Box 8.1), for use in beliefs clarification and decision making. The client describes the costs and the benefits of keeping things as they are and the costs and benefits of changing. As the client then

---

BOX 8.1 Decisional Balance Sheet

Continue to Drink as Before		Abstain from Alcohol	
Benefits	Costs	Benefits	Cost
Helps me relax	Could lose my family	Less family conflict	I enjoy getting high
Enjoy drinking with friends	Bad example for my children	More time with my children	What to do about my friends
	Damaging my health	Feel better physically	How to deal with stress
	Spending too much money	Helps with money problems	
	Impairing my mental ability		
	Might lose my job		
	Wasting my time/life		

Source: From *Motivational Interviewing: Preparing people for change,* 2nd Ed. by William R. Miller & Stephen Rollnick (2001, p. 16). © 2002 Guilford Press. Reprinted with permission of Guilford Press.

---

reflects on each belief listed, the clinician empathizes with how hard it is to feel two ways about something so important, mirroring the feelings and thoughts the client shares on examining the pros and cons.

- *Reflecting to clients an approximation of what they have just said* is another frequently used technique that keeps them in charge of puzzling out how to proceed when seesawing toward and away from change action. This reflective process makes them the drivers of the process and deciders of what they wish to do. Clinican reflection often encourages clients to go deeper in their self-reflection, continually sifting through the benefits and costs of staying the same and stirring things up in very productive ways.

- *A major technique is to create and amplify the discrepancy between present behavior and the broader goals and values.* Clients experience such a discrepancy when we help them contrast what they listed as the cons of staying the same and the benefits of changing, or when they compare the benefits of staying the same and of changing. The dissonance created by these comparisons can bring about a gradual reduction in ambivalence and some movement toward change.

- *Another helpful technique is described as rolling with the resistance.* "The counselor does not impose new views or goals; rather, the person is invited to consider new information and is offered new perspectives. 'Take what you want and leave the rest' is the permissive kind of advice that pervades this approach" (p. 40).

- *Turning the question back to clients* for further comments (rather than answering it or musing on it) is another technique that respects and patiently draws out the insights and capacities of clients to involve them as active fellow problem solvers.
- *Expressing our faith and confidence in the client's ability to make the desired changes supports self-efficacy.* Miller and Rollnick suggest that the gap between present behavior and the desired future behaviors is crucial to keep in mind: the greater the gap is, the greater our efforts must be to understand and support clients so that discouragement and defeatism do not derail their aspirations and activities.

Since the clinician does not take sides in clients' internal debates about what they might gain or lose in changing and in staying the same, they have no one to "resist" but themselves. Clients who highly value self-determination have only themselves to argue with, and the argument can become tiresome after a period of seesawing back and forth.

Miller and Rollnick (2002) remind us that a lot of change takes place without any assistance from professionals or programs. In the past, "recovery" was called a **"spontaneous remission"** of symptoms, as though it were the symptoms who acted by going away. However, human resilience and determination that so often spur improvement and other changes were seen in the survivors of 9/11, of Hurricane Katrina, the South Asian and African tsunamis, and the earthquakes in Turkey and Pakistan. These disasters provide inspiring examples of how people from all walks of life can effect change when professionals and institutions can provide little or no help.

■ Treatment Plan

Once the initial assessment is complete, the clinician and client develop a **treatment plan.** In some settings these plans are called service plans or intervention plans to avoid any implication that the word "treatment" presupposes an illness in a person and to the multiplicity of biopsychosocial factors usually identified in requests for professional help. Treatment plans spell out agreed-upon goals for the work to come and the methods proposed to achieve the goals. Neukrieg and Schwitzer (2006) describe the treatment plan as a "road map [and] tool by which clinicians put their case conceptualization and theoretical perspectives into action" (p. 224).

Treatment plans usually include a number of topics (see Box 8.2). A treatment plan starts with overarching goals as well as more specific goals and objectives for the work. It specifies the participants in the work and their specific roles and responsibilities.

The core of the treatment plan elaborates the specific techniques and methods to be used to accomplish each goal. Included also is the modality or combination of modalities that are to be utilized (individual, family, group). The treatment plan should address important logistics: where the work will take place; the expected length and number of sessions; expected cost and

---

B O X 8.2   Treatment Plans

- Goals
- Participants
- Modalities
- Techniques and strategies
- Logistics
- Other services and resources
- Advocacy
- Evaluation

---

other important contingencies, such as transportation, child care, available space, and the like.

The treatment plan must also acknowledge any constraints that managed care or agency mission and policies place on plans and goals. For example, Mark Young (2005) notes that, in many managed care and agency settings, the client can be seen for only six to ten sessions. Such restraints call for creative planning ahead, making explicit how ancillary services and supports are to be arranged, and by whom, when the brief contacts end but clients still have pressing needs. We appreciate that, in addition to counseling, many other services and resources can be helpful to clients, no matter how extensive our work with them. The treatment plan should be explicit about other services and resources to be utilized—for example, AA, an exercise program or meditation class, a study group at temple, or a GED prep class at a nearby school.

Client problems are not just located in the individual, couple, family, or group; they are often a product of environmental factors and oppressive systems. Thus we believe that a good treatment plan should recommend environmental interventions in the form of advocacy (helping a family get food stamps, helping a single mom get housing) and political activism and work for social justice (fighting for a change in minimum wage laws, working to ensure school programs for the children of undocumented immigrants). Both clients and clinicians can engage in these activities to address systemic issues and to change oppressive systems affecting clients and their attainment of goals.

Treatment plans also include statements about how—by whom, at what intervals, and with what procedures—progress toward goal achievement will be measured and evaluated. Treatment plans should be articulated in clear and specific language. Some people find it helpful to review or utilize treatment planning guides to help them write the plans succinctly and specifically.

In formulating treatment plans with clients, we have an ethical obligation to discuss potential risks or adverse effects that they may experience as part of their work for change. Clients can give informed consent only if they are aware of the potential downsides to their work.

Choosing Strategies and Interventions

How do we choose among the wide variety of strategies, interventions, or techniques that can be included in a treatment plan? Some clinicians base their decisions on a theory of counseling or psychotherapy or on empirically validated methods. Others are eclectic in their choice of theory, selecting what they believe to be effective methods from various theories or weaving empirically validated methods into their preferred theoretical model. Whatever the guiding theories, all treatment plans must be crafted to give full consideration to the unique capacities, supports, and needs of each client and situation.

Theories of Counseling and Psychotherapy

Theoretical models of counseling and therapy are usually taught at advanced levels of clinical education, where students learn theory in class and then practice applying it in their supervised internships. You may be familiar with some widely used theoretical models, including psychodynamic, behavioral, cognitive, humanistic, and family systems models. Recall from Chapter 1 that Prochaska, Norcross, and DiClemente (1994) identified over four hundred different models of therapy in North America alone, each one touting its unique ability to inform and promote change.

In the past, clinicians from a particular theoretical school usually developed a relatively generalizable treatment plan based chiefly on their theoretical orientation. This plan would be utilized with a wide variety of clients, problems, and situations. For example, clinicians using analytically informed psychodynamic theory believed that client symptoms resulted from repressed unconscious conflicts from early childhood or adolescent development. Therefore, the goal of therapy was to make these conflicts conscious to resolve or rework them. The preferred modality was individual therapy. The clinical stance was that of providing a rather blank slate onto which clients could project their unresolved anxieties and conflicts from relationships with past significant others. Techniques might include free association and the analysis of client transferences, resistance, dreams, and slips of the tongue. Meetings might occur two to five times a week, and the work could last for years.

Today, some clinicians still predominantly utilize one theoretical model and adhere to the guiding principles and strategies spelled out in that model with little variance. These colleagues often describe themselves according to the model they are using: as cognitive therapists, as dialectical-behavioral therapists, as family therapists, as holistic therapists, and the like.

In using theory to guide plans and interventions, all clinicians need to guard against culturally biased assumptions that could convert a theoretical lens into a blinder. Sue and Sue (2003) describe a clinician working with an African-American man who could not find a job and wanted help with job search skills. The clinician reported: "Using a humanistic existential approach, I reflected his feelings, paraphrased his thoughts, and summarized his dilemma. This did not seem to immediately help" (p. 63). No wonder! The client was seeking information and advice about how to look for a job. The clinician had his own preferred approach down, and he was going to use it regardless of the client's expectations, preferred help seeking and relating style with professionals, and specific issues and requests.

Evidence-Based Practice

A great deal of evidence for the efficacy of certain models and techniques in use with specific conditions (anxiety, depression, eating disorders, shyness) has emerged in the clinical practice research literature over the past two decades. The term **"evidence-based practice"** (EBP)—sometimes referred to as **empirically supported therapy** (EST)—describes the use of efficacy research in the choice of intervention methods (Chambless et al., 1998; Chambless & Hollon, 1998; Cournoyer, 2004). For example, a clinician who is working with an anxious client is likely familiar with research demonstrating that applied relaxation techniques are useful in reducing generalized anxiety (Barlow, Rapee, & Brown, 1992; Borkovec & Costello, 1993). Accordingly, relaxation training would be a part of the treatment plan. In some circumstances, clinicians using EBP procedures follow a **treatment manual** that spells out step-by-step instructions and techniques to resolve a particular set of problems.

Manualized treatments require prior instruction in the careful use of the procedures and regular supervision to keep the therapist on track in the use of the specified techniques. Some practitioner-researchers believe that the application of manual-based interventions leaves much to be desired (Goldfried & Eubanks-Carter, 2004; Westen, Novotony, & Thompson-Brenner, 2004). Since empirically supported therapies are "clearly specified psychological treatments shown to be efficacious in controlled research with a delineated population" (Chambless & Hollon, 1998, p. 7), by definition EBP has been conducted with a relatively homogeneous sample of participants with similar problems. Thus it may not be generalizable to clients of different ages, genders, races, or cultures differing from the sample population studied.

Eclecticism

Many practitioners today are **eclectic.** They incorporate more than one theoretical perspective into their clinical work because of the utility of concepts and methods gleaned from a variety of theoretical models. For example, psychodynamic therapists may incorporate a number of family therapy principles and techniques, inviting family members and friends to occasional sessions in which systemic exploration may assist all in achieving better understanding and communication. Cognitive techniques for working on distorted ideas and misinterpretations of events to effect changes in mood are also more widely used by clinicians of many persuasions. Clinicians have an ethical responsibility to provide detailed information about their theoretical orientation, what assessment strategies and interventions they offer, what they do not offer, and how the work often unfolds.

Eclecticism requires knowledge and experience. A *New Yorker* cartoon portrays a therapist saying, "I am eclectic. I take a little from Freud, a little from Jung, and a little from my Uncle Harry who is a very wise man." However, clinicians who are eclectic often have a guiding or foundation theory into which they incorporate demonstrably useful techniques from other theoretical models. Many beginning clinicians say they are eclectic because they know a little bit about a lot and wish to apply numerous theories at once in their work with clients. "Loose eclecticism"—using whatever ideas feel right or comfortable for the clinician but have not been well tested out with clients—differs from a considered application of different methods in which one has been educated over time and under excellent supervision.

> *I learned about "miracle questions" at a conference and was taken with the optimism and future possibilities they appeared to generate in clients. So the next week I found myself using miracle questions with all my clients. In my interview with a depressed woman that week, I asked brightly: "What if you woke up tomorrow and a miracle had happened while you slept, and things were changed in the very way you wanted them to be . . . how would they be different?" Then she said in a serious tone, "So you're predicting I'll always wake up tomorrow"—and she began to describe her suicidal thoughts.*

The judicious use of methods from more than one theoretical approach can be quite useful. However, our planning decisions should be based on the client's needs, style, culture, and preferences, not on something that we think is interesting or exciting to do or that is rigidly imposed to control cost of care. Sue and Sue (2003) affirm that, when working with clients from different backgrounds or cultures than our own, we have to be flexible and eclectic, drawing from established strategies and techniques while incorporating new culturally appropriate interventions.

Treatment Plans Should Be Jointly Constructed

We must fully engage clients as active participants in the design of any treatment or intervention plan, employing their own vision and other strengths as partners in the work to come. Their active involvement in planning also tends to keep it grounded in the realities of their capacities and readiness as well as competing situational demands. Active involvement also helps build and sustain co-ownership of the design and implementation of plans, as well as their redesign if they prove less workable than originally anticipated. Prochaska et al. (1994) affirm that people attempting change are more likely to change if they feel they have some choice in the matter as well as choice among several change strategies.

Once assessment and goal setting have taken place, many clinicians write up formal treatment plans in which the specific long-term and short-term goals and objectives are prioritized and specific interventions are laid out.

Contracting

Contracting involves the development of working agreements among clinicians, clients, and any significant others vital to the realization of the goals and objectives. In general, **contracts:**

- Enumerate the goals.
- Describe the roles and responsibilities of all involved parties.
- Include the interventions and methods to be used to attain the goals.
- Describe the frequency, duration, and length of the meetings, and, if applicable, the costs and payment arrangements.
- Include the means for evaluating the work or measuring progress toward the specified goals.
- Include a provision for how the contract can be renegotiated.
- Discuss the consequences of failure of either party to carry out their agreed-upon responsibilities, as well as how to handle unanticipated complications.

Although contracts can be informal or formal, clinicians are increasingly moving to more formalized contracting arrangements based on treatment plans. **Formal contracts** are highly specific and concrete to clarify responsibilities and minimize drift and ambiguity. They enable both client and clinician to judge whether they are accomplishing what is intended. Formal contracts are often written, and they may list each goal and its component objectives, specifying particular tasks and anticipated time lines for achievement of each objective. This form of contracting is intended to lead to more structured **treatment by objectives.**

Issues in Contracting

1. *There are individual session contracts as well as overall contracts.* The clinician and client may agree during the session to focus on certain subjects and to table others. Or they may agree at the end of one session that next week's meeting should include all of the children and be held at the homeless shelter so that the clinician can better appreciate the conditions under which the family is struggling to maintain itself.

2. *Contracts should include all stakeholders whenever possible.* Others significant in the client's life may be involved in the process, and so may other service providers who have a stake in the desired outcomes. Wise clinicians make sure that all these others are included in the contract in some way. If not, clinicians may lose significant input, misattribute problems, weaken alliances, or cause others to impede the implementation of the contract. In constructing a

contract with a young teen mother who lives at home, for example, the clinician should involve the family in order to support them and to be sure that they will be able to provide the teen with transportation to the center. The adjustment counselor who wants to set up a behavioral program for a hyperactive child should make sure that not only the classroom teacher but also the principal, the school, and the family sign on.

3. *Contracts should be specific.*   The more specific the contract is, the more able the parties are to determine whether they are carrying out their roles and moving toward the specified goals. If some steps (for example, "maintain sobriety") must be taken before others can be taken, they should be spelled out in the contract.

> In the adolescent drug treatment program, the kids have specific behavior contracts that are determined each morning at a group meeting. The goals are written up and posted in the dining room. Privileges such as watching TV or playing basketball are earned by achievement of these daily goals. The kids also contract to attend daily group therapy and family meetings weekly.

4. *Contracts should be mutually constructed.*   Both client and clinician should participate in developing the contract, each contributing ideas and preferences as to what should be done and how. Each should be able to specify what is expected from the other.

At times the client may not want or may not be able to be an equal participant in the construction of the contract. For example, the involuntary client (e.g., the man who is forced to see the probation officer) may not have many choices about the contract; he may be told whom he has to see and what he has to work on. In negotiating the contract, the clinician can try to give the client room to negotiate something, such as the time of the meeting. Contracting can be prefaced with the idea that almost everyone has things to talk about or hope for, and, since the client is obliged to attend, why not use the time to to work on something the client is interested in or concerned about?

When working with members from oppressed groups—the poor, immigrants, people who do not speak English very well—we recognize that the client may be feeling fearful or powerless and so may be unable to negotiate a contract but instead simply agrees with whatever the clinician suggests. As Wynetta Devore and Elfriede Schlesinger (1996) note, "the skill of helping people who feel particularly defeated to recognize and believe that they can play a part in determining why and how something is to be done is one that needs to be continually sharpened" (p. 209).

5. *Contracts require informed consent.*   Clients need to be aware of the potential risks and benefits of the work. The woman who is coming to the clinic because she is depressed should be informed that, when people change their behavior and become less depressed, their relationships with others are often affected. Her partner, friends, and family may begin to respond to her differently, and she may want to make other changes in her life. This could be seen as either a benefit or a risk. Optional treatments and their benefits and risks should also be discussed with her.

In addition, clients need to know what other options and resources are available to them to meet their desired outcomes. The couple who is seeing a counselor about marital difficulties should also be informed about other resources, such as pastoral counseling, couples groups, or marital enrichment groups, which they may choose instead of, or in addition to, counseling. Options and resources are very important when counseling lesbian, gay, and transgendered clients who are new to the area or in the process of coming out. You can work to link them with relevant resource centers, social and support groups, health providers, and welcoming and supportive religious or spiritual organizations. Similarly, you can also help isolated or silenced people of color, newly arrived immigrants, and disaster survivors from other locales link up with cultural centers, ethnic mutual aid organizations, health and mental health resources, and work and educational opportunities where they can access other people who are familiar with their customs, languages, and preferred practices.

At times, when working with children or with adults who are not able to give informed consent because of mental retardation, cognitive impairment, or mental illness the clinician is both legally and ethically bound to get consent from the legally authorized guardians. However, even in these instances, the clinician should explain the contract to the client in as clear and detailed a way as possible. Often a friend, guardian, or relative can assist in conveying meaning in ways meaningful to the client.

6. *Contracts should be flexible.*   Brett Seabury speaks of the dynamic nature of contracting, recognizing that people, resources, and situations change (Garvin & Seabury, 1997; Seabury, 1976). The clinician and client should be willing to renegotiate the contract in response to changing circumstances, emerging information, or client growth.

> Gemma and I had a contract that we would work for 12 sessions to help her control her angry outbursts in the classroom. After five meetings, she seemed to really be managing this well. We talked about what we should do with the remaining sessions and decided that she would like to work on becoming less shy. I decided to continue to meet with Gemma even though she had accomplished the original task. Gemma enjoyed our meetings and would be disappointed if they stopped before scheduled. I thought that to end now would not reinforce Gemma's hard work and that it might even result in more angry outbursts on Gemma's part in order to continue our relationship.

7. *Contracts should be realistic.*   Contracts must take into account the resources, capacities, motivation, and opportunity that people and agencies have to meet the contract requirements. Setting up a contract in which a teen mother is expected to come to the agency twice a week for parenting group meetings is unrealistic unless the agency is sure that transportation is available and child care is provided.

> Max resisted having a regularly scheduled weekly appointment, feeling he had been locked into something he couldn't control. So at the end of each session, I'd ask, "Would you like to come again?" We would wind up with the same appointment each week. It was unrealistic for me to expect him to commit to a long-term relationship.

8. ***Contracts should be upheld.*** For example, if the contract contains a specific prohibition against using substances while in the homeless shelter, the shelter worker needs to stand firm, even if it means refusing shelter to the client for the night. In such a circumstance, caring clinicians can offer the client detox or a referral to a "wet" shelter—one that houses those who are actively drunk or on drugs.

9. ***Contracts should avoid built-in problems.*** Charles Garvin and Brett Seabury (1997) discuss three problems with contracting and treatment plans—hidden agendas, corrupt contracts, and sabotage. Contracts can include **hidden agendas**—secret aims of the clinician that are unexpressed to the client. The clinician may believe these goals will greatly improve the client's situation or functioning, but he or she fears that the client will balk at them and hopes that the power of relationship will later make the goals possible to pursue openly. Hidden agendas often doom the work, since "it is close to impossible . . . to change people against their will, especially when they recognize that they have been deceived" (p. 165).

Corrupt contracts occur when multiple service providers, working separately, make different agreements with clients, or clients with them, without all of the parties realizing that different goals or methods have been agreed upon. A client may tell a probation officer that she is attending a weekly support group for former sex workers, while telling the group's leader that her mandated attendance at an AIDS support meeting prevents her attending the sex workers group more than once every other week. Because the group leader and probation officer are not communicating, the treatment plans established with the client are unauthentic for all practical purposes, and the client will attend no meetings whatsoever as a result.

Sabotage can occur when one member of a treatment team encourages a client to act out against the plan because he or she does not believe in the goals and plans the team has established. For example, a counselor might feel sorry for a client and identify with his wish for more freedom. She might help him secretly go off the unit for the day while supposedly working in the laundry because she feels the limits imposed on the particular client are unjust or inappropriate.

10. ***Contracts can be changed if they prove unworkable.*** Sometimes the hopeful plans of enthusiastic clinicians and clients far exceed the time and resources actually available, and they must be revised. Realistic revisions are preferable to pressuring clients to do things that changing circumstances or resources prevent them from doing. Under pressure, clients may feel disappointed in themselves and fear disappointing the clinician too. Compromises or postponements—and sometimes accepting that the planned work is finished-may be necessary to "be where the client is."

> Wrenn and I worked hard together to find public funds to pay for her junior college education so that she could realize her dream of becoming a paralegal. Then, unexpectedly, she got pregnant again "by accident" and was unable to go on with her education. She put off telling me because she expected me to be mad after all that work. I wasn't mad, but in my heart I couldn't help wishing she could have followed her dream. I said that maybe

she could just take an evening course. She smiled sadly and said that, with work and child care for her toddler, those paralegal days were pretty much over. She wanted to continue seeing me to discuss whether she might find a way to set up a child care center in her home, and I agreed.

Holding clients to contracts is one of the hardest things for beginning clinicians to do because they are highly motivated to help others and may feel reluctant to say "no" or apply limits. Many have reported in supervision that they fear losing the client if they do not bend the rules or look the other way. Other clinicians fear the anger of clients when they remain firm in the face of challenges to agreements made in the client's best interest.

We, too, need to be held to our part of the contract. Arriving late, canceling appointments, forgetting tasks between meetings, and not providing agreed-upon resources or services are violations of the contract that should be addressed. Clients may have a difficult time in confronting us about our failures to meet our part of the contract.

Regular review of the contract allows both clinicians and clients to comment on adherence or missteps. Compton, Galaway, and Cournoyer (2005) refer to such reviews as "fidelity checking" to see whether planned steps of change are actually taking place and, if so, to what extent. Fidelity checks can help us keep our commitments to clients and confront them when they, too, have trouble following through with agreed-upon tasks and steps.

EXERCISE 8.1   Contracting

In class, role-play the scenarios in Exercise 7.3 (Freydia, Thomas, and Rad). Negotiate written contracts that follow the principles outlined in this chapter. Decide who should be involved in your contract and make sure that it is specific, mutually constructed, flexible, and realistic. Include a section on informed consent. Think of any circumstances that might require you to adjust or adapt the contract. Role-play the renegotiation.

DVD

CLIP 8.1
Establishing a
Contract

■ Evaluation

Many people confuse the terms "evaluation" and "assessment." We assess clients and their situations. Then we plan our work together. Finally, we evaluate that work to determine its effectiveness. As we noted in Chapter 1, **evaluation** is an ongoing part of all clinical work. We should examine our work session by session to determine the effectiveness of the specific focus, techniques, or uses of self. Progress and process notes, weekly assessment measures and scales, audiocassettes, and videotapes are all helpful in this process. We review our work on a regular basis with supervisors or with outside consultants who have particular areas of expertise. In addition, agencies or insurers often require monthly progress reports or quarterly summaries for management to oversee the extent, nature, and quality of care. In some settings, these evaluation reports are required even more frequently. Computer programs and tools for tracking information and progress are facilitating the evaluation process. At the same time, there is concern that the increasing mechanization of the process may negatively affect the clinical relationship.

Finally, there is a process of evaluation at the end of the working relationship. Clinician and client may use formal outcome measures or simply review the relationship, the work, and what has been accomplished. As managed care and quality assurance become more prevalent, clinicians are more frequently asked to demonstrate the effectiveness of their interventions.

Common Elements in Evaluation

Measurement of progress and effectiveness takes differing forms, but instruments or procedures usually have some common elements.

- *There is an assessment of baseline functioning,* enumerating strengths as well as patterns or problems targeted for change. On this functional baseline, change goals are developed, contracts made, and hoped-for outcomes evaluated.
- *Some form of progress measurement is used consistently.* This can include informal discussion of the work and its effects, the periodic readministration of original assessment measures, or the use of other evaluative measures, such as a symptom checklist like the Beck Depression Inventory that tracks specific behaviors or feeling states over time.
- *The measurement of progress often occurs at specified intervals and certainly at the end of the contracted work together.*
- *In addition, there can be periodic follow-up evaluations* to see whether gains or changes have been maintained or further services are needed.

Principles of Evaluation

The questions to ask in assessment before intervention are very similar to the questions in evaluation after intervention. These include the who, what, when, where, and how issues that can complicate the evaluation of progress, the outcomes, and the postintervention maintenance of well-being.

- *Evaluation is influenced by who does the evaluating.* A risk in evaluation is that clinicians, for motives of self-preservation, may be biased toward finding positive changes and outcomes. Clients can also be inaccurate reporters because they have invested time, energy, and money in the work and quite understandably want to believe that they and their situations have changed for the better. They may also wish to please or reward their clinicians by putting a positive spin on developments and by suppressing questions or doubts. Outside observer-evaluators, including family members, may also be differently motivated to see positive or negative results, depending on the effects of outcomes on them. For all of these reasons, it seems most efficacious to use multiple reporters in the evaluation process.

- *Evaluation should focus not only on problems but also on the strengths of clients and their related systems.* Naturally, evaluations focus on changes in the frequency and duration of the problems targeted for intervention. Just as in assessment, evaluation must also focus on the frequency with which previously identified strengths and resources are used and new strengths and resources are developed.

- *Evaluation should utilize a number of evaluation methods.* Clinicians often utilize standardized tests and self-reports, such as logs and journals, to help clients monitor the effectiveness of their work together. Sometimes direct observation is possible. For example, if a teacher wants a child to be less aggressive with other students or to engage with more people in interactions, an objective observer can actually record the change in behavior frequency before, during, and after an intervention aimed at behavior change.

- *Whenever possible, evaluation should occur in real-life settings.* Clients can make changes that are observable in the clinical setting but not necessarily generalize or translate them to broader areas in their lives. For example, a client may learn to be more assertive in the office or even in the classroom, but not in the playground or at home. The clinician who evaluates the work solely by looking at assertive behavior in the classroom might consider the intervention successful, whereas the clinician who looks at behavior in many settings may report a mixed picture, pointing the way toward specific further work.

- *A follow-up evaluation should be conducted.* Follow-up evaluation can occur one month, two months, or even years after the intervention. Follow-up enables the clinician and client to reevaluate the long-term effectiveness of the work. At times, follow-up evaluations can serve as "booster shots" to the original work, helping clients remember and continue to build on the positive outcomes of their work.

EXERCISE 8.2 Evaluation

Using the cases from Exercise 7.3 (Freydia, Thomas, and Rad), describe the methods you would use to evaluate the effectiveness of your work together. Address the who, what, when, where, and how of evaluation.

■ Conclusion

Planning for and evaluating change is an important part of all clinical work. In preparing and planning for change, we work with clients to construct clear and realistic contracts and to measure progress and outcomes using a variety of reporters and procedures. In designing interventions, we rely on knowledge and theoretical orientation; experience with the clients; assessment of the client's motivation, capacity, and resources; and a sense of the time and professional resources available. We also utilize the professional literature and the findings from clinical efficacy studies that examine and compare various intervention outcomes for specific problems and populations.

Regardless of theoretical orientation or the specific intervention strategies planned, clinicians use a number of the same skills in working with clients. In subsequentchapters, we discuss many of the specific skills and relational processes that clinicians use to help clients think, feel and behave differently—and to achieve their goals.

■ Suggested Readings

Akamatsu, Norma N. (1998). The talking oppression blues: Including the experience of power/powerlessness in the teaching of "cultural sensitivity." In Monica McGoldrick, (Ed.), *Re-visioning family therapy: Race, culture, and gender in clinical practice* (pp. 129–143). New York: Guilford.

Amodeo, Maryann, & Jones, L. Kay. (1998). Using the AOD cultural framework to view alcohol and drug issues through various cultural lenses. *Journal of Social Work Education, 34,* 387–399.

Collin, Kathryn S., Valentine, Deborah, and Welkley, Debra L. (2005). People living with disabilities. In Krishna Guadalupe & Doman Lum (Eds.), *Multidimensional contextual practice: Diversity and transcendence* (pp. 250–269). Belmont, CA: Brooks/Cole.

Cournoyer, Barry R. (2004). *The evidence-based social work skills book.* Boston: Allyn & Bacon.

Miller, William R. and Rollnick, Stephen. (2002). *Motivational interviewing: Preparing people for change* (2nd Ed.). New York: Guilford.

Van Den Bergh, Nan, & Crisp, Catherine. (2004). Defining culturally competent practice with sexual minorities: Implications for social work education and practice. *Journal of Social Work Education, 40,* (2), 221–238.

■ Self-Explorations

1. Develop a decisional balance sheet for a problem you are struggling with. Be sure to be clear about the pros and cons of each side of the dilemma.

2. Recall a time when you decided to make a change and took steps toward it, but then felt sorry that you did. Once you regretted it, what, if anything, did you do then?

3. Have you ever found yourself urging or leaning on friends or family members to change when they were not ready, willing, or able to do so? What were the sources of your zeal? Looking back, what would you do differently now?

■ Essay Questions

1. List some obvious benefits of evaluating outcomes. Discuss three or four cautions when setting out to evaluate outcomes.
2. What are some of the benefits and limitations of evidence-based practice?
3. Some clinicians use assessment tools (such as the BDI or the Symptom Checklist) in the interview to measure progress or outcomes. Discuss the positive and negative effects that their use might have on the interview process or on the relationship.
4. Discuss the criteria for a good evaluation report.

■ Key Terms

Contracts

Corrupt contracts

Decisional balance sheet

Eclectic

Empirically supported therapy

Evaluation

Evidence-based practice

Formal contracts

Hidden agendas

Motivational interviewing

Sabotage

Spontaneous remission

Treatment by objectives

Treatment manual

Treatment plan

CHAPTER 9

Gaining New Perspectives: Helping Clients Feel and See Things Differently

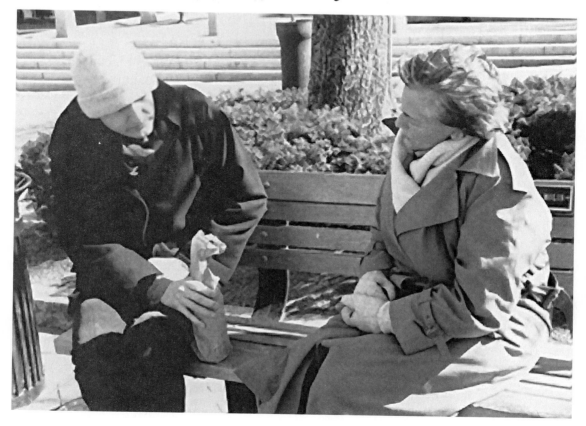

In spite of using a variety of guiding theoretical and practice models, clinicians often draw from a fund of basic counseling skills in implementing interventions with clients. In this chapter, we elaborate on skills commonly used to help clients feel better and develop new perspectives. Developing new perspectives often alters feeling states, and working with feelings often alters perspectives. Distressing thoughts and feelings are often so intertwined that they play off of and feed into each other in powerful ways. Jean Baker Miller and Irene Stiver of the Stone Center use the term **"feeling-thinking"** to describe these interlocking and mutually interacting bundles, believing that "all thoughts are accompanied by emotions and all emotions have a thought content (1997, p. 212).

■ Working with Feelings

Clients often come to see clinicians because of feelings of sadness, anxiety, anger, and hopelessness, or because they are overwhelmed by unusually strong feelings:

"I can't seem to handle my anger."
"I feel so sad all the time."
"I am so easily frightened."

Some clients directly express feelings related to important events, relationships, and conditions in their lives. Others describe emotional distress signaling them that something is wrong, yet when asked for clarification, they cannot be more specific about the feeling or about feelings they lump together as "distress."

"I don't know what's wrong I just don't feel right."

Some come in and recount painful stories without any accompanying feelings, as though numb. Others come in with feelings known to them but wait until some trust is established before sharing them even superficially. Still others come in describing distressing patterns and themes, unaware that unresolved feelings from past events could be affecting current thinking, feeling, and behaviors.

> *Evan came to the counseling center for help because he felt stuck. Evan described himself as cranky a lot of the time and always getting involved with "women who criticize me for the least little thing." He was a talented artist, but drifted from job to job: "I can't seem to settle in and succeed at anything."*
>
> *As we talked about his life, Evan told me that fifteen years ago, after he had just received his driver's license, he was in a terrible accident. An SUV driven by an intoxicated man suddenly crossed into his lane. Evan swerved sharply to avoid a head-on crash, but in doing so, crashed into a nearby traffic signpost. His best friend was thrown through the windshield and died instantly.*
>
> *He was aware that something was wrong, but he wasn't yet aware that feelings of guilt and the distorted idea that he didn't deserve happiness because of the accident might be contributing to his current difficulties.*

Direct Exploration of Feelings

Familiar open-ended questions help in eliciting client feelings. Questions such as "What are you feeling as I explain this?" and "What did you feel when that happened?" help clients focus on their reactions. Questions that probe for a little more detail might include "Did you have other feelings besides shock when Baptiste hit your daughter?" "Who are you most comfortable sharing those feelings with?" If feelings have been openly shared, we might then ask: "Shall we stay with your feelings a bit longer, or get back to what you were saying?" Encouragement to continue can be provided through minimal empathic sounds and prompts "Yes . . . " or "Good . . . " or "Just let the feelings come" or "Try not to fight your natural feelings."

It is important not to judge or criticize the expression of feelings. Clients often stop and ask, "Is this okay for me to say?" or "Are you sure you don't mind my saying how mad I am at the director of this place?" Sometimes during moments of tearfulness they may look down or away. The clinician can universalize about the hesitation that so many people feel when sharing their feelings more deeply with a relative stranger and then appreciate aloud the client's willingness to take this risk. Validating and normalizing human feelings can help relieve the embarrassment or concerns about being strange or odd that people can experience when describing their emotions or feeling patterns.

Sometimes when clients have shared a lot in one session, we check in with them in the next visit about how it was for them to share those feelings. We attempt to avoid overwhelming clients with too much feeling exploration.

Clients often experience relief through the expression of feelings as long as such expression or ventilation is modulated and under control. As discussed in Chapter 11, research on trauma and crisis interventions over the past fifteen years has revealed that, when clients are shocked and overwhelmed in the immediate aftermath of disaster and trauma, intense exploration of their feelings can further destabilize them (Herman, 1997 Knight, 2006; van der Kolk & van der Hart, 1991). But even if the client is not in crisis, we need to think carefully about the potential negative effects of feeling exploration in terms of timing and dosage.

> *I was working with a woman whose mother was dying of cancer. She would talk a lot about how much time it took to take care of her mother and the day-to-day logistics of taking her to the hospital for treatment, arranging visiting nurses, feeding and bathing her mother, going on drugstore runs for supplies, etc. When I asked her about how she felt, her response was, "I don't have time to feel." I wondered if, in fact, that was true—perhaps she was afraid that her feelings of sadness, resentment, pain, and loss would overwhelm her and interfere with her ability to do all that she needed to do to take care of her mother.*

As always, the clinician should be aware of the culture of the client and how it might influence feeling expression. Sue and Sue (1999) describe a situation in which an Asian male client was speaking with a male counselor. It is a long quote but we think it is an excellent example:

White Male Therapist: I sense it's difficult to talk about personal things. How are you feeling right now?

Asian American Client: Oh, all right.

White Male Therapist: That's not a feeling. Sit back and get in touch with your feelings. [Pause] Now tell me how you feel right now?

Asian American Client: Somewhat nervous.

White Therapist: When you talked about your parents and your friends not understanding and the way you said it made me think you feel ashamed and disgraced at having to come. Was that what you felt?

While this exchange appears to indicate that the therapist (a) was able to see the client's discomfort and (b) interpret his feelings correctly, it also points out the therapist's lack of understanding of Asian cultural values. While we do not want to be guilty of stereotyping Asian Americans, many do have difficulty at times expressing feelings publicly to a stranger. The therapist's persistent attempts to focus on feelings and his direct and blunt interpretation of them may indicate to the Asian American client that the therapist lacks the more subtle skills of dealing with a sensitive topic and/or is shaming the client . . . . In many traditional Asian groups, subtlety is a highly prized art and the traditional Asian client may feel much more comfortable when dealing with feelings in an indirect manner (Sue & Sue, 1999, p. 45).

Indirect Exploration of Feelings

Sometimes clients who are not used to expressing feelings directly respond spontaneously when presented stories illustrating situations like their own, in which someone else is having feelings. These situations often facilitate an emotional identification by the client with someone in the story, stimulating a spontaneous sharing of the client's own feelings as he or she relates to personally relevant elements of the story. The following is an example of indirect exploration:

> *When I was a volunteer at the rape crisis center I saw a woman, Darlia. Although she came to the center, she didn't want to talk about being raped. We have a number of books in our library that describe how people coped with being raped and one day I noticed she was reading Maya Angelou's* I Know Why the Caged Bird Sings. *In the book, Angelou gives an account of her own rape and how she was mute for a year or more following the assault. Darlia started to cry as she was reading and when I stopped by her chair, she told me how much it saddened her to think that a woman as strong and outspoken as Angelou had felt silenced and embarrassed about being raped. It led us to a great discussion about how other women might feel about being assaulted.*

Discrimination of One Feeling From Another

People sometimes cry when they are mad and respond irritably when sad. They may be awash with feelings that they lack words to describe. Clients need to learn to recognize and describe their distinct feelings. For many, this feeling clarity is a revitalizing first step in authentic self-acknowledgment and self-assertion. Clinicians and clients can review together the range of feelings and expressive styles manifested in literature, music, and life. Then we move from the general to the particular, asking clients to monitor themselves for authentic reactions to people and events in their lives, becoming more familiar with exactly what they feel, when, and with whom. This feeling discrimination not only helps clients realize and appreciate the richness of their own feeling life, it also helps them become more aware of which particular people, events, and situations trigger specific feelings and which do not.

If culturally appropriate, we can provide journal exercises as homework in which clients monitor, name, and comment on their daily feelings and then bring their findings and observations in for discussion with the clinician. Sometimes clients see movies or hear songs that inspire feeling reflections in them, and these are fertile sources for client work on recognizing, naming, and beginning to express and enjoy feelings. Some clients may write poetry to express their feelings and share it with their clinicians. The important goal is for clients to recognize and honor their real feelings, whether deciding to express them or not.

While we want to help clients discriminate among their feelings, it is important that we do not tell them what they are feeling. If we mistakenly attempt to speak for or second-guess them, they might respond by saying, "I am mad, so please don't try to tell me that what I'm 'really' feeling is sad."

Managing and Containing Feeling

In contrast to people who believe in keeping feelings private, some people express their feelings excessively or impulsively without much regard for context or their impact on others. They may storm out of a meeting when they disagree with their employer or burst into tears at the slightest frustration. They may become demanding of attention when feeling needy or repeatedly yell in a frightening way at their children when overtired. Others may feel overwhelmed by feelings of sadness, anger, or anxiety.

Clinicians can use a number of techniques to help clients manage or contain feelings.

- *Identifying emotional triggers.*   **Triggers** are the people, circumstances, ideas, and events that stimulate emotional reactions. AA and other recovery programs teach clients how to become aware of triggering situations and remain calm and intentional instead of escalating. Clinicians can do the same by asking clients to list the people and situations that most upset them or get them going in a worrisome way. We can discuss ways to avoid or minimize time in triggering situations, as well as helping clients learn strategies for staying calm when in such situations. Clients learn that they can have both clear and strong feelings without letting them rise to their boiling points—the points at which they lose control.
- *Using scaling questions.*   DeJong and Miller (1995) recommend teaching clients how to use **scaling questions** to estimate the extent of their emotional arousal on a scale of 1 to 10. Using 0 to describe having no feelings about a situation and 10 to represent total escalation, clients learn to recognize the degree of feeling stimulated by each situation. If the baseline rating with a certain triggering person is a 9, then a goal is to begin to lower reactivity by a point or two, using strategies such as calming procedures, walking away, or changing the subject. Scaling talk is easily learned and actually enjoyed in its use, because it keeps the client aware, situation to situation, of both progress and slips backward. Both kinds of behavior provide important subjects for discussion. Moreover, when we are not

present, clients can still evaluate their feelings: "Boy, that was a 3 with my landlady—down 2 points, and about a 7.5 with my 'ex'—worse than I expected." These informal reports help reinforce the strategies that *are* working to contain and soothe.

- *Developing a personal "stop" strategy.* Often clients who rapidly escalate need other people to restrain or help calm them down, which is difficult for everyone involved. An early activity with these clients is to help them recognize when they are starting to escalate emotionally and to teach them how to interrupt the escalation with a *"Stop!"* command they say to themselves. Some prefer to picture immediately a brightly colored stop sign. Others learn to picture the word "Stop!" in their minds. The goal is to find a short command and use it the moment they feel themselves getting into their "red zone"—that is, reaching their personal boiling point.

- *Walking away.* Two important skills in containing and deescalating are learning to detour around or walking away from triggering people and situations if feelings continue to escalate. Rehearsal of detouring and walking away helps prepare clients before the inevitable upsetting situations arise.

- *Changing the channel.* Distraction strategies help people switch their minds from painful thoughts and feelings to more calm and pleasing ones. When distressed, clients are encouraged to do something they like that leaves them feeling both calmed, and proud, and able to think of themselves as being more than a set of problems. Baths, reading, listening to music, calling a friend to book time together, playing with a pet, shopping in a favorite store—all such activities have the potential to soothe and affirm. "Turning the page" and "changing the channel" are other names for actions taken to switch quickly from emotional escalation to activities that affirm self-worth.

- *Self-calming strategies.* A number of strategies can be useful to help clients control and contain strong feelings. Many self-calming strategies come from Buddhist mindfulness practices. Many clients are already familiar with and use positive self-calming strategies. They might exercise to work off steam, attend support groups that reinforce self-containment, pray or chant, listen to quieting music, or watch a TV program that makes them laugh. Clients can learn relaxation techniques, self-talk, or self-coaching ("You'll get through this, you always do, so calm down" and "Cool your jets!"). Dialectical Behavioral Therapy programs (Heard & Linehan, 1994) are noted for their self-calming, self-rewarding, self-distracting, and self-assertion strategies, formats, and measured steps toward efficacy. Wellness or **mind/body programs** at many health centers emphasize the connections between physical, spiritual, and emotional states; clients can attend such programs to learn relaxation and meditation practice.

- *Medication.* In some instances, medication may be useful to help people cope with overwhelming feelings. People with mood problems should be evaluated medically for possible use of medication in addition to counseling. Numerous well controlled comparison studies since the 1980s have demonstrated that a combination of medication and counseling focused on enhancing self-efficacy and coping resources is highly effective in reducing depressive and other mood symptoms (Feldman & Feldman, 1997). The clinician has to stay in close contact with the medical staff overseeing the use of medications, so that all helpers are aware of developments and reactions and are aware of potential side effects.

EXERCISE 9.1   Handling Strong Feelings

What do you do to handle strong feelings when you are upset? In groups of three or four, share the various methods you use. Did you learn any new methods from your colleagues?

People sometimes use alcohol and other substances to contain feelings or blunt affect. Substance use and abuse can be an important hidden contributor to the inability of some clients to rein in or modulate moods. Initial and continuing assessment should include direct inquiry about the frequency and amount of drinking and other drug use. Clients may be reluctant to disclose substance use because of dependence, denial, embarrassment, or a wish to continue to use substances in spite of their negative effects on functioning. We recommend that you take advanced coursework in substance abuse assessment and treatment because of the number of people whose lives are affected by substance-related problems.

Clinician Reactions to Client Feelings

As fellow human beings empathizing with clients, we are often deeply moved by their lives and stories. Feelings of pleasure, sadness, worry, disappointment, tenderness, irritation, and fear are not at all unusual as we work with the strengths, problems, and prospects of many people.

> *When a legally blind 9-year-old began to cry about her differentness from other kids, and I had seen how delightful and creative she was in the playroom, I felt tears well up and come down my cheeks.*

> *I felt so much happiness when Kiki got her dream job that the two of us, walking down the school corridor, stopped and jumped up and down with shared joy and excitement for her.*

> *Suleima's story stayed with me for days. She had crossed the desert with her kids and made it to safety. All of that courage and achievement, and here she is now, abused regularly by her American boyfriend. What a hand Fate deals some people.*

Students sometimes worry that being professional and intentional means that these human reactions are now inappropriate. In our experience, these natural reactions are important signals to clients of our humanity and of our ability to join closely with their experiences and feelings. Indeed, Jean Baker

Miller and Irene Stiver (1997) assert that one of the most powerful growth-inducing moments in clinical work is when a client sees that he or she is actually able to affect or move the clinician. Our feelings also make rich topics for supervision and consultation because, while having them is normal, being selective about how, when, and with whom to express them involves a combination of knowledge, timing, relational sensitivity, and caution.

Also, how we register and express our reactions may not be compatible with the client's normative ways, either because of individual variance or cultural norms.

> *Counselor:* Youn, you are not expressing anything about the death of your Grandmother, and I know she has been a huge support for you.
>
> *Youn:* When it is a person's "time," we are respectful of that and of a good life lived. Also, I am relieved to see her out of pain. I believe she may return, and that we will see each other again. I miss her, but I feel at peace, too. I light sticks for her each night to show my love and reverence.

Cautions When Working With Feelings

Working with feelings is an educational objective that many students anticipate eagerly. This work turns out to be some of the most complex work we do, and it can both free people up, when done skillfully, and set them back when we blunder. The following guidelines may provide guidance as you develop and try to apply your new knowledge:

- Do not explore for too much, too soon.
- Notice whether the client's story flowers and deepens or tightens up and suddenly refocuses after intense feeling expression.
- Be ready to provide support and empathy when clients are upset.
- Acknowledge small growth steps in identifying and expressing feelings.
- Note your own reactions to client feelings and reflect on their various sources.
- Discuss in supervision any lingering discomforts you feel in reaction to client feelings.

■ Gaining New Perspectives

When people come for counseling help, they often feel stuck. They may experience or view things in fixed or seemingly immutable ways and feel distressed or hopeless, seeing few options to their situation or perspective.

> *As a boy from a poor part of a large city, Shane thought he had only two options open to him if he was going to "get somewhere": be an athlete or join the army. The idea of completing high school and college was really foreign to him, since no one he was close to ever had done those things. His nickname for me was "Big Dreamer."*

Others may hold tenaciously to a view that feels right to them, and their limited ability to see alternatives may be problematic in helping them approach the future differently.

Angie came from three generations of women who married alcoholic men who beat them when drunk. The women had all stayed in their marriages, believing that "marriage is for life." All of their children had needed counseling for depression or substance abuse, and, when I talked with Angie in detox, she was getting ready to return home to Dougie, an active alcoholic. She hoped that her own sobriety would act as an example for Dougie and that by sticking by him she would influence him to go with her to AA. She said: "I've got to think of Dougie; I can't just think of myself."

One of our major clinical tasks is to help clients develop new perspectives or envision other potentials that may maximize strengths or effect change. **Perspective** refers to viewpoint: the position you take as you envision self, others, and the world. If you change where you stand, things can look quite different. For example, a tree looks very different to you when you are flying over it than it does when you are lying beneath it. Similarly, an alcoholic home can look different to its members than it does to an outside observer, who may focus chiefly on symptoms rather than on the connections between people or on time-honored intergenerational, cultural, or gender norms. In both instances, stance affects perspective and vision.

We frequently work with clients to assist in the development of new dimensions to their understanding—other possibilities that may not have been presented to them, that they may not have previously considered, or that they may have been afraid of entertaining. When clients can safely begin to see things from new perspectives, they often begin to feel or act differently; they may even feel and act for the first time in many years. Having a multiplicity of perspectives gives clients options from which they may choose those that they find to be most useful to them. Some need help to change to more positive and hopeful perspectives regarding themselves, their prospects, and potentials. Others need help facing harsh realities and discovering resources of which they were previously unaware. Our simple encouragement of them to explore, express, examine, challenge, and try out a range of ideas and feelings can itself be novel and inspiring.

Accentuate the Positive

People seeking help often describe themselves as "a loser," "sick," or "hopeless" in reaction to ideas they have taken in from others regarding self or situation. These views may be expressed directly, or they may lurk beneath an exterior of bravado or mock acceptance.

I ran a group for young adults with schizophrenia, and one night I asked them what music best represented the way they felt about themselves. One young man said that the Beatles' song "Nowhere Man" was the song that he identified with. Another responded sadly, "Fool on the Hill."

Highlight Client Efficacy

While recognizing and appreciating a client's perspective, we have to maintain a positive outlook and convey it actively to the client. We *do not* mean ignoring or minimizing the client's very real pain by making simplistic statements like, "Let's look on the brighter side." Rather, we mean that, after empathizing with the client's experience of "being nowhere," we try, when the moment is right, to elicit or highlight instances of efficacy or agency, with special attention to the abilities that the client may not recognize or may trivialize as irrelevant.

DeJong and Miller (1995) recommend the use of exception questions and coping questions to focus on client strengths. **Exception questions** ask about situations or days in which "the problems" have not happened: who or what things helped or were different at that moment, that improved the situation When can those very people and things be brought together again in order to experience positive differences again? What has been learned in those exceptional moments that might be transferred to similar moments and challenges?

Coping questions focus clients on how they have gotten where they are today, given the chronic adversity of their circumstances: "How have you managed [or survived], given all that you're up against?" The client usually notes something that keeps them going when they think all is finished: kids, prayer, a cousin who counts on them. We can then explore these activities or relationships to emphasize their power in the client's life.

Teach Transferability of Skills

We believe in teaching **transferability of skills** in a way that builds a sense of competence and hope. We suggest that what works in situation A could well work in situations B and C.

> *Zarita was down on herself for "being out of control" at home with anxious obsessions that drove her husband crazy. We explored her work as a clerk-magistrate at the court, where she had been through every imaginable thing with unflappable cool: bomb scares, threats to her life from convicted felons, unexpected fights erupting in court, and so on. My anxiety went sky high as I heard her examples from court, and I shared this with her. She explained that her family had always put huge importance on dignity and self-control in public. At home, though, both parents yelled at each other and at the kids, would slam doors, cry—"the works." I said I could appreciate more where these two sides of her came from: the "cool and collected one" in court and the "out of control one" at home. She had never appreciated how in control of her reactions she was at work and was very pleased to see it. "But how," she asked, "can I bring the collected one home?" We went on to identify the skills she used in court to calm herself ("count to 10" or "take deep breaths") and then visualized an upsetting scene at home in which she could practice using the same skills.*

Construct Positive Future Visions

We also accentuate the positive when we help clients construct positive visions of their future lives and selves. Steve de Shazer notes that we can use language to construct a positive reality for clients. "Sentences are constructed in such a way as to create an alternative future. For example, 'When the problem is solved, what will you be doing differently?' . . . instead of 'if' [it is solved] . . . " (cited in Koob, 2003, p. 135).

Steve de Shazer and Insoo Kim Berg, the founders of Solution Focused Brief Therapy (SFBT), have developed the **miracle question** to help clients gain new perspectives on their problems and focus on the positive desired goal rather than just on what is "wrong." De Shazer suggests the clinician say the following:

> I have a strange, perhaps unusual question, a question that takes some imagination. Suppose . . . after we finish here, you go home tonight, watch TV, do your usual chores, etc., and then go to bed and to sleep . . . And, while you are sleeping, a miracle happens . . . And the problems that brought you here are solved, just like that! . . . But, this happens while you are sleeping, so you cannot know that it has happened . . . What will be different that will indicate that the problem is resolved . . . How will your best friend discover that this miracle has happened to you? (1988, p. 5).

Conceptualizing how the subsequently changed reactions of others might affect the client in turn is helpful. De Shazer notes: "When the client imagines feeling better in a wide range of situations involving various other people, then he or she can make the switch from 'I am able to imagine I feel better' to 'I am able to imagine that I am better'" (de Shazer, n.d.).

Act as a Positive Mirror

We seek out and reflect an alternative view of the client—a technique we refer to as acting as a positive mirror. We reflect and credit small achievements the client may have overlooked or undervalued, emphasizing positive connections that clients may already have in their lives.

Beginning clinicians can be tempted to give false reassurance to assuage the client's pain ("Everything will be fine" or "I'm sure that if we work on this, we can make things better for you"). They may not readily understand why this type of reassurance is false because they are urged to maintain and share an optimistic viewpoint with clients. By false reassurance, we simply mean that, given the complexities of everyday life and the changing nature of people and situations, we cannot predict either the future or the utility of imagined interventions.

Use Appropriately Timed Hopefulness

Rosy expectations may be unbelievable to despairing clients. Such expectations may be incorrect or inappropriate for the moment or situation at hand, especially with clients from families or neighborhoods where poverty, violence, and a lack of opportunity and support appear unremitting. What is required instead is the complex skill of communicating appropriately timed hopefulness while maintaining a balancing empathy for the pain, injustice, or stuckness of the moment. We usually empathize in the moment and then later quietly shift to some potential in the person or situation.

> *Stevie was a 20-year-old mother of two girls who had just been denied custody of them because she had hit them while she was drunk. She said she now had a record of child abuse that would likely be checked every time she went for child care jobs, and child care was the thing she always thought she could do best for a living. I asked how it was for her to think that what she'd loved best might be out of her reach in some instances now. I said it sounded like she'd felt alone and down for so long that it must seem futile to hope for anything. She blew off some more anger and then started to cry and said, "I might as well just give up." I said I could see why she would feel that way and that it was an awful feeling to want her girls and her work back, and yet to want to give up sometimes. She nodded.*

Build on Here-and-Now Connections

To be effective, clinicians have to build on here-and-now connections and achievements to help clients develop realistic hopes for a more positive future. This future image may not be totally or even primarily positive, but it is important that clients identify **islands of possibility** that serve to fuel hope for the work. Stevie's story continues:

> *After things had subsided a bit, I reminded Stevie that she had told me earlier of wanting to complete her night school diploma and try for LPN training. This seemed to me within reach while the kids were still in foster care, and I said so. I then said that I had seen other folks like herself get some support and ideas from talking with me like we've done today. I told her that I would love to see her try it, to see if it added anything to help her think through the times she feels so lost and alone. It might not, but on the other hand, what if it did? Stevie said she would consider it, but the main thing she wanted today was to find out if she could visit her two girls in foster care on their birthdays. I asked how she wanted to go about finding out. First she asked if I would call ("Who wants to talk to a con?"). Then she laughed and said, reaching for the phone, "If I can call my sister a million times a day to ask if she's seen my boyfriend, I can work the phone to ask about my kids. If I can't use the phone, how am I ever going to get an LPN job?"*

Creating Alternative Perspectives

Sometimes clients have been exposed to only one way of thinking about things, and their thinking reflects that one way and little else. They may be aware of alternative views but are manifesting loyalty to family, cultural, or religious precepts by adhering inflexibly to a perspective, even though it is not proving useful to them in attempting to resolve tensions or problems at hand. At other times, if clients have been dominated or silenced, they may simply hold on to a perspective to enjoy a rare opportunity to affirm their own way of thinking. Moreover, some clients feel threatened by alternative perspectives that may feel unfamiliar or risky.

At times, we introduce alternative perspectives to broaden clients' sense of possibilities, to heighten and encourage a spirit of curiosity and exploration, or to counter the automatic thinking that we all tend to do under stress. Clients may have a variety of reactions to the introduction of novel explanations or ways of thinking about people and situations. Although some welcome new points of view and feel stimulated by them, not everyone is delighted to explore ideas different from their own.

> *Takis and I had met a few times to talk about his experience in hospice. In about our fourth meeting, I asked him if he had any faith or any belief in anything beyond himself that he could call on to help him through this time. He looked at me with a good deal of sarcasm and said he hoped I was not going to introduce "some kind of spiritual crap" into his quiet little corner here. He said he was raised strictly in the church but had been an atheist for a long time.*

> *Polly Mae had been talking about what a loser her mother was. She was an alcoholic who had spent most of Polly's life in and out of the hospital. Polly hated having such a poor role model and disidentified with her mother. At one point, I noted that at times her mother really seemed to have a way with people. Polly at first said this made her afraid I would be on her mother's side and would be taken in by her like everyone else. After a minute or two, she said, "You know, she was good at 'working' people. I think I have a little of her skill, but I hope I put it to better use."*

There are many ways to introduce or stimulate new perspectives. Some are things that the clinician and client can do together during the session. Others are suggestions for things that the client can do between meetings.

Questioning and Brainstorming to Elicit New Perspectives

Clinicians can help clients elucidate new perspectives simply by asking questions such as:

"How else could we see that?"
"Can you think of any other ways to explain this?"
"What other kinds of things could be going on?"

Sometimes a simple technique of listing alternative explanations or possibilities is useful. The clinician and client can **brainstorm** together, making a list of numerous alternative explanations, sometimes recording them on a flow-chart. No idea is evaluated or judged; each is simply put on the table or chart. Then the clinician and client can review the list to see if any of them are useful.

Using Role-Plays to Expand Perspective

Role-plays are a useful technique with many applications. In Chapter 5, we discussed using role plays to help the clinician gain empathy for the client. In the next chapter, we discuss using role-play techniques to help clients do things differently. Role-plays can also be used in a number of ways to help clients gain new perspectives.

- *Play out the other side.* The clinician may take a position that plays out the other side of an issue, struggle, or ambivalence: "Ayman, you said that you'll never find another job now that you are in a wheelchair, but there are lots of jobs I could imagine for you." When the clinician plays the other side, the risk is that the client gets into a "stuck opposer" role, rejecting any alternative the clinician presents. On the other hand, clinicians must be aware that some clients quickly defer to what they perceive to be the superior knowledge of the clinician. One way to avoid such dilemmas is to reverse things and have the client play the other side: "Ayman, I know that right now it seems impossible for you to think of being able to get another job. If you could take the other side for a moment—pretend you are an optimistic champion of people with disabilities—what kinds of things might you say to a guy who thinks he'll never get another job because he's in a wheelchair?"

- *Take the role of the other.*   When talking about a relationship, people are often so wed to their own point of view that they have a hard time appreciating another's perspective. Role-playing the other can help clients broaden their views of a relationship and offer new insights about another person. We might give the following instruction: "Jeremy, we've been talking a lot about your take on your relationship with your brother Hugh. Let's try having you play Hugh for a moment so you can get some insight into how he might see things. Sit in the chair over there. When you do, you become Hugh." (Client moves to other chair.) We can then interview "Hugh," asking such things as "How do you feel as Hugh?" and "Hugh, what do you think about Jeremy?"

- *Play the outside observer.*   Clients sometimes get a better perspective if they feel removed from the situation. The clinician can help clients see things from a different angle by asking them to bystand the situation: "If you were an outsider, viewing this situation from afar, what different ideas might you have about what is going on? Or if you were reading a novel about these people, how would you understand their story? Would you have any observations about the central characters?"

Using Video to Expand Perspective

One useful way of helping clients take the observer role to get new perspectives is by videotaping the process as they interact with family or group members or with the clinician. Client and clinician can watch the video together and discuss new ideas that may emerge or things they might have missed during the interview. Clients can also take home videotapes and review them to see if they gain any new perspectives while literally observing themselves. We ask the client to make notes on personal observations and reactions that can be addressed during the next meeting. These new perspectives may include observations about the clinician and the relationship, as well as about the client or the current focus of their work together.

Contact with Others

Contact with other people can assist clients in redefining themselves and their stories. Clients can be encouraged to open themselves to the novel, often liberating ideas of others by joining self-help groups such as AA,

Parents Anonymous, and Breast Cancer Support. In communities of color, a black church, an Asian neighborhood, a family improvement association, or the tribal council can all provide opportunities for clients to think about their problems and issues in new ways and gain greater perspectives. We often see rapid changes in thinking following group participation. Clients can move from lonely, discouraged isolation to heightened hopefulness and self-acceptance. Hope and self-regard almost invariably lead to thinking more imaginatively and energetically about life situations and possibilities.

Developing New Metaphors

Another way of helping clients create alternative perspectives is to help them in **developing new metaphors.** Richard Kopp (1995) defines metaphors as "mirrors reflecting our inner images of self, life, and others" (p. xiii). He believes that cultures, families, social groups, and individuals structure reality through the use of guiding images (metaphors), and, by helping clients change the negative or powerless metaphors that structure their versions of reality, we can help them move rapidly toward positive change. He gives an example of a woman who was helped through questioning to shift from describing her husband as an out-of-control locomotive and herself as a tunnel to describing herself as a "derailer" of locomotives. Kopp is discussing his theory of "metaphor therapy"; however, we believe that the skill of helping clients develop new metaphors can be used by all clinicians to help clients broaden their perspectives.

> *Marisol said that trying to date in this country was like swimming with sharks. We talked at length about the risks of dating strange men in a big city. She was used to scuba diving in her country, so I compared our meetings to scuba lessons where she could identify the safety equipment she needs and she could enjoy the coral reefs (club scene) while learning to tell the beautiful fish from the predators.*

Culturally responsive clinicians are aware of the rich metaphoric traditions of the clients with whom we work and can use these metaphors in helping clients enlarge their perspectives. Those working with Native American clients, for example, may make use of some of their traditional stories and "sings."

Caution: Just as we need to be certain that our clients understand the meaning of our words, we have to be particularly careful that they understand the meaning of our metaphors.

> *The other day the clinic director called me into his office to discuss a complaint he had received about me from a family I was seeing. I was surprised that the family had complained because I thought we were doing well. The family had told the director that I showed them no respect. They told the director that as far as I was concerned, their son's problems "could just go up in smoke." When I thought about it, I realized that during our last meeting I had suggested that "we put Frankie's problems on the back burner for a while" while we focused on some other issue in the family. "Putting something on the back burner" to them meant "letting it go up in smoke."*

Using Spiritual Practices

DVD

CLIP 9.1
Developing New
Perspectives

Clients sometimes mention spontaneously that they pray, chant, meditate, or envision conversation with a god, goddess, powerful spirit, or universal presence when feeling lost or defeated and needing to reestablish a hopeful perspective. We ask about, honor, or utilize spiritual inquiry and techniques when working with clients for whom spirituality has a central place in resilience and well-being.

Developing Working Hypotheses or Hunches

Clinicians also help clients develop new perspectives by sharing ideas or hunches about content, affect, themes and patterns, or relationship dynamics of which they may be unaware. **Hunches** are informed guesses, or working hypotheses, about the client and his or her situation.

As discussed in Chapter 5, Gerard Egan (1998) coined the term **advanced level accurate empathy** to describe the process of hypothesizing from experience with the client. For Egan, hunches are based on empathy with the client about themes or feelings the client may not yet have verbalized or even understood. Shulman (2006) refers to this process as "tuning in . . . to hear the client's indirect cues" (p. 57). Following the work of Theodor Reik (1948), others have referred to the activity of hypothesizing by means of empathy as "listening with the third ear." Although we like to think of developing working hypotheses and hunches as trying to understand the unspoken, we must remember that, until the client confirms or disconfirms our hunches, we are at risk of misunderstanding or misattributing meaning. Our hunches must always be tentative, awaiting the client's affirmation or denial.

As noted, we often refer to hunches as intuition, and some clinicians talk about "getting this feeling" when they are with someone, experiencing their intuition as a sensory or visceral event. We believe that clinical intuition and hunches are actually derived from a number of sources:

1. *Clinical theory or research.* The clinician may have a hunch that the client who has recently lost a loved one due to death may be having trouble sleeping, based on research demonstrating a correlation between grief and sleeping problems. The clinician who is trained in psychoanalytic theory may have a hunch that a person with a snake phobia may have repressed unconscious conflict with her father, whereas a cognitive-behavioral therapist might posit a conditioned association between a snake and an anxiety state.
2. *Clinical experience in general.* The intern working with the client who has recently lost a loved one might have a hunch, based on accumulated practice wisdom, that the client may react sensitively to the intern's announcement of an upcoming vacation.
3. *Clinical experience with the specific client.* As the clinician gains information and understanding about the client and his or her situation, hunches develop more easily. The guesses are informed by the clinician's

growing knowledge of the client's idiosyncrasies, of the themes and patterns in the client's story, and of information gleaned from the clinical relationship itself.

4. *Knowledge about larger social issues,* including political and socioeconomic conditions that might have an impact on the client. The clinician might consider that health care policies that limit hospital stays for new mothers might increase the anxiety of the pregnant woman who is about to give birth for the first time.

5. *Personal experience and beliefs.* The clinician who is in recovery from alcoholism may be more alert to clues indicating alcoholism than would other clinicians for whom alcoholism is a more distant issue.

6. *Reading between the lines.* The clinician may develop hunches about things that are unspoken but seem implicit in the client's story.

EXAMPLE: WALLY

Wally is a 60-year-old computer programmer who has had four sessions with the EAP counselor of the computer company where he has worked with moderate success for the past twenty years. The company is downsizing and is offering faithful employees like Wally an adequate early retirement package if they leave within a month. If they opt to stay on board, they have to move with the company to one of two distant states, with no clarity about future security. Wally wants to move and even seems excited about it, but he reports that his wife does not want to move. She said that, if he does not want to retire, he should just get another job in the community where they currently live. He states that his two sons are in computer businesses in nearby towns and seem settled here with their families. His youngest son has just had his third child, and his oldest son has two young infants. His wife, Evelyn, is a paralegal who can probably get work anywhere, but she prefers to stay near the boys and the five grandchildren. The EAP counselor has offered to have a meeting with Wally and his wife to talk about the options, but Wally has said he would rather not bring Evelyn.

Some Hunches About Wally

Hunch 1: Wally seems willing to sacrifice family ties for job security.

Hunch 2: The reason Wally is asking to be seen alone is that he may have a secret that he has not shared with his wife or children. Furthermore, he may be coming to see the counselor about the secret under the guise of asking for help about his job situation.

Hunch 3: Wally is depressed and wants to make a change to feel better.

Hunch 4: Wally feels that he has no choice and must move if he wants to continue working.

Hunch 5: Wally is attempting to protect his wife by not including her in the counseling sessions.

Hunch 6: Wally would welcome the opportunity to put distance between the couple and their children and grandchildren.

Discussion

Hunch 1: Based on theory. The clinician is familiar with life-cycle theory, as well as with recent literature on gender differences. She has learned that men in Wally's age cohort frequently use work achievement as a way of obtaining meaning and purpose, whereas women frequently use family and other relational connections as a way of developing a sense of self-worth. The clinician thinks that Wally's concerns about premature retirement are causing him to sacrifice family ties for job security, in direct conflict with Evelyn's wishes to be near family.

Hunch 2: Based on clinical experience. The counselor has worked with many couples over the years and has noticed that a partner asking to meet with the counselor alone often subsequently discloses a secret in the absence of the other partner.

Hunch 3: Based on established client patterns. Wally has reported that in the past he has often used what the clinician thinks of as "geographic cures"—moving far away from a conflict in the vain hope that such a move will resolve everything. When Wally got out of high school, he said he wanted to get away from the small town where he was born and "start fresh." He had previously reported that, when his young son was having difficulty in school, Wally moved the family to another town "to give him a clean slate." Perhaps Wally is looking to move to make a change that he hopes will help him feel better.

Hunch 4: Based on knowledge of social conditions. The clinician has seen many reports that men in their sixties are unlikely to find another good job when they are laid off. She knows that there have been many plant and company closings in the surrounding area. She thinks that Wally may feel that his only chance of staying employed is to move.

Hunch 5: Based on the clinician's personal experience. The clinician comes from a traditional Polish working-class family and has noticed that in her community the men often do not talk about financial or work issues in front of their wives to protect them. She has often heard the phrase, "We don't want to worry the women and children." Knowing that Wally is Polish, she thinks that his desire to meet alone may have to do with traditional Polish working-class values.

Hunch 6: Based on reading between the lines. Wally has occasionally talked about his wife's involvement with the grandchildren. In previous conversations, he has said things like: "She's always over there";

"Now that the babies take so much of her time . . . "; and "When she finally gets home . . . ." The clinician has stored away all of these phrases, thinking they might indicate that Wally is feeling left out or jealous over the amount of time his wife is spending with the children and grandchildren.

EXERCISE 9.2   Hunches

Develop a number of hunches about the clients in the following vignettes. What is the basis of your hunch (theory, experience, knowledge about social conditions, or other factors)?

Leah is a 13-year-old runaway living on the streets with a group of three other teens. They show up at the food kitchen occasionally, where a counselor has talked with Leah about the possibility of coming back into school and maybe into foster care. Leah actually seems interested in school. She tells the counselor: "I might like to finish school. I was good at it, but there's no way I'm living in another family. I've been on my own too long and I don't want to take orders from anybody. Besides, my friends need me. We do okay."

Arturo is a 34-year-old musician making his living playing in a small quartet that performs at functions like weddings and bar mitzvahs. He is seeing an employment counselor about career training: "I don't know, I guess I should get a real job. I'm 34 and it doesn't look like I'll make it as a classical musician. My wife says it's time for me to quit fooling around. I love what I do, but there's no future in it."

Huston, age 49, has just been released from jail, where he served 11 years for child sexual assault. He's meeting with his probation officer: "Man, I'm uptight about living outside. It's kind of scary after all these years. I have no family left; my only friends are the guys I met in the slammer."

Kimsoo, age 44, came to the United States to undertake religious studies and to become the first woman minister in her village back home. After being here for 4 years, she is experiencing a number of conflicts about returning to Korea: "I feel really torn. I always thought I wanted to be a minister, and my family and church are counting on me. But things here are so different from back home. Plus, I didn't expect to get involved with an American the way I have."

Improving Hypothesis Building Capacity

Intuitions, hunches, and feelings provide rich data for supervision and the enhancement of clinical listening and responding abilities. With experience, these processes can be used in sessions with clients as material for work.

Clinicians can consciously develop and improve their hypothesis-building capacities in the following ways:

- Value your intuitions, speculations, and sensory responses, and make them explicit for further analysis.
- Review your ideas and reactions with supervisors and consultants, exploring many possible alternative views of what the data might mean.
- Attempt to predict from your hunches and guesses what may happen in ensuing sessions, so as to be able to test your thinking against what actually transpires.
- Keep revising your impressions in supervisory discussion because people, events, and transactions keep changing.

Sharing Hunches

There are a number of guidelines for how to share hunches with clients:

Offer hunches tentatively.   Because our hunches are only informed guesses, we must be careful how we present them to clients. We thus offer hunches tentatively, sharing ideas provisionally, as questions or as possibilities rather than certainties:

"Could it be that . . . ?"
"Perhaps . . . "
"I wonder if . . . "
"Is there a chance that . . . ?"

Avoid the pitfall of assumed brilliance.   Clinicians need to avoid the pitfall of assumed brilliance. Some clients may need to have an authority tell them things and may agree too readily with the clinician's hunches, subordinating their own judgment to the clinician's.

On the other hand, clients might reject a clinician's hunch, even if there is some truth in it, because they are reacting against the clinician or because they are not yet ready to make the connection that the clinician has made. It requires a great deal of skill to know when to let go of a hunch and when to store it away. We can come back to an issue later if we feel the client is more ready to "hear" it or deal with it, or we may conclude that we were off base in our speculation.

> *During my third meeting with Graciela, I remember thinking that the trouble she was having with her roommate seemed to be like two sisters fighting over who was most loved. I had a hunch that her relationship with her roommate might be evoking some of the competitive feelings she might have had with her sister. When I mentioned this to her, she said: "You psychologists are all alike . . . always trying to read something into things. I can't believe you could actually be so stereotypic. I thought you were really getting to know me. How could you be so wrong?" I felt stupid and naive. I remember it took me a long time before I was willing to take a risk and share a hunch again.*

> *When I first broached the subject with him, Mustafa rejected the idea that the reason he might not be applying for jobs as an electrician in Boston was because he was fearful of*

entering a "white-dominated trade." He said he just knew there weren't any jobs. A couple of weeks later, he said he had been thinking about it and that he now felt that some of his reluctance was about being a Muslim among all those "Irish Catholic guys."

Well-timed and sensitively shared hunches can help clients develop new perspectives. Sharing hunches also models for clients the process of looking for alternative meanings or possibilities in their thoughts, feelings, or actions.

Share hunches in a way that makes clients think they came up with them. Clinicians can share their hypotheses in a number of ways. We can directly share a hunch using an "I" statement. Often, however, because we want clients to experience a sense of efficacy and to develop their own voices, we may share a hypothesis in such a way that the client feels it came from him or her. In the following example, note the differential responses of the client. With Clinician A, the client attributes the wisdom to the clinician. With Clinician B, the client assumes ownership of the idea.

EXAMPLES

Carrie and Jana have been a couple for two years. They are often fighting but seem to keep getting back together. The clinician, aware of their family histories, has a hunch that they do not stay separated because each of them is afraid of living on her own.

Clinician A: Looks to me like both of you may have some fears of separating. (Clinician directly shares her hunch.)

Client: Yes, you are right. I think we might.

Clinician B: Sounds like you're saying that both she and you might be afraid of separating. (Clinician B is also sharing a hunch but does so in such a way that the client feels that it came from her.)

Client: Yes, I do think so.

Sharing an inaccurate hunch is okay.   Always remember that a hunch can be wrong and sharing an inaccurate hunch is okay. The hunch may help clients clarify an issue or clarify their own perspective as separate from the clinician's. When we offer a hunch in a tentative or provisional way, it encourages clients to correct or amplify it. Clinician tentativeness is expressed in tone and language. It is fine to share a hunch directly, as Clinician A does in the example, but she could also have shared it by saying, "Could it be that . . . ?" or "Have you considered the possibility that . . . ?" These questions make it easier for clients to think about whether the clinician's hunches are accurate.

Know when to hold them.   Clinicians must decide how, when, with whom, and to what extent to share hunches. Such decisions are often a matter of judging how quickly and comfortably clients can correct clinician statements when necessary, especially given the authority that both clients and clinicians tend to attribute to clinician insight and wisdom. Excessive sharing of hunches by the clinician may become tiresome and can stifle the client's voice. We do not and should not always share our hunches. Keep in mind that we wait for more information with which to validate or invalidate speculations and that we put high developmental priority on providing opportunities for clients to author their own narratives. Before sharing any hunch, ask yourself what effects the hunch might have and be prepared to take responsibility for any negative fallout.

> *I remember being in supervision with a young psychology intern who was always sharing his "ideas about what's going on" with the client. He intended to be helpful and was often confused when his clients stopped coming to see him or complained that they felt he was judgmental.*

EXERCISE 9.3 Sharing Hunches

Go back to Exercise 9.2 and frame a response in which you share your hunch with the client. If possible, videotape your response and play it back. What do you notice?

Encouraging Client Hypothesizing

Hunches often come from clients themselves, sometimes well before the clinician ever thinks of the material offered in the hunch. Some clients are more "psychologically minded" than others: They do a great deal of speculating on the meanings and motivations in events and readily develop their own working hypotheses.

Be conscious of how this reflective capacity can be nourished and developed. We can emphasize the importance of thinking about meanings and interrelationships and encourage clients to develop their own working hypotheses by frequently asking what clients think about things or how they understand situations. Clients can be helped to search out their own hunches if the clinician uses appropriate prompts, such as:

"Let's stop for a moment and think about this."
"How could we understand this?"
"What's your take on this?"
"What are your thoughts about this?"
"What might be some different ways to think about this?"

Reinforce constructive introspection. Clients occasionally share their ideas or thoughts or offer insights about things. Clinicians can reinforce clients' constructive introspection by responding positively.

"What an interesting idea."
"So you're trying to figure out where this might come from. Good work!"
"It's so important that you're coming up with these insights."

Silence for pondering.　Another way to encourage clients to respect and develop their own hunches is through a purposeful use of silence—silence for pondering. After the client says something or shares a story, we intentionally leave a brief period of silence, assuming a pensive expression to indicate that we are thinking about implications or contemplating meanings. Here we model for clients the importance of taking time to think things out rather than responding glibly or moving on too quickly. Sitting with the silence is natural for some clinicians, but others may have to consciously develop it so that clients can be left sufficient space to gather and plumb their own thoughts.

Holding our smarts.　Related to the purposeful use of reflective silence is holding our smarts. As clinicians, we can come to value the sound of our personal voices and wisdom too much, too readily offering our personal hunches instead of gently urging clients to risk developing their own. Clinicians may pay lip service to the principle of empowerment by always asking the client to speak first, but, when the client does not respond quickly enough, they may too quickly come in with their own ideas or thoughts. Beginning practitioners often mistakenly define the helping process as the imparting of wisdom, and they worry excessively about not conveying enough to clients to appear competent and helpful. There is great merit in developing knowledge and ideas, and clinicians should develop skills in hypothesis building. However, they have to learn to refrain from sharing their own ideas too quickly when it is more helpful to the client to exercise his or her own thinking.

> *A friend of mine who is a rock climber (and therapist) shared a quote with me from Rebuffat (1965) about guides that I think captures an aspect of clinical helping, too: "With the inevitable repetition of the same ascents, the work of the guide could become tedious, but the guide is not just a machine to climb slopes of ice and walls of rock, to know the weather and the route. He does not climb for himself: He opens the gates of his mountain for his companion. He knows that such and such a climb is interesting, that this particular area is as delicate as a piece of lacework, he knows at which turn there is, suddenly, a wonderful view. He says nothing, but his reward comes with the smile of his companion when he sees it."*

Sometimes clients may not want to develop their own hunches, expecting the clinician to come up with explanations and answers. Laura Uba (1994) notes that Asian-American clients may expect the clinician to figure out what is wrong and tell them what to do differently. It may be tempting to leap in, particularly if we feel that the client's journey is one we know well and can speculate on in helpful ways. Although it may at times be helpful, and even necessary, for the clinician to share hunches and hypotheses, it is important

C L I P 9.2
Sharing Hunches

that clients develop and utilize these skills themselves whenever possible. We try to encourage clients to develop hunches and hypotheses, helping them to affirm their own voices and recognize that they are the experts on their own stories. In this way, they develop skills that they can use long after the clinical relationship ends.

Making Observations About Stuck Patterns

We can help clients enlarge their perspective by making observations about stuck patterns of thinking, feeling, or behaving that seem to get in the way of the client's goals. Sometimes the client is unaware of these patterns, and we gently suggest them in the form of a tentative hunch. For example, a client feels strongly that she will be judged harshly for speaking her mind and, as a result, does not speak up in most situations. The clinician may observe how the client's resultant silence has prevented her from moving up in her job in a company that rewards verbal initiatives. He might offer his observation in the form of a hunch: "I notice something interesting about you. Because you're afraid you'll be criticized, you remain silent and then, ironically, you often get criticized for not speaking up." If the client agrees with the hunch about a pattern holding her back, she might respond with comments such as, "I never realized I did that before" or "I never thought of it from that perspective."

Reflecting Discrepancies

As noted in our discussion of motivational interviewing in Chapter 8, while listening to clients' stories we pay attention to discrepancies or inconsistencies. Among other things, **discrepancies** can manifest as inconsistencies between two statements, between thoughts and feelings, between intentions and actual behaviors, and between verbal and nonverbal communication. It is very human to be unaware of our discrepancies until they are brought to our attention, and they often illuminate struggles, ambivalences, or conflicts we are not quite ready to resolve. Clients are often unaware of their own contradictions or inconsistencies. Clinicians may point out discrepancies to clients to help them examine the several sides of an issue or reaction, so that they can proceed in the work with new perspectives and with more information and clarity about themselves, their situation, and how the mind works when divided about things.

Clinicians try to note discrepancies as they arise. We may then choose to reflect the discrepancy directly, develop unspoken hunches based on observed inconsistencies, or wait to see if a pattern develops that would make a hunch more compelling. Some clinicians refer to pointing out discrepancies as *challenging* the client (Egan, 1994), and others call it *confronting* (Ivey & Ivey, 2003; Kadushin & Kadushin, 1997; Okun, 1997). We believe that **reflecting discrepancies** can serve many functions, depending on the intent of the clinician and the impact on the client. The clinician may *intend* to clarify; the client may *feel* challenged or confronted.

The techniques that clinicians use to point out discrepancies are many and varied. Some common techniques follow:

- *Reflection of discrepancy.*
  "While you described your sadness, you were smiling."
  "You've said that you like school, and you've said that you hate being a student."
- *The "on the one hand . . . on the other hand" technique.*
  "On the one hand, you say that you really like your job; on the other, you are always late for work."
- *Name it directly.*
  "I sense an inconsistency here."
  "I hear two things at once."
  "You seem to be of two minds about this."
- *The "help me understand" technique.*
  "You say that you and your brother don't get along but that you are looking forward to visiting him. Help me understand how these two fit together."

EXERCISE 9.4 Helping Clients See Discrepancies

Divide into groups of three. Using the following examples, role-play various ways of pointing out the discrepancy to the client. Assume the roles of clinician, client, and observer/commentator. Note how it feels to be the client and how you respond to different ways of having discrepancies pointed out to you.

> Nancy, age 55, is talking to an EAP counselor because her boss has said she must: "I don't have a problem with drinking and I don't know why people say I do. Sure, I have a few. Who doesn't? They say it affects my work, but, hey, I give them a good morning's work. Sometimes I have a few drinks with lunch, but that's no big deal. My boyfriend says he doesn't like how I act in public. Half the stuff he accuses me of I don't remember. I'm just having a good time, so what's his beef?"

> Marcel, age 30, a recent widower, says he wants to find a new mother for his young children. He's been going to every church singles event for the last 6 months. He is talking to his pastor: "I miss Gabrielle so much. It's only been 7 months since she died. She was a rare find. I can't imagine anyone taking Gabrielle's place, but the kids really need a woman's touch."

CLIP 9.3
Identifying
Discrepancies

Education or Information Sharing

In clinical work, education and **information sharing** refer to introducing new concepts or information the client may be unaware of as another means of widening possibilities or extending opportunity. Information can be liberating. The abused single mother who is afraid of losing custody of her children if she seeks safety in a homeless shelter, the male teenager who is attracted to other males, and the lonely widower who has few social contacts can all benefit from information and resources.

Information sharing usually occurs in situations in which clients are unaware of resources or of their rights in a particular situation. Clinicians frequently provide information about transportation, respite care, funding sources, training opportunities, elder resources, child care, and preventive health care services. In addition, clinicians need to inform clients about legal rights or protective services. Information sharing may be accomplished in several ways.

Helping Clients Identify Sources of Information

We can directly ask whether the client knows where to get the needed information.

"Do you know where you can get information about TMJ [temporal mandibular joint disease]?"
"How would you find out about legal rights of lesbian mothers?"
"Do you know about mutual aid groups for anorexia in your area?"

Such questions can help the client delineate what information is needed and how to go about getting it. Some clients are able to identify the sources of information and obtain it for themselves. Clients' confidence and resourcefulness are often increased by successfully seeking out their own information, and success at this task can reinforce skills that are useful in the process of locating other needed resources and networks. Elaine Pinderhughes (1989) notes that such empowerment work "shifts the client's perspective from that of self as powerless, to that of self as a member of a valued group using effective strategies to acquire the necessary resources to meet his or her goals" (p. 111).

Providing Materials

Some clinicians, especially those who work in specialized services, have resources and materials readily available for use by clients. A clinician who works in a drug treatment program might have pamphlets about AIDS prevention. Someone who works in a hospital with people who have had spinal cord injury might have brochures from health care companies about home health equipment. Some clinicians have bulletin boards where they post information about mutual aid groups or other supportive services that might be of interest to clients. As technology advances, we should also be aware of information available via the Internet. For example, people can find useful information about depression from the National Institute of Mental Health at *www.nimh.nih.gov/healthinformation/depressionmenu.cfm*. Clinicians can consider posting specialized information and resources on the Internet.

Bibliotherapy is a form of intervention in which the clinician refers clients to specific readings, sometimes lending clients the books. We can also give clients audiotapes or videotapes for their use at home (e.g., relaxation tapes or conference tapes on subjects that would be instructional and supportive for clients). Web resources and educational Web sites may also be suggested.

Directly Imparting Information

Clinicians who have the expertise may at times give clients information directly. The clinician working with a couple who has decided to adopt may directly share information about what to expect during the prescreening interview with the agency social worker, informing the couple that the interviewer often asks to see the room where the child will sleep. The clinician working with a client who is phobic about AIDS may reassure him that he cannot get AIDS through kissing or hugging.

Clients can be very appreciative of the clinician's imparting of information, which can serve as a shortcut when people are especially busy and already stressed. However, when providing information, we should be careful not to have clients see us as "the expert" or "the one with all the know-how." Harry Aponte (1994) aptly observes that the mission of providers "is to serve, not to colonize" (p. 11). Giving direct information can tempt some clients to come back anytime they have a question instead of exercising their own resourcefulness. Teaching people how to get needed answers gives them confidence and skills they can use forever.

Finally, when providing information, clinicians should be careful that the client does not feel pushed toward or into a particular stance or service. For example, if the clinician gives a pregnant 13-year-old information about abortion but not about adoption, she and her parent or guardian may feel that the clinician has tried to guide her in a specific direction.

Accompanying Clients in Seeking Information

Sometimes we may accompany the client who is attempting to get information, offering to go with the client to lend support. At other times, the client may ask the clinician to come along. In some clinical settings, going with clients to obtain information and services is a valued, routine function; in others, it is an exceptional occurrence. Supervisors can help you think carefully about the pros and cons of accompanying the client or of going with one client but not with another.

> *I was working with a client who was dying from bone cancer. He was interested in getting information about dying at home. He asked if I would go with him to a meeting with the people from the local hospice because he was afraid he wouldn't be able to remember what was said and he wanted my help in processing the information and figuring out what to do. I was glad to go with him, and it gave me a chance to meet people in his potential helping network and learn more myself about what they could offer.*

Sharing Information Through Self-Disclosure

Through the selective and judicious sharing of personal information, clinicians can sometimes provide clients with helpful information. For example, with a client about to undergo abdominal surgery and deciding how soon to return to work, the clinician might share that she had similar surgery and felt tired in the afternoons for more than one month after surgery. Information sharing through self-disclosure is often based on learning from life experience and is meant to convey empathy as well as information. Lesbian, gay, and transgendered clients often benefit enormously from having providers who have "been down that road" themselves and who can share both optimistic and cautionary advice and coping strategies.

When sharing information through self-disclosure, we try to be brief and avoid sounding either condescending or self-righteous. Before self-disclosing, we always pay attention to where the client is and to the impact of sharing. Some clients see the disclosure as informative, some may be pleased to know more about the clinician, and others may find that the self-disclosure moves them away from their own issues. In the previous example, the client may find that she is now worrying about the clinician's health, subsequently asking more about the clinician's surgery instead of focusing on her own concerns about surgery. One risk of sharing information through self-disclosure is that the client may feel pressured to act in the way that the clinician did; one benefit is that such sharing may strengthen the mutuality of the relationship. We discuss self-disclosure more fully in Chapter 13.

EXERCISE 9.5   Sharing Information with Clients

In small groups, come up with a number of issues about which you might feel comfortable sharing potentially useful information through self-disclosure. Role-play and videotape scenarios, rotating the roles of client and clinician. Discuss the impact that your sharing information in this way has on the client. Try sharing the same information with the client using the other techniques suggested. Watch the role-plays and notice the differential effects on your client of conveying the same information in different ways.

CLIP 9.4
Sharing
Information

Introducing New Topics

Clinicians always attend to the whole shape of their contacts with clients. Attention is paid to what is being focused on across a series of contacts, not just during each interview. Is the focus too scattered or too limited? Are there repeating or stuck themes or themes that may be digressing from material not yet covered, thus limiting the client's and clinician's perspective?

Clients may work intensely on certain situations, relationships, or themes but never touch on others. Preoccupation with particular stressors or persistent problems is understandable, yet at times it can prove unproductive because the same subjects are discussed over and over without leading anywhere. At other times, clients and clinicians can unwittingly stay narrowly focused to avoid painful or taboo areas. Shulman (2006) regards such conversation as creating an "illusion of work" (p. 152).

In any event, sometimes the clinician has to raise new areas for exploration, to fill out the picture. Introducing new perspectives can help clients enlarge their view of self and context, especially when things have been omitted from a story because the client does not think these topics mattered. Sometimes focusing on a new area highlights the strengths of a client or situation.

> *Lonny and Carla fought like cats and dogs in the office. You name it, they argued about it. Then they would proclaim, "See? All we know how to do is fight." It seemed that there was nothing to hold them together. I realized that we'd been talking, and they'd been arguing, about everything—money, time, sex—but they never talked about their children. When I asked about the kids, their whole demeanor changed. They softened; they agreed with and appreciated each other as parents. The whole feeling in the room changed, and I felt the first glimmer of hope for this couple. Here was something about their "team" to build on.*

New topics need not be introduced abruptly. The clinician usually waits for an appropriate opening—even just a pause for breath—and then gently introduces the new topic.

"We haven't talked much about . . . "
"I'm curious to know more about . . . "
"I realize I don't know anything about . . . "
"We've talked a lot about . . . but not about . . . "
"While we're on that subject . . . "

◼ Working for Social Change

Social forces, including the attitudes of others, account for much of our clients' distress. Far too many people are left feeling that they *are* problems, rather than that they *have* problems, which are often due to socioeconomic and political factors beyond their control. As clinicians, we recognize that, in addition to helping clients gain new perspectives, sometimes the best intervention is to work to change the attitudes and beliefs of others and to change larger systems and institutions, especially those that limit opportunities for others.

> *I was a school counselor who was seeing a couple of high school students who identified themselves as gay. As these two young men talked about their experiences, it became clear that a lot of the stress they felt was in response to the attitudes that some of their teachers seemed to have toward them. I realized that, to help the students, I also had to work with the teachers. I offered an in-service for teachers in which I used a number of techniques including stories by several lesbian/gay/bisexual students about the extent of the pain they experienced in being either ignored or attacked. I shared information about the development of sexual orientation, and I had the teachers role-play scenarios in which they had to experience the plight of lesbian, gay, and bisexual students. Some of the teachers said that the workshop raised some issues that they had never thought about. The students later reported that they felt that some teachers were showing a little more sensitivity after that.*

One of my classmates in social work school was in a wheelchair because of multiple sclerosis. She wanted us to perceive more fully how many barriers there are to mobility in the supposedly enlightened environment of a university. She had several of us experience what it was like to be in a wheelchair for half a day. Because the entrance ramp was blocked by bicycles chained to it, I had to be carried into the building by strangers happening by. Then I had to try to make it across the street in the wheelchair at a stoplight that changed so fast that I couldn't get across. I asked for help from passersby, who would stare at me and walk right on by. Others offered help when I didn't want or ask for it. I returned to the meeting room exasperated and really full of ideas about what should happen differently for people in wheelchairs. We were all quite shocked that we'd never really appreciated what they go through. That one day really shifted my perspective about barriers to access.

Workshops, community trainings, and media presentations all can help change the perspectives of others and may have an indirect effect on clients with whom we work. As clinicians, we work for social change on behalf of clients,. Sometimes clinicians can even find appropriate ways to be present in the same political or social action campaigns and protests as their clients, such as Walk for Hunger, Take Back the Night, or political marches for civil or human rights. These shared events affirm our common humanity and strengths.

EXERCISE 9.6   Broadening the Views of Others

In small groups, make a list of commonly held social attitudes, such as racism, classism, heterosexism, ableism, that you believe may have a negative impact on your clients. Choose one of the problematic attitudes and design a public education campaign around it. What techniques will you use to help people alter or broaden their perspectives? Describe persons or institutions that you believe are likely to respond favorably or unfavorably to your efforts.

■ Conclusion

In this chapter, we reviewed a number of techniques that can help clients develop new perspectives and feel things differently. We noted that it is hard to underestimate the power that develops in clients from learning to name, talk about, and stand up for their own ideas and feelings in the presence of a validating and encouraging other.

Often this work requires that we, too, develop new perspectives and become more aware of our own feeling reactions. As clinicians, we can broaden our own views and expand our range of feelings using the same techniques that have proven useful in helping clients develop new perspectives. Bystanding, brainstorming, observing and working out our own discrepancies, role-playing the part of the other, gathering new information through continuing education, and looking for and changing stuck patterns in ourselves are all ways we can expand our responsiveness.

■ Suggested Readings

There are a number of highly readable self-helps books:

Borysenko, Joan, & Dveirin, Gordon (2006). Say yes to change: Essential wisdom for your journey. Carlsbad, CA: Hay House.

Burns, David D. (1999). *The feeling good handbook.* New York: Plume-Penguin.

Kabat-Zinn, Jon. (1994). *Wherever you go, there you are: Mindfulness meditation in everyday life.* New York: Hyperion.

Spradlin, Scott E. (2003). *Don't let your emotions run your life: How Dialectical behavioral therapy can put you in control.* Oakland, CA: New Harbinger.

The following books provide useful information for clinicians about working with thoughts and feelings:

Beck, Judith. (1995). *Cognitive therapy: Basics and beyond.* New York: Guilford.

Berlin, Sharon. (2002). *Clinical social work practice: A cognitive-integrative perspective.* New York: Oxford.

de Shazer, Steve. (1988). *Clues: Investigating solutions in brief therapy.* New York: Norton.

Kopp, Richard R. (1995). *Metaphor therapy: Using client-generated metaphors in psychotherapy.* NY: Brunner/Mazel.

Padesky, Christine. (1995). *Clinicians' guide to mind over mood.* New York: Guilford

The following readings offer provocative insights on complications in clinicians' efforts to empower others:

Gutierrez, Lorraine M., Parsons, Ruth J, & Cox, Enid (2000). *Empowerment in social work practice: A sourcebook.* Pacific Grove, CA: Brooks/Cole.

Rose, Stephen M. (2000). Reflections on empowerment-based practice. *Social Work, 45,* 403–412.

■ Self-Explorations

1. When you were growing up, what messages did you get from your family, culture, or religion about how you should or should not show feelings? Were certain feelings more acceptable than others? Did you conform to these messages? How do these messages affect your ideas about feeling expression now?

2. How good are you at dealing with confrontations? Do you avoid directly confronting people? Do you feel comfortable in doing so? How did people handle confrontation in your family and culture? Are you more likely to go too far or to be too polite? Too harsh and direct or too avoidant and cautious? (Adapted from Young & Chromy [2005].)

3. Think of a time when you were "stuck" or in a rut. What things did you find helpful in getting a new perspective?

■ Essay Questions

1. People often say it is good to express their feelings. When is it useful to help clients contain their feelings? Describe some of the strategies or techniques clinicians can use to help clients manage or contain their feelings.

2. Describe strategies that clinicians can use to help clients accentuate the positive.

3. Do you think it is unprofessional for a clinician to show emotional reactions with a client? What are the cautions and benefits of clinicians sharing feelings with clients?

4. It is sometimes easier to give clients information than to help them find the information for themselves. If you have the needed information readily available, is it "phony" or just making more work for clients if they have to get information themselves? Discuss some reasons why clinicians might encourage clients to seek information. What are some potential problems of directly imparting information to the client?

5. Describe some of the sources from which clinicians develop hypotheses, and discuss some of the pros and cons of offering a hypothesis to a client.

■ Key Terms

Advanced-level accurate empathy

Bibliotherapy

Brainstorm

Coping questions

Developing new metaphors

Discrepancies

Exception questions

Feeling-thinking

Hunches

Information sharing

Islands of possibility

Mind/body programs

Miracle question

Perspective

Reflecting discrepancies

Scaling questions

Transferability of skills

Triggers

CHAPTER 10

Changing Behaviors: Helping Clients Do Things Differently

Sometimes people come to see clinicians because they want to change patterns of behavior that are not working for them or because they want to learn new skills and new behaviors. Clarinda wants to find new ways of handling her anger rather than yelling. Howard, diagnosed with obsessive-compulsive disorder, wants to learn how to control his compulsive hand washing. Estrella wants to learn how to be more assertive at work. Pete wants to develop better study habits. Lincoln wants to learn the skills he needs to live on his own as an adult with mental retardation.

Sometimes clients come for practical information about how to do things. Bernice wants to know how to adopt a child as a single woman. Yves wants his boys to get green cards so they can help support the extended family. Lana wants a referral to the Reach to Recovery program in her area.

Clients may come to see a clinician because other people are concerned about their behaviors. Chet is referred by his teacher to the school guidance counselor because he calls out in a disruptive way in class. Gilbert is sent by the court to see an alcohol abuse counselor after being convicted for driving while intoxicated. Gladdie is taken to see a neighborhood clinic counselor by her children, who are concerned that she has scarcely left the house since the death of her husband.

Sometimes clients may not be coming to do things differently. Although not initially seeking to change behavior, the client comes to realize that the presenting problem is connected with behaviors that might need to be changed or replaced with new skills. Francesca comes complaining that she is depressed and unhappy. In talking with the psychologist, she discovers that, if she did some things differently (e.g., getting together with others even when she does not feel like it), she might begin to feel better. Selina comes to see a social worker about her boyfriend's abuse of her. In talking with the social worker, Selina realizes that her children have been affected by her boyfriend's violent behavior, and she then wants to learn how to talk to them about it. In due time, she decides to end her relationship with her boyfriend and asks how to get a restraining order.

A clinician often helps clients focus on changing individual personal behaviors. It is also important to work to change patterns of behavior in the larger society. Frederick came to see a pastoral counselor about his plan to volunteer to help reconstruct some of the southern black churches destroyed by arsonists and about his fears about personal safety. Shusei is taking a course on conflict resolution at the local mental health center because she wants to serve as a volunteer mediator in family court. After Selina is successful in moving away from her relationship with her abusive boyfriend, she decides that she wants to help other women overcome what she refers to as *marianismo* (the female counterpart of *machismo*), which she believes contributes to Latina women's willingness to put up with violence from men. She sets up a local educational program and eventually becomes a national Latina spokesperson. Damien attended the 1996 Million Man March in Washington, D.C., to rally men of color to action, and he now reports a heightened sense of belonging, power, and responsibility, which led to a new commitment to be actively involved in parenting his young son. Sometimes working on behavior change leads to social action, as it did for Selina. At other times, social action can lead to personal behavior change, as it did for Damien.

■ Ripples in a Stream

As clients change their behaviors, learn new skills, or accomplish practical tasks, many aspects of their lives are affected. Not only behavior, but also perspective, emotions and feeling states, self-concept, and achievement levels may all change, because all are interrelated. Sometimes people ask: "Does changing one's perceptions change one's behaviors, or vice versa?" "Does changing one's behavior change one's mood, or vice versa?" "Does insight change behavior, or vice versa?" Which occurs first does not matter as much as that something occurs, for we know that change in any domain has a ripple effect on all others.

People often find that, when they do things differently, they see and feel things differently. As clients learn to do things differently, their perspective about themselves—how they envision their potential and place—changes. Successful achievement and connection with others, even in small amounts, can often counteract hopelessness. By achievement, we do not mean scaling life's Everests or winning important posts in government; rather, achievement is finally doing these things in daily life that clients had wished to do but that had seemed impossible. Achievement could mean making just one friend or speaking up for the first time.

As behaviors change, so do relationships. Doing things differently affects not only one's own behavior, but also the behaviors of others with whom the client relates. Working for social change affects the individual's perspective, mood, self-concept, worldview, and activities, but it also affects large groups of others and perhaps society as a whole. Black men like Damien coming together in Washington, D.C., for the Million Man March triggered a much needed nationwide soul searching and commentary regarding persistent discrimination based on race, class, and gender. The march also stimulated a number of organizations to stand up more forthrightly for societal change.

In Chapter 9, we discussed techniques used to help clients see and feel things differently. In this chapter, we focus on techniques that can help clients *do* things differently, building on many principles discussed in previous chapters.

■ Exploring What the Client Is Doing "Right"

To help clients learn new behaviors and skills, it is crucial to elicit client strengths, minor triumphs, and successful adaptive strategies and activities, no matter how small. A natural tendency in clinical work is to focus on what clients want to do differently, especially when using a time-limited or problem-solving approach. However, we recognize the importance of emphasizing what is already working for clients, what clients like, what they want to preserve and expand, as well as what they want to change. It helps to underscore the idea that clients' successes came about not by magic or fate, but through hard work, persistence, and a successful connection with others who care and help.

> *Denny came to see me because he was having difficulties at work. His company was going through a period of retrenchment. There were a lot of layoffs. He had been given more responsibilities since there were fewer people to get tasks done. He felt overwhelmed and was impatient and irritable at home. As we talked, I asked him what he felt good about at work. He spoke of how he was, in fact, pleased with many of the new responsibilities he was being given. He said, with some pride, it was because his boss knew that he could get things done. He had in the past and would do so now.*

Similarly, we explore with clients any problem-solving skills they have learned from struggling, coping, and mastering challenges in the past, emphasizing that these skills can be used to resolve current problems too. Many people undervalue their former experiences because of past mistakes and failures that continue to haunt their thinking. When we see this happening, we emphasize the transferability of skills and behaviors, underscoring as assets those effective behaviors and skills that are already in the client's repertoire.

Alphonse said that, in struggling with his alcoholism, he learned how to relinquish battles over things he cannot change, and now he tries to focus effort on that which he can do something about. This helps him be more patient with his rather rigid supervisor, instead of butting heads with her all the time.

Jobeth learned from raising three teens alone that she has more strength than she ever thought and that, if she just takes one thing at a time, she can get through many challenges without being overwhelmed.

Trish said she learned from the protective services worker how to count to 10 and leave the room before hitting her children. Now she recognizes that counting to 10 and cooling off in another room are also good ways of avoiding angry confrontations with her landlady.

Historically, clinicians have given too little credit to the substantial support their clients might derive (or have been deriving) from spiritual or religious beliefs. Some have been slow to recognize that spiritual beliefs and belongingness can give a sense of purpose and worth to embattled or isolated individuals and groups. For example, from her research in communities of color, Wendy Haight (1998) describes "spiritual socialization" as a protective factor in children's healthy development (p. 213). She found that such socialization provides youth with core experiences of acceptance, dignity, and worth that can counteract stigma and oppression. Similarly, Melvin Delgado (2007) and Robert Taylor and colleagues (Taylor, Ellison, Chatters, Levin, & Lincoln, 2000) discuss the crucial role that **faith-based organizations** play in providing the hope, spiritual and social support, advice, and consolation through which large numbers of underserved people find self-respect and empowerment to counter experiences of marginalization and stigmatization.

DVD

CLIP 10.1
Identifying
Exceptions

Chip was in training to be a firefighter and was talking about how anxious he felt when he had to go into a burning building. I knew that he had participated in the War in Iraq and I asked him if he felt a similar fear then. He said he did. I asked what he did to enable him to get through it. Chip said that in the Gulf War he learned to pray when under fire. I asked if he could use this now. He was surprised, saying he didn't think counselors believed in things like praying. I said that I do and that I was glad if it comforts him. He said that he doesn't tell his buddies, but when he's in a bad fire and is afraid, he prays silently in his head for himself and the others involved.

■ Helping Clients Own Their Part in Things

Now and then, most of us manifest the human tendency to perceive that the causes of our difficulties lie in others or in forces beyond our control. Many people go about their daily lives unaware of their motivations, of particular triggers of happy or sad feelings, of others' effects on them, or of possible ways their histories might be shaping what they say and do. Clients learning to do things differently must assume responsibility for behaviors that may be contributing to problems. They also need to learn to credit themselves for behaviors that result in successful change.

■ Identifying Behaviors to Change and New Skills to Learn

To help clients do things differently, the clinician helps them identify behaviors, relationships, and tasks they wish to work on or new skills they need or want to learn. A number of guidelines facilitate this process:

1. *Clinicians help clients be as concrete and specific as possible in describing what they want to do differently.*   The clearer the clinician's and client's views are of the desired objectives and possible strategies for attaining them, the more likely they are to accomplish them. It helps to develop clear images or metaphors of what the change will look like, so that clinician and client will know when they have achieved it.

2. *Clinicians help clients identify contexts in which the behavior occurs and encourage them to examine when, with whom, and under what circumstances the targeted behaviors occur.*   An awareness of the circumstances in which the behavior occurs can help the clinician and client think about appropriate interventions. Behavior is never separate from its context.

> *Jason was referred to the psychologist for his aggressive behavior with younger children at the residential treatment center. Upon exploration, the psychologist discovered that this behavior was pretty much limited to the residential program and that Jason did not seem to have this difficulty with younger children at school.*

3. *Clinicians help clients identify precipitating events and triggers, or easily pushed emotional "buttons," that seem to set off a habitual behavior pattern or sequence.*   For example, every time Paul's wife asks him if he has stopped for a drink after work, he gets angry and slams the door, goes to the basement workshop, and stays there fuming until after everyone is in bed.

> *Annmarie noticed that she was most likely to be short-tempered with her children when one of them says something about missing their father.*

Sometimes these triggers and sequences are so deeply imbedded and out of awareness that the clinician must patiently retrace with the client circumstances or interactions that precede unhappy moods, behaviors, or preoccupations that the client cannot explain. The clinician has to do detective work with the client to discover and understand the precipitants of the behavior. Bringing into awareness information and understandings previously split off from conscious memory is referred to as **insight development.** Insight can help clients understand and change their behaviors as well as their feeling states and relationships with others.

E X A M P L E

Client: I've been acting very short-tempered all week. On Wednesday, I was in an especially foul mood.

Clinician: Were there any particular things that happened that day?

Client: No.

Clinician: What were your thoughts or feelings on waking?

Client: Nothing special.

Clinician: How about events or people the evening before?

Client: Nope; watched TV, went to bed seemingly okay.

Clinician: Anything on TV that distressed you?

Client: No . . . cop shows, news.

Clinician: Was there anything about this day of the week or date that had any significance for you?

Client: [Hesitates.] There *were* a lot of ads on TV for Father's Day . . .

Clinician: Hmmmm. Father's Day is coming up. Might you be missing your father at this time?

Client: I never think about him . . . [Then she begins to cry.] My mother always told me that it was best if we just got on with our lives: "There's no sense crying over spilt milk." I guess I felt that she was so hurt about my father's death that I shouldn't even miss him, since that would hurt her, too.

---

4. *Clinicians and clients work together to identify the* **consequences** *of the current behavior.* Consequences are responses or contexts that reinforce or encourage the behavior, as well as things that serve as disincentives (reasons the client wants to change the behavior). We also explore the effects of the behavior on others, because the reactions of other people in the client's life are likely to impact the planned work and may serve as encouragers or discouragers of change.

> *Ricardo was referred to the teen shelter counselor because he kept running away. I kept looking to find out what was happening right before he would run away—to see if there was something that triggered his behavior. It took a while for me to ask what the consequences were of his running away. He told me that, when he runs away, it is the only time his parents talk to each other anymore. He said, "Sometimes they even come to get me together."*

5. *Clinicians work with clients to identify exceptions to stated problematic behaviors or behavioral sequences.* We listen for "I've always" and "I never"

statements and then gently challenge them and search for exceptions that represent client strengths. For example, regular visits with the clinician may be used as an exception to the avowal, "I can never make and keep a relationship." It will be important for clients to try to build up more exceptions like these in their daily lives to act as encouragements. We can also explore the possibility that the unwanted behavior does not occur with the same frequency or intensity in some contexts. Then we can encourage clients to frequent those contexts or develop new ones like those to experience more pleasure and less frustration.

EXAMPLE

Client: I never seem to be able to finish things on time. Everybody says that about me, too. I just can't meet deadlines.

Clinician: I could swear you told me when we first met that you had done okay in boot camp—and in fact met your girlfriend at squad leader camp. Did I get that wrong? You must have been doing okay to be chosen as a squad leader.

Client: But that's different. That was the Army. If you screw up there, you lose pay, time off, stuff like that. You can't be late with things there.

Clinician: Since you say you are invariably late, how come you weren't late with stuff then?

Client: Hmmm . . . let me think a minute. Well . . . there were rules and codes that you followed; it was real plain what you had to do and what would happen if you didn't. It was not confusing at all.

Clinician: So then it helped to have things spelled out clearly, have a specified timetable, and be shown how.

Client: I didn't think about it like that. I just followed the rules and did okay. As a matter of fact, I hated to leave the service, but the pay was so low I couldn't support a family on it.

Clinician: I wonder if there are other jobs we could think of where there would be those kinds of codes or instructions that would make it clearer and easier to meet deadlines.

---

6. *It is often useful to ask clients to think about what specific skills or behavioral sequences they would need to learn to do things differently.* The desired goals can be broken up into simpler component skill and behavioral parts so that they seem more ordinary, sensible, and achievable. If the client does not know what steps or skills are required, the clinician can help identify specific behavioral sequences, checking out the client's comfort level with the suggested steps and fine-tuning them as they go along.

For example, the social worker who is working to help Lincoln live on his own might help him list the specific behaviors he needs to learn to achieve his goal: wake up on time, attend to his personal care, set up and use a money management system with family or staff, learn to do his own shopping a step at a time, learn and master bus fares and routes, find out specifics of sheltered work opportunities, and so on. Here we are using the same partializing and prioritizing skills that are applicable to the goal-setting and contracting phase of work.

7. *Clinicians and clients identify the resources that provide support and backup for this difficult work.* Doing things differently can be hard. The client's preexisting skills can be resources, as can other people who may support the client in making the change. If the client has few resources or is under a great deal of stress, it may not be a good time to attempt to make a change. Helping clients improve their situation (for example, getting a green card, getting good permanent housing) may be necessary before they can effect other kinds of behavior change.

As clients talk about how they wish to do things differently, the clinician must assess how realistic their hopes are. An old joke captures the spirit of this exploration very well:

Patient: Doctor, will I be able to play the flute after my hand surgery?

Doctor: Only if you were able to play it before.

We constantly engage in reality checks: (a) the client's *capacity* to change, (b) the client's *motivation* to change, and (c) the *opportunity, time, and resources* to make the desired behavioral change. Because each of these factors may change over time, the clinician and client must periodically reexamine the appropriateness of their behavioral goals. Sometimes both the client and the clinician have to let go, at least temporarily, of overly ambitious expectations and goals.

EXERCISE 10.1 Identifying Behaviors to Change

Think of three problematic behaviors that you would like to change in yourself. Be as concrete and specific as possible. In what contexts does each behavior occur? Note any precipitants or triggers that set off the unwanted behaviors. What are the current consequences of each behavior? What reinforces each behavior, and what makes you want to change it? What specific skills or behavioral sequences would you need to learn to change the behavior? What resources do you have for making the change? After looking at all three behaviors, choose one that you believe would be realistic for you to work on this week. We will come back to this behavior in a later exercise.

■ Normalizing Ambivalence

All of us experience some anxiety and mixed feelings about changing because there is no change without loss. Artists ask, "Will my art be ruined by therapy?" Clients ask, "Will the worker take my kids away when she hears how I really behave sometimes?" Clinical interns ask, "Will I lose my spontaneity and humanness if I take on the discipline of my supervisors?"

Often we forewarn clients that some **ambivalence** is likely to arise as the work proceeds. From time to time they may feel pulled by simultaneously opposing ideas, feelings, or impulses: "I want/don't want to change." "I do/don't trust this clinical social worker" "I will be able to attain my goals/I am pretty hopeless." We should expect pendulum swings in both directions. Mixed feelings often manifest themselves in behaviors such as lateness to meetings, abrupt endings, and sudden struggles with the clinician that are difficult to fathom.

Often people do not adequately anticipate the sense of loss they experience in giving up old ways, even though at times it feels exciting to contemplate or experience the change. Just as we do when contracting with clients initially, we normalize ambivalence and note that sometimes behaviors are like old friends, and they have to be honored and mourned before moving on to the new ones. We can also sympathize, noting that giving up the familiar for the unfamiliar is never easy, because it means giving up some control over our lives as we open them up to others' scrutiny, feedback, and potential influence.

■ Behavioral Techniques for Helping People Change What They Do

Many of the techniques discussed in Chapter 8 and in the last chapter to help clients see and feel things differently can help clients *do* things differently as well. The following are additional techniques.

Setting Priorities

When talking about goals for clinical work, you should help clients prioritize the many things that they would like to do differently. The counselor helps clients set the tasks that they will work on in a reasonable and realistic sequence that gives clients the impetus to continue moving forward with the work to change behavior.

Step by Step

When working for behavior change, clinicians and clients can move slowly through a series of steps sequenced from the easy to the difficult. We often find that the specific objectives require new behaviors and specific skills. These, too, can be broken down into smaller, more readily achievable steps and their component parts (partializing).

Taletha, a shy teen, wanted to work with her school counselor on how to make friends because she was lonely and doubted that anyone would pick her as a friend. She didn't talk to the other girls at school. When she was in a group of girls, she said she felt really self-conscious. She couldn't imagine what to say and thought that the other girls all thought she was stupid. This made her even more anxious and less willing to talk. Therefore, she never went out with the team after games.

The counselor suggested they think about starting small by working toward making one friend. They detailed the things Taletha would have to do to make a friend. As they worked together, the counselor noted and commented that Taletha often looked down and away instead of at her while they talked, and she muffled or fumbled her words when nervous. Taletha agreed to practice a number of times making eye contact and exchanging comments with the counselor to improve her confidence in her social skills.

The counselor went to one of the high school basketball games and noticed that Taletha was quite a good player. When she was on the court, she seemed confident and she certainly was able to make eye contact with her opponents—often staring them down as she drove past them.

Taletha identified "a candidate for friendship" and spelled out the steps of approach: volunteer for the same team in gym, begin to make eye contact and exchange greetings, ask for help with a basketball technique, and so on.

The counselor, borrowing from the way Taletha said she "psyched herself up" for a game, taught Taletha some techniques that she could use to counter her negative self-talk by "psyching herself up."

Obviously, Taletha's counselor attempted to break the large task of establishing new friends into small, easily achievable component parts. Behavioral therapists use the term **shaping** to refer to the process of breaking a task into its component parts and then rewarding successive approximations (small steps) to the desired behavior.

EXERCISE 10.2 Component Parts

Using the following chart, continue the process with Taletha of breaking down behaviors into their component parts. Are there other components that you would want to work on with her? Would you do anything differently from the counselor in the scenario?

Desired Behavior	*Component Parts*	*Subcomponents*
Make new friends	1. Improve self-esteem.	1a. Practice positive self-talk.
		1b. Talk about prior social successes.
		1c. Discuss other things she feels good about.
	2. List possible new friends on the team.	2a. Pick a person likely to be most responsive.
		2b. Discuss approach strategies.
	3. Prepare.	3a. Practice eye contact with the clinician.
		3b. Practice opening lines.

| 4. Approach the new person during a team practice break. | 4a. Use the opening lines.
4b. Continue with small talk.
4c. Use silent self-talk to keep going. |
| 5. Anticipate the team trip. | 5a. Save babysitting money for the trip.
5b. Discuss the details of the trip with her parents.
5c. Ask the new friend if they can sit together on bus. |

CLIP 10.2
Partializing
Behaviors

EXERCISE 10.3   Identifying and Prioritizing New Skills and Their Components

What new skills or behaviors would you have to learn to change the behavior you identified in Exercise 10.1? Break the new behaviors or skills down into smaller component parts. Prioritize the behaviors or skills you would focus on first.

Modeling

A good way for clients to learn new skills or to change behaviors is to watch other people acting in the desired way. **Modeling** is based on the behavioral principle that people learn new behaviors, attitudes, values, or feelings by observing others (Bandura, 1976). People are more likely to imitate the behavior of the model if they feel that the model is similar to themselves or is a respected authority figure or celebrity. TV commercials and advertising campaigns are often based on using a model's influence to get people to behave in certain ways. People are also more likely to imitate the behavior of the model if they see the model being successful and reinforced for the behavior. The behavior must also be desirable to the client.

Clients need to be encouraged to find their own style or way of being, rather than just imitating the model's behavior. Students in a workshop on nonviolent conflict resolution might watch a tape in which they observe other students demonstrating the technique. Yet students must be encouraged not just to parrot what they have seen, but to modify those behaviors to fit their own style. As you continue to observe clinical mentors and models, you, too, need to slightly modify the behaviors you observe so that you can truly "own" and internalize them.

Clinicians are important models, whether or not we intend to be. For example, if the client wants to learn how to be more direct, we can help by modeling directness in the relationship itself. We also model by sharing our own experiences with a particular way of doing things. However, clinicians have to be judicious in self-disclosure. We must always remember the power and authority inherent in the clinical role. Clients may feel that they have to behave exactly as we do, believing that "the clinician knows best." It is important that the client and clinician acknowledge that there are usually many ways to handle a situation and that trial-and-error practice is how we all learn and refine new skills, depending on their effects from situation to situation.

Clients can find other models by joining groups or workshops with others who share a common interest in learning similar skills. Self-help groups are based on the premise of mutual aid, in which participants can model caring and emphasize potentials while providing support and close attention to each other (Gitterman & Shulman, 1994). AA meetings, Widow-to-Widow programs, and religious groups all provide opportunities for clients to observe and practice new behaviors in response to modeling from others who engage or inspire them.

Books, films, commercial videos, and Internet offerings can also help clients learn new ways to be and do. Suggesting that a client read about someone with whom he or she can identify may provide a model for behavioral change as well as offer specific information about steps that can be taken toward the desired change. For example, a young mother can profit from a book or TV show about a woman similar to herself who details how she mastered adversity and went on to establish her own day care center or Neighborhood Crime Watch group.

Rehearsing New Behaviors or Skills

Behavioral rehearsal allows clients to practice new behaviors or skills in the safety of the clinical relationship. Behavioral rehearsal usually takes some of the anticipatory anxiety out of future events. It also gives clients a chance to master behavioral skills by identifying the ones needed and trying them out with the clinician's feedback and encouragement. Then they try out behaviors in the actual situation—"in vivo"—with more ease and confidence than would have been possible without the rehearsal. **Assertiveness training** is a very popular form of behavioral rehearsal, often carried out in groups. Groups afford the benefit of several models with many different styles of self-affirmation in arenas of shared concern and support.

In another form of rehearsal, the clinician and client can **role-play** scenarios or interactions in which the client can practice the new behavior, with the clinician and client working collaboratively. They may exchange roles in the scenario, allowing the clinician to model the desired behavior, or the clinician might play "the other" with whom the client attempts the new behavior. Both clinician and client provide feedback to each other, practicing and fine-tuning potential interactions.

If possible, videotape the role-play and have the client watch it and comment on it. Taping allows clients to observe and critique themselves, commenting on both what works and what does not. Such self-observation can contribute to the building of self-awareness and insight. This work comports with the major premise of our RE-VIEW PRACTICE Method: Interns and clients learn new behaviors most easily when they can (a) see the behaviors enacted by an experienced other, (b) rehearse them, (c) practice them in real-life settings, (d) observe themselves enacting the behaviors, and (e) share their experiences with others for further discussion and reinforcement to fine-tune their behaviors.

In **imaginal rehearsal,** clients rehearse new behaviors mentally, pretending that they are acting in desired ways. Many of us rehearse things mentally to prepare for anticipated events or situations. Carrying around positive images of having worked out a good plan of action can help clients build confidence as a side benefit of rehearsing new behaviors.

Eventually, the goal is to have the client move from behavior rehearsal in the clinical setting to trying the behavior in real life. Clients can be encouraged to try the new behavior gradually, starting out in small ways or safe settings. The client may practice the new behavior in a group therapy setting or try it with people with whom it is easy to take risks. Clinicians should remember that the behaviors learned in a clinical setting are usually harder to execute in the real world, where many complications can arise and reinforcement may be poor or nonexistent. For example, the woman who learns to be more assertive and to express her opinions may find that, even though this behavior is reinforced in school settings, it is frowned upon and even punished in her family.

I was working with a client who was very shy. She said that she often felt uninvolved or like she was standing outside of the conversation when she was in social situations. We talked about what specific things she could do that might help her feel more a part of the conversation. She decided that she could reflect back what the person just said and ask questions as a way to begin to engage. We practiced these skills in the office for a while, with me playing a friend. She said that she would like to try these skills at the next big party. I suggested that she try it one night at dinner with her partner so that she could practice in a safe environment and get some feedback.

EXERCISE 10.4 Practicing New Behaviors

Think of a situation in which you would like to try out a new behavior. It might be the behavior you identified in Exercise 10.1 or a different one. In groups of three, identify a behavior that you would like to practice. Using role-plays, rehearse the new behavior, getting and giving feedback from others.

Use of Reinforcement

Behavioral theory asserts that people tend to act in ways that have been reinforced. **Reinforcers** are consequences or events that occur after a behavior and that increase the probability of the behavior occurring again in the future. We can make use of behavioral knowledge by exploring with clients how they are reinforced for current behaviors, as well as what might be desirable reinforcement for new behaviors (Pryor, 1984). Allysa reports that smoking has always made her feel calmer and that this effect reinforced her smoking. Nick always got attention from the teacher when he clowned around. (Although the teacher was yelling at Nick, he liked the attention.) Carol said that she would buy a new CD if she lost 10 pounds.

What is reinforcing to one person may not be reinforcing to another. Telling a child that if she is good she can have a lollipop works only if the child likes lollipops. Therefore, when working with a client and using reinforcement, remember that, to be effective, reinforcers must be valued by clients and established by them.

> *I was working as a counselor in an alternative school program for adolescents with poor impulse control. One of the students, Damar, refused to sit at the table when the teacher requested that he do so. I decided that I would try to get him to change his disruptive behavior using a reinforcement program. I knew that the student had to determine what would be the best reinforcer. When I sat down with Damar and asked what reward he would want for complying with the teacher's request, he said, "Sex or drugs." Well, needless to say, these were not things we could use as reinforcers. We eventually negotiated that he would be reinforced by being able to sit in "the teacher's chair"—one with wheels. Eventually, Damar wheeled himself closer and closer to the table and stayed there.*

A specific method of using reinforcement is the **contingency contract.** Contingencies are elements of a contract on which the successful attainment of goals depends. Contingency contracts are clearly articulated agreements that say to a client, "If you do this, then you will get that" or "If you do this, you will lose that." These contracts are frequently used in halfway houses, group homes, school settings, and involuntary detention centers.

In working with Steven and his family about his temper outbursts at home, the human service worker helped them decide what kinds of rewards Steven would get for specified behaviors and from whom. They also set up a list of privileges he would have to give up if he engaged in certain identified problematic behaviors.

> *I have my own sort of contingency contract. I tell myself that for every 10 papers I grade I can get a reward—a cookie and a cup of tea.*

Residential settings often employ a **token economy,** a specific kind of contingency contract in which the client actually earns tokens or points for desired behavior and pays tokens for misbehavior. Tokens can be used to buy a desired reinforcer in designated amounts. For example, a teen may trade tokens for a trip to see a movie or a baseball game or play video games an extra half hour after supper. Teaching clients about reinforcement and helping them define their own reinforcements are useful ways of helping them learn how to do things differently with feelings of satisfaction.

Homework

Homework consists of specific behavioral assignments, such as keeping a behavioral log, practicing meditation, going to a meeting, trying to express feelings more directly, recording times when one has self-defeating ideas, and the like. Any work that the client plans to carry out between sessions can also be called homework. Homework can be assigned by the clinician or mutually developed by the client and clinician.

Homework often involves other people. A sister may agree to accompany a woman who has agoraphobia to the supermarket to encourage her and help her use her calming techniques when she feels panicky. The parents of a 10-year-old might be involved in reinforcing his desired behavior of studying for 1 hour after school each night. A friend may role-play a prospective employer in a behavioral rehearsal for a job interview.

Behavior change affects others, whether they are involved in homework or not. The clinician and client need to identify the people in the client's life who may be affected by the client's changes. Because these stakeholders are needed to support the anticipated behavioral changes, clinicians often meet with them to provide education about what helps, reinforcement for their own participation, and support for their efforts to help the client change. Sometimes other people or larger systems are obstructing the work. In that event, the clinician may need to shift the work to engaging the people and systems and trying to agree on goals and roles.

> *Archie was a 48-year-old man with mental retardation whose aging parents called the agency because they were worried about what would happen to him when they died. I began to meet with Archie and attempted to teach him some skills that he would need for living in a group home: doing his laundry, making his bed, cooking his own meals. One day I suggested that Archie practice making his bed each day for the next week and that he tell me how well he did. When I questioned him the next week, he said he didn't make his bed at all. He said that his mother would come in each morning and remake it for him, telling him that he wasn't able to learn how.*

> *I decided to meet with Archie's parents and encourage them to let Archie do things for himself, even if they weren't done perfectly. Otherwise, he would never learn how to be independent. His parents were afraid of losing the role they had played with him for many years; their care of him was their main activity. I helped them redefine their role as teaching him new things. As Archie and I continued our work, I would occasionally meet with his parents to support them in their roles as Archie's teachers.*

Using Direct Influence to Help Clients Do Things Differently

We can sometimes help clients change their behaviors by **using direct influence**. Because of the power inherent in the professional role, this kind of professional activity obviously increases pressure on clients to behave in given ways, and many clinicians do not like to exert such influence because it can feel manipulative, coercive, and contrary to our ethical mandates to ensure clients' maximum self-determination.

However, we may choose to use the power of our role because it is part of a theoretical orientation in which being directive is legitimized. Sometimes we make use of our influence because we believe that clients or their dependents will be adversely affected if certain behaviors recur or if certain actions are not taken. Or we may put our weight behind behaviors or actions when the client refuses to act and we think a specified action will significantly improve the client's life (for example, make a job application to bring in desperately needed income or get needed health care when a medical condition is life-threatening).

The use of direct influence is often mediated by race, class, status, culture, age, and philosophical and religious principles. Sue and Sue (2003) believe that the culturally responsive clinician must recognize that some clients may expect and prefer that a clinician tell them what is wrong and what to do. Some Native Americans and Asians who are used to following the orders of traditional healers may prefer that the clinician give advice and directives. Clinical approaches that are based on Western concepts of client autonomy, independence, and self-discovery may not be useful. At the same time, clinicians must carefully understand the power dynamics of working with clients, particularly those who have been oppressed and marginalized and who consequently feel compelled to go along with whatever the clinician and other authority figures suggest.

The following techniques demonstrate a variety of ways in which clinicians use influence to promote behavior.

- *Offering suggestions.*   At times, the clinician may give suggestions to clients about how to behave in a situation. Advice giving is usually avoided unless people and situations are very "stuck" because it presents the clinician as the knower and the client as the recipient, which is something we try assiduously to avoid. Because clients should feel responsible for their own behaviors, the clinician frequently gives advice in a tentative way, asking clients what they think about the suggestion.

  "Perhaps if you tried [state suggestion]. Do you think that might be helpful?"
  "I have a suggestion. [State it.] Let's see what you think about it."
  "I was wondering if you could [state suggestion]. Might that work?"

- *Giving directives.*   At times, the clinician may directly tell clients what they need to do. For example, the milieu therapist may tell Justin that he must keep his pants zipped. The psychologist on inpatient service may tell Doris that she cannot hit other patients. The social worker may tell a mother that she must attend a jobs skill training program if she is to continue receiving public assistance. Ivey and Ivey (2003) note that, when giving directives, the clinician must be clear and concise and check out whether the directive was understood, as well as determine its impact on the client. In giving directives, the clinician is particularly careful to convey respect and caring for the client. Using directives too frequently can backfire, leaving clients feeling either blamed or controlled, although, as noted, some clients may see the clinician who uses directives as caring and the clinician who does not as neither caring nor helpful.

- *Accompanying the client.*   Clinicians might accompany clients to meetings or to agencies that are important to their well-being. We may go with a client to a crucial legal hearing if our presence facilitates testimony. We may accompany a client to appeal what seems an unfair rejection of application for benefits, when verbal appeals by phone have failed for unclear reasons. We might go with a shy immigrant mother to register her children for nursery school or arrange to give a teen client a ride to his first Alateen meeting.

  Accompanying clients can have many results. Clients can feel incredibly supported by the presence of the clinician. In addition, accompanying clients may help them follow through with an intended behavior because it is hard to wiggle out of something with the clinician right there. When accompanying clients, it is important to check in with them. The clinician might ask, "How is it to have me here?" We might also check in again during the next scheduled meeting: "Looking back, was having me go with you the right decision?"

- *Representing the client.*   Barry Cournoyer (2005) discusses the skill of representing the client with others, using clinician authority to broker services that the client has not been able to obtain alone. For example, a clinician may ask for a meeting with officials from the housing authority to convey a client's desperate situation and help the client get priority housing.

- *Calling on authorities to enforce a behavior change.*   At times, we have to involve others in helping the client change behavior. For example, the mother who is abusing her child may not be able to stop without outside intervention. Yet clinicians are required by law to report cases of suspected abuse or neglect of children, older people, or people with disabilities.

  I'll never forget the first time I had to file a 51A [a report of suspected child abuse]. I was working with Kathy, a young mother who had a 2-year-old daughter. I had observed how the daughter cringed if the mother made any moves toward her. I also knew that the mother was under a great deal of stress and said that at times she was so annoyed with her "selfish" daughter. I informed Kathy that I knew she didn't want to hurt her child and that she was trying to be a really good parent, but it was difficult with so many pressures on her. I told her that I was going to try to get her some help by calling in the Department of Social Services. I hoped that they would do an evaluation and help her get the resources she needed to take care of her child and to avoid hurting her. Kathy was angry at me and asked if DSS would take her daughter away from her. I said that I hoped they wouldn't but that, if they did, I hoped that she would be able to get her back real soon.

  They didn't remove her daughter, but they did offer her some respite care, and she became eligible for job training. I was really scared about what this would do to my relationship with Kathy, but I think she really felt my caring, and the fact that the Department of Social Services didn't remove her child made it easier. We continued our work together. I am not sure what would have happened if they had taken her daughter away, but I would hope that we still could have found a way to continue our work.

- *Warning the client that the relationship will be terminated unless the client meets certain conditions.* Sometimes there are behavioral conditions that must be met for the clinical relationship to continue. Some teen residences require that members be sober to continue living in the house. A clinician may say that she will terminate the clinical relationship if a client does not follow through on an agreed-upon behavior change. An outpatient clinic may have a policy that clients who cut themselves will not be allowed to continue as outpatients. A social worker may assert that she will not continue to meet with a client individually unless the client attends the group therapy session every day.

> *I was seeing a client who had manic depressive illness and he was not taking his medication. He was acting quite manic. I was stuck with a dilemma. I wanted to tell him I couldn't work with him unless he took his medication but I was also afraid that if I stopped seeing him there wouldn't be much hope he would take his meds.*

As harsh as they may seem, requirements can serve as an impetus for change, modeling the structure and seriousness of purpose and succeeding where other methods have failed. Such strategies are controversial, however. Some clinicians worry that such terminations may leave the client stranded without crucial structure and support. Others caution that clinicians are acting out their frustration or anger with the client, often simply reenacting unresolved power struggles from the clinician's and client's earlier lives. Warnings and terminations should never be carried out without considerable conversation with clients beforehand and only under the most thorough supervision.

CLIP 10.3
Using Direct
Influence

EXERCISE 10.5   When All Else Fails

Would you terminate a clinical relationship with a client under certain circumstances? Make a list and discuss the pros and cons of this strategy with your fellow students in class.

Addressing Behavioral Balking

A client sometimes starts to work on a behavior targeted for change (for example, keeping a journal on binge eating) and then suddenly "forgets" either her journal, the correct time of the appointment, or the appointment itself. She might say that this happened "because" the bus came late or she needed to take work home and had no time to write in the journal. In another instance, a clinician might not show up for supervision, saying that he had so much on his mind that he forgot. Sometimes clients do not do what they agreed to do in order to signal that we are pushing in the wrong direction or imposing rules that seem unjust. Sometimes clients need to take a breather or a rest from the work of behavior change.

At other times, the clinician may inadvertently push the work too fast or too deeply, stirring up more anxiety than the client can tolerate. This anxiety may be verbalized, but it can also emerge in behaviors. Cancellations, lateness, forgetting, getting off track, becoming defensive about the return of old nonproductive patterns—all can signal discomfort, a need for a breather, or a reluctance to proceed due to fears of losing more than one may gain by changing behaviors, contexts, or relationships.

At such times, we might simply share the hunch that perhaps the client is feeling divided about proceeding for reasons that need airing and sorting through together. We might reach out by phone or visit someone who has suddenly canceled or dropped out, to process the disconnect. Our main goal is to get things on the table unambiguously so as to clarify and ventilate attitudes or conflicts that are stalling further work together. Part of the disconnect may be due to us and our ways of working, so we must stay open to the possibilities. In addition, we need to consider that changing realities in clients' situations may contribute to this change in commitment.

CLIP 10.4
Addressing
Behavioral Balking

Validating, Commending, and Celebrating Accomplishments

Clinicians should recognize, validate, and celebrate clients' achievements in changing old behaviors and learning new skills. Validation can be an important social reinforcer, encouraging the client to continue the work. In some settings, there are specific rituals that recognize client achievements. In AA groups, for example, clients are given a pin for one year of sobriety. In halfway houses, clients might be "promoted" to a new level based on their upholding their part of a contingency contract. A clinician might share cake and coffee to celebrate a client's success in getting a job after years on welfare.

EXERCISE 10.6   Your Own Behavior Change

Go back to the behavior you chose to work on this week. What techniques would you use to change that behavior? With two colleagues in class, work on changing your behavior. Keep a record of what techniques you used and how effective they were. Did you encounter resistance in yourself as you tried to change? Continue to work on changing the behavior using different techniques until you are successful. Plan a way to celebrate your success.

■ Conclusion

We believe that both clinicians and clients can be helped to learn new ideas and new behaviors by clearly identifying what is to be mastered and breaking it down into tasks and steps, utilizing specific skills. These steps and skills are most readily learned from clear, consistent, and encouraging models with whom there can be good-natured exchanges in the process of rehearsing new behaviors. Planned reinforcers help stoke our persistence, just as it does for clients who are trying to master new ideas, insights, and skills. Interviewing skills are best learned in relationships with others who are prepared and motivated to give informed feedback. Self-observation through journaling, videotaping, and feedback from others help refine skills.

We believe that learning through connection, collegial exchanges, shared risks, and mutual aid are all reinforcements for new learning. These principles underpin all clinical work, including work with clients in crisis, which we discuss in the next chapter.

■ Suggested Readings

Good self-help books on behavior change include:

Prochaska, James O., Norcross, John C., & DiClemente, Carlo, C. (1994). *Changing for good.* New York: Morrow.

Pryor, Karen. (1984). *Don't shoot the dog! How to improve yourself and others through behavioral training.* NY: Bantam.

The following is a useful resource for clinical work on behavior change:

Watson, David L., & Tharp, Roland G. (1993). *Self-directed behavior: Self-modification for personal adjustment.* Pacific Grove, CA: Brooks/Cole.

■ Self-Explorations

1. Think of a behavior that you have learned from someone else's modeling. Who was the model? What did you see him or her do? What were the consequences of the model's behavior? What made that behavior desirable to you? How did you modify the behavior you observed to make it your own? What reinforced the changes you made to be more like the model?

2. You have been engaging in behavioral rehearsals throughout this class as you have practiced interviewing skills in role-plays with your fellow students. What kinds of feedback have been most useful to you? What kinds have been less useful and why?

3. Have you ever participated in a contingency contract or similar situation in which reinforcements (for example, tokens, stars, stickers, prizes, money) were awarded, contingent upon your behavior? How did you feel about that? Do you ever give yourself rewards for particular behaviors?

4. How does it feel for you to be helping clients change things that you yourself have not yet changed but need to? What goes on for you internally when the client's change work surpasses what you personally have been able to do about a needed change of your own?

■ Essay Questions

1. From your reading, list guidelines for helping clients identify behaviors to change and new skills to learn.

2. What do we mean by the "transferability of skills" in clinical work? What helps clients achieve it? Did you yourself come to professional education with any skills that you can see yourself transferring positively into clinical practice techniques for use with clients? Have you had to alter any aspect of your old skill usage in the process of professionalization? Discuss these questions.

3. Discuss the benefits and risks of behavioral modification programs. If you have worked in or observed such a program, describe what you experienced as well as any aspects that created concern for you.

4. From your reading of this chapter, list the numerous techniques clinicians use to help clients change their behaviors. Discuss the pros and cons of each technique.

5. With which change techniques are you the most familiar and comfortable at this point in your learning? Discuss any techniques you would feel less comfortable using, and explain why.

6. In the course of our helping them change, clients often give *us* feedback about our ways, expectations, or statements, and these can have a very positive reshaping effect on our professional development. Have you had such reshaping feedback from a client? What happened, and how did you alter yourself accordingly? Were there any difficulties in doing so?

■ Key Terms

Addressing Behavior Balking
Ambivalence
Assertiveness training
Behavioral rehearsal
Consequences
Contingency contract
Faith-based organizations
Homework
Imaginal rehearsal

Insight development
Modeling
Precipitating events
Reinforcers
Role-play
Shaping
Token economy
Using direct influence

CHAPTER 11

Working with People in Crisis

Crisis intervention has much in common with other forms of clinical work. It requires attending and listening, support and empathy, exploration and elaboration, and careful assessment and working agreements. We use many of the same skills to help clients gain insights, make meaning of events, and change behaviors. As in all clinical work, we pay careful attention to the relationship. However, crisis intervention requires modifications in some of the customary timing, focus, and forms of clinical interviewing.

In this chapter, we begin by describing what is meant by "crisis." We explore crisis intervention and the skills clinicians use in working with individuals and communities in crises. Finally, we discuss how crisis intervention work can create unique stress for clinicians, who must cope with vicarious or secondary trauma.

■ Crisis

Crisis is ubiquitous in the twenty-first century. War, famine, political upheaval, sudden population dislocations, slavery, disasters, accidents, abuse, torture, and widespread violence make crisis an inescapable reality in the lives of millions of people around the globe. Violence, poverty, racism, religious prejudice, large-scale unemployment, and other forms of hardship and oppression also create hazardous conditions that prime people for crisis reactions to precipitating events that easily overwhelm already stressed coping resources. The constant stream of distressing media images of traumatizing domestic and international crises and their focus on dire consequences perpetuate a climate of crisis that is hard to avoid.

The ravages of trauma and crisis cut across all class, color, ethnocultural, political, and international boundaries. No one is immune, whether in large urban areas, small towns and villages, rural settings, desert habitats, or remote islands. From epidemiological research, Martin Deahl (2000) estimates that over two-thirds of the world's population are exposed at some point to traumatizing events severe enough to meet the DSM "stressor" criterion for **Posttraumatic Stress Disorder** (PTSD). Symptoms of PTSD include (1) reexperiencing the traumatic events through intrusive thoughts or dreams; (2) experiencing hyperarousal through difficulty sleeping, hypervigilance, inability to concentrate, irritability, and (3) avoiding reminders of the event through detachment, efforts to avoid thoughts or feeling, numbing, withdrawal from social contact. The reported rate of PTSD among combat veterans and first-line emergency responders is over 30% (Deahl, 2000). It is clear that over the course of our clinical careers, we will be called upon time and again to help people in crisis. All clinicians must be prepared to provide speedy, well crafted, and well coordinated interventions in collaboration with others.

The word "**crisis**" comes from a Greek root meaning "to decide." Murray Levine and David Perkins (1997) state that "the term means a critical turning point in the progress of some state of affairs in which a decisive change, for better or worse, is imminent" (p. 208). The father of crisis intervention, psychiatrist Erich Lindemann, first described crisis reactions after observing the acute grief expressed by persons who survived or were affected by the 1942 Cocoanut Grove nightclub fire in Boston—a sudden conflagration that took the lives of nearly 500 revelers in less than 10 minutes. He also studied and worked with similar reactions in relatives of deceased armed forces personnel and medical patients, and he counseled patients who had lost a relative in the course of psychiatric treatment.

"**Trauma**" is the term often used to describe a catastrophic crisis that involves events so sudden, massive, extraordinary, uncontrollable, or dehumanizing that they overwhelm cognition and meaning making, feeling regulation, biological processes, habitual adaptive mechanisms, and relational capacity. Traumatic events significantly affect overall functioning and can shatter people's assumptions about how the universe operates and how people behave toward one another (Janoff-Bulman, 1992). Judith Herman (1997) notes that:

> Traumatic events call into question basic human relationships. They breach the attachments of family, friendship, love and community. They shatter the construction of the self that is formed and sustained in relation to others. They undermine the belief systems that give meaning to human experience. They violate the victim's faith in a natural or divine order and cast the victim into a state of existential crisis (p. 51).

From an ecological perspective, Patricia Harney, Leslie Lebowitz, and Mary Harvey (1997) believe that there are multiple possible outcomes to trauma, not just psychological harm, depending on the interaction of the traumatic event, individual variables, and the environment in which these factors play out. Among the environmental factors that influence posttrauma adaptation, we emphasize family, cultural, friendship, and spiritual support, plus provision of sufficient emergency income to help people restabilize, rebuild, and mitigate stress with renewing activities.

Jessica Henderson Daniel (2000) has called for a widening of the definition of trauma to include persistently distressing memories or continual experiences of race- or color-based "**microaggressions**" (p. 130). These frequent aggressions include acts of exclusion, victimization, harassment, verbal abuse, stereotyping comments, intimidation, and injustice. Daniel notes that, in addition to the prejudicial policies and practices of organizations and institutions, racism also occurs in subtle and "equally troubling, individual everyday acts" (p. 128), whose cumulative effects are widely traumatizing for people of color and many others identifying with them.

In a similar vein, Joan Hertzberg (1996) speaks of the cumulative traumatizing effects of class-based oppression through both subtle and overt acts of dominance. "The effects of malignant, internalized oppression can be devastating and the cumulative impact can constitute what Root (1992) refers to as **insidious trauma,** one that evolves from the ongoing experience of denigration based on social status or identity" (p. 133). Weaver (1999) discusses the traumatic effects on Native Americans of the "atrocities of the indigenous holocaust in this country and the unresolved pain associated with it" (p. 221), including the forced breakup of families and tribal groups, theft of land and resources, governmental assimilation policies, and forced dependence.

EXERCISE 11.1 Oppression-Based Traumas

In your journal, discuss oppression-based traumas you have either directly experienced or have observed as they happen. Share your experiences in class. Notice how you react to telling or hearing about these incidents. Imagine the feelings and coping strategies of others who may experience these aggressions on a regular basis. How does this exercise improve your clinical understanding of responsiveness with victimized people?

The term "**secondary trauma**" is used to describe a traumatic response to hearing about or witnessing others' traumatic experiences. Charles Figley (1983) first used the term to describe the stressful reactions of families and friends in response to knowing about a traumatic event experienced by a significant other. In addition, individuals can experience secondary trauma in response to events that happen to people they hardly know because these events awaken their own vulnerability.

Shortly after the shooting in Columbine High School, my son Miguel started having nightmares and would awake screaming that "they" were coming after him. He was scared to go to school, and his mother and I didn't know how to reassure him. This lasted for a couple of weeks. Every now and then, he still has the same dreams.

Hate crimes can create secondary trauma for those who are not the direct victims of the attack. Peter Finn and Taylor McNeil (1987) define hate crimes as "words or actions intended to harm or intimidate an individual because of her or his membership in a minority group; they include violent assaults, murder, rape, and property crimes motivated by prejudice, as well as threats of violence and other acts of intimidation" (p. 2). Hate violence is a form of terrorism that traumatizes not only the direct victim but all members of the targeted group. Hate crimes affect the rest of us by reminding us of the sudden malice with which our lives can be ended or turned upside down by forces beyond our control.

The counseling center at the college reported seeing a number of lesbian, gay, bisexual, and transgender students who came in because they were having anxiety symptoms and wanted to talk about what happened to Matthew Shepard, a gay college student who was beaten and left to die hanging on a barbed wire fence in Laramie, Wyoming.

In the weeks following the racially motivated dragging death of James Byrd, Jr., an African American, in rural Texas, the parents of African-American kids at our day care center decided to meet to talk about how to handle the anger, fear, and despair they felt for their children.

■ Common Features of a Crisis

Some suggest that, whenever clients come to us, they are in crisis (James & Gilliland, 2005). Although that may be true on one level, we are referring to a more limited and specific use of the term "crisis." We believe that crises have some very specific features.

1. *There is a precipitating or triggering event.*   People face numerous events that could precipitate a crisis. Crisis theorists describe many different types of crises arising from different **precipitating events.** We find it helpful to delineate four: situational, developmental, environmental, and compound.

Situational crises may be precipitated by extraordinary incidents, such as fires, acts of violence, diagnoses or episodes of mental/physical illnesses, or abrupt changes in established systems in which people feel secure. **Predisposing factors** such as poverty, social isolation, racism, and gender bias put people at risk for specific situational events. For example, living in a poor inner-city neighborhood may put people at higher risk of being exposed to violence and health hazards.

Erik Erikson (1963) notes that normal growth and life cycle developmental events can generate **developmental crises** of adaptation to new people and challenges. Developmental transitions include the birth of a child, marriage, divorce, going to school, finding and developing job opportunities, aging, and death. Of course, different cultures have different developmental transitions and may attribute different meanings to them.

Environmental crises affect groups of people who may share a common living environment. They may be precipitated by **natural disasters** (e.g., storms, tornadoes, floods, hurricanes, tidal waves, earthquakes, volcanoes) or **human-made disasters** (e.g., oil spills, toxic waste dumps, biohazards, nuclear accidents). Richard James and Burl Gilliland (2005) suggest that environmental crises can also include biologically based disasters (disease, epidemics), politically based disasters (war, refugee crisis, "ethnic cleansing"), or economically based disasters (severe economic depression, mass unemployment due to plant closings or job outsourcing).

Many have noted that a crisis often rekindles unfinished business from previous crises (Lindemann, 1965; Parad, 1965). Cynthia Poindexter (1997) refers to this phenomenon as a **compound crisis,** while James and Gilliland (2005) refer to it as a transcrisis state. A person whose mother died when she was 5 may find she reexperiences the crisis at age 60 when her sister dies. Lindemann (1965) writes of "delayed grief reactions," in which survivors of a recent loss may suddenly experience grief from an earlier loss. Sometimes delayed grief reactions occur when people reach the age of the deceased at the time of his or her death.

Precipitating events do not have to be big. "The straw that broke the camel's back"—a small thing that is the last in a series of upsetting events or hazardous circumstances—can overwhelm the individual or system. After nine pregnancies, a tenth may be a crisis. The precipitating event may not be as severe as the events or conditions preceding it, but it can be overwhelming physically, emotionally, or psychologically. A person may be able to cope with numerous hazardous conditions and events. For example, a woman may be able to cope even though she loses her job, becomes ill, and her partner dies, but, like the straw that broke the camel's back, the breakdown of the water heater overcomes her.

2. *The person perceives the event as a danger, loss, or threat.* Howard Parad (1965) notes that the event that precipitates a crisis must be perceived as a threat. The key thing is not the event but the meaning that individuals attribute to it and its anticipated effect on the future. Perception of danger and reactions to it are idiosyncratic. Two people exposed to the same event may perceive the threat quite differently.

> *I worked in a school in which a student brought a gun to class. One of the students, Hunter, was quite frightened at the time, shaking and crying. The next day, his mother said that he didn't want to go to school. He feigned sickness. For weeks after the event, he was jumpy and emotional. Jamil was in the same class. He didn't seem at all anxious at the time, nor did he have any visible follow-up reactions.*

Culture often influences the way people understand and make meaning of events, signaling them about the kind and level of distress they should experience and express in reaction to events. Spiritual beliefs, too, can influence responses. Lindemann discovered that surviving family members who thought events were connected with God's divine plan recovered more quickly than those who could find no way to understand why their loved ones had been taken. Hinduism and Islam teach that life is determined by fate or by the will of God or Allah. It is possible that subscribing to these beliefs may help protect people from the more severe and lasting effects of trauma and crisis.

3. ***Customary coping methods do not work or are inadequate to the degree of threat.*** **Coping mechanisms** are methods people use to overcome, reduce, or accommodate the demands of stress. In a crisis, people often attempt to use their customary coping methods, but, in the face of a novel or extreme situation, they may try new methods. In fact, the failure of familiar or customary coping mechanisms may precipitate a crisis in and of itself or may exacerbate an existing crisis.

Coping mechanisms can be healthy or maladaptive, and they can also be effective or ineffective. During a crisis, a person may try a healthy but ineffectual method of coping. For example, talking to friends can be a helpful coping strategy. But if these friends have not had a similar experience and/or do not grasp its meanings and effects, talking to them may not help.

> *Eileen was a very resilient and social young woman. In times of crisis, she would often talk things through with her family and her boyfriend, get their input, and decide how to proceed. But after she was raped, that coping strategy no longer worked. Her family thought that she shouldn't "dwell on it," and, although her boyfriend was willing to listen, he would soon be shaking with rage at the man who did this to her.*

At the same time, it is possible to have an effective but paradoxically maladaptive response to a crisis.

> *After the fire, Lucas found that he couldn't sleep. He was nervous and jittery. He found that having a couple of drinks helped him feel less anxious and sleep through the night. While he was able to drown out the images of the fire, his drinking began to interfere with his work and family relationships and eventually led to his being fired from his job and to major marital difficulties.*

4. ***The person feels overwhelmed, anxious, disoriented, or uncertain.*** When faced with a crisis, the person is thrown into a state of disequilibrium, feeling overwhelmed, disoriented, anxious, or uncertain. Unsettling reactions are manifest in statements such as:

"I can't breathe."
"I'm on the verge of a nervous breakdown."
"I feel numb, empty, nothingness."
"I'm losing it."
"My world is turned upside down."

"I can't eat, I can't think, I can't feel."
"Why me?"
"Nothing matters anymore."

These reactions to crisis may take the form of a number of common physiological, emotional, cognitive, and relational responses.

- *Physiological:* Tightness in chest and heart palpitations; tiredness; headaches; digestive, appetite changes, and sleep problems; high blood pressure; frequent sighing, blank staring, and hand-wringing.
- *Emotional:* Numbing; feelings of sadness, anxiety, anger, crankiness, and impatience; periods of tearfulness; loss of pleasure in people, things, and activities; feelings of estrangement, of not being like other people.
- *Cognitive:* Distorted thinking; self-blame; inability to concentrate; narrowed perception; foggy thinking and disorganized thoughts; perseveration; expecting the worst.
- *Relational:* Withdrawal from usual social contact to avoid too much stimulation or the expectations of others; or the opposite—having the need to be with, or in touch with, others constantly for reassurance, calming, advice, resources; loss of confidence in authority figures, community leaders, and spiritual groups.

5. *The destabilization inherent in a crisis provides the opportunity to restabilize at a higher or lower level of functioning.*   In every crisis, there exists both danger and opportunity. The destabilization of a crisis provides an opportunity to restabilize at a new level of growth or to decline in functioning. David Finkel (1974) describes the positive effects of coping with stress, pointing out that it is only after time and in hindsight that people can speak of the beneficial effects of stressful events and crises. How one copes with a crisis is mediated by situational factors, such as material and social supports and culture, and psychological factors, such as coping capacities and resilience.

Resilience is the capacity to adapt competently despite or because of adverse or hazardous conditions. Dante Cicchetti and Norman Garmezy (1993) note that resilience is a process, not a trait, and consists of constant and dynamic transactions between internal and family assets and environmental resources. Bonnie Benard (1997) identifies caring, communication skills, humor, and the ability to make and sustain strong peer relationships as important assets of resilient individuals and families. But they need to be supported by caring peers, friends, and environments that offer hope, high expectations with matching resources, and a vision of how goals are achieved.

Richard McNally, Richard Bryant, and Anke Ehlers (2003) describe the surprising post-9/11 underuse of psychological assistance by New Yorkers directly impacted by the Twin Towers disasters. They observe that trauma response planners underestimated the resilience of New Yorkers and their preference for using friends, family, work associates, school-based services, and survivor networks to work through the horrors they experienced and witnessed.

In a crisis, a person can **decompensate,** engaging in self-harm and other maladaptive behaviors. However, a crisis also affords the opportunity to learn, grow, and establish new connections, behaviors, and skills that can be useful in the future. The vulnerability experienced in a crisis may also leave people open to new ideas. In addition, although a new crisis may carry with it the risk of evoking old unresolved crises from the past, it can also provide an opportunity for people to rework those past issues and feelings as they emerge in the present situation (Lindemann, 1965; Parad & Caplan, 1965).

> *Yoshi came to see me when a lover of 7 years left her with very little warning. It turned out that this was the second time someone who seemed so caring and ready to settle down had begun to cool and then left her high and dry, and suddenly seeming so cold in the process. "Where did I miss the warning signs?" she wondered miserably. Over several meetings, it became clear that she had been raised by a distant and work-involved single mom whose premature death in an automobile accident removed any chance for this client, a child at the time, to express her sadness and anger about being so left out in the cold, second fiddle to a job. She came to see that perhaps she had chosen these lovers in an unconscious replay of her feelings of abandonment by her mother. Maybe her antennae were out, searching for another person who couldn't really stay by her over time, in order to have a different ending this time. Yet here she was, "high and dry" again. A lot of our work, then, was to have her revisit her powerful longings for her mom not to leave her, but to hold her close and say that nothing would make mom happier than to spend her days with this lonely child. The client cried a lot and was eventually able to put words to her unexpressed childhood grief about her mom's distance and death.*

6. *There is a window of opportunity during a crisis when the person is particularly amenable to assistance.* There is a period of several weeks following a crisis, during which feelings of vulnerability may make people more open to growth and development. They may reach out to others for assistance or be unusually amenable to help offered by neighbors, community agencies, or emergency service providers. Crisis theorists suggest that after about 8 weeks, people often will find some way to lower or eliminate their stress and tension and that help after that time is less effective. As Lydia Rapoport (1965) states, "A little help, rationally directed and purposively focused at a strategic time, is more effective than more extensive help given at a period of less emotional accessibility" (p. 30).

■ Crisis Intervention

Characteristics of Crisis Intervention

Crisis intervention has much in common with other forms of clinical work, yet due to the rapid and intense nature of crisis work, there are some differences.

1. *Crisis intervention is immediate.* We know that, unless help is provided rapidly, people under significant stress can worsen their situations through impulsive action based on incorrect information, by taking their feelings out on those around them, through the use of substances to numb or express

intense emotions, or by retreating into angry, hopeless isolation. For these reasons, Rapoport (1965) urges that clients and clinicians have "rapid and flexible access to each other" (p. 30) to take best advantage of the window of opportunity that crises often afford for growth and learning.

2. *Crisis intervention is brief.* Crisis intervention involves a rapid evaluation and time-limited provision of services to support coping and the resumption of precrisis relationships and activities. Brief interventions mobilize, reinforce, and focus clients' strengths to reduce the likelihood of becoming anxious, depressed, and helpless under stress. Key needs and activities are identified for short-term interventions, with more long-standing needs and problems identified but often sidelined for now. If they wish, clients may do further work of greater complexity later when the immediate crisis has passed.

3. *Crisis intervention is specifically focused.* The clinician working with a client in crisis often provides more structure than in other types of clinical work. Once there is agreement to meet, work immediately focuses on eliciting a clear, organized description of precipitating events; on discussing related client interpretations and reactions; on planning action to meet any urgent needs for concrete resources, such as shelter, clothing, and food; and on thinking about clear next steps to be taken in the days and weeks ahead. We are less likely to explore for links between current events and those earlier in life unless clients introduce such links and press to discuss them to find some measure of relief.

4. *Crisis intervention may require more frequent meetings and meetings of varying durations.* Meetings are often scheduled at shorter intervals to help calm and organize thinking, to relieve pressure from urgent feelings that might promote impulsive behaviors, and to bring about a speedier resolution of crisis-related problems. Initial sessions may be longer than usual to allow the client to tell the whole story and get some initial relief, while later sessions may take the form of brief check-ins. As the crisis abates, the intervals between sessions usually become increasingly longer, allowing clients continued support while resuming their lives.

5. *Crisis intervention may require more clinician activity than usual.* Clinicians often inform, guide, structure, and advise clients in crisis more than they normally might. We may also accompany clients to meetings or hearings to provide support or take action on behalf of clients too destabilized at present to speak or act for themselves. Because people are sometimes in crisis because they have lost their homes, loved ones, pets, or means of making a living, we are very active in helping them find shelter, food, transportation, links with loved ones near and far, assistance in finding pets, and temporary funds to sustain them until more secure arrangements can be developed.

What Clinicians Do in Crisis Intervention

The clinician's tasks are many in the immediate work of engagement and assessment. All interventions should be carried out with empathy, patience, and carefulness, so as not to further destabilize things, and a commitment to doing all that we can to alleviate stress and feelings of dislocation from the familiar. A major activity of crisis responders in recent natural disasters such as Hurricane Katrina was to provide donated cell phones to separated survivors and arrange for the national media to show photos of separated children and elderly so that survivors can try to locate each other and reestablish supportive communication. Another important activity was to provide legal aid assistance to displaced residents who had encountered racism in some sectors of the real estate industry when seeking temporary apartments until they could rebuild back home.

1. ***Help the client tell the story.***   One of the first tasks of the clinician is to help the client organize a coherent and meaningful narrative of critical events. Initial conversations can be disorganized, emotion laden, and overwhelming for both the client and the clinician. Some clients may be mute, shocked, silent. Bessel van der Kolk, Jennifer Burbridge, and Joji Suzuki (1997) note that certain biological changes affect how clients remember and talk about what occurred: "Because traumatic experiences appear to be stored primarily as somatic sensations and intense affect states, they may be least accessible to semantic processing. It is important to help persons with PTSD find a medium in which they can come to understand and communicate their experience" (p. 110). For example, play therapy and various forms of artwork can help children with expression and relief of anxieties.

We first help clients to talk about the events by providing structure for the conversation. Gentle questions focusing on specifics can help organize the pressured stream of feelings and information. This work is important in helping the client reestablish a sense of capacity and control, even if only by creating a coherent story for self and others.

EXAMPLE

In the following exchange the clinican is working with a teenager who survived a fatal car crash.

Client [weeping]:   I don't know what happened.

Clinician: You were in an accident.

Client: I tried to get Bobby out but I couldn't. Oh, God . . . he was . . . there was . . . I can't do this . . . they were all over the place but him . . .

Clinician: Let's stop for a second. I think it may help to just go back and start by describing the accident itself.

Client: I am so confused. There was all this blood and the horn.

Clinician: Who was in the car with you?

Client: Bobby, Grace, and Jerry.

Clinician: Where were you going?

Client: I don't know . . . to the movies.

Clinician: What road were you on?

Client: Route 128 . . . near Bordenville.

Clinician: Then what happened?

Client: The accident.

Clinician: What do you remember right before it occurred?

EXERCISE 11.2   Helping to Structure the Story

In class, role-play the initial conversations between a client and crisis worker in which the client is disorganized and overwhelmed by feelings and the clinician attempts to help the client structure a coherent story about the event. Use as many clinical skills as you think useful (gentle guiding questions, reflection, clarification, limit setting, calming, empathic statements, changing the subject).

---

2. *Validate events and distress reactions.*   People in a state of crisis often feel uniquely upset, troubled, and different from others because of what has happened to them. They commonly wonder whether they are making up or exaggerating events or overdramatizing effects and reactions. It is thus essential to validate and normalize universal human feelings and behaviors in a crisis to help decrease feelings of differentness and worries about being mentally ill. For example, a message helpful to many men and boys from cultures that celebrate male power and invincibility is that of permission and encouragement to express their feelings directly rather than suppressing them, acting them out aggressively, or using substances to numb them. If feelings are taboo for any individual, family, or group, we can explore for current thoughts, reactions, and possible bodily complaints that may be somatic expressions of pain.

CLIP 11.1
Eliciting and
Validating the
Story

We also validate how normal it is not to want to trigger more upset feelings once people believe they are finally calmer. If the individual's culture or local gender norms discourage the expression of strong emotions, we do not push—the last thing that people need when feeling vulnerable. Rather, we can work with the client on other things while helping them understand that any upsets they feel in future could be the normal remnants of the current crisis and that they may talk with someone in future if they wish.

3. *Focus on safety and concrete needs.*   One of the urgent first tasks of crisis responders is to help people reestablish their resource base through advocacy and action on their behalf. For example, the first task in work with people who have lost everything in a fire is to help them find surviving loved ones following the rush to escape, and then work together to find shelter, food, clothing, and other needed resources.

Concrete needs also include safety from outside harm. Judith Herman (1997) notes that for those who experience violence, rape, and other forms of abuse, the first task is the establishment of safety: "This task takes precedence over all others, for no other therapeutic work can possibly succeed if safety has not been adequately secured" (p. 159). Safety work may involve making sure that the survivor of partner abuse finds a place to stay in a domestic violence shelter with an undisclosed address, that an abused child is never left alone with a known abuser, or that the victim of sexual assault at home installs secure locks on windows and doors.

> *Jacki said it was very hard to leave Aidan and go to the shelter with her daughter Kelly because Aidan would be unable to manage alone, and, in spite of beating her, he could be so thoughtful and loving when sober. We talked many, many times about such a move before she was able to move out. What finally got to her was my underscoring that, if he seriously harmed her or Kelly, he would have to live with the consequences for the rest of his life. She was so centered on his interests that thinking of him in prison or separated from them by a court order moved her to go into the shelter. It also helped to review that he would leave them during benders for days at a time—evidence that he could "manage alone." I knew that her problems of low esteem and inability to protect herself would require longer-term work, but the pressing need was to prevent injury or death at the hands of a violent man.*

CLIP 11.2
Establishing a
Sense of Safety

4. ***Help clients contain feelings and reduce stress.*** When working with clients who have experienced trauma, clinicians need to help clients protect themselves from overwhelming intrusive feelings and thoughts. There is widespread misperception in popular culture that emotional catharsis brings about immediate healing. However, encouragement to ventilate tumultuous feelings may not be indicated until clients have developed better coping strategies for containment and stress reduction.

Workers should be prepared to explain to clients the wisdom of strengthening self-protecting and containing capacities before putting further pressure on already overburdened adaptive capacity. An important message to communicate is that all people need to exercise the capacities to both have and not have emotional reactions because both capacities—expression and self-restraint—are required throughout life. Expression makes sense when people are able to self-soothe and contain extremes of feeling or behavior that would otherwise destabilize them or others around them.

Stress-reducing strategies help cushion the recall of especially disturbing events such as rape, family violence, and massively distressing disasters where life and property are lost in the blink of an eye. Some people forget to breathe when stressed, but they can be coached to find safe and calming images or "places to go" in their minds to contain distress and quickly exit from distressing preoccupations. From prior spiritual or meditative practice, many people already know how to focus on and regulate their breathing to calm and reach meditative states. During any crisis, these practices can be revived and strengthened, first using them with the clinician and then resuming meditative calming on their own. We also discuss and encourage physical self-strengthening through gym activity and other exercise like skating, walking, jogging, and good diet and health practices. We encourage the use of spiritual resources and increasing the time spent with positive people and activities.

We can practice containment and relaxation strategies with the client in our meetings, so that these can also be tried with increasing success and frequency at home or on their own. These strategies include our intervening during a session to limit the subject matter, the feeling reaction, or the amount of time spent on feeling or thinking about upsetting material. Stress reduction strategies can also be taught, practiced together, and applied outside of the meetings, with reports back as to their personal or cultural appropriateness and ease or difficulty of use.

> *I generally tell my clients to start with those relaxing/soothing skills that have worked for them in the past. If they typically use jogging, hot baths, and TV shows to relax or take care of themselves, I encourage them to do that rather than take up a new skill or activity. When faced with the stress of a crisis, clients don't need the added stress of learning a new activity. On the other hand, for some clients, focusing on a new skill may help to distract them from perseverating on the crisis. It depends on the individual client.*

EXAMPLES

Client A: I just keep having these images in my mind of the tornado ripping everything apart, and our sheep flying through the air and then turning up dead, miles away.

Clinician A: Whenever you get those images, you might try focusing on your breath and your breathing. Imagine a calm and comfortable place of complete safety. Keep enlarging this in your mind, screening out all concerns. It's a way of distracting and refocusing your thoughts. The slowing and lengthening of your breathing also calms anxiety all by itself. Let's try it together.

Client B: I can't sleep at night. I feel anxious and scared of being alone in the house.

Clinician B: That's hard. Let's think together about things you could do to feel safer. First tell me what you are doing prior to sleep.

Client B: I watch TV.

Clinician B: That might be a good idea if it isn't violent. Does it help?

Client B: Not really. I find I can't go to sleep.

Clinician B: Doing arduous exercises about an hour before bed can help your body relax.

EXERCISE 11.3   Eliciting and Containing Feelings

In groups of three or four, rotate the roles of interviewer and client. Do two different role plays. In the first, the client recounts a traumatic event, displaying very little affect. The clinician attempts to elicit feelings and validate the feelings as normal. In the second role-play, the client is dramatically spilling thoughts and feelings in a relatively incoherent way. The clinician practices helping the client to contain and self-soothe.

Whenever feasible, we encourage clients in crisis to try to avoid or reduce contact with situations and people who introduce more stress into their lives. Since some work and home stresses are natural and unavoidable, we can suggest ways of minimizing hassles by focusing on one task at a time, getting through one hour or day at a time, and giving maximum attention to activities with others that are likely to minimize conflict. Ironically, volunteering to help others in crisis actually helps people feel better because the recipients are usually grateful for the help and the activity gets them out of their isolation and usual routines. The skill is in finding the right activities that affirm and soothe the self without unduly taxing it.

Following the hurricane that tore through their area and left many homeless, Maxine practically had to be dragged by her sister to help serve turkey dinners to senior citizens on Thanksgiving Day. She felt she had nothing left to give to anybody after many weeks in a shelter and a bout of the flu. She agreed to go and later said it was the best thing she ever did, because she had forgotten that some people were worse off than she was and were thankful for any little thing people did for them. She later went back and offered to do Bible study one day a week to take her mind off things, and reading the Testament with others helped her remember how calming that was.

DVD

CLIP 11.3
Stress Reduction

5. ***Quickly establish a baseline of previous functional capacity.*** To develop a sound assessment of current client assets and realistic goals, we also take a brief history of client relational patterns, educational and work levels, coping strategies, and crisis management experiences prior to the present crisis. Clients' past aspirations and plans, ideas about self, and expectations for the future are also important to elicit, as they often inform the client's current reactions and capacities for readjustment following a destabilization. Since helplessness, confusion, and inadequacy are common reactions to destabilizing events, it is important to ask clients whether these attitudes, feelings, or self-assessments are new or were a pattern prior to the triggering event. If new, they may benefit from focus and countering by the clinician, whereas if they indicate ongoing personality patterns, they may require more work at another time.

This rapidly gathered information constitutes a functional baseline with which to compare important aspects of client functioning during and following the current crisis. For example, if a man is newly using substances to calm himself for sleep since the onset of crisis, planning and goals will be different than if he had a history of episodic problem drinking unrelated to particular stress levels.

6. ***Focus on the effects of the crisis on relationships and feelings of relatedness.*** Because people in crisis often isolate themselves to avoid further emotional stimulation or conflict, clinicians should periodically check in with them about the nature and extent of their relationships with family, friends, and others. It is not unusual for clients to become irritable or sad when encouraged to have more contact with people. At times, relating makes them remember people or things they have lost, so they may feel it is wiser to hunker down alone to avoid remembering.

A good relational experience with a clinician or other compassionate friend/helper is one of the best antidotes for isolation because it can rekindle longings for more contact with others. If ever there were a need for a "holding environment," it is with people recovering from crisis and trauma who have for all intents and purposes given up on themselves and others. If we provide unfailing support, positive regard, carefulness of approach, and sensitivity to mood and timing, it can help restore the client's understanding that, while many bad things happen to people, all people are not bad.

Additionally, the very focus on relating itself brings the importance of human ties back to mind and offers clients a chance to grieve their losses as well as entertain fleeting thoughts of restoring positive ties with others over time. In this work, we listen for subtle signs of disengagement or reengagement (e.g., spending too much time alone or beginning to come out of one's shell one step at a time). Tiny signs of progress can be missed unless there is routine checking in about relationships and activities involving more time outside the home. People who feel damaged often need a longer time to take the risk of reconnecting more openly with others, especially if they have to explain the crisis event to others before reaching some level of understanding, self-acceptance, and peace about it.

7. *Involve family and friends in the intervention.*   Friends and family (biological and chosen) can be rich sources of information about the crisis and about the presence or absence of natural helping resources currently available to the client. Resilient people often return rather rapidly to familiar routines and responsibilities if these make sense and are still available in a daily life altered by crisis. Family, friends, and fellow members of faith communities can all reach out, support, and assist crisis-stressed loved ones in reintegrating themselves into the familiar, thus decreasing feelings of estrangement and "being ill." However, crises may both stress and isolate clients from their usual base of support by virtue of some stigma, fear, or overwhelming sense of separateness caused by triggering events.

> *After some grief work with me right after the loss of her husband, Ida went back to work pretty quickly because she loved lunches with her fellow workers at the counseling center. Yet, even though music had always comforted her, she couldn't bring herself to sing in her church choir again at this time because she wanted to "be mad at God a little longer" for taking her husband from her at too young an age.*

If the crisis is related to or caused by family or friends (domestic violence, sexual abuse, rejection by family for being gay), it may not be appropriate to involve them in the work. It is important to assess with the client whether including family or friends in the work would be more distressing than productive.

Charles Figley (1995) observes that significant others in the person's life may experience "**emotional contagion,**" that is, they may "catch" or absorb the loved one's distress and be in crisis as well. Thus, we try to involve significant others early in any crisis work when family members and friends of the person in crisis may also need support, information, and an opportunity to discuss events and reactions.

8. *Focus on strengths and hope.* A common problem of people in crisis is that they easily forget their strengths and reliable resources, especially if these have not initially led to the immediate resolution of crisis conditions. We thus ask about client strengths—small or large—demonstrated prior to the crisis. We communicate the normalizing beliefs that crisis discombobulates everyone and that the resulting confusion and disequilibrium are not a confirmation of personal deficits or problems too huge to resolve.

Workers responding quickly and knowledgeably to crisis have to be careful to maintain a strengths perspective even while using benign authority to create a sense of calm, orderly process, and hope for change. Overwhelmed and exhausted people often feel better and more competent if they can assist in their own recovery or need-meeting efforts and not just stand by while turmoil unfolds around them. Furthermore, if we become too directive or controlling, clients' feelings of being overwhelmed and out of control may be reinforced rather than dissipated.

9. *Help the client make meaning of the events.* Clinicians help clients use their cognitive skills to make meaning of their crisis experiences. We noted earlier that one of the first tasks is to help the client tell a coherent story. Later, the clinician helps the client create a fuller understanding of the events and situations around the crisis. This often involves challenging perceptual distortions as well as helping clients feel in charge of their lives.

Locus of control refers to one's perceptions of personal power and place in the world. It also concerns the extent to which people see themselves as capable of effectively influencing outcomes and accomplishing their desired goals. When people experience a crisis, when their perceptions and expectations of themselves and their world are shattered, they frequently experience life as essentially out of their control or as controlled by cruel fate, a god, or a karmic destiny playing itself out. People often ask themselves "why me?" and come up with answers that are a fulfillment of their worst suspicions about themselves. Survivors of sexual assault, for example, often describe themselves as damaged goods and can feel somehow responsible for the assault ("I should have left when the others did," "I shouldn't have gone there that late at night"). Lone survivors of accidents almost universally struggle with the question of why they survived and others ("nicer than me") did not.

As we do routinely in our work to help people alter distorted beliefs and perceptions, we can gently challenge posttraumatic harsh self-judgments by exploring the evidence on which they are based, by asking for alternative explanations of why events happened, by actively suggesting other interpretations or implications of events, and by sharing stories of anonymous survivors of similar events to illustrate different conclusions for the client to consider.

> *I find it tricky to talk about others who have been in a similar experience because it may make my clients worry about confidentiality. Clients may worry that "If she is telling me about someone else's story, what does she tell other clients about my story?" Stressing anonymity helps somewhat, but I have chosen to say, "I read about people in a similar situation once . . . ."*

CLIP 11.4
Making Meaning
of Events

Clients also have to find a way to integrate the crisis experience into their lives and identities so that it becomes one part of their story instead of the whole story. Some people may not be able to get beyond the destabilizing event, but many others can be helped by individual, family, or group work after the initial crisis is resolved.

10. *Maintain a here-and-now focus on the present crisis.*   Because of the compound nature of many crises, the discussion of events, reactions, and interpretations often leads naturally to past crises being rekindled by the present one. For example, a stressful job change may remind a man of an earlier crisis he went through when switching from a public to a private high school. Being resettled in public housing near a noisy airport may rekindle a Bosnian family's frightening memories of planes pulverizing their village. Our goal is to find the right balance between here-and-now focus and there-and-then exploration so that clients do not become overwhelmed by the powerful combination of past and present review.

We may speak of past losses if such expression will not destabilize current efforts to cope. Judgments are formed by evaluating the client's emotional stability when talking about the past. If they can tolerate linkages between the past and present, clients need to feel free to grow at times through making useful connections between feelings now and feelings then or through comparing adaptive strategies available in the past with more (or less) sophisticated and helpful resources available now. A clinician's main consideration is to try to confine work to a focus on present concerns, needs, and reactions so that situations are resolved as quickly and constructively as possible.

11. *Check regularly for suicidal or other self-harming behaviors.*   We regularly check in with clients in crisis about their distress levels, moods, and preoccupying thoughts. We listen for signs of despair, hopelessness, wishes to escape or to rejoin lost ones, or for mentions of means of self-harm such as pills, weapons, risky behaviors, or fantasies of driving into bridge abutments or jumping off nearby cliffs. We are also alert for behaviors such as suddenly giving away possessions or money or suddenly presenting as strangely relieved and happy—the result of a decision to end life. Discussions with supervisors may need to be augmented by consultations with appropriate psychiatric staff, with an eye to possible hospitalization if the client cannot persuasively contract for safety and dispose of harmful items or substances that would make impulsive self-harming action all too easy.

> When her husband died suddenly, Micah ingested so much aspirin that it made her sick and she threw up. Interestingly, she did this at the time her best friend was to pick her up for lunch, which suggested to me that she was at least ambivalent about killing herself—a good sign. However, when she was subsequently hospitalized, I did note with the inpatient physician that I thought her gesture had been a serious one and asked if he could only give her very limited prescriptions for antidepressants to make it harder for her to use the medication to kill herself.

12. *Use rituals and other marker events.*   An important reintegrative tool that clinicians have learned from people undergoing recovery from traumatic shock is the importance of rituals in restoring feelings of agency, dignity, and

connections. Some survivors and relatives of those lost in the 9/11 attacks have helped design memorial sites and tributes honoring those lost. Survivors of those lost in the 1995 bombing of the Federal Building in Oklahoma City came together in their grief to have the ruins of the building supplanted by a lasting memorial honoring the victims. Much as the English did following the traumatic loss of Princess Diana in 1997, citizens of Oklahoma City converted a bomb site perimeter fence into a wall of remembrance by weaving thousands of flowers, sympathy notes, and toys into the fence as an ongoing expression of grief and respect. Survivors went on to lobby for and to create a permanent memorial park and museum on the site of the blast. Web sites like those for James Byrd, Jr., and Matthew Shepard offer the opportunities to participate in virtual rituals as well as providing education about hate crimes.

The AIDS Memorial Quilt has achieved a similar result in bringing loved ones and survivors together to honor those lost and to connect thousands of people in support of programs and research to improve victims' lives and chances of survival. Annual services that celebrate the lives of national heroes like the Reverend Martin Luther King, Jr., Cesar Chavez, and Rosa Parks also serve as uniting experiences and beacons of hope for those still struggling for respect, rights, and improved economic opportunities.

When a longtime school administrator died last year, two colleagues devised a touching ritual in which her picture, flowers, and candles were placed on a table around which a large group collected in a remembrance circle, each recalling aloud something precious about the deceased.

EXERCISE 11.4 Rituals For Healing

In class, discuss rituals you have participated in or learned about that help survivors of trauma honor losses and begin to heal. What thinking and planning needs to take place before enacting a ritual? How will you decide who should participate and in what manner? Can you think of any rituals you witnessed that did not appear to serve their stated purpose? How would you have carried out the ritual differently? Has your family passed on to you any rituals of healing that you would like to share with the group?

---

13. *Refer to mutual aid groups.*   It often helps people in crisis to speak with and learn from others like themselves who have been through similar ordeals. Joyce West Stevens (1997) underscores the importance of helping African-American adolescent females develop and sustain strong kinship and reference group connections as they deal with societal devaluations (microaggressions) based on racism and gender bias. Women with new breast cancer diagnoses can benefit from talking with others in Reach to Recovery Programs, and men who have experienced heart attacks may utilize Heart to

Heart groups in rehabilitation settings. The very process of mutual aid—the exchange of caring, coping tips, and reinforcing support for persistence—is revitalizing for all members as they feel themselves able to help others in spite of their own stress and self-doubt (Shulman, 2006).

It has become common for relatives of people lost in jetliner crashes to form support groups following the crash. These groups not only place flowers at the crash site and devise religious services and memorials, but they also have advocated successfully to get airlines to improve their notification and support processes following airline accidents.

In areas without such group programs, clinicians can start mutual aid groups simply by asking clients who need support and education if they would be interested in meeting with other affected people about ways they cope with a shared crisis. Very often, if child or elder care and transportation are provided as needed, men and women are ready to give support groups a try.

These groups are now more frequently referenced in the media, creating more awareness of their benefits in reducing isolation and increasing awareness of resources and coping strategies to help with stress. Katherine Briar-Lawson (1998) estimates that some 25 million people in the United States are served by the "giving and benefiting ethos" of self-help groups promoting "non-elite and non-hierarchical peer power" (p. 546).

14. *Prepare the client for ending.* Usually, crisis intervention is understood by participants to be purposely short term. As the work progresses, the clinician should mention preparation for ending more frequently. He or she moves to a less active stance, encouraging the client to assume more responsibility for the meetings and to devise problem-solving strategies for use in the future. Crisis intervention usually ends when clients have returned to precrisis levels and modes of functioning and have reestablished a reliable base of adequate resources, social support, and work or other meaningful activities.

Bonds can be unusually strong in crisis intervention, so both clinicians and clients should carefully attend to the ending work. Discussions at ending can include honoring the relationship and the work they have done together, as well as their meaning to each participant. They should discuss the client's plans for the future, as well as the support and resources that the client has established. (See Chapter 14 for a fuller discussion of endings and transitions.)

The multiple disasters caused by the 2005 back-to-back hurricanes Katrina and Rita have demonstrated that this benign concept of a well planned ending to crisis intervention is not always accurate. While thousands of people eventually received housing and other resources from shelters and relief centers around the United States, many of those who survived remain in what might rightly be called a "second state" of posttraumatic marginalization, outrage, and despair.

15. *Provide follow-up and ongoing support.* Clinicians and crisis response teams should plan periodic check-ins with "recovered" clients to assess well-being and coping capacities over time. Clients may also reach out to clinicians at anniversaries of important crises, such as deaths or disasters.

Cindy called me every fall, not mentioning what I knew—that this time of year was the anniversary of the deaths of both her mother and father. Often we simply caught up by phone, with her disclosing a new achievement or work stress getting her down. This year, I invited her to come in and see me, and she talked about the fact that I seemed like "good family" to her, and she hated to think of me dying or moving away "out of reach" when I retire, a prospect she's aware of. She herself could tie these feelings in to missing her dad, her closest supporter of many years, and she was able to experience a little more sadness with me over his death. We reviewed with delight her good work in maintaining a happy marriage over many years and the presence of a few really good friends in her life. I made sure she understood how much I've enjoyed working with her and that I am always glad to hear from her about how she is. To ease an eventual transition, I referred her to a younger colleague for some specialized work I don't do, and she agreed.

When Ongoing Clients Experience Crises

Crises can and do arise in the lives of ongoing clients. When they do, they often (not always) displace other work at hand. Clinicians need to shift gears to attend to the crisis, support coping, and mobilize any resources that might assist the client's adaptation to the new circumstances and challenges. Often clients use what has been learned in ongoing work to manage crises more quickly and resourcefully. We can also help them find similarities between a current crisis and upsetting situations they have resolved previously so that the current challenge feels less daunting or unmanageable.

Critical Incident Stress Debriefing (CISD)

Human service workers sometimes use an immediate and brief posttrauma group process known as **Critical Incident Stress Debriefing (CISD)** to help people begin to heal so that they do not go on to develop longer-term psychological difficulties or PTSD (McCammon & Allison, 1995). Chrys Harris (1995) describes critical incident stress debriefing as "a process of education, ventilation, validation, and preparation regarding the psychological and emotional impacts of a traumatic life event" (p. 108).

The education phase involves providing information about normal stress reactions, reassuring participants that their symptoms represent common human reactions under stress and not mental illness or individual "breakdown." Participants are then asked to discuss what they witnessed or experienced, and, in the next phase, what they felt and how they interpreted events and their reactions to these. Their experiences then receive validation and support, and, in a final phase, participants are prepared for what they may learn from the events and what normal reactions may persist for a time. They also learn about resources for ongoing counseling if they need or wish it in future. Positive relationships and coping activities are also encouraged.

Since CISD was first developed in 1983 by paramedic-turned-psychologist Jeffrey Mitchell (following a traumatic event he could not stop reacting to), numerous practitioners have developed variants on the original model. Many realized that in the first few hours and days posttrauma, people are often so numb and preoccupied with major loss and disruption that they either do not want to attend group meetings to ventilate or they drop out of them prematurely, feeling overstimulated by group content and affect. CISD in its various forms has been utilized to assist survivors of industrial accidents, workplace and school violence, fires, bombings, and other widely affecting traumatic events. While many studies and several meta-analyses of studies (Deahl, 2000) have found that participants have often felt relieved and educated from their CISD experiences, other studies have identified complaints of being overwhelmed and "retriggered" by the intensity of the experience. On follow-up, some participants had developed PTSD later anyway, so that the program did not insulate them against it as hoped, while others reported their symptoms greatly reduced and eliminated in three months' time (Irving & Long, 2001; McNally et al. 2003). Marwan Dwairy (2003) studied the use of CISD to help Palestinians with their stress reactions following terrorist events. He concluded that individual debriefing is not appropriate in cultures that are group or family focused. Practitioners considering using CISD programs should be aware of the need for further empirical support, as well as further clarification of what works best across a wide variety of populations and contexts. Individuals and groups should not be forced to attend CISD sessions. Many people prefer to find their own ways of working things through naturally and without outside intervention.

■ Community Crises

James and Gilliland (2005) note that environmental crises usually affect very large groups or communities, as when a flood destroys most of the housing in a village or a toxic waste accident causes terminal illnesses in many people living nearby. Responses to these widely affecting crises vary, depending on the strengths, needs, and resources available in local areas, on the community's beliefs about and access to outside services and helpers, and on the willingness and ability of insiders and outsiders alike to help in ways that feel empowering rather than overwhelming and demeaning.

Characteristics of Community Crises and Interventions

Environmental crises can affect a community in many destabilizing ways. Initially, they shake the fundamental beliefs of all affected regarding the predictability of daily life and the immutability of familiar support networks and resources. Other effects, such as the sudden breakup of families, the loss of pets and livestock, and the loss of most means of making a living, are equally distressing and combine with the following factors to devastate a community and trigger outside intervention.

The Entire Infrastructure of a Community Can Be Lost or Destabilized

Loss of customary support systems.   Often people turn to their friends, families, and social and spiritual networks for help in times of crisis. However, during overwhelming community crises such as tornadoes that destroy everything in a town, their most basic networks may all be experiencing trauma at the same time and unable to help each other as soon or as well as in the past. Television demonstrates this phenomenon graphically through postcrisis images of groups of neighbors and families in shock, staring fixedly at ruins, crying with each other, or digging fruitlessly for personal belongings long gone. Yet within hours or days, communities often pull together collectively to establish communication and order, to help each other with shelter, food, and the rescue of animals, and to seek governmental help for specific collective needs.

Crises have a way of revealing the nature and extent of any community's organization and disorganization, its power centers, and its marginalized groups in need of further inclusion and empowerment. In another apparent race- and class-based microaggression, the poor and many people of color in New Orleans affected by Hurricane Katrina have been largely sidelined again in planning for the safety and reconstruction of their traditional residential areas. It is in just such situations that clinicians can ally with political activists and supportive politicians to work to create an inclusive process for reconstruction of meaningful opportunities and networks when such devastating disasters strike.

Loss of leadership and community resources.   When calamity strikes a whole community, skilled leadership in the community may be disabled or destroyed. Community leaders may be killed, injured, or in a crisis state over their own losses and unable to respond to the needs of the community.

There may be no phone service, electricity, or sanitation, and there may not even be enough food and water for the number of people in need. Roads, bridges, and transportation systems to other people and resources may be out of commission for a long time, meaning that basic supplies and means of sheltering people and communicating have to be flown in on a continuous basis until the foundations of community life are restored. Such effects have been observed in the Southeast Asian and African tsunamis of 2004 and the Pakistani earthquakes of 2005. It has been estimated that it will require two decades to restore community structures, institutions, and resources to those affected by these events.

Political and legal authorities themselves can be paralyzed by the degree of loss and devastation and may have difficulty providing immediate protective and reorganizing responses, causing people to panic about their survival. For example, as floodwaters rose rapidly during Hurricane Katrina, numerous policemen abandoned their posts to save their families from widespread flooding, and others were among the citizens photographed looting local stores for food and water.

Clinicians, too, may be traumatized by losses and unable to respond for a time as helpers of others. In addition, their agencies may no longer be standing or operative, and colleagues may have been injured or killed.

Loss of a sense of agency, purpose, and meaning in life.   Devastating community crises leave members feeling that life is out of their control. They may feel that much of what anchored their lives and gave them meaning and purpose has been lost forever and that little can be trusted or counted on anymore, including people offering support and assistance. This despairing worldview often leads to anguished and aimless pacing or searching for lost people and possessions; to numb passivity, excessive sleep, and bouts of crying; or to angry protests and unreasonable demands for the immediate restoration of life as it used to be. Some members may abandon the community temporarily or permanently, moving away to recover with relatives in another locale, yet finding it hard either to forget or to reclaim their roots.

People from Outside the Community May Come to Help

When damage to people, institutions, and property is severe and widespread, outsiders, including the Red Cross, the Federal Emergency Management Agency (FEMA), the National Guard, the military, and a host of state and regional agencies trained to provide emergency assistance, may be called in to help. The focus of these helpers is on the most basic survival needs of the whole community and on meeting the needs of all people, not just powerful ones or insiders. Clinical professions also participate in community interventions. For example, the American Psychological Association's Disaster Response Network consists of trained volunteer professionals flown into various locales beset by crisis. The Red Cross and many social work and counseling organizations have crisis response training for workers in disasters and school emergencies.

Suspicion of strangers.   James and Gilliland (2001) note that small, isolated, or poor communities may lack the expertise and financial resources to respond adequately to widely affecting crises, yet may be suspicious of outsiders so that "fear, rumor, parochialism, and inaccessibility to services can keep the community traumatized" for a longer period of time than is necessary (p. 660). This is especially true if the outside helpers are from a different cultural, religious, or language group than the affected community or if they treat the community as too inept to engage in meaningful joint assessment and planning.

Under crisis conditions, those affected may knit together more tightly in their behaviors and beliefs to survive with traditions intact and may not be comfortable depending on outsiders to meet most of their basic needs. People can quickly feel sidelined by outsiders and "experts," who may be suspected of not really understanding who the survivors are and what they are up against. A we–they perspective is easy for people to develop under unremitting stress, and families or groups may "circle their wagons" to ward off further distress. It can take a while for people to accept and believe in newcomers, especially when crises have destroyed their faith in other human beings.

Although nonlocal clinicians may be the most experienced and skilled at counseling around certain crises in the life of a community or region, they may be seen as unwelcome intruders. Thus, we must respond with sensitivity to our outsider status, and community leaders should be observed bridging outsiders to insiders through demonstrations of positive regard and gratitude. Indigenous leaders must be seen requesting outsiders' help, welcoming them publicly at a gathering of the community, and familiarizing outsiders with local beliefs about the nature of disasters and the locally sanctioned ways of seeking or receiving help. News of the positive ways outsiders do actually help must be widely disseminated informally to encourage residents to use the help offered.

Utilizing the community's own power. From the onset of crisis, community members must be empowered to act on their own behalf at every opportunity to prevent the malignant effects of passivity and despair in the aftermath of community crises. Restoration of a sense of agency and worth in people who have lost their sense of a secure base, as well as their sense of control over life events, is a first priority in the prevention of further personal, familial, or systemic disorganization. Sometimes large group process is the best and only way to help people ventilate feelings and concerns because it is an efficient means of enabling people to experience their commonalities and provide mutual aid. The more people come to know about each other's feelings, ideas, caring, and coping, the stronger their community can be once it is reconstituted, and the readier it can be to face adversity in the future.

Interventions by both insiders and outsiders must value and ensure the active collaboration of ordinary community members in decision-making, planning, and reconstructive action all along the way. Unfortunately, citizens with power often find it easier to exclude their already marginalized fellow citizens in order to speed the process of reconstruction by allocating planning power and emergency funding to better known, well connected insiders. James and Gilliland (2005) note that a lot of research indicates that, when disaster strikes, a community's natural altruism does not extend as readily to the elderly, poor, less educated, or ethnic minority residents.

Listening and responding, quickly and sympathetically, to all requests for special forms of help signals respect for all those affected, and an appreciation that they often know better than outsiders what is most helpful in restoring their faith in people and in collective action.

> *One thing our community asked for right away and got was an expanded rescue force rowing around the area rescuing beloved pets stranded on barn roofs, housetops, and slabs of high ground. After we insisted, rules designed to maintain healthy environments were changed in the shelters so that families could have their pets with them as familiar sources of support. Some livestock were also rescued and secured in separate areas, representing the promise of restored livelihood over time.*

Many helpers, many complications. Community interventions necessarily involve many helpers and agencies, each providing different but necessary services. Efficiency and the prevention of wasteful duplication require a great degree of close relating, coordination, and trust in each other to follow through as planned. That many strangers can come together in unfamiliar locales and rapidly provide excellent reconstructive and lifesaving services is a testimony to the professional dedication and preparation of so many skilled helpers, including clinicians.

James and Gilliland (2005) describe instances of "too much helping" that can impede or complicate a community's collective efforts to reconsolidate through mutual aid and reorganization. They deplore what they describe as well-intentioned but sometimes misguided "trauma tourism," in which throngs of well-meaning "helpers" and "the trauma industry" flood in, un-invited and uncoordinated, to help people they automatically assume will be panicky, inept at coping, and in need of guidance and protection. McNally et al. (2003) report that more than 9,000 counselors streamed unbidden into New York City following the World Trade Center, setting up counseling sites that very few people used except to get claim forms.

Coordination. The coordination of services and providers is vital to mar-shal quickly a variety of interventions while conserving precious resources. A group of community and agency leaders identifies community needs and designates interventions and roles. A crucial aspect of this coordination is deciding on the goals and steps of various interventions and then collectively assigning and carrying out roles so that efforts are not duplicated or wasted. In this way, people get the timely and appropriate forms of help they need without being deluged with helpers. It is not a good idea to jump into a dis-aster scene doing whatever feels natural.

Uncoordinated emergency interventions can add to the chaos and con-fusion, can send conflicting messages, can wastefully duplicate services for some while others get nothing, and can undermine careful centralized plan-ning and the equitable distribution of resources. Chaotic service provision and lack of accountability also allow unscrupulous people—both survivors and "helpers"—to siphon off resources for their own profit. For example, an entrepreneur in New Orleans actually devised tour bus trips that take curi-ous visitors through the city's ruins as numbed fellow citizens move out trash and try to rebuild.

Communication. Rumor and misinformation are two great destabilizing forces in the period following a community crisis. People can be unsettled by misinformation and begin to react in ways that further destabilize already pressured systems. For example, following a flood, if citizens are mis-takenly informed by a panicky neighbor that their homes are being looted, they may unwisely try to reach their homes alone and be drowned in a subsequent tidal surge.

Emergency communications need to be clear, specific, and limited to the important information people need to feel safe, informed, and heard by authorities. Unless invited to do so and well-informed by the response lead-ership as to what should be communicated, clinicians and other emergency workers should not get involved in speculative discussions with clients about things to come or hoped-for services that have not yet materialized.

Intervention staff members usually establish a centrally located communications center that collaboratively produces and distributes informational reports for leaflet and media distribution. If media infrastructure has not been devastated by the disaster, clarifying reports are broadcast regularly on radio, TV, and the Internet at set intervals and in the multiple languages used in the area. Trusted native language speakers may also be called on to move from area to area, answering questions and providing the latest news. Crisis response leadership may request that clinicians wishing to participate in the crisis intervention be speakers of the area's primary languages. They may also ask willing community members to act as translators once they have been briefed on the counseling process and goals, as well as the need for confidentiality.

James and Gilliland (2005) observe that, when crises strike, we usually do not have the culturally suitable resources needed to help the many people who are suddenly affected. However, each locality should be preparing both human and concrete resources for their specific populations. If disaster response planners are aware that a large number of elderly live in their community, they should include plans for the evacuation of the elderly and disabled. If a community is composed of mostly Spanish-speaking individuals, planners should be sure that information is available in Spanish. Even if no culturally appropriate resources are available, James and Gilliland suggest that establishing a relationship built on hope, trust, and credibility can be a starting point and a key ingredient in helping survivors begin to access resources and to cope. The support of friends, family, and other allies has proved to be remarkably effective in helping people stabilize and develop beneficially after crisis (Tedeschi & Calhoun, 1996).

■ The Clinician in Crisis

Clinicians' reactions to working with people in crisis are commonly observed and have been variously referred to as "**emotional contagion**" (Miller, Stiff, & Ellis, 1988), "secondary traumatic stress" (Figley, 1983), "traumatic countertransference" (Herman, 1997), "compassion fatigue" (Figley, 1995), and "vicarious traumatization" (McCann & Pearlman, 1990). Figley (1995) argues that we get these secondary stress, or **vicarious trauma**, reactions because "the process of empathizing with a traumatized person helps us to understand the person's experience of being traumatized, but, in the process, we may be traumatized as well" (p. 15). He observes that clinicians who have the greatest capacity for empathy may also be at the greatest risk of developing what he calls "compassion stress." We can at times experience symptoms similar to those of our clients in crisis, including difficulty sleeping, nightmares, anxiety, and intrusive thoughts.

For those of us who work with violence and abuse, repeated stories of the brutality people inflict on one another can shake our faith in human relationships. This can affect both professional and personal relationships outside work as we take upset responses home with us. For example, according to Figley (1995), women who work with rape survivors "often develop a general disgust for rapists that extends to all males" (p. 1). As Herman (1997) notes:

> Repeated stories of human rapacity and cruelty inevitably challenge the therapist's basic faith. It also heightens her sense of personal vulnerability. She may become more fearful of other people in general and more distrustful even in close relationships. She may find herself becoming increasingly cynical about the motives of others and pessimistic about the human condition (p. 141).

Workers can experience vicarious trauma from empathizing with clients in crisis but can also experience crises in their professional lives—for example, when their place of employment closes down on short notice, when a client commits suicide, or when there is violence against a colleague in the workplace. In addition, we can experience direct stress and trauma from the hazards of working long hours in stressful or high-risk situations without adequate support and supervision.

Community crises can also affect clinicians, who may be struggling with the loss of their own loved ones, pets, or material goods at the same time as they are trying to help others cope with similar losses. While encouraging others to express themselves freely, we may not think that we, as self-styled models of resilience, should express distress in public. Yet everyone may be staying in close proximity in a public place such as a gym or an armory.

Clinicians who have experienced previous crises in their own lives can have unfinished business stirred up by working with clients in a similar crisis (Figley, 1995). Finally, we may be facing our own current personal life crises, such as the illness or death of loved ones, becoming depressed or distractible, and wondering how we can continue to provide good service to others. As clinicians, we need to attend to how our own crises, past or present, affect our abilities to work effectively with clients in crisis.

> *I took a man on in treatment who had been through a number of things that I had in my own childhood. During one memorable period of time, he began to have nightmares of a man attacking him in the dark. Shortly after that, without realizing that his story had evoked my own childhood trauma, I began to have scary illusions when entering my apartment that an attacker was waiting for me in the shower or the closet. I actually had to go check each time to make sure no one was there and was very embarrassed yet gripped by these ideas, and I distinctly remember wishing that the client generating these fears would drop out of treatment. That would fix everything, I thought.*

Herman (1997) notes that the therapist "empathically shares the patient's experience of helplessness. This may lead the therapist to underestimate the value of her own knowledge and skill, lose sight of the patient's strengths and resources, lose confidence in the power of the therapeutic relationship . . . feel de-skilled" (p. 141). She also believes therapists can experience "profound grief" in working with victims of childhood sexual abuse and trauma.

Mary Ann Dutton and Francine Rubenstein (1995) note that clinicians may detach from clients, distancing by judging, labeling, or pathologizing the traumatic reaction ". . . which creates the illusion that the client's reaction to the traumatic event is in some way different from that of a 'normal' individual. Other forms of detachment include adopting a personal and emotional distance from the client . . . being chronically late or frequently canceling appointments, or allowing frequent interruptions during appointments . . . " (p. 87).

Herman (1997) believes that another way of detaching is "to feel contempt for the patient's helplessness, or paranoid fear of the patient's vindictive rage" (p. 145). A less obvious form of detachment is that of actually taking on so many assignments involving traumatic stress that no one person or story can truly engage us deeply because we are always moving rapidly in and out of contact to serve so many people. Detachment is also observed in those of us who try to identify a domain of practice in which there will—hopefully—be no work with trauma. No such domain exists.

Self-Care to Counter Worker Stress

Clinicians and other crisis responders now recognize that we, too, need help to digest, make meaning of, and move on from the often overwhelming sensory and emotional experiences involved in trauma work. An important aspect of such self-care is setting some limits on the number of clients in severe crisis to be seen at any one time. Some jobs do not permit such a limit because the clinician's role is precisely that of emergency room or neighborhood crisis responder, and crisis is the specific raison d'être and focus of the work. Even then, if we are taxed beyond the ability to perform our duties in a professional manner, it is our ethical responsibility to negotiate with superiors for periodic relief from taking on new clients, if only temporarily.

When an agency does, however, permit more balance in assignments, it is important that we take advantage of the opportunity to *diversify assignments*. Supervision and consultation are musts in crisis and trauma work. Just as clients need help and support in dealing with crises, so do clinicians. Informed, safe, and reliable supervision provides a unique opportunity to ventilate and receive knowledge and support following upsetting experiences with clients and communities. Rescue urges, overidentification, detachment, and judgmentalism can be spotted, identified, and worked on so that workers are less likely to burn out in the work.

Supervisors can normalize periodic feelings of hopelessness, helplessness, anger, or guilt about not having suffered as much as others, not having saved people, and not always providing the "just right" intervention with people deeply in crisis. Whenever working alone with highly stressed and disorganized families presents more challenges than an individual clinician can respond to adequately, supervision can redirect clinicians to *work in teams*. Debriefings, supportive supervision, teamwork, continuing support from friends and family, and periodic respite from work can all play a role in sustaining crisis responders.

CLIP 11.5
Community Crises

■ Conclusion

Crisis affects everyone: No one is immune. When beliefs, familiar people, structures, and resources are suddenly gone, crisis reactions call for brief, immediate, well focused, and sensitive interventions to reestablish a sense of connection and capacity to cope. Only with awareness, information, and care can clients and clinicians alike minimize stress and destabilization from repeated crises and maximize the opportunity for healing and growth. Rituals, social support, and restorative activity with others can refocus survivors' strengths and altruism in empowering ways that rekindle feelings of efficacy and safe belonging.

In all clinical work, including crisis intervention, we pay special attention to relationship dynamics. In Chapter 12, we will discuss the skills that clinicians use to directly address the relationship process.

■ Suggested Readings

Daniel, Jessica H. (2000). The courage to hear: African American women's memories of racial trauma. In Leslie C. Jackson & Beverly Greene (Eds.), *Psychotherapy with African American women* (pp. 126–144). New York: Guilford.

Herman, Judith. (1997). *Trauma and recovery.* New York: Basic Books.

James, Richard, & Gilliland, Burl E. (2005). *Crisis intervention strategies* (5th Ed.). Belmont, CA: Thomson Brooks/Cole.

Knight, Carolyn. (2006). Groups for individuals with traumatic histories: Practice considerations for social workers, *Social Work, 51*, 20–30.

McNally, Richard J., Bryant, Richard A., & Ehlers, Anke. (2003). Does early psychological intervention promote recovery from posttraumatic stress? *Psychological Science in the Public Interest, 4*, (2), 45–79.

van der Kolk, Bessel A., Hopper, James W., and Osterman, Janet E. (2001). Exploring the nature of traumatic memory: Combining clinical knowledge with laboratory methods. *Journal of Aggression, Maltreatment, & Trauma, 4*, (9)–31.

Webb, Nancy Boyd (Ed.) (2004). *Mass trauma and violence: Helping families and children cope.* New York: Guilford.

■ Self-Explorations

1. Have you personally experienced a traumatic event? In your journal, record the event and your reactions to it. Ronnie Janoff-Bulman (1992) believes that trauma shatters people's assumptions about the world. Do you think the trauma you experienced affected your worldview? In what ways?

2. Discuss a traumatic event that happened to someone else but had a significant impact on you. It could be something that happened to a member of your family or someone close to you, or it could be an event that happened to someone you did not know. Discuss how it affected you.

3. Make a list of the common ways you cope with crisis. You might use different coping mechanisms in different situations, but list the ones you use most often. What determines the strategies you use and when you use them?

4. Have you ever experienced a crisis that, at the time, you thought of as a negative event, but from which there later emerged productive outcomes and personal growth? Discuss the events and what came of them for you personally.

■ Essay Questions

1. Define vicarious trauma. How does it affect the clinician's cognitive schemas? List and discuss some ways that clinicians can resolve or balance the vicarious trauma in their lives.

2. Define "environmental traumas" and "human-made traumas." Discuss the differences between them. What local or national factors can cause the two kinds of traumas to occur together? Can you give an example?

3. Describe a specific natural disaster you witnessed, were a part of, or know a lot about. If it were to occur again and you could give advice to intervention teams who are about to go in and try to help, what suggestions and cautions would you give them?

4. In what circumstances would you encourage clients to tell their crisis stories immediately, welcoming whatever feelings were present? In what circumstances would you advise clients to go slowly so as not to be retraumatized by the unsettling content or intense flooding of emotion?

5. This chapter explained that crisis presents both danger and opportunity. Discuss what that means, giving examples of crisis components that illustrate your discussion.

■ Key Terms

Compound crisis	Locus of control
Coping mechanisms	Microaggressions
Crisis	Natural disasters
Critical Incident Stress Debriefing (CISD)	Posttraumatic Stress Disorder (PTSD)
Decompensate	Precipitating events
Developmental crises	Predisposing factors
Emotional contagion	Resilience
Environmental crises	Secondary trauma
Hate crimes	Situational crises
Human-made disasters	Trauma
Insidious trauma	Vicarious trauma

CHAPTER 12

The Clinical Relationship: Issues and Dynamics

■ A Unique Relationship

A client once said to me, "This is the strangest relationship I've ever known. I trust, love, and reveal myself deeply to someone I barely know."

A clinical relationship can be one of the most important and memorable relationships in a person's life, for both client and clinician. Its power and meaning for people are evidenced by its widespread appearance in the popular culture as the subject of numerous jokes and cartoons and as a topic in novels and films. Many people come to count on the professional clinical relationship as a source of support, reflection, information, and activity for meaningful change. The qualities of nonjudgmental acceptance, confidentiality, client-centeredness, and purposefulness render the clinical relationship a unique experience in most people's lives. It feels almost too good to be true, and, for most people, it takes some getting used to.

The clinical relationship not only provides a context in which change can occur, but it is often the means *by* which change occurs. The clinical relationship can be used as an interpersonal laboratory in which developments and issues arising within the relationship can be worked on in vivo to bring about change. Miller and Stiver (1997) suggest that **mutual empathy** is at the core of human development and of all effective work with people, whether with individuals, families, groups, or communities. They assert that mutual empathy in the clinical relationship leads to **mutual empowerment** in both clients and clinicians. Mutual empathy and feeling moved by each other's behaviors and reactions within the work combine with honest process observations and feedback to stimulate mutual growth in clinicians and clients in five ways:

1. *Increased zest and vitality are experienced from the energizing effect of emotional joining.*
2. *Capacity to act is increased by the awareness of one's positive contributions to the ongoing relationship and process.*
3. *Knowledge is enhanced regarding the ways in which relationships can develop.*
4. *The participants' sense of worth increases due to each other's recognition and validation.*
5. *Pleasure in this particular relationship creates a desire for more connection in a gradually widening circle of growth-fostering relationships.*

Developing skills for relational work with clients requires knowledge of common human dynamics and of the relational preferences and patterns of many different cultures. This skill development also requires great self-awareness on the part of clinicians. Clients' lives and stories are precious. Our responsibility for their protection and safety in clinical work includes observing and adjusting our own thoughts, feelings, behaviors, and intentions so that we stay client-centered and purposeful in our professional use of self.

Relational tending is one of the hardest skills we have to learn in life as well as in clinical work. It requires accurately spotting and verbally addressing our mistakes in relationships with clients and others, and then working out together any hurts these mistakes cause. Ongoing self-observation and relational tending are aimed at minimizing the effects on the clinical relationship of clinicians' unresolved issues, personal biases, and blind spots.

We believe that the development of awareness, knowledge, and skills for tending the relationship is one of the most difficult yet satisfying aspects of clinical education. Beginning clinicians often think that, because they are nice people or have had so many good relationships, the relational aspect of work with clients should come easily. You may be surprised to discover how complicated the relationship can become in the course of purposeful work together. The clinician and the client enter into a relationship to work on a task or accomplish designated goals, yet almost inevitably, they also attend to some aspect of their relationship as their work together unfolds.

Most newcomers to clinical work are unaccustomed to the degree of attention to process that is required in clinical interviewing: the noticing and retaining of detail and nuance; the reflecting on meanings; the repeated self-exploration and adjustment in response to client needs; and the complex art of interweaving purposeful self-restraint and self-expression. The beginning clinician takes on the enormous task of learning how to attend to self, other(s), and the process of the relationship, while simultaneously focusing on the purpose and goals that gave rise to the relationship in the first place. There is, in short, much to learn.

In previous chapters, we have focused on many of the skills the clinician uses in the interviewing process. This chapter discusses some special issues in the clinical relationship and elucidates skills useful in addressing the issues as they arise.

■ Relationship Dynamics: The Real and the Symbolic

It is important that we attend to our reactions to clients, since these reactions often provide important information for further consideration. In addition, we pay careful attention to clients' reactions to us. The reactions of client and clinician to each other are dynamic and interactive. Some theorists attempt to distinguish between the "real," in-the-moment encounter between the two people and the "symbolic" relationship—referred to in psychodynamic theory as the transference and countertransference relationship (Coleman, 2000). The following discussion of related psychodynamic concepts of transference and countertransference may be helpful in understanding traditional psychodynamic principles regarding these processes and their importance in therapeutic relationships.

Transference

In psychodynamic theory, **transference** is the unconscious process by which early unresolved relational dynamics or conflicts are unwittingly displaced or "transferred" onto the current relationship with the clinician and then reenacted or expressed as though appropriate or "real" in the moment. It is crucial to remember that transference is an unconscious process and that, when individuals are caught up in it, they are unaware of its distorting influence on their thoughts, feelings, and behaviors in the moment. Remembering this helps us to be more understanding, patient, and less reactive to what would otherwise seem to be irrational or unwarranted behaviors in clients, ourselves, or others.

Psychodynamic theorists postulate both positive and negative transference as expected features of helping relationships. Both positive and negative transference can mobilize unresolved developmental issues for clients and clinicians alike regarding dependence, competence, authority, closeness, trust, and tender and sexual feelings. In **positive transference,** the client idealizes the clinician and may experience him or her as incomparably wise, caring, and helpful. When not extreme, such idealizations are thought to fuel the early stages of most human attachments and to sustain relationships through times of hardship and disappointment.

> *My supervisor told me that a teen client of mine seemed to be viewing me as a "kindly grandfather," even though I was a 26-year-old woman. She noted from an earlier process recording how the boy had fished and hunted with his grandfather, the only positive figure in his grade school years. Now he is frequently asking me to do things with him, things he used to love doing with his granddad.*

Psychodynamic clinicians believe that positive transference helps sustain the **working alliance** in spite of mistakes and disagreements. In the clinical relationship, clients may be unconsciously expressing unsatisfied longings for a wise, caring, and safe helper, from whom to gain soothing and strength for the work at hand. Unfortunately, positive transference can also lend itself to exploitation by unprincipled practitioners, since it tends to blind clients to their clinicians' manipulations and its halo effect can make clinicians seem far more caring and wise than they actually may be.

In **negative transference,** the client is thought to unconsciously express or act out in the moment old, unhappy stuck scenarios with the clinician as though the clinician were actually the exploiter, the abandoner, the molester, or the punisher who has harmed the client in the past. A client may misinterpret what the clinician says or does, may mishear words, or may mistake benign clinician behaviors as uncaring, exploitative, intentionally mean, or belittling. The inherent messages are frequently "You don't really care" or "You hurt me just like X did"—charges that reflect the antithesis of clinical purpose. Negative transference can be hard to tolerate, especially when we are doing our utmost to be available, supportive, and helpful while under attack. It can drive a wedge between the client and clinician unless the latter is conscientious in getting continuing supervision to assist in the management of reactions and of clinical process with the client.

At times, a clinician's manner or style may inadvertently approximate that of someone harmful to the client in the past. Furthermore, clients may even seem as though they are actually trying to get the clinician to harm them—for example, by flirting with or asking the clinician to socialize with them, by offering gifts or bribes, by menacing the clinician, or by openly violating laws the clinician is mandated to uphold. Many trauma theorists believe that severely abused individuals may unwittingly reenact transferential relational behaviors with others—including professional helpers—they believe have malign relational power over them (Chu, 1991; van der Kolk & van der Hart, 1991).

Ethnocultural Transference and Countertransference

Lillian Comas-Diaz and Frederick Jacobsen (1991) speak of **ethnocultural transference,** in which previous inter- or intraethnic cultural experiences are unconsciously displaced onto the clinical relationship. Such a reaction might manifest in a number of ways: A client might be overly compliant or demonstrate mistrust and suspiciousness toward the clinician. Similarly, a clinician might overexplore cultural issues to the detriment of meeting client needs; might deny differences, failing to spot them as salient in the moment; or might communicate pity, guilt, or aggression around ethnocultural issues.

Hierarchical Transference

Lillian Comas-Diaz and Beverly Greene (1994) believe that, in response to clinician authority, many poor female clients with histories of subordination may manifest **hierarchical transference**—feeling powerless and helpless in the relationship. Such feelings need to be noted and worked through as an empowering aspect of relational work. Of course, hierarchical transference can occur with all people, not just poor women.

Countertransference

Freud coined the term **countertransference** to describe the clinician's unconscious reactions to the client. Clinicians today are asked to scrutinize the relational process regularly for countertransference because it can occur in situations that replicate unresolved scenarios in the clinician's past. For example, a normally accepting clinician might begin to loathe or dread a particularly critical client. On reflection, he comes to see that, because of his own early experience of criticism from his perfectionistic father, he is taking the man's criticism personally and is resenting the client for it, as though at this moment he were back in the room with his own critical father. This realization helps him relax with the client and explore his criticisms more empathically.

Beyond Transference: A Feminist Therapy Perspective

Feminist therapist Laura Brown (1994) suggests that the symbolic relationship between clinician and client is more than and different from transference as it is typically described:

> The therapist is not simply defined as a neutral screen upon which internal reality is projected by a client; thus, the client's end of the symbolic exchange is not simply a distortion of the therapist based upon the client's prior experiences. Nor are all the passionate responses of therapist to client and client to therapist defined as necessarily derived from disruptive or disturbed elements in each person's past. Instead, the symbolic relationship in feminist therapy consists of lively and interactive responses to the changing meanings of the various factors that carry symbolic significance to either participant in the therapeutic encounter. While individual past experiences lend significance to the relationship in feminist therapy, the present and its signifiers are considered equally important in shaping and forming the symbolic layers of interaction. In addition, the participants' collective pasts and their positions as members of communities that may have met, touched, and even clashed apart from their individual experiences will inform how they symbolically experience one another (p. 98).

We agree that the clinical relationship is multilayered, complex, and mutually influencing. We think of the clinical relationship as both real and symbolic and as evolving over time as participants influence each other and gradually enhance their relational understanding and skills.

Reflecting on Self in the Relationship

We have found the following questions helpful in reflecting on possible symbolic reactions with clients:

Why am I reacting with this particular client in a way that is unusual for me?
What buttons might this client be pushing in me?
What buttons might I be pushing in this client?
What do critical (seductive, bossy, self-centered, demanding, etc.) people stir up in me?
Are my reactions to this client (or client story) being displaced from another life experience?
Can I identify a pattern of reacting to certain types of people in characteristic ways that are not purposeful or helpful to the client?
Do I think of some clients often and of others almost never?
Am I favoring some clients over others?
Am I regularly reviewing my work with all my clients or only with some?
Is personal reflection enough to change my reactions, or do I need supervision or personal therapy to assist with professionalizing my responses with clients?

It is essential to engage in regular personal reflection and conscientious work in supervision to better understand the dynamics of the clinician-client relationship. Because relationship dynamics have been a central focus of psychodynamic therapy, that focus is often misunderstood by beginning clinicians as the "real meat" of all clinical work. Not only do many of today's time-sensitive working agreements preclude such a focus, but working with the symbolic requires regular process supervision by a highly skilled and thoughtful clinical mentor who is accomplished in this complex work. By no means should inexperienced practitioners simply launch impulsively into speculation with clients on possible past-to-present links underlying behaviors in a session. After reviewing written or taped process recordings over time, supervisors can help you decide if it is useful to undertake any work with clients on symbolic relationship issues and, if so, how to undertake it with proper timing, sensitivity, and clarity.

■ Relationship as Foreground or Background

At times, the relationship serves as the background for clinical work, providing a safety net or holding environment for the work of sustainment or change. At other times, the relationship becomes the foreground, the focus of the work itself. A number of factors determine how the relationship is defined and the extent to which it is purposefully made the foreground or background of the work.

1. *The clinician's theoretical orientation usually suggests what kind of relational activity, style, intensity, and focus constitute an effective and purposeful use of relationship.* Psychodynamic theory, for example, emphasizes the importance of directly addressing the dynamics of the relationship when the client seems to be reenacting unconscious conflicts with significant others in his or her past (transference). The clinician uses interpretations of clinician-client dynamics to help the client "work through the transference." Behaviorally oriented clinicians may see clinician-client interaction chiefly as providing information about the client's repertoire of behaviors. They may directly use the relationship as a means for rehearsing interpersonal skills or modeling the management of future scenarios. Almost all theorists suggest directly focusing on the clinical relationship when problems arise that affect the work—for example, when there is direct conflict or when the client cancels without explanation.

2. *Ethnocultural norms for relationships—and relationships with professionals—are important influences on how and when the clinical relationship will be foreground or background.* There may be no equivalent for client-clinician relationships in many cultures so that, at the beginning and periodically thereafter, a respectful negotiation of relational roles and expectations may be necessary. For example, in some cultures, the social worker is an agent of the state who provides food, money, and housing only. A counselor might be expected to be a wise person who listens to problems and then unilaterally pronounces advice or solutions. Negative comments by the client on the helping process might be conceived of as unthinkable. Focusing on the relationship itself might feel rude or inappropriate. Again, it is important that we ask our clients how they frame the help-seeking process and roles, as well as how they view a professional relationship and its importance or unimportance (Sue & Sue, 2003; Weaver, 2005).

Sharing food and personal talk are important elements of building rapport with many clients. In that sense, these are very much foreground relationship considerations, even though the relationship and its dynamics per se are rarely an explicit focus of the work.

3. *The use and management of the relationship are affected by the clinical goals, the client's capacity and interest, the role of the clinician, and time parameters.* The clinical relationship may be a less direct focus of attention in settings or roles in which clinicians see many people briefly to provide practical information, concrete problem solving, and mobilization of resources. The dynamics of the clinical relationship are more frequently a focus of discussion when the clinician's primary purpose is to provide longer-term counseling or therapy.

4. *The stage of the relationship or of the interview process affects decisions about the use of the relationship.* In initial or brief encounters, the clinician's primary relational tasks are to be warm, attentive, empathically attuned,

responsive, and focused with the client on mutually determined goals for the meetings. As trust and safe experience build, the clinician may focus with greater frequency on the relationship itself to provide feedback, conflict resolution, self-disclosure, and intentional relational skill rehearsal. Later, as the work together draws to a close, developments in the relationship can be used as familiar examples of what happens in relationships and of how awareness and skills can be learned with caring others through thoughtful interchange and feedback.

5. *Factors in the client and the clinician also affect the use of the relationship in clinical work.* Clients' cultural norms, cognitive and emotional capacities, their relationship histories, and their comfort with intimacy and self-exploration all affect the degree to which relationship dynamics can be productively addressed. Clinician factors that can influence the use of relationship include education and skill, openness to insight and client feedback, and willingness to adjust self to the needs of clients. We have affirmed our belief in client and clinician as coevolvers of the story, but we also believe that the clinician remains ethically and practically responsible for knowing when, how, and to what extent to make direct and appropriate use of the relationship in the clinical interview.

■ Directly Addressing the Relationship Process

The clinician may directly address the relationship process for a number of reasons.

1. *To provide the client with the necessary information about what to expect in the clinical relationship at the beginning of work.*

Example

A clinician at the college counseling center clarifies with the client the roles, responsibilities, and conditions of the working relationship: what the client can expect from the clinician and the setting and what is expected of the client. The clinician discusses confidentiality and its limits so that the client knows under what circumstances the clinician might have to report information disclosed. She explains informed consent procedures and invites the client's comments, reactions, or questions about the nature of their relationship.

2. *To help clients accomplish designated tasks.*

Example

A clinician who, as an intake worker, sees a woman once to evaluate her eligibility for food stamps might not normally focus direct attention on the relationship dynamics. However, if the client's style of angry demandingness with the clinician is so disruptive that it might derail the application process at the food stamp office, the clinician shares her own reaction to the behavior and inquires briefly into possible outside sources of the anger to determine if other kinds of intervention are indicated. If not, she alerts the client to the probable effect that the client's anger may have on staff at the food stamp office. She then very briefly explores other ways the client might express her needs and get them met.

3. *To help clients develop relational competencies—the skills necessary to develop and maintain relationships with others.*

Example

A clinician working in a group home with clients who are focusing on loneliness or failed relationships makes reference to ways that the clinician experiences the clients. The clinician then helps the clients explore their reactions to him with the aim of enhancing their interpersonal awareness and feedback skills.

4. *To address problems or issues in the relationship that need to be addressed.*

Examples

A counselor who notices that a talkative parolee suddenly has nothing to say this week wonders aloud about whether his silence has anything to do with the relationship between them.

After announcing a planned vacation, the psychologist spends some time talking with the client about how she feels about this interruption in their work together.

The milieu therapist suggests that the resident and clinician should talk about why things do not seem to be moving in their work together.

A rehab counselor on an inpatient psychiatric service interrupts her explanation of a job application process when she feels that the client's anger and frustration are making him feel unsafe.

A client sees her hospital social worker at the Gay Pride March. In the next session, the worker explores with the client her reactions to seeing him in the march and discovering that he is gay. The social worker asks whether and how this knowledge might affect their working relationship.

The drug counselor whose client has given her an expensive present for Christmas discusses with her client the meaning of the present in their relationship and their work together.

5. *To summarize the work and affirm gains as the relationship is ending.*

Example

At the end of their six months of working together, an employee assistance counselor invites the employee to reflect with him on the nature of their work. He talks with her about his perceptions of her, requests that she share with him her perspective on their work together, and they talk about how they both have been affected by it. They talk about the outcomes of the work and evaluate what they have achieved together.

In addressing the relationship process, the clinician may use the skills of (a) *examining the moment*, (b) *processing the overall process*, and (c) *exploring indirect or parallel references to the relationship.*

Examining the Moment

At times, the clinician will use the skill of **examining the moment**—addressing what is happening in the clinician-client relationship at a given moment in time. This me-and-you-in-the-here-and-now work usually aims at gaining greater understanding of dynamics, of highlighting a repeating dynamic, or of working through tensions or feelings apparent at that moment in the interview. Egan (1998) refers to this skill as **immediacy.** Examining the moment can be particularly useful when something unexpected happens, when some outside event impinges on the relationship, or when the clinician notices something out of the ordinary.

When examining the moment, clinicians have a choice of focus. The focus can be on the client: "I notice this or that about you right now." This centering on client experience or behavior is a way of building the client's self-awareness and modeling the safe, direct expression of feelings.

EXAMPLE

Clinician: Althea, let's stop a minute. I noticed that, just now, when I asked you about your son, you crossed your arms and started to kick your leg. What was going on for you just then?

Client: I guess I felt like you didn't believe what I just told you.

Clinician: Can you help me see what I did or said to leave you feeling that way?

Examining the moment may be used to focus on the relationship itself: "I'm noticing this or that right now about the relationship between us." Such a focus models noting and responding to the nuances of communication and builds skills in tending a relationship. This is particularly important if there appear to be unexplored feelings and issues that might undermine the relationship.

EXAMPLE

Clinician: Things feel so tense here today.

Client: [Silence]

Clinician: This doesn't feel like our usual way of working together. What do you make of it?

Client: I have something to tell you, but I don't know how.

Examining the moment can be used to focus on the clinician's own feelings and reactions: "I'm noticing this or that about myself in relation to you right now." Sometimes this focus is used to model either comfortably revealing oneself or expectable reactions to what is being discussed. It can be important for clients to know that they have an impact on the clinician and can foster a sense of empowerment.

EXAMPLE

Clinician: You weren't looking at me when you told me the story of being in the hospital with Jeddie, so I wanted you to know that your account brought tears to my eyes.

Client: I'm sorry to make you cry. Nobody likes to hear about the death of a child.

Clinician: Please don't apologize. It's so sad, but I'm very glad that you are talking with me about it, and I'm moved by your story and your bravery.

When examining the moment is used to share the clinician's discomfort with the client's behavior, it has to be undertaken very cautiously. Clinicians must carefully monitor their own responses and discuss them with a supervisor before disclosing them to the client. In an emergency situation, however, the use of self-disclosure might be necessary to maintain safety in the moment. Therefore, all clinicians must discuss with their supervisors how they would handle a situation in which they felt unsafe, in case such a situation arises.

EXAMPLE

Clinician: You're scaring me with this shouting and threatening, Knox, and I can't listen and react well when I'm scared. Please sit down with me and try to calm down now so we can keep talking about what's happened.

Examining the moment can be used not only to help the client explore what is currently happening in the relationship, but also as a source of feedback that may have implications for other areas in the client's life.

EXAMPLE

Client: When will I ever have a boyfriend? I feel so-o-o-o awful. Everyone else has had a lover but me. I feel like I just crawl across the ground while everyone else is up and running. It's not fair. My life is awful. [Whining]

Clinician: Sounds like you feel really disappointed that this hasn't happened for you. [Clinician thinks to herself: "She is bright, healthy, financially okay—her life could be so much worse, especially compared to the woman I just saw who is poor and dying of cancer, with two young kids and nobody to take care of them."]

Client: Yeah, when Stephanie [a best friend] got raped, I went to visit her in the hospital and I thought, "Look, she's got her friends and family here, her boyfriend sent her flowers, she's got everything . . . it's not fair."

Clinician: Might you have been feeling a little jealous of all she seemed to have?

Client: Yeah . . . she even had sex! [Referring to the rape]

Clinician: [Feeling appalled by the client's response, the clinician decides to share her reaction to help the client understand something about the effects of her behavior.] Just now when you were talking about how awful you felt about not having a lover, I found myself thinking: "Gee . . . this situation is not all that bad." I was startled by my thinking that . . . it's just not the way I usually respond when a person is hurting. Your pain is very real, so I had to ask myself why I'm having thoughts like that. Then I thought, "Well, maybe it's the way she described her situation so dramatically: 'It's so-o-o awful, I crawl across the ground.'" When you said that you were jealous of your girlfriend who had been raped, I think I found it hard to be supportive of you. I know that you must feel bad about what happened to her and I am sure that you recognize how awful it was for her. It was hard to hear your pain without reacting to the way you phrased it.

Client: Hmmm . . .

Clinician: I've a hunch you could be feeling that no one appreciates how bad you feel. People saw your friend's pain and gathered around her . . . even I took her part in my thoughts. No one seems to hear you.

Client: No one seems to care—everyone acts like I don't have anything to complain about.

Clinician: I wonder if sometimes other people might be responding to you as I did. Instead of giving you their care and support, they seem to minimize your pain—perhaps because of the way you express it . . . ?

Miller and Stiver (1997) describe a **"central relational paradox"** observed in clinical relationships. People who are repeatedly silenced or invalidated may try to connect by holding back important parts of their experience and feelings for fear that disclosure may end the connection. For example, when feeling disappointed or misunderstood by the clinician, such clients may pretend everything is fine or may change the subject if asked for their reactions to specific clinician behaviors. Miller and Stiver affirm the courage it takes for these clients to become more authentic in a relationship of trust and caring.

While the clinician has the responsibility to monitor what is happening in the relationship and make use of important moments, the client is also likely to comment occasionally on what is going on in the moment. Such noticing by the client gives the clinician the opportunity to reinforce the client's ability to tend to relationships—an important skill in all relationships and one for which clients may receive little validation or thanks.

EXAMPLES

Client A: Can we stop for a moment? I just wanted to tell you how nervous I felt when you just said that you will be out of town next week.

Clinician: I'm glad you stopped us to talk about this. Please say more about what happened for you when I said that.

Client B: You look uptight. Do you need a minute?

Clinician: I'm sorry to take your time with this . . . I guess I am worried. When I came in the front door, my cat had dripped blood in the entryway, and I have her on my mind a little. I just cleaned up before you rang the bell.

Client B: Do you need to take five minutes to go check on the cat? I have my crossword puzzle from traveling on the bus.

Clinician: Thanks, I'll just be a minute. Let's make up the time on the other end if that's okay.

Client B: It's okay. I have a cat and I would be just as worried if she were sick.

It is the fortunate clinician who has a client willing to acknowledge when a statement or behavior of the clinician has a negative or worrisome impact. We need to appreciate a client's strength in giving such direct feedback, recognizing that, in many cultures, one does not criticize a "helper" or "wise person."

EXAMPLE

Client: I don't know how to tell you this, but I feel really uncomfortable when you walk me to the door. I get the feeling that you're afraid I won't leave.

Clinician: I had no idea you felt like that. Thanks for telling me. Let's talk some more about your concerns.

Honest acknowledgment of in-the-moment process events can be unique for both clinician and client because many of us have been taught to skirt around interpersonal tensions or blunders should they arise in social conversations (Miller & Stiver, 1997). It takes courage for both clients and workers to stay in connection when experiencing conflict with each other and to own their contributions to difficulties when they arise (Jordan, 1990).

> *Aldana said I could dish it out in the group but not take it. This was a really uncomfortable thing for me to hear, even though I could feel myself blush every time she or other members gave me feedback that was other than positive. I always thanked people for the feedback, but then kept reacting to it visibly. I hadn't known much "good criticism" in the foster home I grew up in, and, thanks to these women, I came to realize how much corrective feedback felt like criticism from the foster home. My supervisor had already suggested something similar in supervision, so when it came up in the group, too, I got myself a therapist to talk with about my reactions and my history.*

EXERCISE 12.1   Examining the Moment

In small groups, practice the skill of examining the moment with clients in the following scenarios. Think of as many ways to express yourselves as you can.

Jermaine, an excellent 19-year-old college basketball player, has come to see the campus counselor to mull over whether to graduate or to drop out now and join a pro team. As you comment on how hard the decision is and review potential options, he begins to glaze over and stare out the window.

Cookie, a depressed, often silent 14-year-old, comes into the session looking unusually bright and animated, although not saying anything.

Edgar, an 80-year-old man seeking to have his wife arrested for physically abusing him, frowns and huffs as you explain that there needs to be a home investigation before further action can be taken.

CLIP 12.1
Examining the
Moment

When you have completed the exercise, talk together in a large group about the usefulness and the complications of examining the moment.

Processing the Overall Process

At times, clinicians **process the process**—discuss the overall course of the relationship with clients. The clinician may do this to point out a theme or pattern, whether positive or negative, in the relationship and to trace its development backward over the course of the work so far. The clinician may sum up in broad strokes developments or achievements of note.

EXAMPLE

Clinician: You know, Van, it's amazing how you've hung in with this relationship in spite of all your fears of people taking control of you.

We had our moments back there when you thought I was trying to make you join that group.

Client: Yeah, I just didn't want to be in any group, and you kept pushing it on me. A few times I thought of quitting.

Clinician: Yes, and it was important—so different for you—that you could say you'd rather see me alone because you needed the privacy.

Client: I thought you'd be mad.

We can also invite the client to process the process with an invitation to examine it, such as "Could we look at how things have been going in the relationship these last six weeks?" The client may be able to respond to such an invitation easily, may require more time or support, or may not be able to make process observations. Clinicians support all reasonable client efforts to make process comments because it is important for them to develop the skill of observing and commenting on relational processes. In addition, clients may not be used to people "telling it like it is" in relationships or receiving critical feedback gratefully (because of its power to alter clinician behaviors productively).

We can help the client anticipate possible problems in other relationships in the future if the relational behavior exhibited in the clinical relationship is enacted with others.

EXAMPLE

Clinician: During our work together, I've noticed how quickly you interrupt me if you feel that I am going to say something appreciative about you. You will often stop me before I can give you a compliment, or you denigrate what you've done. For example, last week when I said that you were very generous to have volunteered to work overtime over the Jewish holidays, you said, "Anyone would have done the same thing."

Client: Yeah, I get embarrassed when someone tells me I do something well.

Clinician: I can imagine that other people notice your discomfort and then don't tell you about their positive perceptions of you. One of the results is that you often feel that you don't get much feedback.

Client: I just get so embarrassed.

Clinician: That might be a problem in the new job you're taking, since you have to have quarterly reviews with your supervisor. Can we talk a little about that embarrassment? Maybe I can help you with that.

The clinician can use overall process comments to strengthen client awareness regarding the process of relationship building. Surrey (1991b) believes that the mutual empowerment from honest relational feedback and tending leads to greater relational **"response-ability"**—a growing appreciation of what relationships mean and require and how to remain faithful to them when it is not always easy to do so.

EXAMPLE

> *Clinician:* One of the things I appreciate most about you is the way that you have of stepping back and looking at what is going on in our relationship. You've often helped to focus our attention on things that we should be talking about . . . things that sometimes I hadn't thought about. I think that that must be what makes your friends appreciate you so much.

EXERCISE 12.2   Processing the Process

In small groups, practice the skill of processing the process with the clients in the following vignettes.

Olandra always pressures for advice, but then responds with "Yes, but . . . " to everything the clinician suggests.

Kenny has been skipping every second or third session, saying he "just forgot."

Jerri has been great at going out and trying things, no matter how hard, and keeps at it, even though feeling discouraged at times.

CLIP 12.2
Processing the
Process

Exploring Indirect References to the Relationship

The clinician always listens for parallel patterns or themes in the client's comments. For example, sometimes after clients lose someone to death, they find themselves losing keys, gloves, and so on. In **exploring indirect references** to the relationship, the clinician wonders whether the client may be responding to issues or feelings arising in the clinical relationship.

EXAMPLE

> *Client:* I am so tired of people asking me questions. My mother-in-law keeps asking me how I'm doing and I'm sick of her nosing around in my business

Clinician: Is that how you feel with me sometimes?

Client: Well, now that you mention it ... I know that I am here to talk about how I feel about my sister's accusations of sexual abuse by my father, but sometimes I just want to forget about it. When I see you each week, it is a constant reminder.

Clinician: So at times it feels like I'm pushing you to think about things you would rather forget?

Client: I guess I would be worrying about it anyway, but it's easier to think that, if I weren't seeing you and you weren't asking me questions, I wouldn't think about it at all.

In the preceding example, the clinician addresses a reference to something outside the relationship (reactions to questions by her mother-in-law) to see whether it paralleled anything that might be going on in the clinical relationship (reactions to the clinician's questions). Conversely, a clinician could explore things going on *inside* the clinical relationship that may relate to relationships or events outside it.

EXAMPLE

Clinician: You'd rather not have to think about it at all.

Client: I find myself getting mad at you.

Clinician: It feels like I'm making you do something you don't want to do.

Client: I don't want to be mad at my father . . . that's really what I'm feeling . . . How could he do that—how could he force her?

In this example, the clinician intentionally chose her words, recognizing that they parallel how the client may feel about her father "making" her sister do things she "didn't want to do." This kind of attention to parallel themes requires very careful monitoring and is part of the careful attention paid to relationship issues.

Cautions About Addressing the Relationship Process

Clinician genuineness in thought and feeling expression can model a more open way of being that builds relationships. For example, we can show sadness about a loss, irritation at repeated insults from a client, surprise at being accused of not doing something. We can spell out mistakes we think we made with the client, apologizing for them and inquiring about their impact.

We can patiently encourage the client to go more deeply into reactions while affirming the risk people often feel in self-revelation. We can also specify feedback from clients that has changed our way of thinking and working, thanking them for the courage to speak up. As often as is appropriate, we try not to pretend in relation, because this inauthenticity only repeats what many clients have already experienced over and over again.

There can be complications in examining the moment, processing the process, or reflecting on indirect references to the relationship. No matter how useful it feels to us, focusing on the relationship displaces other topics or work at hand. We have to compare the expected benefit with the cost of such a focus: Will the time the discussion takes truly forward the agreed-upon work? Furthermore, being noticed in such detail may prove too intense for some clients (just as it does for some clinicians) who are more comfortable simply focusing on agreed-upon goals or tasks.

Examining what is happening in the moment, in the process, and in indirect references to the relationship is an ongoing part of our thinking. However, it does not have to be made manifest with clients for "good" clinical work to happen. In fact, a problem can arise when clinicians overvalue focusing on the moment, either processing the process or examining indirect references to the relationship so frequently that the exchange risks becoming a "Woody Allen type" of parody of clinical conversation. In addition, if the content of the work is painful or uncomfortable for the client or the clinician, either may be tempted to divert the focus to the relationship to avoid discomfort with the content. The clinical relationship should never be the center of the universe.

■ Addressing Issues of Difference, Power, and Influence

Addressing Client-Clinician Differences

In Chapter 2, we talked about race, class, gender, culture, sexual orientation, age, physical ability, and other differentiating attributions and their implications for the clinical relationship. Differences are often fraught with concerns about dignity, respect, power, voice, the honoring of valued strengths and traditions, and the right to determine one's own fate as often as possible.

Very often it is appropriate to put issues of difference on the table right away to demonstrate the clinician's awareness of widespread concerns about such differences and willingness to tackle difficult subjects. At other times, a clinician may wait until remarks or behaviors suggest that a discussion of differences is indicated. We may address the issues in a number of ways.

1. *Examining the moment.*   Clinicians may use their skill in examining the moment to directly address differences between the client and themselves. This is most easily done when the subject comes up, often in response to the clinician's naiveté or lack of knowledge.

EXAMPLE

The clinician is Catholic and the client is Jewish:

Client: My sister suggested that I join a *havurah.*

Clinician: A hurrah?

Client: No, a *havurah.*

Clinician: Tell me more about that.

Client: [Client explains the *havurah.*]

Clinician: What was it like for you that I didn't know about a *havurah?*

Client: I wouldn't expect you to know.

Clinician: You know, this helps me remember that we haven't talked about what it means for you to see someone who isn't Jewish—that's such an important part of your identity.

Sometimes a clinician raises the issue of difference to open channels of communication when the client has signaled a reaction to difference. Taking time out to examine things in the moment often strengthens the alliance and signals to the client that everything is grist for the mill of examination and sorting through. Clinicians need to develop both understanding and composure, since clients' behaviors and statements around differences can sometimes make it hard to remain empathic and nonjudgmental.

EXAMPLE

The couselor is African-American and the client is white:

Clinician: I noticed that when you walked in and saw me, your jaw dropped.

Client: Uh . . . I was surprised you were a man. I thought with the name "Lacy," you would be a woman.

Clinician: Some of my white clients have told me that initially they reacted to my being African-American. They say they worried I couldn't help them the way a white person could.

Client: People actually said that to you? Didn't that hurt your feelings?

Clinician: As a matter of fact, I think it's really important that people be able to speak their minds here so that we can talk about things and try to work them out together. Counseling doesn't work too well if people sit on things they feel strongly about.

Client: Well . . . to tell you the truth, you're the first black professional I ever got help from. I don't know how it will be.

Clinician: How what will be?

Client: How it will be to tell my friends at the mill that I have a black psychologist.

Clinician: Could you say more about your concerns?

2. ***Commenting on a client's indirect reference to the relationship.*** Clients often lack experience in confronting differences and realizing that differences have an impact on relationships of all kinds, including the clinical one. They may address differences only obliquely, but this gives the attentive clinician an opportunity to make the latent manifest.

EXAMPLE

This is an exchange between a woman in a battered women's shelter and a male human services worker:

Client: You'll never again find me anywhere near a man for long.

Clinician: Since I'm a man, let's take a minute to see how it is for you to be talking with me. Sometimes clients feel they have to take whoever they get as a counselor, but that's not true here. I want to make sure you're in the best situation for you.

Client: I do hold back. You'd hate me if you knew what was on my mind half the time.

Clinician: I am so glad you let me know about holding back, although I'm not surprised, given what guys have done to you. I'd like to hear more about what you've been thinking, if you feel okay telling me.

Client: I've thought of asking for a woman to talk to.

Clinician: What are your thoughts about that?

EXAMPLE

The social worker is white, the client is Jamaican:

Client: I hate those white folk at work who keep saying that they wish they could have dreads like mine.

Clinician: What do you hate?

Client: The way they pick some stupid part of me like my hair to talk about. I feel like their pet sometimes.

Clinician: I'm sorry that happened to you. Do those feelings ever come up between you and me?

3. *The clinician introduces the difference into the conversation.* If the client does not offer, the clinician often brings the subject up because clients may fear the consequences of broaching differences with a clinician. This is especially true if the clinician is a member of a group that the client thinks of as powerful and potentially harmful or about whom the client has strong antipathies or feelings from past experience. It is essential to explore the relational and political implications of differences, because they are often intertwined with issues of racism, class privilege, power, and inequality that need to be recognized and discussed.

EXAMPLE

The clinician is male and straight; the client is lesbian:

Clinician: Darcy, we have never talked about the fact that I'm straight and you're lesbian.

Client: It never seemed to come up since I was just talking about work and stuff.

Clinician: A lesbian woman might feel that her sexual orientation does affect how people react to her at work. I was wondering if you had any thoughts about that.

CLIP 12.3
Addressing Indirect References

Clinician Power and Influence

Closely related to client–clinician differences are issues of power and influence. Clinicians do have real power: We are not simply benign, caring others. In reality, a professional whose assessments, reports, or testimony contribute to life-affecting custody determinations or judicial proceedings has real state-sanctioned power to which clients may understandably respond with anxiety, uncertainty, and defensiveness. Relationships benefit when this clinician power is addressed directly and with respect for client feelings about it.

Sometimes, directly or indirectly, the client brings up the subject of the clinician's power. In such instances, it is important to attend to the underlying messages and intensity of affect attached to the client's communications.

EXAMPLES

"You could get my kids back for me if you really wanted to—just like that!"

"You people think you know everything and can make other people do anything you want with your psychological tricks."

"I don't like you to look in my eyes; it makes me feel like you're trying to read my mind."

"You can go on vacation whenever you feel like it, but I have to get the approval of the whole team, my parents, the school. Would you like it?"

"You're the doctor—you tell me!"

"I liked you because I could tell right away that you knew what I was feeling without me really having to tell you."

"Well, I suppose you are going to go right out of here and report me. So go ahead; I'm not afraid of inquisitioners."

The clinician responds to such statements with empathy, acknowledging a power differential in the clinical relationship and perhaps asking the client what it is like to think of the clinician as having more power. For some people, to see the clinician as powerful can be unpleasant; for others, it can be reassuring. The clinician explores both sides of the client's reactions, as well as past experiences with people who may have exploited power over the client.

EXAMPLES

Client A: You could get me my kids back if you wanted to.

Clinician: What's it like to think I have that kind of power and am not using it for you?

Client A: I feel mad about it sometimes.

Clinician: I would feel mad, too, if I thought somebody could help me but wasn't. When you're mad with me about it, what thoughts come to mind?

Client A: I picture you talking secretly to my family worker and telling her I'm not fit to have my own kids.

Clinician: Oh . . . this helps me begin to understand why you seem so tense with me sometimes . . .

Client B: So go on and report me; I'm not afraid of inquisitors.

Clinician: Am I sounding like an inquisitor?

Client B: You got that right.

Clinician: That's not what I ever meant to sound like . . . you've had so much meddling in your affairs over the years. Can you help me do a better job here? Can you show me how I sounded?

Client B: You said three weeks ago that you have to report any intended crimes, and today I said I felt like knocking Max's block off.

Clinician: It could be hard to trust me if you're worried I'm going to think of the angry things you say here as crimes. Where did you get the idea that your angry thoughts are crimes?

In addition to real authority invested in certain clinical roles, clinicians often have **symbolic power**—the power, expertise, and influence attributed to them by clients. They also have the power that comes from the different activities of clinicians and clients, such as who keeps notes on whom, who sets the schedule, who sits in the waiting room, who pays for the visit, who sets the boundaries, and so on. At times, the clinician elects to address this symbolic power directly, as when the client attributes any good things that occur in the work to the clinician's knowledge and skills rather than to his or her own hard work.

EXAMPLE

Client: Thanks to you I can now get my kids back, get some child care, and go get that high school equivalency offered at the school up the street.

Clinician: Thanks to me? Mostly what I did was encourage and believe in you. You're the one who did the hard work every day of the last year and a half. You went to the meetings, you worked with the homebuilders, you met with the protective worker, and you got counseling with Esteban.

Clients may also blame all their misfortunes on the clinician's interventions or mere presence in their lives. This premise, too, can be addressed as it arises in client statements, such as, "My last worker had real good luck getting me jobs; you must not have the kind of connections she did."

As discussed in Chapter 10, sometimes clinicians assert or address the use of their power or influence with the client to set limits or to move work forward in a particular way. When intentionally choosing to use direct influence, it is important to attend to the resulting effects on the client and on the relationship.

EXAMPLE

Clinician: Last week, I said that you had to go to five AA meetings a week in order for us to continue working together. I wanted to check in with you first thing today to see how that sat with you.

Our ethical stance can also be novel for clients who are used to seeing people with power exploit it for their own gain. Worker ethics may be tested time and again to see if they hold up.

Curtis saw me smoking not far from a sign that said "No smoking." He asked me if it would be okay if he went up to the neighborhood bar and just had one beer, since he'd been clean of all street drugs for almost five weeks now. I asked him if this request could be connected to my smoking where I wasn't supposed to. He grinned and said that what's good for the goose should be good for the gander. I realized I was living in a fishbowl here where the things I did and said could really matter, so I said that I had a saying to match his: Two wrongs don't make a right. He laughed. I said I regretted smoking in the house, and that even one wrong is wrong. He asked me if I wanted to go shoot some baskets now, and I said I did. On the way, he said solemnly that smoking could be dangerous to my health. I was affected by his worry, realizing that I simply hadn't stopped to think through the impact of my behavior on him and our other clients. I honestly hadn't realized either that a resident would actually care that much if I lived or died.

EXERCISE 12.3 Power

In your journal, record your answers to the following questions.

Have you seen a professional use power over a client?

What were the circumstances?

What were the effects?

Have you ever used the power of your professional role with a client?

What were the circumstances?

What were the effects?

Client Power and Influence

One of the goals of the clinical relationship is to help clients feel and experience their own power in the world. Since the clinical relationship acts as a microcosm of human experience in the world, clinicians can help clients experience and assert more power by recognizing, examining, and increasing the client's power in the clinical relationship itself.

Clients actually have a lot of different kinds of power in the relationship. They can approve or disapprove of clinician responses, activities, and ideas. They can continue or drop out whenever they wish, even if mandated (they can elect to take the consequences rather than see a clinician, and many do). They can pay or refuse to pay for the relationship, and they can keep clinicians and agencies waiting for payment by not filling out or mailing in the necessary forms. They can complain to agency heads and boards, to local and state elected officials, and through letters to newspapers or appearances in the media. They can say complimentary or disparaging things about the clinician to other clients and professionals without speaking directly to the clinician, and they can sue the clinician for perceived damages if they feel harmed by the care given.

Clinicians can be awed by clients who have socially perceived status and power, particularly the rich and famous—the VIPs. Rules and limits can be stretched in ways that do not help such clients cope with ordinary frustrations.

In addition, we can fail to be as searching in our exploration or as frank in our feedback as we might with non-VIPs. Often only senior personnel are allowed to interact with "important" clients, so beginning clinicians rarely have an opportunity to learn about how to deal with the entitlement or very real vulnerabilities of these clients. Confidentiality can also be violated when clinicians cannot resist boasting about a famous person who was seen at their agency.

> *A wealthy elderly man came into rehab for physical therapy for serious injuries from a fall while intoxicated. His wife would sneak bottles of liquor into him in her knitting bag. He would come to afternoon physical therapy sessions somewhat high. The wife was a very impressive person. Her brother had donated a lot of money to the hospital, and no one wanted to confront her about bringing in liquor.*

Regardless of social status, all clients have very real power in the clinical relationship. Just as clients may be deeply affected by their interactions with clinicians, so, too, are clinicians often deeply moved and changed by interactions with clients. Just as we may help clients "see and do things differently," so do clients affect how we perceive things, feel things, and act. Our ways of viewing and experiencing the world can be radically changed by our experience with them, and almost every clinician's empathy, listening skills, and capacity to respond quickly have been improved by client feedback. Although clinical supervision often focuses on the things clinicians are doing helpfully, it often focuses just as much on verbal or nonverbal signals from clients that the clinician missed, detoured around, or dismissed as not so important.

While we bring clinical skills and expertise to the relationship, clients bring their own self-knowledge and expertise. Although the roles in the clinical relationship are not equal, the clinical relationship is an egalitarian relationship in that we try to develop and maintain equal respect and value, even though there are differences in roles and responsibilities. The goal is to help the client achieve more power, both in the relationship and in the world (Brown, 1994). However, Julie Mencher (Eldridge, Mencher, & Slater, 1997) asserts that the asymmetries of power in the clinician-client relationship disqualify it from being the "egalitarian" relationship we say it is and wish it could be.

Overvaluing the Power and Influence of the Clinical Relationship

As clinicians, we can put so much stock in ourselves, our skills, and our theories that we overvalue the clinical relationship and what it can achieve. We can even begin to believe that events and realities in the client's life should be subordinate to the clinical work and relationship. A client's tardiness or sudden absences may automatically be interpreted as related to the client-clinician relationship dynamics, when we know that children really do get sick at the last minute and buses actually do run late sometimes. We try to avoid putting clients in the position of feeling guilty about their behaviors in the relationship because this relationship, while meaningful, is only one of the important forces in their busy lives. The more connections they have with others, the more this is likely to be true.

> *A psychiatrist told my friend that, if her parents who lived in England should die suddenly, she should plan not to spend more than a few days in England or it would interfere with the "level of caring" in their work together. . . .*
>
> *My client, a really poor single mom, called to say she needed to miss a week because it was three days until her next check and, if she spent the money for bus fare, she wouldn't be able to buy peanut butter and jelly to keep the kids fed the next few days. My supervisor told me that "anybody can afford $1.00 for the bus." Later I came to know better.*

Beginning clinicians can also undervalue the power and meaning of their relationships with clients. They may rebuff praise when it would be good for the client to give it, or they may minimize the importance of what they say with clients or the importance of clients' latenesses or absences. They may skim over learning, as though clinical education were just more courses to be gotten through. Striking some balance, it is probably fair to say that this unique relationship is very important to many people but not the be-all and end-all that some professionals wish it were.

■ Aversions to Clients

Dislike of a client is one of the hardest things to recognize, own, and talk about with a supervisor because of our blinders and our guiding ethical principle of nonjudgmental and unconditional acceptance of all people. Dislike can sometimes be triggered by unconscious countertransference (reacting to a client as though he or she were a person in the past who was disliked). However, dislike can also be a product of prejudice, bias, and stereotyping by the clinician.

When aversive reactions remain unspoken and unresolved, clients can be left with a clinician who may never come to like or respect them. Clients are thus stuck—sometimes for a long time—with someone with whom they may never experience the growth-producing mutual empowerment, described by Miller and Stiver (1997) as an enormous unheralded benefit of clinical encounters. It helps to recall that we can all be hard to like sometimes, yet find common ground and goals for respectful work together. Supervisory review of aversions when they arise can greatly assist in understanding and resolving them for purposes of growth in both clinician and client.

■ Conclusion

The clinical relationship provides not only the context *in* which change can occur but also the means *by* which change occurs. As a real human relationship, it provides the client and the clinician with the opportunity to develop relational competencies, including how to tend and discuss process in a relationship, how to resolve interactional problems when they arise, and how to increase respect and mutuality in a relationship with another.

Although each of the parties in the relationship has preferences as to how much relational focus there should be in the work together, the clinician is charged with a fiduciary responsibility, for ensuring that the relationship is safe, effective, and appropriately centered on the client's needs.

In Chapter 13, we will address how the clinician deals with the disclosure of personal information and other specific boundary issues in the relationship.

■ Suggested Readings

The following book has an excellent discussion of issues of power and influence in the clinical relationship.

Brown, Laura. (1994). "The Relationship in Feminist Therapy" (Chapter 4). In *Subversive dialogues: Theory in feminist therapy.* New York: Basic Books.

Other excellent resources are:

Chu, James A. (1991). The repetition compulsion revisited: Reliving dissociated trauma. *Psychotherapy, 28,* (2), 327–332.

Jackson, Leslie C., & Greene, Beverly (Eds.). (2000). *Psychotherapy with African American women: Innovations in psychodynamic perspectives and practice.* New York: Guilford.

Miller, Jean B., & Stiver, Irene P. (1997). *The healing connection: How women form relationships in therapy and in life.* Boston: Beacon.

Walker, Maureen, & Rosen, Wendy B. (Eds.). (2004). *How connections heal: Stories from relational-cultural therapy.* New York: Guilford.

■ Self-Explorations

1. Have you ever met someone, and, without knowing much about the person, had a strong initial reaction (positive or negative), but later, as you got to know the person, changed your initial reaction? Do you think that your initial reaction may have been due to some sort of transference on your part? Discuss.

2. How comfortable are you interacting with people from a financial or class group different from your own? Have class differences ever caused you to feel less at ease and competent than you usually do? Discuss.

3. Think about a time in your life when you had real power over someone. How did you feel about that power? Compare this with a time when someone attributed "symbolic power" to you? How did you feel about that attribution?

■ Essay Questions

1. What is meant by transference? Briefly explain how the ethnocultural and feminist approaches differ from psychodynamic theorists regarding this concept. What do you think about the concept of transference?

2. Briefly describe two methods that clinicians can use to directly address relationship process with clients. How are these methods different? Discuss the challenges of each.

3. From your reading, discuss the five types of growth and change that mutual empathy stimulates in both clients and clinicians.

4. Detail the ways in which the various clinicians you watched on the DVD manifested warmth, empathy, and caring. In your view, was any clinician more—or less—successful in showing empathy? Why?

■ Key Terms

Central relational paradox

Countertransference

Ethnocultural transference

Examining the moment

Exploring indirect references

Hierarchical transference

Immediacy

Mutual empathy

Mutual empowerment

Negative transference

Positive transference

Process the process

Relational tending

Response-ability

Symbolic power

Transference

Working alliance

CHAPTER 13

The Clinical Relationship: Addressing Self-Disclosure and Other Boundary Issues

Professional boundaries are the lines of demarcation between clinician and client as they come together in a work-focused relationship. Theoretical models may describe in some detail what they construe to be the ideal arrangements, behaviors, and operating procedures in a professional clinical relationship. As discussed in Chapter 2, professions, agencies, institutions, and individual states have standards of practice or ethics and regulatory codes defining the dimensions of a professional relationship and describing the behaviors and practices that are and are not permitted between professional and client.

Traditionally observed boundaries in the clinical relationship have included the following understandings. The relationship remains centered on the client's work needs, not on the clinician's needs. The contract itself acts as a quasi boundary around the conversation, suggesting focus and direction for the work and minimizing drift. Specific time constraints on the number and length of meetings provide further structure. Planned contacts outside the office should be for the express purpose of forwarding contracted clinical work, not to develop other forms of relationship. The clinical relationship, while friendly in tone, is to be maintained as a working one, not as a friendship and not as a prelude to a friendship. Unavoidable outside contacts are discussed in session to resolve potential complicating effects on the clinical relationship and on other people. In smaller communities and less formal neighborhood service settings, outside contact as neighbors or fellow participants in community activities is expected and usually regarded as normal and not a complication of clinical work as long as clinician conduct is guided by professional norms and values.

Sexual contact between clients and clinicians is strictly prohibited by professional codes of ethics and punishable by law in many states. These traditions and ethical standards are common to most service professions today, to ensure the well-being of clients and to protect both the public and the professions from unprincipled providers.

In the last chapter, we explored some of the situations in which the relationship becomes foreground, and we elucidated skills useful in addressing issues that arise in the relationship process itself. Boundary issues frequently arise that also might require the clinical relationship to become foreground. In this chapter, we focus on boundary issues including (1) disclosure of personal information about the clinician, (2) confidentiality issues, (3) limits on conversation, (4) out-of-office contacts, (5) requests for more time, (6) gift giving and receiving, (7) sexual attraction, and (8) limit setting.

■ Disclosure of Personal Information About the Clinician

Clients may obtain information about clinicians in a number of ways:

1. The clinician may choose to share personal information with the client, who can also receive information from others about the clinician.
2. The client may unwittingly discover something about the clinician from a public source, perhaps by reading a newspaper report that the clinician had a car accident or got married. The client may see the clinician on TV or during a community service project or an activist demonstration.
3. The client may ask the clinician personal questions.
4. The client may purposefully seek out information about the clinician from other sources, such as the Internet.

Self-Disclosure

Self-disclosure refers to the clinician's sharing of demographic information or personal experience with the client. You may have heard that clinician self-disclosure is always frowned upon as narcissistic or disruptive, but we believe that judicious self-disclosure can help develop trust, especially for clients who are not comfortable with what may seem like artifical distance and anonymity. Melba Vasquez (2005) notes that information is a form of power, and that receiving information from and about us gives clients more power in the relationship than they would otherwise have with less transparent clinicians. She observes that shared clinician information also allows clients to reciprocate empathy with us from time to time (an empowering feature of relational tending discussed in Chapter 12). Vasquez notes that feminist therapists of the 1970s–1980s were among the first to provide guidelines for periodic, well thought-out self-disclosure to reduce the power differential in therapeutic relationships.

Self-disclosure can be used in many ways as a part of other skills:

1. *Information sharing.* In an example in Chapter 9, the clinician was working with a client who is about to undergo abdominal surgery and who was not sure when she would be able to return to work. The clinician, who also had had abdominal surgery, shared the information that she was tired for about six weeks.
2. *Modeling.* In Chapter 10, we talked about how the clinician can help clients do things differently by modeling, one form of which is through self-disclosure: "When I was studying for the licensing exam, I found that one thing that worked for me was to put aside two hours every morning before everyone else got up."
3. *Empathy building.* In Chapter 5, we discussed how judicious self-disclosure could help the client feel joined and understood: "I've been thinking about all the things you may be feeling right now. I myself was divorced earlier in life and I know it can trigger a lot of feelings."
4. *Examining the moment.* As discussed in Chapter 12, when addressing what is happening in the relationship at the moment, the clinician can reveal what he or she is thinking as a form of feedback: "As you were talking about how you had to take care of your brother, I found that I was feeling sad—you were such a little girl and there was no one taking care of *you.*"

Self-disclosure can be particularly important when working with members of oppressed or isolated groups. Sue and Sue (2003) believe that "a culturally diverse client may not open up (self-disclose) until you, the helping professional, self-disclose first. Thus, to many minority clients, a therapist who expresses his or her thoughts and feelings may be better received in a counseling situation" (p. 147). Many lesbian, gay, and bisexual clients have expressed their gratitude for having clinicians who were "out" to them and provided healthy models of affirming their lesbian, gay, or bisexual identity (Dillon, 1999). Pinderhughes (1989) affirms the importance of shared personal information and mutual experience in rapport building with many clients of color. Clinicians may elicit more trust if they use some self-disclosure and demonstrate cultural sensitivity before asking Native American clients personal questions (La Fromboise, Coleman, and Hernandez 1991; Weaver, 2005).

Many Asians believe that it is improper to talk with strangers (Weijun Zhang, as cited in Ivey, 1994, pp. 282–283) and that they should discuss their problems only with family members. Thus, the clinician is often assigned an honorary kinship role and is referred to as aunt, uncle, or elder brother or sister (Lum, 2004). Lum also notes that many cultural groups have relationship protocols that guide intergenerational, interpersonal, and intercultural exchanges. All of these situations require that clinicians be flexible in disclosing personal information to their clients. From their research on client preferences regarding therapist self-disclosures, Craig Cashwell, Julia Scherbakova, and Tammy Cashwell (2003) found that both Caucasian and African-American respondents preferred some counselor self-disclosure, especially when the counselor's ethnicity was different from their own. These researchers suggest that clinicians use a brief "trial self-disclosure" in the first session, carefully noting whether clients signal interest or disinterest in the information. A main point in self-disclosure is that clients should experience it as a client-centered sharing rather than a clinician-centered or irrelevant diversion from the work. We should pay careful attention to verbal and nonverbal signals from the client about any brief self-disclosure.

Whenever and for whatever reasons we consider using self-disclosure, we should begin by asking ourselves the following questions:

Why am I considering self-disclosure around this issue?

Why am I using self-disclosure at this moment?

Is it in the client's best interest?

Is there any way I could accomplish the same goal without using self-disclosure?

What are the potential effects on the client of my self-disclosure?

How might this help our relationship? What possible negative effects might it have?

Am I sure that I am not doing this to meet my own needs at the expense of the client?

How will I feel if the client tells other people what I have disclosed? (Remember the paradox of confidentiality: While the clinician may not discuss the client, the client is completely free to disclose information about the clinician.)

The clinician should evaluate the effects of self-disclosure and directly check in with the client about the information revealed. Clinicians should also personally reflect on the following questions after self-disclosure.

How did the client make sense of what I have shared?

Did the client have feelings about or reactions to what I disclosed?

How do I notice the self-disclosure affecting the relationship?

Did it have the intended effect?

Have I asked the client what it was like for him or her to have me share that information?

If I had to do it over, would I disclose in the same way or not at all?

EXERCISE 13.1 Self-Disclosure

In small groups, discuss the pros and cons of sharing personal information, and discuss the differences between offering the information and being asked questions. In what ways do you think this kind of sharing is similar or different for clients? How do clients come to "know" clinicians without actually hearing much specific information about us?

Disclosure by Others

Clients may learn something about the clinician because it is revealed accidentally or by others.

EXAMPLES

> A client may see a clinician attending an AA meeting.
>
> A client may learn that a clinician has breast cancer when he learns that she will be speaking as a breast cancer survivor at a public hearing on funding for cancer research.
>
> A client may discover that her daughter is working in the same law firm as the clinician's gay male partner and that they are considering adopting a child.

As with intentional self-disclosure, the clinician must evaluate what effects the information might have on the client and then directly address these with the client. In addition, the clinician might explore what it was like for the client to learn the information indirectly or from someone else.

EXAMPLES

> *Clinician A:* Todd, we haven't talked about what it was like for you to learn that I was a member of AA.
>
> *Client B:* My friend Ginger told me that you will be talking at the breast cancer rally.
> *Clinician B:* and . . . ?
> *Client B:* Well . . .
> *Clinician B:* Do you know what I will be talking about? [To determine if the client has the information that the clinician has had breast cancer already.]

Client B: No.

Clinician B: [Clinician decides that she had better tell the client directly.] I have had breast cancer, and I will be speaking at the rally about the need for more funding.

Client B: Oh.

Clinician B: What's it like for you to learn that about me?

Client B: I'm glad you're an activist.

Clinician B: And what's it like for you to hear I have had breast cancer?

Client B: I guess it scares me. I didn't know you were sick.

Clinician B: [Deciding to share more information to alleviate the client's fear.] I had a very small tumor removed two years ago, and I have been fine since then. My prognosis is excellent.

Client B: I'm glad to hear that.

Clinician B: [Letting client know it's okay to talk about it.] Given your history of people who have left you by dying, I can see how this might raise some strong feelings for you. I want you to feel comfortable talking to me about those feelings as they come up for you. Let's go back and talk more about your being scared.

Clinician C: I just found out that your daughter Carrie is working at the same law firm as my partner, Len.

Client C: Yeah. That's something, huh?

Clinician C: That kind of puts you in an interesting position. You may be finding out things about me that I haven't told you and that you haven't asked.

Client C: Yeah.

Clinician C: I hope that you will feel comfortable talking to me about anything that comes up for you. I am confident that we can handle it together. Has anything come up that you want to mention?

Client C: Well, now that you mention it, Carrie said that she was going to a baby shower for Len.

Clinician C: Yes, Len and I are adopting a son. What was it like for you to find out this information from someone else?

Client C: It's odd because I think I know you so well, and yet here is this important thing that's happening in your life and you hadn't told me.

Responding to Personal Questions

Sometimes clients ask personal questions: How old are you? Are you married? Have you ever had an abortion? Whether the clinician chooses to answer depends on a number of factors, including theoretical orientation, personal comfort in sharing information, agency preferences or policies, and the anticipated effects on the client. Feminist therapists, for example, often use judicious self-disclosure to try to reduce unequal power in the relationship.

Clinicians think carefully about the effects of both answering and not answering client questions. Not answering is a traditional psychodynamic strategy, designed to allow the client to project any anxieties, frustrations, or fantasies onto the "blank screen" of the clinician, indicating earlier unconscious issues that might need to be recognized and explored. Nonpsychodynamic clinicians may not respond to personal questions in order to encourage the client to search for other possible meanings or motivations in their questions. Others simply answer questions they are comfortable with and then bring the focus back to the client. This may be done without leaving the client feeling criticized for asking.

EXAMPLES

"Rather than spending more of your time on *me*, could we get back to what you were saying just before that question? You seemed worried."

"Let's get back to *you* now. That's the most important focus."

"You get so little time just to focus on *you* . . . shall we get back to why you're thinking about dropping your nurses' aide training program?"

Disclosures are always a subject for continuing review. Sometimes clients say they are glad or relieved to hear things, but later they share more complex reactions of which they were not initially aware. Similarly, a clinician may sometimes feel that disclosure is right and comfortable but at other times feel overexposed or prodded to reveal more than he or she is comfortable with.

Sometimes clinicians do not want to answer a client's direct question. It takes skill and finesse not to answer a direct question without leaving the client feeling embarrassed and rejected. We have found that it is often helpful to reflect back to the client what the underlying purpose of the question might be and to address that—or simply explain why we are not answering.

EXAMPLES

Client A: [During a first interview.] I was wondering how old you are.

Clinician A (Example 1): Might you be wondering if I have enough experience to work with you on the issues you've mentioned?

Clinician A (Example 2): I am wondering what reasons you might have for asking me my age. [To stimulate exploration by the client of the meanings behind the question]

Client B: I don't know much about you. Are you married? Lesbian? Where do you live? Do you have kids?

Clinician B: It's natural that you would want to know more "facts" of my life. Therapy is an unusual relationship that in some ways is imbalanced. I know a lot about you and the facts of your life, while you know very little about mine. However, I do think that in one sense you know me quite well. Over the last four weeks, you have gotten a sense of me in a very real and genuine way, even though some of those facts might be missing. Do you know what I mean?

Client C: Last week, when you told me you were pregnant, you asked me if I had any reactions. I didn't then, but now I do have a question.

Clinician C: Okay . . .

Client C: Are you going to put the baby in child care?

Clinician C: Could you also be wondering if I will still be working with you or putting you in someone else's care?

Client C: Hmmm . . . I never thought of that. Maybe I am.

Sometimes the clinician chooses not to answer the question but wants to explore the client's fantasies about the clinician. These fantasies may provide useful information about how the client sees and experiences things.

EXAMPLE

Client: [Office is in clinician's home.] Do you live here by yourself or what? I didn't mean to pry . . . just curious about it.

Clinician: What thoughts have you had about it?

Client: Not many. Just wondered.

Clinician: I'm interested in what you imagined.

EXERCISE 13.2   Responding to Personal Questions

CLIP 13.1
Information About the Clinician

In teams of three or four, role-play a client and clinician. Have the client ask the clinician personal questions. In the role of the clinician, practice different ways of responding. Note how you feel when the client asks you a question. Observers take notes on what occurs. If possible, videotape the role-plays. As you watch the video, note both your verbal and nonverbal behavior in response to the client's questions. Discuss with your team what you have observed.

■ Confidentiality

We have already mentioned that at the beginning of the relationship, the clinician discusses with the client confidentiality and its limitations. We also discussed some ethical dilemmas about confidentiality in Chapter 2. Now, we explore exactly how clinicians can directly address confidentiality issues and their impact on the relationship as they arise.

EXAMPLES

Clinician A: Delma, I wanted to let you know that I have just received a request from your insurance company to fill out a form about our work together.

Client A: Oh yeah, I remember you said you might have to do that.

Clinician A: Let me tell you what they are asking and what I will say. [The clinician goes on to describe what information is requested and what information he will provide.] Do you have any questions about it?

Client A: No, I think that's okay.

Clinician A: If you have any concerns about it, please let me know.

Client A: Well, will you tell them what I told you about my brother? [Client had disclosed that her brother was a drug addict.]

Clinician A: I don't have to reveal that information at all.

Client A: Good, I was worried he might get fired.

Client B: I just saw someone from my church in your waiting room.

Clinician B: What was that like for you?

Client B: I don't want her to know that I'm coming here.

Clinician B: Tell me what you're worried about.

Client B: I don't want her to know my business.

Clinician B: What do you think she might think about your being here?

Client B: [Responds with her fears.]

Clinician B: [Clinician explores the client's concerns and then reaffirms the confidentiality.] It's true she will know that you are here and she may have her fantasies about why, but no one here will say anything about what you and I talk about.

CLIP 13.2
Confidentiality as
a Boundary Issue

■ Limits on Clinical Conversations

In addition to the boundaries (confidentiality, time) *around* the entire clinician-client conversation, there are boundaries *within* the conversation, including (1) the focus that structures, concentrates, and clarifies the conversation and (2) any existing proscriptions against certain topics of conversation in particular settings.

The Focused Conversation

The clinician helps the client stay focused on the topic at hand to avoid getting sidetracked by other issues the client may raise. For example, if a client and an employment counselor contracted specifically to work on job skills, but the client continually brings up concerns about his relationship with his son, the clinician may either (1) explore the issue in more detail to see if there is a possible connection between the client's concerns and the issue they have contracted to work on or (2) help the client refocus on the task at hand but consider talking with a family specialist about parent-child concerns. Unless the ongoing agreement is to talk about anything that arises for the client, the clinician usually tries to help the client stay focused to make the most of their time together.

E X A M P L E

> *Clinician:* Luis, I know you're worried about your relationship with your son, but we had agreed that your need to work is so urgent that right now our main job is to help you figure out how to get ready for tomorrow's interview. I hear your worries about Luisito, though, so let's get you hooked up with one of our family life counselors as soon as we end today to talk about your relationship with your boy. I feel that it's important today to stay on course with our work.

The Proscribed Conversation

Proscribed conversation occurs when an agency prohibits clinicians from discussing certain topics with clients. The social worker at a faith-based agency may be prohibited from discussing abortion as one of the options for an adult woman who is facing an unwanted pregnancy. The high school counselor may be told that, because of a vote by the school board, she is not permitted to discuss issues of sexual orientation with any of the students.

E X E R C I S E 13.3   Restricted Conversations

In small groups, discuss whether you believe that an agency has a right to restrict the topic of conversation between a clinician and client? Under what circumstances? How would you handle a situation if the agency you worked for proscribed an area of clinical conversation?

When clinicians are prohibited from discussing certain issues, they must clearly articulate the limits to the client and offer a referral to an appropriate professional if the client would like to discuss that topic further. This process should be suffused with the same acceptance, empathy, and caring we demonstrate with any client. Particularly important is the need to offer the referral in a manner that does not suggest that the issues that the client wants to discuss are bad, wrong, or taboo.

EXAMPLES

Clinician A: Nancy, this is a Catholic family agency, and I am not permitted to talk with you about abortion as an option for handling this pregnancy. If you want to consider that, I can refer you to a counselor I know at Family Planning who can explore that alternative with you.

Clinician B: Thomas, it sounds like you are thinking you might be gay. I am glad you were able to come to me about this. Unfortunately, the policy in our town doesn't allow school counselors to talk about issues of sexual orientation with students. But I know a great youth worker in town who has had lots of experience talking with kids about gay issues. I can refer you to him if you'd like. I want to be sure you understand that my not being able to work with you on this has nothing to do with how I feel about the subject or about you.

EXERCISE 13.4   Restricted Conversation Role-Play

In teams of four, role-play the following scenarios, in which you are prohibited from discussing certain topics with clients. Discuss the ethical issues that such a prohibition might raise for you. How would you handle a situation in which you disagreed with the stated policy of the agency for which you worked? In your discussion, remember the ethical principle of upholding contractual agreements with employer agencies, as well as working for the best interests of your client. Record your reactions in your journal, and prepare to discuss them in class.

As a high school guidance counselor in a Catholic school, you are forbidden to join students who have asked you to march with them in the local Gay Pride March.

A 27-year-old mother who is receiving welfare assistance asks if you think it is okay that she is working two nights a week as a waitress and not reporting the income to the government. She says that she couldn't pay for food and heat if she didn't have this little extra income.

A managed care plan prohibits you from discussing with your clients your view that their son needs to be in a day treatment program, which the plan has rejected as too costly.

■ Out-of-Office Contacts

Not all clinicians see their clients in offices. However, we use the phrase "out-of-office contact" to refer to times when the clinician sees clients in settings outside their normal meeting place.

Planned Contact Outside the Office

Contact outside of the normal meeting place may be a planned part of the work together. Planned out-of-office contacts include home, hospital, and institutional visits. These places may be the normal settings for meetings—the hospital social worker routinely sees her clients in their hospital rooms—or they may constitute an unusual event, as when the counselor who usually meets with a client at the clinic suggests a home visit. The clinician might also accompany someone to an AA meeting, go with someone to the welfare office, or drive a client to the battered women's shelter. These types of activities are clearly related to easing the way for the client to get needed services.

Some clinicians may attend commitment or marriage ceremonies, christenings, graduations, healing services, or funerals. Sometimes they provide a supportive presence for lonely or isolated people. At other times, they may join with family and friends to help celebrate or honor an occasion that marks special achievements related to the aims of clinical contact.

E X E R C I S E 13.5   I Do . . . or Maybe Not

In your journal, record your thoughts about whether you might attend a client's wedding. Under what circumstances, if any, would you do so? What factors would go into your decision? What might be the advantages of your attendance? The disadvantages? Discuss your responses in class. What watchwords might guide your behaviors while there?

In the situation in Exercise 13.5, the clinician bases the decision on whether to see the client outside the normal meeting place by thinking about whether it furthers the work they are doing together. Sometimes clients ask to see us in other situations, but we usually do not enter into activities and relationships with clients outside the office without compelling professional reasons to do so. Though a friendly tone may characterize the working relationship, the clinical relationship is not a friendship. Putting some boundaries around the relationship clarifies its work purpose and focus and removes from the client the onus of trying to guess how far the relationship can be taken or what motivates the clinician's attention and caring.

I remember when I was working at the group home, I went with the residents to see a movie as part of their recreational activity. For me, it was work; for them, it was fun. One of the residents asked me if I would go to the movies with him the next week when he was out on a pass. I had to explain the difference that when I went with the group, it was part of my role as a resident counselor. I wasn't just going out with the group as a friend.

When a client asks to see us in a setting other than the normal meeting place, we need to carefully consider the request and discuss it with a supervisor. If the decision is not to go, we should support the client while clearly articulating the reason for the refusal.

EXAMPLE

A clinician has helped the client cope with depression so serious that she had lost a job as an accountant as a result of it. Over the last six months, they discussed the client's desire to open her own accounting office. She had been discussing how excited she was about having a party to celebrate her "return to the real world."

Client: I want to ask you if you would come to my office warming.

Clinician: How were you picturing it would be with me there?

Client: You've been so important to my improvement. I guess I want you to see what I've made of myself.

Clinician: It's really a celebration for you of overcoming your depression as well as of opening the office.

Client: That's why I want you there.

Clinician: It's nice that you want to include me. I, too, share your excitement in being able to go back to work—and to set up your own office at that. You have every right to feel proud.

Client: I know. Thanks, I do feel proud.

Clinician: Unfortunately, I won't be able to come. I don't see clients outside the office. Maybe we could celebrate your success here. I will, however, be thinking about you that day. Would you like to bring in pictures of your office?

Client: Yeah, I'd like to bring in pictures of the party, too.

Clinician: Great.

When meeting purposefully with clients outside the customary meeting place, it is important to be careful that roles are clear and that boundaries, though flexible, are still well defined.

EXAMPLE

The client is a teenager who dropped out of high school. He has met with the youth worker regularly over the last three years. They have worked together to help him get back into an alternative school program, and, after many difficulties, the client is going to graduate.

Client: So—you gonna come to my graduation?

Clinician: I'd be happy to be there.

Client: We're gonna have one big party after.

Clinician: Well, I'll be at the ceremony, but I won't be coming to the party.

Client: Why not, man?

Clinician: We've spent a lot of time working together to get to this day. I am delighted that you did it, and I want to be there to celebrate your success, so I'll be at the school. But I'm your counselor, and counselors don't usually go to parties with their clients.

Client: Why not?

Clinician: Well, that's one of the rules about this relationship. It's part of what makes it different from other relationships that you have in your life. A little distance helps me think more clearly about the people I work with. That may be one of the things that helps us work so well together.

Client: So what are you gonna do, stay in the back of the auditorium?

Clinician: Well, how should we handle this? I'd be happy to meet your mom and your aunt or anyone else right after the ceremony if you want to introduce me, but you don't need to.

Client: Yeah, I want you to meet them.

Clinician: Well, let's talk about how we can do that and what it'll be like.

We must always think about the implications of our presence for clients and directly address the topic with them, particularly when there is a change in setting. However, we believe it is always important to explore the client's reactions to the clinician's encounters with other people or places in the client's life. The clinician might ask questions such as:

"How was it for you, my coming to your home for us to meet last week?"

"How was it for you when I met your sister?"

"What was it like for you when I went with you to the hospice?"

"Now that you're seeing me in the clinic instead of in the shelter, how does it feel?"

EXERCISE 13.6   Outside Contact

Outside contact can be complicated, as clinicians sometimes have flexible inter-viewing strategies, such as talking with a client at a coffee shop where conditions are less formal or having a meal with a family in their home. What, then, would be the difference if clinicians and clients went to the movies, if it gives the clients good feelings about themselves? Would you think it is ethical? Record your response in your journal and then discuss this topic in class.

Unplanned Contact

Sometimes the clinician and client happen to see each other outside their nor-mal meeting place. A clinician may see a client at a party, on the street, or in the bank. These **unplanned contacts** are not part of the work together, but they should be briefly addressed in the relationship.

EXAMPLE

> *Clinician:* Bumping into you at the market was the first time we've seen each other outside the office.
>
> *Client:* Yeah . . . I didn't know what to say.
>
> *Clinician:* I thought we handled it well by just saying "hi." Have you had any other thoughts about it?
>
> *Client:* No. Now I know that if we bump into each other again, we can just say "hi" and move on.
>
> *Clinician:* That would be fine. We can also talk in our session about any-thing that comes up for you if we meet.

Because it is always possible that clinicians and clients may have un-planned out of office contact, clinicians should ask clients in advance how they would like to handle such contact.

I routinely discuss with clients how we want to handle the situation if we see each other outside the office. Some clients would like me to say "Hi, how are you?" and move on. Others would prefer that I ignore them so they are not in the position of having to explain to friends who I am or how they know me.

We must put clients' needs first and try to avoid specific situations where clients might be uncomfortable in our presence. Some clinicians believe they should avoid any contact with clients outside the office, even if the client is okay with it. This belief may be derived from their theoretical perspectives or their wish to keep their work and private lives separate.

A couple of times, I have had to leave a small party or even a restaurant because I knew a client was there and that she would feel uncomfortable seeing me dancing, talking, or socializing with others.

I live in a very small town, and I have to be careful about what dinner invitations I accept. Twice in the past year, I have been invited to a dinner where a client of mine would have been present. I have learned to ask the host who is coming, and if a client is, I find an excuse not to attend.

Sometimes clinicians cannot avoid interacting with their clients outside the clinical relationship.

I live in a village of 1,750 people and bump into my clients everywhere—market, gas station, beauty shop, gym. There's one Catholic church, and we attend it pretty often at the same time. I have to be extremely careful in protecting confidentiality, but there is no way I could not have contact outside. Once people see I don't tell their stuff, we relax about it. . . .

When I walk through campus, I often bump into students I have seen in the counseling center. I don't initiate contact or conversation with a client outside the office. I take my cue from the client. If he or she says "hi," I will say "hi" back. Some clients readily say "hi" in front of their friends, some ignore me completely, and others acknowledge with a nod of the head or eye contact that no one else will notice. And then, of course, I'll check in about our contact at the next session.

Without the client's permission, the clinician may not reveal anything about the nature of his or her relationship with the client. If we bump into someone we have worked with and a friend asks who it is or how we know him or her, we have to find a way to answer that does not disclose the clinical relationship. We have used the following responses.

"I know her from town."
"Just someone I know."
"We've known each other for a while."
"I know her through work."

These vague responses can feel awkward, but it is crucial to maintain client confidentiality.

I've told people I know that if we're walking along and I suddenly turn my back on them and don't introduce them, just walk ahead and I'll catch up. In one funny instance, a charming teen client of mine saw me walking in the square, followed me, and jumped out of the bushes, doing a little song and dance. My friend and I laughed, and I just said, "Go ahead and I'll catch up in a minute." My client said, "He's cute . . . is that your main squeeze?" I just laughed and asked what she was up to. She filled me in briefly, and let me go on. What can you do? A clinician's friends learn not to ask when things like this happen.

C L I P 13.3
Out-of-Office
Contacts

■ Addressing Requests for More Clinical Time

Clients sometimes ask for more time than has been agreed to. They may ask for extra meetings, phone calls, or extensions of the length of regularly scheduled meetings. Clients who request more time may be upset, anxious, in need of anchoring contact or assessment, or they may even be testing the clinician's caring by pushing on the limits of the relationship. The clinician's response should be flexible, and it depends on a number of factors:

1. *The clinician's practice framework shapes the response.* For example, clinicians using a brief treatment framework might confine all contact to the given sessions and encourage clients to hold material until the next session. Crisis intervention specialists might be available 24 hours a day for a given number of weeks or months. Many clinicians use a combination of variable personal availability and local emergency resources to provide a ready response to reasonable client requests for more time.

2. *The agency's rules and procedures regarding coverage for clients' needs govern the clinician's decisions about offering extra time.* For example, some have emergency services that they prefer clients use outside scheduled appointments; others do not wish staff to take client calls at home.

3. *The clinician's assessment of the client's agenda, capacities, needs, and availability of other supports influences the response to requests for more time.* Clinicians carefully assess how requests for more time do or do not seem to complement the agreed-upon goals for client functioning and growth. Extending time to some clients is a necessary lifeline in crisis, but for others it can be an invitation to exploit the clinician or to undercut their own new strengths. Only when the clinician and client have experience with each other can they determine what is truly in the best interest of the client's functioning, and the decisions may vary from time to time. The degree of seriousness of an emergency arising in the client's situation also determines response.

4. *The clinician's response also depends on the amount of time and energy the clinician can reasonably devote to requests for extra time, particularly after hours and between sessions that are booked one after another.* Clinicians sometimes develop "calling times"—specific times for telephoning during the day or evening—whose limits clients are asked to respect so that clinicians can renew themselves.

Whether or not we agree to requests for extra time or phone contact, we must carefully address the meaning for the particular client of both the request and the response. Any change in the originally agreed-upon contract needs to be carefully considered. Upholding reasonable conditions and limits may help clients get the work done more efficiently and, for clients with a poor sense of boundaries and time, may assist in the internalization of structure.

Time constraints are one of the unusual aspects of the clinical relationship, and they differentiate it from many other types of relationships with which clients are familiar. Holding to set times leaves the clinician time for work with many clients; it also structures the work so that clinician and client are less likely to exhaust themselves with too much data, analysis, or emotional intensity. But this clinical sense of time may be at variance with that of clients. As Tafoya (1989) noted, "Many native languages do not measure time in standard units. The Sioux language has no translatable equivalents for words like late, waiting, or time. The term 'Indian time,' often interpreted as being late, in fact refers to doing something when 'it [the time] is right'" (cited in La Fromboise et al., 1994, p. 33).

Changing the rules suddenly, while perhaps necessary in serious emergencies, can confuse clients. For example, regularly extending the session for extra time and then suddenly ending on time may leave clients feeling that they have lost something special or have done something wrong.

EXAMPLES

Client A: Could you see me every other day? I'm so panicky . . . I don't think I can make it through the days.

Clinician A: I can hear how rough things feel to you just now and I'd like to hear more. I am not going to be able to see you more often, but let's see if we can find other supports for you.

Client B: Can I have your number in case I get depressed over the weekend?

Clinician B: What kinds of things are you worried about? [After the clinician explores in depth what the client's concerns are and ways the client might handle it—like calling friends, going out, positive self-talk—he might say the following.] Yolanda, I don't accept calls at home, but, if you feel it's an emergency and you feel you need to talk to one of our staff, we have on-call workers you can reach by phone, 24 hours a day. If you want, I will tell them that you might call.

Clients may not ask for additional contact in advance. They may just call the clinician or appear at the agency for unscheduled meetings.

EXAMPLE

Client: I got your number from the phone book and I hope it's okay that I'm calling. I couldn't wait until our next appointment to tell you that Gordon said I shouldn't call him at work anymore. I'm so mad and I just didn't feel like waiting until Tuesday to tell you.

Clinician: I am sorry to hear that you are having such a hard time, but it's pretty late. I don't usually take calls at home, but I want to make sure you're okay.

Client: I'm fine. I just wanted to tell you.

Clinician: Okay. We can talk more about what happened on Tuesday.

If clinicians agree to see a client for extra sessions or to receive calls at home, at some point they must clarify any time limits on this service. They should also clarify who is available to the client when the clinician is not.

EXAMPLES

> *Clinician A:* Pietro, I can talk with you for 10 minutes on Wednesday morning, but we have to stop at 11:00 sharp. Can you do that?

> *Clinician B:* Francis, we can have an extra half-hour meeting this week, but we won't be able to do that on a regular basis.

Like everything else we do, providing extra time or contact requires careful consideration. Extra contact can be justified as appropriate support for clients under unusual stress, but it can also undermine client resourcefulness if the client does not attempt to seek other sources of support. In addition, the clinician can sometimes feel helpful and even "heroic" providing extra contact but may feel resentful at other times, thus sending clients mixed messages about what is okay.

■ Gift Giving and Receiving

Sometimes clients give clinicians gifts. Gifts may represent messages about the relationship, and it can be useful to explore what clients were thinking and feeling when they thought of giving the clinician a gift, how they picked the gift, and how they pictured the clinician reacting when the gift was presented. It is not unusual for clients to give clinicians gifts they wish they could have for themselves. In the case of someone who has been taught throughout life to do things for others in order to earn love, the clinician may help the client more by discussing the gift and asking the client to keep it than by accepting it. On the other hand, some people may try to control clinicians by showering us with gifts, and others may be uncomfortable either giving or receiving presents.

The acceptance of a small gift (a Hanukkah card, flowers in thanks for special help) is often appropriate and respectful of the client's need to honor the relationship and its meaning. In such circumstances, the clinician thanks the client for the thoughtfulness and responds with courtesy—tasting an edible treat only if the client will share it or putting the flowers in water. The use or placement of the gift should not make other clients feel they are expected to give gifts as well. A clinician may accept small tokens from some clients and not from others, and all responses should be carefully thought out and based on the client's specific needs.

Sometimes clinicians do not accept gifts. Regarding **gifts as symbolic messages** about dynamics in the clinical relationship, the clinician may talk about the meanings and intentions behind gifts rather than accepting them. In these instances, the refusal has to be couched in a respectful and plausible discussion of the reasons for declining the gift.

A client gave me "an Easter present" of a gold crucifix right when she was the maddest at me. I said she seemed to be mad (she was glowering and seething), so I wondered why she would want to give me something. She asked whether I was going to give it back, and I said that, to me, the important thing was to understand what she was mad about. She said she wasn't mad. She looked at the crucifix, then at me, and said, "I guess I was picturing you on the cross in a lot of pain, so you could finally feel like I do." I wondered if she was feeling that I didn't appreciate her pain, and she said she didn't think I did.

Clinicians try not to accept expensive gifts so as not to get caught up in anything seductive or anything that compromises their clinical judgment by making them feel somehow beholden. Yet sometimes we can reinforce a client's faltering sense of self-worth by simply accepting the gift and appreciating the client's thoughtfulness.

When I was leaving the agency, a client brought me a gift. She was poor and I didn't want to take a gift from her. I said that I knew she appreciated our work together and that I would always remember her. I wasn't sure if I should take the gift, but because she begged me to take it in thanks for our work, I decided that I should at least open it. It was a pen with my name on it, and so I decided that I couldn't give it back to her. I told her that I would always remember her for the specialness of herself—even without the gift.

It is important to think about the client's culture and how that may affect the meaning of your refusal to accept a gift. In many cultures, a gift is always given to thank another person for services rendered or to show respect for another. Rejecting a gift might be taken as evidence of extreme disrespect for another's way of being. However, repeated gifts should be explored. For example, a client who regularly brings in "surprises" like coffee or donuts may unwittingly be repeating the relational pattern that was reinforced throughout her life—that of serving, feeding, or pleasing powerful others. Rather than ignoring such gifts, it is helpful to explore the meaning of the gift-giving pattern.

An Irish client of mine, the caretaking oldest of 11 children, always knocked herself out at the holidays baking cakes and cookies for others. She had even been in a convent, where she baked for the pleasure of others. This was a woman who asked for nothing and who got scarcely anything from others—something we were working to improve. Lo and behold, at Christmas, she brought me a huge pudding that she'd stayed up all night to make. She mentioned that, after our meeting, she was going home to bake some more of these for cousins. When I refused the pudding for the sake of helping her to see her self-abnegating pattern, she burst into tears and got very mad with me. These were unpleasant, yet very important, feelings to get on the table. She was able to grasp the point I was trying to make with her, and the next Christmas she sent me a note of relief and gratitude that she wasn't baking for many people any more and it relieved so much pressure.

Supervisors can help beginning clinicians frame a variety of responses to gifts deemed inappropriate. Often, simple statements can be effective.

EXAMPLES

"I appreciate your thoughtfulness in bringing me this coffee, but I want this to be a place where you can finally get for yourself and give to just you."

"I get plenty from the work with you without your having to bring me anything else."

"I like to think of this as a relationship where you can finally take instead of give for a change. Could you stand that kind of switch, do you think? It would be interesting to see what happens."

"Staff aren't allowed to accept gifts, but if you feel you want to say thanks for the work we do here, donations to the Tiny Tots program can be left with the secretary."

EXERCISE 13.7 Gift Role-Play

In groups of three or four, make up scenarios in which a client brings a gift to the clinician. Role-play different ways of handling the situation and, if possible, video-tape them. Under what conditions did you feel comfortable accepting a gift? Under what conditions did you think it would be unwise? How did you address the issues with the client? What did you learn from watching each other and from watching the video?

Sometimes the clinician gives the client a gift. A gift may serve as a symbol—something that the client can keep with him or her as a symbol of the connection with the clinician.

When I was to be away for surgery, a client who'd had a lot of losses in her life gave me a soothing tape to play during the post-op period. She said she knew she couldn't visit me in the hospital, but she wanted to "be there," to do something to help me as I had helped her. When she later left for a six-week trip to Asia, I in turn gave her a tape of soothing music to play, saying I would be thinking of her, wishing her a safe journey, and picturing her having a great, relaxing time with her friends.

■ Sexual Attraction

Sexual attractions can occur in the intimacy of the clinical relationship. A client can be attracted to a clinician, and a clinician can be attracted to a client. However, as discussed in Chapter 2, romantic or sexual interaction between client and clinician is strictly forbidden by the ethical codes of all of the helping professions, and it is a criminal offense in a number of states.

If a client expresses romantic feelings or sexual attraction toward you, you should always consult with a supervisor before addressing the issue in the relationship. A clinician who feels sexual attraction toward a client should discuss it with a supervisor rather than mentioning it to the client. Gerald Schamess (1999) believes that attractions in therapy are frequent, human, and some of the least discussed experiences in professional practice. He underscores the importance of open discussion with supervisors to develop understanding and skill in managing such attractions.

Clinicians may respond to a client's sexual attraction in any number of ways. How and why we choose a particular response is beyond the scope of this chapter. Suffice it to say that the issue is complex and depends on a number of factors, which include theoretical orientation, the clinician's understanding of the client and what the sexual attraction may represent, the type of work the client and clinician are engaged in, and how the client raises the issue. Clinicians should also consider the possibility that maybe their own behaviors are stimulating the client's sexual feelings.

The following are some relevant practice principles when sexual feelings arise:

1. *The clinician can explore the client's sexual attraction and related fantasies.* Some clinicians believe that this exploration provides useful information about the client's dynamics and is therefore appropriate for their work together. The skills of exploration and elaboration are used to obtain more information about the attraction the client has expressed.

E X A M P L E S

Client A: I had a weird dream about you last night. We were having sex. It's so embarrassing.

Clinician A: I am glad that you told me about it. Counseling is an intimate experience in which lots of feelings can arise, including sexual ones. Would you feel comfortable telling me more about the dream, and let's see if we can understand this better?

Clinician B: Lauren, I notice that right now you are leaning forward toying with the top two buttons of your blouse in a way some people might describe as seductive. Let's talk about it.

Client B: [Straightens out skirt and sits back.] I wasn't aware of it. But I have to admit, I do find you sexy.

Clinician B: Sometimes when people feel close to their counselors, they can start to feel attracted to them, especially if they learned as kids that sex often comes with closeness.

Client B: Wow, so I'm just like a textbook "patient" . . .

Clinician B: Did I leave you feeling that way?

Client B: I wasn't asking you for a date. I just said I think you are sexy. No big deal.

> *Clinician B:* This isn't easy to talk about, I know, but it could help us understand how you get into sexual relationships with people without really knowing them and then get hurt.
>
> *Client B:* Do you mean that maybe I come on to people without being aware of it?
>
> *Clinician B:* Do you think that could be so?

---

2. *The clinician can reassure the client about how commonly tender and sexual feelings arise in situations of intense personal sharing.* Clients often report feeling attraction to clinicians because of the intimacy of the clinical relationship. They may feel frightened or confused by these feelings, especially if they have experienced sexual abuse at the hands of intimates or have come from strict religious backgrounds that expected sexual feelings to be suppressed.
3. *The clinician can refocus the conversation on the contracted work.* Sometimes clients may raise sexual feelings as a distraction from the work at hand if the work is too difficult for them at the moment.
4. *The clinician can let the client know that he or she would never act on romantic or sexual feelings.* Whether the clinician explores the issue in more detail, reassures the client about the commonness of the experience, or refocuses the conversation back to the topic, it is always important to clearly state the boundaries so that there is no confusion.
5. *The clinician should carefully document any discussion of sexual feelings, both for review in supervision and as a protection against future misinterpretation by clients or others.*
6. *It is wise to have a general conversation with a supervisor about how to handle sexual attractions.* It is important to be prepared since we can never predict whether or when romantic feelings or sexual attraction will come up in our work.

In the preceding example, the clinician explored feelings appearing in the moment as they may relate to other experiences in the client's life. He also reassured her that such experiences are common in clinical work. He affirmed safe boundaries that would allow them to talk about feelings without acting on them. This very capacity to feel, examine, and discuss things *without acting on them* is a goal of both good clinical learning and sound clinical practice. On rare occasions, the client may become sexually assertive, gazing at the clinician's breasts or genitals while talking, rubbing against the clinician provocatively on entering or exiting the room, or attempting other forms of physical contact such as "surprise" kisses or hugs. Clients frequently exhibit these behaviors when they have grown up in an atmosphere of inappropriate sexualized intimacy and violence or when they doubt their attractiveness and urgently need it validated.

Paradoxically, some clients who fear closeness may actually cross boundaries to distance the clinician, whose repulsion they fully anticipate. For other clients, sexualized encounters may be a cultural or gender norm on which the client is acting at the moment. Following supervisory review of the behavior, the clinician may be helped to directly address it and its inappropriateness to the professional relationship. As with most boundary issues, the clinician can follow up by exploring the meaning of the behavior from the client's perspective and experience.

EXAMPLES

Clinician A: I've noticed that, when we talk, you often seem to be staring at my breasts. That makes me uncomfortable, and I wonder if you could try making eye contact with me or looking someplace else instead. Am I the first woman to mention this?

Clinician B: Birch, when you leave the room, you always lay your hand on my back as you go out. I'd rather you not do that, but I'm also interested in what that's about for you?

Directly addressing sexualized behaviors can help clients begin to develop boundaries appropriate to the context of clinical working environments. At the same time, we must be professional in our own dress, manner, language, and tone so that we do not elicit the very behaviors we then confront.

EXERCISE 13.8 Talking About Attraction

In small groups, take turns role-playing a client either talking about or manifesting sexual attraction. Practice how you would respond to the client without acting. Talk with your team about how to do that in a way that neither demeans the client nor encourages the fantasies or behaviors.

■ Limit Setting

Beginning clinicians may mistakenly feel that the principles of acceptance and nonjudgmentalism prevent our ever acting in ways that limit the client's freedom or cause unpleasant feelings. They may ask whether **limit setting** on client behaviors is a clinician-centered rather than a client-centered activity. We believe that it is both. Clinicians cannot work productively in an atmosphere that threatens their fundamental sense of comfort and well-being, and clients can usually read rather accurately a clinician's negative reactions to things they do. Limit setting is also important for client growth. Letting clients persist in demeaning or offensive behaviors gives them a confusing double message about what we think is appropriate in relationships, and it models the kind of denial or trivializing of abuse that many clients have already experienced too much of. Limit setting helps clients learn self-containment, an important developmental step in human relationships.

■ Conclusion

In this chapter, we have given numerous examples of the clinician's setting limits with clients about such things as time, topics of conversation, privacy of the clinician, and sexual behaviors to maintain clear and comfortable boundaries in the clinical relationship. When setting limits, the clinician unfailingly conveys respect and caring for the client.

We believe that the process of establishing, tending, and maintaining the clinical relationship contributes fundamentally to helping clients change. This relationship not only provides a context in which change can occur, but it is often the means by which change occurs in the client and in the clinician. Learning to care about, tend, and authentically participate in a relationship builds skills that benefit both participants in their future connections and work with others. Ironically, the relationship itself can become so important that, while it often reinforces change efforts, it can also inhibit them. It can feel so rare and so good that the participants may unwittingly slow down change to postpone losing this very special relationship when work is completed and the relationship ends.

In the next chapter, we review the major principles and techniques of the ending phase of work, including relational issues that can arise when terminating work together.

■ Suggested Readings

There are a number of excellent readings on multiple relationships and sexual attractions in clinicial work:

Bridges, Nancy. (2005). *Moving beyond the comfort zone in psychotherapy*. Lanham, MD: Jason Aronson.

Lazarus, Arnold, and Zur, Ofur. (2002). *Dual relationships and psychotherapy*. New York: Springer.

Schamess, Gerald. (1999). Therapeutic love and its permutations. *Clinical Social Work Journal, 27*, 9–26.

The following are useful readings on self-disclosure:

Brown, Laura S., & Walker, Lenore E. A. (1990). Feminist therapy perspectives on self-disclosure. In George Stricker & Martin Fisher (Eds.), *Self-disclosure in the therapeutic relationship* (pp. 135–155). New York: Plenum.

Goldstein, Eda. (1997). To tell or not to tell: The disclosure of events in the therapist's life to the patient. *Clinical Social Work Journal, 25*, 41–57.

Pope, Kenneth S., Sonne, Janet L., & Greene, Beverly. (2006). *What therapists don't talk about and why: Understanding taboos that hurt us and our clients*. Washington, DC: American Psychological Association.

■ Self-Explorations

1. How comfortable are you about revealing personal information to others? Is this related to your family or cultural values? Have you ever disclosed something to a person and later wished you had not? What did you disclose and why did you regret it? How has the experience affected your comfort with self-disclosure?

2. Describe some situations in which you have had to set limits on others. How comfortable are you in limit setting in your relationships with others?

3. Do you know anyone who has been involved in a sexual or romantic relationship with an authority figure, such as a coach, teacher, priest, relative, or other? How did it happen and what were the effects?

■ Essay Questions

1. What factors should a clinician consider if a client requests more meeting time?

2. From your reading in Chapter 2 about ethics, and in this chapter about boundary maintenance, discuss the benefits and risks of getting to know clients in nonwork-related ways.

3. How should a clinician respond if a client directly raises his or her romantic feelings toward the clinician?

■ Key Terms

Gifts as symbolic messages

Limit setting

Professional boundaries

Proscribed conversation

Self-disclosure

Unplanned contact

CHAPTER 14

Endings and Transitions

Inevitably, clinical work comes to an end. As often as possible, endings are planned and are a natural part of a stated contract. For example, the clinician and client in an employee assistance program may agree to meet for a fixed number of sessions, a social worker in a halfway house may agree to meet with a client only as long as the client is attending other specified programs, or a college student may graduate and no longer be eligible for services at the college counseling center. But endings can also happen in an unplanned way. They may be the result of unanticipated circumstances, as when the client has to move away, the clinician becomes too ill to work, the client discontinues the relationship, or the agency closes.

Either the client or the clinician may initiate endings. Endings may seem to be a natural and timely closure to the work together, or they may seem precipitous. Regardless of the reason, we try to undertake a formal process of ending to assist the client in summarizing and integrating the work with the clinician and to assist in planning for the future. This formal termination process may be brief or carried out over a number of sessions.

Termination is the term traditionally used in clinical work to describe the process of ending. The term was conceived in a much earlier era of practice that was heavily influenced by the psychoanalytic theory of therapy. Traditional psychoanalytic theory anticipated so thorough and productive a therapeutic restructuring of client dynamics, defenses, and character that work could be terminated with the expectation of little future need for further work.

We believe that termination represents a transitioning process through which clients gradually move to other systems of support and problem solving, such as family; ethnocultural and spiritual networks and practices; and mutual aid, political action, and recreational groups. Clients often take the work and the relationship away with them, as sustaining inner resources available for use in the future. But we also recognize that termination may not be the last time the clinician sees the client. Clients with few resources, complex problems, or new objectives for work together sometimes came back to see the same clinician with whom they ostensibly "terminated" or finished up. Therefore, although clinicians often use words such as "termination," "ending," and "transition," we believe that the process is often one of finishing work "for now." If we think of life and circumstances as forever fluid and dynamic, then the idea of cycles of work at different points in time makes perfect sense in the lives of many people.

■ Even Before We End: Foreshadowing

It is important that clinicians and clients have as much lead time as possible to discuss ending and to allow for the processing and digestion of the transition from this special form of caring and collaboration. Thus, whether or not there is a specified plan for ending, we occasionally **foreshadow the ending** during the working relationship. This is particularly true in work with clients whose many prior relational losses make separations or endings difficult.

An agreed-upon, planned ending is the best way to wrap up work together because it provides many opportunities to review, compare expectations with realities, look ahead, and both regret and celebrate concluding this cycle of work. When there is a projected date for an ending, we foreshadow it by occasionally noting the date so that all can be alert to it and can plan the focus and pace of the discussion accordingly.

EXAMPLES

Clinician A: Before we begin work today, I wanted to review with you that it's the end of March, just seven weeks before my placement ends and I leave here to continue my education.

Clinician B: We said we would finish up after Christmas, and since Christmas is just three weeks away, I thought it might be good today to look at where we are and whether that still seems to be a good idea. If so, let's figure out how we can plan ahead for it so it doesn't just suddenly happen without us getting ready for it, especially here at the holidays.

Clinician C: This is our fifth of eight sessions; what would you like to accomplish by the time our meeting ends today?

CLIP 14.1
Foreshadowing the Ending

When the contract is somewhat more open and continues over time, clinicians may periodically review goals, accomplishments, and remaining issues and more frequently mention "when our work together is finished" to help clients keep the relationship and work in perspective.

Here time is well used as both a boundary and an incentive for efficient use of work.

Initiating Endings and Transitions

Whatever the reason for or the nature of the ending, clinicians can use several skills to ease the process of change for the client, maximize gains to date, and help make the transition to other supportive connections and activities. Because the skills used to end the work are much the same as those used in transitions and breaks, we begin by elaborating ending skills and then demonstrate how these skills can be adapted for planned and unplanned transitions and interruptions in the work.

EXERCISE 14.1 When Clinicians Should Initiate Endings

Before reading more about endings, pause to identify some of your ideas about them. In your journal, describe the circumstances in which you think the clinician should initiate the ending of the clinical relationship.

Clinician-Initiated Endings

Sometimes clinicians initiate the process of ending. This may be appropriate in a number of situations. For example, a clinician may initiate ending because the goals have been accomplished and it is simply time to end work together. Beginning clinicians should always consult with supervisors as to the appropriateness of ending before raising the subject with the client.

Whenever possible, initiate the conversation about ending early in a given session so that the client does not feel that you want to end the relationship because of something the client has just revealed or done. Whenever suggesting the possibility of ending for now, it is important to leave room for the client's responses and, in the absence of any immediate ones, keep an eye out for nonverbals and indirect themes. The following are several useful ways of introducing the topic of ending when the goals of the relationship have been met.

EXAMPLES

Clinician A: Anna, things have gone so well for a while now. Is it time for us to think about the possibility of our bringing our work together to a close?

Clinician B: Miguel, you've been wondering when our work will be through. Should we decide on a date, far enough away to give you a few more weeks to reestablish yourself back in the community?

Clinician C: By spring, Brian, I expect you'll be ready to try things without seeing me every week. I'd like us to keep things as they are for now, to support you through the holidays, but we might plan on ending our work together in March.

We may also initiate ending the relationship if we believe that, although the client could still use some assistance, we are unable to help because we do not have the expertise necessary to work with the client on a specific issue.

I was working with a woman at the family planning clinic. We were meeting about birth control methods and STD prevention. She disclosed that she had been sexually abused. I knew that this would be an important topic for her to explore, but I certainly wasn't trained to work with it. I referred her to a more knowledgeable mental health counselor at the clinic.

When we feel that we can no longer work with a client because the client's issues are beyond our expertise, we must carefully make a **referral.** This can be difficult because the client may feel rejected or reluctant to see another clinician. Using the prior example, the clinician might proceed in the following way.

EXAMPLE

Clinician: Serafina, I was thinking about what you told me at our last meeting about what happened to you in your family.

Client: Yeah.

Clinician: I think that having been sexually abused must have been an awful experience that you haven't gotten much help for.

Client: You're the first one I told about it.

Clinician: I appreciate your confidence in me.

Client: Yeah, I couldn't believe that I told you.

Clinician: What does it feel like to have told me?

Client: It felt okay . . . but I've been thinking about it a lot.

Clinician: You know, I think it would be really good if you could talk about what happened to you with a colleague of mine who has a lot of experience helping women who have been abused.

Client: I couldn't imagine talking to anyone but you. Can't you help me with it?

Clinician: Serafina, I really want to help you, but I haven't had any experience working with women who have been sexually abused. I think the best thing I could do for you would be to help you talk to Brenda. She is a wonderful counselor whom I like a lot.

Client: Do you mean I can't see you anymore?

Clinician: Well, we were finishing up our work about birth control and safe sex practices, so we would be stopping anyway. I know it can be hard to think about saying good-bye to someone with whom you've shared so much.

Client: Yeah. I always hate good-byes.

Clinician: What I would like to do is to set up a meeting for you with Brenda. I would meet with you for one last time after you've seen her to find out how it goes and to say good-bye.

EXERCISE 14.2   Thinking About Ending

In your journal, record your reactions to the preceding scenario. How do you think the client feels? How do you think the clinician feels? What would you have done differently?

EXERCISE 14.3   Referral Role-Plays

Role-play a scenario in which you discuss referring a client to another person or agency because you are unable to help the client with the issues he or she has uncovered. Videotape the role-play. Watch the video with your team and then debrief: Discuss what it felt like to be the clinician and what it felt like to be the client.

Clinicians may need to initiate the end of the relationship if they feel that a client is not making use of the relationship. This is a very complex and difficult issue, and such an ending should be undertaken only after careful review with a supervisor.

EXAMPLE

Clinician: Leo, we've been meeting for a while about your problems finding a job, and we don't seem to have accomplished much. I am not sure that our continued meeting would be helpful to you.

Client: Well, I like meeting.

Clinician: I don't think it is a good use of your time and money. I have the feeling that you aren't sure that you really do want to work on getting a job.

Client: Yeah, I do.

Clinician: Well, I've noticed that you haven't followed through on any of the assignments we've agreed might help. We've explored this a lot, and I'm still not sure why that is. However, why don't we stop meeting for a while. Then, if you feel ready to practice job hunting skills, I'll be happy to work with you again.

Client-Initiated Endings

Clients, too, can initiate endings for a variety of reasons. They may feel that the goals of the relationship have been met and that they are ready to try things on their own or to transition to another kind of work. Clients may also suggest ending if they feel that the clinician is getting ready to end the relationship and they themselves want to be the first to leave. In addition, clients can end work because they are at odds with the clinician or agency, because the issue being addressed in the work makes them feel uncomfortable, or because they feel they are not being helped. The clinician may or may not agree with the client's decision and must carefully explore the situation with the client to make sure that he or she is not initiating ending because of discontent with the clinician or clinical process. We attempt to explore the issue while respecting a client's right to decide.

I remember a client who came in quite angry one week and said that he was leaving our counseling sessions. He said I hadn't helped him and he decided that he was through. My first instinct was to say, "Okay." I felt like I didn't want to seem defensive by pushing him as to why he wanted to go, and I worried that maybe I hadn't helped him. But then I remembered my supervisor saying, "You have to explore it." So I did and kept saying to myself, "Don't be defensive . . . keep the focus on him . . . try to be empathic . . . this is a learning opportunity." It worked. He really felt I listened, and then he said he was mad at me for something I had said that had pushed his buttons. We explored those buttons and continued our work. I was glad I hadn't given in to my first instinct to say, "Fine, bye."

Sometimes it becomes clear that the client wants to end, even against the clinician's best judgment. In such situations, we believe that, after carefully exploring the issues, the clinician should help the client end as well as is feasible, highlighting any positives to date and not being punitive about the decision to leave. This avoids contributing to the client's potential feelings of failure or guilt. In addition, we try to keep the door open for future work or referrals.

EXAMPLE

Clinician: Well, it sounds as if you're really feeling that this is the time to stop. You've used the relationship well [summarizing way client has used it]. While you may want to do some more work later, this feels to you like it is enough for now. I'd be happy to help you or make a referral if you decide that you want to do more work on this in the future.

At times we become concerned that the client is self-sabotaging or playing out an old pattern of breaking off relationships just when they are working. A clinician might want to raise the possibility that such dynamics may be at work. The client may disagree but at least the clinician has left him or her with something to think about. We may not feel good about this sort of ending, but it is important to recognize that decisions still rest with the client. Maximizing client self-determination is always important. Sometimes clients learn things through the process of ending that they have not been able learn in the relationship.

EXAMPLE

Clinician: Wayne, I'm worried that you may be doing with me what you've described doing so many times before: that whenever you get close to somebody, you take off.

Client: What's it to you?

Clinician: If at some point you don't let someone in and keep them in, I worry you're going to be lonely for the rest of your life. You've already told me how much that hurts.

Client: I have to see on my own how it goes.

Outside Forces May Precipitate Ending

Clients or counselors may also have to initiate ending because of external circumstances. Insurance limits may necessitate an ending. Clients may no longer be able to afford the care being offered. A significant other may insist that the client end the relationship. Unexpected events can result in a client or clinician having to move away or change jobs (Penn, 1990). Participants can become too ill to attend meetings, or an agency might close with very little notice.

When an agency is closing, restructuring, or discontinuing some services, both clinician and client may feel displaced and upset. At times, our own anger or fears may seep into the clinical work with clients, escalating their worries and feelings of loss. We need to find other places to work out our own distress so that our work remains centered on the client's experience rather than on our own. Supervisors can indicate any instances in which it might be useful to share clinicians' own reactions to changes in the agency.

> I was working in a methadone clinic in a hospital where there was some talk of a merger with a larger teaching hospital. The clients picked up on it somehow. There were lots of rumors that the clinic would be closed. I remember Philip saying, "I'm just gonna go back to using when they close this place." We had to spend lots of time reassuring them that we weren't closing.

> I know that closing an agency is tough on the staff as well as on the clients, but I was shocked to hear that some of the staff just started not showing up and began using their sick time right before the agency closed. I felt so bad for the clients. It wasn't their fault, but they were the ones who were losing out. They didn't even get to say good-bye to some of the staff.

When external circumstances necessitate a transition or ending, the client and clinician may both feel that things are beyond their control, especially if their work is not completed or if it is at a crucial point. Some people are barely fazed by ending this kind of relationship, but others—clinicians included—may need to grieve the loss of the relationship, at the same time appreciating all that they have been able to accomplish in whatever time they have had. In a classic work on endings, Hilliard Levinson (1977) describes the grief process that some clients and clinicians go through over endings, particularly unexpected ones.

> Nonie and I had worked together for a couple of years on maintaining her at home in spite of a history of episodes of bipolar disorder. She was in her early thirties, had a child by someone she had had a fling with at the mental hospital, and was being supported by Rehabilitation funds to go back and finish college. Right at the point when she was trying to enter school and worrying about being accepted by her peers, I was offered a job that I could not resist at another agency. It meant moving from a mental health to a medical setting, where I would not be allowed to see my current clients. I loved Nonie, and we had been through so much together with her getting in jams and then out again. It gets to you to have to step away from someone you care about and who is counting on you to be there with them. We did some work on ending well in advance of my leaving, but Nonie went off her meds, as I feared, and landed back in the hospital just when I left the agency. I felt terrible and poured this out fairly regularly in supervision. My supervisor helped me to see

that Nonie had probably gotten herself readmitted to have familiar people around to help her with her sadness. The staff at the hospital confirmed that this was what she was absorbed with in their meetings with her. As life would have it, a month after I left, I was shopping in the area market when I wheeled my cart around an aisle and literally ran smack into Nonie. I was so happy to see her again, but she burst into tears and could not stop crying. We sort of went off into an empty corner and did more talking about moving on to her new worker at the clinic, someone I knew would be great with her. Over the next six months, she called me twice at home to ask me to please see her, and I just continued gently to underscore her strengths and encourage her back to her new worker. She did follow through as hoped.

Initiating Ending Too Soon or Too Late

Sometimes either a client or a clinician may suggest ending the relationship too soon. Clinicians might be tempted to end the clinical relationship prematurely when a client is constantly hostile, demanding, critical, or "manipulative." **Client abandonment** is the unethical and thinly disguised process of "dumping" or deserting clients who are still in obvious need of service but with whom the clinician finds it difficult to work. A clinician who is frustrated with a difficult or angry client might be all too willing to initiate an end to the relationship and may try to justify this termination with impressive clinical formulations. Clinicians can be subject to licensing board investigation and civil suits for client abandonment.

Clients who are feeling anxious about the work might suggest ending just when things are "getting hot" or when they are on the verge of making a significant change. They, too, may use compelling language to justify their leaving.

Lorinda was a woman who came to the women's center for counseling about her relationship with an abusive husband. She was beginning to talk about the possibility of leaving him and had even asked me to look into some shelters for women who were victims of domestic violence. Lorinda and I had been meeting for about three weeks when she announced that she thought she needed to stop coming because she couldn't get a babysitter for her 1-year-old child and there was "just no way I can keep coming." We talked about the difficulty she was facing (it was true that she had no sitter), but as we explored it in more detail, Lorinda said that perhaps she didn't want to come because she was scared she was on the verge of making a major change in her life.

On the other hand, both clinician and client may enjoy the work and the relationship and may want to hold on to the relationship for longer than necessary. Sometimes the clinician may continue to see a client for financial reasons because of the income the client provides or because the client is an "easy" client—someone the clinician likes and enjoys working with. Some clinicians find the work of ending so painful that they repeatedly delay talking about an approaching ending, thus shortening the time for the important reflection and conversation that could greatly benefit the client.

Moreover, clinicians and clients may not want to give up the caring warmth and wonderful experience of having someone who is there to listen in such a relationship-centered way. It is no favor to clients, however, to delay the modeling and development of a necessary life skill: concluding a relationship knowing that there will be other important relationships and that important aspects of this one can be stored forever in the hearts and minds of the participants.

> *I had seen Simcha off and on for several years for various problems related to leaving home, getting established in a career, and partnering in a big city full of risks for young adults. We had become as comfortable in our work together as two old shoes and clearly enjoyed each other. When it finally felt right not to come anymore, Simcha said laughingly that there must be some ethical rule that a social worker can't say no if a client wants to pay to come and be with the worker because it just feels so good, period.*

Sometimes clients can feel dependent on professionals, as though unable to make it alone. Others may have suffered serial losses and may understandably resist experiencing another. For some clients, contact with the clinician is perhaps the most interesting experience they have all week. Isolated individuals refusing referrals to other groups and activities outside their homes may even tell the clinician that, when he or she stops home visiting, they will have little other human contact, which makes ending very painful. Periodic conversations with clinical supervisors can help ensure that clinicians and clients end relationships in a compassionate but timely manner.

EXERCISE 14.4 Your Own Experiences with Endings

In your journal, discuss a time in the past when you ended a relationship. It might have been the ending of your own work with a clinician or the day you graduated from school or had a school friend who moved very far away. Record the circumstances of the ending and the things you experienced or said during the ending process. Looking back, what thoughts and feelings come to mind now about the ending process?

The Tasks of Endings and Transitions

The tasks and skills involved in ending are many, and you may have noted some of them as you recorded your part in the endings you wrote about in Exercise 14.4. Although we discuss the skills of ending in a particular order, they often overlap and ebb and flow. The work around endings can occur purposefully over a number of sessions, weeks, months—even in one meeting, if that meeting is all we have.

Announcing the Process: "Now We Are Ending"

Whether at the end of an interview or at the end of the work, the responsibility for verbally marking the ending time rests with the clinician. Because clinicians are responsible for marking the end of a session, they may say: "We have to be finishing shortly, so let's take a moment to review what we've said today, where we are, and what's ahead." Similarly, and using many of the same skills, the clinician has to say at a designated point in the work that, because the work and relationship are ending soon, it is time to acknowledge the ending and to do some work together specifically about ending. The subject of ending is gently yet confidently broached as a natural and inevitable part of life and work.

Clients with serious cognitive limitations may not be able to grasp the concept of ending or understand the nuances of a discussion focused on ending. Sometimes the best that the clinician can do is to mark off the sessions on a calendar or chart, as a visual indicator of time moving ahead and finally running out. Often a loved one close to the client and skilled in communication with him or her can accompany the client and translate the clinician's intent and tasks to be done.

As time and ability permit, the clinician notes with clients that they can still take beneficial steps during the ending time: dealing with reactions, reviewing accomplishments and remaining issues, planning ahead, and making any necessary arrangements to ease the way for the client. Sometimes the introduction of focused ending work is an occasion for relief and excitement; at other times, the client may react with shock or dismay.

EXAMPLE

Clinician: Well, Roland, we are coming to the end of our work together.

Client: I can't believe how quickly the time has gone.

Clinician: Me either.

Client: So we're "terminating." What do we do when we're finishing?

Clinician: Well, I think it's a good time to remember where you were when we first met, to think about what we have done and where you are now in relation to the issues you came in with. It's also a time to think about how you may handle things in the future. We get to see if there are any loose ends that we want to talk about before you leave, and finally we say good-bye.

Acknowledging and Exploring Reactions to Ending: "How Does It Feel?"

Clients who see a dentist or an internist a number of times do not usually "work through" the ending of their work together. Even after a lengthy hospital stay, the staff do not usually ask, "How do you feel about our discharging you?" or "Did you have feelings about the people who assisted you while you were here?" A formal termination process is a phenomenon particular to clinical relationships, and many clients may not be used to focusing so intensely on ending a professional relationship. In addition, both clients and clinicians may be surprised at the intensity of their emotional reactions to ending—the more so if the contacts were initially mandated by others or laden with other complexities. For many clients, the ending phase of work is a great opportunity to celebrate their achievements, to honor a valued relationship, and then to move on (Fortune, 1987). Joseph Walsh (2003) notes that in solution-focused and narrative therapies, in which the whole emphasis of the work is on helping clients author more positive and hopeful narratives that look toward more empowering futures, the focus at ending is celebrating the success of these activities and how they are already playing out constructively in everyday life.

We can help by normalizing feelings and reactions related to endings and by helping clients express these feelings as the process of ending unfolds. Some clients take endings in stride and have few reactions beyond mild regret at ending contact with someone they respect. Other clients, especially those who are loss sensitive or isolated, may feel sad and apprehensive as they imagine ending work with the clinician. Feelings may be overwhelming or intolerable, especially when the ending stirs up many unresolved losses from the past.

Some clients may threaten to harm themselves or others in response to the clinician's leaving, sending up an unmistakable **"cry for help."** Clinicians are alert to these possibilities, particularly in clients who may have had a history of harming themselves or others before undertaking clinical work. Many people use the term **regression under stress** to describe the familiar phenomenon of outgrown behaviors returning under pressure because they are familiar, almost knee-jerk outlets for distress that cannot at the moment be expressed verbally.

Clinicians wisely discuss with supervisors a range of potential responses in case client emergencies arise during ending work. Sometimes client action takes the simpler form of losing things: schedule books, keys to the house or car, important papers, and so on. We can use the skills of examining the moment, processing the process, or directly addressing indirect references to the ending process. If we can help clients see connections between their unusual behaviors during ending and certain unexamined feelings underlying them, in the future they may be able to recognize their customary distress signals sooner and perhaps speak out, rather than acting out, their feelings.

EXAMPLE

Clinician: Roland, have you noticed that you have started to lose things a lot lately? Last week, you said you lost your car keys and today you lost your gloves.

Client: Yeah, I'm scattered.

> *Clinician:* Do you think it could have anything to do with losing our relationship soon? Sometimes it's easier to have feelings about lost things than about lost people.

Some clients may miss a session or two at this time, perhaps to abbreviate or draw out the process of ending, to avoid pain of reflecting on loss, or perhaps even to register protest. In such instances, it is often helpful to reach out by phone or letter, suggesting a possible link between the missed sessions and the process of ending. Here the clinician can gently ask the client to try to come back in so that things can be discussed together rather than thought about alone (the way that many clients have learned to deal with unhappy events).

> *Gary had suffered from a serious form of schizophrenia, but over a 3-year period, he let me in so that we developed very good talks about his hopes for the future. It came time for me to make a change, and I moved to another town. I could not get Gary to come in to talk with me about this. Instead, he took off for Florida on his motorcycle and sent me a note on a restaurant napkin to say, "Hi there." In response, I sent a letter to his parents' home, telling him what my last day would be and hoping to see him. He just appeared in the waiting room that day, in motorcycle leather and helmet, and when we sat together to say good-bye, he pulled his helmet visor down over his face and talked with me through it. I could see the tears running down his cheeks behind the visor but did not comment, as I knew how hard this was for him. He was able to say that, when you lose friends, it is sad. At the end, we hugged each other good-bye and wished each other well. For a time, I could see him sitting on his bike outside the agency, loudly racing his motor. I was sorry to end with him, and he saw it in me as I saw it in him.*

Reactions to ending provide an important opportunity for clinician and client to attend to the client's way of dealing with change and, time permitting, to explore unresolved feelings from past losses, educating the client as to how these feelings may be emerging in current reactions to ending. Clients who can appreciate human reactions to loss and change, as well as the possibility of taking good experiences with them in memory, are helped to cope better with loss and change. They can learn to anticipate common reactions to future changes and develop in advance good alternatives for managing their reactions with a minimum of harm to self or others.

Remembering: "Where Were You When We Began?"

Client and clinician review goals and accomplishments in relation to the client's issues and circumstances when the work began: "Let's go back and look at where you were when we first met." Some clients remember very accurately, and others not so well. In some situations, it can be useful to bring in process notes from early encounters and review them together to refresh the clients' memory of what they described as their situation and what feelings they had when they first came in. If they filled out an intake problem list or were asked to provide a written narrative regarding problems and goals, these materials can also be reviewed. A discussion of the goals and accomplishments can be the source of much pleasure, as clients remember how stuck they felt and how much further along they feel now.

E X A M P L E

Clinician: Roland, I was thinking about where you were when we first met. You were having anxiety attacks.

Client: Yeah. I was having about three a week. It was awful.

Clinician: And it was affecting your work and home life.

Client: I kept missing work and I thought Brenda was going to leave me.

Reviewing Highlights of the Work Together: "What Have We Gotten Done?"

Client and clinician review salient developments during their work together for the purpose of identifying changes, honoring persistence and achievement, affirming client strengths, and discussing the transferability of developed skills. Embedded in this generally upbeat review is the notion that change in concert with others is now clearly possible. This review also gives the clinician a chance to note that the client's convictions about hopelessness and "stuckness" have lost some of their power. Perhaps the future can now be tackled more hopefully and assertively. During this review, clinician and client may also explore the main features and dynamics of their relationship, particularly where changes or improvements have occurred that augur well for the client's future efforts to relate with others.

E X A M P L E

Clinician: You did a lot of work here.

Client: I remember during our first meeting when you said that you thought you could help. I didn't really believe it.

Clinician: Well, you really worked hard at it in spite of that.

Client: I remember when we started those relaxation tapes . . . [They continue to discuss events in the course of their work together, including setbacks or failures.]

Evaluating Current Status: "Where Are You Now?"

In evaluating the current status of the client and his or her situation and prospects, the clinician and client discuss where the client is in relation to the originally described issues, assets, and problems. They may also evaluate the client's current functioning, outlook, and circumstances, highlighting the client's strengths and supports and checking for any risks to well-being. These discussions act as a reminder of the gains the client has made during their work together.

EXAMPLE

> *Clinician:* So, how would you say you're doing with the anxiety attacks at this point?
>
> *Client:* Well, you know . . . I haven't had one in almost two months.
>
> *Clinician:* Nice work! And how would you describe things with Brenda?
>
> *Client:* Well, we still have our tensions. I thought she would be so relieved that my anxiety attacks were gone that everything would be great with her. But she still gets on my case sometimes. [They continue to talk about his home and work life.]

Foreshadowing the Future: "Where Are You Heading?"

As part of the ending process, the clinician and client explore what the client anticipates and what kinds of issues might arise in the future. They discuss how the client might respond to old familiar challenges if they should arise again. To double-check on shared understandings, the clinician often asks the client to recount what he or she will do in a particular crisis and to review more specifically whom he or she will rely on in the future for support, advice, and comfort to buttress and maintain growth.

EXAMPLE

> *Clinician:* What will you do two months from now if you find that the anxiety attacks come back?
>
> *Client:* Well, I certainly hope they don't. I thought I was better.
>
> *Clinician:* I hope they don't, too, but in case they do, it's important to know what you would do to handle them.
>
> *Client:* Well, I guess I would go back to that self-talk exercise you gave me and I would use the tapes.
>
> *Clinician:* And if that doesn't work?
>
> *Client:* I would call you. Would that be okay?
>
> *Clinician:* Of course it would

Checking for Unfinished Business: "Is There Anything We Should Cover Before We End?"

The clinician and client always double-check to see whether they need to take care of anything before ending. We keep an eye out for things that might need saying or doing—things the client might not have mentioned or thought of.

> *I have a little visualization I use with clients when we are ending. I ask them to imagine that they are walking down the stairs after leaving my office for the last time and to think about whether or not there is anything else they would have liked to have said to me but didn't. I invite them to say it now.*

Giving and Eliciting Feedback About the Meaning of the Relationship: "What Has This Meant?"

As we mentioned in our discussion of the skills of examining the moment and processing the process, the clinical relationship provides an opportunity to talk about the relationship itself. In the ending phase of the work, we often give clients direct feedback about how we have experienced and valued them and their work with us.

EXAMPLE

Clinician: One of the things I noticed about you, Roland, is how persistent you are. Things would look pretty gloomy, and you were still having lots of anxiety attacks, but you kept at it. You continued to use the relaxation exercises and self-talk when a lot of people would have given up.

Client: Some people would say I'm stubborn.

Clinician: I think hanging in there is a very important thing when it works for you. Are there times when it doesn't?

Client: Well, sometimes I have a hard time knowing when it's a matter of persistence that will get me somewhere and when it's a matter of something that I am too rigid to let go of. [Clinician and client explore.]

The clinician purposely sets time aside to review with the client special aspects of their relationship and what it has meant to them both. This is often a time when both clinicians and clients share what they have appreciated about each other. We advise clinicians to hold off on these discussions for a time, lest any resulting "love fest" prevent clients from telling clinicians about any anger they may have about ending, especially when a circumstance in the clinician's life is making termination necessary. Exploration could be initiated using a number of different statements or questions.

EXAMPLES

"Before we finish, Ed, I'd like us to have a chance to talk about our relationship and what it's meant to both of us."

"We have gone over just about everything except how it's been for us to work together, Dan. Can we do that this morning?"

"Graciela, should we take some time now to review the relationship we've had here and what it says about your new ability to work closely with someone?"

"One of the things we haven't said much about, Denise, is the relationship we've developed. It's special, and I'm going to miss working with you."

"It was an honor to work with you, Kwame. Your courage in getting your family here from your homeland during wartime and carving out a new life for all of you has touched me deeply."

"Chou, you have really taught me a lot about the benefits of silence! I have even started to meditate, thanks to the little book you gave me. I am very grateful."

We make a point of expressing what we have gotten from the work with the client because we unfailingly learn or grow from parts of the experience. If the relationship has been difficult, we may not say that in parting but instead say, for example, "Even though we've had our moments, I'm glad we kept working together and were able to get some things done that you felt helped your son." We try never to fake goodwill or meaning that clearly has not characterized the meetings. Inauthenticity does not feel right, and clients can usually see through it. Instead, we try to remain cordial and polite, no matter what has happened.

EXERCISE 14.5   Giving Positive Feedback

Divide into small groups. Think about a person in your life with characteristics that you find unpleasant. Briefly describe the relationship, as well as the negative characteristics that make this relationship unpleasant for you. Think of one honest, positive piece of feedback that you could give to this person. Role-play giving this positive feedback to that person. Discuss whether the statements were well framed and believable.

Addressing Issues Around Future Contact

Both clients and clinicians may have a hard time parting. Clients may express this difficulty by asking whether, now that clinical work is ending, the clinician can become a friend: "You're just the kind of person I like" or "You and I have so much in common . . . can't we do anything together after this? It seems such a shame."

Clients often picture the client-centered relationship occurring in social settings—a far cry from the mutuality of real friendships. Moreover, once clients come to experience the "warts and all" of the real person who is the clinician out of role, they may be surprised or regretful.

> When I told a beloved therapist that I often wished we knew each other in some other ways, she recounted a lunch she'd had with a therapist of hers after finishing up their clinical work. She was appalled to see how slovenly his dress was, and how his tie was covered with soup stains, and that he droned on a lot about himself. She reminded me that we see what we want to in people. That was the last contact she ever wanted with that therapist. I wondered what this hinted I might see in my own therapist if she became a friend, and I pretty much gave up the idea.

One of the good things about leave-takings is that, when done well, they teach us how to develop ending skills. Joan Fleming and Therese Benedek (1966) suggest that current clinical experience can be "metabolized into a memory" (p. 174) so that energy invested in it can be released to other relationships and activities. Moreover, this memory can act as a precious resource to be called upon when people face future adversity or challenge.

Clients sometimes ask if they can call or write the clinician in the future. Clinicians are of many minds about this request, and it is helpful to talk over options and their implications with a supervisor. Often the very idea that one can have contact makes the contact unnecessary: The idea itself is the comfort. Decisions have to be made individually. When working in smaller settings or locales, be careful not to choose some clients to favor with continued contact, denying others whose feelings may be quite hurt should they learn of the distinction.

Since we believe that much clinical work is ongoing, we often choose to let clients know that they can attempt to contact us in the future if they decide that they would like to do further work. However, we must be careful that we do not make promises we cannot keep. Aware of how situations and schedules can change, we do not promise that we will always be available to work with clients in the future. Ideally, we can suggest that the agency and others like ourselves will be available if we are not, giving the client alternatives in case the familiar service or agency closes for good.

Giving and Receiving Mementos

Sometimes the clinician gives a gift to the client at the end of the relationship as a memento or symbol of the work together. For example, we may give a client who is beginning to feel her own strength a magic wand representing the client's power, or we may give a book of nature poetry to a client who uses nature as a comfort during times of loss. The gifts that clinicians give to clients need not be concrete. A gift could be the sharing of a blessing (e.g., the Irish blessing "May the wind be always at your back . . ."). It could be a memory of something strong or soothing (watching the sunset at water's edge) or a mental picture of a significant scene from the client's life (imagining being held by a beloved parent).

Clients may ask for a picture or for mementos of the work together. Again, depending on the client's cultural traditions, the agency's and worker's theoretical orientation, the agency policy, and the worker's and client's individual styles, pictures or mementos may or may not be given. Clinicians—especially those who work with children, teens, or groups—may join clients for a photograph that acts as memory of a cherished experience together. If the clinician and client have been videotaped during their work, the client may request a copy of the tape: "You know how we did that videotaping? Well, could I get you and me on videotape so I can have something to remember what we did? Or "Can I get a shot on my cell phone?" It would be wise to consult with a supervisor before acting on such requests and prepare in advance for things that may come up that might require an immediate response.

It may at times be validating to send a client a letter or card underscoring the client's accomplishments and wishing him or her well on the road ahead.

> *When Moses left the residence, I wanted him to have something to hang onto if things got tough when he went home. I wrote him the following letter:*
>
> *Dear Moses,*
> *It was good yesterday to watch you leave the house—and our work together—with such good confidence and skills for your life back in your "real" home. I could see how excited your dad was to get you back. You said you never got a letter, so I thought I would send this short note to say, "Way to go!" I want you to hang onto this and check it out if you get low. We all think you have what it takes to make it, and we're wishing you luck and courage every step of the way.*
>
>   *High fives from all of us at The Grove,*
>   *Your Counselor,*
>   *Kareem Batts*

Clients may bring ending gifts to us. People from many cultures believe that gifts symbolize a natural and well deserved thank-you for services rendered by a hardworking professional. As with other gifts, carefully address their suitability and meaning.

> *I don't ask, "Why did you feel you needed to bring me a gift?" But as I open the gift, I do ask the client what they were thinking when they decided to bring me a gift. They always have interesting and useful things to say without it becoming a big deal. I always open the gift and am thankful for it with the client present. If it's food and the client asks me to taste it on the spot, I say that I will only eat some if the client will join me, and they usually do.*

Some community agencies may have bulletin boards on which pictures of clients and activities are displayed. Clinicians need to think carefully about confidentiality and get clients' permission before displaying any pictures in which clients are visible. We should also think about the effects on all clients if only some clients' pictures are displayed or if gifts from some clients are visible.

In many collective societies and cultures, showing and sharing come naturally. Thinking back on endings he regrets, Walsh (2003) describes a very traumatized and isolated Burmese war veteran he encouraged to use his good cooking skills to connect with a roommate. He did so and felt much better. When gains were made and the time came to end, this young man invited Walsh to share a meal at his apartment, which the clinician declined due to his sense of his code of ethics. The client was crushed, and Walsh now believes he conveyed a double message about food and relating. Now he wishes he had at least asked the man what cooking for Walsh would have meant to him and whether he would like to bring in some food that they could share in the office together.

Saying Good-Bye

In time-limited or task-focused clinical work, saying good-bye is a fairly straightforward and simple task that occurs much as it does in regular good-byes following any association. Participants acknowledge the end of the meeting or meetings, appreciate what each has contributed, and wish each other well. Handshakes and light hugs are often exchanged, the counselor walks the client to the door or waiting room, observing their customary practice of leave-taking. Deeply emotional reactions and protests about ending are rarely anticipated, since the focus of ending work has been on a review of the work, the tasks accomplished, and the client's reliance on self, family, and community resources more than it has been on the counselor's presence.

By contrast, when the clinical relationship itself has been a primary focus or an important therapeutic holding environment, the last meeting may follow searching and wide-ranging discussions of achievements, regrets, work yet to be done, past losses, gains, and readiness to proceed without the clinician. Whereas earlier ending discussions may have had a graver or more affective coloration, the final good-bye is usually more interactive and upbeat—a positive send-off after much good work together. Sometimes a quiet celebration or other ritual (e.g., an exchange of small gifts) is used to focus on the good-bye as a kind of celebratory launching.

While we recognize that the final good-bye may be sad, we always attempt to refocus clients on achievements and possibilities (Epston & White, 1995; Fortune, 1987). We find it helpful to say that we will be picturing them doing something they have longed for and intended to do, such as graduate, stay clean and sober, or parent successfully. We attempt to have clients remember us as someone who is permanently in their corner, who believes in them, and who is rooting for them.

DVD

CLIP 14.2
Tasks and Skills
of Ending

EXERCISE 14.6   Saying Good-Bye

Divide into small groups. Practice in pairs the final moments of saying good-bye and exiting. Practice several kinds of good-byes, including from public places, from office settings, from a client's apartment, or after a shared subway ride following a meeting at another agency. Discuss your experience and feelings as both clinician and client. What have you learned from this exercise?

■ Follow-Up and Evaluation

Many clinicians and agencies conduct **follow-up evaluations** after the end of clinical work. These evaluations may be formal, involving tests and other assessment measures as discussed in Chapter 8, or they may be informal check-ins. Follow-up evaluations can occur a month, six months, or even years after the initial work. At times, these follow-up meetings may serve as a reinforcement of the previous work together, reminding clients of the strengths and resources they have and the skills they developed during the course of the clinical relationship. As a side benefit, follow-up evaluations give the client a chance to discuss and honor how he or she is able to use the learning from the clinical relationship in other arenas with other problems.

EXAMPLE

Client: Well, it's been six months since I saw you.

Clinician: How's it been going, Roland? [The clinician explores Roland's anxiety attacks and how he is doing at work and with Brenda.]

Client: You know, Brenda has gone back to school. The other night she was a wreck about an exam she had to take. I taught her those relaxation exercises you taught me, and she calmed down. It was neat to be the helper for once.

Clinician: I'm glad they were helpful. What a great thing you did for her.

Client: Yeah, I'm pretty proud that I can use what I learned here.

■ Planned Breaks, Interruptions, Transfers, and Abrupt Endings

Planned Breaks

Sometimes a clinician and client decide together that a great deal has been accomplished and that it is now time for a **planned break,** during which the client goes for a time without face-to-face visits with the clinician. In advance of the break, they schedule a future appointment in which to review the client's interim experience and to decide only then whether further professional assistance is indicated. Sometimes these planned breaks are a part of the termination process.

> At the clubhouse, a day program for people who have been in an inpatient psychiatric hospital, we have a gradual termination process. We slowly decrease the number of days that the client comes to the clubhouse until they are coming only once a week. After a while, we will suggest that the member take a one-month "vacation" from the center, but we always set up a follow-up visit to see what the experience was like. Often a client will take repeated "vacations" before he or she finally feels ready to leave for good.

Interruptions

Sometimes the work between clinician and client is interrupted, occasioning a need for immediate work on the process of ending contact, either temporarily or permanently. A clinician or client may become ill, pregnant, take a long trip—all of which may require an interruption, although a return is anticipated.

> I had been working as a rehabilitation counselor at a nursing home for three years when my husband got a sabbatical from his college teaching job. He was offered a six-month fellowship in Montana, and we decided that I would join him there. I took a leave from my job, and let me tell you, it was hard to say good-bye to all the clients. I wasn't sure which of them would still be there when I returned. I reassured the clients that I would be returning in September. I told them where I was going, and I said I would think of them.

The use of a symbolic **transitional object** is helpful in sustaining a feeling of connection between the client and the clinician. This is especially true with children, who may need a concrete reminder of the clinician's existence, but it is often supportive for adults as well.

> When the college interns leave the preschool for winter break, we actually use it as a learning experience. Kalina was going home to Hawaii, so we took out a world map and showed the children where Kalina was going. We brought in pictures of Hawaii and had Kalina send postcards each week. That way the children would remember her when she returned.

Even when the interruption or break is anticipated or time limited, client and clinician may go through a process similar to other endings. We prepare the client for the interruption, leave room to talk about the feelings the interruption evokes, and attempt to get some closure for the work completed. Although we plan to return, the client may not be there when we do so. In fact, a clinician might not return.

> A couple of years ago, two therapists were murdered while they were on vacation. I was one of a team of clinicians who stepped in to work with their clients after their deaths. It really brought home to me how important it is to realize that you can never promise you will be back. You can promise you will try, but never that you will always be there.

In a similar vein, when a clinician is suddenly diagnosed with a life-threatening illness and subject to periods of treatment absence, of low energy, and of low emotional availability, the clinician is faced with tough choices about whether and how to keep working with clients. Careful work with supervisors and regular support from a group of supportive colleagues can help guide decision making about the disclosure of the illness, as well as temporary or ongoing needs for scheduling changes (Morrison, 1997; Philip, 1994).

Clients are usually very understanding and accommodating, yet the question lingers with the clinician as to whether they would be better served by another clinician. If the illness is serious or life-threatening, clients are often helped to say goodbye and transfer to another colleague or group if further work remains to be done. For the client's sake, the transfer work is usually done before the clinician's functioning deteriorates markedly. It is not unusual for clients to attend memorial or funeral services whose rituals afford an opportunity to get some closure on the loss an important relationship. Public processes also help clients mourn without having to disclose the nature of their relationship with the clinician.

Transitions to Another Clinician

On other occasions the client may be transferred to another clinician. This can happen during a planned interruption, as with illnesses, in which case it is anticipated that the original clinician and client will reconnect. It can also happen when the client sees another clinician after terminating with the original one. If the client is terminating, the clinician can offer to speak with the new clinician. This can facilitate the new work, help the clinician learn about the client, and perhaps avoid old pitfalls. Some clients like to have a sense of continuity in the work, and they may hope that this conversation will prevent them from having to repeat everything with the new clinician. Other clients may refuse permission for the clinicians to speak with each other, preferring to start with a clean slate.

When the client is seeing another clinician, the original clinician can help the client prepare for work with the new clinician.

E X A M P L E

> *Clinician:* Last week you told me that you and Brenda are going to see a couples therapist after we finish our work together.
>
> *Client:* Yeah, Brenda wants to work on "our communication," as she calls it.
>
> *Clinician:* What do you think that will be like? [They explore Roland's anticipations and fears.]
>
> *Clinician:* Do you think you will talk about our work together?

Client: I don't know.

Clinician: I want you to know that I feel fine about your talking about what worked and didn't work in our relationship. Sometimes people feel that they are betraying their old counselor if they talk to their new counselor about stuff they did or feelings they had with their old counselor. It can help future work to explore with your new counselor—both the things that helped and those that didn't.

If the client is seeing another clinician only temporarily and anticipates continuing with the original clinician, the two clinicians usually speak but, again, only after the client has given written permission, which is kept in the client's file. It can ease transitions if the original clinician introduces the client to the **covering clinician** before leaving.

The covering clinician can often feed useful information about the relationship back to the original clinician, although being careful never to compete to be the "better helper." Any concerns or questions that the covering clinician has about the work should be shared directly with the clinician rather than with the client. The covering clinician becomes a team member and assumes the same ethical and legal obligations as though he or she were the primary clinician.

> When one of my partners was taking an extended vacation, she asked me to see a client of hers. She described the client as someone who was very shy and had a hard time talking. I was quite surprised when I met the client, who seemed anything but shy. After I had met with him a couple of times, I told him that I had expected him to be much more reticent because that was how his therapist had described him to me. He told me that he felt very uncomfortable talking to any women, specifically professional women. He was comfortable talking with me because I was a man. We explored the issue and discussed how he might raise the issue with his therapist when she returned. When she did return, she told me how great it was that her client had seen me. He had talked with her about what we had discussed, and it really changed the nature of their work together. She threatened to go away again so that I could "do consultations" with all her clients.

Transitions to Family and Community Support Systems

When clients end therapy, they often continue to receive support and caring from their natural helping networks, such as family, friends, neighborhood resource centers, religious or spiritual communities, or mutual aid groups. As noted previously, Taylor and colleagues (Taylor, et al., 2000) have delineated the vital roles that black churches play in providing connections, activities, emotional support, and guidance. Delgado (1997) has noted that small businesses and Latino-owned beauty parlors act as social and informational support centers in Latino communities. Community centers and clubs, afterschool programs, literacy and citizenship initiatives, cultural associations, and neighborhood action groups also offer opportunities to lessen isolation and strengthen individual and family esteem and pride.

A clinician's knowledge of and solid relationship with a wide variety of these resources are important in helping clients connect with them as they transition from the clinical relationship. Some of these programs and support centers may have staff who reach out to clients. Sometimes the clinician may explain what services are offered and even accompany clients to their first contacts with community resources. Doman Lum (2004) considers the ability to connect clients with meaningful resources to be a bedrock of clinical competence in working cross-culturally. Ideally, the clinician uses these resources throughout the work together, not only as the clinical relationship draws to a close.

Abrupt Endings

The client may abruptly leave a session, simply not show up, or cancel future appointments. If a client stops coming, we usually attempt some sort of **outreach:** a phone call, a letter, or, in some cases, a home visit. Decisions about outreach should be discussed with a supervisor. If the client does not return, we can try to get some closure through a **letter of termination.**

EXAMPLE

Dear Juan,

I haven't heard from you since our last meeting on July 23. I have tried to contact you by phone and letter. I will assume that you have made the decision to stop our work at this time.

If you decide that you would like to return to get more closure on our work or if you feel that I can be of help to you in the future, please feel free to contact me at the agency.

It has been a pleasure getting to know you. I hope that you will have success in getting your GED as you planned.

Sincerely,
Davra Nawan

We all need to prepare ourselves for the fact that sometimes clients suddenly drop out of the work and never call or write to explain why. They may not respond to any of our outreach to them. These unexplained exits can leave us blaming ourselves, doubting our abilities, and feeling upset that a client we have worked hard to engage has just left us high and dry. Sometimes reviewing our work with a supervisor can help us understand problems that we did not see or subtle messages from the client that might have signaled ambivalence or intention to stop.

At a day treatment center, when a member dropped out, we would hold what we called a "group autopsy "We would discuss the member, his history in the program, and his relationship with staff and peers. Sometimes we could figure out why the member left—for example, because he was having difficulty with another member or one of the staff, or because of things changing at home. Sometimes there was no way of knowing. At least in these meetings, we could identify we needed to change to respond more effectively to our members or we could console each other that we had done the best we could.

We can fret for a long time about what we did or did not do to make things end this way, and doing so can make it hard to get closure. While it is good to explore which of our actions may have contributed to this sudden ending, we have to be able to let go and move on.

I remember one supervisor telling me that it was narcissistic to think that the reason a client left was because of something I had done. He reminded me how small we actually are in a client's extremely complicated life.

■ The Clinician Feels the Loss

Abrupt endings are particularly difficult for a clinician, but all endings evoke feelings in us. As the time to end approaches, we may find that, like the client's feelings, our own feelings may come out in behavior. We may lose our appointment books, double-book a client who is ending, or find ourselves feeling sad, anxious, or relieved. Clinicians working in health or hospice settings often encounter the very moving experience of working closely with clients with terminal health conditions. These clients know they have little time left and understandably do not want to lose a clinician with whom they are able to share whatever they wish about their dying.

Under special circumstances, a clinician who wishes to do so may arrange with the agency to continue to meet with a dying client even after leaving the agency and other clients. Consultation with a supervisor can help resolve dilemmas about whether and with whom to continue and how to arrange to keep seeing a client until death occurs. This is clinical work at its most human, characterized by flexibility, availability, and respectful adaptation to the needs of clients and their loved ones.

As clinicians, we form attachments to our clients and can have a great investment in their well-being, just as they are often strongly invested in the work with us and in our presence, caring, and encouragement. This is a human relationship of some intensity as well as a working partnership, and its attenuation or ending affects clinicians as well as clients.

CLIP 14.3
Clinicians'
Reflections

I hated ending with Charysse. I had literally watched her grow up. She had been in the after-school program at the center when I was a rec counselor, and I had coached her on the basketball team. Then she'd been one of the kids in the alcohol and drug group, and she eventually became a peer counselor. Now, she was having a baby and moving to Des Moines with Raffie. (I knew him, too.) When our last meeting was over, I walked into my supervisor's office and just cried. I was so happy for her and for the new life she was starting, but it was so sad to see her go.

■ Conclusion

Whether planned or unplanned and whether initiated by client, clinician, or outside forces, the ending of the clinical relationship provides an opportunity for new learning and growth. Good endings can help clinicians and clients increase their relational capacity, knowledge, and sensitivity. Both can take the work and the relationship away with them as internalized and sustaining inner resources, available for use as long as there is memory.

Chapter 15 highlights the ongoing education and self-care that clinicians need to remain fit and effective in work with clients. It elaborates many professional issues and challenges that await clinicians over the course of a long and active career.

■ Suggested Readings

A theoretically inclusive book that discusses ethnocultural considerations in ending is:

Walsh, Joseph. (2003). *Endings in clinical practice: Effective closure in diverse settings*. Chicago: Lyceum.

Further readings about endings include:

Fair, Susan M., & Bressler, Joanna M. (1992). Therapist-initiated termination of psychotherapy. *The Clinical Supervisor, 10,* 171–189.

Fortune, Anne E. (1987). Grief only? Client and social worker reactions to termination. *Clinical Social Work Journal, 15,* 159–171.

Gutheil, Irene A. (1993). Rituals and termination procedures. *Smith College Studies in Social Work, 63,* 163–176.

■ Self-Explorations

1. Recall a time when you were part of an ending that was not done well. What happened? Why? How do you think you or the other person could have handled it better?

2. Do you think you would be more likely to end a relationship too soon or too late? Why?

3. How do you deal with endings at this point in your life? What are your strengths in this area? What are the challenges for you?

4. Sometimes people do funny things during a period of transition in their lives—acting in ways that may be considered expressions of loss—misplacing keys, locking themselves out, leaving a personal item behind so that they have to go back to retrieve it. Has this ever happened to you? How do you understand it?

■ Essay Questions

1. List and briefly describe five major tasks of ending the clinical relationship and work.

2. Discuss the benefits and risks of giving and receiving mementos at the end of the work or the construction of an ending ritual (a celebration, a drawing, a picture taking, or a videotaping) with the client.

3. Discuss mistakes clinicians can make when ending clinical relationships and work.

4. What are the steps clinicians take to ensure the best possible referral for a client with ongoing needs for service? What things can clinicians do to determine whether an agency they have never used before is one that would provide effective follow-through with the client?

■ Key Terms

Client abandonment	Outreach
Covering clinician	Planned break
"Cry for help"	Referral
Follow-up evaluation	Regression under stress
Foreshadow the ending	Termination
Letter of termination	Transitional object

CHAPTER 15

Professional Issues: Ongoing Education and Self-Care

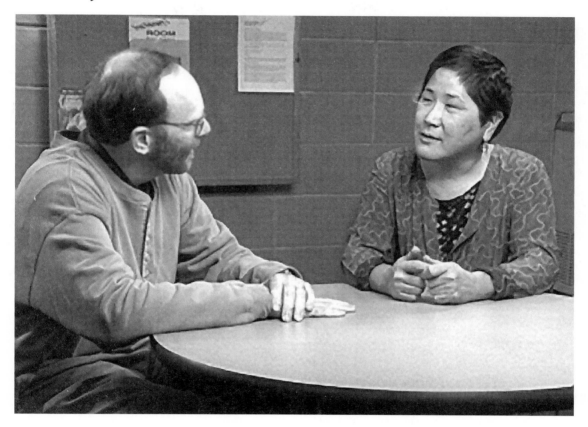

In previous chapters, we have elaborated on the foundation knowledge, values, skills, and activities that constitute clinical practice as it addresses human prospects, problems, and processes. To be effective, clinicians have to develop and sustain high degrees of understanding, compassion, skill, and commitment. Refining these capacities—what Egan calls "moving from smart to wise" (Egan, 1998, p. 7)—requires lifelong education, personal growth, and careful attention to the care of the professional self. This chapter addresses numerous ways in which self-care and ongoing education can be assured over the course of a long and fulfilling career.

■ Self-Care: Taking Care While Giving Care

If you believe in quality clinical work and the contributions it can make to a better world, then it is important that you not only survive, but also thrive as compassionate, effective, and ethical providers. Only then can you perpetuate clinical practice at high levels of commitment and competence. You must come to the work with your eyes wide open, prepared to nourish and renew yourselves and to connect with others for support, validation, relaxation, and enjoyment.

Stresses of Clinical Work

All work is stressful to some degree. In complex societies, most working people have to contend with the stresses of time and resource pressures, of complex communication networks, of working within systems of unequal power and privilege, and of compromises to ideals that must be made to get work done.

Certain stresses are unique to clinical work in the human services. Assignment loads can be very large and call for work both within and outside the agency, often separating clinicians from their collegial support for many hours of the week. Agencies may call on us for evening and weekend beeper coverage too. It is often hard to put the work down at day's end, especially when emergencies suddenly arise that only worsen if left unattended to. Consequent reductions in rest and relaxation with family and friends can be very wearing on relational people.

Michael Sussman (1992) summarizes research indicating that many clinicians learn early in life to overdo for others to earn love or to avoid conflict in their troubled families of origin. To help the family stay organized when parents were absent or dysfunctional, these youngsters were inducted into self-sacrificing roles carried out for the good of others. The influence of these early roles may underlie much of the workaholism that seems to characterize the working style of many clinicians. The very other-centeredness that is the hallmark of so much good clinical work can also strain our resources and draw our attention away from our own survival needs.

> *I used to tell people that I worked two or three jobs because I needed the money, but really, I think now that it was because I didn't know any other way of being. In visiting my siblings more, I began to notice that none of us could really just sit still for long and talk with each other. We had to get up while talking and be busy "doing something useful." We regularly drove each other crazy asking repeatedly, "Are you hungry?. . . can I get you anything while I'm up?. . . if you need anything, please just say."*

Historically, most clinicians have been underpaid, undervalued, and undersupported, especially during economic downturns. At the same time, we are very aware that many other professions and occupations enjoy greater pay, benefits, and respect than we do. This occurs in spite of our years of education and experience, the importance of our services to communities, our advanced degrees, and our willingness and commitment to work with populations that are often marginalized by other professions.

> *After a master's degree and 30 years of experience, I am making less money than my nephew, who's a year out of college and working in a big accounting firm. It does bug me sometimes, but I always try to remember why I chose to do this work in the first place. I still love it—but I do fret about pay inequities.*

Clinicians often work with stories of tragedy, violence, cruelty, and human indifference to suffering. These stories can continue disconcertingly to haunt our thoughts—sometimes even our dreams. As noted in Chapter 11, clinicians repeatedly exposed to traumatic stories may absorb clients' experiences so extensively that they develop symptoms of vicarious traumatization (McCann & Pearlman, 1990).

Burnout, or **compassion fatigue,** is an occupational hazard in the helping professions (Figley, 1995). It often results from clinicians' interacting intensely with people with many severe problems over a long period and with poor support. The symptoms of compassion fatigue include physical, mental, and emotional exhaustion ("I'm worn out"); insensitivity to others ("I don't care anymore"); a sense of futility or hopelessness about one's actions ("Going out there to visit them will change nothing"); and a sense of isolation and invalidation ("Who cares what we do anyway?"). At times you may experience a kind of disempowerment, lack of control, and disenchantment similar to that experienced by many of our clients when they work hard under tough conditions.

Work stresses often compromise the immune system, contributing to emotional and physical disorders and symptoms, such as head, stomach, and back pain; insomnia; and a pervasive feeling of uneasiness or tension (Benson & Klipper, 1976; Borysenko, 1987). Over the years, some clinicians turn to substance use to cope with the pressures of the job and develop addictions and serious relationship problems at home. In extreme circumstances, some find release in unethical activities or relationships with clients involving financial or sexual exploitation. The stresses of clinical work can take their toll unless we are vigilant about our own well-being. All professions now have confidential help lines for impaired colleagues, and some urban AA groups are specifically for clinicians, so that they can participate in mutual aid without encountering clients.

EXERCISE 15.1   Stresses in Clinical Work

In your journal, record the major stresses that affect clinicians in your agency or area. What impact have you seen these stresses have on colleagues? What stresses have affected *you* so far? What can you do to diminish their impact on your own life and work?

Strategies of Self-Care

Whereas the physician uses the stethoscope and X-ray or the plumber a wrench and pliers, clinicians use the professionally developed self to relate with clients, conduct assessments, and develop meaningful responses and interventions. Personal awareness, attunement, empathy, and readiness to listen and respond to others are a clinician's basic "tools of the trade." To preserve the precious instrument of self, we have to become as responsive to ourselves as we are to our clients.

1. *You need to identify clearly the people, activities, and forces that sustain you and those that do not.*   Work to find work settings and colleagues that can consistently appreciate and support you while helping you learn how to set some limits on what you are able to do with and for others—and stay on this side of exhaustion. Unless you take these important steps of self-advocacy with the same concern and energy with which you would advocate for any client, your gifts of attunement, caring, empathy, and responsiveness can actually become hazards to your long-term well-being. The overuse or misuse of an instrument leads to its deterioration. Furthermore, when we are tired, distracted, or resentful of work's burdens, clients can see this and then quietly suffer from diminished caring, attention, and responsiveness just as we do when we see that our usual support is "not there" due to stressful preoccupations.

2. *We need to develop and sustain self-empathy.*   Judith Jordan (1991b) describes **self-empathy** as the capacity to notice, care about, and respond to our own felt needs as generously as we attend to the needs of others. Just as with clients, the strategies of self-care involve valuing yourself, thinking about your needs differently, and connecting with others in order to experience rest and renewal, support and validation, self-actualization, and effectiveness at home and at work.

3. *We need to be good to ourselves and to take time and space for ourselves without feeling selfish and guilty, or that we are wasting time.*   We often find out the hard way that overworking and overgiving always have a physical and emotional price, often paid in physical symptoms and relational disconnects. It is important to relax and nurture yourself, rather than to feel driven to always be doing something for others. Since doing for others is also a very rewarding part of our lives and work, what we are urging is more self-care and balance in how you organize your life. We would like to see self-care become routine in the lives of caregivers rather than incidental to "more important things."

> *I get up an hour earlier than I used to, in order to do yoga stretches in the quiet of the morning before the others come down. Everyone knows this is "mama's time."*

> *Every day I pretend to get on a scale that shows how much my burdens weigh today instead of how much I do. If they weigh a lot, I laugh and plan what little treat I can work into the day to pick up my spirit. It is usually something chocolate!*

> *I thank my angels every morning for love and strength, and again every night. You can never have too many angels.*

4. *Fundamental to self-care are good health practices, which sustain both energy and the body's natural immune responses to protect against physical, mental, and emotional problems.*   You can stay fit through regular exercise and healthy dietary practices, minimizing the use of substances like caffeine, nicotine, alcohol, or drugs, which trigger high-low cycles that in turn affect energy, concentration, and mood. When work is largely confined to interior or closed spaces with poor air quality and artificial lighting, take very brief

breaks outside in fresh air and sunlight, and bike or walk to and from work whenever feasible. You can also carve out a few moments to walk down hallways or between floors instead of always phoning or e-mailing colleagues. Just a little bit of exercise refreshes mind and body between tasks, but we have to make a habit of it.

> *A neighbor, who walks, helped me get started walking daily with her. It didn't have to be far or long; it just had to be. Then the trick was to set up my own workday so that there would be time for walking in it. If the weather was bad, I learned to walk the five floors of my agency.*

5. ***Using the power of humor to sustain and refresh is another useful strategy in reclaiming efficacy.***   Clinicians often develop shared bulletin boards on which they post favorite cartoons or sayings that make everyone laugh and reflect on the follies of the human condition or the pomposities some people are capable of. We are always careful not to use humor that hurts or offends.

6. ***Connections with others, especially those not talking about workplace stress all the time, are also crucial to good self-care.***   These connections can be with friends and family, or they can occur through activities in which people with similar interests come together to share or create. Some clinicians take great satisfaction in working together in social action and public health campaigns aimed at changing social conditions. Singing and theater arts groups, dance, exercise, and meditation groups—all can provide channels for creative expression, feedback, and friendship.

> *Some of our staff go out dancing on Friday nights—one loves to salsa dance. Four play bridge once a month. One man sings in a gospel choir, and another plays trombone in a little jazz café the next town over. All of them say how much this eases them up and helps them be more present for clients all week.*

7. ***Many clinicians find that spiritual connections through meditation or formalized religious practice help them when stressed.***   Meditation programs, videos, workshops, and literature are widely available for use in relaxation and stress reduction, and you can practice physically relaxing activities at the beginning or end of a day or during a lunch break. In any 24-hour period, there are 96 fifteen-minute blocks, leaving us few excuses for not relaxing. Just 10 to 15 minutes of focused meditation can induce a peacefulness and bodily rest that help alleviate sleep problems due to worry as well as daytime stress on the job.

8. ***You must also purposely make time for doing creative things you are good at and find especially pleasing.***   Gardening, working out, sports, painting and drawing, quilting or knitting, listening to music or playing an instrument, cooking special foods, writing and poetry, and reading are some of the many ways that people find to enjoy themselves through self expression.

> *I saved up and got a keyboard and told my friends about how much I liked writing little songs for people's birthdays—it was so different from my usual routines, in which I encourage others' creativity and growth. Occasionally I play simple duets with a friend who's just now taking cello lessons at 70.*

9. *When you feel depleted, use staff or professional meetings to talk more about your positive feelings about your work and the things that are going well.*   Although angry or negative ventilation in peer groups may be a good release, too much negative ventilation can also leave participants feeling cynical or hopeless. Always try to find a way to balance excessive negativism with recall of *what you like and value* in the work and things you admire in special people with whom you work.

10. *In hard times, remember your competencies and contributions, and relate to an ongoing base of support that revives your spirit.*   Too much isolation when distressed can dismantle your energy, spirit, and perspective on the world and your place in it. Mind/body specialists Alice Domar and Henry Dreher (2000) emphasize that, to maintain health and spirit, self-care always has to have "two aspects: one in solitude, one in relationship" (p. 11).

> *Sometimes I like to eat my lunch by myself outside the school, looking out at the nearby lake. This is when I'm tired of listening and talking and I just want to have some private, silent time to get myself together before I go back to class. Other times I like to go eat Thai food up the street with my program friends. We get silly together and catch up on news and gossip.*

EXERCISE 15.2 Preventing Compassion Fatigue

In small groups, discuss how you recognize compassion fatigue in yourselves, and describe some of the things you do successfully, alone and with others, to prevent it.

■ Ongoing Education

Clinical education does not end with a diploma; it is a lifelong learning process. It is your professional obligation to continue your education through supervision, consultation, personal therapy, reading about current clinical research and intervention techniques, and attending continuing education and professional development courses. All of these collaborative activities contribute to an important maturational process that you are likely already beginning to experience.

Supervision

Clinical internships usually provide weekly supervision. In some settings, you may have two or more supervisors, who select and assign cases that advance learning, arrange coverage, oversee the general work of clinicians, and attend to the development of students' values, knowledge, and skills in clinical practice with clients. Agencies sometimes have group supervision in which all interns gather to review their work with each other.

Supervision is an essential part of your continuing growth throughout your career. We believe that all clinicians should have some form of ongoing supervision, whether it is individual, group, or peer supervision.

Individual Supervision

Good individual clinical supervision parallels a good clinical relationship in several respects. It provides a sustaining environment for learning and growth; it helps potentiate the learner's strengths, skills, and development; and it models relational, assessment, and problem-solving skills. While primarily task focused, a worker and supervisor may also examine the moment or process the process of their relationship. Because of supervisors' considerable ongoing knowledge of a worker's clients, goals, and stories to date, they often cover with clients when their supervisees are away, occasionally seeing a client or two who may need support during the worker's absence. Supervisors act as a backstop in times of crisis, and they frequently model critical thinking, composure, and purposeful behavior under fire.

> *I remember the first time I was working with a client who was suicidal. I felt quite out of my depth. I called my supervisor to tell him what my client had just said about thinking about killing herself. His response was, "Well, let's think how we should respond." I can't tell you how relieved I felt with his use of the word "we." It made me feel that I wasn't alone. I felt I could relax into the comfort of our team. He was in this with me.*

Your supervisors also help you learn professional values and work with you to resolve contradictions and dissonance between the values of your upbringing and those of the profession you have chosen (Cascio & Gasker, 2001). Supervisors are often selected because of their sound values and standards and their effective role modeling of well thought-out approaches to complex problems.

Regular supervision is one of a clinician's best ways to monitor clients' progress toward goals and personal actions and reactions in relation to clients and client material (Kadushin & Kadushin, 1997). Clay Graybeal and Elizabeth Ruff (1995) state that reviewing the content and sequencing of clinician-client exchanges in interviews also helps us develop reflective practice skills. That is, you will come to see that moment-to-moment transactions between you and clients generate knowledge about the both of you and can provide direction for the next steps in the interview, in the overall work, and for your clinical learning. The process of good supervision is similar to the clinical skills learning process suggested in this text, with a parallel focus on examining and trying out skills and receiving feedback from others that enhances understanding and skill execution.

Supervisors will help you recognize and attend to subtleties of themes and expression in your conversations with clients, supervisor, colleagues, and others. They often model the attitudes, reactions, and listening/responding skills that they hope you incorporate into your developing practice repertory. Certainly, effective supervisors listen closely to the supervisory process, trying to join with both your perspective and that of the client (Dean, 1984).

Your supervisors may also focus on steps in the overall problem-solving work with clients: What is or is not being resolved, and where agreed-on plans may have gotten derailed. Thinking things out together can generate new goals or strategies. Before the meeting closes, you and the supervisor summarize plans for next sessions. You will be asked often to hazard guesses about what may occur next, to develop your capacity accurately to anticipate events so as to be more prepared to work with them. In time you will become more comfortable and adept at spotting problems *as* they occur and able to take corrective action.

Although **"therapizing" supervisees** (probing for painful details of personal history) is avoided, supervisors are usually open to hearing a brief outline of a clinician's problems or experiences if they are disrupting learning or work with clients. Because problems with interviewing inevitably arise as a result of the complex dynamics of human exchange, supervisors try to find the right blend of minimal exploration of the learner's story and respect for the learner's privacy and personal boundaries (Kaiser, 1997).

> *Cora was a 42-year-old woman who came to the clinic to get some help with child rearing. While I was seeing her, her father was diagnosed with bone cancer, adding even more stress to her caregiving responsibilities. I didn't specifically talk about the issue with Duane, my supervisor, but it came up in passing as I said something about how Cora was late because she stopped at the hospital to visit her father. Duane started asking me questions, and it became clear that I hadn't talked with Cora enough about how her father's illness was affecting her. My supervisor said he was curious about my lack of follow-through on this, and then I told him about my mother's recent cancer diagnosis.*
>
> *We talked a little about how my own feelings as a daughter of someone who was dying of cancer may have gotten in the way of my attending to an important issue for Cora. Throughout the conversation, I thought Duane was being careful to look at the interface but not to push me too hard to talk about my mother. While he was caring, he made it clear that he was interested in talking about my mother's illness only to the extent that it might be affecting my work. At the end of our meeting, he said that I might want to talk to a counselor myself about all the stresses I was coping with. I started to cry and said I thought he had a good point.*

To normalize the struggles of the learning process, clinical supervisors may occasionally share some of their own missteps and dilemmas as continuing learners. They may also periodically assign readings about the process of clinical work or learning. Supervisory discussions may incorporate learning from the intern's concurrent course readings or training programs, and supervisees may bring in materials that give the supervisor new information or perspective, heightening a feeling of reciprocal influence and respect.

> *I brought in an article from my clinical class for my supervisor to read, about new research detailing the effects of trauma on children's neurology. After we looked at the research in relation to two kids I'm working with, she brought in an article for me to read, about research on love and empathy that shows that they have the potential to alter neurological development favorably.*

Sometimes supervision is really hard; for example, when a supervisor may have to tell you that something you have said or done is inappropriate and that you must change your behavior. This might occur if your continuing statements or work practices demonstrate unethical bias or prejudice; if you consistently miss client appointments; or if several colleagues complain that your approach to them is rude or offensive. Limit setting is designed to help you realign your behaviors with the standards of the profession. You will come to appreciate how professional guidance and limits help you work with others more productively.

The diversity of students and clients today reflects the changing demographics of the twenty-first century in ways that practicum supervisors, training faculties, and agency staff may not because the human services have been as slow as other sectors of the economy in hiring and promoting ethnocultural minorities. Students thus may or may not be able to find the range of diversity in colleagues and mentors that they might wish to have as models (e.g., people of color, gay or lesbian persons, people with disabilities). Whether supervision is intra- or intercultural, supervisors work to help learners develop a range of models and provide students the opportunity to speak frankly about problems the setting may pose for them (McRoy, Freeman, Logan, & Blackmon, 1986).

> *I always wished I had a gay or lesbian supervisor with whom I could talk over my questions about whether and how I might come out to my clients, and whether it would be okay to talk in the lunchroom about activities with my partner when everybody else talked about their weekends. I had heard there were other gay people in the agency, but they weren't out, and I couldn't be sure of correctly identifying them by myself, so I didn't know what to do.*

EXERCISE 15.3   Reactions to Supervision

In your journal, record your positive and negative reactions to supervision you have received in the past. Based on your experience, make a list of guidelines or watchwords that you would give to a new supervisor. Note any special needs that arose for you in your work and whether your supervision was helpful or unhelpful. Be prepared to discuss your experiences in class.

Group Supervision

You can also benefit greatly from weekly **group supervision**—education and support meetings in which discussions of clinician–client dialogues, learning dilemmas, techniques, and case-planning concerns affirm the mutuality of the learning process. This kind of back-and-forth exchange of knowledge and practical tips can help to build both your comfort and "voice" in groups and get feedback from trusted colleagues.

Supervisors can often arrange for interns and counselors in several neighboring agencies to come together at intervals for education and support. The agency may also be able to arrange for you to be supervised by more than one person or discipline to vary the learning experience, tap many sources of expertise, and enrich the feedback and exchange process between individuals and disciplines.

> *Isaac was a great individual supervisor. He taught me tons of stuff about how to work with clients. I felt like I could share all my concerns with him and that he would help me figure out what to do. But I was also glad that I was in group supervision. I liked hearing about how other people were doing things. The group gave me an opportunity to get lots of different feedback, and then with Isaac, I could sit down and see which felt right to me.*

Peer Supervision

Following completion of formal education, clinicians continue to use supervision to enhance their effectiveness. You can establish **peer supervision** groups, in which two or more clinicians share their work and offer feedback and support as they would do in an agency supervision group. Many such groups last for 20 years or more.

> *When I worked at the community mental health agency, about four of us were considered senior clinicians. We were the supervisors to the new staff and student interns, but we realized that we also wanted support and help with our own work. We set up a peer supervision group where we took turns presenting our cases to each other.*

EXERCISE 15.4   Peer Supervision

Many of the exercises in this book have suggested that you get feedback from peers. In small groups, give positive feedback to your colleagues about the peer supervision you have received. Be as specific as possible about what you have gained from them.

The amount and quality of supervision beginning clinicians can anticipate after completing formal degree studies are varied, depending on local resources and developments in managed care. There is a widespread impression that the quality and extent of supervision are diminishing in many settings because of agency cutbacks and administrative demands that supervisors provide more direct service or case management functions and devote less time to nonincome-producing supervision, staff education, and interagency collaborations.

State licensure in the helping professions usually mandates specified hours per week of advanced clinical supervision, but finding employment in agencies that reliably provide it is another matter entirely. Some clinical job applicants make supervision a bargaining chip in employment negotiations when they can. Others ask that part of their hiring package be money for outside supervision at the requisite level to assist them in meeting licensing requirements.

Many recently graduated clinicians must purchase private supervision or settle for inconsistent supervision on the job. Whether supervision is provided at work or not, it is still your responsibility to continue advancing your knowledge and skills through supervision, specialized training, and workshops. Local and state clinical societies and organizations can be very helpful in locating appropriate resources.

Consultation

Consultation is a process whereby clinicians at all levels of experience reach outside their normal learning and supervisory relationships to benefit from the perspective and advice of a seasoned mentor, who is valued for special knowledge and skills in certain areas of practice. Consultation is often sought when the clinician feels unusually stuck or confused in work with a client. The consultation may focus on the client, on the clinician, on the relationship, or on the surrounding systems influencing care.

The contact with the consultant is often short term, for purposes of ad hoc brainstorming and the formulation of strategies for problem resolution. The clinician or other involved parties present a thumbnail sketch of the client, the ongoing work, the relationship, and the reason for consultation. The consultant may interview the client separately, with the clinician, or in front of a staff group to elicit information or demonstrate strategy. Consultation has several different uses.

EXAMPLES

- A clinician in a group home for latency-aged children seeks a consultation on how to handle a specific client's bed-wetting. Others on the staff ask to attend to learn more about the problem in general.

- A teen client assigned to a clinical intern is showing signs of psychotic thinking. The intern's supervisor has not worked with psychosis before and so refers the intern to a colleague in the clinic's outpatient psychiatric services for consultation about the client. The consultant may advise additional outpatient evaluation of the client to see whether medication or further family involvement is indicated.

- A Cambodian psychologist makes monthly medical rounds at a neighborhood health clinic, commenting on any special ethnic issues or concerns arising in work with Cambodian patients of the clinic.

- After an unexpected client death upsets many staff, a practitioner specializing in trauma work with teams is invited to consult with the staff as a group, with an agenda of dealing with the death and the staff's sense of loss and failure.

If you seek outside consultation about a client, remember that ethically you must protect the client's right to confidentiality. You are ethically required to conceal all identifying information about the client, and, if the consultant is to see a videotape or hear an audiotape recording of a session, you must obtain the client's written approval first.

Sometimes the consultant focuses entirely on your concerns and needs, sometimes on the teaching of a new skill, and at other times on dealing with an issue that has arisen in the course of work with a client. Finally, you and your supervisor might seek informal consultation with experienced colleagues if tensions between you disrupt the supervisory learning process. While you are in school, you and your supervisor can usually consult directly about problems with faculty liaisons to placement sites. In such instances, to assure just process, be sure to ascertain that the liaison is not a close friend of any of the participants in the problem resolution. Agencies and supervisors may be legally and ethically responsible for your behaviors, and therefore they usually have the final say in the conduct of professional practice. An exception is an agency asking staff to carry out unethical practices. In such circumstances, contact your local, state, or national professional association or licensing board for information about available resources for assistance.

Personal Therapy as a Learning Experience

Your own therapy might make a significant contribution to your clinical education and practice. In fact, some graduate programs suggest that interns have personal therapy. Furthermore, interns often seek therapy because their clinical learning stimulates curiosity and interest in exploring their own stories further.

The experience of being a client can also heighten your appreciation of the dynamics and skills involved in the helping process. In addition, you can use your own therapy to explore the personal dynamics and blind spots that may interfere with your effective use of self in relationships with clients. Finally, you might decide to seek therapy if a client's issue stimulates unresolved issues of your own that affect your functioning both on the job and in your private life. A supervisor may help identify such issues; then you can decide whether you want to explore them more thoroughly in therapy. In rare instances, a student or clinician who becomes unable to discharge duties because of serious impairment can be asked to take a leave to get help in order to meet professional responsibilities. In fact, clinicians have an ethical responsibility to assist colleagues whose physical, mental, or emotional problems affect their work.

A supervisee of mine was having difficulties at work. I began to wonder if she was drunk. She sometimes slurred her speech, she came late to meetings and missed two sessions with clients. I asked her what was happening. At first she said she was fine but I persisted (using all my clinical skills of reflection and confrontation). She eventually told me that she was hooked on narcotics. I told her that she needed to get help for lots of reasons, but one was that it was clearly affecting her ability to be a responsible social worker and that, if she didn't, she could lose her job. She was admitted to a detox hospital. When she came back in about six weeks, she seemed different and motivated to live a clean and sober life. She carried out responsibilities well after that, and saw an addictions specialist to learn more about herself. It turns out that, while she was in detox, someone told her about a group for impaired social workers sponsored by our local association and she joined that group.

Clinicians usually seek therapy outside their work environments because professional codes of ethics and standards for practice prohibit dual relationships with supervisors. In addition, we are likely to relate our own problems more comfortably and fully with therapists than with workplace supervisors who participate in performance evaluations and periodic administrative discussions of how students and staff are handling their responsibilities.

Professional Resources

An important way to keep up with advances in the fields of counseling and psychotherapy is by continuing to read the professional literature. Clinicians often subscribe to the major professional journals in their discipline, some of which are provided as a benefit of membership in professional organizations. The *Journal of Counseling and Development* is a benefit of membership in the American Counseling Association, just as the journal *Social Work* comes with membership in the National Association of Social Workers. All members of the American Psychological Association receive the *American Psychologist.*

Clinicians working in specific fields often subscribe to journals whose subject matter ranges from child welfare, alcohol and drug abuse, family therapy, and multicultural practice, to school guidance counseling, vocational and rehabilitation counseling, and health and hospital practice. These journals give us the opportunity to stay abreast of innovative developments and model projects in practice and research in our fields. Professional organizations often have newsletters and magazines (e.g., *Counseling Today, The NASW Newsletter,* and the *APA Monitor*) that provide current information about what is happening in the professions.

In addition to journals and newsletters, we read books about special areas of treatment and topics of interest. Reading is a vital part of the professional's ongoing responsibility to maintain expertise and to practice competently.

I have a growing library of books and articles. While I was a student, I started a file folder in which I put articles that I found particularly helpful. Over the years, that file folder has become a file cabinet! We often share articles at the clinic. There's a space on the bulletin board where we can post something we find useful.

The Internet increasingly eases our access to a great deal of information. The major clinical professional organizations have Web sites, and there are listserves and online discussion groups on numerous topics of interest to clinicians. You need to carefully check the credentials of the people involved in these lists and the accuracy of postings and articles making impressive claims.

With the advent of the World Wide Web, when I want information about a particular topic, I can do a PsychInfo search. But I also belong to a number of psychology listserves. I was looking for a good article on termination the other day and put my request on the listserve. I got back some great leads from colleagues across the country.

Continuing Education

Most states require clinicians to take specific amounts of approved continuing clinical education to maintain their licenses. **Continuing education** programs may focus on working with particular client populations (the elderly, refugees), with specific problems or disorders (sexual abuse, personality disorders, compulsive behaviors, depression), or with specific methods or techniques (short-term interventions, eye movement desensitization techniques, play therapy, journal writing).

Continuing education affords an ongoing opportunity to grow in understanding, self-awareness, and the purposeful use of self; to learn new skills; and to develop our competencies. Courses often address problems and recommend techniques for use in a specialized area of practice (methamphetamine abuse, Alzheimer's dementia, postdivorce kids with three sets of parents to relate with). They also provide very useful practice-related bibliographic resources. After some presentations, learners divide into small discussion or role-play groups in much the same way that formal educational programs ask students to do.

Continuing education programs also provide important venues for networking with other clinicians.

Continuing education programs have given me wonderful opportunities for new knowledge and skills, and they have also given me unexpected chances to meet and learn from leading clinical figures I thought I would only ever encounter in books and articles. Over the last couple of years, I have taken continuing education institutes on DBT with Marsha Linehan, on ADD with Ted Hallowell, on cognitive behavioral therapy with Dave Barlow, and on multiracial identity with Maria Root. Now when I read their work, I feel like I know them.

A special form of continuing education is offered by advanced certificate programs, postgraduate internships, fellowships, and specialty training. These programs sometimes allow enrollees to see clients with designated problems (domestic violence, alcoholism, trauma) at specialized sites and under senior supervision for the advancement of knowledge and skills.

Contributing to the Education of Others

As clinicians we are not just consumers of education; we also contribute to the education of others through teaching, research, public speaking, consultation, writing for the media, supervision, and academic scholarship. These pursuits may begin while individuals are still in school, and are often carried out with colleagues or mentors. Educational exchange and feedback among clinicians (as when attending and presenting papers at annual professional meetings) provide rich satisfaction and can be a stimulating addition to work.

> *When three colleagues and I presented at a statewide conference on gay adoption, two respected therapists from the West Coast were there to hear more about issues and research in this area of interest. After our presentation, they asked to meet with us over coffee to talk more about our topic. It was great giving them information for a change— we have used so many of their articles about counseling adolescent parents.*

There will be many more international exchanges over the decades ahead, as technological advances narrow the distances between human service providers, clients, researchers, and educators around the world.

■ Conclusion: What Lies Ahead

A graduation is called a "commencement" with good reason because it marks the beginning of learning for life. Completing a course or text on clinical interviewing is also a commencement; it marks the beginning of lifelong learning about clinical knowledge, methods, and roles. We believe that the most effective clinical learning is embedded in relationship. Working alone, you cannot see your blind spots and therefore cannot get help from others about them. You also miss the "aha!" moments that occur with colleagues and mentors in the lively exchange of confirming and opposing ideas. In addition, you miss chances to develop comfort in giving and receiving feedback.

Contact with others also increases the probability of generating completely novel possibilities that none of us think of alone. Empathy, intuition, perception, judgment, and timing are also improved by feedback from colleagues. Because we often work behind closed doors and supervisors can know only what we and others tell them, our learning and work call for a high degree of integrity, respect for the rights of others, the exercise of self-restraint, and a readiness to act to protect others from harm.

Advancing your clinical knowledge and skills always involves re-view, re-view, re-view and practice, practice, practice. Nothing beats being seasoned through the mastery of a variety of learning challenges with the help of wise and caring mentors and colleagues. In addition to your own personal advocacy to obtain the best teaching available, you can seek out the help of professional organizations to obtain the needed resources and advanced training and education. Ultimately you, too, may be one of their continuing education presenters in your own specialty.

We believe that informal learning is equally important as formal education in the intentional refinement of clinical skills. A crucial part of informal learning is widening the influences to which you let yourself be exposed. You will need more shared neighborhood, friendship, workplace, and family experiences across color, language, and other cultural divisions. The history of human service organizations sadly demonstrates that these experiences will not be handed to you. You will have to make them happen with the same courage and caring that brought you into clinical education in the first place. Getting "out there" with many different kinds of people and belief systems and interacting with human suffering, struggle, and triumph will almost always stir you to social action on some level. Becoming involved in political action campaigns, working for justice and equality, and extending your ethic of care to all living things and resources on our planet are also natural extensions of your clinical work and professional values.

Another major influence on the shaping of your professional self and skills is your interactions with clients as teachers. Clinical work is never just a simple process of thinking ahead that "she'll do this and then I'll do that." It is precisely the relationship between the participants, and the effects of relationship dynamics on the evolution of each conversation and activity, that play such an important role in both clinical work and learning. Clients teach and shape us by their comments, by their looks and other nonverbal messages, by their complaints or requests that things be said or done differently, and by their refusals to go down useless pathways that look so good to us as outsiders to their stories. They also beam and credit us when we "get it right," commend our faithfulness in making important visits after hours, and acknowledge the importance of our concern and efforts as they work to improve their situations and relationships. They will teach you to laugh and cry with them, to persist when it is hard to go on, to take a look at yourself while you are looking at them. They will help you change, and these changes sharpen your vision and soften your edges. Some clients will stay within you forever, as they have for us, just as some of who you are stays within them.

So clinical skill and relational capacity are much, much more than what we *do* at work; they are importantly who we *become* through work, thanks to the way clients affect us through the interactive process that is the clinical relationship. Thus, clinical learning will be a life-changing process for you. No one participating in a process of human exchange can emerge from that exchange unaltered in important ways. Once you get "clinical ears"—the ability to hear and read the metacommunication in human transactions—you are likely to become more sensitive and attuned listeners and responders in your personal relationships. Furthermore, meeting new and varied people throughout your career usually stimulates heightened curiosity and interest in others and may impel you into domains of practice you might never have imagined yourself engaging in when you started out. While many challenges await you as clinicians, so do the many rewards and benefits of working with and for others.

CLIP 15.1
Conclusion

■ Suggested Readings

Ames, Natalie. (1999). Social work recording: A new look at an old issue. *Journal of Social Work Education, 35,* 2, 227–237.

Dean, Ruth G. (1984). The role of empathy in supervision. *Clinical Social Work Journal, 12,* 129–139.

Dillon, Carolyn. (2003) *Learning from mistakes in clinical practice.* Pacific Grove, CA: Brooks/Cole.

Domar, Alice & Dreyer, Henry. (2000). Self-nurture: Learning to care for yourself as effectively as you care for everyone else. New York: Penguin Books.

Figley, Charles (Ed.). (1995). *Compassion fatigue: Coping with secondary traumatic stress disorder in those who treat the traumatized.* New York: Brunner/Mazel.

Jansson, Bruce S. (1999). *Becoming an effective policy advocate: From policy practice to social justice.* Pacific Grove, CA: Brooks/Cole.

Kaiser, Tamara. (1997). *Supervisory relationships: Exploring the human element.* Pacific Grove, CA: Brooks/Cole.

McCann, Lisa, & Pearlman, Laurie Ann. (1990). Vicarious traumatization: A framework for understanding the psychological effects of working with victims. *Journal of Traumatic Stress Studies, 3,* 131–149.

■ Self-Explorations

1. What originally attracted you to clinical work? Describe the differences between what you expected and some of the realities in professional life and work of which you are now more aware.

2. List the activities in your personal life that can help balance out the stresses in your professional or student life. Discuss the activities you actually make time for now, as well as the ones you need to carve out time for in the future so that you stay fit and smart over the long haul.

3. What do you find are your most common missteps at this point in your clinical learning? What are the sources of these mistakes, and how can you remedy them? Discuss situations or techniques that are proving especially challenging for you at this point?

4. List your own personal qualities that you will work assiduously to preserve. Discuss any personal qualities you want to alter, soften, or eliminate to be more effective as a clinician. Finally, what aspects of the clinical professions make personal qualities so important?

■ Essay Questions

1. Discuss clinician burnout. Define "burnout" and elaborate its major causes. Is burnout inevitable for all human service workers? Why or why not? What are the signs of burnout in a professional clinician? Finally, discuss the numerous things human service workers can do to prevent burnout in spite of ongoing stresses and challenges in the work.

2. What are the benefits of and differences between individual and group supervision?

3. Discuss the advantages and disadvantages of peer group supervision. Should friends join a group where they will be giving supervision to each other? Discuss the "dual roles" concept and its implications for this situation.

4. Debate the premise that all clinicians should show evidence that they have had personal therapy. Should educational programs mandate therapy for students? Why or why not?

■ Key Terms

Burnout

Consultation

Continuing education

Group supervision

Peer supervision

Self-empathy

"Therapizing" supervisees

Multicultural Counseling Competencies

The following *guidelines* were developed by the Association for Multicultural Counseling and Development and have been endorsed by the ACA and many training programs across the country. Reprinted with permission from ACA.

I. Counselor Awareness of Own Cultural Values and Biases

A. Attitudes and Beliefs

1. Culturally skilled counselors believe that cultural self-awareness and sensitivity to one's own cultural heritage is essential.
2. Culturally skilled counselors are aware of how their own cultural background and experiences have influenced attitudes, values, and biases about psychological processes.
3. Culturally skilled counselors are able to recognize the limits of their multicultural competency and expertise.
4. Culturally skilled counselors recognize their sources of discomfort with differences that exist between themselves and clients in terms of race, ethnicity and culture.

B. Knowledge

1. Culturally skilled counselors have specific knowledge about their own racial and cultural heritage and how it personally and professionally affects their definitions and biases of normality/abnormality and the process of counseling.
2. Culturally skilled counselors possess knowledge and understanding about how oppression, racism, discrimination, and stereotyping affects them personally and in their work. This allows individuals to acknowledge their own racist attitudes, beliefs, and feelings. Although this standard applies to all groups, for White counselors it may mean that they understand how they may have directly or indirectly benefited from individual, institutional, and cultural racism as outlined in White identity development models.
3. Culturally skilled counselors possess knowledge about their social impact on others. They are knowledgeable about communication style differences, how their style may clash with or foster the counseling process with persons of color or others different from themselves based on the A, B, and C Dimensions and how to anticipate the impact it may have on others.

C. Skills

1. Culturally skilled counselors seek out educational, consultative, and training experience to improve their understanding and effectiveness in working with culturally different populations. Being able to recognize the limits of their competencies, they (a) seek consultation, (b) seek further training or education, (c) refer out to

more qualified individuals or resources, or (d) engage in a combination of these.

2. Culturally skilled counselors are constantly seeking to understand themselves as racial and cultural beings and are actively seeking a nonracist identity.

II. Counselor Awareness of Client's Worldview

A. Attitudes and Beliefs

1. Culturally skilled counselors are aware of their negative emotional reactions toward other racial and ethnic groups that may prove detrimental to the counseling relationship. They are willing to contrast their own beliefs and attitudes with those of their culturally different clients in a nonjudgmental fashion.

2. Culturally skilled counselors are aware of their stereotypes and preconceived notions that they may hold toward other racial and ethnic minority groups.

B. Knowledge

1. Culturally skilled counselors possess specific knowledge and information about the particular group with which they are working. They are aware of the life experiences, cultural heritage, and historical background of their culturally different clients. This particular competency is strongly linked to the "minority identity development models" available in the literature.

2. Culturally skilled counselors understand how race, culture, ethnicity, and so forth may affect personality formation, vocational choices, manifestation of psychological disorders, help-seeking behavior, and the appropriateness or inappropriateness of counseling approaches.

3. Culturally skilled counselors understand and have knowledge about sociopolitical influences that impinge upon the life of racial and ethnic minorities. Immigration issues, poverty, racism, stereotyping, and powerlessness may impact self-esteem and self concept in the counseling process.

C. Skills

1. Culturally skilled counselors should familiarize themselves with relevant research and the latest findings regarding mental health and mental disorders of various ethnic and racial groups. They should actively seek out educational experiences that enrich their knowledge, understanding, and cross-cultural skills for more effective counseling behavior.

2. Culturally skilled counselors become actively involved with minority individuals outside of the counseling setting (e.g. community events, social and political functions, celebrations, friendships, neighborhood groups, and so forth) so that their perspective of minorities is more than an academic or helping exercise.

III. Culturally Appropriate Intervention Strategies

A. Attitudes and Beliefs

1. Culturally skilled counselors respect clients' religious and/or spiritual beliefs and values, including attributions and taboos, because they affect worldview, psychosocial functioning, and expressions of distress.

2. Culturally skilled counselors respect indigenous helping practices and respect minority community intrinsic help-giving networks among communities of color.

3. Culturally skilled counselors value bilingualism and do not view another language as an impediment to counseling (monolingualism may be the culprit).

B. Knowledge

1. Culturally skilled counselors have a clear and explicit knowledge and understanding of the generic characteristics of counseling and therapy (culture bound, class bound, and monolingual) and how they may clash with the cultural values of various cultural groups.

2. Culturally skilled counselors are aware of institutional barriers that prevent minorities from using mental health services.

3. Culturally skilled counselors have knowledge of the potential bias in assessment instruments and use procedures and interpret findings keeping in mind the cultural and linguistic characteristics of the clients.

4. Culturally skilled counselors have knowledge of family structures, hierarchies, values, and beliefs from various cultural perspectives. They are knowledgeable about the community where a particular cultural group may reside and the resources in the community.

5. Culturally skilled counselors should be aware of relevant discriminatory practices at the social and community level that may be affecting the psychological welfare of the population being served.

C. Skills

1. Culturally skilled counselors are able to engage in a variety of verbal and nonverbal helping responses. They are able to send and receive both verbal and non-verbal messages accurately and appropriately. They are not tied down to only one method or approach to helping but recognize that helping styles and approaches may be culture bound. When they sense that their helping style is limited and potentially inappropriate, they can anticipate and modify it.

2. Culturally skilled counselors are able to exercise institutional intervention skills on behalf of their clients. They can help clients determine whether a "problem" stems from racism or bias in others (the concept of health paranoia) so that clients do not inappropriately personalize problems.

3. Culturally skilled counselors are not averse to seeking consultation with traditional healers and religious and spiritual leaders and

practitioners in the treatment of culturally different clients when appropriate.

4. Culturally skilled counselors take responsibility for interacting in the language requested by the client and, if not feasible, make appropriate referrals. A serious problem arises when the linguistic skills of a counselor do not match the language of the client. This being the case, counselors should (a) seek a translator with cultural knowledge and appropriate professional background or (b) refer to a knowledgeable and competent bilingual counselor.

5. Culturally skilled counselors have training and expertise in the use of traditional assessment and testing instruments. They not only understand the technical aspects of the instruments but are also aware of the cultural limitations. This allows them to use test instruments for the welfare of culturally different clients.

6. Culturally skilled counselors should attend to as well as work to eliminate biases, prejudices, and discriminatory contexts in conducting evaluation and providing interventions, and should develop sensitivity to issues of oppression, sexism, heterosexism, elitism, and racism.

7. Culturally skilled counselors take responsibility for educating their clients to the processes of psychological intervention, such as goals, expectations, legal rights, and the counselor's orientation.

Glossary

Advanced empathy   The process of hypothesizing (after some experience with the client) about themes, patterns, or feelings of the client that he or she may not yet have verbalized or even been aware of.

Advocacy   Clinicians' work with social action groups, service agencies, and institutions to increase benefits, access, opportunities, justice, and rights for people.

Ambivalence   Having two or more opposing ideas, feelings, or impulses simultaneously, which often leads to feeling stuck and immobilized.

Anticipatory empathy   Before meeting with clients, we think about the information we have about them, anticipate their feelings and reactions, and adjust our ways of interacting accordingly.

Assertiveness training   Learning to develop greater self-affirmation and voice through education, support, and new skills rehearsal to prepare for challenging or formerly disempowering interactions.

Assessment summary   A psychological report summarizing assessment findings and case conceptualization.

Behavioral rehearsal   The clinical technique of practicing new behaviors in the safety of the clinical interview, trying them out with the clinician's feedback and encouragement before trying them out elsewhere.

Bibliotherapy   The clinical strategy of referring clients to specific readings, books, articles, or Web sites relevant to issues they are working on.

Borrowed environment   Any nonoffice setting or locale adopted for interviewing purposes.

Brainstorm   Putting numerous alternative explanations or possibilities on the table for discussion without judging them as they emerge.

Bubble of calm   A circumscribed and focused atmosphere of quiet and safety conducive to clinical conversation and reflection on the work.

Burnout   An occupational hazard in the helping professions (often called compassion fatigue) resulting from repeated intense interactions with people with many severe problems. Symptoms include exhaustion, insensitivity to others, hopelessness, irritability, and frequent absences from work.

Case conceptualization   The integration and analysis of assessment data from which hypotheses about the person, situation, and possible interventions are based.

Central relational paradox   The Stone Center principle asserting that individuals accustomed to invalidation or rejection often try to connect with others by holding back parts of their experience and feelings for fear that disclosure of these parts of themselves will lead to more rejection.

Certification   A process by which a professional group confirms that a practitioner has met a set of advanced educational and practice standards established by the certification agency or board.

Checking-in   A sustaining technique in which the clinician asks how things feel or seem to the client after a period of exploration.

Circular causality   A principle of systems theory asserting that events in complex systems often exist as both causes and effects of each other.

Client abandonment   The unethical practice of "dumping" or deserting clients with whom the clinician has found it hard to work.

Client gestalt   A client's values, beliefs, and personal background in the larger social, cultural, and familial contexts.

Client information variables   Important information about client demographics including age, gender, ethnicity, and presenting problem.

Client rights   Principles of client care to ensure a mutually respectful partnership, including the right to information necessary to make decisions about treatment options, confidentiality, and professional courtesy.

Clinical interviewing   The process of structured, purposeful, client-centered, ethically guided conversations with clients aimed at identifying problems as well as assets and resources that may help in problem resolution.

Clinical intuition   A clinician's informed hypotheses, combined with preconceived ideas and feelings about clients and their narratives.

Clinical judgment   Informed decision making about how to proceed clinically, based on client data, relevant theory and research, hunches, intuition, and cumulative experience with situations such as the one at hand for the client and the team.

Clinical listening   A form of attending closely to verbal and nonverbal communication, to themes and patterns, and to the context in which clients' stories take place. This process includes attending to the relationship and to the clinician's own inner process.

Clinical repose   The relaxed, attentive, reassuring steadiness of the clinician, which helps the client to relax and feel confident of the clinician's reliability.

Clinician gestalt   A clinician's values, beliefs, and past experiences, mediated by familial and cultural background.

Closed-ended questions   Focused questions that can usually be answered with a word or two.

Complementary medicine   Holistic health specializations whose techniques are designed to bring about the harmonious integration of mind and body resources. Complementary practices include acupuncture, meditation, herbal remedies, homeopathy, naturopathy, reflexology, and chiropractic.

Compound crisis   Situations in which a current crisis rekindles unfinished business from previous crises.

Confidentiality   A professional ethical standard ensuring the privacy of client-clinician communications with special exceptions designed to protect both the public and professionals from specified perils.

Congruence Clinicians are genuine and authentic with clients, free of pretense and hypocrisy, and not hiding behind a mask of professionalism.

Consequences Responses that reinforce or encourage a behavior, or that serve as disincentives to it.

Consultation A clinical learning process in which clinicians reach outside their normal supervisory relationships to benefit from the perspective and advice of a seasoned practitioner or expert valued for special knowledge and skills in certain areas of practice.

Content of assessment Identifying the specific problems, participants, incentives, and goals for the change process, while also elaborating clients' strengths and resources for use in problem solving.

Contingency contract A clearly articulated behavioral plan that outlines roles, responsibilities, action steps, and rewards and consequences to promote and maintain specified behaviors.

Continuing education Advanced clinical learning programs continuously required for licensure and often focused on enhancing knowledge and skills for work with particular populations, on problems or disorders, or on specialized or newly developing methods and techniques.

Contracts Working agreements that enumerate goals, roles, and responsibilities; proposed intervention methods; duration and costs of meetings; and plans for measuring progress and evaluating outcomes.

Coping mechanisms The methods people use to overcome, reduce, or accommodate the demands of stress.

Coping questions Clinical questions that focus clients on how they have been successful in the face of adverse circumstances.

Corrupt contracts Contracts in which multiple service providers, working separately and without communicating with each other, make different or conflicting working agreements with clients (or clients with them) that are thus inauthentic for all practical purposes.

Countertransference A term from psychodynamic theory to describe an unconscious process in which the clinician views the client as a representative of an important figure from the clinician's past, then behaves toward the client as thought he or she *were* that person.

Covering clinician A clinician who carries out supportive work with a client whose primary clinician is away for a time and who later provides the primary clinician with useful feedback about the client's reactions and work during the absence.

Crediting client strengths The technique of stopping conversation to give clients deserved appreciation for their courage, determination, and accomplishments to sustain them at hard points of the work.

Crisis An important turning point in events when action must be taken to avoid disaster or significant distress. The destabilization in a crisis provides an opportunity to restabilize at a higher or lower level of functioning.

Critical Incident Stress Debriefing (CISD) The immediate and brief posttrauma process of education, ventilation, and validation of personal experiences, along with the preparation of survivors for ongoing coping around the complex aftereffects of the trauma.

Critical thinking A form of theoretical critique that divides theories into their conceptual constructs, assumptions, and hypotheses; attempts to understand the history and context that inform these constructs; and evaluates their strengths, limitations, and practice implications.

"Cry for help" A client's self-harming or threatening behaviors that signal a need to elicit a response from the clinician or others. This may occur during the ending process and reflect strong reactions to the clinician's anticipated departure.

Culturagram A clinical assessment matrix elaborating the complexities and interwoven influences of family, cultural, and contextual relationships, as well as the family's efforts to engage with cultural institutions for support.

Cultural competencies Professional guidelines addressing specific values, attitudes, techniques, and strategies for working with people in culturally responsive ways.

Cultural formulation A DSM-IV-TR listing and brief discussion of cultural issues to consider before a clinician from one culture diagnoses and plans treatment for apparent "disorders" manifested by someone from another culture.

Cultural relativism A philosophical perspective asserting that diagnostic categories are social constructions used to explain Western psychiatric phenomena, with limited applicability in diverse settings around the world.

Cultural universalism A philosophical perspective that asserts the Western biomedical diagnostic framework as universal and attempts to identify similarities in illness patterns across cultures.

Culture A group's shared history, language, behaviors, traditions, customs, symbolic expressions, rituals, and expectations of one another, transmitted from generation to generation.

Culture-bound The sociological principle asserting that human behaviors are shaped by the culture in which they are lodged and that their meanings can be understood only in the context of that culture.

Culture-bound syndromes Recurrent and locality-specific patterns of behavior and experience that are considered to be illnesses or afflictions but that do not seem to have an attributable and identifiable organic base. It is assumed that these behaviors are influenced by local cultural factors.

Decisional balance sheet A Motivational Interviewing tool for clarifying a client's beliefs and readiness for change through a cost-benefit analysis that weighs the client's investment in current troubling behaviors against proposed new behaviors.

Decompensate The gradual process of becoming less organized and able to cope with adversity.

Developmental crises Crises triggered by normal but stressful growth and life cycle transitions.

Diagnosis A shorthand summary of a complex set of human behaviors and characteristics, often using medical or psychological terms to describe disorders and important related social factors for purposes of intervention planning and ongoing research.

Diagnostic reliability The level of agreement between two or more clinicians about whether individuals meet criteria for psychiatric (or other) diagnoses, and about which diagnosis is the primary one.

Discrepancies Inconsistencies between two statements, between thoughts and feelings, between intentions and behaviors, and between verbal and nonverbal communication.

Discrimination The unfair treatment of people because of prejudice, usually based on color, class, age, gender, sexual orientation, size, or ability or on racial, ethnic, or religious group membership.

Diversity The rich variations, permutations, and complex overlaps within the multiple identities of people.

Dot-dot-dot reflection An interview response in which the clinician repeats back the last thing said and hangs it, unfinished, in midair for the client to complete.

Double questions Clinician questions that confuse clients by asking them to reply to a stream of two or more questions at once.

DSM-IV-TR The American Psychiatric Association's classification system in which symptoms are organized into relatively homogenous groups. The Diagnostic and Statistical manual is used for diagnosis and record keeping by most mental health clinicians in the United States.

Duty to warn A therapist's legal and ethical responsibility to warn intended victims of any serious threat to their life or safety that is expressed by a client of the therapist. In addition, the clinician may be required to notify police and other authorities of such a threat.

Eclectic A clinical practice approach incorporating aspects of more than one theoretical perspective and requiring knowledge and experience to implement effectively.

Ecological A systems perspective describing the interactive and interdependent relationships between people, all other living and nonliving things, and the systems of which they are all a part.

Ecomap A clinical assessment tool that reflects the nature and extent of reciprocity in client relationships with others.

Empathic echo A verbal reflection of both the content and the affect within a client's story, to signal that the clinician is attending closely to what the client says and does in the moment.

Empathic failures Clinical interactions in which clinicians reflect the wrong content, feeling, or meaning; miss important themes; pile on too much sympathy; confuse one client's story with another; or seem disingenuous.

Empathy The process of experiencing the world from another's subjective perspective while maintaining one's own perspective as an outside observer. Clinical empathy involves a constant oscillation between observing the client, feeling and thinking as if one *were* the client, and then feeling and thinking *about* the client's experience in order to develop hypotheses about it.

Empirically supported therapy (EST) Another term used to describe evidence-based practice.

Environmental crises Incidents in which natural disasters, biologically based, politically based, and economically based disasters seriously destabilize those who share a common living environment.

Ethical dilemmas Conflicts arising between institutional and professional policies and ethics; between parts of an ethics code; between law and ethics; or between a professional's personal and professional values and an ethics code.

Ethical principles Ethics code statements that describe overarching professional values, aspirational in nature, that are to serve as enduring benchmarks for professional conduct with clients and colleagues.

Ethical standards Ethics code statements that clearly elaborate professional behaviors that are prescribed as well as specific professional conduct that is proscribed.

Ethics A branch of philosophy that deals with moral judgments and perceptions of right and wrong.

Ethnicity The common ancestral, cultural, linguistic, religious, geographic, or national characteristics by which large groups of people distinguish and organize themselves.

Ethnocultural transference A relational process in which previous inter- or intracultural experiences are unconsciously displaced onto the clinical relationship by both the client and the clinician, distorting their interactions.

Evaluation The measurement of the appropriateness, progress, and effectiveness of clinical work both during and following interventions.

Evidence-based practice (EBP) The use of findings from efficacy research to guide the selection and implementation of proposed treatment methods.

Examine the moment The technique of addressing what is happening in the clinician-client relationship at a given point in time.

Exception questions A solution-focused technique of eliciting information about situations or days in which the client's usual behaviors or problems have not occurred.

Exploring indirect references The technique of addressing a client's remarks about other situations or experiences that the clinician thinks may obliquely refer to the clinical relationship or represent issues or feelings arising in it.

Faith-based organizations Religious organizations that provide community services, support, and activities.

Feeling-thinking A term developed by Relational-Cultural theorists to describe the intertwined bundles of thoughts and feelings that play off of and feed into each other powerfully and inseparably.

Fiduciary relationship A safe, reliable realtionship that enables the client to have confidence that the clinician is trustworthy.

Focal opening lines A clinician's opening remarks that lend structure to initial clinician-client interactions and often provide a conversational framework, agenda, and tone.

Follow-up evaluations Interviews, tests, and other assessment measures used to determine how well client strengths, resources, and prospects are holding up over time after the termination of the clinical relationship.

Foreshadow the ending The technique of forecasting an ending so that both clinician and client can prepare and pace their discussion accordingly.

Formal contracts Written, highly specific, and concrete agreements that specify each goal's component objectives and the tasks, steps, participants, and timelines for accomplishing each.

Formal diagnosis The process of determining if the client's problems or symptoms meet the specific criteria for a disorder.

Formulation Summary statements that condense and attribute meaning to all the rich data emerging from the assessment process, providing a practical and meaningful guide for work.

Genogram A clinical assessment tool (like a family tree) that reflects multigenerational family relationships, patterns, and intergenerational transmission of assets and issues.

Gifts as symbolic messages Client gifts to the clinician may often express subtle or unconscious client needs, dynamics, or hopes in regard to the clinician.

Goals The desired results or outcomes of the clinical work and relationship.

Group supervision A group of clinicians hire a supervisor for regular meetings focusing on education and support, where discussions of clinician-client dialogues, learning dilemmas, techniques, and case-planning concerns affirm the mutuality of the learning process.

Hate crimes Hateful words or actions intended to harm or intimidate an individual because of her or his membership in a minority group. Actions include violent assaults, murder, rape, and property crimes motivated by prejudice, as well as threats of violence and other acts of intimidation meant to terrorize all members of the targeted group as accounts of the violence spread.

Heterosexism A value system that prizes heterosexuality, assumes that it is the only appropriate manifestation of love and sexuality, and that devalues homosexuality and all that is not heterosexual.

Hidden agendas Secret aims of the clinician or client that are unexpressed and that can negatively affect the work together.

Hierarchical transference A relational process in which many people with histories of subordination may manifest feelings of powerlessness and helplessness in response to perceived clinician power and authority whether the power is real or not.

Holding environment The anchored, client-centered, and caring clinician presence that allows the client to stay self- and problem-focused without distraction or fear of judgment or abandonment.

Homework Client work assigned between sessions, such as journaling, meditation, behavior logs, and meeting attendance, to support client strengthening beyond the presence of the clinician.

Homophobia The hostility, contempt, or hateful speech and acts directed toward gay men and lesbian women because of their real or perceived sexual orientation.

Human-made disasters Events such as oil spills, toxic waste dump or biohazard lab leaks, nuclear accidents, global transmission of viruses, and wartime use of chemical weapons that leave widespread illness, disability, and fear of death.

Hunches Informed guesses or working hypotheses about the client and his or her situation.

ICD The World Health Organization's International Classification of Diseases, which is often used by clinicans outside the United States.

Identity An individual's self-conceptualization as well as the ways in which one defines oneself as part of larger groups or communities.

Imaginal rehearsal Mentally practicing new behaviors and developing plans of action and new skills for responding to future challenges.

Immediacy Gerard Egan's term for examining the moment.

Indigenous helpers Individuals in a culture who are prized for their gifts of wisdom, spirituality, and healing and to whom community members turn for advice, healing, and consolation.

Information sharing The introduction of new concepts or information the client may be unaware of, as a means of widening possibilities or extending opportunity.

Informed consent A professional ethical standard requiring that clients be fully informed about the benefits and risks of specific recommended interventions before these may be implemented.

Insidious trauma A kind of trauma that steadily evolves from the ongoing experience of denigration based on color, social status, or some devalued aspect of one's identity.

Insight development Gaining a new or clearer perspective on complex issues, dynamics, feelings, or relationships.

Intentional use of self The clinical process of acting in a self-aware, considered, deliberate, and goal-focused manner with clients.

Interpreters Trained translators knowledgeable about the client's culture, the counseling process, and confidentiality, who are prepared to translate both words and their meaning in a culturally sensitive way.

Interrater reliability The level of agreement between two appropriately qualified observers rating the same behaviors.

Introspection The reflective process of looking within oneself to appraise the nature, intensity, and meanings of feelings, thoughts, and dynamics that can affect interpersonal behaviors and relationships.

Islands of possibility Small client successes that can be amplified through review and discussion that kindles hope and further work toward goals.

Labeling Reducing the rich complexity of a person to a few behaviors, then categorizing the person based on those behaviors.

Letter of termination   A letter the clinician writes to a client after the client's abrupt and unexplained disconnect from clinical work, reassuring the client that the clinician's agency will be available for future contact if needed.

Levels of inference   Proximity of clinical inferences and conclusions to the data on which they are presumed to be based. Low levels of inference stick close to the facts while high levels of inference are more hypothetical.

Life chart   A clinical assessment tool that provides a birth-to-present-day timeline of dates and ages at which major life experiences impacted the client, both positively and negatively.

Life records   Previous treatment records or notes, school records and reports, health reports, and other written documents describing client development and performance of everyday tasks.

Lifespace interviews   Observations of and conversations with clients in their everyday environments.

Limit setting   The technique of restricting, with respect and caring, a client's inappropriate or destructive comments, behaviors, or requests in order to maintain clear and comfortable boundaries.

Locus of control   A psychological principle referring to one's perception of personal power and place in the world, and the extent to which people see themselves as capable of effectively influencing outcomes and accomplishing desired goals.

Long-term goals   Desired results that require extended time, work, and resources to accomplish.

Managed care   A cost-driven structure of health and mental health service provision limiting the number, length, and type of visits for defined health or mental health problems.

Mental disorder   A behavior or psychological syndrome associated with (1) emotional distress, (2) impaired functioning or disability, or (3) behavior that puts the person at risk of pain, suffering, disability, death, or loss of freedom.

Metacommunication   Implicit messages about the communication, as well as about the relationship between the communicators.

Metaphor   A word or phrase (not meant literally) that clients or clinicians can use as a symbolic representation of experience.

Microaggressions   Acts of exclusion, victimization, harassment, verbal abuse, stereotyping comments, intimidation, and injustice, including everyday acts of racism whose cumulative effects are widely traumatizing.

Mind/body programs   Wellness-oriented programs that emphasize and work to harmonize the connections between people's physical, spiritual, and emotional states.

Minority status   A term denoting the social position of a numerically smaller or politically powerless group in relation to a larger, controlling, and politically dominant majority.

Miracle question   Steve DeShazer's solution-focused technique of asking clients: "If a presenting problem were magically resolved while you were sleeping, what would be different on waking that would indicate that the problem is resolved?"

Mirroring   A physical form of reflection in which the clinician subtly matches the client's posture, facial expression, and gestures, careful not to mimic or parrot.

Modeling   The principle that people will learn new behaviors, attitudes, values, and feelings by observing others who seem similar to themselves or who are respected authorities.

Motivational Interviewing   Miller and Rollnick's structured process for increasing motivation for change by helping clients understand and resolve their ambivalences and patiently structure and time their change activities.

Multiaxial diagnostic system   The use of the five axes or domains of human experience of a DSM diagnostic system to represent relevant health and mental health diagnoses, past and present levels of personal and social functioning, and social or other stresses affecting functioning.

Multicultural practice   Clinical practice within and between a wide variety of cultures and backgrounds.

Multidisciplinary team   A collaborative group representing a variety of clinical disciplines whose case conceptualizations and formulations benefit from the specialized knowledge, skills, and biopsychosocial perspectives that each member contributes to the evaluation and planning process.

Multiethnic   A term denoting that an individual's or group's identity incorporates more than one ethnic heritage.

Multiple dimensions of identity   An individual's core sense of personal identity develops in the context of various identity dimensions, including family background, sociocultural conditions, and other social influences.

Multiple realities   A principle of systems theory positing that each participant in a transaction will have unique and sometimes conflicting views of what is occurring, how and why it developed, and the way it "ought" to evolve.

Multiple relationships   A clinical boundary crossing in which a clinician has more than one kind of relationship with a client or a client's family members or friends.

Multiracial   A term indicating that an individual's or group's identity incorporates more than one race.

Mutual empathy   The relational process of reciprocal caring and attending that leaves both clinician and client feeling seen, understood, and moved by the other.

Mutual empowerment   The relational process wherein clinician and client both develop better relational skills through mutual empathy and the exchange of authentic feedback about what happens between them.

Mutuality   The interview process phenomenon in which client and clinician come to affect each other's ideas and behaviors, growing and changing through authentic give-and-take.

Natural disasters   Widely unsettling events in nature such as severe storms, tornadoes, floods, hurricanes, tidal waves, earthquakes, and volcanic eruptions.

Natural helper An instinctively attuned, empathic, and responsive person to whom others easily turn for help and support.

Negative transference An unconscious relational process in which a client expresses or reenacts in the moment old, unhappy, stuck scenarios with the clinician, as though the latter were actually the punisher, exploiter, molester, or indifferent parent of the past. The client, feeling angry or betrayed, may proceed to misinterpret the clinician's motives and behaviors.

Nondirective opening lines A clinician's opening remarks that are deliberately open-ended to give clients greater opportunity to set agenda, pace, focus, and tone.

Nonverbal communication A form of communication that includes physical appearance, body posture, gestures, movements, and facial expressions.

Not-knowing perspective A viewpoint expressing two important aspects of clinical knowledge building: (1) It is okay not to know, and (2) clients often know more than we do about the realities of their experience and of everyday life.

Objectives The specific and concrete component parts of goals that are observable and measurable and that can be used in assessing the effectiveness of interventions.

Observation A method of clinical assessment in which the clinician evaluates the client's behaviors and interactions in the interview setting, a lab, or a natural lifespace.

Open-ended questions Nondirective questions that keep clients in the driver's seat of the conversation by giving them more opportunity or flexibility in responding and elaborating.

Outreach The technique of reaching out to clients by phone, letter, or Internet. Outreach can be used to try to bring closure and reassurance to the client when he or she has abruptly stopped coming before or during the ending process.

Overidentification A psychological process in which clinicians emphasize the similarities between themselves and their clients, while minimizing or denying things that would reveal differences between them.

Paralinguistic cues How things are said—the culturally influenced tone and pitch of voice, rate of speech, emphasis, stuttering, sighing, and other vocalizations that give nuance and meaning to interpersonal communication.

Partialize The technique of breaking broad goals down into their concrete and measurable component parts.

Patterns Repeated behavioral or affective sequences.

Peer supervision A gathering in which two or more clinicians meet regularly to share their work and offer feedback and support about their clinical dilemmas and concerns.

Personal space An invisible area around people that serves as a protective emotional barrier against the unwanted approaches of others.

Perspective The viewpoint or position one takes when envisioning self in relation to others and to the wider world.

Planned break A period of time in which the client purposely goes without face-to-face contact with a clinician, often used as "a dry run" before ending.

Positive transference A relational process in which the client idealizes the clinician and may experience him or her as incomparably wise, caring, and helpful.

Posttraumatic Stress Disorder (PTSD) A reaction to a serious or life-threatening event in which the person (1) reexperiences the traumatic event through dreams, intrusive thoughts, or flashbacks, (2) avoids stimuli associated with the event, and (3) has persistent symptoms of arousal such as sleep disturbances and hypervigilance.

Posture of attention The physical manifestation or embodiment of the clinician's interest in and openness to the client, the story, the relationship, and the work together.

Precipitating events The incidents or circumstances that set off a crisis. They may be catastrophic incidents or small things that are the last in a series of upsetting circumstances that leave the person feeling overwhelmed and unable to cope.

Predisposing factors Poverty, health hazards, social isolation, marginalization, racism, widespread prejudice, and other conditions that leave people vulnerable to traumatic events and crisis states.

Prejudice Positive or negative bias, poorly informed opinions, or unjustified assumptions about individuals who belong to a certain group or who fit into a particular socially constructed category.

Prioritize The technique of ranking goals and objectives in the order of their urgency, importance, and likelihood of achievement.

Privileged communication Federal or state legal protections of confidentiality for certain types of client-clinician relationships or in specified situations.

Process of assessment The use of exploration techniques to gather, organize, and analyze client-situation information relevant to the problems presented and to the strengths and resources available for use in problem resolution.

Process recording Written or recorded verbatim transcripts of clinician-client interviews, useful in clinician-supervisor reflection on both the unfolding work and relationship, and on the skill development of the clinician.

Process the process The technique of discussing the overall course of the relationship to point out themes, patterns, or notable developments in the work.

Professional boundaries Lines of demarcation between clinician and client as they come together in a work-focused relationship.

Professional clinicians Practitioners who have completed formal clinical education at or beyond the bachelor's or master's degree, who are appropriately licensed, and whose work is guided by clinical theory, research findings, ethics, and laws.

Professional code of ethics A formal set of principles and standards of conduct that elucidate the values of a discipline or profession, prescribing certain behaviors and specifically forbidding others.

Professional license A certification by a state demonstrating the practitioner's completion of required advanced course work and a set number of hours of advanced practice under supervision, in addition to successful testing in advanced clinical knowledge and competencies in specialized areas of practice.

Projection A psychodynamic term to describe the clinical process in which clinicians disavow and repress their own unpleasant or taboo feelings, then attribute these feelings to clients or others. ("I'm not angry, she is!")

Prompts Minimal interview responses by the clinician that encourage the client to continue with the story or to add to what has already been said.

Proscribed conversation An interview in which there are external restrictions on topics or content areas that clinicians can discuss with clients.

Pseudoquestions Clinician directives or commands disguised as questions.

Psychological attending The discipline of putting aside personal distractions, worries, and self-concerns and setting up radar to receive the signals the client is sending.

Psychological report A term often used to describe an assessment summary.

Race A social construct often used to classify people based on geographic origin and presumed shared physical characteristics like skin color, hair texture, and facial features. While the concept of race is socially meaningful, there is no biological basis for racial categorization.

Racism A powerful force of race-based prejudice and discrimination with institutional power behind it that can be found in individuals, families, cultures, and sociopolitical structures and institutions.

Ratatat questions Clinician questions that barrage the client with one rapid-fire question after another. No topic is pursued long enough to develop any real depth or meaning.

Reciprocal influences A principle of systems theory describing the ways in which every member of an interaction affects and is affected by the other participants.

Referral Giving the client names of particular providers or agencies that can meet a client's specific needs, either during their work together or after the work ends.

Reflecting discrepancies The technique of pointing out to clients perceived inconsistencies between two statements, between thoughts and feelings, between intentions and behaviors, and between verbal and nonverbal communication.

Reflection of affect Clinician statements that accurately represent the client's stated or implied feelings.

Reflection of content Clinician statements that accurately represent the client's statements about behaviors, thoughts, and interactions, as well as about the contexts in which they are embedded.

Refocusing The technique of returning the client to a desired topic by gently intruding on client remarks and inserting the topic into the conversation once again.

Regression under stress A psychological process in which clients return to outgrown behaviors under pressure because they are familiar, knee-jerk outlets for distress.

Reinforcers Consequences or events that occur after a behavior, increasing the probability of its recurrence.

Relational tending A relational technique of accurately noticing, addressing, and working through issues in the clinical relationship.

Reliability The degree to which an assessment measure is consistent over time or in different settings.

Resilience The capacity to adapt competently to adverse or hazardous conditions.

Resistance A psychodynamic term referring to unconscious defenses against, or familial or cultural prohibitions regarding, the recognition and expression of painful or forbidden material.

"Response-ability" Janet Surrey's term for understanding what relationships require, developing relational skills, and, remaining faithful to relationships even it is not always easy to do so.

RE-VIEW PRACTICE Method The authors' suggested method of mastering clinical practice knowledge and skill application by reading about clinical concepts and techniques, seeing them applied by clinicians, then trying them out and receiving useful feedback from instructors and colleagues.

Role-play Relational behavior simulations in which clinicians help clients prepare for difficult interactions with others by alternating roles and feedback in a brief scenario of exchanges similar to those the client faces elsewhere.

Sabotage An act in which one member of a treatment team, who does not believe in the goals and plans that the team has established, encourages a client to undermine or act against the treatment plan.

Salience of identity The importance and meaning of an individual's or group's identity varies depending on the situation.

Scaling questions Clinical questions that ask clients to estimate the intensity of their emotional arousal, desire for change, or other variables on a scale of 1 to 10 or 1 to 100.

Scientist/practitioner model Clinicians conduct research, develop and carry out interventions, and evaluate treatment procedures and programs to determine best practices. They also stay abreast of current developments in psychology and human services, medical and psychiatric services, and political and economic spheres.

Secondary trauma A traumatic response to hearing about or witnessing others' traumatic experiences that awaken one's sense of vulnerability, sometimes causing the witness to develop posttraumatic symptoms too.

Self-disclosure Clinicians' purposeful sharing of their own personal demographic information, experiences, and reactions with clients.

Self empathy The capacity to notice, care about, and respond to our own felt needs as generously as we attend to the needs of others.

Shaping Breaking a task into its component parts then rewarding successive approximations (small steps) in the direction of the desired behavior.

Short-term goals   Desired results that can be accomplished relatively quickly in the near term.

Silence   A form of communication, not just a blank space between communications. It may serve as a natural breather between topics or as a period of thoughtful reflection, and it can indicate comfort, discomfort, anger, calm, or many other things.

Situational crises   Crises triggered by ordinary events such as fires, acts of violence, diagnoses or episodes of mental/physical illness, or abrupt changes in established systems in which people feel secure.

Slowdowns   A sustaining technique in which the clinician "taps the brakes" on the interviewing process, modeling patience and carefulness with self by signaling clients that there is no need to rush the unfolding story or feelings.

Social justice perspective   A point of view asserting that clinicians have a primary social responsibility to work for equal rights, resources, and opportunities for all people. Clinicians should also nourish structures and processes that encourage growth and development while opposing all forms of oppression and environmental degradation.

Socially constructed   Meanings are created and recreated though human interactions and use of language. A shift in power often leads to a redefinition of meaning.

Societal norms   Widely held standards and expectations of conduct, often codified into laws, to which all members of society are expected to adhere.

SOLER   Psychologist Gerard Egan's acronym for sitting squarely in an open posture, leaning forward, making eye contact, and relaxing into the moment.

Spontaneous remission   The natural process by which client symptoms end or improve greatly without any assistance from professionals or programs.

Stakeholders   Friends, family, and others important to the client and to the problem-solving process and who have vested interests in the outcomes of the intervention.

Statused   A term asserting that groups to which people belong have particular social worth. Some groups are valued more than others, and those in higher-status groups often have the power to define and assign social meanings and privilege.

Stereotype   A fixed, oversimplified, often biased collective image of members of a particular group based on its characteristics, beliefs, practices, aspirations, or capacity to threaten established power arrangements.

Stigma   The negative assumptions and prejudices attached to people because of their membership in particular devalued groups.

Strength-based genogram   A clinical assessment tool that clarifies important intergenerational models and sources of individual, family, and group assets and accomplishments.

Strengths perspective   A view of human development and functioning that highly values client strengths. Clinicians identify and underscore the often undervalued or unnoticed strengths that clients have used successfully to resolve problems, as well as highlighting and supporting new strengths.

Summarizing   An interview technique in which the clinician pulls together in condensed form the major ideas, themes, or patterns that have just been discussed and reflects them back to the client.

Supportive sounds   Brief utterances and encouragements that mark the clinician's active listening and close following of the client's narrative.

Sustaining techniques   Interviewing strategies that offer clients support as they explore and elaborate more deeply.

Symbolic power   The power, expertise, and influence clients may attribute to clinicians by virtue of their roles and authority.

Synchrony   A response to rapport in which people involved in ongoing conversation begin without awareness to manifest similar tones, postures, gestures, and other nonverbal behaviors.

Systemic   A systems perspective asserting that people are best understood in the context of the relationships, resources, opportunity systems, and barriers to well-being in their lives.

Tangential Questions   Clinician questions that veer from the main topic of the interview, taking side roads without good reason and creating an aura of aimless or poorly focused conversation.

Termination   The term traditionally used in clinical work to describe the process of ending.

Testing   A method of clinical assessment in which the clinician uses intelligence and personality tests, symptom checklists, and other evaluative tools to measure client capacities and problems in functioning.

Test-retest reliability   The scores a person receives on a test should be consistent even if the test is given by different examiners or administered at different times.

Themes   Repeated or recurring sets of ideas and beliefs reflecting an underlying organizing principle.

Theory   A systematic set of principles used to understand and explain observable phenomena and to guide clinical work with clients.

"Therapizing" supervisees   A supervisor's inappropriate probing for painful details of a supervisee's personal history that could be related to current interviewing missteps.

Timing   A clinician's developed instinct and cultural sensitivity for what and how much to ask, when to ask it, and whom to ask.

Token economy   A specific form of contingency contract in which clients "earn" tokens or points for desired behavior and "pay" tokens for designated misbehavior. Self-defined reinforcements can be purchased with tokens or points.

Transferability of skills   The clinical concept asserting that one's strengths, talents, or methods of coping in one situation might work well in others.

Transference   A psychodynamic term referring to an unconscious relational process in which a client's earlier unresolved relational dynamics or conflicts are unwittingly displaced or "transferred" onto the current relationship with the clinician and then reenacted or expressed as though appropriate or "real" in the moment.

Transitional object A symbolic representation of the clinical relationship or work, often given to the client at ending to sustain a feeling of connection and support.

Trauma An extraordinary, overwhelming event in which a person's usual coping mechanisms are insufficient to meet the challenge or threat. Trauma can shatter people's assumptions about how the universe operates.

Treatment by objectives An intervention structured by partialized, prioritized, and measurable objectives and by the particular tasks, steps, timelines, and responsibilities for accomplishing each objective.

Treatment manual An empirically validated treatment guide that spells out step-by-step instructions, timing, and techniques to resolve a particular set of problems.

Treatment plan An intervention or service proposal that elucidates the participants, goals, and methods proposed to achieve the goals of clinical work.

Triggers People, circumstances, ideas, feelings, and events that stimulate behavioral reactions.

Unconditional positive regard The appreciation and affirmation of clients as people of worth. The clinician communicates nonjudgmental acceptance and genuine care for the client.

Underlining An interview response in which the clinician underscores important content or experience by the strategic use of verbal or nonverbal emphasis, often rendered through tone, facial expressions, or emphatic gestures.

Universalizing A technique in which the clinician verbally situates the client in a community of people sharing similar feelings, experiences, or opinions.

Unplanned contact Unintended encounters between clinicians and clients when they see each other outside their usual meeting place.

Using direct influence Employing the symbolic power of clinical roles to pressure clients, subtly and overtly, to behave in given ways deemed important to their well-being or safety.

Validation of the client's story The clinician's endorsement and appreciation of the realities of the client's story.

Validation of the difficulty of disclosure The sustaining technique of recognizing and appreciating personal and cultural reluctance to share private matters with an outsider such as a professional interviewer.

Validity How well an assessment measures what it intends to measure and how accurate a picture it gives of the person(s) assessed.

Value differences Often unseen and unspoken differences in the way people attribute meaning and worth to other people, events, institutions, cultural practices, beliefs, group aspirations, and the like.

Vicarious trauma Clinicians' secondary trauma reactions due to empathizing with and absorbing the stories and symptoms of numerous traumatized people. It is also known as compassion fatigue or emotional contagion.

Watchwords Helpful "reminders" for clinicians of simple do's and don'ts regarding specific behaviors, relational dynamics, or reactions they anticipate in an upcoming interview.

Working alliance The form of clinician-client bond that is focused on problem-solving work.

References

Addams, Jane. (1910). *Twenty years at Hull House.* New York: Macmillan.

Akamatsu, Norma N. (1998). The talking oppression blues: Including the experience of power/powerlessness in the teaching of "cultural sensitivity." In Monica McGoldrick (Ed.), *Revisioning family therapy: Race, culture, and gender in clinical practice* (pp. 129–143). New York: Guilford.

American Counseling Association. (2002). *Multicultural counseling competencies.* Alexandria, VA: Author.

American Counseling Association. (2005). *The American Counseling Association code of ethics.* Alexandria, VA: Author

American Psychiatric Association. (2000). *Diagnostic and statistical manual of mental disorders* (4th Ed.–TR). Washington, DC: Author.

American Psychological Association. (2002a). *Ethical principles of psychologists and code of conduct.* Washington, DC: Author.

American Psychological Association. (2002b). *Guidelines on multicultural education, training, research, practice, and organizational change for psychologists.* Washington, DC: Author.

American Psychological Association. (1990). *Guidelines for providers of psychological services to ethnic, linguistic, and culturally diverse populations.* Washington, DC: Author.

Ames, Natalie. (1999). Social work recording: A new look at an old issue. *Journal of Social Work Education, 35,* 2, 227–237.

Amodeo, Maryann, & Jones, L. Kay. (1997). Viewing alcohol and other drug use cross-culturally: A cultural framework for practice. *Families in Society: The Journal of Contemporary Human Services, 227,* 240–254.

Amodeo, Maryann, & Jones, L. Kay. (1998). Using the AOD cultural framework to view alcohol and drug issues through various cultural lenses. *Journal of Social Work Education, 34,* 387–399.

Amodeo, Maryann, Grigg-Saito, Dorcas, & Robb, Nancy. (1997). Working with foreign language interpreters: Guidelines for substance abuse clinicians and human service practitioners. *Social Work, 15,* 75–87.

Anderson, Harlene, & Goolishian, Harry. (1992). The client is the expert: A not-knowing approach to therapy. In Sheila McNamee & Kenneth Gergen (Eds.), *Therapy as a social construction* (pp. 25–39). Newbury Park, CA: Sage.

Aponte, Harry. (1994). *Bread and spirit: Therapy with the new poor—diversity of race, culture, and values.* New York: Norton.

Arredondo, Patricia, & Glauner, T. (1992). *Personal dimensions of identity model.* Boston: Empowerment Workshops, Inc.

Arredondo, Patricia, Toporek, Rebecca, Brown, Sherlon P., Jones, Janet, Locke, Don C., Sanchez, Joe, & Stadler, Holly. (1996). Operationalization of the multicultural counseling competencies. *Journal of Multicultural Counseling and Development, 24,* 42–78.

Atkinson, Donald R. (2004). *Counseling American minorities* (6th Ed.). New York: McGraw-Hill.

Atkinson, Donald R., Bui, Uyen, & Mori, Sakurako. (2001). Multiculturally sensitive empirically supported treatments—an oxymoron? In Joseph G. Ponterotto, J. Manuel Casas, Lisa A. Suzuki, & Charlene M. Alexander (Eds.), *Handbook of multicultural counseling* (pp. 542–574). Thousand Oaks, CA: Sage.

Baird, Brian. (2004). *The internship, practicum, and field placement handbook: A guide for helping professionals* (4th ed.). Upper Saddle River, NJ: Prentice Hall.

Baker, F. M. (2001). Diagnosing depression in African-Americans. *Community Mental Heath Journal, 37,* 31–38.

Bandura, Albert. (1969). *Principles of behavior modification.* New York: Holt Rinehart & Winston.

Bandura, Albert. (1976). Effecting change through participant modeling. In John Krumboltz & Carl Thorenson (Eds.), *Counseling methods* (pp. 248–265). New York: Holt, Rinehart & Winston.

Barlow, David, Rapee, R. M., & Brown, T. A. (1992). Behavioral treatment of generalized anxiety disorder. *Behavior Therapy, 23,* 551–570.

Barlow, David, & Durand, Mark. (1999). *Abnormal psychology.* Belmont, CA: Wadsworth.

Barlow, David (Ed.). (2001). *Clinical handbook of psychological disorders: A step-by-step treatment manual* (3rd Ed.). New York: Guilford.

Barrett, Janie Porter. (1926). The Virginia Industrial School. *Southern Workman, 55,* 353–361.

Baruth, Leroy G & Manning, M. Lee. (2003). *Multicultural counseling and psychotherapy: A lifespan perspective* (3rd Ed.). Upper Saddle River, NJ: Pearson Education.

Bateson, Gregory. (1972). *Steps to an ecology of mind.* New York: Chandler.

Bateson, Gregory. (1979). *Mind and nature.* New York: Dutton.

Bateson, Gregory, Jackson, Don, & Weakland, John. (1963). A note on the double bind. *Family Processes, 2,* 154–161.

Beck, Judith. (1995). *Cognitive therapy: Basics and beyond.* New York: Guilford.

Benard, Bonnie. (1997). Fostering resiliency in children and youth: Promoting protective factors in school. In Dennis Saleebey (Ed.), *The strengths perspective in social work practice* (pp. 167–182). White Plains, NY: Longman.

Benson, Herbert, & Klipper, Miriam. (1976). *The relaxation response.* New York: Morrow.

Berlin, Sharon. (2002). *Clinical social work practice: A cognitive-integrative perspective.* New York: Oxford.

Birdwhistell, Ray L. (1970). *Kinesics and context.* Philadelphia: University of Pennsylvania Press.

Borkovec, T. D., & Costello, Ellen. (1993). Efficacy of applied relaxation and cognitive-behavioral therapy in treatment of generalized anxiety disorder. *Journal of Consulting Clinical Psychology, 61,* 611–619.

Borys, Debra, & Pope, Kenneth. (1989). Dual relationships between therapist and client: A national study of psychologists, psychiatrists, and social workers. *Professional Psychology: Research and Practice, 30,* 283–293.

Borysenko, Joan. (1987). *Minding the body, mending the mind.* New York: Addison-Wesley.

Borysenko, Joan, & Dveirin, Gordon. (2006). *Saying yes to change: Essential wisdom for your journey.* Carlsbad, CA: Hay House.

Bradshaw, Carla K. (1994). Asian and Asian American women: Historical and political considerations in psychotherapy. In Lillian Comas-Diaz & Beverly Greene (Eds.), *Women of color: Integrating ethnic and gender identities in psychotherapy* (pp. 72–113). New York: Guilford.

Briar-Lawson, Katherine. (1998). Capacity building for integrated family-centered practice. *Social Work, 43,* 539–550.

Bridges, Nancy. (2005). *Moving beyond the comfort zone in psychotherapy.* Lanham, MD: Jason Aronson.

Bronfenbrenner, Urie. (1979). *The ecology of human development: Experiments by nature and design.* Cambridge, MA: Harvard University Press.

Brown, Laura S. (1994). *Subversive dialogues: Theory in feminist therapy.* New York: Basic Books.

Brown, Laura S., & Walker, Lenore E. A. (1990). Feminist therapy perspectives on self-disclosure. In George Stricker & Martin Fisher (Eds.), *Self-disclosure in the therapeutic relationship* (pp. 135–155). New York: Plenum.

Burns, David D. (1999). *The feeling good handbook.* New York: Plume-Penguin.

Canda, Edward R. (1997). Spirituality in social work. In *Encyclopedia of social work supplement, 1997* (pp. 299–309).

Canda, Edward, & Furman, Leola. (1999). *Spiritual diversity in social work practice: The heart of helping.* New York: Free Press.

Caplan, Paula J. (1995). *They say you're crazy: How the world's most powerful psychiatrists decide who's normal.* Reading, MA: Addison-Wesley.

Cascio, Toni. (1998). Incorporating spirituality into social work practice: A review of what to do. *Families in Society: The Journal of Contemporary Human Services,* (September/October), 523–531.

Cascio, Toni, and Gasker, Janice. (2001). Everyone has a shining side: Computer-mediated mentoring in social work education. *Journal of Social Work Education, 37* (2), 283–293.

Cashwell, Craig S., Scherbakova, Julia, & Cashwell, Tammy H. (2003). Effect of client and counselor ethnicity on preference for counselor disclosure. *Journal of Counseling and Development, 81* (2), 196–202.

Chambless, Dianne L., & Hollon, Steven D. (1998). Defining empirically supported therapies. *Journal of Counseling and Clinical Psychology, 66* (1), 7–18.

Chambless, Dianne L., Baker, Mary J., Baucom, Donald H., Beutler, Larry E., Calhoun, Karen S., Crits-Christoph, Paul, Daiuto, Anthony, DeRubeis, Robert, Detweiler, Jerusha, Haaga, David A. F., Johnson, Susan Bennett, McCurry, Susan, Mueser, Kim T., Pope, Kenneth S., Sanderson, William C., Shoham, Varda, Stickle, Timothy, Williams, David A., & Woody, Sheila R. (1998). Update on empirically validated therapies, II. *The Clinical Psychologist, 51* (1), 3–16.

Chan, Sam, & Lee, Evelyn. (2004). Families with Asian roots. In Eleanor W. Lynch & Marci J. Hanson (Eds.), *Developing cross-cultural competence: A guide for working with children and their families* (3rd Ed.) (pp. 219–298). Baltimore, MD: Brookes.

Chao, Christine M. (1992). The inner heart: Therapy with Southeast Asian families. In Luis Vargas & Joan D. Koss-Chioino (Eds.), *Working with culture: Psychotherapeutic interventions with ethnic minority children and adolescents* (pp. 157–181). San Francisco: Jossey-Bass.

Chu, James. (1991). The repetition compulsion revisited: Reliving dissociated trauma. *Psychotherapy, 28* (2), 327–332.

Cicchetti, Dante, & Garmezy, Norman. (1993). Prospects and promises in the study of resilience. *Development and Psychopathology, 5,* 497–502.

Coleman, Daniel. (2000). The therapeutic alliance in multicultural practice. *Psychoanalytic Social Work, 7* (2), 65–90.

Collin, Kathryn S., Valentine, Deborah, and Welkley, Debra L. (2005). People living with disabilities. In Krishna Guadelupe & Doman Lum (Eds.), *Multidimensional contextual practice: Diversity and transcendence* (pp. 250–269). Belmont, CA: Brooks/Cole.

Comas-Diaz, Lillian, & Greene, Beverly (Eds.). (1994). *Women of color: Integrating ethnic and gender identities in psychotherapy.* New York: Guilford.

Comas-Diaz, Lillian, & Jacobsen, Frederick M. (1991). Ethnocultural transference and countertransference in the therapeutic dyad. *American Journal of Orthopsychiatry, 61,* 392–402.

Combs, Arthur. (1989). *A theory of therapy: Guidelines for counseling practice.* Newbury Park, CA: Sage.

Comstock, Dana. (2004). Reflections on life, loss, and resilience. In Maureen Walker & Wendy B. Rosen (Eds.), *How connections heal: Stories from relational-cultural therapy* (pp. 83–101). New York: Guilford.

Compton, Beulah, Galaway, Burt, & Cournoyer, Barry. (2005). *Social work processes* (7th Ed.). Belmont, CA: Brooks/Cole.

Congress, Elaine. (1994). The use of culturagrams to assess and empower culturally diverse families. *Families in*

Society: The Journal of Contemporary Human Services, 75, 531–539.

Constantine, Madonna, & Sue, Derald Wing (Eds.). (2005). *Strategies for building multicultural competence in mental health and educational settings.* Hoboken, NJ: John Wiley.

Corey, Gerald. (2005). *Theory and practice of counseling and psychotherapy* (7th Ed.). Belmont, CA: Wadsworth.

Corey, Gerald, & Corey, Marianne Schneider. (2003). *Becoming a helper* (4th Ed.). Pacific Grove, CA: Brooks/Cole.

Corey, Gerald, Corey, Marianne Schneider, & Callanan, Patrick. (2003). *Issues & ethics in the helping professions* (6th Ed.). Pacific Grove, CA: Brooks/Cole.

Cournoyer, Barry R. (2004). *The evidence-based social work skills book.* Boston: Allyn & Bacon.

Cournoyer, Barry. (2005). *The social work skills workbook* (4th Ed.). Pacific Grove, CA: Brooks/Cole.

Cowger, Charles. (1997). Assessing client strengths: Assessing client empowerment. In Dennis Saleebey (Ed.), *The strengths perspective in social work practice* (pp. 59–73). New York: Longman.

Cross, William E., Jr. (1971). The Negro-to-Black conversion experience: Towards a Psychology of Black liberation. *Black World, 20,* 13–27.

Cross, William E., Jr. (1991). *Shades of black: Diversity in African American identity.* Philadelphia: Temple University Press.

Cross, William E., Jr., & Fhagen-Smith, Peony. (2001). Patterns of African American identity development: A life-span developmental perspective. In Charmaine J. Wijeyesinghe & Bailey W. Jackson III (Eds.), *Reflections on racial identity development: Essays on theory, practice, and discourse* (pp. 243–270). New York: New York University Press.

Cross, William E., Jr., Smith, Lakesha, & Payne, Yasser. (2002). Black identity: A repertoire of daily enactments. In Paul B. Pedersen, Juris G. Draguns, Walter J. Lonner, & Joseph E. Trimble (Eds.), *Counseling across cultures* (pp. 93–108). Thousand Oaks, CA: Sage.

Cross, William E., Jr., & Vandiver, Beverly J. (2001). Negrescence theory and measurement: Introducing the Cross Racial Identity Scale (CRIS). In Joseph G. Ponterotto, J. Manuel Casas, Lisa A. Suzuki, & Charlene M. Alexander. (Eds.). (2001). *Handbook of multicultural counseling* (pp. 371–393). Thousand Oaks, CA: Sage.

Daniel, Jessica H. (2000). The courage to hear: African American women's memories of racial trauma. In Leslie C. Jackson & Beverly Greene (Eds.), *Psychotherapy with African American women* (pp. 126–144). New York: Guilford.

Darwin, Charles. (1859). *On the origin of the species.* London: John Murray.

De La Cancela, Victor, Jenkins, Yvonne M., & Chin, Jean Lau. (1993). Diversity in psychotherapy: Examination of racial, ethnic, gender, and political issues. In Jean Lau Chin, Victor De La Cancela, & Yvonne M. Jenkins (Eds.), *Diversity in psychotherapy: The politics of race, ethnicity, and gender* (pp. 5–15). Westport, CT: Praeger.

Deahl, Martin. (2000). Psychological debriefing: Controversy and challenge. *Australian and New Zealand Journal of Psychiatry, 34* (6), 929–939.

Dean, Ruth G. (1984). The role of empathy in supervision. *Clinical Social Work Journal, 12* (2), 129–139.

DeJong, Peter, & Miller, Scott D. (1995). How to interview for client strengths. *Social Work, 40,* 729–736.

Delgado, Melvin. (1997). Role of Latina-owned beauty parlors in a Latino community. *Social Work, 42,* 445–453.

Delgado, Melvin. (1999). *Social work practice in nontraditional settings.* New York: Oxford University Press.

Delgado, Melvin. (2007). *Social work practice with Latinos: A cultural assets paradigm.* New York: Oxford University Press.

DePoy, Elizabeth, & Gilson, Stephen French. (2004). *Rethinking disability: Principles for professional and social change.* Belmont, CA: Thomson-Brooks/Cole.

de Shazer, Steve. (1988). *Clues: Investigating solutions in brief therapy.* New York: Norton.

de Shazer, Steve. (n.d.). The Miracle Question. Available at: http://www.brief-therapy.org/steve_miracle.htm. Accessed February 1, 2006.

Devore, Wynetta, & Schlesinger, Elfriede G. (1996). *Ethnic-sensitive social work practice* (4th Ed.). Boston: Allyn & Bacon.

Diller, Jerry V. (2007). *Cultural diversity: A primer for the human services (3rd Ed.).* Belmont, CA: Brooks/Cole.

Dillon, Carolyn. (1999). A relational perspective on mutuality and boundaries in clinical practice with lesbians. In Joan Laird (Ed.), *Lesbians & lesbian families: Reflections on theory and practice* (pp. 283–303). New York: Columbia University Press.

Dillon, Carolyn. (2003). *Learning from mistakes in clinical practice.* Pacific Grove, CA: Brooks/Cole.

Domar, Alice, & Dreher, Henry. (2000). *Self-nurture: Learning to care for yourself as effectively as you care for everyone else.* New York: Penguin.

Dutton, Mary Ann, & Rubenstein, Francine L. (1995). Working with people with PTSD: Research implications. In Charles R. Figley (Ed.), *Compassion fatigue: Coping with secondary traumatic stress disorder in those who treat the traumatized* (pp. 82–100). New York: Brunner/Mazel.

Dwairy, Marwan. (2005). Stress management among collective societies: The case of the Palestinian Arabs in Israel. *Australian Journal of Disaster and Trauma Studies* (Electronic peer review journal), ISBN 1174-4707, 2005 (1).

Egan, Gerard. (1994). *The skilled helper: A problem-management approach to helping* (5th Ed.). Pacific Grove, CA: Brooks/Cole.

Egan, Gerard. (1998). *The skilled helper: A problem-management approach to helping* (6th Ed.). Pacific Grove, CA: Brooks/Cole.

Egan, Gerard. (2006). *Essentials of skilled helping: Managing problems, developing opportunities.* Belmont, CA: Brooks/Cole.

Eldridge, Natalie S., Mencher, Julie, & Slater, Suzanne. (1997). The conundrum of mutuality: A lesbian dialogue. In Judith V. Jordan (Ed.), *Women's growth in diversity: More writings from the Stone Center* (pp. 107–137. New York: Guilford.

Ellis, Albert, & MacLaren, Catharine. (1998). *Rational emotive behavior therapy: A therapist's guide.* Atascadero, CA: Impact.

Ellis, Priscilla, & Murphy, Bianca Cody. (1994). The impact of misogyny and homophobia in therapy with women. In Marsha Mirkin (Ed.), *Women in context: Toward a feminist reconstruction of psychotherapy with women* (pp. 48–93). New York: Guilford Press.

Epston, David, & White, Michael. (1990). Narrative means to therapeutic ends. New York: Norton.

Epston, David, & White, Michael. (1995). Termination as a rite of passage: Questioning strategies for a therapy of inclusion. In Robert A. Neimeyer & Michael J. Mahoney (Eds.), *Constructivism in psychotherapy* (pp. 277–313). Washington, DC: American Psychological Association.

Erikson, Erik. (1963). *Childhood and society.* New York: Norton.

Fadiman, Anne. (1997). *The spirit catches you and you fall down.* New York: Farrar, Straus & Giroux.

Fair, Susan M., & Bressler, Joanna M. (1992). Therapist-initiated termination of psychotherapy. *The Clinical Supervisor, 10,* 171–189.

Feldman, Larry B., & Feldman, Sandra L. (1997). Integrating psychotherapy and pharmacotherapy in the treatment of depression. *In Session: Psychotherapy in Practice, 3,* 23–38.

Ferdman, Bernado M., and Gallegos, Placida I. (2001). Racial identity development and Latinos in the United States. In Charmaine L. Wijeyesinghe & Bailey W. Jackson III (Eds), *New perspectives on racial identity development: A theoretical and practical anthology.* (pp. 32–66). New York: New York University Press.

Fhagen-Smith, Peony E. (2003). Mixed Ancestry Racial/Ethnic Identity Development (MAREID) model. Wellesley College Centers for Women Working Paper #413. Wellesley, MA: Wellesley College Centers for Women.

Figley, Charles. (1983). Catastrophe: An overview of family reactions. In Charles R. Figley & Harris I. McCubbin (Eds.), *Stress and the family: Vol 2. Coping with catastrophe* (pp. 3–20). New York: Brunner/Mazel.

Figley, Charles (Ed.). (1995). *Compassion fatigue: Coping with secondary traumatic stress disorder in those who treat the traumatized.* New York: Brunner/Mazel.

Finkel, David. (1974). Stress and traumas: An attempt at categorization. *American Journal of Community Psychology, 2,* 265–273.

Finn, Peter, & McNeil, Taylor. (1987). *The response of the criminal justice system to bias crime: An explanatory review.* Cambridge, MA: Abt Associates.

Fisher, Roger, Ury, William L., & Patton, Bruce. (1991). *Getting to yes: Negotiating agreement without giving in* (2nd Ed.). New York: Penguin.

Fleming, Joan, & Benedek, Therese. (1966). *Psychoanalytic supervision.* New York: Grune & Stratton.

Fortune, Anne E. (1987). Grief only? Client and social worker reactions to termination. *Clinical Social Work Journal, 15* (2), 159–171.

Garbarino, James, & Abramowitz, Robert. (1992). Sociocultural risk and opportunity. In James Garbarino (Ed.), *Children and families in the social environment* (2nd Ed., pp. 35–70). New York: Aldine de Gruyter.

Garcia Coll, Cynthia, Cook-Nobles, Robin, & Surrey, Janet. (1997). Building connection through diversity. In Judith V. Jordan. (Ed.), *Women's growth in diversity: More writings from the Stone Center* (pp. 176–198). New York: Guilford.

Garvin, Charles, & Seabury, Brett. (1997). *Interpersonal practice in social work: Promoting competence and social justice.* Boston: Allyn & Bacon.

Gelman, Sheldon R., Pollack, Daniel, & Weiner, Adele. (1999). Confidentiality of social work records in the computer age. *Social Work, 44,* 243–252.

Germain, Carel B., & Gitterman, Alex. (1996). *The life model of social work practice.* New York: Columbia University Press.

Gitterman, Alex, & Shulman, Lawrence (Eds.). (1994). *Mutual aid groups, vulnerable populations, and the life cycle.* Itasca, IL: F. E. Peacock.

Goffman, Erving. (1963). *Stigma: Notes on the management of spoiled identity.* Englewood Cliffs, NJ: Prentice Hall.

Goldfried, Marvin, & Eubanks-Carter, Catherine. (2004). On the need for a new psychotherapy research paradigm: Comment on Westen, Novotny, and Thompson-Brenner (2004). *Psychological Bulletin, 130,* 669–673.

Goldstein, Eda. (1997). To tell or not to tell: The disclosure of events in the therapist's life to the patient. *Clinical Social Work Journal, 25,* 41–57.

Gorden, Robert, & Kline, Paul. (1997). Should social workers enroll as preferred providers with for-profit managed care groups? In Eileen Gambrill & Robert Pruger (Eds.), *Controversial issues in social work ethics, values, and obligations* (pp. 52–62). Boston: Allyn & Bacon.

Graybeal, Clay, & Ruff, Elizabeth. (1995). Process recording: It's more than you think. *Journal of Social Work Education, 31* (3), 169–181.

Griffin, William. (1995). Social worker and agency safety. In Richard L. Edwards (Ed.), *Encyclopedia of social work, Vol. 3* (pp. 2293–2305). Washington, DC: National Association of Social Workers Press.

Grisso, Thomas, & Applebaum, Paul S. (1998). *Assessing competence to consent to treatment: A guide for physicians and other health professionals.* New York: Oxford University Press.

Guadelupe, Krishna L., & Lum, Doman. (2005). *Multidimensional contextual practice: Diversity and transcendance*. Belmont, CA: Brooks/Cole.

Guilmet, G., & Whited, D. (1987). Cultural lessons for clinical mental health practice in the Payallup tribal community. *American Indian and Alaska Native Mental Health Research, 1*, 32–49.

Gutheil, Irene A. (1993). Rituals and termination procedures. *Smith College Studies in Social Work, 63* (2), 163–176.

Gutierrez, Lorraine M., Parsons, Ruth J., & Cox, Enid O. (2000). *Empowerment in social work practice: A sourcebook*. Pacific Grove, CA: Brooks/Cole.

Haight, Wendy L. (1998). "Gathering the spirit" at First Baptist Church: Spirituality as a protective factor in the lives of African American children. *Social Work, 43*, 213–221.

Hall, Edward. (1959). *The silent language*. New York: Fawcett.

Harney, Patricia A., Lebowitz, Leslie, & Harvey, Mary R. (1997). A stage by dimension model of trauma recovery: Application to practice. *In Session: Psychotherapy in Practice, 3* (4), 91–104.

Harper, Robert G., Wiens, Arthur N., & Matarazzo, Joseph D. (1978). *Nonverbal communication: The state of the art*. New York: John Wiley.

Harris, Chrys. (1995). Sensory-based therapy for crisis counselors. In Charles R. Figley (Ed.), *Compassion fatigue: Coping with secondary traumatic stress disorder in those who treat the traumatized* (pp. 101–114). New York: Brunner/Mazel.

Harris, Daniel. (1997). *The rise and fall of gay culture*. New York: Hyperion.

Hartman, Ann. (1978). Diagrammatic assessment of family relationships. *Social Casework, 59*, 465–476.

Heard, Heidi L., & Linehan, Marsha M. (1994). Dialectical behavior therapy: An integrative approach to the treatment of borderline personality disorder. *Journal of Psychotherapy Integration 4*, 55–82.

Hecker, Jeffrey E., & Thorpe, Geoffrey L. (2005). *Introduction to clinical psychology: Science, practice, and ethics*. Boston: Allyn & Bacon.

Helms, Janet E. (1985). Cultural identity in the treatment process. In Paul B. Pedersen (Ed.), *Handbook of cross-cultural counseling and therapy* (pp. 239–245). Westport, CT: Greenwood.

Helms, Janet E. (1990). *Black and White racial identity: Theory, research, and practice*. New York: Praeger.

Helms, Janet E. (1995). An update of Helms's white and people of color racial identity models. In Joseph Pontoretto, J. Manual Casas, Lisa Suzuki, & Charlene Alexander (Eds.), *Handbook of multicultural counseling* (pp. 181–191). Thousand Oaks, CA: Sage.

Hepworth, Dean H., Rooney, Ronald H., Rooney, Glenda Dewberry, Strom-Gottfried, Kimberley, & Larsen, Jo Ann. (2006). *Direct social work practice: Theory and skills* (7th Ed.). Pacific Grove, CA: Brooks/Cole.

Herdt, Gilbert (Ed.). (1992). *Gay culture in America: Essays from the field*. Boston: Beacon.

Herek, Greg M. (1986). The social psychology of homophobia: Toward a practical theory. *Review of Law and Social Change, 14*, 923–934.

Herman, Judith. (1997). *Trauma and recovery*. New York: Basic Books.

Hernstein, Richard, & Murray, Charles. (1994). *The bell curve: Intelligence and class structure in American life*. New York: Free Press.

Hertzberg, Joan F. (1996). Internalizing power dynamics: The wounds and the healing. In Marcia Hill & Esther Rothblum (Eds.), *Classism and feminist therapy: Counting costs* (pp. 129–148). New York: Harrington Park.

Hill, G. William, IV. (1998). Activities and videos for teaching cross-cultural issues. Available at: http://www.lemoyne.edu/OTRP/otrpresources/otrp_ccissues.html.

Hill, Marcia, & Rothblum, Esther D. (Eds.). (1996). *Classism and feminist therapy: Counting costs*. New York: Harrington Park.

Hill, Marcia. (2004). *Diary of a country therapist*. Binghamton, NY: Haworth.

Hodge, David R. (2003). *Spiritual assessment handbook for professionals*. Botsford, CT: North American Association of Christians in Social Work.

Hodges, Vanessa G., & Blythe, Betty J. (1992). Improving service delivery to high-risk families: Home-based practice. *Families in Society: The Journal of Contemporary Human Services*, May, 259–265.

Horse, Perry G. (2001). Reflections on American Indian identity. In Charmaine M. Wijeyesinghe & Bailey W. Jackson III (Eds), *New perspectives on racial identity development: A theoretical and practical anthology* (pp. 91–107). New York: New York University Press.

Iglehart, Alfreda P., & Becerra, Rosina M. (1995). Ethnicity, race, reform, and the evolution of social work. In Alfreda P. Iglehart & Rosina M. Becerra (Eds.), *Social services and the ethnic community* (pp. 107–148). Boston: Allyn & Bacon.

Irving, P., & Long, A. (2001). Critical incident stress debriefing following traumatic life experiences. *Journal of Psychiatric & Mental Health Nursing, 8* (4), 307–314.

Ivey, Allen E. (1994). *Intentional interviewing and counseling: Facilitating client development in a multicultural society*. Pacific Grove, CA: Brooks/Cole.

Ivey, Allen E., & Ivey, Mary Bradford. (2003). *Intentional interviewing and counseling: Facilitating client development in a multicultural society* (5th Ed.). Pacific Grove, CA: Brooks/Cole.

Ivey, Allen E., Ivey, Mary B., & Simek-Morgan, Lynn. (2002). *Counseling and psychotherapy: A multicultural perspective*. Needham Heights, MA: Allyn & Bacon.

Jackson, Leslie C., & Greene, Beverly (Eds.). (2000). *Psychotherapy with African American women: Innovations in psychodynamic perspectives and practice*. New York: Guilford.

Jacobson, Wendy B. (2001). Beyond therapy: Bringing social work back to human services reform. *Social Work 46*, 51–61.

James, Richard K., & Gilliland, Burl E. (2001). *Crisis intervention strategies* (4th Ed.). Belmont, CA: Thomson-Brooks/Cole.

James, Richard K., & Gilliland, Burl E. (2005). *Crisis intervention strategies* (5th Ed.). Belmont, CA: Thomson-Brooks/Cole.

Janoff-Bulman, Ronnie. (1992). *Shattered assumptions: Towards a new psychology of trauma.* New York: Free Press.

Jansson, Bruce S. (1999). *Becoming an effective policy advocate: From policy practice to social justice.* Pacific Grove, CA: Brooks-Cole.

Jensen, Arthur R. (1969). How much can we boost IQ and school achievement? *Harvard Educational Review, 39,* 1–123.

Joe, Jennie R., & Malach, Randi S. (2004). Families with American Indian roots. In Eleanor W. Lynch & Marci J. Hanson (Eds.), *Developing cross-cultural competence: A guide for working with children and their families* (3rd Ed., pp. 109–134). Baltimore: Brookes.

Jones, James (1996), Prejudice and racism. New York: McGraw-Hill.

Jones, Susan R., & McEwen, Marylu K. (2000). A conceptual model of multiple dimensions of identity. *Journal of College Student Development, 41,* 405–414.

Jordan, Catheleen, & Franklin, Cynthia (Eds.). (2003). *Clinical assessment for social workers: Quantitative and qualitative methods* (2nd Ed.). Chicago: Lyceum.

Jordan, Judith V. (1990). *Courage in connection: Conflict, compassion, creativity. Work in Progress #45.* Wellesley College, MA: Stone Center Working Paper Series.

Jordan, Judith V. (1991a). The meaning of mutuality. In Judith V. Jordan, Alexandra G. Kaplan, Jean Baker Miller, Irene Stiver, & Janet Surrey (Eds.), *Women's growth in connection: Writings from the Stone Center* (pp. 81–96). New York: Guilford.

Jordan, Judith V. (1991b). Empathy and self-boundaries. In Judith V. Jordan, Alexandra G. Kaplan, Jean Baker Miller, Irene Stiver, & Janet Surrey (Eds.), *Women's growth in connection: Writings from the Stone Center* (pp. 67–80). New York: Guilford.

Jordan, Judith V. (2004a). Relational resilience. In Judith V. Jordan, Maureen Walker, and Linda M. Hartling (Eds.), *The complexity of connection: Writings from the Stone Center's Jean Baker Miller Training Institute.* New York: Guilford.

Jordan, Judith V. (2004b). Relational awareness. In Judith V. Jordan, Maureen Walker, and Linda M. Hartling (Eds.), *The complexity of connection: Writings from the Stone Center's Jean Baker Miller Training Institute.* New York: Guilford.

Jordan, Judith V., Kaplan, Alexandra G., Miller, Jean Baker, Stiver, Irene P., & Surrey, Janet L. (Eds.). (1991). *Women's growth in connection: Writings from the Stone Center* (pp. 81–96). New York: Guilford.

Jordan, Judith V., Walker, Maureen, & Hartling, Linda M. (2004). *The complexity of connection: Writings from the Stone Center's Jean Baker Miller Training Institute.* New York: Guilford.

Kabat-Zinn, Jon. (1994). *Wherever you go, there you are: Mindfulness meditation in everyday life.* New York: Hyperion.

Kadushin, Alfred, & Kadushin, Goldie. (1997). *The social work interview.* New York: Columbia University Press.

Kaiser, Tamara. (1997). *Supervisory relationships: Exploring the human element.* Pacific Grove, CA: Brooks/Cole.

Kazdin, Alan E. (2001). Behavior modification in applied settings (6th Ed.). Pacific Grove, CA: Wadsworth.

Kilpatrick, Allie C., & Holland, Thomas P. (Eds.). (2003). *Working with families: An integrative model by level of need* (3rd Ed.). Boston: Allyn & Bacon.

Kim, Bok-Lim C. (1996). Korean families. In Monica McGoldrick, Joseph Giordano, & John Pearce (Eds.), *Ethnicity and family therapy* (pp. 349–362). New York: Guilford.

Kim, Jean. (2001). Asian American identity development theory. In Charmaine Wijeyesinghe & Bailey W. Jackson III (Eds.), *New perspectives on racial identity development: A theoretical and practical anthology* (pp. 67–90). New York: New York University Press.

Kiselica, Mark S., & Robinson, Michelle. (2001). Bringing advocacy counseling to life: The history, issues, and human drama of social justice work in counseling. *Journal of Counseling and Development, 79* (Fall 2001), 387–397.

Knight, Carolyn. (2006). Groups for individuals with traumatic histories: Practice considerations for social workers, *Social Work, 51* (1), 20–30.

Koob, Jeffrey J. (2003). Solution-focused family interventions. In Allie C. Kilpatrick & Thomas P. Holland (Eds), *Working with families: An integrative model by level of need* (3rd Ed.). Boston: Pearson Education.

Kopp, Richard R. (1995). *Metaphor therapy: Using client-generated metaphors in psychotherapy.* New York: Brunner/Mazel.

Kutchins, Herb, & Kirk, Stuart. (1995). Should *DSM* be the basis for teaching social work practice in mental health? No! Response to Janet Williams and Robert Spitzer. *Journal of Social Work Education, 31* (2), 153–158.

Kutchins, Herb, & Kirk, Stuart. (1997). *Making us crazy: DSM: The psychiatric bible and the creation of mental disorder.* New York: Free Press.

Kwan, Karl, & Kwong-Liem. (2001). Models of racial and ethnic identity development: Delineations of practice implications. *Journal of Mental Health Counseling, 23* (3), 269–279.

La Fromboise, Teresa D., Berman, Joan Saks, & Sohi, Balvindar K. (1994). American Indian women. In Lillian Comas-Diaz & Beverly Greene (Eds.), *Women of color: Integrating ethnic and gender identities in psychotherapy* (pp. 30–71). New York: Guilford.

La Fromboise, Teresa D., Coleman, H., & Hernandez, A. (1991). Development and factor structure of the Cross-Cultural Counseling Inventory—Revised. *Professional Psychology: Research and Practice, 22,* 380–388.

Lazarus, Arnold. (1981). *The practice of multimodal therapy.* New York: McGraw-Hill.

Lazarus, Arnold, & Zur, Ofur. (2002). *Dual relationships and psychotherapy.* New York: Springer.

Levine, Murray, & Perkins, David. (1997). *Principles of community psychology: Perspectives and applications.* New York: Oxford University Press.

Levinson, Hilliard. (1977). Termination of psychotherapy: Some salient issues. *Social Casework, 58,* 480–489.

Lindemann, Erich. (1965). Symptomatology and management of acute grief. In Howard J. Parad (Ed.), *Crisis intervention: Selected readings* (pp. 7–21). New York: Family Service Association of America.

Loewenberg, Frank M., Dolgoff, Ralph, & Harrington, Donna. (2000). *Ethical decisions for social work practice* (6th Ed.). Itasca, IL: Peacock.

Lowen, Alexander. (1975). *Bioenergetics.* New York: Penguin.

Luey, Helen Sloss, Glass, Laurel, & Elliot, Holly. (1995). Hard of hearing or deaf: Issues of ears, language, culture, and identity. *Social Work, 40,* 177–182.

Lum, Doman. (2004). *Social work practice and people of color: A process-stage approach* (5th Ed.). Belmont, CA: Thomson-Brooks/Cole.

Lynch, Eleanor W., & Hanson, Marci J. (Eds.). (2004). *Developing cross-cultural competence: A guide for working with children and their families* (3rd Ed.). Baltimore, MD: Brookes.

Mackelprang, Romel, & Salsgiver, Richard. (1999). *Disability: A diversity model approach in human service practice.* Pacific Grove, CA: Brooks/Cole.

Malgady, Robert G., & Zayas, Luis H. (2001). Cultural and linguistic considerations in psychodiagnosis with Hispanics: The need for an empirically informed process model. *Social Work, 46,* 39–49.

Maslow, Abraham. (1968). *Toward a psychology of being.* Princeton, NJ: Van Nostrand.

Maturana, Humberto. (1978). Biology of language: The epistomology of reality. In G. A. Miller & E. Lennonberg (Eds.), *Psychology and biology of language and thought.* New York: Academic Press.

McCammon, Susan L., & Allison, E. Jackson. (1995). Debriefing and treating emergency workers. In Charles R. Figley (Ed.), *Compassion fatigue: Coping with secondary traumatic stress disorder in those who treat the traumatized* (pp. 115–130). New York: Brunner/Mazel.

McCann, Lisa, & Pearlman, Laurie Ann. (1990). Vicarious traumatization: A framework for understanding the psychological effects of working with victims. *Journal of Traumatic Stress Studies, 3,* 131–149.

McCarty, Dawn, & Clancy, Catherine. (2002). Telehealth: Implications for social work practice. *Social Work, 47* (2), 153–162.

McGoldrick, Monica, & Shellenberger, Sylvia. (1999). *Genograms: Assessment & intervention.* New York: Norton.

McIntosh, Peggy. (1989). White privilege: Unpacking the invisible knapsack. *Peace and Freedom,* (July/August), 10–12.

McNally, Richard J., Bryant, Richard A., & Ehlers, Anke. (2003). Does early psychological intervention promote recovery from posttraumatic stress? *Psychological Science in the Public Interest, 4* (2), 45–79.

McRoy, Ruth, Freeman, Edith, Logan, Sadye, & Blackmon, B. (1986). Cross-cultural field supervision: Implications for social work education. *Journal of Social Work Education, 22,* 50–56.

Meichenbaum, Donald. (1996). Stress inoculation training for coping with stressors. *The Clinical Psychologist, 49,* 4–10.

Mezzich, Juan, & Kleinman, Arthur (Eds.). (1996). *Culture and psychiatric diagnosis: A DSM-IV perspective.* Arlington, VA: American Psychiatric Press.

Meichenbaum, Donald. (1977). *Cognitive behavior modification: An integrative approach.* New York: Plenum.

Middleton, Renee A., Stadler, Holly A., Simpson, Carol, Guo, Yuh-Jen, Brown, Michele J., Crow, Germayne, Schuck, Kelly, Alemu, Yared, & Lazarte, Alejandro A. (2005). Mental health practitioners: The relationship between White racial identity attitudes and self-reported multicultural competencies. *Journal of Counseling & Development, 83,* 444–456.

Miller, Dusty. (1996). Challenging self-harm through transformation of the trauma story. *Journal of Sexual Addiction and Compulsivity 3,* 213–227.

Miller, Jean Baker, Jordan, Judith V., Stiver, Irene P., Walker, Maureen, Surrey, Janet L., & Eldridge, Natalie. (2004). Therapists' authenticity. In Judith V. Jordan, Maureen Walker, & Linda M. Hartling. (Eds.), *The complexity of connection: Writings from the Stone Center's Jean Baker Miller Training Institute* (pp. 64–89). New York: Guilford.

Miller, Jean B., & Stiver, Irene P. (1997). *The healing connection: How women form relationships in therapy and in life.* Boston: Beacon.

Miller, K. I., Stiff, J. B., & Ellis, B. H. (1988). Communication and empathy as precursors to burnout among human service workers. *Communication Monographs, 55,* 336–341.

Miller, William R., & Rollnick, Stephen. (2002). *Motivational interviewing: Preparing people for change* (2nd Ed.). New York: Guilford.

Miltenberger, R. G. (2004). *Behavior modification: Principles and procedures* (3rd Ed.). Pacific Grove, CA: Brooks/Cole.

Mio, Jeffery Scott, Barker-Hackett, Lori, & Tumambing, Jaydee. (2006). *Multicultural psychology: Understanding our diverse communities.* Boston: McGraw-Hill.

Morrison, Amy L. (1997). Ten years of doing psychotherapy while living with a life-threatening illness: Self-disclosure and other ramifications. *Psychoanalytic Dialogues, 7* (1), 225–241.

Mumm, Ann Marie, & Kersting, Robert C. (1997). Teaching critical thinking in social work practice courses. *Journal of Social Work Education, 33,* 75–84.

Murphy, Bianca Cody. (1994). Difference and diversity: Gay and lesbian couples. *Journal of Gay and Lesbian Social Services 1,* 5–31.

National Association of Social Workers. (1999). *Code of ethics of the National Association of Social Workers.* Washington, DC: Author.

National Association of Social Workers. (2001). *Standards for cultural competence in social work practice.* Washington, DC: Author.

National Organization for Human Services. (1996). *Ethical standards for human service professionals.* Austin, TX: Author.

Netting, F. Ellen, Kettner, Peter M., & McMurtry, Steven L. (2003). *Social work macro practice* (3rd Ed.). Boston, MA: Allyn & Bacon.

Neukrug, Edward S., & Schwitzer, Alan M. (2006). *Skills and tools for today's counselors and psychotherapists: From natural helping to professional counseling.* Belmont, CA: Brooks/Cole.

Nietzel, Michael, Bernstein, Douglas, Milich, Richard, & Kramer, Geoff. (2002). *Introduction to clinical psychology* (6th Ed.). Englewood Cliffs, NJ: Prentice-Hall.

Okun, Barbara F. (1997). *Effective helping: Interviewing and counseling techniques.* Pacific Grove, CA: Brooks/Cole.

Okun, Barbara, Fried, Jane, & Okun, Marcia. (1999). *Understanding diversity: A learning-as-practice primer.* Pacific Grove, CA: Brooks/Cole.

Padden, C. (1989). The deaf community and the culture of deaf people. In S. Wilcox (Ed.), *American deaf culture: An anthology* (pp. 1–16). Burtonsville, MD: Linstock.

Padesky, Christine. (1995). *Clinician's guide to mind over mood.* New York: Guilford.

Parad, Howard J. (Ed.). (1965). *Crisis intervention: Selected readings.* New York: Family Service Association of America.

Parad, Howard, & Caplan, Gerald. (1965). A framework for studying families in crisis. In Howard J. Parad (Ed.), *Crisis intervention: Selected readings* (pp. 53–72). New York: Family Service Association of America.

Parker-Oliver, Debra, & Dimiris, George. (2006). Social work informatics: A new specialty. *Social Work, 51,* 127–134.

Parker, Robin, & Chambers, Pamela Smith. (2005). *The antiracist cookbook: A recipe guide for conversations about race that goes beyond covered dishes and "Kum-bah-yah."* Roselle, NJ: Crandall, Dostie, & Douglass.

Pedersen, Paul. (1991). Multiculturalism as a generic approach to counseling. *Journal of Counseling and Development, 70* (1), 6–12.

Peebles Wilkins, Wilma. (1995). Janie Porter Barrett and the Virginia Industrial School for Colored Girls: Community response to the needs of African American children. *Child Welfare,* LXXIV (1), 143–161.

Penn, L. S. (1990). When the therapist must leave: Forced termination of psychodynamic psychotherapy. *Professional Psychology: Research and Practice, 21,* 379–384.

Perez, Ruperto, DeBord, Kurt, & Bieschke, Kathleen. (2000). *Handbook of counseling and psychotherapy with lesbian, gay, and bisexual clients.* Washington, DC: American Psychological Association.

Philip, Claire E. (1994). Letting go: Problems with termination when a therapist is seriously ill or dying. *Smith College Studies in Social Work, 64* (2), 169–179.

Pinderhughes, Elaine. (1989). *Understanding race, ethnicity, and power: The key to efficacy in clinical practice.* New York: Free Press.

Plante, Thomas G. (1999). *Contemporary clinical psychology.* New York: John Wiley.

Poindexter, Cynthia C. (1997). In the aftermath: Serial crisis intervention for people with HIV. *Health & Social Work Journal, 22,* 125–132.

Ponterotto, Joseph G., Casas, J. Manuel, Suzuki, Lisa A., & Alexander, Charlene M. (Eds.). (2001). *Handbook of multicultural counseling.* Thousand Oaks, CA: Sage.

Pope, Kenneth S., Sonne, Janet L., & Greene, Beverly. (2006). *What therapists don't talk about and why: Understanding taboos that hurt us and our clients.* Washington, DC: American Psychological Association.

Pope, Kenneth S., & Vasquez, Melba J. T. (1998). *Ethics in psychotherapy and counseling: A practical guide* (2nd Ed.). San Francisco: Jossey-Bass.

Prochaska, James O., & Norcross, John C. (2007). *Theories of psychotherapy: A transtheoretical approach.* Belmont, CA: Brooks/Cole.

Prochaska, James O., Norcross, John C., & DiClemente, Carlo C. (1994). *Changing for good.* New York: Morrow.

Pryor, Karen. (1984). *Don't shoot the dog! How to improve yourself and others through behavioral training.* New York: Bantam.

Ram Dass & Gorman, Paul. (1985). *How can I help? Stories and reflections on service.* New York: Knopf.

Rapoport, Lydia. (1965). The state of crisis: Some theoretical considerations. In Howard J. Parad (Ed.), *Crisis intervention: Selected readings* (pp. 22–31). New York: Family Service Association of America.

Rappaport, Julian. (1987). Terms of empowerment/exemplars of prevention: Toward a theory for community psychology. *American Journal of Community Psychology, 15,* 121–148.

Reamer, Frederic. (1995). Malpractice claims against social workers: First facts. *Social Work, 40,* 595–601.

Rebuffat, Gaston. (1965). *Between heaven and earth.* New York: Oxford University Press.

Reik, Theodor. (1948). *Listening with the third ear.* New York: Farrar & Straus.

Reynolds, Amy L., & Pope, Raechele L. (1991). The complexity of diversity: Exploring multiple oppressions. *Journal of Counseling and Development, 70* (1), 174–180.

Roazen, Paul. (1992). *Freud and his followers.* New York: Da Capo.

Robinson, Tracy L. (2005). *The convergence of race, ethnicity, and gender: Multiple identities in counseling* (2nd Ed.). Upper Saddle River, NJ: Pearson.

Rock, Barry, & Congress, Elaine. (1999). The new confidentiality for the 21st century in a managed care environment. *Social Work, 44,* 253–262.

Rogers, Carl. (1957). The necessary and sufficient conditions of therapeutic personality change. *Journal of Consulting Psychology, 21,* 95–103.

Rogers, Carl. (1958). The characteristics of a helping relationship. *Personnel and Guidance Journal, 37,* 6–16.

Rogers, Carl. (1980). *A way of being.* Boston: Houghton Mifflin.

Rogers, Carl, & Sanford, R. C. (1985). Client-centered psychotherapy. In Harold Kaplan, Benjamin Sadock, & Arthur M. Friedman (Eds.), *Comprehensive textbook of psychiatry* (pp. 1374–1388). Baltimore: Williams & Wilkins.

Rollock, David, & Gordon, Edmund W. (2000). Racism and mental health into the 21st century: Perspectives and parameters. *American Journal of Orthopsychiatry, 70* (1), 5–13.

Romero, J. T. (1983). The therapist as social change agent. In Guadalupe Gibson (Ed.), *Our kingdom stands on brittle glass* (pp. 86–95). Silver Springs, MD: National Association of Social Workers.

Root, Maria P. P. (1990). Resolving the "other" status: Identity development of biracial individuals. *Women & Therapy, 9,* 185–205.

Root, Maria P. P. (1992). The impact of trauma on personality: The second reconstruction. In Laura Brown & Mary Ballou (Eds.), *Theories of personality and psychopathology: Feminist reappraisal.* New York: Guilford.

Root, Maria P. P. (1996). *The multiracial experience.* Thousand Oaks, CA: Sage.

Root, Maria P. P. (2001). Negotiating the margins. In Joseph G. Ponterotto, J. Manuel Casas, Lisa. A. Suzuki, & Charlene M. Alexander (Eds.), *Handbook of multicultural counseling* (pp. 113–121). Thousand Oaks CA: Sage.

Rose, Stephen M. (2000). Reflections on empowerment-based practice. *Social Work, 45,* 403–412.

Rosenhan, David L. (1973). On being sane in insane places. *Science, 179,* 250–257.

Roszak, Theodore, Gomes, Mary E., & Kanner, Allen D. (Eds.). (1995). *Ecopsychology: Restoring the earth, healing the mind.* San Francisco: Sierra Club Books.

Royal, Germain, & Dunstan, Georgia. (2004). Changing the paradigm from "race" to human genome variation. *NatureGenetics, 36* (11), S5–S7. Available at: http://www.nature.com/ng/journal/v36/n11s/pdf/ng1454.pdf. Accessed April 15, 2006.

Ryan, William. (1976). *Blaming the victim.* New York: Vintage.

Saleebey, Dennis. (2001). The Diagnostic Strengths Manual *Social Work, 46* (2), 183–192.

Saleebey, Dennis. (2005) *The strengths perspective in social work practice* (4th Ed.). Upper Saddle River, NJ: Pearson.

Schamess, Gerald. (1999). Therapeutic love and its permutations. *Clinical Social Work Journal, 27,* 9–26.

Schutz, William. (1967). *Joy: Expanding human awareness.* New York: Grove.

Seabury, Brett. (1976). The contract: Uses, abuses, and limitations. *Social Work, 21,* 16–21.

Sharifzadeh, Virginia-Shirin. (2004). Families with Middle Eastern roots. In Eleanor W. Lynch & Marci J. Hanson (Eds.), *Developing cross-cultural competence: A guide for working with children and their families* (3rd Ed., pp. 373–410). Baltimore: Brookes.

Sheafor, Bradford, Horejsi, Charles, & Horejsi, Gloria. (1997). *Techniques and guidelines for social work practice.* Boston: Allyn & Bacon.

Shih, Margaret J., & Sanchez, Diana T. (2005). Perspectives and research on the positive and negative implications of having multiple racial identities. *Psychological Bulletin, 131,* 569–591.

Shulman, Lawrence. (2006). *The skills of helping individuals, families, groups, and communities* (5th Ed.). Belmont, CA: Brooks/Cole.

Slattery, Jeanne M. (2004). *Counseling diverse clients: Bringing context into therapy.* Belmont, CA: Brooks/Cole.

Smith, Janna Malamud. (2000). Psychotherapy with people stressed by poverty. In Alex N. Sabo & Leston Havens (Eds.), *The real world guide to psychotherapy practice* (pp. 71–92). Cambridge, MA: Harvard University Press.

Snowden, Lonnie R., & Cheung, F. K. (1990). Use of inpatient mental health services by members of ethnic minority groups. *American Psychologist, 45,* 347–355.

Snowden, Lonnie R. (1993). Emerging trends in organizing and financing human services: Unexamined consequences of ethnic minority populations. *American Journal of Community Psychology, 21,* 1–13.

Sperry, Len. (2007). *Ethical and professional issues in counseling and psychotherapy practice.* Boston: Allyn & Bacon.

Spickard, Paul R., Fong, Rowena, & Ewalt, Patricia L. (1995). Undermining the very basis of racism—its categories. *Social Work, 40,* 581–584.

Spradlin, Scott E. (2003). *Don't let your emotions run your life: How dialectical behavioral therapy can put you in control.* Oakland, CA: New Harbinger.

Stevens, Joyce West. (1997). African American female adolescent identity development: A three-dimensional perspective. *Child Welfare, 76* (1), 145–172.

Stiver, Irene P. (1991). The meaning of care: Reframing treatment models. In Judith V. Jordan, Alexandra Kaplan, Jean Baker Miller, Irene P. Stiver, & Janet Surrey (Eds.), *Women's growth in connection: Writings from the Stone Center* (pp. 250–267). New York: Guilford.

Stokoe, W. (1989). Dimensions of difference: ASL and English-based cultures. In S. Wilcox (Ed.), *American deaf culture: An anthology* (pp. 49–59). Burtonsville, MD: Linstock.

Stone, Michael. (1997). *Healing the mind: A history of psychiatry from antiquity to the present.* New York: Norton.

Sue, Derald Wing. (2003). *Overcoming our racism: The journey to liberation.* San Francisco, CA: Jossey-Bass.

Sue, Derald W., Arredondo, Patricia, & McDavis, Roderick. (1992). Multicultural counseling competencies and standards: A call to the profession. *Journal of Counseling & Development, 70,* 477–484.

Sue, Derald Wing, & Sue, David. (1999). *Counseling the culturally different: Theory and practice* (3rd Ed.). New York: John Wiley.

Sue, Derald Wing, & Sue, David. (2003). *Counseling the culturally diverse* (4th Ed.). New York: John Wiley.

Sue, Derald W., Ivey, Allen E., & Pedersen, Paul B. (1996). *A theory of multicultural counseling and therapy.* Pacific Grove, CA: Brooks/Cole.

Surrey, Janet. (1991a). Relationship and empowerment. In Judith V. Jordan, Alexandra G. Kaplan, Jean Baker Miller, Irene P. Stiver, & Janet L. Surrey (Eds.), *Women's growth in connection: Writings from the Stone Center* (pp. 51–66). New York: Guilford.

Surrey, Janet. (1991b). The self-in-relation: A theory of women's development. In Judith V. Jordan, Alexandra G. Kaplan, Jean Baker Miller, Irene P. Stiver, & Janet L. Surrey (Eds.), *Women's growth in connection: Writings from the Stone Center* (pp. 51–66). New York: Guilford.

Sussman, Michael. B. (1992). *A curious calling: Unconscious motivations for practicing psychotherapy.* Northvale, NJ: Jason Aronson.

Swenson, Carol R. (1998). Clinical social work's contribution to a social justice perspective. *Social Work 43,* 6, 527–537.

Szasz, Thomas. (1960). The myth of mental illness. *American Psychologist, 15,* 113–118.

Szasz, Thomas. (1993). Curing, coercing, and claims-making: A reply to critics. *British Journal of Psychiatry, 162,* 797–800.

Tafoya, Terry. (1989). Circles and cedar: Native Americans and family therapy. *Journal of Psychotherapy and the Family, 6,* 71–98.

Tatum, Beverly Daniel. (1997) "Why are all the black kids sitting together in the cafeteria": And other conversations about race. New York: BasicBooks.

Taylor, Robert, Ellison, Christopher, Chatters, Linda, Levin, Jeffrey, & Lincoln, Karen. (2000). Mental health services in faith communities: The role of clergy in Black America. *Social Work, 45,* 73–87.

Tedeschi, Richard, & Calhoun, Lawrence. (1996). The Post-Traumatic Growth Inventory: Measuring the positive legacy of trauma. *Journal of Traumatic Stress, 9* (3), 455–471.

Thakker, Joanne, & Ward, Tony. (1998). Culture and classification: The cross-cultural application of the DSMIV. *Clinical Psychology Review, 18,* 501–529.

Torrey, E. Fuller. (1972). What western psychotherapists can learn from witchdoctors. *American Journal of Orthopsychiatry, 42* (1), 69–76.

Uba, Laura. (1994). *Asian Americans: Personality patterns, identity, and mental health.* New York: Guilford.

Valle, Ramon. (1980). Social mapping techniques: A preliminary guide for locating and linking to natural networks. In Ramon Valle & William Vega (Eds.), *Hispanic natural support systems: Mental health promotion perspectives* (pp. 113–121). Sacramento: State of California Department of Mental Health.

Van Den Bergh, Nan, & Crisp, Catherine. (2004). Defining culturally competent practice with sexual minorities: Implications for social work education and practice. *Journal of Social Work Education, 40* (2), 221–238.

van der Kolk, Bessel A., Burbridge, Jennifer A., & Suzuki, Joji. (1997). The psychobiology of traumatic memory: Implications of neuroimaging studies. *Annals of the New York Academy of Sciences, 821,* 99–113.

van der Kolk, Bessel A., Hopper, James W., & Osterman, Janet E. (2001). Exploring the nature of traumatic memory: Combining clinical knowledge with laboratory methods. *Journal of Aggression, Maltreatment, & Trauma, 4* (9), 9–31.

van der Kolk, Bessel A., & van der Hart, Onno. (1991). The intrusive past: The flexibility of memory and the engraving of trauma. *American Image, 48* (4), 425–454.

Vasquez, Melba J. T. (2005). Independent practice settings and the multicultural guidelines. In Madonna G. Constantine & Derald Wing Sue (Eds.), *Strategies for building multicultural competence in mental health and educational settings* (pp. 91–108). Hoboken, NJ: John Wiley.

Vinson, T. S., & Neimeyer, G. T. (2000). The relationship between racial identity development and multicultural counselor training. *Journal of Multicultural Counseling and Development, 28* (3), 177–193.

von Bertalanffy, Ludwig. (1968). *General systems theory: Foundation, development, application.* New York: Braziller.

von Foerster, Heinz. (1981). *Observing systems.* Seaside, CA: Intersystems Publications.

Wachtel, Paul. (1993). *Therapeutic communication: What to say when.* New York: Guilford.

Walker, Maureen, & Rosen, Wendy B. (Eds.). (2004). *How connections heal: Stories from relational-cultural therapy.* New York: Guilford.

Walsh, Froma (Ed.). (1999). *Spiritual resources in family therapy.* New York: Guilford.

Walsh, Joseph. (2003). *Endings in clinical practice: Effective closure in diverse settings.* Chicago: Lyceum.

Watson, David L., & Tharp, Roland G. (1993). *Self-directed behavior: Self-modification for personal adjustment.* Pacific Grove, CA: Brooks/Cole.

Weaver, Hilary N. (1999). Indigenous people and the social work profession: Defining culturally competent services. *Social Work, 44,* 217–225.

Weaver, Hilary N. (2005). *Explorations in cultural competence: Journey to the four directions.* Belmont, CA: Brooks/Cole.

Webb, Nancy Boyd (Ed.). (2004). *Mass trauma and violence: Helping families and children cope.* New York: Guilford.

Weick, Ann, Rapp, Charles, Sullivan, W. Patrick, & Kisthardt, Walter. (1989). A strengths perspective for social work practice. *Social Work, 34,* 350–354.

Weick, Ann. (1983). Issues in overturning a medical model of social work practice. *Social Work, 28,* 467–471.

Weinger, Susan. (2001). *Security risk: Preventing client violence against social workers.* Washington, DC: National Association of Social Workers Press.

Westen, Drew, Novotny, Catherine, & Thompson-Brenner, Heather. (2004). The empirical status of empirically supported psychotherapies: Assumptions, findings, and reporting in controlled clinical trials. *Psychological Bulletin, 130* (4), 631–663.

White, Michael, & Epston, David. (1990). *Narrative means to therapeutic ends.* New York: Norton.

White Kress, Victoria, Eriksen, Karen, Rayle, Andrea Dixon, & Ford, Stephanie J. W. (2005). The DSM-IV-TR and cultures: Considerations for counselors. *Journal of Counseling and Development, 83,* 97–105.

Wijeyesinghe, Charmaine L. (2001). Racial identity in multiracial people: An alternative paradigm. In Charmaine L. Wijeyesinghe & Bailey W. Jackson III (Eds.), *New perspectives on racial identity development: A theoretical and practical anthology* (pp. 129–152). New York: New York University Press.

Williams, Janet B., & Spitzer, Robert. (1995). Should *DSM* be the basis for teaching social work practice in mental health? Yes. *Journal of Social Work Education, 11,* 148–153.

Wise, Tim. (2005). *White like me: Reflections on race from a privileged son.* Brooklyn, NY: Soft Skull Press.

Young, Mark E. (2005). *Learning the art of helping: Building blocks and techniques.* Upper Saddle River, NJ: Pearson.

Young, Mark, & Chromy, Samantha. (2005). *Exercises in the Art of Helping.* Upper Saddle River, NJ: Pearson.

Index

Note: Figures are indicated by an *f* following the page number.